Software Quality Assurance

Software Quality Assurance

From theory to implementation

Daniel Galin

PEARSON

Addison
Wesley

Harlow, England • London • New York • Boston • San Francisco • Toronto • Sydney • Singapore • Hong Kong
Tokyo • Seoul • Taipei • New Delhi • Cape Town • Madrid • Mexico City • Amsterdam • Munich • Paris • Milan

Pearson Education Limited
Edinburgh Gate
Harlow
Essex CM20 2JE
England

and Associated Companies around the world

Visit us on the World Wide Web at:
www.pearsoned.co.uk

First published 2004

ISBN 0201 70945 7

British Library Cataloguing-in-Publication Data
A catalogue record for this book is available from the British Library

Library of Congress Cataloging-in-Publication Data

Galin, Daniel,
   Software quality assurance / Daniel Galin.
      p. cm.
   Includes bibliographical references and index.
   ISBN 0-201-70945-7
      1. Computer software--Quality control. I. Title.

QA76.76.Q35G35 2003
005.1'068'5--dc21

                                                      2003050668

10 9 8 7 6 5 4 3 2 1
09 08 07 06 05 04

Typeset in 10/12pt Sabon by 30.
Printed and bound in Great Britain by Biddles Ltd, Guildford and King's Lynn

The publisher's policy is to use paper manufactured from sustainable forests.

To my parents,
Blima and Elchanan,
who inspired me with their love of learning,
scholarship, and teaching

Contents

Preface

The opening of the new Denver International Airport (DIA) in February 1995 was a day of celebration for Colorado citizens but it was certainly the end of a traumatic period for the information technology industry. DIA was planned to be the largest airport in the United States, to serve 110 000 000 passengers annually by 2020, to handle 1750 flights daily through 200 gates and 12 operating runways. Operations at DIA were delayed by 16 months, mainly due to the failure of the software-based baggage handling system, causing estimated total losses of $2 billion. Moreover, the baggage handling system finally put into service was substantially downscaled in comparison to the system originally specified. Although several other colossal failures of software systems unfortunately have been recorded since 1995, the failure of IT technology at DIA was especially traumatic to the profession, whether due to the scale of the losses or the public interest and criticism it raised.

Many SQA professionals, including the author, believe that had appropriate software quality assurance systems been applied to the project at its start, a failure of this scale would not have occurred or, at least, its losses would have been dramatically reduced. The methods and tools discussed in this book, especially the risk management procedures, could have identified the severity of the situation at very early stages and enabled timely employment of the appropriate corrective measures throughout the project. Other SQA tools could probably have assured completion of the system on schedule and in full compliance with its specifications.

According to the author's conception of software quality assurance, an acceptable level of software quality can be achieved by:

- Combined application of a great variety of SQA components.
- Special emphasis on quality in the early phases of software development, including the pre-project phase.
- Performance of comprehensive SQA activities to control the quality of the work carried out by external participants (subcontractors, suppliers of reused software modules and COTS software products, and the customers themselves in cases where they carry out parts of the project).
- Extension of SQA activities to project schedules and budget control, based on the expectation that functional requirements, schedule and budget plans behave according to the *principle of communicating vessels*, that is, a failure (or reduced level of achievement) in one of these three fluid components induces immediate failure in the others.

This conception of software quality assurance guides us throughout the book.

Unique features of this text

The following features of this book are of special importance:

- A broad view of SQA
- Comprehensive discussion of SQA implementation issues
- Comprehensive coverage of SQA topics
- State-of-the-art topics.

A detailed discussion of these features follows.

A broad view of SQA

The book extends discussion of SQA issues much beyond the classic boundaries of custom-made software development by large established software houses. It dedicates significant attention to the other software development and maintenance environments that reflect the current state of the industry:

- **In-house software development by information systems departments**. The book discusses SQA of in-house projects, situations where traditional customer–supplier relations are missing or vague, and outlines recommended solutions to the attendant risks (see Sections 5.6 and 6.4.2).
- **COTS software packages**. COTS software packages represent a growing proportion of software packages used throughout the industry. Assurance of the quality of these packages, which are integrated directly into the customer's software systems, has become an important issue (see Chapter 12).
- **Small projects and small organizations**. Issues related to software development by small organizations and the execution of small software projects are likewise dealt with in the book (see Section 6.4.1).

Comprehensive discussion of SQA implementation issues

Stress is placed throughout the book on organization, control and other aspects arising in the implementation of SQA components:

- **Specialized chapter sections** and subsections dealing with implementation processes.
- **Examples** that refer to real-life situations, especially those involving implementation issues, are integrated into the text.
- **Implementation tips** related to special implementation problems are integrated into most of the chapters.
- **Topics for discussion**, found at the conclusion of each chapter, encourage the reader to suggest innovative solutions to implementation issues.

Comprehensive coverage of SQA topics

The book is very comprehensive in the range of SQA subjects covered. It includes topics rarely if ever covered in other SQA texts. These topics include:

- **Procedures and work instructions,** their preparation, implementation and updating (Chapter14).
- **Supporting quality devices,** that is, templates and checklists, their preparation, implementation and updating (Chapter 15).
- **Costs of software quality,** estimated according to the classic quality costs model in addition to a new extended model that better represents the special nature of software quality costs (Chapter 22).
- **The SQA unit and other actors in the SQA framework,** specifically the activities and responsibilities of active and occasional bodies that promote SQA issues within the organization: the SQA unit, SQA trustees, SQA committees and SQA forums (Chapter 26).

State-of–the-art topics

The text emphasizes up-to-date SQA topics:

- **Automated testing,** including a discussion of the various types of automated tests and their implementation, concluding with a review of the advantages and disadvantages of automated testing (Section 10.3).
- **Computerized SQA tools,** discussed in conjunction with almost all SQA components mentioned in the book. A special chapter (Chapter 13), entirely dedicated to computerized tools, reviews CASE tool issues. Special emphasis is placed on techniques that dramatically improve the performance of SQA tools, such as automated testing, software configuration management and documentation control.
- **International SQA standards.** Two chapters (Chapters 23 and 24) are dedicated to a survey of recent developments in software quality management standards and project process standards.

A downloadable *Instructor's Guide, PowerPoint Slides* and additional testing material are also available free of charge to lecturers and tutors adopting the main book. They can be accessed at www.booksites.net/galin.

The book's audience

The book is intended to meet the needs of a wide audience of readers interested in software quality assurance. We can identify four main groups of such readers, as follows:

- Managers of software development departments, project managers and others
- Those attending or presenting vocational training courses
- University and college students
- Practitioners involved in quality issues of software development and maintenance.

In addition, there are special groups of readers who are addressed on page xxiii.

Acknowledgements

This book has benefited from comments by software consumers as well as questions from students in the many courses I have taught at the Technion, Israel Institute of Technology, the Ruppin Academic Center and elsewhere. They helped me improve my explanations and inspired many of my examples. Others helped by directly answering questions or supplying valuable articles, books and other material. Their numbers prevent my mentioning all their names. I am grateful to each.

Special thanks to Andrea Shustaritch, representative of Pearson Education in Israel, who encouraged me to write this book and followed its progress. My editor, Keith Mansfield, a senior acquisition editor at Pearson Education in the UK, also deserves special recognition for his cooperation, continuous guidance and valuable advice throughout the long months of writing. I would especially like to express my appreciation to Nicola Chilvers, responsible for production of this book at Pearson Education, whose efficiency and amiable manner made working together such pleasure. In addition, I wish to express my appreciation to Nina Reshef, who edited my drafts with devotion and contributed substantially to the book's readability and accuracy.

Finally, I wish to say how grateful I am to my family, my wife Amira Galin, my daughter Michal Nisanson and my son Yoav Galin for their continuous support and encouragement as well as for their important comments on the book's drafts.

Publisher's acknowledgements

We are grateful to the following for permission to reproduce copyright material:

Figure 7.1 adapted from Royce, W.W. (1970) Managing the Development of large Software Systems: Concepts and Techniques, *Proceedings* of the IEEE WESCON, August 1970 and *Software Engineering Economics* by Boehm, B.W. © 1981. Reprinted by permission of Pearson Education, Inc., Upper Saddle River, NJ. Figure 7.3 adapted from Boehm, B.W. (1988) A Spiral Model of Software Development and Enhancement, *Computer*, Vol. 21, No. 5, pp. 61–72; Figure 7.4 adapted from Boehm, B.W. (1998) Using the Win-Win Spiral Model: A case study, *Computer*, Vol. 31, No. 7, pp. 33–44; Table 8.3 and Table 21.11 from *Japan's Software Factories: A Challenge to U.S. Management* by Michael A. Cusumano, copyright 1991 by Oxford University Press, Inc. Used by permission of Oxford University Press, Inc.; Table 10.6 adapted from Dustin/Rashka/Paul, *Automated Software Testing: Introduction, Management and Performance*, Table 2.4 (p. 53), © Pearson Education, Inc. Reprinted by permission of Pearson Education, Inc.; Table 23.1 and Table 23.2 reproduced with the permission of BSI under licence no. 2003SK/0025. British Standards can be obtained from BSI Customer Services, 389 Chiswick High Road, London W4 4AL (Tel. +44 (0) 208 996 9001). Figure 23.2 Capacity Maturity Model by Paulk et al. © Reprinted by permission of Pearson Education, Inc., Upper Saddle River, NJ. Table 23.5 and 23.6 adapted from Jung, H.-W., Hunter, R., Goldenson, D.R. and El-Eman, K. (2001) Finding the Phase 2 of the SPICE Trials, *Software Process Improvement and Practice*, 7(6) pp. 205–42. © John Wiley & Sons Limited. Reproduced with permission. Figure 24.1 reprinted with permission from IEE Std 1045-19992 by IEEE. The IEEE disclaims any responsibility or liability resulting from the placement and use in the described manner.

BSI for the eight principles of ISO 9000.3 and the structure of the ISO/IEC TR 15504 Standard (under licence number 2003DH0143), and IEEE for IEEE Std. 10278 (reviews) © 1994 IEEE and list of IEEE Software Engineering Standards.

In some instances we have been unable to trace the owners of copyright material, and we would appreciate any information that would enable us to do so.

About the author

Dr Daniel Galin received his B.Sc. in Industrial and Management Engineering, and his M.Sc. and D.Sc. in Operations Research from the Faculty of Industrial and Management Engineering, the Technion, Israel Institute of Technology, Haifa, Israel. He serves on the faculty of the Ruppin Academic Center, where he is the current Head of Information Systems Studies.

Dr Galin acquired his expertise in SQA through teaching, writing and consulting in the field. He teaches courses in software quality assurance and information systems at the Ruppin Academic Center, Information Systems Studies, at the Faculty of Computer Sciences, the Technion, Haifa and at the College of Administration, Tel-Aviv.

Dr Galin co-authored (with Dr Z. Bluvband) the book *Software Quality Assurance*. His many papers have been published in professional journals, the majority in English-language journals. All his former books on analysis and design of information systems and software quality assurance were written in Hebrew and published by Israel's leading publishers.

Dr Galin's professional experience of over 20 years includes consulting on numerous projects in software quality assurance as well as analysis and design of information systems.

Guides for special groups of readers

Among the readers interested in software quality assurance, one can distinguish two special groups:

- Readers interested in ISO 9000-3 requirements
- Readers interested in the American Society for Quality's (ASQ) CSQE (Certified Software Quality Engineer) body of knowledge.

The following tables direct the reader to the chapters and sections relevant to their interests.

Guide to readers interested in ISO 9000-3 requirements

The reader interested in ISO 9000-3 requirements will find a comprehensive discussion of standard ISO issues in Chapter 23. In addition, related material is spread throughout the book, as detailed in the following table. The ISO 9000-3 requirements numbers quoted are taken from the outline of ISO/IEC 9000-3:2001 (final draft).

ISO 9000-3 requirements: chapter	ISO 9000-3 requirements: subject	Book references (chapter/section)
4. Quality management system	4.1 General requirements 4.2 Documentation requirements	Ch. 4 Ch. 19
5. Management responsibilities	5.1 Management commitments 5.2 Customer focus 5.3 Quality policy 5.4 Planning 5.5 Responsibility authority and communication 5.6 Management review	Sec. 25.1 Sec. 25.1.1 Sec. 25.1.1 Ch. 25 Ch. 25 Sec. 25.1.3
6. Resource management	6.1 Provision of resources 6.2 Human resources 6.3 Infrastructure 6.4 Work environment	Sec. 25.1.1 Ch. 16 Secs 10.3, 11.4, Chs 13, 14, 15, Secs 18.7, 19.5, 20.4 Sec. 1.2

ISO 9000-3 requirements: chapter	ISO 9000-3 requirements: subject	Book references (chapter/section)
7. Product realization	7.1 Planning of product realization	Chs 6, 23, 24
	7.2 Customer-related processes	Chs 3, 5, 6, 12, 20
	7.3 Design and development	Chs 7, 8, 9, 10, Sec. 18.3
	7.4 Purchasing	Ch. 12
	7.5 Production and service provision	Chs 11, 12, Secs 18.4–18.6, Ch. 20
	7.6 Control of monitoring and measuring devices	Sec. 18.1
8. Measurement, analysis and improvement	8.1 General	Secs 21.1, 21.2, 22.1–22.3
	8.2 Monitoring and measurement	Secs 21.3, 21.4, 22.4, 22.5
	8.3 Control of non-conforming product	Secs 21.5, 22.4, 22.5, 26.1
	8.4 Analysis of data	Sec. 17.6
	8.5 Improvement	Ch. 17

Guide to readers interested in ASQ's CSQE body of knowledge

Almost all the elements of the CSQE (Certified Software Quality Engineer) body of knowledge, as outlined in ASQ (American Society for Quality) Item B0110, are included in the book. The following table directs the reader to the relevant chapters and sections.

CSQE body of knowledge: chapter	CSQE body of knowledge: subject	Book references (chapter/section)
I. General knowledge, conduct, and ethics	A. Standards	Sec. 2.1, Ch. 23
	B. Quality philosophy and principles	Secs 2.4, 2.5
	C. Organizational and interpersonal techniques	Ch. 25
	D. Problem-solving tools and processes	Secs 6.2, 6.3, App. 6A
	E. Professional conduct and ethics	–
II. Software quality management	A. Planning	Ch. 6, Secs 7.4, 17.2, 17.3
	B. Tracking	Ch. 6, Secs 17.4–17.8, Ch. 18
	C. Organizational and professional software quality training	Sec. 11.4, Ch. 16
III. Software processes	A. Development and maintenance methods	Sec. 7.1, Chs 8, 11, 13, 19
	B. Process and technology change management	Secs 18.3–18.7, Ch. 25

CSQE body of knowledge: chapter	CSQE body of knowledge: subject	Book references (chapter/section)
IV. Software project management	A. Planning	Chs 3, 5, 6, Secs 7.2, 12.2, App. 21A
	B. Tracking	Chs 20, 22, 25
	C. Implementation	Secs 7.4, 12.3, 12.4, Ch. 20, Sec. 22.4
V. Software metrics, measurement and analytical methods	A. Measurement methods	Secs 21.1, 21.2
	B. Analytical methods	Sec. 21.5
	C. Software measurement	Ch. 21
VI. Software inspection, testing, verification and validation	A. Inspection	Ch. 8, Sec. 25.1.3
	B. Testing	Chs 9+10
	C. Verification and validation	Sec. 7.3, Chs 8, 10, Sec. 18.3, Ch. 24
VII. Software audits	A. Audit types	Secs 23.3, 26.1.4
	B. Audit methodology	Ch. 17, Secs 23.3, 26.1.4
	C. Audit planning	Secs 23.3, 26.1.4
VIII. Software configuration management	A. Planning and configuration identification	Secs 18.1, 18.2, 18.4
	B. Configuration control, status accounting and reporting	Secs 18.3, 18.5

Guides for special groups of readers

Introduction

The software quality challenge

Two basic questions should be raised before we proceed to list the variety of subjects and details of the book:

(1) Is it justified to devote a special book to software quality assurance (SQA) or, in other words, can we not use the general quality assurance textbooks available that are applicable to numerous areas and industries?

(2) Having decided to develop specialized books for software quality assurance, at which of the various environments of software development, from amateurs' hobby to professionals' work, should we aim our main efforts? Put simply, what are the unique characteristics of the SQA environment?

The objective of this chapter is to answer these questions by exploring the related issues.

After completing this chapter, you will be able to:

■ Identify the unique characteristics of software as a product and as production process that justify separate treatment of its quality issues.

■ Recognize the characteristics of the environment where professional software development and maintenance take place.

■ Explain the main environmental difficulties faced by software development and maintenance teams as a result of the environment in which they operate.

1.1 The uniqueness of software quality assurance

"Look at this," shouted my friend while handing me **Dagal Features**'s Limited Warranty leaflet. "Even **Dagal Features** can't cope with software bugs." He pointed to a short paragraph on page 3 of the leaflet that states the conditions of the warranty for **AMGAL**, a leading Software Master product sold all over the world. The leaflet states the following:

LIMITED WARRANTY
Dagal Features provides no warranty, either expressed or implied, with respect to **AMGAL**'s performance, reliability or fitness for any specified purpose. **Dagal Features** does not warrant that the software or its documentation will fulfil your requirements. although **Dagal Features** has performed thorough tests of the software and reviewed the documentation, **Dagal Features** does not provide any warranty that the software and its documentation are free of errors. **Dagal Features** will in no case be liable for any damages, incidental, direct, indirect or consequential, incurred as a result of impaired data, recovery costs, profit loss and third party claims. the software is licensed "as is". the purchaser assumes the complete risk stemming from application of the **AMGAL** program, its quality and performance.

If physical defects are discovered in the documentation or the CD on which **AMGAL** is distributed, **Dagal Features** will replace, at no charge, the documentation or the CD within 180 days of purchase, provided proof of purchase is presented.

"Is the AMGAL software really so special that its developers are incapable of meeting the challenge of assuring a bug-free product?" continued my friend. "Do other software packages limit their warranties in the same way?"

Though **Dagal Features** and AMGAL are fictitious, an examination of the warranties offered by other software developers reveals a similar pattern. No developer will declare that its software is free of defects, as major manufacturers of computer hardware are wont to do. This refusal actually reflects the essential elemental differences between software and other industrial products, such as automobiles, washing machines or radios. These differences can be categorized as follows:

(1) **Product complexity**. Product complexity can be measured by the number of operational modes the product permits. An industrial product, even an advanced machine, does not allow for more than a few thousand modes of operation, created by the combinations of its different machine settings. Looking at a typical software package one can find millions of software operation possibilities. Assuring that the multitude of operational possibilities is correctly defined and developed is a major challenge to the software industry.

(2) **Product visibility**. Whereas the industrial products are visible, software products are invisible. Most of the defects in an industrial product can be detected during the manufacturing process. Moreover the absence of a part in an industrial product is, as a rule, highly visible (imagine a door missing from your new car). However, defects in software products (whether stored on diskettes or CDs) are invisible, as is the fact that parts of a software package may be absent from the beginning.

(3) **Product development and production process**. Let us now review the phases at which the possibility of detecting defects in an industrial product may arise:

(a) **Product development**. In this phase the designers and quality assurance (QA) staff check and test the product prototype, in order to detect its defects.

(b) **Product production planning**. During this phase the production process and tools are designed and prepared. In some products there is a need for a special production line to be designed and built. This phase thus provides additional opportunities to inspect the product, which may reveal defects that "escaped" the reviews and tests conducted during the development phase.

(c) **Manufacturing**. At this phase QA procedures are applied to detect failures of products themselves. Defects in the product detected in the first period of manufacturing can usually be corrected by a change in the product's design or materials or in the production tools, in a way that eliminates such defects in products manufactured in the future.

In comparison to industrial products, software products do not benefit from the opportunities for detection of defects at all three phases of the production process. The only phase when defects can be detected is the development phase. Let us review what each phase contributes to the detection of defects:

(a) **Product development**. During this phase, efforts of the development teams and software quality assurance professionals are directed toward detecting inherent product defects. At the end of this phase an approved prototype, ready for reproduction, becomes available.

(b) **Product production planning**. This phase is not required for the software production process, as the manufacturing of software copies and printing of software manuals are conducted automatically. This applies to any software product, whether the number of copies is small, as in custom-made software, or large, as in software packages sold to the general public.

(c) **Manufacturing**. As mentioned previously, the manufacturing of software is limited to copying the product and printing copies of the software manuals. Consequently, expectations for detecting defects are quite limited during this phase.

The differences affecting the detection of defects in software products versus other industrial products are shown in Table 1.1 and Frame 1.1.

It should be noted that significant parts of advanced machinery as well as of household machines and other products include embedded software components (usually termed "firmware") that are integrated into the product. These software components (the firmware) share the same characteristics of the software products mentioned above. It follows that the comparison shown above should actually be that of software products versus other industrial products and non-software components of industrial products that include firmware. Hereinafter, when mentioning software, we will mean software products as well as firmware.

The fundamental differences between the development and production processes related to software products and those of other industrial products warrant the creation of a different SQA methodology for software. The need for special tools and methods for the software industry is reflected in the professional publications as well in special standards devoted to SQA, such as ISO 9000-3, "Guidelines for the application of ISO 9001 to the development, supply and maintenance of software". This point is supported by the fact that targeted guidelines have not been prepared by ISO for other industries,

Table 1.1: Factors affecting defect detection in software products vs. other industrial products

Characteristic	Software products	Other industrial products
Complexity	Usually, very complex product allowing for very large number of operational options	Degree of complexity much lower, allowing at most a few thousand operational options
Visibility of product	Invisible product, impossible to detect defects or omissions by sight (e.g. of a diskette or CD storing the software)	Visible product, allowing effective detection of defects by sight
Nature of development and production process	Opportunities to detect defects arise in only one phase, namely product development	Opportunities to detect defects arise in all phases of development and production: ▪ Product development ▪ Product production planning ▪ Manufacturing

---

Frame 1.1   **The uniqueness of the software development process**

▪ **High complexity,** as compared to other industrial products

▪ **Invisibility of the product**

▪ **Opportunities to detect defects ("bugs")** are limited to the product development phase and the only other targeted guidelines have been prepared for services (ISO 9004-2, "Quality management and quality systems elements: Guidelines for the services").

The great complexity as well as invisibility of software, among other product characteristics, make the development of SQA methodology and its successful implementation a highly professional challenge.

1.2 The environments for which SQA methods are developed

The software developed by many individuals and in different situations fulfills a variety of needs:

- Pupils and students develop software as part of their education.
- Software amateurs develop software as a hobby.
- Professionals in engineering, economics, management and other fields develop software to assist them in their work, to perform calculations, summarize research and survey activities, and so forth.
- Software development professionals (systems analysts and programmers) develop software products or firmware as a professional career objective while in the employment of software houses or by software development and maintenance units (teams, departments, etc.) of large and small industrial, financial and other organizations.

All those who participate in these activities are required to deal with software quality problems ("bugs"). However, quality problems in their most severe form govern the professional software development.

This book is devoted, therefore, to defining and solving many of the software quality assurance (SQA) problems confronted by software development and maintenance professionals. However, all other types of software developers can find portions of the book applicable to and recommended for their own software development efforts.

Let us begin with the examination of the environment of professional software development and maintenance (hereafter "the SQA environment"), as it is a major consideration in the development of SQA methodologies and their implementation. The main characteristics of this environment are as follows:

(1) **Contractual conditions**. As a result of the commitments and conditions defined in the contract between the software developer and the customer, the activities of software development and maintenance need to cope with:

- A defined list of functional requirements that the developed software and its maintenance need to fulfill.
- The project budget.
- The project timetable.

The managers of software development and maintenance projects need to invest a considerable amount of effort in the oversight of activities in order to meet the contract's requirements.

(2) **Subjection to customer–supplier relationship**. Throughout the process of software development and maintenance, activities are under the oversight of the customer. The project team has to cooperate continuously with the customer: to consider his request for changes, to discuss his criticisms about the various aspects of the project, and to get his approval for changes initiated by the development team. Such relationships do not usually exist when software is developed by non-software professionals.

(3) **Required teamwork**. Three factors usually motivate the establishment of a project team rather than assigning the project to one professional:

■ Timetable requirements. In other words, the workload undertaken during the project period requires the participation of more than one person if the project is to be completed on time.
■ The need for a variety of specializations in order to carry out the project.
■ The wish to benefit from professional mutual support and review for the enhancement of project quality.

(4) **Cooperation and coordination with other software teams**. The carrying-out of projects, especially large-scale projects, by more than one team is a very common event in the software industry. In these cases, cooperation may be required with:

■ Other software development teams in the same organization.
■ Hardware development teams in the same organization.
■ Software and hardware development teams of other suppliers.
■ Customer software and hardware development teams that take part in the project's development.

An outline of cooperation needs, as seen from the perspective of the development team, is shown in Figure 1.1.

(5) **Interfaces with other software systems**. Nowadays, most software systems include interfaces with other software packages. These interfaces allow data in electronic form to flow between the software systems, free from keying in of data processed by the other software systems. One can identify the following main types of interfaces:

■ Input interfaces, where other software systems transmit data to your software system.
■ Output interfaces, where your software system transmits processed data to other software systems.
■ Input and output interfaces to the machine's control board, as in medical and laboratory control systems, metal processing equipment, etc.

Salary processing software packages provide good examples of typical input and output interfaces to other software packages – see Figure 1.2. First let us look at the input interface. In order to calculate salaries, one needs the employees' attendance information, as captured by the time

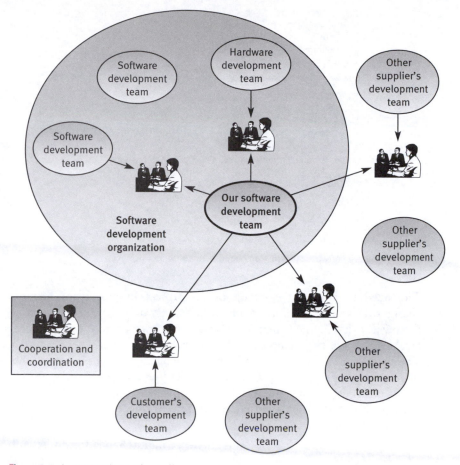

Figure 1.1: A cooperation and coordination scheme for a software development team of a large-scale project

clocks placed at the entrance to the office building and processed later by the attendance control software system. Once a month, this information (the attendance lists including the overtime data) is transmitted electronically from the attendance control system to the salary processing system. This information transmission represents an input interface for the salary processing software system; at the same time it represents an output interface to the attendance control system. Now, let us examine the output interface of our system. One of the outputs of the salary processing system is the list of "net" salaries, after deduction of the income tax and other items, payable to the employees. This list, including the employees' bank account details, has to be sent to the banks. The transmission of the list of salary payments is done electronically, representing an output interface for the salary processing system and an input interface for the bank's account system.

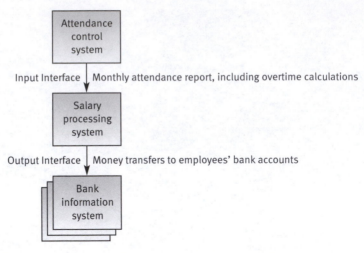

Figure 1.2: The salary software system – an example of software interfaces

(6) **The need to continue carrying out a project despite team member changes.** It is quite common for team members to leave the team during the project development period, whether owing to promotions to higher level jobs, a switch in employers, transfers to another city, and so forth. The team leader then has to replace the departing team member either by another employee or by a newly recruited employee. No matter how much effort is invested in training the new team member, "the show must go on", which means that the original project contract timetable will not change.

(7) **The need to continue carrying out software maintenance for an extended period.** Customers who develop or purchase a software system expect to continue utilizing it for a long period, usually for 5–10 years. During the service period, the need for maintenance will eventually arise. In most cases, the developer is required to supply these services directly. Internal "customers", in cases where the software has been developed in-house, share the same expectation regarding the software maintenance during the service period of the software system.

The environmental characteristics create a need for intensive and continuous managerial efforts parallel to the professional efforts that have to be invested in order to assure the project's quality, in other words to assure the project's success.

A summary of the main characteristics of the SQA environment is shown in Frame 1.2.

A significant amount of software as well as firmware development is not carried out subject to formal contracts or formal customer–supplier relationships, as mentioned in the first two SQA environment characteristics. This type of activity usually concerns software developed in-house for internal use

Frame 1.2 Summary of the main characteristics of SQA environment

1. Being contracted
2. Subjection to customer–supplier relationship
3. Requirement for teamwork
4. Need for cooperation and coordination with other development teams
5. Need for interfaces with other software systems
6. Need to continue carrying out a project while the team changes
7. Need to continue maintaining the software system for years

or for marketing as software packages and in-house development of firmware. The relationships between the marketing department that initiates and defines the qualifications of a new product and the respective in-house software development department often resemble a contract and customer–supplier relationship. The same applies to internal requests for a new software system or for the upgrading of current software or firmware to be implemented by the organization's software department. Actual relationships between the internal "customers" and the development departments are found to vary greatly when measured by a formal–informal scale. Some managers claim that the closer the relationships to the formal form, the greater the prospects for the project's success.

Summary

(1) The uniqueness of software quality assurance.

The fundamental differences between software products (including firmware) and other products are caused by the higher product complexity, by the invisibility of software and by the nature of the product development and production process. These differences create the need for an SQA methodology and tools for SQA that will meet the special and different challenges for the development and operation of quality assurance for software.

(2) The environments for which SQA methods were developed.

The SQA methods and tools discussed in this book are specially aimed at the needs of professional software development and maintenance, activities where quality problems appear in their most severe form, and where the most painful losses are expected. Therefore any method or tool to be applied is subject to the environmental characteristics of their activities, namely:

- Contract conditions and commitments defining the contents and timetable.
- The conditions of the customer–supplier relationship, as realized by the need for consultation with the customer and the acquisition of his approval.

- Teamwork requirements.
- Need for cooperation and coordination with other software and hardware development teams both internally and externally.
- Need for interfaces with other software systems.
- Need to continue carrying out a project when team members change.
- Need to conduct maintenance of the software system for several years.

These environmental characteristics also apply to internal development of software and firmware, though only informal contract or informal customer–supplier relationships exist in these cases. These characteristics demand that intensive and continuous managerial efforts be expended in parallel to the professional efforts that have to be invested in order to ensure the project's quality or, in other words, to assure the project's success.

Review questions

1.1 There are three major differences between software products and other industrial products.

(1) Identify and describe the differences.
(2) Discuss the ways in which these differences affect SQA.

1.2 It is claimed that no significant SQA activities are expected to take place during the phase of production planning for software products.

(1) Discuss this claim.
(2) Compare the required production planning for a new automobile model with the production planning efforts required for a new release of a software product.

1.3 Seven issues characterize the professional software development and maintenance environment.

(1) Identify and describe these characteristics.
(2) Which of these environmental characteristics mainly affect the professional efforts required for carrying out software development and maintenance projects? List the characteristics and explain why a professional effort is needed.
(3) Which of these environmental characteristics mainly affect the managerial efforts required for carrying out software development and maintenance projects? List the characteristics and explain why such efforts are needed.

Topics for discussion

1.1 Educational systems are assumed to prepare the students to cope with real-life conditions. Examine the procedural requirements of a software development project or final software project, and determine which of the requirements could be considered as preparatory to professional life situations as discussed above.

1.2 Referring to the seven environmental characteristics of software development and

maintenance, consider the characteristics of future software products, discussing
whether the professional and managerial burden of coping with these characteristics in future is expected to be higher or lower when compared with the current
performance of these activities.

1.3 The interfaces of a salary processing system are exhibited in Figure 1.2.

(1) Suggest what are the main benefits of applying computerized interfaces
instead of transferring printouts.

(2) Give two additional examples where input interfaces are applied.

(3) Give two additional examples where output interfaces are applied.

(4) Suggest additional situations where the use of input and output interfaces is
not applied and should be recommended.

(5) Would you advise all information transfers from one organization to another
be performed by computerized interface? Discuss the reasons behind your
answer.

1.4 The need to carry out work by a team demands additional investment in coordination of the team members. Discuss whether these managerial efforts could be
saved if the work were performed as a "one-man job".

1.5 It is clear that a software development project carried out by a software house for
a specific customer is carried out under content and timetable obligations, and is
subject to the customer–supplier relationship.

(1) Discuss whether a customer–supplier relationship is expected when the software developed is to be sold to the public as a software package.

(2) Discuss whether a customer–supplier relationship is expected when software
is developed for in-house use, as in the case where a software development
department develops an inventory program for the company's warehouses.

(3) Some managers claim that the closer relationships are to a formal pattern, the
greater the prospects are for the project's success. Discuss whether implementing customer–supplier relationships in the situations mentioned in (1)
and (2) are a benefit for the company (referring to the internal customer and
supplier) or an unnecessary burden to the development team.

1.6 It has been claimed that environmental characteristics create the need for intensive and continuous managerial efforts parallel to the professional efforts that
have to be invested in order to ensure the project's quality or, in other words, to
assure the project's success. Discuss the reasons behind this claim, including an
analysis of the managerial effort created by each of the SQA environmental characteristics.

chapter 2

What is software quality?

Before we proceed to study the components of the SQA system, the basic concepts and objectives of software quality assurance should be discussed. Later, it will be possible to examine how and to what extent various methodologies and tools conform to these concepts and objectives.

After completing this chapter, you will be able to:

- Define software, software quality and software quality assurance.
- Distinguish between software errors, software faults and software failures.
- Identify the various causes of software errors.
- Explain the objectives of software quality assurance activities.
- Distinguish and explain the difference between software quality assurance and quality control.
- Explain the relationship between software quality assurance and software engineering.

Intuitively, when thinking about software, we imagine an accumulation of programming language instructions and statements or development tool instructions, that together form a program or software package. This program or software package is usually referred to as the "code". Is it enough to take care of the code in order to assure the quality of the services provided by the software program? Are additional elements necessary to assure their quality and thus assure the operational success of the software system?

As a preliminary answer, let us review the IEEE definition for "software" (IEEE, 1991), shown in Frame 2.1.

Frame 2.1   Software – IEEE definition

Software is:
Computer programs, procedures, and possibly associated documentation and data pertaining to the operation of a computer system.

The IEEE definition of software, which is almost identical to the ISO definition (ISO, 1997, Sec. 3.11 and ISO/IEC 9000-3 Sec. 3.14), lists the following four components of software:

- Computer programs (the "code")
- Procedures
- Documentation
- Data necessary for operating the software system.

All four components are needed in order to assure the quality of the software development process and the coming years of maintenance services for the following reasons:

- Computer programs (the "code") are needed because, obviously, they activate the computer to perform the required applications.
- Procedures are required, to define the order and schedule in which the programs are performed, the method employed, and the person responsible for performing the activities that are necessary for applying the software.
- Various types of documentation are needed for developers, users and maintenance personnel. The development documentation (the requirements report, design reports, program descriptions, etc.) allows efficient cooperation and coordination among development team members and efficient reviews and inspections of the design and programming products. The user's documentation (the "user's manual", etc.) provides a description of the available applications and the appropriate method for

their use. The maintenance documentation (the "programmer's software manual", etc.) provides the maintenance team with all the required information about the code, and the structure and tasks of each software module. This information is used when trying to locate causes of software failures ("bugs") or to change or add to existing software.

■ Data including parameters, codes and name lists that adapt the software to the needs of the specific user are necessary for operating the software. Another type of essential data is the standard test data, used to ascertain that no undesirable changes in the code or software data have occurred, and what kind of software malfunctioning can be expected.

To sum up, software quality assurance always includes, in addition to code quality, the quality of the procedures, the documentation and the necessary software data.

2.2 Software errors, faults and failures

■ "We've used the Simplex HR software in our Human Resources Department for about three years and we have never had a software failure."

■ "I started to use Simplex HR two months ago; we had so many failures that we are considering replacing the software package."

■ "We have been using the same software package for almost four years. We were very satisfied throughout the period until the last few months, when we suddenly faced several severe failures. The Support Center of the software house from which we bought the package claims that they have never encountered failures of the type we experienced even though they serve about 700 customers who utilize Simplex HR."

All these views, expressed by participants in a human resources management conference, refer to the same software package. Is it possible for such a variation in users' experience with failure to appear with the same software package? Can a software package that successfully served an organization for a long period "suddenly" change its nature (quality) and become "bugged"?

The answer to these questions is *yes*, and it is rooted in the characteristics of software.

The origin of software failures lies in a **software error** made by a programmer. An error can be a grammatical error in one or more of the code lines, or a logical error in carrying out one or more of the client's requirements.

However, not all software errors become **software faults**. In other words, in some cases, the software error can cause improper functioning of the software in general or in a specific application. In many other cases, erroneous code lines will not affect the functionality of the software as a whole; in *a part* of these cases, the fault will be corrected or "neutralized" by subsequent code lines.

We are interested mainly in the software failures that disrupt our use of the software. This requires us to examine the relationship between software faults and **software failures**. Do all software faults end with software failures? Not necessarily: a software fault becomes a software failure only when it is "activated" – when the software user tries to apply the specific, faulty application. In many situations, a software fault is never activated due to the user's lack of interest in the specific application or to the fact that the combination of conditions necessary to activate the fault never occurs.

Example 1: The "Pharm-Plus" software package
"Pharm-Plus", a software package developed for the operations required of a pharmacy chain, included several software faults, such as the following:

(a) The chain introduced a software requirement to avoid the current sale of goods to customers whose total debts will exceed $200 upon completion of the current sale. Unfortunately, the programmer erroneously put the limit at $500, a clear software fault. However, a software failure never occurred as the chain's pharmacies do not offer credit to their customers, that is, sales are cash sales or credit card sales.

(b) Another requirement introduced was the identification of "super customers". These were defined as those customers of the pharmacy who made a purchase at least once a month, the average value of that purchase made in the last M months (e.g., 12 months) being more than N times (e.g., five times) the value of the average customer's purchase at the pharmacy. It was required that once "super customers" reached the cashier, they would be automatically identified by the cash register. (The customers could then be treated accordingly, by receiving a special discount or gift, for example.) The software fault (caused by the system analyst) was that "super customers" could be identified solely by the value of their current purchase. In other words, customers whose regular purchases consisted of only one or two low-cost items could mistakenly be identified as "super customers".

At this particular chain, this software fault never turned into a software failure because its pharmacies, which allow for cash sales or credit card sales only, were unconcerned about identifying their customers, and were thus uninterested in applying the "super customer" option. This was the case for several years until the management of a new pharmacy decided to promote sales by developing customer–pharmacy relationships, and chose to implement the "super customer" option offered by "Pharm-Plus". The pharmacy defined a "super customer" to be a person whose average purchase in the last three months ($M = 3$) was over 10 times ($N = 10$) the value of the average purchase made in the pharmacy. In order to execute their marketing strategy, management began to distribute a pharmacy ID card to their customers, who were asked to show the card to the cashier. The cashiers were instructed to give special treatment to customers who were identified by the cash register as "super customers". It was soon observed that customers who entered the pharmacy for the first time as well as those who were recognized as frequent purchasers of only one or two items were identified as "super customers". In this case, the severe software fault turned into a severe software failure. Obviously, circumstances could have hidden this serious case of a severe software fault forever.

Example 2: The "Meteoro-X" meteorological equipment firmware
The software requirements for "Meteoro-X" meteorological equipment firmware (software embedded in the product) were meant to block the equipment's operation when its internal temperature rose above 60°C. A programmer error resulted in a software fault when the temperature limit was coded as 160°. This fault could cause damage when the equipment was subjected to temperatures higher than 60°. Because the equipment was used only in those coastal areas where temperatures never exceeded 60°, the software fault never turned into a software failure.

These examples should adequately make the point that only a portion of the software faults, and in some cases only a small portion of them, will turn into software failures in either the early or later stages of the software's application. Other software faults will remain hidden, invisible to the software users, yet capable of being activated when the situation changes.

Figure 2.1 illustrates the relationships between software errors, faults and failures. In this figure, the development process yields 17 software errors, only eight of which become software faults. Of these faults, only three turnout to be software failures.

Importantly, developers and users have different views of the software product regarding its internal defects. While developers are interested in software errors and faults, their elimination, and the ways to prevent their generation, software users are worried about software failures.

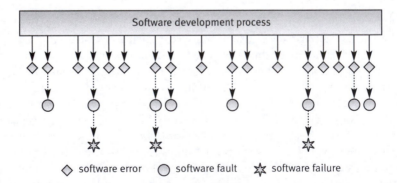

Figure 2.1: Software errors, sotware faults and software failures

As software errors are the cause of poor software quality, it is important to investigate the causes of these errors in order to prevent them. A software error can be "code error", a "procedure error", a "documentation error", or a "software data error". It should be emphasized that the causes of all these errors are human, made by systems analysts, programmers, software testers, documentation experts, managers and sometimes clients and their representatives. Even in rare cases where software errors may be caused by the development environment (interpreters, wizards, automatic software generators, etc.), it is reasonable to claim that it is human error that caused the failure of the development environment tool. The causes of software errors can be further classified as follows according to the stages of the software development process in which they occur.

(1) Faulty definition of requirements
The faulty definition of requirements, usually prepared by the client, is one of the main causes of software errors. The most common errors of this type are:

- Erroneous definition of requirements.
- Absence of vital requirements.
- Incomplete definition of requirements. For instance, one of the requirements of a municipality's local tax software system refers to discounts granted to various segments of the population: senior citizens, parents of large families, and so forth. Unfortunately, a discount granted to students was not included in the requirements document.
- Inclusion of unnecessary requirements, functions that are not expected to be needed in the near future.

(2) Client–developer communication failures
Misunderstandings resulting from defective client–developer communication are additional causes for the errors that prevail in the early stages of the development process:

- Misunderstanding of the client's instructions as stated in the requirement document.
- Misunderstanding of the client's requirements changes presented to the developer in written form during the development period.
- Misunderstanding of the client's requirements changes presented orally to the developer during the development period.
- Misunderstanding of the client's responses to the design problems presented by the developer.

■ Lack of attention to client messages referring to requirements changes and to client responses to questions raised by the developer on the part of the developer.

(3) Deliberate deviations from software requirements

In several circumstances, developers may deliberately deviate from the documented requirements, actions that often cause software errors. The errors in these cases are byproducts of the changes. The most common situations of deliberate deviation are:

■ The developer reuses software modules taken from an earlier project without sufficient analysis of the changes and adaptations needed to correctly fulfill all the new requirements.

■ Due to time or budget pressures, the developer decides to omit part of the required functions in an attempt to cope with these pressures.

■ Developer-initiated, unapproved improvements to the software, introduced without the client's approval, frequently disregard requirements that seem minor to the developer. Such "minor" changes may, eventually, cause software errors.

(4) Logical design errors

Software errors can enter the system when the professionals who design the system – systems architects, software engineers, analysts, etc. – formulate the software requirements. Typical errors include:

■ Definitions that represent software requirements by means of erroneous algorithms.

■ Process definitions that contain sequencing errors. For example, the software requirements for a firm's debt-collection system define the debt-collection process as follows. Once a client does not pay his debts, even after receiving three successive notification letters, the details are to be reported to the sales department manager who will decide whether to proceed to the next stage, referral of the client to the legal department. The systems analyst defined the process incorrectly by stating that after sending three successive letters followed by no receipt of payment, the firm would include the name of the client on a list of clients to be handled by the legal department. The logical error was caused by the analyst's erroneous omission of the sales department phase within the debt-collection process.

■ Erroneous definition of boundary conditions. For example, the client's requirements stated that a special discount will be granted to customers who make purchases more than three times in the same month. The analyst erroneously defined the software process to state that the discount would be granted to those who make purchases three times or more in the same month.

- Omission of required software system states. For example, a real-time computerized apparatus is required to react according to a combination of temperatures and pressures. The analyst did not define the needed reaction when the temperature is over 120°C and the pressure is between 6 and 8 atmospheres.

- Omission of definitions concerning reactions to illegal operation of the software system. For example, in a computerized theater ticketing system operated by the customer with no human operator interface, the software system is required to limit the sales to 10 tickets per customer. Accordingly, any request for the purchase of more than 10 tickets is "illegal". In his design, the analyst included a message stating that sales are limited to 10 tickets per customer, but did not define the system's reaction to the case where a customer (who might not have listened carefully to the message) keys in a number higher than 10. When performing the illegal request, a system "crash" is to be expected as no computerized reaction was defined for this illegal operation.

(5) Coding errors

A broad range of reasons cause programmers to make coding errors. These include misunderstanding the design documentation, linguistic errors in the programming languages, errors in the application of CASE and other development tools, errors in data selection, and so forth.

(6) Non-compliance with documentation and coding instructions

Almost every development unit has its own documentation and coding standards that define the content, order and format of the documents, and the code created by team members. To support this requirement, the unit develops and publicizes its templates and coding instructions. Members of the development team or unit are required to comply with these requirements.

One may ask why non-compliance with these instructions should cause software errors. The quality risks of non-compliance result from the special characteristics of the software development environment, discussed in Chapter 1. Even if the quality of the "non-complying" software is acceptable, future handling of this software (by the development and/or maintenance teams) is expected to increase the rate of errors:

- Team members who need to coordinate their own codes with code modules developed by "non-complying" team members can be expected to encounter more than the usual number of difficulties when trying to understand the software developed by the other team members.

- Individuals replacing the "non-complying" team member (who has retired or been promoted) will find it difficult to fully understand his or her work.

- The design review team will find it more difficult to review a design prepared by a non-complying team.

- The test team will find it more difficult to test the module; consequently, their efficiency is expected to be lower, leaving more errors undetected. Moreover, team members required to correct the detected errors can be expected to encounter greater difficulties when doing so. They may leave some errors only partially corrected, and even introduce new errors as a result of their incomplete grasp of the other team members' work.

- Maintenance teams required to contend with the "bugs" detected by users and to change or add to the existing software will face difficulties when trying to understand the software and its documentation. This is expected to result in an excessive number of errors and the expenditure of an excessive amount of maintenance effort.

(7) Shortcomings of the testing process

Shortcomings of the testing process affect the error rate by leaving a greater number of errors undetected or uncorrected. These shortcomings result from the following causes:

- Incomplete test plans leave untreated portions of the software or the application functions and states of the system.

- Failures to document and report detected errors and faults.

- Failure to promptly correct detected software faults as a result of inappropriate indications of the reasons for the fault.

- Incomplete correction of detected errors due to negligence or time pressures.

(8) Procedure errors

Procedures direct the user with respect to the activities required at each step of the process. They are of special importance in complex software systems where the processing is conducted in several steps, each of which may feed a variety of types of data and allow for examination of the intermediate results.

For example, "Eiffel", a chain of construction materials stores, has decided to grant a 5% discount to customers, who are billed once a month. The discount is offered to customers whose total purchases in the last 12 months exceed $1 million. Nevertheless, Eiffel's management has decided to withdraw this discount from customers who returned goods valued in excess of 10% of their purchases during the last three months. The chain's billing system is decentralized, so that every store processes the monthly invoices independently. Table 2.1 presents a comparison of correct and incorrect procedures regarding application of the discount.

(9) Documentation errors

The documentation errors that trouble the development and maintenance teams are errors in the design documents and in the documentation

Correct procedure	Incorrect procedure
At the beginning of each month, Eiffel's central information processing department:	At the end of each year, Eiffel's central information processing department:
(1) Collects the sales data and returned goods data for the previous month for each of its customers from all the stores in the chain. (2) Calculates the cumulative purchases of each customer for the last 12 months in all the chain's stores. (3) Calculates the percentage of returned goods for the last 3 months of each customer in all the chain's stores. (4) Prepares a list of all the customers who deserve the 5% discount and distributes it to each store before the end of the month.	(1) Collects the previous year's sales data for each of the customers from all the chain's stores. (2) Calculates the cumulative purchases of each customer for the previous year in all the chain's stores. (3) Prepares a list of all customers whose purchases exceed $1 million and distributes it to all the stores.
At the beginning of the month the individual store's information processing unit:	At the end of the each quarter, the individual store's information processing unit:
(1) Processes the monthly purchases for each of the customers. (2) Calculates the discount according to the updated list that was received at the end of the previous month.	(1) Calculates the percentage of goods returned during the last quarter for each customer. (2) Prepares a list of all customers whose returned goods for the last quarter exceed 10% of that quarter's purchase.
	At the beginning of the month, the store's information processing unit:
	(1) Processes the monthly purchases for each of the customers. (2) Calculates the discount according to the last year's purchase data in all the stores, and according to the store's records of returns in the last quarter.

integrated into the body of the software. These errors can cause additional errors in further stages of development and during maintenance.

Another type of documentation error, one that affects mainly the users, is an error in the user manuals and in the "help" displays incorporated in the software. Typical errors of this type are:

- Omission of software functions.
- Errors in the explanations and instructions given to users, resulting in "dead ends" or incorrect applications.
- Listing of non-existing software functions, that is, functions planned in the early stages of development but later dropped, and functions that were active in previous versions of the software but cancelled in the current version.

Frame 2.2 summarizes the causes of software errors.

Frame 2.2   The nine causes of software errors

1. Faulty requirements definition
2. Client–developer communication failures
3. Deliberate deviations from software requirements
4. Logical design errors
5. Coding errors
6. Non-compliance with documentation and coding instructions
7. Shortcomings of the testing process
8. Procedure errors
9. Documentation errors

2.4 Software quality – definition

Our introduction to software components and to errors and their causes, and our knowledge that errors harm the quality of the software, have prepared us to define our target – software quality.

The definition suggested by IEEE (IEEE, 1991) shown in Frame 2.3 is the definition we have chosen to apply in this text.

Frame 2.3   Software quality – IEEE definition

Software quality is:
1. The degree to which a system, component, or process meets specified requirements.
2. The degree to which a system, component, or process meets customer or user needs or expectations.

Frame 2.3 offers two alternative definitions of software quality, held by the founders of modern quality assurance, Philip B. Crosby and Joseph M. Juran. Each definition reflects a different conception of software quality:

- "Quality means conformance to requirements" (Crosby, 1979).
- "(1) Quality consists of those product features which meet the needs of customers and thereby provide product satisfaction.
  (2) Quality consists of freedom from deficiencies" (Juran, 1988).

Crosby's definition of software quality refers to the degree to which the written software meets the specifications prepared by the customer and his professional team. This means that errors included in the software specification are not considered and do not reduce the software quality, a characteristic that can be considered the approach's deficiency.

Juran's definition is aimed at achieving customer satisfaction, and views the fulfillment of customers' real needs as the true goal of software quality. Adopting the second definition demands that the developer invest significant professional efforts in examining and correcting, if necessary, the customer's requirements specifications. The main deficiency of this definition is the fact that it frees the customer of any professional responsibility for the accuracy and completeness of the software specifications. Also, following this conception, the customer is allowed to express his real needs, which may differ from the project specifications on one or more issues, at a very late stage of the project, even at the final stage. As a result, difficulties are expected to arise during the development process of the project, especially when attempting to prove how well the program fulfills the user's needs.

Additional aspects of software quality are included in the definition suggested by Pressman (Pressman, 2000, sec. 8.3), shown in Frame 2.4.

Frame 2.4	Software quality – Pressman's definition

Software quality is defined as:
Conformance to explicitly stated functional and performance requirements, explicitly documented development standards, and implicit characteristics that are expected of all professionally developed software.

Pressman's definition suggests three requirements for quality assurance that are to be met by the developer:

- Specific functional requirements, which refer mainly to the outputs of the software system.
- The software quality standards mentioned in the contract.
- Good Software Engineering Practices (GSEP), reflecting state-of-the-art professional practices, to be met by the developer even though not explicitly mentioned in the contract.

In effect, Pressman's definition provides operative directions for testing the degree to which the requirements are met.

2.5 Software quality assurance – definition and objectives

In this section we discuss:

- The alternative SQA definitions
- Software quality assurance compared with software quality control
- The objectives of SQA.

2.5.1 Software quality assurance definitions

One of the most commonly used definitions of software quality assurance (SQA) is offered by the IEEE Glossary (IEEE, 1991), cited in Frame 2.5.

Frame 2.5 **Software quality assurance – The IEEE definition**

Software quality assurance is:
1. A planned and systematic pattern of all actions necessary to provide adequate confidence that an item or product conforms to established technical requirements.
2. A set of activities designed to evaluate the process by which the products are developed or manufactured. Contrast with quality control.

This definition may be characterized in the following:

■ Plan and implement systematically. SQA is based on planning and the application of a variety of actions that are integrated into all the stages of the software development process. This is done in order to substantiate the client's confidence that the software product will meet all the technical requirements.
■ Refer to the software development process.
■ Refer to the specifications of the technical requirements.

Despite its emphasis on planning and systematic implementation, the IEEE definition restrains the scope of SQA in several directions, excluding maintenance and timetable and budget issues. This author adopts a broader conception of SQA that, of course, affects its definition. A broader definition, though placing additional burdens on the SQA function, is expected to yield better results and greater customer satisfaction. The main deviations from the IEEE definition are:

■ SQA should not be limited to the development process. Instead, it should be extended to cover the long years of service subsequent to product delivery. Adding issues directly related to the software product introduces quality issues that integrate software maintenance functions into the overall conception of SQA.
■ SQA actions should not be limited to the technical aspects of the functional requirements, but should include also activities that deal with scheduling and the budget. The reasoning behind this expansion in scope is the close relationship between timetable or budget failure and the meeting of functional technical requirements. Very often, when projects are under severe time constraints, professionally "dangerous" changes that can seriously harm the prospects of meeting the functional requirements are made in the project schedule. Similar undesirable results can be expected with projects that are under budgetary constraints and unable to cope with the inadequate resources allocated to the project and its maintenance.

The resulting expanded SQA definition is shown in Frame 2.6.

27

> **Frame 2.6   SQA – expanded definition**
>
> Software quality assurance is:
> A systematic, planned set of actions necessary to provide adequate
> confidence that the software development process or the maintenance
> process of a software system product conforms to established functional
> technical requirements as well as with the managerial requirements of keeping
> the schedule and operating within the budgetary confines.

The expanded SQA definition corresponds strongly with the concepts at the foundation of the ISO 9000 standards regarding SQA (see the various requirements of ISO 9000-3, 1997). The expanded definition also corresponds to the main outlines of the Capacity Maturity Model (CMM) for software (Paulk *et al.*, 1993; Tingey, 1997).

Table 2.2 compares elements of the expanded SQA definition with:

- The IEEE SQA definition
- The relevant ISO 9000-3 sections
- CMM requirements.

This book adopts the expanded definition of SQA, which will serve as the basis for the inclusion and evaluation of various components of the SQA system.

Table 2.2 The expanded SQA definition – comparisons with other versions

No.	SQA expanded definition	IEEE SQA definition	Relevant sections from ISO 9000–3	Relevant SEI-CMM requirements
1	Systematic, planned actions are required	+	Management responsibilities (4.1) Quality system (4.2) Contract review (4.3)	Software quality management Requirement management Software project planning Software tracking and oversight
2	Deals with the process of software development	+	Contract review (4.3) Design control (4.4) Control of customer-supplied product (4.7) Process control (4.9) Inspection and testing (4.10) Control of non-conforming product (4.13) Control of quality records (4.16) Statistical techniques (4.20)	Requirement management Software project planning Software tracking and oversight Software configuration management Software product engineering Peer review Software subcontractor management Quantitative process management Software quality management

Table 2.2 Continued

No.	SQA expanded definition	IEEE SQA definition	Relevant sections from ISO 9000–3	Relevant SEI-CMM requirements
3	Deals with software maintenance (re. the product)		Contract review – management concerns (4.3.2c) Process control (4.9) Servicing (4.19) Statistical techniques (4.20)	Requirement management Software project planning Software tracking and oversight Software product engineering Quantitative process management Software quality management
4	Deals with functional technical requirements	+	Contract review (4.3) Design control (4.4) Control of customer-supplied product (4.7) Inspection and testing (4.10) Control of non-conforming product (4.13)	Requirement management Software project planning Software tracking and oversight Software configuration management Software product engineering Peer reviews Software subcontractor management
5	Deals with scheduling requirements		Contract review – management concerns (4.3.2c) Identifying the schedule (4.4.2g) Suppliers' review of progress of software development (4.4.3)	Requirement management Software project planning Software tracking and oversight
6	Deals with budgetary controls		Identifying the schedule (4.4.2g)	Requirement management Software project planning Software tracking and oversight

2.5.2 Software quality assurance vs. software quality control

Two phrases are constantly repeated within the context of software quality: "Quality control" and "quality assurance". Are they synonymous? How are they related? According to the IEEE software quality assurance definition (see Frame 2.5), "quality control" is to be contrasted with "quality assurance".

These two terms represent separate and distinct concepts:

- **Quality control** is defined as "a set of activities designed to evaluate the quality of a developed or manufactured product" (IEEE, 1991); in other words, activities whose main objective is the withholding of any product that does not qualify. Accordingly, quality control inspection and other activities take place as the development or manufacturing of the product is completed yet before the product is shipped to the client.

■ The main objective of **quality assurance** is to minimize the cost of guaranteeing quality by a variety of activities performed throughout the development and manufacturing processes/stages. These activities prevent the causes of errors, and detect and correct them early in the development process. As a result, quality assurance activities substantially reduce the rate of products that do not qualify for shipment and, at the same time, reduce the costs of guaranteeing quality in most cases.

In sum:

(1) Quality control and quality assurance activities serve different objectives.

(2) Quality control activities are only a part of the total range of quality assurance activities.

2.5.3 The objectives of SQA activities

The objectives of SQA activities refer to the functional, managerial and economic aspects of software development and software maintenance. These objectives are listed in Frame 2.7.

Frame 2.7 **The objectives of SQA activities**

Software development (process-oriented):

1. Assuring an acceptable level of confidence that the software will conform to functional technical requirements.

2. Assuring an acceptable level of confidence that the software will conform to managerial scheduling and budgetary requirements.

3. Initiating and managing of activities for the improvement and greater efficiency of software development and SQA activities. This means improving the prospects that the functional and managerial requirements will be achieved while reducing the costs of carrying out the software development and SQA activities.

Software maintenance (product-oriented):

1. Assuring with an acceptable level of confidence that the software maintenance activities will conform to the functional technical requirements.

2. Assuring with an acceptable level of confidence that the software maintenance activities will conform to managerial scheduling and budgetary requirements.

3. Initiating and managing activities to improve and increase the efficiency of software maintenance and SQA activities. This involves improving the prospects of achieving functional and managerial requirements while reducing costs.

2.6 Software quality assurance and software engineering

According to the IEEE (1991), **software engineering** is defined as follows:

(1) The application of a systematic, disciplined, quantifiable approach to the development, operation and maintenance of software; that is, the application of engineering to software.

(2) The study of approaches as in (1).

The characteristics of software engineering, especially the systematic, disciplined and quantitative approach at its core, make the software engineering environment a good infrastructure for achieving SQA objectives. The methodologies and tools that are applied by software engineering determine, to a considerable extent, the level of quality to be expected from the software process and the maintenance services. Therefore, it is desirable that when making decisions about software methodologies and tools, SQA considerations be added to the efficiency and economy considerations associated with software engineering.

It is commonly accepted that cooperation between software engineers and the SQA team is the appropriate way to achieve efficient and economic development and maintenance activities that, at the same time, assure the quality of the product of these activities.

Summary

(1) Define software, software quality and software quality assurance.

- **Software**, from the SQA perspective, is the combination of computer programs (the "code"), procedures, documentation, and data necessary for operating the software system. The combination of all four components is needed to assure the quality of the development process as well as the ensuing long years of maintenance.
- **Software quality**, according to Pressman's definition, is the degree of conformance to specific functional requirements, specified software quality standards, and Good Software Engineering Practices (GSEP).
- **Software quality assurance:** this book adopts an expanded definition of the widely accepted IEEE definition of software quality assurance. According to the expanded definition, software quality assurance is the systematic, planned set of actions necessary to provide adequate confidence that a software development or maintenance process conforms to established functional technical requirements as well as the managerial requirements of keeping to schedules and operating within the budget.

(2) Distinguish between software errors, software faults and software failures.

- **Software errors** are sections of the code that are partially or totally incorrect as a result of a grammatical, logical or other mistake made by a systems analyst, a programmer, or another member of the software development team.

- **Software faults** are software errors that cause the incorrect functioning of the software during a specific application.
- **Software faults** become **software failures** only when they are "activated", that is, when a user tries to apply the specific software section that is faulty. Thus, the root of any **software failure** is a **software error.**

(3) Identify the various causes of software errors.

There are nine causes of software errors: faulty requirements definition, client–developer communication failures, deliberate deviations from software require-ments, logical design errors, coding errors, non-compliance with documentation and coding instructions, shortcomings of the testing process, procedure errors, and documentation errors. It should be emphasized that all causes of error are human, the work of systems analysts, programmers, software testers, documentation experts, and even clients and their representatives.

(4) Explain the objectives of software quality assurance activities.

The objectives of SQA activities for software development and maintenance are:

(1) Assuring, with acceptable levels of confidence, conformance to functional tech-nical requirements.
(2) Assuring, with acceptable levels of confidence, conformance to managerial requirements of scheduling and budgets.
(3) Initiating and managing activities for the improvement and greater efficiency of software development and SQA activities.

(5) Distinguish and explain the differences between software quality assurance and quality control.

Quality control is a set of activities carried out with the main objective of withhold-ing products from shipment if they do not qualify. In contrast, **quality assurance** is meant to minimize the costs of quality by introducing a variety of activities through-out the development and maintenance process in order to prevent the causes of errors, detect them, and correct them in the early stages of development. As a result, quality assurance substantially reduces the rates of non-qualifying products.

(6) Explain the relationship between software quality assurance and software engineering.

Software engineering is the application of a systematic, disciplined, quantifiable approach to the development, operation and maintenance of software. The charac-teristics of software engineering, especially its systematic, disciplined and quantitative approach, make software engineering a good environment for achiev-ing SQA objectives. It is commonly accepted that cooperation between software engineers and the SQA team is the way to achieve efficient and economic develop-ment and maintenance activities that, at the same time, assure the quality of the products of these activities.

Selected bibliography

1. Crosby, P. B. (1979) *Quality is Free*, McGraw-Hill, New York.
2. IEEE (1991) "IEEE Std 610.12-1990 – IEEE Standard Glossary of Software Engineering Terminology", Corrected Edition, February 1991, in *IEEE Software Engineering Standards Collection*, The Institute of Electrical and Electronics Engineers, New York.
3. ISO (1997) *ISO 9000-3:1997(E), Quality Management and Quality Assurance Standards – Part 3: Guidelines for the Application of ISO 9001:1994 to the Development, Supply, Installation and Maintenance of Computer Software*, 2nd edn. International Organization for Standardization (ISO), Geneva.
4. ISO/IEC (2001) "ISO 9000-3:2001 Software and System Engineering – Guidelines for the Application of ISO 9001:2000 to Software, Final draft", International Organization for Standardization (ISO), Geneva, unpublished draft, December 2001.
5. Juran, J. M. (1988) *Juran's Quality Control Handbook*, 4th edn, J. M. Juran, Editor in Chief; I. M. Gryne, Associate Editor. McGraw-Hill, New York.
6. Paulk, M. C., Curtis, B., Chrissis, M. B. and Weber, C. V. (1993) *Capability Maturity Model for Software, Version 1.1*, CMU/SEI-93-TR-24, ESC-TR-93-177, Software Engineering Institute, Carnegie Mellon University, Pittsburgh, PA.
7. Pressman, R. S. (2000) *Software Engineering – A Practitioner's Approach*, European adaptation by D. Ince, 5th edn, McGraw-Hill International, London.
8. Tingey, M. O. (1997) *Comparing ISO 9000, Malcolm Baldridge, and the SEI CMM for Software. A Reference and Selection Guide*, Prentice Hall, Upper Saddle River, NJ.

Review questions

2.1 A software system comprises four main components.

  (1) List the four components of a software system.
  (2) How does the quality of each component contribute to the quality of the developed software?
  (3) How does the quality of each component contribute to the quality of the software maintenance?

2.2 (1) Define software error, software fault and software failure. Explain the differences between these undesirable software statuses.

  (2) Suggest a situation where a new type of software failure ("bug") appears in a software package that has been serving 300 clients for the first time six years since the software package was first sold to the public.

2.3 (1) List and briefly describe the various causes of software errors.

  (2) Classify the causes of error according to the groups responsible for the error: the client's staff, the systems analysts, the programmers, the testing staff – or is it a shared responsibility belonging to more than one group?

2.4 What are the differences between the IEEE definition of SQA and the expanded definition used in this book?

2.5 Mr Johnson is a customer of the Adams and Lincoln stores belonging to the Eiffel chain (see Section 2.3). His purchase records and returned goods records are as follows:

Month	Adams Store Purchases ($000)	Adams Store Returned goods ($000)	Lincoln Store Purchases ($000)	Lincoln Store Returned goods ($000)
Jan 2000	100	20	60	5
Feb 2000	120	10	40	–
Mar 2000	10	–	30	10
Apr 2000	80	5	50	10
May 2000	30	–	20	–
Jun 2000	60	20	30	10
Jul 2000	10	–	40	–
Aug 2000	60	5	10	–
Sep 2000	20	–	20	5
Oct 2000	20	5	40	10
Nov 2000	40	–	20	–
Dec 2000	20	–	60	5
Jan 2001	30	10	40	–
Feb 2001	60	5	30	5
Mar 2001	20	5	40	10

(1) Find for which of the months – Jan. 2001, Feb. 2001 or Mar. 2001 – does Mr Johnson qualify for the 5% discount? What is the sum discounted? Calculate according to the correct procedure.

(2) According to the erroneous procedures, find for which of the months – Jan. 2001, Feb. 2001 or Mar. 2001 – does Mr Johnson qualify for the 5% discount in the Adams store and in the Lincoln store? What is the sum discounted?

2.6 According to the IEEE definition of SQA, quality control (QC) is not equated with quality assurance (QA).

(1) In what respects does QC vary from QA?

(2) Why can QC be considered part of QA?

2.7 Examine the definitions of SQA and the objectives of SQA activities.

(1) Is there a correspondence between the two definitions?

(2) If yes, show how the objectives of SQA activities aim at the implementation of the SQA concepts.

Topics for discussion

2.1 A programmer claims that because only a small proportion of software errors turn into software failures, it is unnecessary to make substantial investments in the prevention and elimination of software errors.

(1) Do you agree with this view?

(2) Discuss the outcome of accepting these views.

2.2 George Wise is an exceptional programmer. Testing his software modules reveals very few errors, far fewer than the team's average. He keeps his schedule promptly, and only rarely is he late in completing his task. He always finds original ways to solve programming difficulties, and uses an original, individual version of the coding style. He dislikes preparing the required documentation, and rarely does it according to the team's templates.

A day after completing a challenging task, on time, he was called to the office of the department's chief software engineer. Instead of being praised for his accomplishments (as he expected), he was warned by the company's chief software engineer that he would be fired unless he began to fully comply with the team's coding and documentation instructions.

(1) Do you agree with the position taken by the department's chief software engineer?
(2) If yes, could you suggest why his or her position was so decisive?

2.3 Pressman's definition of quality requires the client to specify the software requirements because only documented requirements are binding for the developer. Any omissions or errors made by the client are considered as his or her fault, and not listed among the developer's errors.

(1) How can a client be sure that his or her organization has the professional capabilities to cope with this issue?
(2) In what ways can the developer support the client in this matter?
(3) Suggest pro and con arguments to Pressman's definition of the client's responsibility.

2.4 It is claimed that the expanded definition of SQA supports those who are interested in increasing client satisfaction.

(1) Do you agree with this claim?
(2) If yes, provide arguments to substantiate your position.

2.5 (1) Examine the correct and erroneous procedures determining the discount qualification outlined in Table 2.1.
(2) List the procedure errors.

Software quality factors

We have already established (see Chapter 2) that the requirements document is one of the most important elements for achieving software quality. Here we ask: What is a "good" software requirements document? We want to explore what subjects and aspects of software use should be covered in the document.

This chapter is, therefore, dedicated to the review of the wide spectrum of aspects of software use that may be operative throughout the life cycle of software systems. Some SQA models suggest that the wide spectrum of requirements should be classified into 11 to 15 factors (subject areas) that can be amalgamated into three or four categories.

After completing this chapter, you will be able to:

■ Explain the need for comprehensive requirements documents and characterize the contents of such documents.
■ Explain the structure (categories and factors) of McCall's classic factor model.

- List the factors, other than those included in McCall's model, that are suggested by the alternative SQA models.
- Identify who is interested in the definition of quality requirements.

3.1 The need for comprehensive software quality requirements

- "Our new sales information system seems okay, the invoices are correct, the inventory records are correct, the discounts granted to our clients exactly follow our very complicated discount policy, **but** our new sales information system frequently fails, usually at least twice a day, each time for twenty minutes or more. Yesterday it took an hour and half before we could get back to work . . . . Imagine how embarrassing it is to store managers . . . . Softbest, the software house that developed our computerized sales system, claims no responsibility . . . ."

- "Just half a year ago we launched our new product – the radar detector. The firmware RD-8.1, embedded in this product, seems to be the cause for its success. **But,** when we began planning the development of a European version of the product, we found out that though the products will be almost similar, our software development department needs to develop new firmware; almost all the design and programming will be new."

- "Believe it or not, our software package 'Blackboard' for schoolteachers, launched just three months ago, is already installed in 187 schools. The development team just returned from a week in Hawaii, their vacation bonus. **But** we have been suddenly receiving daily complaints from the 'Blackboard' maintenance team. They claim that the lack of failure-detection features in the software, in addition to the poor programmer's manual, have caused them to invest more than the time estimated to deal with bugs or adding minor software changes that were agreed as part of purchasing contracts with clients."

- "The new version of our loan contract software is really accurate. We have already processed 1200 customer requests, and checked each of the output contracts. There were no errors. **But** we did face a severe unexpected problem – training a new staff member to use this software takes about two weeks. This is a real problem in customers' departments suffering from high employee turnover . . . . The project team says that as they were not required to deal with training issues in time, an additional two to three months of work will be required to solve the problem."

There are some characteristic common to all these "but's":

- All the software projects satisfactorily fulfilled the basic requirements for correct calculations (correct inventory figures, correct average class's score, correct loan interest, etc.).
- All the software projects suffered from poor performance in important areas such as maintenance, reliability, software reuse, or training.

■ The cause for the poor performance of the developed software projects in these areas was the lack of predefined requirements to cover these important aspects of the software's functionality.

The need for a comprehensive definition of requirements

There is a need for a comprehensive definition of requirements that will cover all attributes of software and aspects of the use of software, including usability aspects, reusability aspects, maintainability aspects, and so forth in order to assure the full satisfaction of the users.

The great variety of issues related to the various attributes of software and its use and maintenance, as defined in software requirements documents, can be classified into content groups called *quality factors*. We expect the team responsible for defining the software requirements of a software system to examine the need to define the requirements that belong to each factor. Software requirement documents are expected to differ in the emphasis placed on the various factors, a reflection of the differences to be found among software projects. Thus, we can expect that not all the factors will be universally "represented" in all the requirements documents.

The next sections deal with the classification of quality requirements into quality factors. Obviously, only the major approaches to this topic will be covered.

3.2 Classifications of software requirements into software quality factors

Several models of software quality factors and their categorization in factor categories have been suggested over the years. The classic model of software quality factors, suggested by McCall, consists of 11 factors (McCall *et al.*, 1977). Subsequent models, consisting of 12 to 15 factors, were suggested by Deutsch and Willis (1988) and by Evans and Marciniak (1987). The alternative models do not differ substantially from McCall's model. The McCall factor model, despite the quarter of a century of its "maturation", continues to provide a practical, up-to-date method for classifying software requirements (Pressman, 2000).

McCall's factor model

McCall's factor model classifies all software requirements into 11 software quality factors. The 11 factors are grouped into three categories – product operation, product revision and product transition – as follows:

■ **Product operation factors:** Correctness, Reliability, Efficiency, Integrity, Usability.
■ **Product revision factors:** Maintainability, Flexibility, Testability.
■ **Product transition factors:** Portability, Reusability, Interoperability.

McCall's model and its categories are illustrated by the McCall model of software quality factors tree (see Figure 3.1).

The next three sections are dedicated to a detailed description of the software quality factors included in each of McCall's categories.

3.3   Product operation software quality factors

According to McCall's model, five software quality factors are included in the product operation category, all of which deal with requirements that directly affect the daily operation of the software. These factors are as follows.

Correctness
Correctness requirements are defined in a list of the software system's required outputs, such as a query display of a customer's balance in the sales accounting information system, or the air supply as a function of temperature specified by the firmware of an industrial control unit. Output specifications are usually multidimensional; some common dimensions include:

■   The output mission (e.g., sales invoice printout, and red alarms when temperature rises above 250°F).

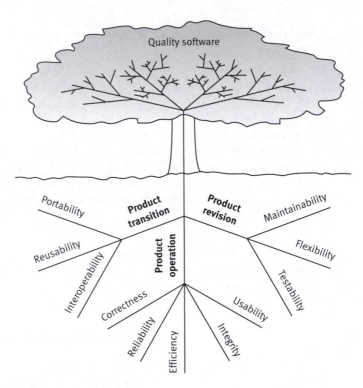

Figure 3.1: McCall's factor model tree
Source: Based on McCall *et al.*, 1977

- The required accuracy of those outputs that can be adversely affected by inaccurate data or inaccurate calculations.
- The completeness of the output information, which can be adversely affected by incomplete data.
- The up-to-dateness of the information (defined as the time between the event and its consideration by the software system).
- The availability of the information (the reaction time, defined as the time needed to obtain the requested information or as the requested reaction time of the firmware installed in a computerized apparatus).
- The standards for coding and documenting the software system.

Example
The correctness requirements of a club membership information system consisted of the following:

- The output mission: A defined list of 11 types of reports, four types of standard letters to members and eight types of queries, which were to be displayed on the monitor on request.
- The required accuracy of the outputs: The probability for a non-accurate output, containing one or more mistakes, will not exceed 1%.
- The completeness of the output information: The probability of missing data about a member, his attendance at club events, and his payments will not exceed 1%.
- The up-to-dateness of the information: Not more than two working days for information about participation in events and not more than one working day for information about entry of member payments and personal data.
- The availability of information: Reaction time for queries will be less than two seconds on average; the reaction time for reports will be less than four hours.
- The required standards and guidelines: The software and its documentation are required to comply with the client's guidelines.

Reliability
Reliability requirements deal with failures to provide service. They determine the maximum allowed software system failure rate, and can refer to the entire system or to one or more of its separate functions.

Examples
(1) The failure frequency of a heart-monitoring unit that will operate in a hospital's intensive care ward is required to be less than one in 20 years. Its heart attack detection function is required to have a failure rate of less than one per million cases.

(2) One requirement of the new software system to be installed in the main branch of Independence Bank, which operates 120 branches, is that it will not fail, on average, more than 10 minutes per month during the bank's office hours. In addition, the probability that the off-time (the time needed for repair and recovery of all the bank's services) be more than 30 minutes is required to be less than 0.5%.

Efficiency

Efficiency requirements deal with the hardware resources needed to perform all the functions of the software system in conformance to all other requirements. The main hardware resources to be considered are the computer's processing capabilities (measured in MIPS – million instructions per second, MHz or megahertz – million cycles per second, etc.), its data storage capability in terms of memory and disk capacity (measured in MBs – megabytes, GBs – gigabytes, TBs – terabytes, etc.) and the data communication capability of the communication lines (usually measured in KBPS – kilobits per second, MBPS – megabits per second, and GBPS – gigabits per second). The requirements may include the maximum values at which the hardware resources will be applied in the developed software system or the firmware.

Another type of efficiency requirement deals with the time between recharging of the system's portable units, such as, information systems units located in portable computers, or meteorological units placed outdoors.

Examples

(1) A chain of stores is considering two alternative bids for a software system. Both bids consist of placing the same computers in the chain's headquarters and its branches. The bids differ solely in the storage volume: 20 GB per branch computer and 100 GB in the head office computer (Bid A); 10 GB per branch computer and 30 GB in the head office computer (Bid B). There is also a difference in the number of communication lines required: Bid A consists of three communication lines of 28.8 KBPS between each branch and the head office, whereas Bid B is based on two communication lines of the same capacity between each branch and the head office. In this case, it is clear that Bid B is more efficient than Bid A because fewer hardware resources are required.

(2) An outdoor meteorological unit, equipped with a 1000 milli-ampere hour cell, should be capable of supplying the power requirements of the unit for at least 30 days. The system performs measurements once per hour, logs the results, and transmits the results once a day to the meteorological center by means of wireless communication.

Integrity

Integrity requirements deal with the software system security, that is, requirements to prevent access to unauthorized persons, to distinguish between the majority of personnel allowed to see the information ("read permit") and a limited group who will be allowed to add and change data ("write permit"), and so forth.

Example

The Engineering Department of a local municipality operates a GIS (Geographic Information System). The Department is planning to allow citizens access to its GIS files through the Internet. The software requirements include the possibility of viewing and copying but not inserting changes in the maps of their assets as well as any other asset in the municipality's area ("read only" permit). Access will be denied to plans in progress and to those maps defined by the Department's head as limited access documents.

Usability

Usability requirements deal with the scope of staff resources needed to train a new employee and to operate the software system. For more about usability see Juristo *et al.* (2001), Donahue (2001) and Ferre *et al.* (2001).

Example

The software usability requirements document for the new help desk system initiated by a home appliance service company lists the following specifications:

(a) A staff member should be able to handle at least 60 service calls a day.

(b) Training a new employee will take no more than two days (16 training hours), immediately at the end of which the trainee will be able to handle 45 service calls a day.

3.4   Product revision software quality factors

According to the McCall model of software quality factors, three quality factors comprise the product revision category. These factors deal with those requirements that affect the complete range of software maintenance activities: corrective maintenance (correction of software faults and failures), adaptive maintenance (adapting the current software to additional circumstances and customers without changing the software) and perfective maintenance (enhancement and improvement of existing software with respect to locally limited issues). These are as follows.

Maintainability

Maintainability requirements determine the efforts that will be needed by users and maintenance personnel to identify the reasons for software failures, to correct the failures, and to verify the success of the corrections. This factor's requirements refer to the modular structure of software, the internal program documentation, and the programmer's manual, among other items.

Example
Typical maintainability requirements:

(a) The size of a software module will not exceed 30 statements.
(b) The programming will adhere to the company coding standards and guidelines.

Flexibility

The capabilities and efforts required to support adaptive maintenance activities are covered by the flexibility requirements. These include the resources (i.e. in man-days) required to adapt a software package to a variety of customers of the same trade, of various extents of activities, of different ranges of products and so on. This factor's requirements also support perfective maintenance activities, such as changes and additions to the software in order to improve its service and to adapt it to changes in the firm's technical or commercial environment.

Example
TSS (teacher support software) deals with the documentation of pupil achievements, the calculation of final grades, the printing of term grade documents, and the automatic printing of warning letters to parents of failing pupils. The software specifications included the following flexibility requirements:

(a) The software should be suitable for teachers of all subjects and all school levels (elementary, junior and high schools).
(b) Non-professionals should be able to create new types of reports according to the schoolteacher's requirements and/or the city's education department demands.

Testability

Testability requirements deal with the testing of an information system as well as with its operation. Testability requirements for the ease of testing are related to special features in the programs that help the tester, for instance by providing predefined intermediate results and log files. Testability requirements related to software operation include automatic diagnostics performed by the software system prior to starting the system, to find out whether all components of the software system are in working order and to obtain a report about the detected faults. Another type of these requirements deals with automatic diagnostic checks applied by the maintenance technicians to detect the causes of software failures.

Example
An industrial computerized control unit is programmed to calculate various measures of production status, report the performance level of the machinery, and operate a warning signal in predefined situations. One testability

requirement demanded was to develop a set of standard test data with known system expected correct reactions in each stage. This standard test data is to be run every morning, before production begins, to check whether the computerized unit reacts properly.

3.5 Product transition software quality factors

According to McCall, three quality factors are included in the product transition category, a category that pertains to the adaptation of software to other environments and its interaction with other software systems.

Portability

Portability requirements tend to the adaptation of a software system to other environments consisting of different hardware, different operating systems, and so forth. These requirements make it possible to continue using the same basic software in diverse situations or to use it simultaneously in diverse hardware and operating systems situations.

Example

A software package designed and programmed to operate in a Windows 2000 environment is required to allow low-cost transfer to Linux and Windows NT environments.

Reusability

Reusability requirements deal with the use of software modules originally designed for one project in a new software project currently being developed. They may also enable future projects to make use of a given module or a group of modules of the currently developed software. The reuse of software is expected to save development resources, shorten the development period, and provide higher quality modules. These benefits of higher quality are based on the assumption that most of the software faults have already been detected by the quality assurance activities performed on the original software, by users of the original software, and during its earlier reuses. The issues of software reuse became a subject of software industry standards (see IEEE, 1999).

Example

A software development unit has been required to develop a software system for the operation and control of a hotel swimming pool that serves hotel guests and members of a pool club. Although the management did not define any reusability requirements, the unit's team leader, after analyzing the information processing requirements of the hotel's spa, decided to add the reusability requirement that some of the software modules for the pool should be designed and programmed in a way that will allow its reuse in the spa's future software system, which is planned to be developed next year.

These modules will allow:

- Entrance validity checks of membership cards and visit recording.
- Restaurant billing.
- Processing of membership renewal letters.

Interoperability
Interoperability requirements focus on creating interfaces with other software systems or with other equipment firmware (for example, the firmware of the production machinery and testing equipment interfaces with the production control software). Interoperability requirements can specify the name(s) of the software or firmware for which interface is required. They can also specify the output structure accepted as standard in a specific industry or applications area.

Example
The firmware of a medical laboratory's equipment is required to process its results (output) according to a standard data structure that can then serve as input for a number of standard laboratory information systems.

3.6 Alternative models of software quality factors

Two factor models, appearing during the late 1980s, considered to be alternatives to the McCall classic factor model (McCall *et al.*, 1977), deserve discussion:

- The Evans and Marciniak factor model (Evans and Marciniak, 1987).
- The Deutsch and Willis factor model (Deutsch and Willis, 1988).

3.6.1 Formal comparison of the alternative models

A formal comparison of the factor models reveals:

- Both alternative models exclude only one of McCall's 11 factors, namely the testability factor.
- The Evans and Marciniak factor model consists of 12 factors that are classified into three categories.
- The Deutsch and Willis factor model consists of 15 factors that are classified into four categories.

Taken together, five new factors were suggested by the two alternative factor models:

- Verifiability (by both models)
- Expandability (by both models)

- Safety (by Deutsch and Willis)
- Manageability (by Deutsch and Willis)
- Survivability (by Deutsch and Willis).

The factors included in the various factor models are compared in Table 3.1. The additional factors are defined as follows.

Verifiability (suggested by Evans and Marciniak)

Verifiability requirements define design and programming features that enable efficient verification of the design and programming. Most verifiability requirements refer to modularity, to simplicity, and to adherence to documentation and programming guidelines.

Expandability (suggested by Evans and Marciniak, and Deutsch and Willis)

Expandability requirements refer to future efforts that will be needed to serve larger populations, improve service, or add new applications in order to improve usability. The majority of these requirements are covered by McCall's flexibility factor.

Safety (suggested by Deutsch and Willis)

Safety requirements are meant to eliminate conditions hazardous to operators of equipment as a result of errors in process control software. These errors can result in inappropriate reactions to dangerous situations or to the failure to provide alarm signals when the dangerous conditions to be detected by the software arise.

Table 3.1: Comparison of McCall's factor model and alternative models

No.	Software quality factor	McCall's classic model	Alternative factor models	
			Evans and Marciniak	Deutsch and Willis
1	Correctness	+	+	+
2	Reliability	+	+	+
3	Efficiency	+	+	+
4	Integrity	+	+	+
5	Usability	+	+	+
6	Maintainability	+	+	+
7	Flexibility	+	+	+
8	Testability	+		
9	Portability	+	+	+
10	Reusability	+	+	+
11	Interoperability	+	+	+
12	Verifiability		+	+
13	Expandability		+	+
14	Safety			+
15	Manageability			+
16	Survivability			+

Example
In a chemical plant, a computerized system controls the flow of acid according to pressure and temperature changes occurring during production. The safety requirements refer to the system's computerized reactions in cases of dangerous situations and also specify what kinds of alarms are needed in each case.

Manageability (suggested by Deutsch and Willis)
Manageability requirements refer to the administrative tools that support software modification during the software development and maintenance periods, such as configuration management, software change procedures, and the like.

Example
"Chemilog" is a software system that automatically logs the flows of chemicals into various containers to allow for later analysis of the efficiency of production units. The development and issue of new versions and releases of "Chemilog" are controlled by the Software Development Board, whose members act according to the company's software modifications procedure.

Survivability (suggested by Deutsch and Willis)
Survivability requirements refer to the continuity of service. These define the minimum time allowed between failures of the system, and the maximum time permitted for recovery of service, two factors that pertain to service continuity. Although these requirements may refer separately to total and to partial failures of services, they are especially geared to failures of essential functions or services. Significant similarity exists between the survivability factor and the reliability factor described in McCall's model.

Example
Taya operates a national lottery, held once a week. About 400 000 to 700 000 bets are placed weekly. The new software system the customer (the Taya National Lottery) has ordered will be highly computerized and based on a communication system that connects all the betting machines to the central computer. To its other high reliability requirements, Taya has added the following survivability requirement: The probability that unrecoverable damage to the betting files will occur in case of any system failure is to be limited to less than one in a million.

3.6.2 Comparison of the factor models – content analysis

After comparing the contents of the factor models, we find that two of the five additional factors, Expandability and Survivability, actually resemble factors already included in McCall's factor model, though under different names, Flexibility and Reliability. In addition, McCall's Testability factor can be considered as one element in his own Maintainability factor.

47

3.7 Who is interested in the definition of quality requirements?

This implies that the differences between the three factor models are much smaller than initially perceived. That is, the alternative factor models add only three "new" factors to McCall's model:

- Both models add the factor Verifiability.
- The Deutsch and Willis model adds the factors Safety and Manageability.

3.6.3 Structure of the alternative factor models

Nevertheless, despite their similarities, the categories employed by the alternative factor models and the classification of the specific factors into these categories differ from those offered by McCall's model. Table 3.2 compares the structure of the three models according to the factors and their classification into the categories.

3.7 Who is interested in the definition of quality requirements?

Naturally, one might think that only the client is interested in thoroughly defining his requirements in order to assure the quality of the software product he contracted. The requirements document he prepares does indeed serve as a fundamental protection against low quality. However, our analysis of the various quality factors indicates how the software developer can add requirements that represent his own interest. Following are some examples:

(1) **Reusability requirements.** In cases where the client anticipates development in the near future of an additional software system having strong similarities to the present software, the client will himself initiate reusability requirements. In other cases, the client is interested in reusing parts of software systems that were developed earlier in a new system. However, it is more likely that the developer, who serves a great variety of clients, will recognize the potential benefits of reuse, and will enter reusability into the list of requirements to be fulfilled by the project team.

(2) **Verifiability requirements.** These requirements are meant to improve the design reviews and software tests carried out during software development. Their aim is to save development resources and they are, therefore, of interest to developers. The client, however, is usually uninterested in placing requirements that deal with the internal activities of the developer team.

Some quality factors not included in the typical client's requirements document may, in many cases, interest the developer. The following list of quality factors usually interest the developer whereas they may raise very little interest on the part of the client:

- Portability
- Reusability
- Verifiability.

Table 3.2: Comparison of the structure of McCall's factor model *vis-à-vis* the three alternative models

McCall's model categories	Software quality factors	Deutsch and Willis model categories				Evans and Marciniak model categories		
		Functional	Performance	Change	Management	Design	Performance	Adaptation
Product operation	Correctness		x			x		
	Reliability	x					x	
	Efficiency		x				x	
	Integrity	x					x	
	Usability	x					x	
Product revision	Maintainability			x		x		
	Flexibility			x				x
	Testability							
Product transition	Portability			x				x
	Reusability			x				x
	Interoperability		x					x
Factors of the alternative models	Verifiability					x		
	Expandability			x	x			x
	Safety		x					
	Manageability				x			
	Survivability	x						

requirements documents:

- The client's requirements document
- The developer's additional requirements document.

3.8 Software compliance with quality factors

Throughout the software development process, the extent to which the process complies with the requirements of the various quality factors is examined by design reviews, software inspections, software tests, and so forth. Comprehensive discussions of design reviews, software testing, software quality metrics and other tools for verifying and validating the quality of software are provided in the balance of this book.

Furthermore, the software product's compliance to the requirements belonging to the various quality factors is measured by software quality metrics, measures that quantify the degree of compliance. In order to allow for valid measurements of compliance, sub-factors have been defined for those quality factors that represent a wide range of attributes and aspects of software use. Software quality metrics are suggested for each of these sub-factors. Chapter 21 is dedicated to the subject of software metrics.

Table 3.3 presents some of these sub-factors, the majority of which were suggested by Evans and Marciniak (1987).

Table 3.3: Factors and sub-factors

Factor model	Software quality factors	Sub-factors
McCall's model: Product operation category	Correctness	Accuracy Completeness Up-to-dateness Availability (response time) Coding and documentation guidelines compliance (consistency)
	Reliability	System reliability Application reliability Computational failure recovery Hardware failure recovery
	Efficiency	Efficiency of processing Efficiency of storage Efficiency of communication Efficiency of power usage (for portable units)
	Integrity	Access control Access audit
	Usability	Operability Training

Table 3.3 Continued

Factor model	Software quality factors	Sub-factors
McCall's model: Product revision category	Maintainability	Simplicity Modularity Self-descriptiveness Coding and documentation guidelines compliance (consistency) Document accessibility
	Flexibility	Modularity Generality Simplicity Self-descriptiveness
	Testability	User testability Failure maintenance testability Traceability
McCall's model: Product transition category	Portability	Software system independence Modularity Self descriptive
	Reusability	Modularity Document accessibility Software system independence Application independence Self descriptive Generality Simplicity
	Interoperability	Commonality System compatibility Software system independence Modularity
Factors of the alternative models	Verifiability	Coding and documentation guidelines compliance (consistency) Document accessibility Traceability Modularity
	Expandability	Extensibility Modularity Generality Simplicity Self-descriptiveness
	Safety	Avoidance of hazardous operating situations Unsafe conditions alarm reliability
	Manageability	Completeness and ease of support of infrastructure services for software modification in the development process Completeness and ease of support of infrastructure services for software modification in the maintenance activities
	Survivability	System reliability Application reliability Computational failure recovery Hardware failure recovery

As you have probably noticed, several sub-factors relate to more than one factor. This reflects the fact that some attributes contribute to successful compliance in more than one aspect of software use. For example, simplicity (a sub-factor) contributes to maintainability, flexibility, reusability and expandability factors.

Summary

(1) The need for comprehensive requirements documents and their contents.

Many cases of low customer satisfaction are situations where software projects have satisfactorily fulfilled the basic requirements of correctness, while suffering from poor performance in other important areas such as maintenance, reliability, software reuse, or training. One of the main causes for these lapses is the lack of defined requirements pertaining to these aspects of software functionality. Therefore, there is a need for the comprehensive definition of requirements that will cover all aspects of software use throughout all stages of the software life cycle.

Factor models define the broad spectrum of software requirements. We expected that those individuals who define software requirements will refer to each factor and, accordingly, examine the need to incorporate the respective requirements in their requirements documents.

(2) The structure (categories and factors) of McCall's classic factor model.

McCall's factor model classifies all software requirements into 11 software quality factors. The 11 factors are grouped into three categories – product operation, product revision and product transition – as follows:

- **Product operation factors:** Correctness, Reliability, Efficiency, Integrity, Usability.
- **Product revision factors:** Maintainability, Flexibility, Testability.
- **Product transition factors:** Portability, Reusability, Interoperability.

(3) The additional factors suggested by alternative factor models.

The two factor models from the late 1980s, alternatives to the McCall classic factor model, are:

- The Evans and Marciniak factor model.
- The Deutsch and Willis factor model.

These alternative models suggest adding five factors to McCall's model. Two of these factors are very similar to two of McCall's factors; only three factors are "new":

- Both models add the factor Verifiability.
- The Deutsch and Willis model adds the factors Safety and Manageability.

(4) Those interested in defining software quality requirements.

The client is not the only party interested in thoroughly defining the requirements that assure the quality of the software product. The developer is often interested in adding requirements that represent his own interests, such as reusability, verifiability and portability requirements. These may not, however, be of interest to the client. Thus, one can expect that a project will be carried out according to two requirements documents:

■ The client's requirements document
■ The developer's additional requirements document.

Selected bibliography

1. Deutsch, M. S. and Willis, R. R. (1988) *Software Quality Engineering, A Total Technical Management Approach*, Ch. 3, Prentice Hall, Englewood Cliffs, NJ.
2. Donahue G. M. (2001) "Usability and the bottom line", *IEEE Software*, 18 (1), 31–37.
3. Evans, M. W. and Marciniak, J. J. (1987) *Software Quality Assurance and Management*, Chs 7 and 8, John Wiley & Sons, New York.
4. Ferre, X., Juristo, N., Windl, H. and Constantine, L. (2001) "Introducing usability", *IEEE Software*, 18 (1), 20–21.
5. IEEE (1999) "IEEE Std 1517-1999 – IEEE Standard for Information Technology – Software Life Cycle Processes – Reuse Processes", in *IEEE Software Engineering Standards Collection*, The Institute of Electrical and Electronics Engineers, New York.
6. Juristo, N., Windl, H. and Constantine, L. (2001) "Usability basics for software developers", *IEEE Software*, 18 (1), 22–29.
7. McCall, J., Richards, P. and Walters, G. (1977) *Factors in Software Quality*, Vols 1–3, NTIS AD-A049-014, 015, 055, November 1977.
8. Pressman, R. S. (2000) *Software Engineering – A Practitioner's Approach*, European adaptation by D. Ince, 5th edn, Ch. 19, McGraw-Hill International, London.
9. Vincent, J., Waters, A. and Sinclair, J. (1988) *Software Quality Assurance*, Vol. 2, *A Program Guide*, Appendix B, Prentice Hall, Englewood Cliffs, NJ.

Review questions

3.1 (1) What are the three factor categories belonging to McCall's factor model?
(2) What factors are included in each of the categories?

3.2 The software requirement document for the tender for development of "Super-lab", a software system for managing a hospital laboratory, consists of chapters according to the required quality factors as follows: correctness, reliability, efficiency, integrity, usability, maintainability, flexibility, testability, portability, reusability and interoperability. In the following table you will find sections taken from the mentioned requirements document. For each section, fill in the name of the factor that best fits the requirement (choose only one factor per requirements section).

No.	Section taken from the software requirements document	Requirements factor
1	The probability that the "Super-lab" software system will be found in a state of failure during peak hours (9 am to 4 pm) is required to be below 0.5%.	
2	The "Super-lab" software system will enable direct transfer of laboratory results to those files of hospitalized patients managed by the "MD-File" software package.	
3	The "Super-lab" software system will include a module that prepares a detailed report of the patient's laboratory test results during his or her current hospitalization. (This report will serve as an appendix to the family physician's file.) The time required to obtain this printed report will be less than 60 seconds; the level of accuracy and completeness will be at least 99%.	
4	The "Super-lab" software to be developed for hospital laboratory use may be adapted later for private laboratory use.	
5	The training of a laboratory technician, requiring no more than three days, will enable the technician to reach level C of "Super-lab" software usage. This means that he or she will be able to manage reception of 20 patients per hour.	
6	The "Super-lab" software system will record a detailed users' log. In addition, the system will report attempts by unauthorized persons to obtain medical information from the laboratory test results database. The report will include the following information: network identification of the applying terminal, system code of the employee who requested that information, day and time of attempt, and type of attempt.	
7	The "Super-lab" subsystem that deals with billing patients for their tests may eventually be used as a subsystem in the "Physiotherapy Center" software package.	
8	The "Super-lab" software system will process all the monthly reports for the hospital departments' management, the hospital management, and the hospital controller according to Appendix D of the development contract.	
9	The software system should be able to serve 12 work-stations and eight automatic testing machines with a single model AS20 server and a CS25 communication server that will be able to serve 25 communication lines. This hardware system should conform to all availability requirements as listed in Appendix C.	
10	The "Super-lab" software package developed for the Linux operating system should be compatible for applications in a Windows NT environment.	

Review questions

3.3 What differentiates the Evans and Marciniak model from the Deutsch and Willis model?

3.4 Consider McCall's model and the Deutsch and Willis model.

(1) What are the formal differences between the models?
(2) What are the content differences between the models?
(3) What new subjects were actually added by the Evans and Marciniak model to McCall's model?

3.5 Southcottage Inc. is a manufacturer of washing machines and dishwashers. The requirements document for the new control unit included the following specifications:

(a) The firmware should be suitable for all six variations of model 2002 washing machines.
(b) The water level control module of the washing machine should be suitable for use as a water level control module in the new model 2002 dishwasher.

(1) To which of the factors do the above requirements belong?
(2) Explain your answer.

3.6 Some people claim that testability and verifiability are actually different names for the same factor.

(1) Do you agree?
(2) If not, could you explain why?

Topics for discussion

3.1 Four "but" complaints are mentioned in Section 3.1. All of them reflect items missing from the requirement documents.

(1) To which factors do the missing requirements belong?
(2) Can you suggest software quality requirements that could fill the gap?

3.2 Some professionals claim that increased software usability necessarily involves decreased efficiency. Others claim no dependence between software efficiency and usability.

(1) Do you agree with the first or the second group?
(2) Discuss your answer.

3.3 The City of Mountain View has decided to develop a software package that will serve the youth clubs operated by the city. The software's main tasks will be:

■ Follow-up of monthly payments of the members.
■ Preparing lists of participants in the various courses offered by the clubs.
■ Production of reminder notices to course participants who fail to appear regularly.
■ Statistical reports about membership and participation in club activities.

The city already implements the following software packages:

■ Tax collection
■ Public library

- School follow-up and achievements control
- Water consumption billing.

The City Council has asked the Information Technology Unit to report to the council about the possibilities for reuse of the city software packages already available to the city in the youth club software package.

(1) Could you suggest which modules of the existing city software packages could be reused in the new software? List your assumptions about the contents of the existing software packages and the required new software.

(2) Could you grade the reused modules suggested in (1) according to the scope of adaptation efforts required to apply the reused module in the youth club software package?

3.4 It is said that failure to meet the interoperability requirements can negatively affect the correctness level of the software system, and even can cause non-conformance with correctness requirements.

(1) Elaborate on the above statement and explain the mentioned interconnections between factors.

(2) Provide an example of a situation where such effects are to be expected.

3.5 It is claimed that with respect to subjects where qualitative and quantitative requirements can be defined, the quantitative alternatives should be preferred.

(1) Provide three examples each of alternative qualitative and quantitative requirements.

(2) Explain why the customer should prefer the quantitative option.

(3) Explain why the software developer should prefer the quantitative option.

chapter 4

The components of the software quality assurance system – overview

This chapter, the final chapter of the introductory portion of the text, is dedicated to a schematic overview of the wide range of SQA components available to planners of an intra-organizational SQA system. As a local system, an intra-organizational SQA system bears "local colors", which are affected by the characteristics of the organization, its development projects, software maintenance activities, and professional staff. The concise description of SQA components is followed by a discussion of the considerations guiding construction of an organization's SQA system. This glimpse will allow you to obtain some preliminary understanding about the potential contribution of each component, about the entire range of components, and about the system as a defined entity.

4.1 The SQA system – an SQA architecture

An SQA system always combines a wide range of SQA components, all of which are employed to challenge the multitude of sources of software errors and to achieve an acceptable level of software quality. As stated in Chapter 1, the task of SQA is unique in the area of quality assurance due to the special characteristics of software. In addition, the environment in which software development and maintenance is undertaken directly influences the SQA components (see Chapter 1).

SQA system components can be classified into six classes:

- **Pre-project components.** To assure that (a) the project commitments have been adequately defined considering the resources required, the schedule and budget; and (b) the development and quality plans have been correctly determined.

- **Components of project life cycle activities assessment.** The project life cycle is composed of two stages: the development life cycle stage and the operation–maintenance stage.

  The development life cycle stage components detect design and programming errors. Its components are divided into the following four sub-classes:

  - Reviews
  - Expert opinions
  - Software testing.

  The SQA components used during the operation–maintenance phase include specialized maintenance components as well as development life cycle components, which are applied mainly for functionality improving maintenance tasks.

  An additional sub-class of SQA project life cycle components deals with assuring the quality of project parts performed by subcontractors and other external participants during project development and maintenance.

- **Components of infrastructure error prevention and improvement.** The main objectives of these components, which are applied throughout the entire organization, are to eliminate or at least reduce the rate of errors, based on the organization's accumulated SQA experience.

■ **Components of software quality management.** This class of components is geared toward several goals, the major ones being the control of development and maintenance activities and the introduction of early managerial support actions that mainly prevent or minimize schedule and budget failures and their outcomes.

■ **Components of standardization, certification, and SQA system assessment.** These components implement international professional and managerial standards within the organization. The main objectives of this class are (a) utilization of international professional knowledge, (b) improvement of coordination of the organizational quality systems with other organizations, and (c) assessment of the achievements of quality systems according to a common scale. The various standards may be classified into two main groups: (a) quality management standards, and (b) project process standards.

■ **Organizing for SQA – the human components.** The SQA organizational base includes managers, testing personnel, the SQA unit and practitioners interested in software quality (SQA trustees, SQA committee members and SQA forum members). All these *actors* contribute to software quality; their main objectives are to initiate and support the implementation of SQA components, detect deviations from SQA procedures and methodology, and suggest improvements.

The entire range of SQA system components by its classes is presented in Frame 4.1.

Frame 4.1   **SQA system component classes**

Pre-project quality components

Project life cycle quality components

Infrastructure error preventive and improvement components

Software quality management components

Standardization, certification and SQA assessment components

Organizing for SQA – the human components

The spectrum of SQA components presented in this book reflects the comprehensive conception of SQA adopted by the author (see Frame 2.6). Accordingly, several of the SQA components presented here are unique to this volume, and not found in other SQA texts.

A graphic illustration of SQA system components as the SQA architecture is presented in Figure 4.1. Included are references to the chapters that discuss each component in detail. An overview of the system immediately follows.

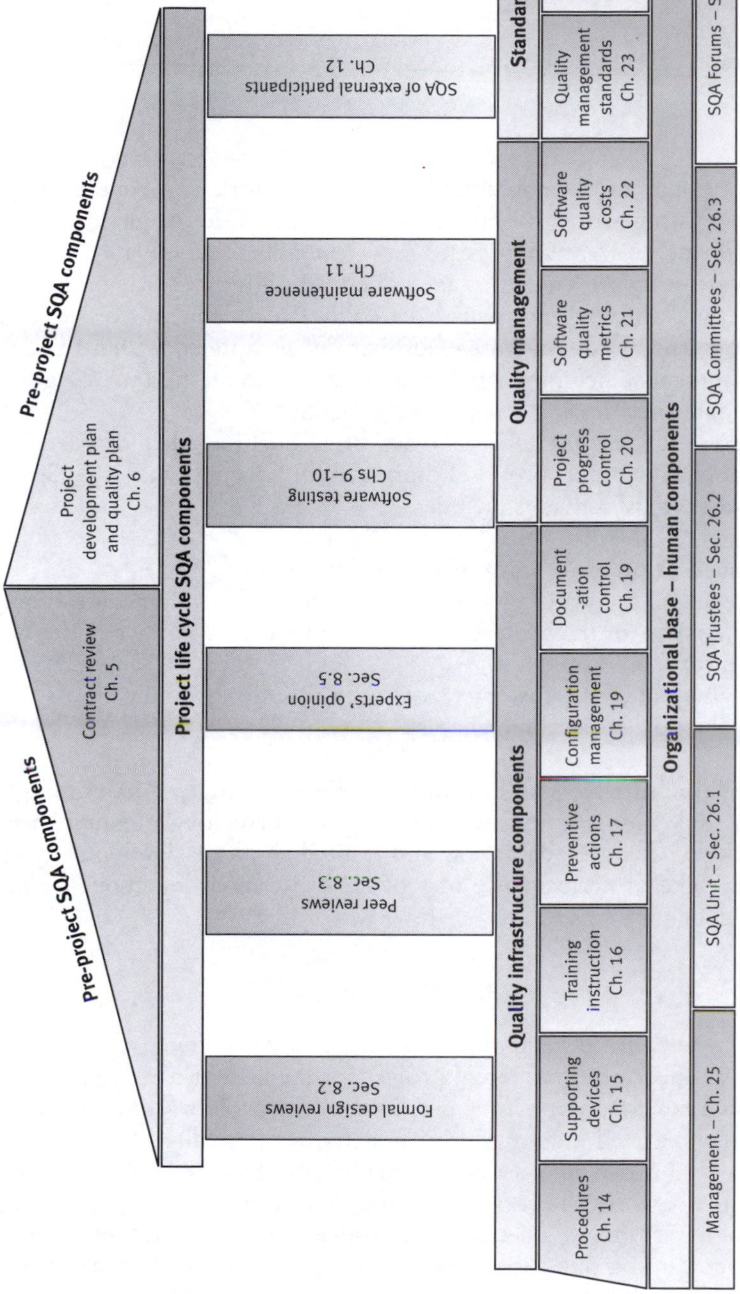

Figure 4.1: "The software quality shrine" – the SQA architecture

4.2 Pre-project components

The SQA components belonging here are meant to improve the preparatory steps taken prior to initiating work on the project itself:

- Contract review
- Development and quality plans.

4.2.1 Contract review

Software may be developed within the framework of a contract negotiated with a customer or in response to an internal order originating in another department. An internal order may entail a request for developing a firmware software system to be embedded within a hardware product, an order for a software product to be sold as a package, or an order for the development of administrative software to be applied within the company. In all these instances, the development unit is committed to an agreed-upon functional specification, budget and schedule.

Accordingly, contract review activities must include a detailed examination of (a) the project proposal draft and (b) the contract drafts. Specifically, contract review activities include:

- Clarification of the customer's requirements
- Review of the project's schedule and resource requirement estimates
- Evaluation of the professional staff's capacity to carry out the proposed project
- Evaluation of the customer's capacity to fulfill his obligations
- Evaluation of development risks.

A similar approach is applied in the review of maintenance contracts. Such reviews take into account that besides error corrections, maintenance services include software adaptation and limited software development activities for the sake of performance improvement (termed "functionality improvement maintenance").

4.2.2 Development and quality plans

Once a software development contract has been signed or a commitment made to undertake an internal project for the benefit of another department of the organization, a plan is prepared of the project ("development plan") and its integrated quality assurance activities ("quality plan"). These plans include additional details and needed revisions based on prior plans that provided the basis for the current proposal and contract. It is quite common for several months to pass between the tender submission and the signing of the contract. During this period, changes may occur in staff availability, in professional capabilities, and so forth. The plans are then revised to reflect the changes that occurred in the interim.

The main issues treated in the project development plan are:

- Schedules
- Required manpower and hardware resources
- Risk evaluations
- Organizational issues: team members, subcontractors and partnerships
- Project methodology, development tools, etc.
- Software reuse plans.

The main issues treated in the project's quality plan are:

- Quality goals, expressed in the appropriate measurable terms
- Criteria for starting and ending each project stage
- Lists of reviews, tests, and other scheduled verification and validation activities.

4.3 Software project life cycle components

The project life cycle is composed of two stages: the development life cycle stage and the operation–maintenance stage.

Several SQA components enter the software development project life cycle at different points. Their use should be planned prior to the project's initiation. The main components are:

- Reviews
- Expert opinions
- Software testing
- Software maintenance
- Assurance of the quality of the subcontractors' work and the customer-supplied parts.

4.3.1 Reviews

The design phase of the development process produces a variety of documents. The printed products include design reports, software test documents, software installation plans and software manuals, among others. Reviews can be categorized as formal design reviews (DRs) and peer reviews.

Formal design reviews (DRs)
A significant portion of these documents requires formal professional approval of their quality as stipulated in the development contract and demanded by the procedures applied by the software developer. It should be emphasized that the developer can continue to the next phase of the development process only on receipt of formal approval of these documents.

Ad hoc committees whose members examine the documents presented by the development teams usually carry out formal design reviews (widely known as "DRs"). The committees are composed of senior professionals, including the project leader and, usually, the department manager, the chief software engineer, and heads of other related departments. The majority of participants hold professional and administrative ranks higher than the project leader. On many occasions, the customer's representative will participate in a DR (this participation is generally indicated among the contractual arrangements).

The DR report itself includes a list of required corrections (termed "action items"). When a design review committee sits in order to decide upon the continuation of the work completed so far, one of the following options is usually open for consideration:

■ Immediate approval of the DR document and continuation to the next development phase.
■ Approval to proceed to the next development phase after all the action items have been completed and inspected by the committee's representative.
■ An additional DR is required and scheduled to take place after all the action items have been completed and inspected by the committee's representative.

Peer reviews

Peer reviews (inspections and walkthroughs) are directed at reviewing short documents, chapters or parts of a report, a coded printout of a software module, and the like. Inspections and walkthroughs can take several forms and use many methods; usually, the reviewers are all peers, not superiors, who provide professional assistance to colleagues. The main objective of inspections and walkthroughs is to detect as many design and programming faults as possible. The output is a list of detected faults and, for inspections, also a defect summary and statistics to be used as a database for reviewing and improving development methods.

Because a peer's participation is usually voluntarily and viewed as a supplement to the regular workload, "reciprocity" considerations frequently enter. Thus, a current participant is expected to initiate a future inspection or walkthrough in which other colleagues will probably exchange roles regarding the inspection activities.

4.3.2 Expert opinions

Expert opinions support quality assessment efforts by introducing additional external capabilities into the organization's in-house development process. Turning to outside experts may be particularly useful in the following situations:

■ Insufficient in-house professional capabilities in a given area.
■ In small organizations in many cases it is difficult to find enough suitable candidates to participate in the design review teams. In such situations, outside experts may join a DR committee or, alternatively, their expert opinions may replace a DR.

- In small organizations or in situations characterized by extreme work pressures, an outside expert's opinion can replace an inspection.
- Temporary inaccessibility of in-house professionals (waiting will cause substantial delays in the project completion schedule).
- In cases of major disagreement among the organization's senior professionals, an outside expert may support a decision.

4.3.3 Software testing

Software tests are formal SQA components that are targeted toward review of the actual running of the software. The tests are based on a prepared list of test cases that represent a variety of expected scenarios. Software tests examine software modules, software integration, or entire software packages (systems). Recurrent tests (usually termed "regression tests"), carried out after correction of previous test findings, are continued till satisfactory results are obtained. The direct objective of the software tests, other than detection of software faults and other failures to fill the requirements, is the formal approval of a module or integration setup so that either the next programming phase can be begun or the completed software system can be delivered and installed.

Software testing programs are constructed from a variety of tests, some manual and some automated. All tests have to be designed, planned and approved according to development procedures. The test report will include a detailed list of the faults detected and recommendations about the performance of partial or complete recurrent tests following a subsequent round of corrections based on the test findings. (The advantages and disadvantages of automated testing are discussed later.) It is recommended that software tests be carried out by an independent, outside testing unit rather than by the project team, as the project team will naturally find it difficult to detect faults they failed to detect during development as well as to avoid conflicts of interest.

4.3.4 Software maintenance components

Software maintenance services vary in range and are provided for extensive periods, often several years. These services fall into the following categories:

- **Corrective maintenance** – User's support services and correction of software code and documentation failures.
- **Adaptive maintenance** – Adaptation of current software to new circumstances and customers without changing the basic software product. These adaptations are usually required when the hardware system or its components undergo modification (additions or changes).
- **Functionality improvement maintenance** – The functional and performance-related improvement of existing software, carried out with respect to limited issues.

Software maintenance services should meet all kinds of quality requirements, particularly functionality and scheduling requirements (generally decided together with the customer) as well as budget limitations (determined by the service provider). The provision of ongoing maintenance services involves the application of a great variety of SQA components. The main SQA components employed in the quality assurance of the maintenance system are as follows.

Pre-maintenance components
- Maintenance contract review
- Maintenance plan.

Software development life cycle components
These components are applied for functionality improvement and adaptive maintenance tasks, activities whose characteristics are similar to those of the software development process.

Infrastructure SQA components
- Maintenance procedures and instructions
- Supporting quality devices
- Maintenance staff training, retraining, and certification
- Maintenance preventive and corrective actions
- Configuration management
- Control of maintenance documentation and quality records.

Managerial control SQA components
- Maintenance service control
- Maintenance quality metrics
- Maintenance quality costs.

The above corresponding SQA components for the software development process have been described briefly in other sections of this overview. We will return to them in greater detail in the chapters dedicated to the individual topics.

4.3.5 Assurance of the quality of the external participant's work

Subcontractors and customers frequently join the directly contracted developers (the "supplier") in carrying out software development projects. The larger and more complex the project, the greater the likelihood that external participants will be required, and the larger the proportion of work transmitted to them (subcontractors, suppliers of COTS software and the customer). The motivation for turning to external participants lies in any number of factors, ranging from the economic to the technical to personnel-related interests, and reflects a growing trend in the allocation of the work involved with completing complex projects. The contribution of external participants may therefore vary. The assignment may thus concern carrying out phased tasks such as programming or testing, or the entire range of tasks required by a development stage of the project.

Most of the SQA controls applied to external participants are defined in the contracts signed between the relevant parties. If an external participant's work is performed using software assurance standards below those of the supplier's, risks of not meeting schedule or other requirements are introduced into the project. Hence, special software assurance efforts are required to establish effective controls over the external participant's work. Special SQA efforts are needed to assure the quality of the hardware, software, staff and training supplied by the customer.

4.4 Infrastructure components for error prevention and improvement

The goals of SQA infrastructure are the prevention of software faults or, at least, the lowering of software fault rates, together with the improvement of productivity. SQA infrastructure components are developed specifically to this end. These components are devised to serve a wide range of projects and software maintenance services. During recent years, we have witnessed the growing use of computerized automatic tools for the application of these components. This class of SQA components includes:

- Procedures and work instructions
- Templates and checklists
- Staff training, retraining, and certification
- Preventive and corrective actions
- Configuration management
- Documentation control.

4.4.1 Procedures and work instructions

Quality assurance procedures usually provide detailed definitions for the performance of specific types of development activities in a way that assures effective achievement of quality results. Procedures are planned to be generally applicable and to serve the entire organization. Work instructions, in contrast, provide detailed directions for the use of methods that are applied in unique instances and employed by specialized teams.

Procedures and work instructions are based on the organization's accumulated experience and knowledge; as such, they contribute to the correct and effective performance of established technologies and routines. Because they reflect the organization's past experience, constant care should be taken to update and adjust those procedures and instructions to current technological, organizational, and other conditions.

4.4.2 Supporting quality devices

One way to combine higher quality with higher efficiency is to use supporting quality devices, such as templates and checklists. These devices, based as they are on the accumulated knowledge and experience of the organization's development and maintenance professionals, contribute to meeting SQA goals by:

- Saving the time required to define the structure of the various documents or prepare lists of subjects to be reviewed.
- Contributing to the completeness of the documents and reviews.
- Improving communication between development team and review committee members by standardizing documents and agendas.

4.4.3 Staff training, instruction and certification

The banality of the statement that a trained and well-instructed professional staff is the key to efficient, quality performance, does not make this observation any less true. Within the framework of SQA, keeping an organization's human resources knowledgeable and updated at the level required is achieved mainly by:

- Training new employees and retraining those employees who have changed assignments.
- Continuously updating staff with respect to professional developments and the in-house, hands-on experience acquired.
- Certifying employees after their knowledge and ability have been demonstrated.

4.4.4 Preventive and corrective actions

Systematic study of the data collected regarding instances of failure and success contributes to the quality assurance process in many ways. Among them we can list:

- Implementation of changes that prevent similar failures in the future.
- Correction of similar faults found in other projects and among the activities performed by other teams.
- Implementing proven successful methodologies to enhance the probability of repeat successes.

The sources of these data, to mention only a few, are design review reports, software test reports, and customers' complaints. It should be stressed, however, that for these data to make a substantial contribution to quality, they must be systematically collected and professionally analyzed.

4.4.5 Configuration management

The regular software development and maintenance operations involve intensive activities that modify software to create new versions and releases. These activities are conducted throughout the entire software service period (usually lasting several years) in order to cope with the needed corrections, adaptations to specific customer requirements, application improvements, and so forth. Different team members carry out these activities simultaneously, although they may take place at different sites. As a result, serious dangers arise, whether of misidentification of the versions or releases, loss of the records delineating the changes implemented, or loss of documentation. Consequently failures may be caused.

Configuration management deals with these hazards by introducing procedures to control the change process. These procedures relate to the approval of changes, the recording of those changes performed, the issuing of new software versions and releases, the recording of the version and release specifications of the software installed in each site, and the prevention of any changes in approved versions and releases once they are issued. Most configuration management systems implement computerized tools to accomplish their tasks. These computerized systems provide the updated and proper versions of the installed software for purposes of further development or correction. Software configuration procedures generally authorize an administrator or a configuration management committee to manage all the required configuration management operations.

4.4.6 Documentation control

SQA requires the application of measures to ensure the efficient long-term availability of major documents related to software development ("controlled documents"). The purpose of one type of controlled document – the quality record – is mainly to provide evidence of the SQA system's performance. Documentation control therefore represents one of the building blocks of any SQA system.

Documentation control functions refer mainly to customer requirement documents, contract documents, design reports, project plans, development standards, etc. Documentation control activities entail:

- Definition of the types of controlled documents needed
- Specification of the formats, document identification methods, etc.
- Definition of review and approval processes for each controlled document
- Definition of the archive storage methods.

Controlled documents contain information important to the long-term development and maintenance of the software system, such as software test results, design review (DR) reports, problem reports, and audit reports. Quality records mainly contribute to the system's ability to respond to customer claims in the future.

4.5 Management SQA components

Managerial SQA components support the managerial control of software development projects and maintenance services. Control components include:

- Project progress control (including maintenance contract control)
- Software quality metrics
- Software quality costs.

4.5.1 Project progress control

The main objective of project progress control components is to detect the appearance of any situation that may induce deviations from the project's plans and maintenance service performance. Clearly, the effectiveness and efficiency of the corrective measures implemented is dependent on the timely discovery of undesirable situations.

Project control activities focus on:

- Resource usage
- Schedules
- Risk management activities
- The budget.

4.5.2 Software quality metrics

Measurement of the various aspects of software quality is considered to be an effective tool for the support of control activities and the initiation of process improvements during the development and the maintenance phases. These measurements apply to the functional quality, productivity, and organizational aspects of the project.

Among the software quality metrics available or still in the process of development, we can list metrics for:

- Quality of software development and maintenance activities
- Development teams' productivity
- Help desk and maintenance teams' productivity
- Software faults density
- Schedule deviations.

4.5.3 Software quality costs

The quality costs incurred by software development and application are, according to the extended quality costs model, the costs of control (prevention costs, appraisal costs, and managerial preparation and control costs) combined with the costs of failure (internal failure costs, external failure costs, and managerial failure costs). Management is especially interested in the total sum of the quality costs. It is believed that up to a certain level, expanding the resources allocated to control activities yields much larger savings in failure costs while reducing total quality costs. Accordingly, management tends to exhibit greater readiness to allocate funds to profitable proposals to improve application of existing SQA system components and further development of new components.

With respect to the specific SQA strategy applied, analysis of software quality costs can direct SQA efforts to the improvement of activities that cause significant failures with their attendant high failure costs or, alternatively, to make expensive control activities more efficient. This analysis, by directing attention to the teams whose activities keep their quality costs substantially below the average, enables others to learn from them and reproduce their success. Concomitantly, quality cost analysis can help identify those teams whose ineffective quality assurance efforts result in higher than average quality costs. The results can then be used to help the teams improve.

4.6 SQA standards, system certification, and assessment components

External tools offer another avenue for achieving the goals of software quality assurance. Specifically, the main objectives of this class of components are:

(1) Utilization of international professional knowledge.
(2) Improvement of coordination with other organizations' quality systems.
(3) Objective professional evaluation and measurement of the achievements of the organization's quality systems.

The standards available may be classified into two main sub-classes: quality management standards and project process standards. Either or both of the two sub-classes can be required by the customer and stipulated in the accompanying contractual agreements.

4.6.1 Quality management standards

The organization can clearly benefit from quality standards of the second sub-class that guide the management of software development, maintenance, and infrastructure. These standards focus on *what* is required and leave the decision about *how* to achieve it to the organization. The application of a managerial quality system provides a fairly objective assessment of the organization's achievements. Organizations that comply with quality achievement requirements can then seek SQA certification. The most familiar examples of this type of standard are:

- SEI CMM assessment standard
- ISO 9001 and ISO 9000-3 standards.

4.6.2 Project process standards

Project process standards are professional standards that provide methodological guidelines (dealing with the question of "how") for the development team. Well-known examples of this type of standards are:

- IEEE 1012 standard
- ISO/IEC 12207 standard.

4.7 Organizing for SQA – the human components

The preceding section pointed out that SQA components cannot be applied in an organizational vacuum: they require an organizational base. This base includes the organization's management, software testing personnel and SQA units in addition to professionals and other practitioners interested in software quality (SQA trustees, SQA committee members and SQA forum members). All these form the organizational software quality framework or, in our terms, the SQA organizational base. The main objectives of the SQA organizational base are as follows:

- To develop and support implementation of SQA components.
- To detect deviations from SQA procedures and methodology.
- To suggest improvements to SQA components.

Although the entire SQA organizational base shares these objectives, each segment of the organizational base concentrates on specific tasks.

4.7.1 Management's role in SQA

The responsibilities of top management (through the executive in charge of software quality), departmental management and project management include the following:

- Definition of the quality policy
- Effective follow-up of quality policy implementation

- Allocation of sufficient resources to implement quality policy
- Assignment of adequate staff
- Follow-up of compliance of quality assurance procedures
- Solutions of schedule, budget and customer relations difficulties.

4.7.2   The SQA unit

This unit and software testers are the only parts of the SQA organizational base that devote themselves full-time to SQA matters. All other segments of the SQA organizational base (managerial and professional staff) contribute only some of their time to software quality issues. Thus, the SQA unit's task is to serve as the main moving force, initiator, and coordinator of the SQA system and its application. This task can be broken down into a number of primary roles:

- Preparation of annual quality programs
- Consultation with in-house staff and outside experts on software quality issues
- Conduct of internal quality assurance audits
- Leadership of quality assurance various committees
- Support of existing quality assurance infrastructure components and their updates, and development of new components.

4.7.3   SQA trustees, committees and forums

SQA trustees are members of development and maintenance teams who have a special interest in software quality and are prepared to devote part of their time to these issues. Their contributions include:

- Solving team or unit local quality problems
- Detecting deviations from quality procedures and instructions
- Initiating improvements in SQA components
- Reporting to the SQA unit about quality issues in their team or unit.

SQA committee members are members of various software development and maintenance units, and are usually appointed for term or *ad hoc* service. The main issues dealt with by the committees are:

- Solution of software quality problems.
- Analysis of problem and failure records as well as other records, followed by initiation of corrective and preventive actions when appropriate.
- Initiation and development of new procedures and instructions; updating existing materials.
- Initiation and development of new SQA components and improvement of existing components.

SQA forums are composed of professionals and practitioners who meet and/or maintain an Internet site on a voluntary basis for discussion of quality issues pertaining to development and maintenance processes. They share their experiences and difficulties as well as try to initiate improvements in the software process. The forums can therefore be considered as important sources of information and SQA initiatives.

4.8   Considerations guiding construction of an organization's SQA system

Software quality assurance systems differ among themselves, showing the flexibility inherent in the construction of such systems. Moreover, variations in the characteristics of the particular organizations using SQA systems are reflected in the considerations applied, which means that different organizations employ different SQA systems.

Decisions regarding the organization's software quality management system fall into two main categories:

(a) The SQA organizational base
(b) The SQA components to be implemented within the organization and the extent of their use.

These decisions are affected by a number of fundamental considerations that reflect the characteristics of (a) the organization, (b) the software development projects and maintenance services to be performed, and (c) the organization's professional staff. The main considerations are as follows.

Organizational considerations:

■ **The type of software development clientele.** Possible clienteles include buyers of software packages, customers of custom-made software packages, and internal clientele (the organization's departments and sub-units).

■ **The type of software maintenance clientele.** The maintenance clienteles may differ substantially from the software development clienteles. For example, an internal maintenance unit may serve purchased software packages or custom-made software specially developed for the organization's departments by software houses. Also, a software house may employ a subcontractor to maintain its software packages sold to clients during the warranty period and afterwards.

■ **The range of products.** The possible situations vary from a wide range of products to a limited range that includes specialized products and/or services.

■ **The size of the organization.** A common measure of the size of an organization is the number of professionals employed. In general, the larger the number of professionals occupied by the organization, the greater the number of different specializations, and the greater the variety of SQA components developed and applied.

- **The degree and nature of cooperation with other organizations carrying out related projects.** The range of cooperative options available covers organizations that carry out entire projects independently (no cooperation), organizations that undertake projects with partners, and organizations that employ subcontractors to complete specific parts of a project. Usually, the greater the cooperation the greater the number of required SQA components.

- **Optimization objectives.** The organization is required to select SQA components while taking into account the optimal combined contribution in the following areas: (a) software quality, (b) team productivity, (c) process efficiency, and (d) financial savings.

Project and maintenance service considerations:

- **The level of software complexity and difficulty.** Complexity and difficulties can be caused by the algorithms applied, the project's size, the variety of development tools used, interfaces to other software and firmware systems required, and so forth.

- **The degree of staff experience with project technology.** Experience can reduce the resources required, the rate of software errors, and the time required for project completion. Usually, the greater the staff's experience, the fewer the SQA components required.

- **The extent of software reuse in new projects.** Higher proportions of software reuse allow for the reduction of SQA efforts (staff, finances, time, etc.) and the employment of fewer SQA components within the project.

Professional staff considerations:

- **Professional qualifications.** In general, a highly qualified professional staff usually enables a reduction in the SQA efforts required to complete and maintain a project.

- **Level of acquaintance with team members.** How well acquainted the team members are with each other and the level of acquaintance of the department with the team members represents an oft-neglected SQA consideration. Teams can be composed of individuals who have worked together for a long time, or who have only recently met. At the same time, teams may contain differing proportions of recently hired employees. Projects performed by teams who have not worked together or have served the organization for only a short time require greater and more intense SQA efforts due to the uncertainty surrounding the members' ability to cooperate and coordinate among themselves as well as the uncertainty about their professional experience and qualifications.

Frame 4.2 summarizes the main considerations listed above.

Frame 4.2 **The main considerations affecting the use of the SQA components**

Organizational considerations

- Type of software development clientele
- Type of software maintenance clientele
- Range of software products
- Size of the organization
- Degree and nature of cooperation with other organizations carrying out related projects
- Optimization objectives

Project and maintenance service considerations

- Level of complexity and difficulty
- Degrees of experience with the project technology
- Extent of software reuse in the new projects

Professional staff considerations

- Professional qualifications
- Level of acquaintance with team members

part II

Pre-project software quality components

Contract review

Chapter outline

A bad contract is always an undesirable event. From the viewpoint of SQA, a bad contract – usually characterized by loosely defined requirements, and unrealistic budgets and schedules – is expected to yield low-quality software. So, it is natural for an SQA program to begin its preventive quality assurance efforts with a review of the proposal draft and, later, the contract draft ("contract review" covers both activities). The two reviews are aimed at improving the budget and timetable that provide the basis for the proposal and the subsequent contract, and revealing potential pitfalls at an early enough stage (in the proposal draft and in the contract draft).

This chapter is dedicated to the study of the objectives of contract review and the wide range of review subjects that correspond to these objectives. The contract review process originates in the customer–supplier relationship, and is expected to make a substantial contribution to internal projects as well.

After completing this chapter, you will be able to:

- Explain the two contract review stages.
- List the objectives of each stage of the contract review.
- Identify the factors that affect the extent of the review.
- Identify the difficulties in performing a major contract review.
- Explain the recommended avenues for implementing a major contract review.
- Discuss the importance of carrying out a contract review for internal projects.

5.1 Introduction: the CFV Project completion celebration

A happy gathering of the CFV project team at a popular restaurant down-town was called to celebrate the successful completion of a 10-month project for Carnegie Fruits and Vegetables, a produce wholesaler. The new information system registers product receipts from growers, processes clients' orders and produce shipments to clients (greengrocers and supermarkets), bills clients, and calculates payments made to the growers.

The team members were proud to emphasize that the project was conducted in full as originally scheduled. The team was especially jubilant as earlier that morning each member had received a nice bonus for finishing on time.

The third speaker, the software company's Vice President for Finance, altered the pleasant atmosphere by mentioning that this very successful project had actually lost about $90 000. During his remarks, he praised the planners for their good estimates of the resources needed for the analysis and design phase, and for the plans for broad reuse of software from other systems that were, this time, completely realized. "The only phase where our estimates failed was one of the project's final phases, the client's instruction, that where the client's staff are instructed on how to use the new information system. It now appears that no one had read the relevant RFP (requirement for proposal) section carefully enough. This section stated in a rather innocuous manner that the personnel in all the CFV branches where the software was to be installed would be instructed in its use by the software supplier." After a short pause he continued thus: "Nobody tried to find out how many branches our client operates. Nobody mentioned that CFV operates 19 branches – six of them overseas – before signing the contract!" He continued: "We tried to renegotiate the installation and instruction budget items with the client, but the client insisted on sticking to the original contract." Though no names were mentioned, it was clear that he blamed the sales negotiating team for the loss.

Similar, and in many cases much heavier, losses stem from sloppily written proposals or poorly understood contracts. Shallow and quick resource estimates, as well as exaggerated software sales efforts, have led to unrealistic schedules and budgets, or to unrealistic professional commitments. A proposal suffering from one of these faults or, worse, a combination of them and that later becomes a contract provides a certain recipe for project or service failure. It is clear that unrealistic professional commitments lead to failure to achieve the required software quality. Furthermore, in most cases, schedule and budget failures are accompanied by lower than acceptable software quality, due to pressures exerted on team members by management "to save time" and "to save resources". We can quite unrestrictedly state that such excessive pressures eventually lead to high rates of software failure.

Contract review is the software quality element that reduces the probability of such undesirable situations. Contract review is a requirement by the ISO 9001 standard and ISO 9000-3 Guidelines (see Sec. 4.3 of ISO (1997) and Sec. 7.2 of ISO/IEC (2001)). See Oskarsson and Glass (1996) for a discussion of some application aspects of contract review.

5.2 The contract review process and its stages

Several situations can lead a software company ("the supplier") to sign a contract with a customer. The most common are:

(1) Participation in a tender.

(2) Submission of a proposal according to the customer's RFP.

(3) Receipt of an order from a company's customer.

(4) Receipt of an internal request or order from another department in the organization.

Contract review is the SQA component devised to guide review drafts of proposal and contract documents. If applicable, contract review also provides oversight of the contacts carried out with potential project partners and subcontractors. The review process itself is conducted in two stages:

- **Stage One – Review of the proposal draft prior to submission to the potential customer** ("proposal draft review"). This stage reviews the final proposal draft and the proposal's foundations: customer's requirement documents, customer's additional details and explanations of the requirements, cost and resources estimates, existing contracts or contract drafts of the supplier with partners and subcontractors.

- **Stage Two – Review of contract draft prior to signing** ("contract draft review"). This stage reviews the contract draft on the basis of the proposal and the understandings (including changes) reached during the contract negotiations sessions.

The processes of review can begin once the relevant draft document has been completed. The individuals who perform the review thoroughly examine the draft while referring to a comprehensive range of review subjects. A checklist is very helpful for assuring the full coverage of relevant subjects (see Appendices 5A and 5B).

After the completion of a review stage it is required that the necessary changes, additions and corrections are introduced by the proposal team (after the proposal draft review) and by the legal department (after the contract draft review).

5.3 Contract review objectives

As can be expected, the two contract review stages have different objectives, which we detail in the following.

5.3.1 Proposal draft review objectives

The objective of the proposal draft review is to make sure that the following activities have been satisfactorily carried out.

(1) **Customer requirements have been clarified and documented.**

RFP documents and similar technical documents can be too general and imprecise for the project's purposes. As a result, additional details should be obtained from the customer. Clarifications of vague requirements and their updates should be recorded in a separate document that is approved by both the customer and the software firm.

(2) **Alternative approaches for carrying out the project have been examined.**

Often, promising and suitable alternatives on which to present a proposal have not been adequately reviewed (if at all) by the proposal team. This stipulation refers especially to alternatives encompassing software reuse, and partnerships or subcontracting with firms that have specialized knowledge or staff that can qualify for meeting the proposal's terms.

(3) **Formal aspects of the relationship between the customer and the software firm have been specified.**

The proposal should define formalities that include:
- Customer communication and interface channels
- Project deliverables and acceptance criteria
- Formal phase approval process
- Customer design and test follow-up method
- Customer change request procedure.

(4) **Identification of development risks.**

Development risks, such as insufficient professional know-how regarding the project's professional area or the use of required development tools, need to be identified and resolved. For a comprehensive description of identification of software risk items and methods for risk management actions, see Appendix 6A.

(5) **Adequate estimation of project resources and timetable.**

Resources estimation refers to professional staff as well as the project's budget, including subcontractors' fees. Scheduling estimates should take into account the time requirements of all the parties participating in the project.

Implementation tip

In some situations, a supplier deliberately offers a *below*-cost proposal, considering factors such as sales potential. In these cases, where the proposal is based on realistic estimates of schedule, budget and professional capabilities, the loss incurred is considered to be a calculated loss, not a contract failure.

(6) **Examination of the company's capacity with respect to the project.**

This examination should consider professional competence as well as the availability of the required team members and development facilities on the scheduled time.

(7) **Examination of the customer's capacity to meet his commitments.**

This examination refers to the customer's financial and organizational capacities, such as personnel recruitment and training, installation of the required hardware, and upgrading of its communications equipment.

(8) **Definition of partner and subcontractor participation.**

This covers quality assurance issues, payment schedules, distribution of project income/profits, and cooperation between project management and teams.

(9) **Definition and protection of proprietary rights.**

This factor is of vital importance in cases where reused software is inserted into a new package or when rights for future reuse of the current software need to be decided. This item also refers to the use of proprietary files of data crucial for operating the system and security measures.

The objectives of a proposal draft review are summarized in Frame 5.1.

Frame 5.1 Proposal draft review objectives

The nine proposal draft review objectives that make sure the following activities have been satisfactorily carried out:

1. Customer requirements have been clarified and documented.
2. Alternative approaches for carrying out the project have been examined.
3. Formal aspects of the relationship between the customer and the software firm have been specified.
4. Identification of development risks.
5. Adequate estimation of project resources and timetable have been prepared.
6. Examination of the firm's capacity with respect to the project.
7. Examination of the customer's capacity to fulfill his commitments.
8. Definition of partner and subcontractor participation conditions.
9. Definition and protection of proprietary rights.

5.3.2 Contract draft review objectives

The objectives of the contract draft review are to make sure that the following activities have been performed satisfactorily:

(1) No unclarified issues remain in the contract draft.

(2) All the understandings reached between the customer and the firm are to be fully and correctly documented in the contract and its appendices. These understandings are meant to resolve all the unclarified issues and differences between the customer and the firm that have been revealed so far.

(3) No changes, additions, or omissions that have not been discussed and agreed upon should be introduced into the contract draft. Any change, whether intentional or not, can result in substantial additional and unanticipated commitments on the part of the supplier.

The objectives of a contract draft review are summarized in Frame 5.2.

Frame 5.2   **Contract draft review objectives**

The three contract draft review objectives that make sure the following activities have been satisfactorily carried out:

1. No unclarified issues remain in the contract draft.

2. All understandings reached subsequent to the proposal are correctly documented.

3. No "new" changes, additions, or omissions have entered the contract draft.

5.4 Implementation of a contract review

Contract reviews vary in their magnitude, depending on the characteristics of the proposed project. This complexity may be either technical or organizational. Accordingly, different levels of professional effort are justified for the various contract reviews. Special professional efforts are required for major proposals.

5.4.1 Factors affecting the extent of a contract review

The most important project factors determining the extent of the contract review efforts required are:

- **Project magnitude,** usually measured in man-month resources.
- **Project technical complexity.**

- **Degree of staff acquaintance with and experience in the project area.** Acquaintance with the project area is frequently linked with software reuse possibilities; in cases where a high proportion of software reuse is possible, the extent of the review is reduced.

- **Project organizational complexity.** The greater the number of organizations (i.e., partners, subcontractors, and customers) taking part in the project, the greater the contract review efforts required.

We may therefore assume that "simple" contract reviews will be carried out by one reviewer, who will focus on a few subjects and invest little time in his review. However, a large-scale contract review may require the participation of a team to examine a wide range of subjects, a process demanding the investment of many working hours.

5.4.2 Who performs a contract review?

The task of contract review can be completed by various individuals, listed here in ascending order, according to the complexity of the project:

- The leader or another member of the proposal team.

- The members of the proposal team.

- An outside professional or a company staff member who is not a member of the proposal team.

- A team of outside experts. Usually, a contract review team composed of outside experts is called in, especially for major proposals (see Section 5.4.3). Outside experts may be called also for contract reviews in small software development organizations that are unable to find enough adequate team members in their staff.

5.4.3 Implementation of a contract review for a major proposal

Major proposals are proposals for projects characterized by at least some of the following: very large-scale project, very high technical complexity, new professional area for the company, and high organizational complexity (realized by a great number of organizations, i.e., partners, subcontractors, and customers, that take part in the project). Implementation of a contract review process for a major project usually involves substantial organizational difficulties. Some avenues for overcoming these difficulties are suggested here, following a review of the factors that introduce difficulties to a smooth completion of the task.

The difficulties of carrying out contract reviews for major proposals
Almost everybody agrees that contract review is a major procedure for reducing the risks of major project failures. Several substantial, fundamental,

and inherent difficulties in performing the contract review exist, especially for those situations requiring a review of a major proposal.

■ **Time pressures.** Both stages of the contract review, proposal draft review and contract draft review are usually performed when the tender team is under considerable time pressures. As a result, each stage of the contract review has to be completed within a few days to allow for the subsequent corrections of documents to take place.

■ **Proper contract review requires substantial professional work.** Professional performance of each stage of the contract review requires investment of substantial professional expertise (the amount of time required varies, of course, according to the nature of the project).

■ **The potential contract review team members are very busy.** The potential members of the contract review team are often senior staff members and experts who usually are committed to performing their regular tasks at the very time that the review is needed. Freeing professional staff can therefore be a significant logistical problem.

Recommended avenues for implementing major contract reviews
The careful planning of contract reviews is required for their successful completion. As should be clear by now, this holds doubly for major contract reviews. It is recommended that the following steps be taken to facilitate the review process.

■ **The contract review should be scheduled.** Contract review activities should be included in the proposal preparation schedule, leaving sufficient time for the review and the ensuing corrections to be made.

■ **A team should carry out the contract review.** Teamwork makes it possible to distribute the workload among the team members so that each member of the contract review team can find sufficient time to do his or her share (which may include preparing a written report that summarizes his or her findings and recommendations).

■ **A contract review team leader should be appointed.** It is important that the responsibility for organizing, managing and controlling the contract review activities be defined, preferable by appointing a team leader. The activities of the team leader include:

– Recruitment of the team members
– Distribution of review tasks among the team's members
– Coordination between the members of the review team
– Coordination between the review team and the proposal team
– Follow-up of activities, especially compliance with the schedule
– Summarization of the findings and their delivery to the proposal team.

Implementation tip

As contract reviews may impose a substantial workload and additional pressures on the proposal team, thought should be given to when it may be appropriate to abstain from conducting a contract review. Such situations may occur with small-scale projects, or small- to medium-scale cost-plus projects. Contract review procedures should therefore define those types of projects for which a contract review is not obligatory.

For other defined types of "simple" projects, it is recommended that authority be given to a senior manager to make the decision as to whether to perform the review.

5.5 Contract review subjects

Contract reviews examine many subjects, based on the contract review objectives. Checklists are useful devices for helping review teams to organize their work and achieve high coverage of the relevant subjects. It is clear that many of the subjects on these lists are irrelevant for any specific project. At the same time, even a comprehensive checklist may exclude some important subjects relevant to a given project proposal. It is the task of the contract review team, but especially of its leader, to determine the list of subjects pertinent for the specific project proposal.

Lists of contract review subjects, classified according to contract review objectives, are presented in the appendices to this chapter:

- Appendix 5A: Proposal draft review – subjects checklist
- Appendix 5B: Contract draft review – subjects checklist.

5.6 Contract reviews for internal projects

A substantial number, if not the majority, of software projects are internal projects — "in-house" projects – carried out by one unit of an organization for another unit of the same organization. In such cases, the software development unit is the supplier, while the other unit can be considered the customer. Typical internal projects and their in-house customers are listed in Table 5.1.

Frequently, internal software development projects are not based on what would be considered a complete customer–supplier relationship. In many cases, these projects are based on general agreements, with goodwill playing an important role in the relationships between the two units. It follows that the developing unit will perform only a short and "mild" contract review, or none at all.

Table 5.1: Typical internal projects and their in-house customers

Type of internal project	The in-house customers	Project examples
(1) Administrative or operative software to be applied internally	Administration and operating units	■ Sales and inventory systems ■ Financial resource management systems ■ Human resource management systems
(2) Software packages originally intended to be sold to the public as "off-the-shelf" packages	Software marketing department	■ Computer games ■ Educational software ■ Word processors ■ Sales and inventory management software packages
(3) Firmware to be embedded in the company's products	Electronic and mechanical product development departments	■ Electronic instrumentation and control products ■ Household amusement equipment and machinery ■ Advanced toys

Unfortunately, loose relationships are usually characterized by insufficient examination of the project's requirements, its schedule, resources and development risks. As a result, the following problems are likely to arise:

(1) Inadequate definition of project requirements.

(2) Poor estimates of required resources.

(3) Poor timetable/scheduling.

(4) Inadequate awareness of development risks.

As this list indicates, we can easily conclude that in-house projects performed for internal customers are more prone to failure than are outside-contracted projects. The potential disadvantages of the loose relationships evidenced by internal projects are shown in Table 5.2.

It could be concluded that the customer–supplier relationship and contract review which proved to be fruitful for external projects should be applied for internal projects as well. The chances of avoiding the above-mentioned potential problems can be considerably improved by implementing procedures that will define:

■ An adequate proposal for the internal project
■ Applying a proper contract review process for internal projects
■ An adequate agreement between the internal customer and the internal supplier.

Subject	Disadvantages to the internal customer	Disadvantages to the internal developer
(1) Inadequate definition of project requirements	Implementation deviates from needed applications Low satisfaction	Higher than average change requirements Wasted resources due to introducing avoidable changes
(2) Poor estimate of required resources	Unrealistic expectations about project feasibility	Substantial deviations from development budget Friction between units induced by requirements for budget additions
(3) Poor timetable	Missing scheduled dates for beginning distribution of new products	Development activities are under time pressures and tend to suffer from low quality Late project completion causes delays in freeing staff for their next project
(4) Inadequate awareness of development risks	Customer unprepared for project risks and their consequences	Tardy initiation of efforts to overcome difficulties

Summary

(1) Explain the two contract review stages.

- **Proposal draft review**. This stage reviews the final proposal draft and the documents on which it is based: customer documents and customer's detailed explanations of the requirements, resource and financial estimates, existing contracts with partners and subcontractors, etc.
- **Contract draft review**. This stage reviews the contract draft on the basis of the proposal and the understandings reached during the *subsequent* negotiations.

(2) List the objectives of contract review.

The objectives of the proposal draft review are to make sure that the following activities have been completed satisfactorily:

- Customer requirements have been clarified and documented.
- Alternatives for carrying out the project have been examined.
- A formal relationship with the customer has been defined.
- Development risks have been identified.
- Resources and schedules for the project have been adequately estimated.
- The company's capacity to perform the project has been examined.
- The customer's capacity to fulfill his commitments has been examined.
- Partner and subcontractor participation has been defined.
- Proprietary rights have been defined and protected.

The objectives of the contract draft review are to guarantee satisfactory completion of the following activities:

- No unclarified issues remain in the contract draft.
- All understandings subsequent to the proposal are correctly documented.
- No changes, additions, or omissions are to be found.

(3) Identify the factors that affect the extent of the contract review.

The efforts to be expended on the contract review depend on the characteristics of the project. The most important factors are the project magnitude and complexity, the staff's acquaintance with and experience in the project area, and the number of additional organizations carrying out the project (partners, subcontractors, and the customer).

(4) Identify the difficulties in performing a major contract review.

The main difficulties are the pressures of time and the need to invest substantial professional working hours when the contract review team member is already occupied by other commitments.

(5) Explain the recommended avenues for implementing a major contract review.

To conduct a proper major contract review, one should abide by the following guidelines:

- The contract review should be part of the proposal preparation schedule.
- The contract review should be carried out by a team.
- A contract review leader should be appointed.

(6) Discuss the importance of carrying out a contract review for internal projects.

The loose relationships maintained between the internal customer and the internal developer increase the probability of project failure. This trend can be reduced by adequate procedures that will define the preparation and by applying the same guidelines used for external project contract review.

Selected bibliography

1. ISO (1997) *ISO 9000-3:1997(E), Quality Management and Quality Assurance Standards – Part 3: Guidelines for the Application of ISO 9001:1994 to the Development, Supply, Installation and Maintenance of Computer Software*, 2nd edn, International Organization for Standardization, Geneva.
2. ISO/IEC (2001) "ISO 9000-3:2001 Software and System Engineering – Guidelines for the Application of ISO 9001:2000 to Software, Final draft", International Organization for Standardization (ISO), Geneva, unpublished draft, December 2001.
3. Oskarsson, O. and Glass, R. L. (1996) *An ISO 9000 Approach to Building Quality Software*, Ch. 3, Prentice Hall, Upper Saddle River, NJ.

5.1 The CFV case is described at the beginning of this chapter. From the Vice President's short speech, it can be understood that the proposal preparation was conducted as follows: (a) a negotiating team was appointed by the management, (b) a proposal was prepared by the negotiating team, (c) management approved the proposal before it was presented to the customer, (d) management signed the contract.

(1) Can you suggest steps that would reduce the possible losses caused by a faulty contract?
(2) What relevant contract review subjects, listed in Appendices 5A and 5B, could have revealed the contract faults described in the CFV case?

5.2 List the various aspects involved with the examination of the customer's capabilities.

5.3 One of the objectives of a contract review is to examine development risks.

(1) List the most common types of development risks.
(2) What proposal team activities are required regarding each of the revealed development risks?

5.4 The extent of a contract review depends on the project's characteristics.

(1) Describe an imaginary project that requires an intensive and comprehensive contract review.
(2) Describe an imaginary project where a small-scale contract review would be adequate.

5.5 Performing a contract review raises many difficulties.

(1) List the "built-in" difficulties to carrying out a large-scale contract review.
(2) List the steps that should be taken to make a large-scale contract review feasible.

5.6 List those issues involved with estimating the resources required for a project that should be considered by the contract review team.

5.7 List the supplier's capability issues that should be considered by the contract review team.

5.8 List the partner and subcontractor participation issues that should be considered by the contract review team.

Topics for discussion

5.1 MJS, Mount Jackson Systems, signed a contract to develop a comprehensive CRM (Customer Relations Management) system for a large food preparation corporation. In order to fulfill the project's requirements, MJS employed three subcontractors. MJS's experience with the subcontractors turned out to be troublesome, especially in regard to not keeping timetables, high rates of software faults of all kinds, and many interface faults with system parts developed by other participants in the project. The head of the software quality assurance unit stated that if his unit had carried out the contract review procedure, most of the described problems would have been averted.

(1) What contract review subject is relevant to this case?
(2) What process would you recommend when applying a contract review in this case?

5.2 An SQA professional claims: "I find all the reasons given for a proposal draft review to be justified. I also believe that a review contributes to the quality of the proposal, especially in clarifying and precisely defining requirements, and in preparing more realistic estimates, among other issues. However, once the proposal has been presented to the customer, there is no need for a contract draft review. The task of reviewing the final negotiations results and the final version of the contract should be left to the legal department and to management."

(1) Do you agree with the above statement? List your arguments.
(2) In what situations is a contract draft review not necessary?
(3 In what situations is a contract draft review absolutely necessary?

5.3 Many organizations do not apply their contract review procedures to internal projects even though they perform comprehensive contract reviews for all their external projects.

(1) List arguments that support this approach.
(2) List arguments that oppose this approach.
(3) Suggest types of internal projects where omission of a contract review could result in severe damage to the organization (mention the main components of damage listed for each project type).

5.4 One of the objectives of a contract review is to examine the customer's capability of fulfilling his commitments. Accordingly, a comprehensive list of contract review subjects is suggested in Appendix 5A. Some managers believe that because the supplier can sue the customer in the event that he does not fulfill his commitments, there is no justification to invest resources in reviewing the customer's capabilities.

(1) Do you agree with these managers?
(2) If you disagree, list your arguments in favor of a comprehensive examination of the customer's capabilities.
(3) Can you describe a real or imaginary situation where a customer's capability failures *could* create substantial direct and indirect damages to the software developer ("the supplier")?

5.5 A contract draft review of a properly prepared contract document is expected to yield no negative findings. Still, in reality, discrepancies in contracts do appear frequently.

(1) List real cases and common situations where such discrepancies could arise.
(2) In what situations are discrepancies in the contract draft expected to be least likely?

5.6 The examination of alternatives is one of the major tasks of a proposal team, especially for tender proposals. However, in many cases, important alternatives are omitted or neglected by the proposal team.

(1) List real cases and common situations where negligence in defining and examining important alternatives can be expected.
(2) In what situations are these types of discrepancies least likely to occur?

5.7 National Software Providers is very interested in the newly developing area of BI (Business Intelligence) for electronic commerce firms. As the company is very keen to gain experience in this area, they were especially interested in winning a tender issued by one of the leading cosmetics manufacturers. The proposal team estimated that in order to win the contract, their proposal should not exceed the sum of $650 000. Accordingly, their quotation was $647 000. As all the team members were aware that the cost of completing the project by the company's inexperienced development department would substantially exceed this sum, they decided that there was little use in investing efforts to estimate the actual costs of the project.

(1) Do you agree with the team's decision not to estimate the project's costs?
(2) If you disagree, what are your arguments in favor of estimating the costs?

5.8 Consider the case of a custom-made software package developed by a supplier according to the unique RFP (request for proposal) specifications of the customer.

(1) What proprietary issues are expected in such a project?
(2) What security issues related to the proprietary rights listed in your answer to (1) should be examined?

5.9 Contract review subjects include a variety of financial issues.

(1) Why should an SQA activity such as contract review be so heavily involved in financial issues?
(2) Is it likely that an SQA unit member will be able to review the financial issues? Who do you believe should do it, and how should the review be organized?

5.10 A contract review can be performed by "insiders" (members of the organization's proposal team or other staff members) or by "outsiders".

(1) What are the advantages and disadvantages of employing outsiders compared with insiders for a proposal draft review?
(2) What are the advantages and disadvantages of employing outsiders compared with insiders for a contract draft review?

5.11 A medium-sized firm submits 5–10 proposals per month, 10%–20% of which eventually evolve into development contracts. The company takes care to perform a thorough project draft review for each of the proposals.

(1) Do the proposal draft reviews performed for each of the individual projects guarantee that the company will be capable of carrying out all the proposals that eventually evolve into development contracts? List your arguments.
(2) If your answer to (1) is negative, what measures should be taken to reduce the risk of being unable to perform the contracts?

Appendix 5A Proposal draft reviews – subjects checklist

Proposal draft review objective	Proposal draft review subjects
1. Customer requirements have been clarified and documented	1.1 The functional requirements. 1.2 The customer's operating environment (hardware, data communication system, operating system, etc.). 1.3 The required interfaces with other software packages and instrument firmware, etc. 1.4 The performance requirements, including workloads as defined by the number of users and the characteristics of use. 1.5 The system's reliability. 1.6 The system's usability, as realized in the required training time for an operator to achieve the required productivity. The total of training and instruction efforts to be carried out by the supplier, including number of trainees and instructed stuff, locations and duration. 1.7 The number of software installations to be performed by the supplier, including locations. 1.8 The warranty period, extent of supplier liability, and method of providing support. 1.9 Proposals for maintenance service provision extending beyond the warranty period, and its conditions. 1.10 Completion of all the tender requirements, including information about the project team, certification and other documents, etc.
2. Alternative approaches for carrying out the project have been examined	2.1 Integrating reused and purchased software. 2.2 Partners. 2.3 Customer's undertaking to perform in-house development of some project tasks. 2.4 Subcontractors. 2.5 Adequate comparison of alternatives.
3. Formal aspects of the relationship between the customer and the software firm have been specified	3.1 A coordination and joint control committee, including its procedures. 3.2 The list of documentation that has to be delivered. 3.3 The customer's responsibilities re provision of facilities, data, and answers to the team's inquiries. 3.4 Indication of the required phase approval by the customer and the approval procedure. 3.5 Customer participation (extent and procedures) in progress reviews, design reviews, and testing. 3.6 Procedures for handling customer change requests during development and maintenance stages, including method of costing introduction of changes. 3.7 Criteria for project completion, method of approval, and acceptance. 3.8 Procedures for handling customer complaints and problems detected after acceptance, including non-conformity to specifications detected after the warranty period.

Proposal draft review objective	Proposal draft review subjects
	3.9 Conditions for granting bonuses for earlier project completion and penalties for delays.
	3.10 Conditions to be complied with, including financial arrangements if part of or the entire project is cancelled or temporarily halted upon the customer's initiative. (Issues include the expected damages to the firm if such actions are taken at various stages of the project.)
	3.11 Service provision conditions during warranty period.
	3.12 Software maintenance services and conditions, including customer's obligation to update his version of the software as per supplier's demands.
4. Identification of development risks	4.1 Risks re software modules or parts that require substantial acquisition of new professional capabilities.
	4.2 Risks re possibility of not obtaining needed hardware and software components according to schedule.
5. Adequate estimation of resources and timetable	5.1 Man-days required for each project phase and their cost. Do the estimates include spare resources to cover for corrections following design reviews, tests, and so forth?
	5.2 Do the estimates of man-days include the required work to prepare the required documentation, especially the documentation to be delivered to the customer?
	5.3 Manpower resources needed to fulfill warranty obligations and their cost.
	5.4 Does the project schedule include time required for reviews, tests, etc. and making the required corrections?
6. Examination of the firm's capacity to perform the project	6.1 Professional pool of knowledge.
	6.2 Availability of specialized staff (on schedule and in the required numbers).
	6.3 Availability of computer resources and other development (including testing) facilities (on schedule and in the required numbers).
	6.4 Ability to cope with the customer requirements demanding use of special development tools or software development standards.
	6.5 Warranty and long-term software maintenance service obligations.
7. Examination of customer's capacity to fulfill his commitments	7.1 Financial capability, including contract payments and additional internal investments.
	7.2 Supply of all the facilities, data and responses to staff queries as they arise.
	7.3 Recruitment and training of new and existing staff.
	7.4 Capacity to complete all task commitments on time and to the requisite quality.

Proposal draft review objective	Proposal draft review subjects
8. Definition of partner and subcontractor participation conditions	8.1 Allocation of responsibility for completion of tasks by the partners, subcontractors, or the customer, including schedule and method of coordination. 8.2 Allocation of payments, including bonuses and penalties, among partners. 8.3 Subcontractor payment schedule, including bonuses and penalties. 8.4 Quality assurance of work performed by subcontractors, partners and the customer, including participation in SQA activities (e.g., quality planning, reviews, tests).
9. Definition and protection of software proprietary rights	9.1 Securing proprietary rights to software purchased from others. 9.2 Securing proprietary rights to data files purchased from others. 9.3 Securing proprietary rights to future reuse of software developed in custom-made projects. 9.4 Securing proprietary rights to software (including data files) developed by the firm (the supplier) and his subcontractors during the development period and while in regular use by the client.

Appendix 5B Contract draft review – subjects checklist

Contract draft review objective	Contract draft review subjects
1. No unclarified issues remain in the contract draft	1.1 Supplier's obligations as defined in the contract draft and its appendices. 1.2 Customer's obligations as defined in the contract draft and its appendices.
2. All understandings reached subsequent to the proposal are correctly documented	2.1 Understandings about the project's functional requirements. 2.2 Understandings about financial issues, including payment schedule, bonuses, penalties, etc. 2.3 Understandings about the customer's obligations. 2.4 Understandings about partner and subcontractor obligations, including the supplier's agreements with external parties.
3. No "new" changes, additions, or omissions have entered the contract draft	3.1 The contract draft is complete; no contract section or appendix is missing. 3.2 No changes, omissions and additions have been entered into the agreed document, regarding the financial issues, the project schedule, or the customer and partners' obligations.

Development and quality plans

Imagine that you have just been appointed head of a sizable project. As is often the case in the software industry, you come under serious time pressures from the very first day. Because you were a member of the proposal team and participated in most of the meetings held with the customer's representatives, you are confident that you know all that is necessary to do the job. You intend to use the proposal plans and internal documents that the team had prepared as your development and quality plans. You are prepared to rely on these materials because you know that the proposal and its estimates, including the timetable, staff requirements, list of project documents, scheduled design reviews, and list of development risks have all been thoroughly reviewed by the contract review team.

You are therefore a bit disappointed that at this crucial point of the project, the Development Department Manager demands that you immediately prepare new and separate project development plans ("development plan") and project quality plans ("quality plan"). When you claim that the completed proposal and its appendices could serve as the requested plans, the manager insists that they be updated, with new and more comprehensive topics added to guarantee the plans' adequacy. "By the way," the manager mentions almost as an aside, "don't forget that a period of seven months has elapsed between the proposal preparation and the final signing of the contract. Such a period is a hell of time in our trade . . . ."

You should expect that your department manager is right. The effort invested in preparing the development and quality plans will certainly be beneficial. You may discover that some team members will not be available at the scheduled dates due to delays in completion of their current assignments, or that the consulting company that had agreed to provide professional support in a highly specialized and crucial area has suffered heavy losses and gone bankrupt in the interim. These are just two of the types of problems that can arise.

To sum up, the project needs development and quality plans that:

■ Are based on proposal materials that have been re-examined and thoroughly updated.

■ Are more comprehensive than the approved proposal, especially with respect to schedules, resource estimates, and development risk evaluations.

■ Include additional subjects, absent from the approved proposal.

■ Were prepared at the beginning of the project to sound alerts regarding scheduling difficulties, potential staff shortages, paucity of development facilities, problems with meeting contractual milestones, modified development risks, and so on.

Development and quality plans are major elements needed for project compliance with 9000.3 standards (see Sections 4.2 and 4.4 of ISO (1997) and Sections 7.1 and 7.3 of ISO/IEC (2001), and with the IEEE 730 standard (IEEE, 1998). It is also an important element in the Capability Maturity Model (CMM) for assessment of software development organization maturity (see Paulk *et al.*, 1995, Sec. 7.2; Humphrey, 1989; Felschow, 1999). Given their importance, these plans deserve a special chapter.

Therefore, this chapter is dedicated to the study of project development and quality plans, their objectives and elements.

After completing this chapter, you will be able to:

■ Explain the objectives of a development plan and a quality plan.
■ Identify the elements of a development plan.
■ Identify the elements of a quality plan.

■ Identify the major software risk items.
■ Explain the process of software risk management.
■ Discuss the importance of development and quality plans for small projects.
■ Discuss the importance of development and quality plans for internal projects.

6.1 Development plan and quality plan objectives

Planning, as a process, has several objectives, each of which is meant to prepare adequate foundations for the following:

(1) Scheduling development activities that will lead to the successful and timely completion of the project, and estimating the required manpower resources and budget.

(2) Recruiting team members and allocating development resources (according to activity schedules and manpower resource requirement estimates).

(3) Resolving development risks.

(4) Implementing required SQA activities.

(5) Providing management with data needed for project control.

6.2 Elements of the development plan

Based on the proposal materials, the project's development plan is prepared to fulfill the above objectives. The following elements, each applicable to different project components, comprise a project development plan.

(1) **Project products**
The development plan includes the following products:

■ Design documents specifying dates of completion, indicating those items to be delivered to the customer ("deliverables")
■ Software products (specifying completion date and installation site)
■ Training tasks (specifying dates, participants and sites).

(2) **Project interfaces**
Project interfaces include:

■ Interfaces with existing software packages (software interface)
■ Interfaces with other software and/or hardware development teams that are working on the same system or project (i.e., cooperation and coordination links)
■ Interfaces with existing hardware (hardware interface).

(3) **Project methodology and development tools** to be applied at each phase of the project

> **Implementation tip**
>
> When evaluating the suitability of proposed project methodology and development tools, one should also take into account the professional experience of the staff, including the subcontractors' personnel, even if temporary.

(4) **Software development standards and procedures**
A list should be prepared of the software development standards and procedures to be applied in the project.

(5) **The mapping of the development process**
Mapping of the development process involves providing detailed definitions of each of the project's phases. These descriptions include definitions of inputs and outputs, and the specific activities planned. Activity descriptions include:

(a) An estimate of the activity's duration. These estimates are highly dependent on the experience gained in previous projects.

(b) The logical sequence in which each activity is to be performed, including a description of each activity's dependence on previously completed activities.

(c) The type of professional resources required and estimates of how much of these resources are necessary for each activity.

> **Implementation tip**
>
> SQA activities, such as design review and software tests, should be included among the scheduled project activities. The same applies to the design and code correction activities. Failing to schedule these activities can cause unanticipated delays in the initiation of subsequent activities.

Several methods are available for scheduling and graphically presenting the development process. One of the most commonly used methods is the GANTT chart, which displays the various activities by horizontal bars whose lengths are proportional to the activity's duration. The bars represent the activities themselves, and are placed vertically, according to their planned initiation and conclusion. Several computerized tools can prepare GANTT charts in addition to producing lists of activities by required time for their beginning and conclusion, and so forth.

More advanced scheduling methodologies, such as CPM and PERT, both of which belong to the category of critical path analysis, take sequence dependencies into account in addition to duration of activities. They enable calculation of the earliest and latest acceptable start times for each activity. The difference between start times determines the activity's scheduling flexibility. Special attention is awarded to those activities lacking scheduling flexibility (which explains their being called "critical path" activities), and whose tardy completion may cause delay in the conclusion of the entire project.

Several software packages, used in conjunction with these methodologies, support the planning, reporting and follow-up of project timetables. An example of a software package of this type is *Microsoft Project™*. For a more detailed discussion of scheduling, refer to the literature dealing with project management.

(6) **Project milestones**
For each milestone, its completion time and project products (documents and code) are to be defined.

(7) **Project staff organization**
The organization plan comprises:

- Organizational structure: definition of project teams and their tasks, including teams comprised of a subcontractor's temporary workers.

- Professional requirements: professional certification, experience in a specific programming language or development tool, experience with a specific software product and type, and so forth.

- Number of team members required for each period of time, according to the activities scheduled. It is expected that teams will commence their activities at different times, and that their team size may vary from one period to the next, depending on the planned activities.

- Names of team leaders and team members. Difficulties are expected to arise with respect to the long-term assignment of staff members to teams because of unanticipated changes in their current assignments. Therefore, the names of staff are required to help keep track of their participation as team members.

Implementation tip

The long-term availability of project staff should be carefully examined. Lags in completing former assignments may result in delays in joining the project team, which increases the risk of failing to meet project milestones. In addition, staff "evaporation" caused by resignations and/or promotions, phenomena that are particularly frequent in the software industry, can cause staff shortages. Therefore, estimates of staff availability should be examined periodically to avoid "surprises". Early warning of unforeseen staff shortages makes it easier to resolve the problem.

(8) **Development facilities**

Required development facilities include hardware, software and hardware development tools, office space, and other items. For each facility, the period required for its use should be indicated on the timetable.

(9) **Development risks**

Development risks are inherent in any project. To understand their pervasiveness, and how they can be controlled, we should first define the concept. A development risk is "a state or property of a development task or environment, which, if ignored, will increase the likelihood of project failure" (Ropponen and Lyytinen, 2000). Typical development risks are:

- Technological gaps – Lack of adequate and sufficient professional knowledge and experience to carry out the demands of the development contract.
- Staff shortages – Unanticipated shortfalls of professional staff.
- Interdependence of organizational elements – The likelihood that suppliers of specialized hardware or software subcontractors, for example, will not fulfill their obligations on schedule.

The top 10 major software risk items, as listed by Boehm and Ross (1989), are shown in the Appendix to this chapter in Table 6A.1. Systematic risk management activities should be initiated to deal with them. The risk management process includes the following activities: risk identification, risk evaluation, planning of risk management actions (RMAs), implementation of RMAs, and monitoring of RMAs. Software RMAs are incorporated in the development plan.

For further discussion of software development risks and software risk management, see Appendix 6A.

The growing importance of software risk management is expressed in the spiral model for software development. To cope with this type of risk, a special phase dedicated to software risk assessment is assigned to every cycle of the spiral (Boehm, 1988, 1998).

(10) **Control methods**

In order to control project implementation, the project manager and the department management apply a series of monitoring practices when preparing progress reports and coordinating meetings. A comprehensive discussion of project control methods is found in Chapter 19.

(11) **Project cost estimation**

Project cost estimates are based on proposal costs estimates, followed by a thorough review of their continued relevance based on updated human resource estimates, contracts negotiated with subcontractors and suppliers, and so forth. For instance, part of the project, planned to be carried out by an internal development team, needs to be performed by a subcontractor, due to unavailability of the team. A change of this nature is usually involved in a substantial additional budget.

The elements comprising a development plan are listed in Frame 6.1.

101

6.3 Elements of the quality plan

Frame 6.1   **The elements comprising a development plan**

1. Project products, specifying "deliverables"
2. Project interfaces
3. Project methodology and development tools
4. Software development standards and procedures
5. Map of the development process
6. Project milestones
7. Project staff organization
8. Required development facilities
9. Development risks and risk management actions
10. Control methods
11. Project cost estimates

Development plan approval

Development plan review and approval is to be completed according to the procedures applied within the organization.

6.3 Elements of the quality plan

All or some of the following items, depending on the project, comprise the elements of a project quality plan:

(1) **Quality goals**

The term "quality goals" refers to the developed software system's substantive quality requirements. Quantitative measures are usually preferred to qualitative measures when choosing quality goals because they provide the developer with more objective assessments of software performance during the development process and system testing. However, one type of goal is not totally equivalent to the other. The possible replacement of qualitative with quantitative measures is illustrated in the following example.

Example

A software system to serve the help desk operations of an electrical appliance manufacturer is to be developed. The help desk system (HDS) is intended to operate for 100 hours per week. The software quality assurance team was requested to prepare a list of quantitative quality goals appropriate to certain qualitative requirements, as shown in Table 6.1.

Table 6.1: Help desk requirements and quantitative goals

HDS qualitative requirements	Related quantitative quality goals
The HDS should be user friendly	A new help desk operator should be able to learn the details of the HDS following a course lasting less than 8 hours, and to master operation of the HDS in less than 5 working days.
The HDS should be very reliable	HDS availability should exceed 99.5% (HDS downtime should not exceed 30 minutes per week).
The HDS should operate continuously	The system's recovery time should not exceed 10 minutes in 99% of cases of HDS failure.
The HDS should be highly efficient	An HDS operator should be able to handle at least 100 customer calls per 8-hour shift.
The HDS should provide high quality service to the applying customers	Waiting time for an operator response should not exceed 30 seconds in 99% of the calls. Achievement of this goal depends on the combination of software features and number of workstations installed and operated.

The quality goals should reflect the major acceptance criteria indicated in the customer's requirement document (i.e., the RFP document). As such, quality goals serve as measures of the successful achievement of the customer's quality requirements.

(2) **Planned review activities**

The quality plan should provide a complete listing of all planned review activities: design reviews (DRs), design inspections, code inspections, and so on, with the following determined for each activity:

- The scope of the review activity
- The type of the review activity
- The schedule of review activities (as defined by its priority and the succeeding activities of the project process)
- The specific procedures to be applied
- Who is responsible for carrying out the review activity?

(3) **Planned software tests**

The quality plan should provide a complete list of planned software tests, with the following designated for each test:

- The unit, integration or the complete system to be tested
- The type of testing activities to be carried out, including specification of computerized software tests to be applied
- The planned test schedule (as defined by its priority and the succeeding activities of the project process)

- The specific procedures to be applied
- Who is responsible for carrying out the test.

(4) **Planned acceptance tests for externally developed software**

A complete list of the acceptance tests planned for externally developed software should be provided within the quality plan. Items to be included are (a) purchased software, (b) software developed by subcontractors, and (c) customer-supplied software. The acceptance tests for externally developed software should parallel those used for internally developed software tests.

(5) **Configuration management**

The quality plan should specify configuration management tools and procedures, including those change-control procedures meant to be applied throughout the project.

The required software quality plan elements are listed in Frame 6.2.

Frame 6.2	**Elements of a software quality plan**

1. List of quality goals
2. Review activities
3. Software tests
4. Acceptance tests for software externally developed
5. Configuration management tools and procedures

The quality plan document, its format and approval

The quality plan may be prepared as part of the development plan or as an independent document. In some cases, the plan is divided into several documents by item category, such as DR plan, testing plan, and plan for externally developed software acceptance tests. Review and approval of the quality plan should be conducted according to the organization's standard procedures for such plans.

6.4 Development and quality plans for small projects and for internal projects

It is quite natural for project leaders to try to evade the "hassle" of preparing a development plan and a quality plan (and the hustle surrounding reviews and plan approvals). This behavior reflects the tendency to avoid "bureaucracy work" and the sweeping control that customers may attempt to exercise. This tendency is especially common in two different situations: small projects and internal projects. The argument for preparing these plans for such projects is discussed in the following two sections.

6.4.1 Development plans and quality plans for small projects

- Does a project of only 40 working days' duration, to be performed by one professional and completed within 12 weeks, justify the investment of a man-day in order to prepare full-scale development and quality plans?
- Does a project to be implemented by three professionals, with a total investment of 30 man-days and completed within five weeks, require full-scale plans?

It should be clear that the development and quality plan procedures applicable to large projects cannot be automatically applied to small projects. Special procedures are needed. These procedures determine how to treat the project in question with respect to the plans:

(1) Cases/situations where neither development nor quality plans are required, e.g. projects requiring 15 man-days.

(2) Cases/situations where the decision to prepare the plans is left to the project leader's discretion. One example could be a project requiring less than 50 man-days where no significant software risk item had been identified – in this case it might be decided that no plans will be prepared. Another example could be a small but complicated project that has to be completed within 30 days, in which there is a heavy penalty on not being completed on time. In this case, planning is needed in order to cope with the project difficulties.

(3) Cases/situations where development and quality plans are obligatory.

A list of elements recommended for inclusion in development and quality plans for small projects is shown in Frame 6.3.

Frame 6.3 **Recommended elements of development and quality plans for small projects**

The development plan:

- Project products, indicating "deliverables"

- Project benchmarks

- Development risks

- Estimates of project costs

The quality plan:

- Quality goals

Several advantages to "planned" small projects over "unplanned" projects can be identified, even for "reduced" plans:

(1) A more comprehensive and thorough understanding of the task is attained.
(2) Greater responsibility for meeting obligations can be assigned.
(3) It becomes easier for management and customers to share control of the project and to identify unexpected delays early on.
(4) Better understandings with respect to the requirements and timetable can be reached between the developer and the customer.

6.4.2 Development plans and quality plans for internal projects

Internal projects are those projects intended for use by other departments in the organization or by the entire organization, as well as those projects dealing with software package development for the software market. Common to all these project types is the fact that no external body participates as customer in their development. Internal projects can be of medium or large scale. Yet even in these cases, there is a tendency to avoid preparation of adequate development and quality plans. The following example illustrates the negative consequences of an "unplanned" internal project.

Example
The Marketing Department of Toyware Ltd, a new computer games manufacturer, had planned to hit the market with "Super-Monster 2000", the firm's new, advanced computer game, during the upcoming Christmas season. The Software Development Department claimed that work on the game should commence immediately in order to complete the project on time. Therefore, preparation of a proposal for discussion by the Marketing and Software Development Departments, and the subsequent preparation of development and quality plans, were not viewed as necessary. The Development Department estimated the project budget at $240 000, which was transferred to the Department. According to the marketing timetable, system tests were to be completed no later than 1 October so as to allow the Marketing Department to carry out the required promotion and advertising campaigns in time for the Christmas sales season.

As the project progressed, it appeared that there might be a delay, but only at the end of June was it obvious that a three-month delay could not be avoided. The promotional and advertising activities that had taken place before 30 June thus became worthless. The project was finally completed at the end of February. The project's cost overrun was significant – actual costs exceeded $385 000 – but most painful was the company's lost opportunity to exploit the Christmas market. Last week, the company's management decided to avoid any future internal computer game development projects.

This example makes clear that preparation of full-scale development and quality plans for internal projects – in addition to regular monitoring – can be highly beneficial for implementation of internal projects as well.

Software development departments can enjoy the following advantages of plan preparation:

(1) Avoiding budget overruns. This is of special importance where the profit center system is applied.
(2) Avoiding damage to other projects caused by delays in release of professionals occupied in an internal project.
(3) Avoiding loss of market status, especially regarding the firm's reputation, caused by delayed completion of external projects triggered by late completion of internal projects.

Internal "customers" can enjoy the following advantages:

(1) Smaller deviations from planned completion dates and smaller budget overruns.
(2) Better control over the development process, including earlier identification of possible delays that enables the search for and resolution of their causes.
(3) Fewer internal delay damages.

The organization can enjoy these advantages:

(1) Reduced risk of market loss (i.e., opportunity window) due to late arrival of the product.
(2) Reduced risk of being sued for late supply of products; hence, reduced penalties for non-compliance with contract demands.
(3) Reduced risk of impairing the firm's reputation as a reliable software developer.
(4) Reduced risk of requesting a budget supplement.

Summary

(1) Explain the objectives of development and quality plans.

The plans' objectives are to provide the basis for:
- Scheduling development activities
- Recruiting team members and allocating development facilities
- Resolving development risks
- Implementing required SQA activities
- Providing management with needed data for project control.

(2) Identify the elements of a development plan.

Eleven types of elements constitute a development plan:
(1) Project products
(2) Project interfaces
(3) Project methodology and development tools
(4) Software development standards and procedures
(5) Mapping of the development process
(6) Project milestones
(7) Project staff organization
(8) Required development facilities
(9) Development risks
(10) Control methodology
(11) Project cost estimates.

(3) Identify the elements of a quality plan.

Five elements constitute a quality plan:
(1) Quality goals
(2) Planned review activities
(3) Planned software tests
(4) Planned acceptance tests for externally developed software
(5) Planned configuration management.

(4) Identify the major software risk items.

Typical development risks are:
- Technological gaps – lack of adequate and sufficient professional knowledge
- Staff shortages
- Interdependence on other organizations: suppliers, subcontractors, etc.

(5) Explain the process of software risk management.

The activities involved in risk management include planning, implementation, and monitoring of implementation. The pertinent planning activities are identification of SRIs, evaluation of those SRIs, and planning RMAs to resolve the SRIs.

(6) Discuss the benefits of preparing development and quality plans for small projects

For small development projects (of not less than 15 man-days), preparation of development and quality plans is optional. However, one should consider the substantial advantages obtained by the plan's developer. The main advantages of plan preparation are improvements in the developer's understanding of the task, and greater commitment to complete the project as planned. In addition, the plan documents contribute to a better understanding between the developer and the customer, and easier and more effective project control.

(7) Discuss the benefits of preparing development and quality plans for internal projects.

It is recommended that internal projects, undertaken on behalf of other departments and for development of software packages geared toward the market, be treated as "regular projects". This implies that full-scale development and quality plans are to be prepared. Their benefits include:

(a) **The development department** will avoid losses incurred by unrealistic timetables and budgets, as well as the consequent damage to other projects and to the firm's reputation.

(b) **The internal "customer"** will enjoy reduced risk of late completion and budget overruns in addition to and by improved project control and coordination with the developer.

(c) **The firm** will enjoy reduced risk of its software product's late entry into the market, reduced risk of a decline in its reputation resulting from late supply, and reduced risk of budget overruns.

Selected bibliography

1 Barki, H., Rivard, S. and Talbot, J. (1993). "Toward an assessment of software development risk", *Journal of Management Information Systems*, 10(2), 203–225.

2 Boehm, B. W. (1988). "A spiral model of software development and enhancement", *Computer*, 21(5), 61–72.

3 Boehm, B. W. (1991). "Software risk management: principles and practices", *IEEE Software*, January, 32–41.

4 Boehm, B. W. (1998). "Using the Win-Win spiral model: a case study", *Computer*, 31(7), 33–44.

5 Boehm, B. W. and Ross, R. (1989). "Theory-W project management: principles and examples", *IEEE Transactions on Software Engineering*, 15, 902–916.

6 Carnegie-Mellon University Software Engineering Institute (1994) *The Capability Maturity Model: Guidlines for Improving the Software Process*, Addison-Wesley, Reading, MA.

7 Felschow, A. (1999). "Understanding the Capability Maturity Model (CMM) and the role of SQA in Software Development Maturity", in G. G. Schulmeyer and J. I. McManus (eds), *Handbook of Software Quality Assurance*, 3rd edn, Prentice Hall, Upper Saddle River, NJ, pp. 329–350.

8 Hall, E. M. (1998) *Managing Risk – Methods for Software Systems Development*, Addison-Wesley, Reading, MA.

9 Humphrey, W. S. (1989) *Managing the Software Process*, Addison-Wesley, Reading, MA.

10 IEEE (1998) "IEEE Std 730-1998 – IEEE Standard for Software Quality Assurance Plans", in *IEEE Software Engineering Standards Collection*, The Institute of Electrical and Electronics Engineers, New York,

11 IEEE (2001) "IEEE Std 1540-2001 – IEEE Standard for Software Life Cycle Processes - Risk Management", in *IEEE Software Engineering Standards Collection*, The Institute of Electrical and Electronics Engineers, New York.

12 ISO (1997) *ISO 9000-3:1997(E), Quality Management and Quality Assurance Standards – Part 3: Guidelines for the Application of ISO 9001:1994 to the*

Development, Supply, Installation and Maintenance of Computer Software, 2nd edn. International Organization for Standardization (ISO), Geneva.

13 ISO/IEC (2001) "ISO 9000-3:2001 Software and System Engineering – Guidelines for the Application of ISO 9001:2000 to Software, Final draft", International Organization for Standardization (ISO), Geneva, unpublished draft, December 2001.

14 Jones, C. (1994) *Assessment and Control of Software Risks*, Yourdon Press, Prentice Hall, Upper Saddle River, NJ.

15 Karolak, D. W. (1996) *Software Engineering Risk Management*, IEEE Computer Society Press, Los Alamitos, CA.

16 Keil, M., Cule, P. C., Lyytinen, K. and Schmidt, R. C. (1998). "A framework for identifying software project risks", *Communications of the ACM*, 41(11), 76–83.

17 Oskarsson, O. and Glass, R. L. (1996) *An ISO 9000 Approach to Building Quality Software*, Ch. 3, Prentice Hall. Upper Saddle River, NJ.

18 Paulk, M. C., Weber, C. V., Curtis, B. and Chrissis, M. B. (1995). *The Capability Maturity Model: Guidelines for Improving the Software Process*, Addison-Wesley, Reading, MA.

19 Ropponen, J. and Lyytinen, K. (2000) "Components of Software Development Risk: How to Address Them? A Project Manager Survey", IEEE Transactions on Software Engineering, 26 (2), pp. 98–111.

Review questions

6.1 Significant similarity exists between the proposal draft review and the development plan.

(1) Compare these documents with reference to the subjects reviewed.
(2) Compare these documents while referring to the aim of preparing the individual documents.

6.2 Development and quality plans have five objectives.

(1) Can you list the objectives?
(2) Suggest ways in which each objective contributes to the successful and timely completion of the project.

6.3 Some development elements are included in the requirement document, yet are not compiled by development planners.

(1) Which elements of the development plan belong to this category?
(2) Explain the importance of gathering this information from the customer's documents.

6.4 Development process mapping is one of the most important elements of the development plan.

(1) List the possible phases of the development process.
(2) List possible inputs and outputs for each of the phases suggested in (1).
(3) What components of each activity, as associated with each project phase, should be described in the development plan?

6.5 The project's organization is an important element of the development plan.

(1) List the components of the organization element.
(2) Which of the components in (1) are based on components of project mapping?
(3) Why is it necessary to mention team members by name? Isn't it sufficient to list the number of team members by their expertise as required for each phase of the project?

6.6 Boehm and Ross (1989) mentioned 10 major software risk items.

(1) Can you list the 10 SRIs?
(2) For each of the SRIs mentioned in (1), suggest the three most effective RMAs for handling them (refer to Table 6A.2 in the Appendix to this chapter). Explain your choice.

6.7 Only four out of the 11 elements of a development plan and only one out of five of the quality plan are considered obligatory for small projects.

(1) Do you agree with this choice? If yes, list your main arguments.
(2) If you do not agree with this choice, present your improved list and explain your choice.

6.8 "Preparing full-scale development and quality plans for internal projects, and applying regular full customer–supplier relationships for the implementation of internal projects, is highly beneficial to both sides."

(1) Explain the benefits of these procedures to the developer.
(2) Explain the benefits to internal customers.

Topics for discussion

6.1 "As long as the proposal was properly prepared and approved, following an adequate contract review, there is no justification for redoing all this work. Its resource estimates and schedule can serve as the project's plan . . . ." You often hear claims like this one.

(1) Do you agree with this claim? If not, list your arguments against it.
(2) Suggest situations where it is clear that the proposal and its materials can serve as development and quality plans.
(3) Suggest situations where it is clear that the proposal and its materials cannot serve as development and quality plans.

6.2 Martin Adams, an experienced project leader at David's Software Ltd, a medium-sized software house, has been appointed project leader for development of an advanced help desk software system for a leading home appliance maintenance service. This is the 12th help desk system developed by his department in the last three years.

The current project is somewhat special with respect to its timetable. The contract with the customer was signed six days after submission of the proposal, and the development team is scheduled to begin working at full capacity, with eight team members, 10 days later. The contract offers a significant early completion bonus for each week below 26 weeks, but determines high late completion penalties for each week after 30 weeks.

In a meeting with his superior, Adams claims that the comprehensive proposal documentation "as is", which has been thoroughly checked by the contract review team, should serve as the project's development and quality plans. His superior does not agree with him and demands that he immediately prepare comprehensive project and quality plans, according to company procedures.

(1) Do you agree with Adams? If yes, list the arguments that support his claim.
(2) Do you agree with his superior? If yes, list the arguments that support the superior's claim.
(3) Considering the circumstances of the project, what, in your opinion, should be done in this case?
(4) Comparing the circumstances described here to those of the opening anecdote, are there any justifications for different recommendations?

6.3 This topic refers to Section 6A.3 in the Appendix to this chapter. An experienced project leader has identified six SRIs inherent in his project and estimated their Est(dam) and Prob(mat). The results are listed in the following table:

No.	SRIs	Prob(mat)	Est(dam) ($)
1	Networking at the customer's 23 sites will not be completed on time	0.2	150 000
2	Subcontracted modules will fail the acceptance tests	0.5	12 000
3	The programming team will be 2–3 programmers short for more than 2 months	0.7	50 000
4	The software quality assurance activities will fail to detect major software errors in the complicated discount module; these errors will be discovered by the customer during the guarantee period	0.05	600 000
5	The final test of the user's guide will detect significant errors that will cause a delay of more than 2 weeks in delivery to the customer	0.3	2500
6	The planned server's capacity will be found insufficient in the final system tests	0.25	40 000

(1) Determine the priorities for these SRIs, using the formula given in Section 6A. 3.
(2) Can you suggest an alternative method for prioritizing the SRIs?
(3) Determine the SRI priorities according to the alternative method. Compare the resulting priority list with that obtained in (1), and discuss the implications of the differences, if any.

6.4 It is said that three of the quality plan's elements must be coordinated with an element of the development plan – the mapping of the development process.

(1) Can you identify these elements?
(2) Explain the nature of the required coordination.

6.5 Quoting from Section.6.3: "Quantitative measures are usually preferred to qualitative measures when choosing quality goals because they provide the developer with more objective assessments of software performance during the development process and system testing. However, one type of goal is not totally equivalent to the other."

(1) How are quantitative goals applied during the development process?
(2) Explain in what way quantitative goals enable more objective evaluation of performance when compared with qualitative goals.

Appendix 6A Software development risks and software risk management

6A.1 Software development risks

Several lists of potential software development risks ("software risk items" or SRIs) are mentioned in the literature. Ropponen and Lyytinen (2000) have classified software risk items into the following six classes:

(1) Scheduling and timing risks
(2) System functionality risks
(3) Subcontracting risks
(4) Requirement management risks
(5) Resource usage and performance risks
(6) Personnel management risks.

Boehm and Ross (1989) suggest a list of the 10 major software risk items. Table 6A.1 shows how this list can be integrated with the six risk classes proposed by Ropponen and Lyytinen (2000).

Methodologies for identification of software risk items have been offered by Boehm (1991), Keil *et al.*, (1998), Ropponen and Lyytinen (2000), Barki *et al.*, (1993) and IEEE (2001). One of the most effective tools for identifying and evaluating software risk items is specialized checklists, also mentioned by several authors.

Karolak (1996) and Jones (1994) have broadened the scope of software risk items to include strategic risk, such as marketing risks and financial risks. This author believes that despite the importance of strategic risks, they are beyond the scope of software quality assurance and thus beyond the scope of this book.

Table 6A.1: The top 10 software risk items

No.	Software risk class (Ropponen and Lyytinen)	No.	Software risk item (Boehm and Ross)	Description
1	Personnel management risks	1	Personnel shortfalls	Lack and turnover of qualified personnel
2	Scheduling and timing	2	Unrealistic schedules and budgets	Incorrectly estimated (too low) development time and budget
3	System functionality	3	Developing wrong software functions	Development of software functions that are not needed or are incorrectly specified
		4	Developing wrong user interface	Inadequate or difficult user interface (GUI)
4	Requirement management	5	Gold plating	Addition of unnecessary features ("whistles and bells") due to professional interests, pride, or user demands
		6	Continuing stream of requirement changes	Uncontrolled and unpredictable changes in system functions and features
5	Subcontracting	7	Shortfalls in externally furnished components	Poor quality of externally delivered system components
		8	Shortfalls in externally performed tasks	Poor quality or unpredictable accomplishment of externally performed tasks
6	Resource usage and performance	9	Real-time performance shortfalls	Poor system performance
		10	Straining computer science capabilities	Inability to implement the system due to lack of technical solutions and/or computing power

6A.2   Risk management activities and measures

Various activities and measures (usually termed "risk management actions" or RMAs) can be taken. The purposes of RMAs are to prevent software risks, to achieve early identification of software risk items, and to resolve them.

Boehm and Ross (1989), Boehm (1991), Ropponen and Lyytinen (2000), and Karolak (1996), among others, have suggested a wide variety of risk management actions (see Table 6A.2).

Table 6A.2: Commonly recommended risk management actions and their contributions

No.	Software risk management action (RMA)	Contribution of the RMA		
		Prevention	Early identification of SRI	Resolution of SRI
	Internal RMA			
1	Application of detailed and thorough analysis to requirements and estimated schedules and costs	x		
2	Efficient project organization, adequate staff and team size	x		
3	Personnel training	x		
4	Arranging for and training replacements to take over in case of turnover and unanticipated workloads	x		
5	Arranging for user participation in the development process	x		
6	Applying efficient change control (change requests screening)	x		
7	Applying intensive software quality assurance measures such as inspections, design reviews, and benchmarking	x		
8	Periodic checking for timely availability of firm professionals currently occupied with other projects		x	
9	Arranging for participation of professional staff members having knowledge and experience with SRIs			x
10	Scheduling SRI-related activities as early as possible to provide leeway in case of difficulties			x
11	Prototyping SRI-related modules or project applications			x
12	Preparing scenarios for complicated SRI-related modules or project applications			x
13	Simulating SRI-related modules or project applications			x
	Subcontracting RMA			
1	Preparing comprehensive and thorough contracts with subcontractors and suppliers, including contract reviews	x		
2	Participating in internal progress control and software quality assurance activities of subcontractors to be incorporated in the contract		x	

No.	Software risk management action (RMA)	Contribution of the RMA		
		Prevention	Early identification of SRI	Resolution of SRI
3	Arranging for "loans" of professionals with specialized knowledge and experience if the need arises			x
4	Hiring consultants to support the team in the absence of sufficient know-how and experience			x
	Customer RMA			
1	Formulating comprehensive and thorough contracts with customers, including contract reviews	x		
2	Negotiating with the customer to change requirements re risky parts of the project			x
3	Negotiating with the customer to change schedules re risky parts of the project			x

These risk management actions can be grouped into the following classes:

- Internal risk management actions, applied within the software developing organization.
- Subcontracting risk management actions, dealing with the relationship between the software developer and his subcontractors and suppliers.
- Customer risk management actions, dealing with the relationship between the software developer and the customer.

Implementation tip

In planning RMAs, one should be aware that:

- Some RMAs can prevent, identify or resolve SRIs of various types.
- Some SRIs can be treated by several RMAs.
- The efficiency of an RMA varies significantly with different projects and in different environments.

6A.3   The risk management process

The risk management process combines planning activities, implementation activities and monitoring activities. Elaine M. Hall (1998) has written a book dedicated mainly to this process.

Planning activities

Several planning activities are aimed to initiate those risk management actions that can respond to the software risks identified and evaluated earlier. Similar planning activities (although not to the same degree of thoroughness) are part of the proposal draft review process (see Chapter 5).

The respective planning activities include:

■ **Identification of software risk items**

The main tool supporting identification of SRIs is those checklists that specify the team, project and customer situations that are likely to bring about software risks. Checklists of this type have been suggested by Boehm and Ross (1989), Boehm (1991), Barki *et al.* (1993), and Ropponen and Lyytinen (2000).

Identification of software risk items should begin with the actual start of the project (pre-project stage) and be repeated periodically throughout the project until its completion.

■ **Evaluation of the identified SRIs**

Evaluation of the identified SRIs is concerned mainly with:

– Estimating the probability that a software risk will materialize if no RMA is taken – i.e., Prob(mat)

– Estimating damages in case an SRI does materialize – i.e., Est(dam).

Estimates of Prob(mat) and Est(dam) can be based on experience gained in earlier projects, by means of simulation models, and so forth.

Evaluation should be followed by determination of priorities regarding the SRIs and their resolution. It should be clear that an SRI displaying a high Prob(mat) and high Est(dam) is of high priority and that an SRI displaying a low Prob(mat) and low Est(dam) is of low priority.

One common method used to prioritize SRIs is by calculating their expected damage, termed "risk exposure" – Exp(risk) – where:

$$Exp(risk) = Est(dam) \times Prob(mat)$$

■ **Planning RMAs**

It is incumbent upon the software risk team to consider alternative ways to resolve the identified SRIs. RMAs include a range of internal, subcontractor and customer actions. Table 6A.2 provides a list of possible RMAs and their contributions to the prevention or resolution of SRIs.

In preparing the recommended list of RMAs, the planning team should consider:

– The priority assigned to the SRI

– The expected results of a planned RMA (complete or partial resolution)

– The costs and organizational efforts required for implementation of the RMA.

Implementation

Implementation of a risk management plan requires that the staff members be assigned personally responsible for each RMA and its implementation schedule.

Monitoring implementation of the risk management plan

Systematic, periodic activities are required to monitor implementation of the risk management plan. The aim of the monitoring activities is to:

■ Determine the efficiency of the RMAs
■ Update the risk evaluation by considering newly identified SRIs.

The process of software risk management is illustrated in Figure 6A.1.

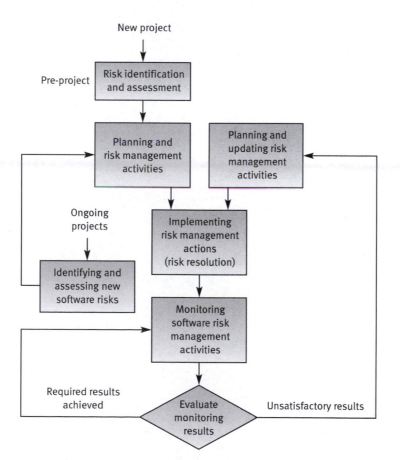

Figure 6A.1: The software risk management process

SQA components in the project life cycle

The project life cycle encompasses two stages: the development life cycle stage and the operation–maintenance stage. Most of the SQA components to be reviewed in Part III support at least one of the phases comprising these stages.

Development life cycle SQA components are meant to detect design and programming errors in the design and programming (coding) phases. The components applied in this stage belong to one of the following four sub-classes:

- Formal design reviews
- Peer reviews
- Expert opinions
- Software testing.

Operation–maintenance stage SQA components include special components to be applied for corrective maintenance but also development life cycle SQA components that can also be used for functionality improvement maintenance tasks.

An additional sub-class of SQA components, other than those listed above, deals with assuring the quality of project parts performed by subcontractors and other external participants during the project life cycle. The importance of this sub-class stems from the high risks associated with functional failures and the failure to keep to the project timetable. Both types of risk are directly related to the difficulty of controlling the external participants' performance.

The project characteristics determine which SQA components enter the project life cycle at any particular point. To guarantee their effectiveness, the choice of components is decided upon prior to the project's initiation.

The first chapter of this part, Chapter 7, is dedicated to a general discussion of the integration of software quality assurance components within each phase of the project's life cycle. A model for assessing the effectiveness and costs of integration is also presented in this chapter.

Chapter 8 discusses the review components of the design phase: formal design reviews, peer review and expert opinions.

Chapters 9 and 10 are dedicated to software testing issues, with Chapter 9 focusing on testing strategies and Chapter 10 on software testing implementation. Among the implementation issues discussed are manual and automated testing.

Chapter 11 deals with SQA components appropriate to the operation–maintenance stage. Although functionality improvement and adaptive maintenance tasks employ primarily development life cycle SQA components (see Chapters 8–10), corrective maintenance, the subject of this chapter, has distinctive requirements and special SQA components.

Chapter 12, the final chapter in this part, explores the SQA issues raised by the participation of external participants in a project.

chapter 7

Integrating quality activities in the project life cycle

The first part of this chapter is dedicated to the various software development models in current use. The remaining sections deal with the objectives of the software quality assurance activities conducted throughout the project life cycle, their integration in the development process, and the factors considered before applying them.

One might inquire why not begin with SQA activities and omit the discussion of the software development models? This question is not simply rhetorical. Software development models provide a coordinated set of concepts and methodologies needed to implement software development. As such, they include definitions of the main activities needed for development, the appropriate sequence for their performance, and their milestones. By deciding what models are to be applied, the project leader determines how the project will be carried out. Most quality assurance activities take place in conjunction with the completion or examination of activity milestones, which require review of the product development activities previously completed. Therefore, SQA professionals should be acquainted with the various software engineering models in order to be able to prepare a quality plan that is properly integrated into the project plan.

The rest of the first part of the chapter deals with the factors affecting the choice of software quality activities to be integrated in the development process. The following four chapters (Chapters 8 to 11) deal with the specific software quality methodologies to be applied at each phase of the development stage and in the operation–maintenance stage.

The second part of the chapter is dedicated to a model for assessing a plan for SQA defect-removal effectiveness and cost. The model, a multiple filtering model, is based on data acquired from a survey of defect origins, percentages of defect removal achieved by various quality assurance activities, and the defect-removal costs incurred at the various development phases. The model enables quantitative comparison of quality assurance policies as realized in quality assurance plans.

After completing this chapter, you will be able to:

■ Describe the various software development models and discuss the differences between them.

■ Explain the considerations affecting intensity of applying quality assurance activities.

■ Explain the different aspects of verification, validation and qualification associated with quality assurance activities.

■ Describe the model for the SQA plan's defect-removal effectiveness and cost.

■ Explain possible uses for the model.

7.1   Classic and other software development methodologies

Four models of the software development process are discussed in this section:

■ The Software Development Life Cycle (SDLC) model
■ The prototyping model
■ The spiral model
■ The object-oriented model.

The models presented here are not merely alternatives; rather, they represent complementary view of software development or refer to different development contexts.

The Software Development Life Cycle model (the SDLC model) is the classic model (still applicable today); it provides the most comprehensive description of the process available. The model displays the major building blocks for the entire development process, described as a linear sequence. In the initial phases of the software development process, product design documents are prepared, with the first version of the computer program completed and presented for evaluation only at quite a late stage of the process. The SDLC model can serve as a framework within which the other models are presented.

The prototyping model is based on replacement of one or more SDLC model phases by an evolutionary process, where software prototypes are used for communication between the developer and the users and customers. Prototypes are submitted to user representatives for evaluation. The developer then continues development of a more advanced prototype, which is also submitted for evaluation. This evolutionary process continues till the software project is completed or the software prototype has reached the desired phase. In this case, the rest of the development process can be carried out according to a different methodology, for example the classic SDLC model.

The spiral model provides a methodology for ensuring effective performance at each of the SDLC model phases. It involves an iterative process that integrates customer comments and change requirements, risk analysis and resolution, and software system planning and engineering activities. One or more iterations of the spiral model may be required to complete each of the project's SDLC phases. The associated engineering tasks may be performed according to any one model or a combination of them.

The object-oriented model incorporates large-scale reuse of software by integrating reusable modules into new software systems. In cases where no reusable software modules (termed objects or components) are available, the developer may perform a prototyping or SDLC process to complete the newly developed software system.

All four models will be presented in detail in the next four sections. Detailed discussions of the respective methodologies are available in the software engineering and system analysis literature, particularly Pressman (2000) and Kendall and Kendall (1999).

7.1.1 The software development life cycle (SDLC) model

The classic Software Development Life Cycle (SDLC) model is a linear sequential model that begins with requirements definition and ends with regular system operation and maintenance. The most common illustration of the SDLC model is the waterfall model, shown in Figure 7.1.

The model shown in Figure 7.1 presents a seven-phase process, as follows:

- **Requirements definition**. For the functionality of the software system to be developed, the customers must define their requirements. In many cases the software system is part of a larger system. Information about the other parts of the expanded system helps establish cooperation between the teams and develop component interfaces.
- **Analysis**. The main effort here is to analyze the requirements' implications to form the initial software system model.

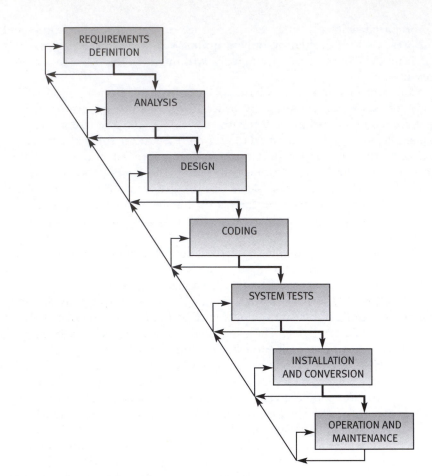

Figure 7.1: The waterfall model
Source: After Boehm (1981) and Royce (1970) (© 1970 IEEE)

- **Design.** This stage involves the detailed definition of the outputs, inputs and processing procedures, including data structures and databases, software structure, etc.
- **Coding.** In this phase, the design is translated into a code. Coding involves quality assurance activities such as inspection, unit tests and integration tests.
- **System tests.** System tests are performed once the coding phase is completed. The main goal of testing is to uncover as many software errors as possible so as to achieve an acceptable level of software quality once corrections have been completed. System tests are carried out by the software developer before the software is supplied to the customer. In many cases the customer performs independent software tests ("acceptance tests") to assure him or herself that the developer has fulfilled all the commitments and that no unanticipated or faulty software reactions are anticipated. It is quite common for a customer to ask the developer to

join him or her in performing joint system tests, a procedure that saves the time and resources required for separate acceptance tests.

■ **Installation and conversion.** After the software system is approved, the system is installed to serve as firmware, that is, as part of the information system that represents a major component of the expanded system. If the new information system is to replace an existing system, a software conversion process has to be initiated to make sure that the organization's activities continue uninterrupted during the conversion phase.

■ **Regular operation and maintenance.** Regular software operation begins once installation and conversion have been completed. Throughout the regular operation period, which usually lasts for several years or until a new software generation appears on the scene, maintenance is needed. Maintenance incorporates three types of services: corrective – repairing software faults identified by the user during operation; adaptive – using the existing software features to fulfill new requirements; and perfective – adding new minor features to improve software performance.

The number of phases can vary according to the characteristics of the project. In complex, large-scale models, some phases are split, causing their number to grow to eight, nine or more. In smaller projects, some phases may be merged, reducing the number of phases to six, five or even four phases.

At the end of each phase, the outputs are examined and evaluated by the developer and, in many cases, by the customer as well. Possible outcomes of the review and evaluation include:

■ Approval of the phase outputs and progress on to the next phase, or
■ Demands to correct, redo or change parts of the last phase; in certain cases, a return to earlier phases is required.

The width of the lines connecting the rectangular boxes in the illustration reflects the relative probabilities of the different outcomes. Thus, the most commonly performed process is a linear sequence (no or only minor corrections). We should note, however, that the model emphasizes direct development activities and does not indicate customer stakes in the development process.

The classic waterfall model was suggested by Royce (1970) and later presented in its commonly known form by Boehm (1981). It provides the foundations for the majority of the major software quality assurance standards employed, such as IEEE Std 1012 (IEEE, 1998) and IEEE Std 12207 (IEEE, 1996, 1997a, 1997b), to mention just two.

7.1.2 The prototyping model

The prototyping methodology makes use of (a) developments in information technology, namely, advanced application generators that allow for fast and easy development of software prototypes, combined with (b) active participation in the development process by customers and users capable of examining and evaluating prototypes.

When applying the prototyping methodology, future users of the system are required to comment on the various versions of the software prototypes prepared by the developers. In response to customer and user comments, the developers correct the prototype and add parts to the system on the way to presenting the next generation of the software for user evaluation. This process is repeated till the prototyping goal is achieved or the software system is completed. A typical application of the prototyping methodology is shown in Figure 7.2.

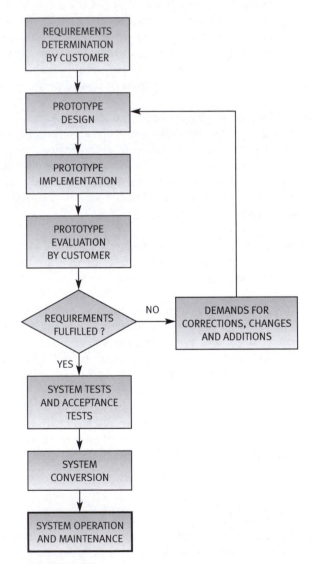

Figure 7.2: The prototyping model

Prototyping can be applied in combination with other methodologies or as a "stand alone" methodology. In other words, the extent of prototyping can vary, from replacement of one SDLC (or other methodology) phase up to complete prototyping of the entire software system.

Prototyping as a *software development* methodology has been found to be efficient and effective mainly for small- to medium-sized software development projects. The main advantages and deficiencies of prototyping over the complete SDLC methodology, summarized in Frame 7.1, result from the user's intense involvement in the software development process. Such involvement facilitates the user's understanding of the system while it limits the developer's freedom to introduce innovative changes in the system.

Frame 7.1	Prototyping versus SDLC methodology – advantages and disadvantages (mainly for small to medium-sized projects)

Advantages of prototyping:

■ Shorter development process

■ Substantial savings of development resources (man-days)

■ Better fit to customer requirements and reduced risk of project failure

■ Easier and faster user comprehension of the new system

Disadvantages of prototyping:

■ Diminished flexibility and adaptability to changes and additions

■ Reduced preparation for unexpected instances of failure

7.1.3 The spiral model

The spiral model, as revised by Boehm (1988, 1998), offers an improved methodology for overseeing large and more complex development projects displaying higher prospects for failure, typical of many projects begun in the last two decades. It combines an iterative model that introduces and emphasizes risk analysis and customer participation into the major elements of SDLC and prototyping methodologies.

According to the spiral model, shown in Figure 7.3, software development is perceived to be an iterative process; at each iteration, the following activities are performed:

■ Planning
■ Risk analysis and resolution
■ Engineering activities according to the stage of the project: design, coding, testing, installation and release
■ Customer evaluation, including comments, changes and additional requirements, etc.

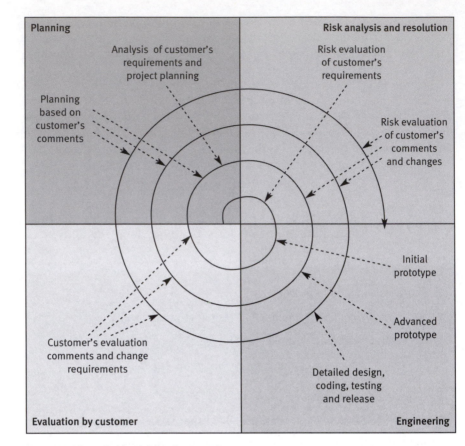

Figure 7.3: The spiral model (Boehm, 1988)
Source: After Boehm (1988) (© 1988 IEEE)

An advanced spiral model, the Win–Win Spiral model (Boehm, 1998), enhances the Spiral model (Boehm, 1988) still further. The advanced model places extra emphasis on communication and negotiation between the customer and the developer. The model's name refers to the fact that by using this process, the customer "wins" in the form of improved chances to receive the system most satisfying to his needs, and the developer "wins" in the form of improved chances to stay within the budget and complete the project by the agreed date. This is achieved by increasing emphasis on customer participation and on engineering activities. These revisions in the development process are shown graphically by two sections of the spiral dedicated to customer participation: the first deals with customer evaluation and the second with customer comments and change requirements. Engineering activity is likewise shown in two sections of the spiral: the first is dedicated to design and the second to construction. By evaluating project progress at the end of each of these sections, the developer is able to better control the entire development process.

Accordingly, in the advanced spiral model, shown in Figure 7.4, the following six activities are carried out in each iteration:

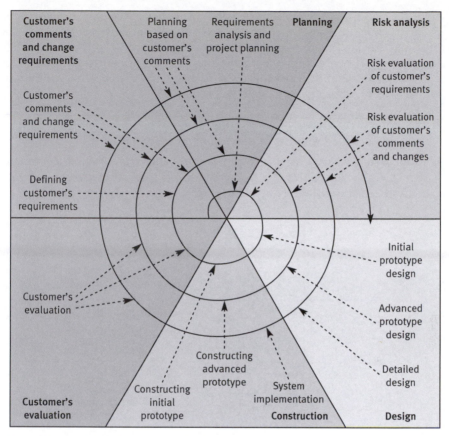

Figure 7.4: The advanced spiral model (Boehm, 1998)
Source: After Boehm (1988) (© 1988 IEEE)

- Customer's specification of requirements, comments and change demands
- Developer's planning activities
- Developer's risk analysis and resolution
- Developer's design activities
- Developer's construction activities pertaining to coding, testing, installation and release
- Customer's evaluation.

7.1.4 The object-oriented model

The object-oriented model differs from the other models by its intensive reuse of software components. This methodology is characterized by its easy integration of existing software modules (called objects or components) into newly developed software systems. A software component library serves this purpose by supplying software components for reuse.

So, according to the object-oriented model as shown in Figure 7.5, the development process begins with a sequence of object-oriented analyses and designs. The design phase is followed by acquisition of suitable components from the reusable software library, when available. "Regular" development is carried out otherwise. Copies of newly developed software components are then "stocked" in the software library for future reuse. It is expected that the growing software component stocks in the reusable software library will allow substantial and increasing reuse of software, a trend that will allow taking greater advantage of resources as follows:

- Economy – The cost of integrating a reusable software component is much lower than the cost of developing new components.
- Improved quality – Used software components are expected to contain considerably fewer defects than newly developed software components due to detection of faults by former users.

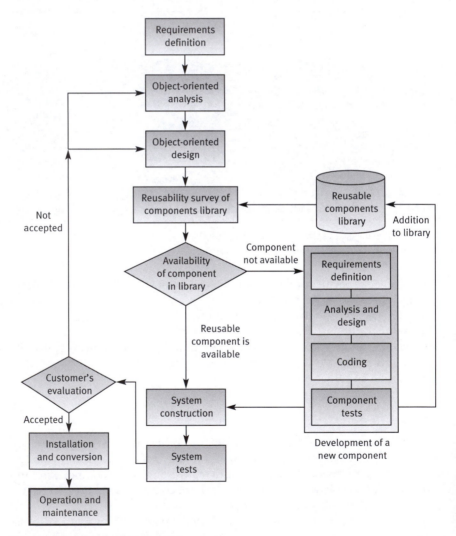

Figure 7.5: The object-oriented model

■ Shorter development time – The integration of reusable software components reduces scheduling pressures.

Thus, the advantages of the object-oriented methodology over other methodologies will grow as the storage of reusable software grows.

7.2 Factors affecting intensity of quality assurance activities in the development process

Project life cycle quality assurance activities are process oriented, in other words, linked to completion of a project phase, accomplishment of a project milestone, and so forth. The quality assurance activities will be integrated into the development plan that implements one or more software development models – the waterfall, prototyping, spiral, object-oriented or other models.

Quality assurance planners for a project are required to determine:

■ The list of quality assurance activities needed for a project.
■ For each quality assurance activity:
  – Timing
  – Type of quality assurance activity to be applied
  – Who performs the activity and the resources required. It should be noted that various bodies may participate in the performance of quality assurance activities: development team and department staff members together with independent bodies such as external quality assurance team members or consultants
  – Resources required for removal of defects and introduction of changes.

Implementation tip

In some development plans, one finds quality assurance activities spread throughout the process, but without any time allocated for their performance or for the subsequent removal of defects. Someone probably assumed that a late afternoon meeting would be sufficient for performing the quality assurance activities and the corrections to be made. As nothing is achieved without time, the almost guaranteed result is delay, caused by the "unexpectedly" long duration of the quality assurance process. Hence, the time allocated for quality assurance activities and the defects correction work that follow should be examined.

The intensity of the quality assurance activities planned, indicated by the number of required activities, is affected by project and team factors, as shown in Frame 7.2.

| Frame 7.2 | **Factors affecting the required intensity of quality assurance activities** |

Project factors:

■ Magnitude of the project

■ Technical complexity and difficulty

■ Extent of reusable software components

■ Severity of failure outcomes if the project fails

Team factors:

■ Professional qualification of the team members

■ Team acquaintance with the project and its experience in the area

■ Availability of staff members who can professionally support the team

■ Familiarity with the team members, in other words the percentage of new staff members in the team

The following two examples can illustrate how these factors can influence quality assurance activities.

Example 1

A software development team has planned the quality assurance activities for its new consumer club project. The current project contract, signed with a leading furniture store, is the team's 11th consumer club project dealing in the last three years. The team estimates that about seven man-months need to be invested by the two team members assigned to the project, whose duration is estimated at four months. It is estimated that a reusable components library can supply 90% of the project software.

Three quality assurance activities were planned by the project leader. The quality assurance activities and their duration are listed in Table 7.1.

Table 7.1: Duration of quality assurance activities – the consumer club example

No.	Quality assurance activity	Duration of quality assurance activity (days)	Duration of corrections and changes (days)
1	Design review of requirements definition	0.5	1
2	Inspection of the design	1	1
3	System test of completed software package	4	2

The main considerations affecting this plan are:

- Degree of team acquaintance with the subject
- High percentage of software reuse
- Size of the project (in this case, medium)
- Severity of failure results if the project fails.

Example 2

The real-time software development unit of a hospital's information systems department has been assigned to develop an advanced patient monitoring system. The new monitoring unit is to combine of patient's room unit with a control unit. The patient's room unit is meant to interface with several types of medical equipment, supplied by different manufacturers, which measure various indicators of the patient's condition. A sophisticated control unit will be placed at the nurses' station, with data to be communicated to cellular units carried by doctors.

The project leader estimates that 14 months will be required to complete the system; a team of five will be needed, with an investment of a total of 40 man-months. She estimates that only 15% of the components can be obtained from the reusable component library. The SDLC methodology was chosen to integrate application of two prototypes of the patient's room unit and two prototypes of the control unit for the purpose of improving communication with the users and enhancing feedback of comments at the analysis and design phases.

The main considerations affecting this plan are:

- High complexity and difficulty of the system
- Low percentage of reusable software available
- Large size of the project
- High severity of failure outcomes if the project fails.

The quality assurance activities and their duration, as defined by the project leader, are listed in Table 7.2.

7.3 Verification, validation and qualification

Three aspects of quality assurance of the software product (a report, code, etc.) are examined under the rubrics of verification, validation and qualification.

IEEE Std 610.12-1990 (IEEE, 1990) defines these aspects as follows:

- "**Verification** – The process of evaluating a system or component to determine whether the products of a given development phase satisfy the conditions imposed at the start of that phase."

Table 7.2: Duration of quality assurance activities – the patient monitoring system example

No.	Quality assurance activity	Duration of quality assurance activity (days)	Duration of corrections and changes (days)
1	Design review of requirements definition	2	1
2	Design review of analysis of patient's room unit	2	2
3	Design review of analysis of control unit	1	2
4	Design review of preliminary design	1	1
5	Inspection of design of patient's room unit	1	2
6	Inspection of design of control unit	1	3
7	Design review of prototype of patient's room unit	1	1
8	Design review of prototype of control unit	1	1
9	Inspection of detailed design for each software interface component	3	3
10	Design review of test plans for patient's room unit and control unit	3	1
11	Unit tests of software code for each interface module of patient's room unit	4	2
12	Integration test of software code of patient's room unit	3	3
13	Integration test of software code of control unit	2	3
14	System test of completed software system	10	5
15	Design review of user's manual	3	2

■ **"Validation** – The process of evaluating a system or component during or at the end of the development process to determine whether it satisfies specified requirements."

■ **"Qualification** – The process used to determine whether a system or component is suitable for operational use."

According to the IEEE definitions, *verification* examines the consistency of the products being developed with products developed in previous phases. When doing so, the examiner follows the development process and assumes that all the former development phases have been completed correctly, whether as originally planned or after removal of all the discovered defects. This assumption forces the examiner to disregard deviations from the customer's original requirements that might have been introduced during the development process.

Validation represents the customer's interest by examining the extent of compliance to his or her original requirements. Comprehensive validation reviews tend to improve customer satisfaction from the system.

Qualification focuses on operational aspects, where maintenance is the main issue. A software component that has been developed and documented according to professional standards and style and structure convention procedures is expected to be much easier to maintain than one that provides marvelous coding improvisations yet does not follow known coding style procedures and so forth.

Planners are required to determine which of these aspects should be examined in each quality assurance activity.

7.4 A model for SQA defect removal effectiveness and cost

The model deals with two quantitative aspects of an SQA plan consisting of several defect detection activities:

(1) The plan's total effectiveness in removing project defects.
(2) The total costs of removal of project defects.

The plan itself is to be integrated within a project's development process.

7.4.1 The data

The application of the model is based on three types of data, described under the following headings.

Defect origin distribution
Defect origins (the phase in which defects were introduced) are distributed throughout the development process, from the project's initiation to its completion. Surveys conducted by major software developers, such as IBM and TRW, summarized by Boehm (1981, Chapter 24) and Jones (1996, Chapter 3), reveal a similar pattern of defect distribution. Software development professionals believe that this pattern has not changed substantially in the last two decades. A characteristic distribution of software defect origins, based on Boehm (1981) and Jones (1996), is shown in Table 7.3.

Table 7.3: A characteristic distribution of software defect origins

No.	Software development phase	Average percentage of defects originating in phase
1	Requirements specification	15%
2	Design	35%
3	Coding (coding 30%, integration 10%)	40%
4	Documentation	10%

Defect removal effectiveness

It is assumed that any quality assurance activity filters (screens) a certain percentage of existing defects. It should be noted that in most cases, the percentage of removed defects is somewhat lower than the percentage of detected defects as some corrections (about 10% according to Jones, 1996) are ineffective or inadequate. The remaining defects, those undetected and uncorrected, are passed to successive development phases. The next quality assurance activity applied confronts a combination of defects: those remaining after previous quality assurance activities together with "new" defects, created in the current development phase. It is assumed that the filtering effectiveness of accumulated defects of each quality assurance activity is not less than 40% (i.e., an activity removes at least 40% of the incoming defects). Typical average defect filtering effectiveness rates for the various quality assurance activities, by development phase, based on Boehm (1981, Chapter 24) and Jones (1996, Chapters 3 and 5), are listed in Table 7.4.

Cost of defect removal

Data collected about development project costs show that the cost of removal of detected defects varies by development phase, while costs rise substantially as the development process proceeds. For example, removal of a design defect detected in the design phase may require an investment of 2.5 working days; removal of the same defect may require 40 working days during the acceptance tests. Several surveys carried out by IBM, TRW, GTE, Boehm and others, summarized by Boehm (1981, Chapter 4), estimate the relative costs of correcting errors at each development phase. Estimates of effectiveness of software quality assurance tools and relative costs of defect removal are provided by Boehm and Basili (2001). Although defect removal data are quite rare, professionals agree that the proportional costs of defect removal have remained constant since the surveys conducted in the 1970s and 1980s. Representative average relative defect-removal costs, based on Boehm (1981) and Pressman (2000, Chapter 8), are shown in Table 7.5.

Table 7.4: Average filtering (defect removal) effectiveness by quality assurance activities

No.	Quality assurance activity	Average defect filtering effectiveness rate
1	Requirements specification review	50%
2	Design inspection	60%
3	Design review	50%
4	Code inspection	65%
5	Unit test	50%
6	Unit test after code inspection	30%
7	Integration test	50%
8	System tests / acceptance tests	50%
9	Documentation review	50%

Table 7.5: Representative average relative defect-removal costs

No.	Software development phase	Average relative defect cost (cost units)
1	Requirements specification	1
2	Design	2.5
3	Unit tests	6.5
4	Integration tests	16
5	System tests / acceptance tests / system documentation review	40
6	Operation by customer (after release)	110

7.4.2 The model

The model is based on the following assumptions:

- The development process is linear and sequential, following the waterfall model.
- A number of "new" defects are introduced in each development phase. For their distributions, see Table 7.3.
- Review and test software quality assurance activities serve as filters, removing a percentage of the entering defects and letting the rest pass to the next development phase. For example, if the number of incoming defects is 30, and the filtering efficiency is 60%, then 18 defects will be removed, while 12 defects will remain and pass to be detected by the next quality assurance activity. Typical filtering effectiveness rates for the various quality assurance activities are shown in Table 7.4.
- At each phase, the incoming defects are the sum of defects not removed by the former quality assurance activity together with the "new" defects introduced (created) in the current development phase.
- The cost of defect removal is calculated for each quality assurance activity by multiplying the number of defects removed by the relative cost of removing a defect (see Table 7.5).
- The remaining defects, unfortunately passed to the customer, will be detected by him or her. In these circumstances, full removal entails the heaviest of defect-removal costs.

In the model, each of the quality assurance activities is represented by a filter unit, as shown for Design in Figure 7.6.

The model presents the following quantities:

- POD = Phase Originated Defects (from Table 7.3)
- PD = Passed Defects (from former phase or former quality assurance activity)

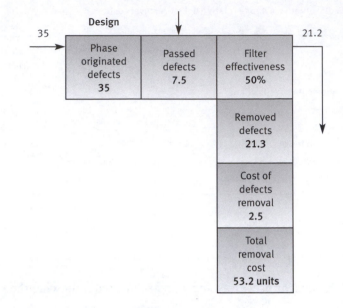

Figure 7.6: A filter unit for defect-removal effectiveness: example

- %FE = % of Filtering Effectiveness (also termed % screening effectiveness) (from Table 7.4)
- RD = Removed Defects
- CDR = Cost of Defect Removal (from Table 7.5)
- TRC = Total Removal Cost: TRC = RD × CDR.

The first illustration of the model applies to a standard quality assurance plan ("standard defects filtering system") that is composed of six quality assurance activities (six filters), as shown in Table 7.6.

A process-oriented illustration of the standard quality assurance plan model is provided in Figure 7.7.

Table 7.6: Standard quality assurance plan

No.	Quality assurance activity	Defect removal effectiveness	Cost of removing a detected defect (cost units)
1	Requirement specification review	50%	1
2	Design review	50%	2.5
3	Unit test – code	50%	6.5
4	Integration test	50%	16
5	Documentation review	50%	16
6	System test	50%	40
7	Operation phase	100%	110

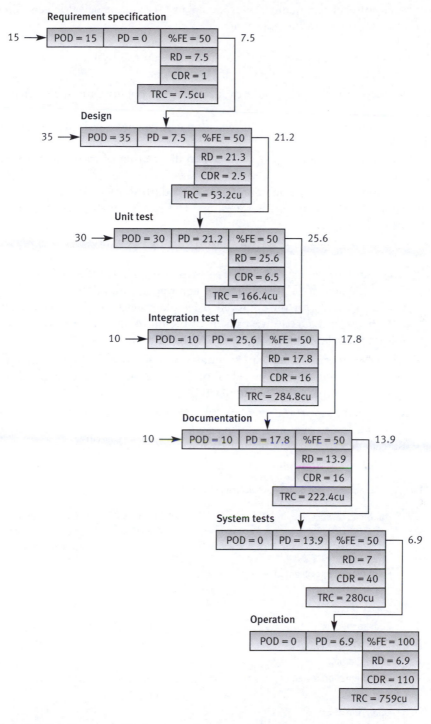

Figure 7.7: Defect-removal effectiveness and costs — standard plan model of the process of removing 100 defects

A comprehensive quality assurance plan ("comprehensive defects filtering system") achieves the following:

(1) Adds two quality assurance activities, so that the two are performed in the design phase as well as in the coding phase.

(2) Improves the "filtering" effectiveness of other quality assurance activities.

The comprehensive quality assurance plan can be characterized as shown in Table 7.7.

Figure 7.8 provides a process-oriented illustration of the comprehensive plan model.

A comparison of the outcomes of the standard software quality plan versus the comprehensive plan is revealing. The results of the comparison are shown in Table 7.8.

The main conclusions drawn from the comparison are:

(1) The standard plan successfully removes only 57.6% (28.8 defects out of 50) of the defects originated in the requirements and design phase, compared to 90.2% for the comprehensive plan, before coding begins. This is to be expected as a direct result of the more intensive defect-removal efforts that characterize the comprehensive plan.

(2) The comprehensive plan, as a whole, is much more economical than the standard plan as it saves 41% of total resources invested in defect removal, compared to the standard plan.

(3) Compared to the standard plan, the comprehensive plan makes a greater contribution to customer satisfaction by drastically reducing the rate of defects detected during regular operations (from 6.9% to 2.6%).

Table 7.7: Comprehensive quality assurance plan

No.	Quality assurance activity	Defect-removal effectiveness	Cost of removing a detected defect (cost units)
1	Requirement specification review	60%	1
2	Design inspection	70%	2.5
3	Design review	60%	2.5
4	Code inspection	70%	6.5
5	Unit test – code	40%	6.5
6	Integration test	60%	16
7	Documentation review	60%	16
8	System test	60%	40
9	Operation phase	100%	110

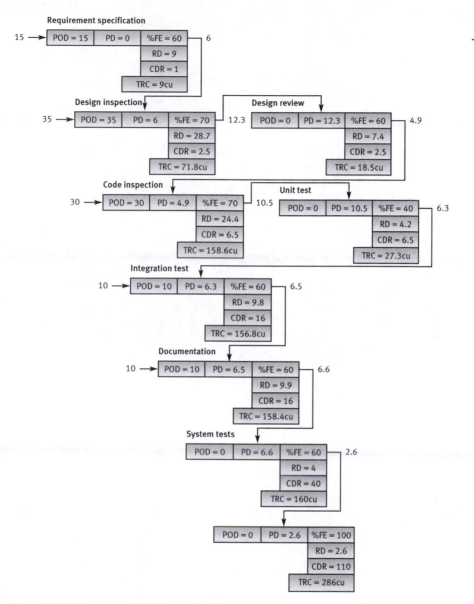

Figure 7.8: Defect-removal effectiveness and costs – comprehensive plan model of the process of removing 100 defects

In general, the quantitative results of the comparison comply nicely with the SQA approach. The comparison also supports the belief that additional investments in quality assurance activities yield substantial savings in defect removal costs.

Alternative models dealing with the cumulative effects of several quality assurance activities are discussed by Pressman (2000, Chapter 8) and Perry (1995, Chapter 2).

Table 7.8: Comparison of the standard and comprehensive quality assurance plans

No.	Quality assurance activity	Standard plan		Comprehensive plan	
		Percentage of removed defects	Cost of removing defects (cost units)	Percentage of removed defects	Cost of removing defects (cost units)
1	Requirements specification review	7.5%	7.5	9%	9
2	Design inspection	–	–	28.7%	71.8
3	Design review	21.3%	53.2	7.4%	18.5
4	Code inspection	–	–	24.4%	158.6
5	Unit test – code	25.6%	166.4	4.2%	27.3
6	Integration test	17.8%	284.8	9.8%	156.8
7	Documentation review	13.9%	222.4	9.9%	158.4
8	System test	7.0%	280	4%	160
	Total for internal quality assurance activities	**93.1%**	**1014.3**	**97.4%**	**760.4**
	Defects detected during operation	6.9%	759	2.6%	286
	Total	**100.0%**	**1773.3**	**100.0%**	**1046.4**

(1) Describe the various software development models and discuss the differences between them.

Four models of software development process are discussed in this chapter:
- The Software Development Life Cycle (SDLC) model
- The prototyping model
- The spiral model
- The object-oriented model.

The classic SDLC model is a linear sequential model comprising several phases, beginning with requirements definition and concluding with regular system operation and maintenance.

At the end of each phase, outputs are reviewed and evaluated by the developer as well as, in many cases, by the customer. The outcomes range from approval of the phase results and continuation to the next phase, to demands to correct, redo or alter parts of the respective phase.

The waterfall model can be viewed as the basic framework for the other models, which can be considered as complementary and represent different perspectives of the process, or as referring to diverse development contexts.

According to the prototyping methodology, the developed system's users are required to comment on versions of the software prototypes prepared by the developers. The developers thereafter correct the prototype and incorporate additional parts into the system. This process is repeated till the software system is completed or till the goal of prototyping is achieved.

The main advantages of the prototyping over the SDLC model, for small to medium-sized projects, are the shorter development process, substantial savings in development resources, better fit to customer requirements, reduced risk of project failure, and clearer user comprehension of the new system.

The spiral model provides an improved methodology for larger and more complex projects. This improvement is achieved by introducing and emphasizing elements of risk analysis and customer participation in the development process. Each of the model's iterations includes planning, risk analysis and resolution, engineering, and customer evaluation.

The advanced spiral model (the Win–Win model) places extra emphasis on communication and negotiation between customer and developer. The customer wins by improving chances to receive a system that satisfies most of his needs while the developer wins by improving chances of completing the project within budgetary and timetable constraints.

The object-oriented model deals with the situation of intensive reuse of software components. According to this model, the development process begins with a sequence of object-oriented analysis and design activities. The design phase is followed by acquisition of a reusable software library together with "regular" development of the unavailable software components. Copies of newly developed software components are "stocked" in the library for future reuse.

(2) Explain the considerations affecting application of quality assurance activities.

The decision about the number of quality assurance activities to be applied is affected by project and team factors. Project factors include project magnitude, its complexity and difficulty, extent of reusable software components, and the severity of the outcomes if the project fails. Team factors include its professional qualifications as well as acquaintance with the project and related experience, availability of professional support, and staff familiarity with team members.

(3) Explain the different aspects of verification, validation and qualification for quality assurance activities.

Quality assurance activities examine three different aspects of quality by means of software product verification, validation and qualification.

- **Verification** examines the consistency of current development activities with the products from previous phases. Doing so enables the examiner to confirm whether the developer has fulfilled his requirements while disregarding deviations from the original requirements that may have arisen during development.
- **Validation** represents the customer's interests by examining the extent to which the customer's original requirements have been fulfilled.
- **Qualification** focuses on operational aspects, where maintenance is the main issue. Qualification reviews project application of professional standards and coding procedures, based on the assumption that applying these standards facilitates maintenance.

Quality assurance activity planners are required to determine which of these aspects should be examined in each of the planned quality assurance activities.

(4) Describe the model for SQA defect removal effectiveness and cost.

The model deals with two quantitative aspects of an SQA plan designed for a specific project:

(1) Total effectiveness of defect removal.
(2) Total cost of defect removal.

The model is based on the following assumptions:

- The development process is linear and sequential (the waterfall model).
- A number of "new" defects are introduced in each development phase.
- Various review and test software assurance activities serve as filters, removing a percentage of the entering defects while allowing the rest to pass to the next software assurance activity.
- Incoming defects are the sum of defects passed from the former quality assurance activity together with "new" defects created in the current development phase.
- The cost of defect removal is calculated by multiplying the number of defects removed by the relative cost of removing a defect.
- Defects passed to the customer will be detected by him or her; their full removal at this phase will incur heavy costs.

(5) Explain possible uses for the model.

The model allows calculating estimates of the cost of decisions regarding the quality assurance plan, e.g.:

■ Addition or elimination of a quality assurance activity from a given plan.

■ Application of current quality assurance procedures activity versus application of a more efficient yet more costly procedure.

Utilization of the model thus enables comparison of SQA policies/strategies and activity plans.

Selected bibliography

1. Boehm, B. W. (1981) *Software Engineering Economics*, Ch. 4 Prentice Hall, Upper Saddle River, NJ.
2. Boehm, B. W. (1988) "A spiral model of software development and enhancement", *Computer*, 21(5), 61–72.
3. Boehm, B. W. (1998) "Using the Win–Win spiral model: a case study", *Computer*, 31(7), 33–44.
4. Boehm, B. and Basili, V. R. (2001) "Software defect reduction – Top 10 list", *Computer*, 34(1) 135–137.
5. IEEE (1990) "IEEE Std 610.12-1990 – IEEE Standard Glossary of Software Engineering Terminology", in *IEEE Software Engineering Standards Collection*, The Institute of Electrical and Electronics Engineers, New York.
6. IEEE (1996) "IEEE/EIA Std 12207.0-1996 – IEEE/EIA Standard – Industry Implementation of International Standard ISO/IEC 12207:1995", in *IEEE Software Engineering Standards Collection*, The Institute of Electrical and Electronics Engineers, New York.
7. IEEE (1997a) "IEEE/EIA Std 12207.1-1997 – IEEE/EIA Guide – Industry Implementation of International Standard ISO/IEC 12207:1995, Software Life Cycle Processes – Life Cycle Data", in *IEEE Software Engineering Standards Collection*, The Institute of Electrical and Electronics Engineers, New York.
8. IEEE (1997b) "IEEE/EIA Std 12207.1-1997 – IEEE/EIA Guide – Industry Implementation of International Standard ISO/IEC 12207:1995, Software Life Cycle Processes – Implementation Considerations", in *IEEE Software Engineering Standards Collection*, The Institute of Electrical and Electronics Engineers, New York.
9. IEEE (1998) "IEEE Std 1012-1998 – IEEE Standard for Software Verification and Validation", in *IEEE Software Engineering Standards Collection*, The Institute of Electrical and Electronics Engineers, New York.
10. Jones, C. (1996) *Applied Software Measurement – Assuring Productivity and Quality*, 2nd edn, McGraw-Hill, New York.
11. Kendall, K. E. and Kendall, J. E. (1999) *Systems Analysis and Design*, 4th edn, Prentice Hall, Upper Saddle River, NJ.
12. Perry, W. (1995) *Effective Methods for Software Testing*, John Wiley & Sons, New York.
13. Pressman, R. S. (2000) *Software Engineering – A Practitioner's Approach*. European adaptation by D. Ince, 5th edn, McGraw-Hill International, London.
14. Royce, W. W. (1970) "Managing the development of large software systems: concepts and techniques", *Proceedings of IEEE WESCON*, August 1970.

Review questions

7.1 Referring to the SDLC model:

(1) What are the seven basic phases of the development process suggested by the model?

(2) Suggest situations where the number of process phases should be reduced.

(3) Suggest situations where the number of process phases should be increased.

7.2 With respect to the prototyping methodology:

(1) List the conditions necessary for the prototyping model to be applied.

(2) Can you suggest an imaginary project ideally suitable for the prototyping methodology?

(3) Can you suggest an imaginary project that is obviously unsuitable for the prototyping methodology?

7.3 Comparing the SDLC and prototyping methodologies:

(1) List the advantages of prototyping compared to the SDLC methodology for development of small to medium-sized projects.

(2) Explain why the advantages of prototyping cannot be realized for large software systems.

(3) In what ways can prototyping support the development of large-scale projects?

7.4 Referring to the spiral model:

(1) Describe the four activities to be repeated in each iteration of the development process. Explain why the four activities designated are to be repeated in each iteration of the development process.

(2) What new activities were added to the classic SDLC model and what is their main contribution to the success of projects?

7.5 Comparing the SDLC and spiral models:

(1) Explain the advantages of the spiral model as compared with the SDLC model.

(2) What characteristics of a project enable these advantages to be best realized?

(3) Provide three examples of projects that would obviously benefit from application of the spiral model.

7.6 With respect to verification, validation and qualification:

(1) Explain the differences between these three aspects of SQA activities.

(2) Can a project that successfully passed verification and validation reviews but failed part of the qualification review adequately supply users with the information needed? Explain your answer.

(3) In which respects is the project described in (2) inferior to a project that passed all three reviews? In what way will this difference affect operation of the software system?

7.7 Theoretically, verification reviews should be sufficient. Still, SQA professionals recommend performance of validation and qualification reviews as well.

  (1) What do they expect to gain by adding a validation review?
  (2) What do they expect to gain by adding a qualification review?

7.8 Referring to the model for defect removal efficiency and costs:

  (1) What assumptions rest at the foundations of the model?
  (2) Which three of the model's data components are based on published survey results?

Topics for discussion

7.1 Consider the expected severity of software system failure.

  (1) What are the main issues that cause the degree of severity?
  (2) Referring to your answer to (1), can you list three examples of software development projects displaying highly severe failures?
  (3) Referring to your answer to (1), can you list three examples of software development projects displaying low-severity failures?

7.2 A software development firm is planning a new airport luggage control project. The system is to control luggage transfer from the terminal to the planes, from the planes to the terminal's luggage release system, and from plane to plane (for transit passengers). The airport requires the highest reliability for the system and wishes to initiate several new applications that have yet to be implemented in another airport.

  (1) What SQA methodology should be implemented for this project? List your arguments.
  (2) Would you recommend integration of additional methodologies in the plan? If yes, what are they and what are their main contributions to the project?

7.3 HRS Ltd is a software house that specializes in human resource management packages sold mainly to small and medium-sized organizations. Its incentive control and management recruitment software packages are already very popular.

  (1) What methodology should be applied by HRS? List your arguments.
  (2) The company wishes to penetrate the area of custom-made human resource management software systems for large organizations such as banks and government agencies. What methodology or combination of methodologies can best fit their new needs?

7.4 Software reuse has become an important factor in the software development industry.

  (1) Explain the advantages of software reuse.
  (2) How can a software development firm organize for efficient software reuse?
  (3) What similar trends can you identify in manufacturing industries (automobiles, home appliances, etc.)?

7.5 Finding herself under time and budget pressures, a project leader has decided to introduce an "economy plan" that limits the quality assurance activities to a standard design review, as required by the contract with the customer (50% filter), and a comprehensive system test (60% filter). Considering the model's contribution to defect-removal efficiency and costs:

(1) What are the expected savings, if any, in resources invested for defect removal during the development process as opposed to the standard quality assurance plan?

(2) What are the expected effects of the "economy plan" on customer satisfaction? Support your answer with a quantitative comparison to the standard plan.

(3) Compare the overall results of the "economy plan" to the results of the standard and comprehensive plans.

(4) Based on your answer to (3), can you suggest some general rules about choosing the preferred quality assurance plan?

Reviews

A common product of the software development process, especially in its analysis and design phases, is a design document in which the progress of the development work performed is recorded. The system analyst or analysts who prepared the document will check it repeatedly, it is to be assumed, in order to detect any possible error that might have entered. In addition, development team leaders are also expected to examine this document and its details so as to detect any remaining errors before granting their approval.

However, it is clear that because these professionals were involved in producing the document, they are unlikely to detect some of their own errors irrespective of the number of checks. Therefore, only others – such as peers, superiors, experts, and customer's representatives (those having different experiences and points of view, yet not directly involved in creating the document) – are capable of reviewing the product and detecting the errors unnoticed by the development team.

As defined by IEEE (1990), a review process is:

"A process or meeting during which a work product, or set of work products, is presented to project personnel, managers, users, customers, or other interested parties for comment or approval."

As these documents are products of the project's initial phases, reviews acquire special importance in the SQA process because they provide early detection and prevent the passing of design and analysis errors "downstream", to stages where error detection and correction are much more intricate, cumbersome, and therefore costly.

Several methodologies can be implemented when reviewing documents. In this chapter, the following methods will be discussed:

- Formal design reviews
- Peer reviews (inspections and walkthroughs)
- Expert opinions.

Standards for software reviews are the subject of IEEE Std 1028 (IEEE, 1997).

It should be noted that successful implementations of inspections and walkthroughs also detect defects in the coding phase, where the appropriate document reviewed is the code printout.

A case study of the contribution of formal design reviews and inspections to software quality is presented by MacFarland (2001).

After completing this chapter, you will be able to:

- Explain the direct and indirect objectives of review methodologies.
- Explain the contribution of external experts to the performance of review tasks.
- Compare the three major review methodologies.

8.1 Review objectives

Several objectives *motivate* reviews. The review's *direct objectives* deal with the current project, whereas its *indirect objectives*, more general in nature, deal with the contribution *of the review proper* to the promotion of team members' professional knowledge and the improvement of the development methodologies applied by the organization.

Frame 8.1   **Review objectives**

Direct objectives

- To detect analysis and design errors as well as subjects where corrections, changes and completions are required with respect to the original specifications and approved changes.

- To identify new risks likely to affect completion of the project.

- To locate deviations from templates and style procedures and conventions. Correction of these deviations is expected to contribute to improved communication and coordination resulting from greater uniformity of methods and documentation style.

- To approve the analysis or design product. Approval allows the team to continue to the next development phase.

Indirect objectives

- To provide an informal meeting place for exchange of professional knowledge about development methods, tools and techniques.

- To record analysis and design errors that will serve as a basis for future corrective actions. The corrective actions are expected to improve development methods by increasing effectiveness and quality, among other product features. (For more about corrective actions, see Chapter 17.)

The various review methods differ in the emphasis attached to the different objectives and in the extent of success achievable for each objective. Therefore, for better "filtering out" of errors and greater long-term impacts, a double or even triple "net", constructed from among the range of review methods available, should be applied.

Reviews are not activities to be conducted haphazardly. Procedural order and teamwork lie at the heart of formal design reviews, inspections and walk-throughs. Each participant is expected to emphasize his or her area of responsibility or specialization when making comments. At each review session, one individual is assigned the task of inscribing mutually agreed remarks. The subsequent list of items should include full details of defect location and description, documented in a way that will later allow full retrieval by the development team. However, because of the human propensity to try to design solutions on the spot and, often, to digress to tangential issues or, even worse, to personal matters during the course of a meeting, a coordinator is needed to maintain control of the discussion and keep it on track.

In general, the knowledge that an analysis or design product will be reviewed stimulates the development team to work at their maximum. This represents a further contribution of reviews to improved product quality.

In the following, the various review methods are presented. A comparison of team review methods is the subject of Section 8.4; expert opinions are discussed in Section 8.5.

8.2 Formal design reviews (DRs)

Formal design reviews, variously called "design reviews", "DRs" and "formal technical reviews (FTR)", differ from all other review instruments by being the only reviews that are necessary for approval of the design product. Without this approval, the development team cannot continue to the next phase of the software development project. Formal design reviews may be conducted at any development milestone requiring completion of an analysis or design document, whether that document is a requirement specification or an installation plan. A list of common formal design reviews is given in Frame 8.2.

Frame 8.2   **Some common formal design reviews**

DPR – Development Plan Review

SRSR – Software Requirement Specification Review

PDR – Preliminary Design Review

DDR – Detailed Design Review

DBDR – Data Base Design Review

TPR – Test Plan Review

STPR – Software Test Procedure Review

VDR – Version Description Review

OMR – Operator Manual Review

SMR – Support Manual Review

TRR – Test Readiness Review

PRR – Product Release Review

IPR – Installation Plan Review

Sauer and Jeffery (2000) discuss a broad range of factors affecting the effectiveness of DRs, based on research results and a wide-ranging survey of the literature. Our discussion of formal design reviews will focus on:

■ The participants
■ The prior preparations
■ The DR session
■ The recommended post-DR activities.

All DRs are conducted by a review leader and a review team. The choice of appropriate participants is of special importance because of their power to approve or disapprove a design product.

The review leader

Because the appointment of an appropriate review leader is a major factor affecting the DR's success, certain characteristics are to be looked for in a candidate for this position:

- Knowledge and experience in development of projects of the type reviewed. Preliminary acquaintance with the current project is not necessary.
- Seniority at a level similar to if not higher than that of the project leader.
- A good relationship with the project leader and his team.
- A position external to the project team.

Thus, appropriate candidates for review team leadership include the development department's manager, the chief software engineer, the leader of another project, the head of the software quality assurance unit and, in certain circumstances, the customer's chief software engineer.

Implementation tip

In some cases, the project leader is appointed as the review leader, the main justification for this decision being his or her superior knowledge of the project's material. In most cases, this choice proves to be undesirable professionally. A project leader who serves as the review team leader tends, whether intentionally or nor, to limit the scope of the review and avoid incisive criticism. Review team members tend to be chosen accordingly. Appointments of this type usually undermine the purpose for the review and only delay confrontation with problems to a later, more sensitive date.

Small development departments and small software houses typically have substantial difficulties finding an appropriate candidate to lead the review team. One possible solution to this predicament is the appointment of an external consultant to the position.

The review team

The entire review team should be selected from among the senior members of the project team together with appropriate senior professionals assigned to other projects and departments, customer–user representatives, and in some cases, software development consultants. It is desirable for non-project staff to make up the majority of the review team.

An important, oft-neglected issue is the size of the review team. A review team of three to five members is expected to be an efficient team, given the proper diversity of experience and approaches among the participants are assured. An excessively large team tends to create coordination problems, waste review session time and decrease the level of preparation, based on a natural tendency to assume that others have read the design document.

8.2.2 Preparations for a DR

Although preparations for a DR session are to be completed by all three main participants in the review – the review leader, the review team and the development team – each participant is required to focus on distinct aspects of the process.

Review leader preparations

The main tasks of the review leader in the preparation stage are:

- To appoint the team members
- To schedule the review sessions
- To distribute the design document among the team members (hard copy, electronic file, etc.).

It is of utmost importance that the review session be scheduled shortly after the design document has been distributed to the review team members. Timely sessions prevent an unreasonable length of time from elapsing before the project team can commence the next development phase and thus reduce the risk of going off schedule.

Review team preparations

Team members are expected to review the design document and list their comments prior to the review session. In cases where the documents are sizable, the review leader may ease the load by assigning to each team member review of only part of the document.

An important tool for ensuring the review's completeness is the checklist. In addition to the general design review checklist, checklists dedicated to the more common analysis and design documents are available and can be constructed when necessary. Checklists contribute to the design review's effectiveness by reminding the reviewer of all the primary and secondary issues requiring attention. For a comprehensive discussion of checklists, see Chapter 15.

Development team preparations

The team's main obligation as the review session approaches is to prepare a short presentation of the design document. Assuming that the review team members have read the design document thoroughly and are now familiar

with the project's outlines, the presentation should focus on the main professional issues awaiting approval rather than wasting time on description of
the project in general.

> **Implementation tip**
>
> One of the most common techniques used by project leaders to avoid
> professional criticism and undermine review effectiveness is the
> comprehensive presentation of the design document. This type of
> presentation excels in the time it consumes. It exhausts the review team and
> leaves little time, if any, for discussion. All experienced review leaders know
> how to handle this phenomenon.
>
> In cases where the project leader serves as the review leader, one can observe
> especially potent tactics aimed at stymieing an effective review: appointment
> of a large review team combined with a comprehensive and long presentation.

8.2.3 The DR session

The review leader's experience in leading the discussions and sticking to the
agenda is the key to a successful DR session. A typical DR session agenda
includes:

(1) A short presentation of the design document.

(2) Comments made by members of the review team.

(3) Verification and validation in which each of the comments is discussed
     to determine the required actions (corrections, changes and additions)
     that the project team has to perform.

(4) Decisions about the design product (document), which determines the
     project's progress. These decisions can take three forms:

   - *Full approval* – enables immediate continuation to the next phase
     of the project. On occasion, full approval may be accompanied
     by demands for some minor corrections to be performed by the proj-
     ect team.
   - *Partial approval* – approval of immediate continuation to the next
     phase for some parts of the project, with major action items (correc-
     tions, changes and additions) demanded for the remainder of the
     project. Continuation to the next phase of these remainder parts will
     be permitted only after satisfactory completion of the action items.
     This approval can be given by the member of the review team
     assigned to review the completed action items, by the full review team
     in a special review session, or by any other forum the review leader
     thinks appropriate.
   - *Denial of approval* – demands a repeat of the DR. This decision is
     applied in cases of multiple major defects, particularly critical defects.

8.2.4 Post-review activities

Apart from the DR report, the DR team or its representative is required to follow up performance of the corrections and to examine the corrected sections.

The DR report

One of the review leader's responsibilities is to issue the DR report immediately after the review session. Early distribution of the DR report enables the development team to perform the corrections earlier and minimize the attendant delays to the project schedule.

The report's major sections contain:

- A summary of the review discussions.
- The decision about continuation of the project.
- A full list of the required actions – corrections, changes and additions that the project team has to perform. For each action item, the anticipated completion date and project team member responsible are listed.
- The name(s) of the review team member(s) assigned to follow up performance of corrections.

The form shown in Appendix 8A presents the data items that need to be documented for an inclusive DR report.

The follow-up process

The person appointed to follow up the corrections, in many cases the review leader him or herself, is required to determine whether each action item has been satisfactorily accomplished as a condition for allowing the project to continue to the next phase. Follow-up should be fully documented to enable clarification of the corrections in the future, if necessary.

Implementation tip

Unfortunately, the entire or even parts of the DR report are often worthless, whether because of an inadequately prepared review team or because of intentional evasion of a thorough review. It is fairly easy to identify such cases from the characteristics of the review report:

- An extremely short report, limited to documented approval of the design product, listing no detected defects.

- A short report, approving continuation to the next project phase in full, listing several minor defects but no action items.

- A report listing several action items of varied severity, but no indication of follow-up (correction schedule, etc.), and no available documented follow-up activities.

Pressman (2000, Chapter 8) lists guidelines for completing a successful DR, while focusing on infrastructure, preparations for a DR, and conduct of a DR session are summarized in Frame 8.3. Pressman's golden "guidelines" for formal design reviews also apply to inspection and walkthrough sessions.

Frame 8.3	Pressman's 13 "golden guidelines" for a successful design review (based on Pressman 2000, Chapter 8)

Design review infrastructure

- Develop checklists for each type of design document, or at least for the common ones.

- Train senior professionals to treat major technical as well as review process issues. The trained professionals serve as a reservoir for DR teams.

- Periodically analyze past DR effectiveness regarding defect detection to improve the DR methodology.

- Schedule the DRs as part of the project activity plan and allocate the needed resources as an integral part of the software development organization's standard operating procedures.

The design review team

- Review teams should be limited in size, with 3–5 members usually being the optimum.

The design review session

- Discuss professional issues in a constructive way while refraining from personalizing those issues. This demands keeping the discussion atmosphere free of unnecessary tension.

- Keep to the review agenda. Drifting from the planned agenda usually interferes with the review's efficiency.

- Focus on detection of defects by verifying and validating the participants' comments. Refrain from discussing possible solutions to the detected defects so as to save time and avoid wandering from the agenda.

- In cases of disagreement about the significance of an error, it is desirable to end the debate by noting the issue and shifting its discussion to another forum.

- Properly document the discussions, especially details of the participants' comments and the results of their verification and validation. This step is especially important if the documentation is to serve as input or a basis for preparation of the review report.

- The duration of a review session should not exceed two hours.

The formal design review process is illustrated in Figure 8.1.

The next section deals with peer review methods, and discusses the two most commonly used methods: inspection and walkthrough.

8.3 Peer reviews

Two peer review methods, inspections and walkthroughs, are discussed in this section. The major difference between formal design reviews and peer review methods is rooted in their participants and authority. While most participants in DRs hold superior positions to the project leader and customer representatives, participants in peer reviews are, as expected, the project leader's equals, members of his or her department and other units. The other major difference lies in degree of authority and the objective of each review method. Formal design reviews are authorized to approve the design document so that work on the next stage of the project can begin. This authority is not granted to the peer reviews, whose main objectives lie in detecting errors and deviations from standards.

Today, with the appearance of computerized design tools, including CASE tools, on the one hand, and systems of vast software packages on the other hand, some professionals tend to diminish the value of manual reviews such as inspections and walkthroughs. Nevertheless, past software surveys as well as recent empirical research findings provide much convincing evidence that peer reviews are highly efficient as well as effective methods.

What differentiates a walkthrough from an inspection is the level of formality, with inspection the more formal of the two. Inspection emphasizes the objective of corrective action. Whereas a walkthrough's findings are limited to comments on the document reviewed, an inspection's findings are also incorporated into efforts to improve development methods *per se*. Inspections, as opposed to walkthroughs, are therefore considered to contribute more significantly to the general level of SQA.

Inspection is usually based on a comprehensive infrastructure, including:

■ Development of inspection checklists developed for each type of design document as well as coding language and tool, which are periodically updated.

■ Development of typical defect type frequency tables, based on past findings, to direct inspectors to potential "defect concentration areas".

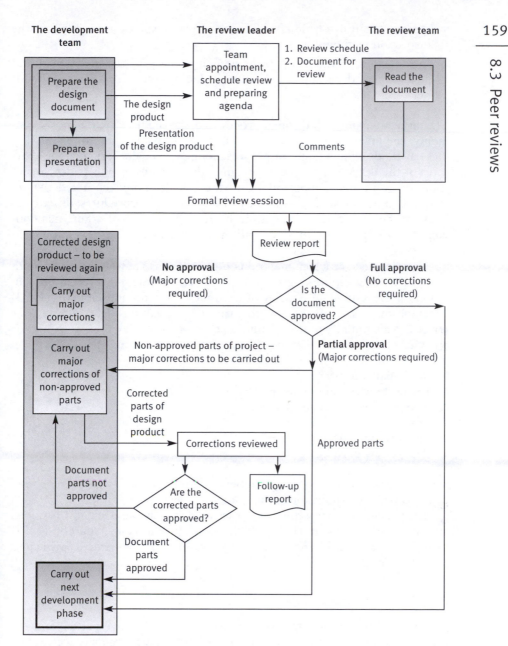

Figure 8.1: The formal design review process

■ Training of competent professionals in inspection process issues, a process that makes it possible for them to serve as inspection leaders (moderators) or inspection team members. The trained employees serve as a reservoir of professional inspectors available for future projects.

- Periodic analysis of the effectiveness of past inspections to improve the inspection methodology.
- Introduction of scheduled inspections into the project activity plan and allocation of the required resources, including resources for correction of detected defects.

The inspection and walkthrough processes described here are the more commonly employed versions of these methods. Organizations often modify these methods, with adaptations representing "local color", that is, the character of the development and SQA units, the software products developed, team structure and composition, and the like. It should be noted that in response to this variability, especially in walkthrough procedures, differences between the two methods are easily blurred. This state of affairs has convinced some specialists to view walkthroughs as a type of inspection, and vice versa.

The debate over which method is preferable has yet to be resolved, with proponents of each arguing for the superiority of their favored approach. Based on their survey of studies of each method, Gilb and Graham (1993) conclude that as an alternative to inspections, walkthroughs display "far fewer defects found but at the same cost".

Our discussion of peer review methods will thus focus on:

- Participants of peer reviews
- Requisite preparations for peer reviews
- The peer review session
- Post-peer review activities
- Peer review efficiency
- Peer review coverage.

With minor adaptations, the principles and process of design peer reviews can also be successfully applied to code peer reviews.

Design and code inspections, as procedural models, were initially described and formulated by Fagan (1976, 1986). As to walkthroughs, Yourdon (1979) provides a thorough and detailed discussion of the related principles and processes.

8.3.1 Participants of peer reviews

The optimal peer review team is composed of three to five participants. In certain cases, the addition of one to three further participants is acceptable. All the participants should be peers of the software system designer-author. A major factor contributing to the success of a peer review is the group's "blend" (which differs between inspections and walkthroughs).

A recommended peer review team includes:

- A review leader
- The author
- Specialized professionals.

The review leader

The role of review leader ("moderator" in inspections, "coordinator' in walkthroughs) differs only slightly by peer review type. Candidates for this position must:

(1) Be well versed in development of projects of the current type and familiar with its technologies. Preliminary acquaintance with the current project is not necessary.

(2) Maintain good relationships with the author and the development team.

(3) Come from outside the project team.

(4) Display proven experience in coordination and leadership of professional meetings.

(5) For inspections, training as a moderator is also required.

The author

The author is, invariably a participant in each type of peer review.

Specialized professionals

The specialized professionals participating in the two peer review methods differ by review. For inspections, the recommended professionals are:

- **A designer:** the systems analyst responsible for analysis and design of the software system reviewed.

- **A coder or implementer:** a professional who is thoroughly acquainted with coding tasks, preferably the leader of the designated coding team. This inspector is expected to contribute his or her expertise to the detection of defects that could lead to coding errors and subsequent software implementation difficulties.

- **A tester:** an experienced professional, preferably the leader of the assigned testing team, who focuses on identification of design errors usually detected during the testing phase.

For walkthroughs, the recommended professionals are:

- **A standards enforcer.** This team member, who specializes in development standards and procedures, is assigned the task of locating deviations from those standards and procedures. Errors of this type substantially affect the team's long-term effectiveness, first because they cause extra difficulties for new members joining the development team, and later because they will reduce the effectiveness of the team that will maintain the system.

- **A maintenance expert** who is called upon to focus on maintainability, flexibility and testability issues (see Chapter 3), and to detect design defects capable of impeding correction of bugs or performance of future changes. Another area requiring his or her expertise is documentation, whose completeness and correctness are vital for any maintenance activity.

- **A user representative.** Participation of an internal (when the customer is a unit in the same firm) or an external user's representative in the walk-through team contributes to the review's validity because he or she examines the software system from the point of view of the user-consumer rather than the designer–supplier. In cases where a "real" user is not available, as in the development of a COTS software package, a team member may take on that role and focus on validity issues by comparing of the original requirements with the actual design.

Team assignments

Conducting a review session requires, naturally, assignment of specific tasks to the team members. Two of these members are the presenter of the document and the scribe, who documents the discussions.

- **The presenter.** During inspection sessions, the presenter of the document is chosen by the moderator; usually, the presenter is not the document's author. In many cases the software coder serves as the presenter because he or she is the team member who is most likely to best understand the design logic and its implications for coding. In contrast, for most walk-through sessions, it is the author, the professional most intimately acquainted with the document, who is chosen to present it to the group. Some experts claim that an author's assignment as presenter may affect the group members' judgement; therefore, they argue that the choice of a "neutral" presenter is to be preferred.
- **The scribe.** The team leader will often – but not always – serve as the scribe for the session, and record the noted defects that are to be corrected by the development team. This task is more than procedural; it requires thorough professional understanding of the issues discussed.

8.3.2 Preparations for a peer review session

The review leader and the team members are to assiduously complete their preparation, with the type of review determining their scope.

Peer review leader's preparations for the review session

The main tasks of the review leader in the preparation stage are:

- To determine, together with the author, which sections of the design document are to be reviewed. Such sections can be:
  - The most difficult and complex sections
  - The most critical sections, where any defect can cause severe damage to the program application and thus to the user
  - The sections prone to defects.
- To select the team members.

■ To schedule the peer review sessions. It is advisable to limit a review session to two hours; therefore, several review sessions should be scheduled (up to two sessions a day) when the review task is sizable. It is important to schedule the sessions shortly after the pertinent design document sections are ready for inspection. This proximity tends to minimize the scope and/or number of design additions based on parts of the document that might be found defective later in the scheduled review. Moreover, for the process to unfold smoothly, the inspection's review leader should schedule an overview meeting for his team.

■ To distribute the document to the team members prior to the review session.

Peer review team's preparations for the review session
The preparations required of an inspection team member are quite thorough, while those required of a walkthrough team member are brief.

Inspection team members are expected to read the document sections to be reviewed and list their comments before the inspection session begins. This advance preparation is meant to guarantee the session's effectiveness. They will also be asked to participate in an overview meeting. At this meeting, the author provides the inspection team members with the necessary relevant background for reviewing the chosen document sections: the project in general, the logic, processes, outputs, inputs, and interfaces. In cases where the participants are already well acquainted with the material, an overview meeting may be waived.

An important tool supporting the inspector's review is a checklist. In well-established development departments, one can find specialized checklists dedicated to the more common types of development documents (see Chapter 15).

Prior to the walkthrough session, team members briefly read the material in order to obtain a general overview of the sections to be reviewed, the project and its environment. Participants lacking preliminary knowledge of the project and its substantive area will need far more preparation time. In most organizations employing walkthroughs, team participants are not required to prepare their comments in advance.

8.3.3 The peer review session

A typical peer review session takes the following form. The presenter reads a section of the document and adds, if needed, a brief explanation of the issues involved in his or her own words. As the session progresses, the participants either deliver their comments to the document or address their reactions to the comments. The discussion should be confined to identification of errors, which means that it should not deal with tentative solutions. Unlike inspection sessions, the agenda of the typical walkthrough session opens with the author's short presentation or overview of the project and the design sections to be reviewed.

During the session, the scribe should document each error recognized by location and description, type and character (incorrect, missing parts or extra parts). The inspection session scribe will add the estimated severity of each defect, a factor to be used in the statistical analysis of defects found and for the formulation of preventive and corrective actions. The error severity classification appearing in Appendix C of MIL-STD-498 (DOD, 1994) and presented in Table 8.1, provides an accepted framework for classifying error severity.

Concerning the length of inspection and walkthrough sessions, the same rules apply as to DRs: sessions should not exceed two hours in length, or schedule for more than twice daily. Pressman's "golden guidelines" for conducting successful DR sessions are also helpful here (see Frame 8.3).

Session documentation

The documentation produced at the end of an inspection session is much more comprehensive than that of a walkthrough session.

Two documents are to be produced following an inspection session and subsequently distributed among the session participants:

(1) **Inspection session findings report.** This report, produced by the scribe, should be completed and distributed immediately after the session's closing. Its main purpose is to assure full documentation of identified errors for correction and follow up. An example of such a report is provided in Appendix 8B.

Table 8.1: Classification of design errors by severity

Severity	Description
5 (critical)	(1) Prevents accomplishment of essential capabilities. (2) Jeopardizes safety, security or other critical requirements.
4	(1) Adversely affects the accomplishment of essential capabilities, where no work-around solution is known. (2) Adversely affects technical, cost or schedule risks to project or system maintenance, where no work-around solution is known.
3	(1) Adversely affects the accomplishment of essential capabilities, where a work-around solution is known. (2) Adversely affects technical, cost or schedule risks to the development project or to the system maintenance, where a work-around solution is known.
2	(1) User/operator inconvenience that does not affect required mission or operational essential capabilities. (2) Inconvenience for development or maintenance personnel, but does not prevent the realization of those responsibilities.
1 (minor)	Any other effect.

Source: After DOD (1994)

(2) **Inspection session summary report.** This report is to be compiled by the inspection leader shortly after the session or series of sessions dealing with the same document. A typical report of this type summarizes the inspection findings and the resources invested in the inspection; it likewise presents basic quality and efficiency metrics. The report serves mainly as input for analysis aimed at inspection process improvement and corrective actions that go beyond the specific document or project. An example of an inspection session summary report appears in Appendix 8C.

At the end of a session or series of walkthrough sessions, copies of the error documentation – the "walkthrough session findings report" – should be handed to the development team and the session participants.

8.3.4 Post-peer review activities

A fundamental element differentiating between the two peer review methods discussed here is the issue of post-peer review.

The inspection process, contrary to the walkthrough, does not end with a review session or the distribution of reports. Post-inspection activities are conducted to attest to:

■ The prompt, effective correction and reworking of all errors by the designer/author and his team, as performed by the inspection leader (or other team member) in the course of the assigned follow-up activities.

■ Transmission of the inspection reports to the internal Corrective Action Board (CAB) for analysis. This action initiates the corrective and preventive actions that will reduce future defects and improve productivity (see Chapter 17).

A comparison of the peer review methods, participants and process elements is presented in Figure 8.2.

8.3.5 The efficiency of peer reviews

The issue of defect detection efficiency of peer review methods proper and in comparison to other SQA defect detection methods is constantly being debated. Some of the more common metrics applied to estimate the efficiency of peer reviews, as suggested in the literature, are:

■ Peer review detection efficiency (average hours worked per defect detected).
■ Peer review defect detection density (average number of defects detected per page of the design document).
■ Internal peer review effectiveness (percentage of defects detected by peer review as a percentage of total defects detected by the developer).

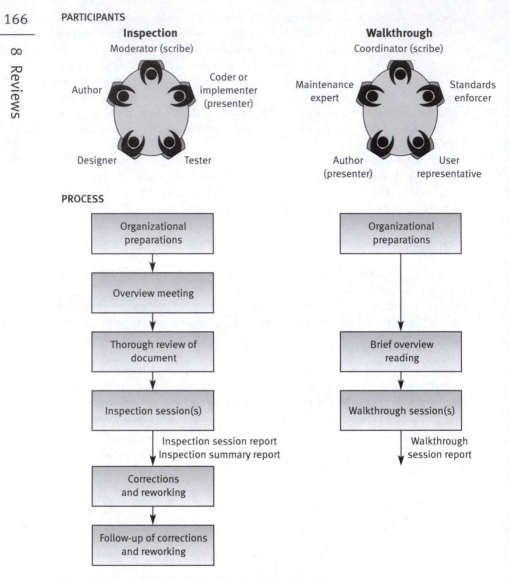

Figure 8.2: Inspection vs. walkthrough – participants and processes

The literature provides rather meager indications about findings inspection effectiveness. Dobbins (1998) quotes Madachy's findings from an analysis of the design and code inspections conducted on the Litton project. Madachy's findings regarding the first two metrics cited above are presented in Table 8.2.

Dobbins (1998) also cites Don O'Neill's 1992 National Software Quality Experiment, conducted in 27 inspection laboratories operating in the US. This experiment provides some insight into the code inspection process, especially at the preparation stage. A total of 90 925 source code lines were code-inspected, with the following results:

Table 8.2: The Litton project's inspection efficiency according to Madachy

Type of document	No. of inspections	Total number of defects and major defects	No. of pages	Inspection resouces invested (work hours)	Inspection efficiency metrics	
					Defect detection density (defects/ page)	Inspection detection efficiency (work-hours/ major defect)
Design inspections						
Requirements description	21	1243 (89 major)	552	328	2.25	3.69
Requirements analysis	32	2165 117 major	1065	769	2.03	6.57
High-level design	41	2398 (197 major)	1652	1097	1.45	5.57
Test procedures	18	1495 (121 major)	1621	457	0.92	3.78
Code inspections						
Code	150	7165 (772 major)	5047*	4612	1.42	5.97

*276 422 lines of code.
Source: After Dobbins (1998)

- Total number of defects detected   1849
- Number of major defects detected   242
- Total preparation time (minutes)   22 828

Accordingly:

- Average preparation time per detected defect

  12.3 minutes (0.2 hours)
- Average preparation time per detected major defect

  94.3 minutes (1.57 hours)

Considering the different environments, a comparison of the defect densities detected in the National Software Quality Experiment and those found in the Litton project reveal relatively small differences, as shown below:

	National Software Quality Experiment	Litton Project
Total defect detection density (defects per KLOC*)	20.3	25.9
Major defect detection density (defects per KLOC*)	2.66	2.80

*KLOC = 1000 lines of code.

The internal effectiveness of inspections is discussed by Cusumano (1991, pp. 352–353), who reports the results of a study on the effectiveness of design review, code inspection and testing at Fujitsu (Japan) for the period 1977–1982. After two decades, the findings are still of interest, even though no efficiency metrics are provided. A comparison by year of inspection, presented in Table 8.3, shows substantial improvement in software quality associated with an increased share of code inspection and design reviews and a reduced share of software testing. The software quality is measured here by the number of defects per 1000 lines of maintained code, detected by the users during the first six months of regular software system use.

Though quantitative research results refer only to the inspection method, we can expect to obtain similar results after application of the walkthrough method. This assumption will one day have to be verified empirically for us to be certain.

8.3.6 Peer review coverage

Only a small percentage of the documents and total volume of code ever undergoes peer review. Coverage of about 5–15% of document pages still represents a significant contribution to total design quality because the factor that determines the benefits of peer review to total quality is not the percentage of pages covered but the choice of those pages. Importantly, with the increased usage of reused software, the number of document pages and code lines demanding inspection is obviously declining. Frame 8.4 lists those document sections that are recommended for inclusion in a peer review as well as those that can be readily omitted.

8.4 A comparison of the team review methods

For practitioners and analysts alike, a comparison of the three team review methods discussed in this chapter should prove interesting. Table 8.4 presents such a comparison.

Table 8.3: Code inspection effectiveness at Fujitsu according to Cusumano

| Year | Defect detection method | | | Defects per 1000 |
	Test %	Design review %	Code inspection %	lines of maintained code
1977	85	–	15	0.19
1978	80	5	15	0.13
1979	70	10	20	0.06
1980	60	15	25	0.05
1981	40	30	30	0.04
1982	30	40	30	0.02

Source: After Cusumano (1991)

Frame 8.4	Sections recommended to be included in or omitted from peer reviews

Sections recommended for inclusion

- Sections of complicated logic
- Critical sections, where defects severely damage essential system capability
- Sections dealing with new environments
- Sections designed by new or inexperienced team members

Sections recommended for omission

- "Straightforward" sections (no complications)
- Sections of a type already reviewed several times by the team in similar past projects
- Sections that, if faulty, are not expected to affect functionality
- Reused design and code
- Repeated parts of the design and code

Table 8.4: Comparison of the review methodologies

Properties	Formal design reviews	Inspections	Walkthroughs
Main direct objectives	(1) Detect errors (2) Identify new risks (3) Approve the design document	(1) Detect errors (2) Identify deviations from standards	Detect errors
Main indirect objectives	Knowledge exchange	(1) Knowledge exchange (2) Support corrective actions	Knowledge exchange
Review leader	Chief software engineer or senior staff member	Trained moderator (peer)	Coordinator (peer, the project leader on occasion)
Participants	Top-level staff and customer representatives	Peers	Peers
Project leader participation	Yes	Yes	Yes; usually as the review's initiator
Specialized professionals in the team	–	(1) Designer (2) Coder or implementer (3) Tester	(1) Standards enforcer (2) Maintenance expert (3) User representative
Process of review:			
Overview meeting	No	Yes	Yes
Participants' preparations	Yes – thorough	Yes – thorough	Yes – brief

Table 8.4: Continued

	Formal design reviews	Inspections	Walkthroughs
▪ Review session	Yes	Yes	Yes
▪ Follow-up of corrections	Yes	Yes	No
Infrastructure:			
▪ Formal training of participants	No	Yes	No
▪ Use of checklists	No	Yes	No
Error-related data collection	Not formally required	Formally required	Not formally required
Review documentation	Formal design review report	(1) Inspection session findings report (2) Inspection session summary report	Walkthrough session findings report

8.5 Expert opinions

The last review method we will discuss is the use of expert opinions. Expert opinions, prepared by outside experts, support quality evaluation by introducing additional capabilities to the internal review staff. The organization's internal quality assurance activities are thereby reinforced. Outside experts transmit their expertise by either:

▪ Preparing an expert's judgement about a document or a code section.

▪ Participating as a member of an internal design review, inspection or walkthrough team.

An outside expert's judgement as well as his or her participation as an external member of a review team is most beneficial in the following situations:

▪ Insufficient in-house professional capabilities in a specialized area.

▪ Temporary lack of in-house professionals for review team participation due to intense workload pressures during periods when waiting will cause substantial delays in the project completion schedule.

▪ Indecisiveness caused by major disagreements among the organization's senior professionals.

▪ In small organizations, where the number of suitable candidates for a review team is insufficient.

(1) Explain the direct and indirect objectives of the review methodologies.

The direct objectives are:
- To detect analysis and design errors.
- To identify new risks expected to affect the completion of the project.
- To identify deviations from templates and style procedures.
- To approve the analysis or design product, allowing the team to continue to the next development phase.

The indirect objectives are:
- To serve as an informal meeting place for the exchange of knowledge about development tools, techniques, experience with new tools, methods and related items.
- To promote and support the improvement of development methods by supplying new data for analysis of design errors.

(2) Explain the contribution of outside experts to the performance of review tasks.

An outside expert can support quality assessment efforts by evaluating a document or a code section or by participating in an internal review team. Turning to outside experts is useful in situations where in-house capabilities are insufficient in specialized areas, the professionals needed to form a review team are temporarily unavailable, an insufficient number of suitable candidates are available (such as in small organizations), and in cases when professional disagreements make it impossible to reach a decision.

(3) Compare the objectives and participants of the three team review methods.

Three team review methods were discussed: formal design reviews, inspections and walkthroughs. The direct objective common to all these methods is error detection. Other objectives, specific to formal design reviews, are identification of new risks and, for inspections, identification of deviation from standards and support of corrective actions. An additional objective, exclusive to DRs, is the approval of design documents, meaning completion of the associated design stages. Another indirect objective shared by all review methods is the exchange of professional knowledge between participants.

The project leader participates in the review teams of every method. However, while the other participants in the DR are superior, professionally or administratively, to the team leader and customer representatives, participants in the other review methods are all peers. Another major difference between the DR and the peer review methods is the inclusion of specialized professionals in the team: designers, coders or implementers and testers in inspections; standards enforcers, maintenance experts and user representative in walkthroughs.

Selected bibliography

1. Biffi, S. (2000) "Using inspection data for defect estimation", *IEEE Software*, 17(6), 36–43.
2. Cusumano, M. A. (1991) *Japan's Software Factories – A challenge to U.S. Management*, Oxford University Press, New York.
3. Dobbins, J. H. (1998) "Inspections as an up-front quality technique", in G.G Schulmeyer and J. I. McManus (eds), *Handbook of Software Quality Assurance*, Prentice Hall, Harlow, Essex, UK.
4. DOD (1994) *MIL-STD-498*, US Department of Defense.
5. Fagan, M. E. (1976) "Design and code inspections to reduce errors in program development", *IBM Systems Journal*, 15(3), 182–211.
6. Fagan, M. E. (1986) "Advances in software inspections", *IEEE Transactions on Software Engineering*, SE-12, (7), 744–751.
7. Gilb, T. and Graham, D. (1993) *Software Inspection*, Addison-Wesley, Harlow, Essex, UK.
8. Hollocker, C. P. (1990) *Software Reviews and Audits Handbook*, John Wiley & Sons, New York.
9. IEEE (1990) "IEEE Std 610.12-1990 – IEEE Standard Glossary of Software Engineering Terminology", in *IEEE Software Engineering Standards Collection*, The Institute of Electrical and Electronics Engineers, New York.
10. IEEE (1997) "IEEE Std 1028-1997 – IEEE Standard for Software Reviews", in *IEEE Software Engineering Standards Collection*, The Institute of Electrical and Electronics Engineers, New York.
11. MacFarland, R. (2001) "Case study of an improvement program featuring reviews and inspections", *Software Quality Professional* (ASQ), 3(3), 26–29.
12. Pressman, R. S. (2000) *Software Engineering – A Practitioner's Approach*, European adaptation by D. Ince, 5th edn, McGraw-Hill International, London.
13. Sauer, C. and Jeffery, D. R. (2000) "The effectiveness of software development technical reviews: behaviorally motivated program of research", *IEEE Transactions on Software Engineering*, 26(1), 1–14.
14. Shull, F., Rus, I. and Basili, V. (2000) "How perspective-based reading can improve requirement inspections", *Computer*, 33(7), 73–79.
15. Yourdon, E. (1979) *Structured Walkthrough*, 2nd edn, Prentice Hall International, London.

Review questions

8.1 There are four direct objectives and two indirect objectives attached to the various review methods.

   (1) List the direct and indirect objectives of each review method surveyed.
   (2) For each objective, indicate the review technique or techniques that contribute(s) the most to achieving that objective.

8.2 One of the objectives of reviews is to identify deviations from templates and style procedures and conventions.

   Explain the importance of enforcing templates and sticking to style procedures and conventions.

8.3 Some people claim that one of the justifications for a small design review team is the need to schedule the review session within a few days after the design product has been distributed to the team members.

(1) Could you list additional reasons for preferring small DR teams apart from the anticipated delays in convening a DR session composed of large teams?

(2) What reasons motivate attempts to schedule the review session as soon as possible after distribution of the design reports to the team members?

8.4 One can expect that in many cases, participants in an inspection session are able to suggest solutions for a detected defect or, at least, point out possible directions for its solution. While it is clear that these suggestions are crucial for the development team, it is commonly recommended to avoid any discussion about solutions during the inspection session.

(1) List your arguments in favor of this recommendation.

(2) What other kinds of cooperation between the moderator and the review team would you prefer to observe in a session?

8.5 It is quite natural to expect participation of the document's author (the designer) in a review of any type.

(1) What are the arguments in favor of his or her participation?

(2) What are the differences in the part played and the status of the author in each of the review methods discussed?

8.6 The preparations made by members of inspection teams are considered to be of greater depth and thoroughness when compared with the preparations for walkthroughs.

(1) What activities are included in such high levels of preparation?

(2) Do you think that inspection teams having 15 members can achieve similarly high levels of preparation?

8.7 Pressman lists 13 golden guidelines for successful design review (see Frame 8.3).

(1) Four of the golden rules deal with design review infrastructure. Can you list these golden guidelines and elaborate on the importance of the infrastructure elements and how they affect software quality?

(2) It is often claimed that the six golden guidelines dealing with the design review session are as applicable to inspection as they are to walkthrough sessions. Can you list these common golden guidelines and explain the reasons for their broad applicability?

Topics for discussion

8.1 A proposal for changing an inspection procedure involves adding a new reporting requirement, as follows: "At the end of the session or the series of sessions, the inspection leader will submit to management a copy of the inspection session findings report and a copy of the inspection session summary report".

(1) Consider the proposal and list possible arguments, pro and con, regarding the change.
(2) What is your recommendation – to add the new reporting requirement or not? Explain.

8.2 David Martin has just finished his inspection coordinator course. After obtaining his first appointment, he plans to add his personal secretary, who is not an IT professional, to the inspection team for the purpose of serving as session scribe and producing the required reports. He assumes that her participation will free him for the coordination tasks and enable him to conduct the session successfully.

Is it advisable to employ a secretary who is not an information technology professional as a scribe in an inspection session? List your arguments pro and con.

8.3 Compare the various review techniques.

(1) In what aspects are design reviews more formal than inspections?
(2) In what aspects are inspections more formal than walkthroughs?

8.4 The chapter offers three different methodologies for team review of design documents.

(1) Which of the methodologies should a software development organization choose?
(2) Can more than one method be chosen and applied for the same document? Alternatively, is it recommended to apply all three methods? List your arguments.

Design Review Report

DR date: _____ The report was prepared by: _____

Project name: _____

The review document: _____ Version: _____

The review team: _____

1 Summary of the discussions

#	Discussion subject	Number of action items

2 The action items

#	Action items to be performed	Responsible employee	Completion date	Approval of completion	
				Date	Signature

3 Decision regarding the design product

☐ Full approval

☐ Partial approval. Approval granted for continuation to the next phase of the following parts:

☐ Denial of approval

Comments:

The report was approved by:

Name of participant	Date	Signature	Name of participant	Date	Signature

Approval of sucessful completion of all action items

Comments:

Name: Signature: Date:

Inspection Session Findings Report

Session dates: _____ The report was prepared by: _____

Project name: _____

The inspected document: _____ Version: _____

The inspected document sections: _____

The inspection team: _____

_____

1 The error list

#	Error type	Error nature (W/M/E)*	Error description	Error location	Error severity

2 Follow-up decisions

a	Follow-up will be carried out by:
b	Re-inspection is recommended: Yes/No
c	

3 Comments

*W = Wrong M = Missing E = Extra

Goldenbug Ltd.
Inspection Session Summary Report

Session date: _17/5_

Project name: _Oak Center_

The inspected document: _Detailed Design_ _____ Version: _3_

The inspected document sections: _Ch. 5, Sec. 6.2–6.5_ Total: (A) _31 pages_ pages/k text lines

The inspection team: _Anita McMahon (inspection leader), John Woo, Ben Kinker_

1 Resources invested (hours worked)

#	Team member	Overview meeting	Preparation	Inspection session	Total (hours)	Comments
1	Inspection leader Anita	1	3	2.5	6.5	including report preparation
2	John	1	4	2	7	
3	Ben	1	4	2	7	
4						
5						
	Total	**3**	**11**	**6.5**	**(B) 20.5**	

2 Error summary

Error severity	Error nature W	M	E*	Total Errors	Severity factor	Total errors (standardized)	Comments
5 – critical	1			1	16	16	
4			2	2	8	16	
3	3			3	4	12	
2		2		2	2	4	
1 – minor	4	1	2	7	1	7	
Total	**8**	**3**	**4**	**(C) 15**		**(D) 53**	

3 Defect detection metrics

(1) Average defects per page = $C/A = \frac{15}{31} = 0.48$

(2) Average defects per page (standardized) = $D/A = \frac{53}{31} = 1.71$

(3) Defects detection efficiency (hours per defect) = $B/C = \frac{20.5}{15} = 1.37$

(4) Standardized defect detection efficiency (hours per standardized defect) = $B/D = \frac{20.5}{53} = 0.39$

Prepared by: _Anita McMahon_ _____ Signature: _Anita McMahon_ _____ Date: _8/5_

*W = Wrong M = Missing E = Extra

Software testing – strategies

Software testing (or "testing") was the first software quality assurance tool applied to control the software product's quality before its shipment or installation at the customer's premises. At first, testing was confined to the final stage of development, after the entire package had been completed. Later, as the importance of early detection of software defects penetrated quality assurance concepts, SQA professionals were encouraged to extend testing to the partial in-process products of coding, which led to software module (unit) testing and integration testing.

Common to all testing activities is their application through the direct running of code, free of review of development documents. Some authors tend to broaden the scope of testing even further and consider all software life cycle quality assurance activities as types of testing activities. In this book, we limit the scope of testing to quality assurance activities performed by running code.

Software testing is undoubtedly the largest consumer of software quality assurance resources. In a survey performed in November 1994, Perry (1995) found that on average, 24% of the project development budget was allocated to testing. In addition, 32% of the project management budget was slated for testing activities. With respect to time resources, an average of 27% of project time was schedule for testing. The survey's participants also indicated that they planned to allocate substantially more time (45% on average) to testing but that the pressures typically arising toward the close of projects generally forced project managers to reduce the testing time scheduled.

Testing is certainly not the only type of SQA tool applied to software code. Additional tools are code inspections and code walkthroughs, methods implemented on code printout without actually running the program. These procedures, which are similar to those applied in design inspection and walkthroughs, yield good results in identifying code defects. Nevertheless, these tools, because they are based solely on the review of documents, can never replace testing, which examines the software product's functionality in the form actually used by the customer. For further discussion of these software quality tools see Chapter 8.

This chapter is dedicated to testing strategies and test classifications. After defining testing and its objectives, the chapter discusses testing strategies and classifies them according to requirement types.

Additional material on testing can be found in the numerous papers and books dealing with software testing. A sample of these sources are the books by Beizer (1984), Perry (1995), Kit (1995), Jorgensen (1995), Kaner *et al.* (1999), Rubin (1994) and Perry and Rice (1997). Another valuable source of material on software testing can be found in the software engineering and software quality assurance literature, such as Pressman (2000), Sommerville (2001) and Hamlet and Maybee (2001), to mention but a few.

After completing this chapter, you will be able to:

- Explain testing objectives.
- Discuss the differences between the various testing strategies, their advantages and disadvantages.
- Describe the concepts of black box testing and white box testing as well as discuss their advantages and disadvantages.
- Define path coverage versus line coverage.
- Describe the various types of black box tests.

9.1 Definition and objectives

The variety of definitions for software testing found in the literature reveals the varied scope of the process, which may be constricted or broadened.

Quite broad in scope is Myers' (1979, Chapter 10) classic definition:

> "Testing is the process of executing a program with intention of finding errors."

According to this rather inclusive definition, activities ranging from code checks performed by a team leader to trial runs of the software performed by a colleague, as well as tests carried out by a testing unit, can all be considered testing activities.

Much more formal and controlled are the two definitions for testing suggested by IEEE Std 610.12 (IEEE, 1990):

> "(1) The process of operating a system or component under specified conditions, observing or recording the results, and making an evaluation of some aspect of the system or component. (2) The process of analyzing a software item to detect the differences between existing and required conditions (that is, bugs) and to evaluate the features of the software item."

It should be noted that according to the second definition, running the program as part of the testing process is not required.

The definition applied in this book stresses the formal operative characteristics of testing. See Frame 9.1.

Frame 9.1 **Software tests – definition**

Software testing is a **formal** process carried out by a **specialized testing team** in which a software unit, several integrated software units or an entire software package are examined by **running the programs on a computer**. All the associated tests are performed according to **approved test procedures** on **approved test cases**.

The words and phrases stressed in the definition allow us to compare the key characteristics of software testing with those of other software quality assurance life cycle tools:

- **Formal** – Software test plans are part of the project's development and quality plans, scheduled in advance and often a central item in the development agreement signed between the customer and the developer. In other words, *ad hoc* examination of software by a colleague or regular checks by the programming team leader cannot be considered software tests.

- **Specialized testing team** – An independent team or external consultants who specialize in testing are assigned to perform these tasks mainly in order to eliminate bias and to guarantee effective testing by trained professionals. In addition, it is generally accepted that tests performed by the developers themselves will yield poor results, as those individuals who developed the original product will find it difficult to reveal errors that they were unable to identify earlier. Still, unit tests continue to be performed by developers in many organizations.

- **Running the programs** – Any form of quality assurance activity that does not involve running the software, for example code inspection, cannot be considered as a test.

- **Approved test procedures** – The testing process performed according to a test plan and testing procedures that have been approved as conforming to the SQA procedures adopted by the developing organization.

- **Approved test cases** – The test cases to be examined are defined in full by the test plan. No omissions or additions are expected to occur during testing. In other words, once the process has begun, the tester is not allowed to exercise discretion by omitting a test case he or she considers redundant or by adding a new test case, promising though it may be.

Now that software testing has been defined and the substantial efforts and resources involved have been recognized, we can turn to a discussion of the objectives of software testing. These objectives are shown in Frame 9.2.

Frame 9.2 **Software testing objectives**

Direct objectives

- To identify and reveal as many errors as possible in the tested software.

- To bring the tested software, after correction of the identified errors and retesting, to an acceptable level of quality.

- To perform the required tests efficiently and effectively, within budgetary and scheduling limitations.

Indirect objective

- To compile a record of software errors for use in error prevention (by corrective and preventive actions).

It should be noted that omission of the frequently stated goal "to prove that the software package is ready" is not accidental. This goal inherently contradicts the first operative objective mentioned, and may influence or, stated more accurately, bias the choice of tests and/or test cases. Myers (1979) neatly summarized the issue: "If your goal is to show the absence of errors you won't discover many. If your goal is to show the presence of errors, you will discover a large percentage of them."

The wording of the second objective reflects the fact that bug-free software is still a utopian aspiration. Therefore, we prefer the phrase "acceptable level of quality", meaning that a certain percentage of bugs, tolerable to the users, will remain unidentified upon installation of the software. This percentage obviously varies by software package and user, but must be lower for high failure risk packages.

9.2   Software testing strategies

Although test methodologies may vary, often greatly, these are applied within the framework of two basic testing strategies:

- To test the software in its entirety, once the completed package is available; otherwise known as "big bang testing".
- To test the software piecemeal, in modules, as they are completed (unit tests); then to test groups of tested modules integrated with newly completed modules (integration tests). This process continues until all the package modules have been tested. Once this phase is completed, the entire package is tested as a whole (system test). This testing strategy is usually termed "incremental testing".

Furthermore, incremental testing is also performed according to two basic strategies: bottom-up and top-down. Both incremental testing strategies assume that the software package is constructed of a hierarchy of software modules. In top-down testing, the first module tested is the main module, the highest level module in the software structure; the last modules to be tested are the lowest level modules. In bottom-up testing, the order of testing is reversed: the lowest level modules are tested first, with the main module tested last.

Figure 9.1 illustrates top-down and bottom-up testing of an identical software development project composed of 11 modules. In the upper part, Figure 9.1(a), the software development process and its subsequent testing are carried out bottom-up, in four stages, as follows:

- Stage 1: Unit tests of modules 1 to 7.
- Stage 2: Integration test A of modules 1 and 2, developed and tested in stage 1, and integrated with module 8, developed in the current stage.
- Stage 3: Two separate integration tests, B, on modules 3, 4, 5 and 8, integrated with module 9, and C, for modules 6 and 7, integrated with module 10.
- Stage 4: System test is performed after B and C have been integrated with module 11, developed in the current stage.

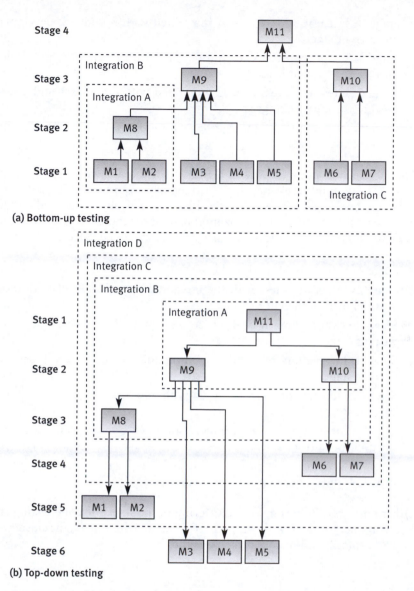

Figure 9.1: Bottom-up (a) and top-down (b) testing – an illustration

In Figure 9.1(b), software development and testing are carried out top-down in six stages. It should be apparent that the change of testing strategy introduces major changes into the test schedule. The testing will be performed as follows:

- Stage 1: Unit tests of module 11.
- Stage 2: Integration test A of module 11 integrated with modules 9 and 10, developed in the current stage.

- Stage 3: Integration test B of A integrated with module 8, developed in the current stage.
- Stage 4: Integration test C of B integrated with modules 6 and 7, developed in the current stage.
- Stage 5: Integration test D of C integrated with modules 1 and 2, developed in the current stage.
- Stage 6: System test of D integrated with modules 3, 4 and 5, developed in the current stage.

The incremental paths shown in Figure 9.1 are only two of many possible paths. The path in the examples is "horizontally sequenced" ("breadth first"), although one could choose a path that is "vertically sequenced" ("depth first"). If we were to alter the horizontal path of the top-down sequence shown in Figure 9.1(b), to a vertical sequence, testing would be performed thus:

- Stage 1: Unit tests of module 11.
- Stage 2: Integration test A of the integration of module 11 with module 9, developed in the current stage.
- Stage 3: Integration test B of A with module 8, developed in the current stage.
- Stage 4: Integration test C of B with modules 1 and 2, developed in the current stage.
- Stage 5: Integration test D of C with module 10, developed in the current stage.
- Stage 6: Integration test E of integration D with modules 6 and 7, developed in the current stage.
- Stage 7: System test is performed after E has been integrated with modules 3, 4 and 5, developed in the current stage.

Other path possibilities involve clustering of modules into one testing stage. For example, for the top-down path of Figure 9.1(b), one might cluster modules 8, 1 and 2, and/or modules 10, 6 and 7.

Stubs and drivers for incremental testing

Stubs and drivers are software replacement simulators required for modules not available when performing a unit or an integration test.

A stub (often termed a "dummy module") replaces an unavailable lower level module, subordinate to the module tested. Stubs are required for top-down testing of incomplete systems. In this case, the stub provides the results of calculations the subordinate module, yet to be developed (coded), is designed to perform. For example, at stage 3 of the top-down example shown in Figure 9.1(b), upper module 9, which activates module 8, is available; it has been tested and corrected at stage 2 of the testing. Stubs are required to substitute for the subordinate level modules 1 and 2, which have not been completed. This test setting is presented in Figure 9.2(a).

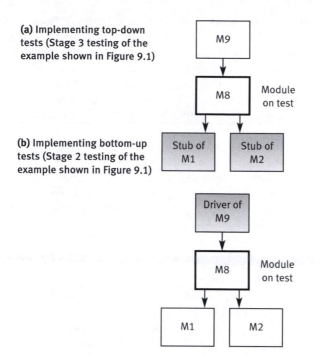

(a) Implementing top-down tests (Stage 3 testing of the example shown in Figure 9.1)

(b) Implementing bottom-up tests (Stage 2 testing of the example shown in Figure 9.1)

Figure 9.2: Use of stubs and drivers for incremental testing – examples

Like a stub, a driver is a substitute module but of the upper level module that activates the module tested. The driver is passing the test data on to the tested module and accepting the results calculated by it. Drivers are required in bottom-up testing until the upper level modules are developed (coded). For example, at stage 2 testing of the bottom-up example shown in Figure 9.1(a), the lower level subordinate modules 1 and 2 are available; they have been tested and corrected at stage 1 of the testing. A driver is required to substitute for upper level module 9, which has not been completed. This test setting/scenario is shown in Figure 9.2(b).

Implementation tip

Substantial savings of resources can be achieved by maintaining a stubs and drivers' library for future reuse.

Bottom-up versus top-down strategies
The main advantage of the bottom-up strategy is the relative ease of its performance, whereas the main disadvantage is the lateness at which the program as a whole can be observed (that is, at the stage following testing of the last module). The main advantage of the top-down strategy is the possibilities it offers to demonstrate the entire program functions shortly after

activation of the upper-level modules has been completed. In many cases, this characteristic allows for early identification of analysis and design errors related to algorithms, functional requirements, and the like. The main disadvantage of this strategy is the relative difficulty of preparing the required stubs, which often require very complicated programming. Another disadvantage is the relative difficulty of analyzing the results of the tests.

Testing experts continue to debate over which strategy is preferable – bottom-up or top-down. While the positions taken vary, it seems that the strategy chosen is actually determined in most cases by the developers' choice of development – not test – strategy, that is, bottom-up or top-down. Clearly, testers should follow the developers' approach because it is crucial that testing will be performed immediately after a module has been coded. Implementation of a testing strategy that differs from the development strategy will cause substantial delays in scheduling of the tests.

Big bang versus incremental testing

Unless the program is very small and simple, application of big bang testing strategies displays severe disadvantages. Identification of error becomes quite cumbersome with respect to immense quantities of software. Despite the vast resources invested, the effectiveness of this approach is relatively meager. The relatively low rate of big bang error identification justifies this conclusion. Moreover, when confronted with an entire software package, error correction is often an onerous task, requiring consideration of the possible effects of the correction on several modules at one and the same time. These constraints obviously make estimation of the required testing resources and testing schedule a rather fuzzy endeavor. This also implies that prospects of keeping on schedule and within the budget are substantially reduced when applying this testing strategy.

In contrast to big bang testing, incremental testing presents several advantages, the main ones being as follows:

(1) Incremental testing is usually performed on relatively small software modules, as unit or integration tests. This makes it easier to identify higher percentages of errors when compared with testing the entire software package.

(2) Identification and correction of errors is much simpler and requires fewer resources because it is performed on a limited volume of software.

To sum up, in incremental testing, a great part of the errors are identified and corrected at an earlier stage of development and testing, which prevents "migration" of escaped defects to a later, more complex stage in the development where their correction would require significantly greater resources.

The main disadvantage of incremental testing is the quantity of programming resources required for preparation of stubs and drivers for the unit and integration tests. Another major disadvantage is the need to carry out numerous testing operations for the same program (big bang testing requires only a single testing operation).

It is generally accepted that incremental testing should be preferred despite its disadvantages.

5

9.3 Software test classifications

9.3 Software test classifications

Software tests may be classified according to the testing concept or to the requirements classification in effect (see Chapter 3).

9.3.1 Classification according to testing concept

There is an ongoing debate over whether testing the functionality of software solely according to its outputs is sufficient to achieve an acceptable level of quality. Some claim that the internal structure of the software and the calculations (i.e., the underlying mathematical structure, also known as the software "mechanism") should be included for satisfactory testing. Based on these two opposing concepts or approaches to software quality, two testing classes have been developed:

- **Black box (functionality) testing.** Identifies bugs only according to software malfunctioning as they are revealed in its erroneous outputs. In cases that the outputs are found to be correct, black box testing disregards the internal path of calculations and processing performed.
- **White box (structural) testing.** Examines internal calculation paths in order to identify bugs. Although the term "white" is meant to emphasize the contrast between this method and black box testing, the method's other name – "glass box testing" – better expresses its basic characteristic, that of investigating the correctness of code structure.

The IEEE (1990) definitions of both testing classes are shown in Frame 9.3.

Frame 9.3 Black box and white box testing – IEEE definitions

Black box testing:

(1) Testing that ignores the internal mechanism of a system or component and focuses solely on the outputs generated in response to selected inputs and execution conditions.

(2) Testing conducted to evaluate the compliance of a system or component with specified functional requirements.

White box testing:

Testing that takes into account the internal mechanism of a system or component.

When implemented, each concept approaches software testing differently, as we shall see in Sections 9.4 and 9.5. In many cases both concepts are applicable, although for some SQA requirements only one class of tests is suitable. Due to cost considerations, most of the testing carried out currently is black box testing, which is relatively less costly.

9.3.2 Classification according to requirements

Chapter 3 presents McCall's classic model for classification of software quality requirements. His model has been extended here to the classification of the tests carried out to ensure full coverage of the respective requirements. The requirements and their corresponding tests are shown in Table 9.1.

Table 9.1: Software quality requirements and test classification

Factor category	Quality requirement factor	Quality requirement sub-factor	Test classification according to requirements
Operation	1. Correctness	1.1 Accuracy and completeness of outputs, accuracy and completeness of data	1.1 Output correctness tests
		1.2 Accuracy and completeness of documentation	1.2 Documentation tests
		1.3 Availability (reaction time)	1.3 Availability (reaction time) tests
		1.4 Data processing and calculations correctness	1.4 Data processing and calculations correctness tests
		1.5 Coding and documentation standards	1.5 Software qualification tests
	2. Reliability		2. Reliability tests
	3. Efficiency		3. Stress tests (load tests, durability tests)
	4. Integrity		4. Software system security tests
	5. Usability	5.1 Training usability 5.2 Operational usability	5.1 Training usability tests 5.2 Operational usability tests
Revision	6. Maintainability 7. Flexibility 8. Testability		6. Maintainability tests 7. Flexibility tests 8. Testability tests
Transition	9. Portability 10. Reusability 11. Interoperability	11.1 Interoperability with other software 11.2 Interoperability with other equipment	9. Portability tests 10. Reusability tests 11.1 Software interoperability tests 11.2 Equipment interoperability tests

Application of white box and black box testing in the performance of
requirements tests has revealed the advantages and disadvantages of each
testing concept. More specifically, as already implied, white box tests of data
processing and calculation correctness can be replaced by black box tests of
output correctness. Maintainability tests can be implemented by both white
box and black box tests, as the findings of each testing concept are complementary. Tests for the other requirements, however, because of their specific
characteristics, can be implemented according to only one or the other concept. The applicability of each testing concept for the various requirement
factors is presented in Table 9.2.

9.4 White box testing

Realization of the white box testing concept requires verification of every
program statement and comment. As shown in Table 9.2, white box testing
enables performance of data processing and calculations correctness tests,
software qualification tests, maintainability tests and reusability tests.

In order to perform *data processing and calculation correctness tests*
("white box correctness test"), every computational operation in the
sequence of operations created by each test case ("path") must be examined.
This type of verification allows us to decide whether the processing operations and their sequences were programmed correctly for the path in

Table 9.2: White box and black box testing for the various classes of tests

Test classification according to requirements	White box testing	Black box testing
1.1 Output correctness tests		+
1.2 Documentation tests		+
1.3 Availability (reaction time) tests		+
1.4 Data processing and calculations correctness tests	+	
1.5 Software qualification tests	+	
2. Reliability tests		+
3. Stress tests (load tests and durability tests)		+
4. Software system security tests		+
5.1 Training usability tests		+
5.2 Operational usability tests		+
6. Maintainability tests	+	+
7. Flexibility tests		+
8. Testability tests		+
9. Portability tests		+
10. Reusability tests	+	
11.1 Software interoperability tests		+
11.2 Equipment interoperability tests		+

question, but not for other paths. Turning to *software qualification*, the focus here shifts to the examination of software code (including comments) compliance with coding standards and work instructions. *Maintainability tests* refer to special features, such as those installed for detection of causes of failure, module structures that support software adaptations and software improvements, etc. *Reusability tests* examine the extent that reused software is incorporated in the package and the adaptations performed in order to make parts of the current software reusable for future software packages.

Given these objectives of SQA tests and the orientation adopted by white box testing, this section will deal with:

■ White box data processing and calculations correctness tests and the number of test cases required
■ McCabe's cyclomatic complexity metrics
■ The performance of software qualification and reusability tests
■ The advantages and disadvantages of white box testing.

9.4.1 Data processing and calculation correctness tests

Applying the concept of white box testing, which is based on checking the data processing for each test case, immediately raises the question of coverage of a vast number of possible processing paths and the multitudes of lines of code. Two alternative approaches have emerged:

■ "Path coverage" – to plan our test to cover all the possible paths, where coverage is measured by percentage of paths covered.
■ "Line coverage" – to plan our tests to cover all the program code lines, where coverage is measured by percentage of lines covered.

These two approaches are discussed in the following sections.

9.4.2 Correctness tests and path coverage

Different paths in a software module are created by the choice in conditional statements, such as IF–THEN–ELSE or DO WHILE or DO UNTIL. Path testing is motivated by the aspiration to achieve complete coverage of a program by testing all its possible paths. Hence, the "path coverage" metrics gauging a path test's completeness is defined as the percentage of the program paths executed during the test (activated by the test cases included in the testing procedure).

While the concept of path testing naturally flows from application of the white box testing concept, it is impractical in most cases because of the vast resources required for its performance. Just how costly these applications can be is illustrated in the following example.

Let us now calculate the number of possible paths created by a simple module containing 10 conditional statements, each allowing for only two options (e.g., IF–THEN–ALSO and DO WHILE). This simple module contains 1024 different paths. In other words, in order to obtain full path coverage for this module (probably 25–50 lines of code) one should prepare at least 1024 test cases, one for each possible path. A straightforward calculation of the number of test cases required to test a software package that contains 100 modules of similar complexity (a total of 102 400 test cases) readily indicates the impracticality of wide use of path testing. Hence, its application is directed mainly to high risk software modules, where the costs of failure resulting from software error fully warrant the costs of path testing.

This situation has encouraged development of an alternative yet weaker coverage concept – line coverage. The line coverage concept requires far fewer test cases but, as expected, leaves most of the possible paths untested. The subject of line coverage is discussed next.

9.4.3   Correctness tests and line coverage

The line coverage concept requires that, for full line coverage, every line of code be executed at least once during the process of testing. The line coverage metrics for completeness of a line-testing ("basic path testing") plan are defined as the percentage of lines indeed executed – that is, covered – during the tests.

To better grasp the essence of basic path testing of a program, reference to a flow chart and a program flow graph can be helpful. In a flow chart, diamonds present the options covered by conditional statements (decisions), whereas rectangles or a succession of rectangles represent the software sections connecting those conditional statements. In program flow graphs, nodes represent software sections and thus replace one or more flow chart rectangles. The edges indicate the sequence of software sections. Nodes having two or more leaving edges represent conditional statements. The following example demonstrates a flow chart and a program flow graph for a taximeter software module that calculates the taxi fares.

Example – the Imperial Taxi Services (ITS) taximeter
Imperial Taxi Services (ITS) serves one-time passengers and regular clients (identified by a taxi card). The ITS taxi fares for one-time passengers are calculated as follows:

(1) Minimal fare: $2. This fare covers the distance traveled up to 1000 yards and waiting time (stopping for traffic lights or traffic jams, etc.) of up to 3 minutes.
(2) For every additional 250 yards or part of it: 25 cents.
(3) For every additional 2 minutes of stopping or waiting or part thereof: 20 cents.
(4) One suitcase: no charge; each additional suitcase: $1.
(5) Night supplement: 25%, effective for journeys between 21.00 and 06.00.

Regular clients are entitled to a 10% discount and are not charged the night supplement.

When planning the basic path testing plan of the new taximeter module, a flow chart and a program flow graph for the taxi fare calculation process were prepared. Each figure represents a calculation process that includes five decisions, as shown in Figure 9.3.

A review of the ITS flow chart and program flow graph demonstrates the difference between path testing and basic path testing as well as comparing the testing requirements of path coverage with those of line coverage.

As mentioned above, full path coverage requires that all the possible paths be executed at least once. In the ITS flow chart (Figure 9.3), 24 different paths may be indicated. In other words, in order to achieve full path coverage of the software module we have to prepare at least 24 test cases, which we list in Table 9.3.

Table 9.3: The Imperial Taxi example – the full list of paths

No.	The path
1	1-2-3-5-6-8-9-11-12-17
2	1-2-3-5-6-8-9-11-13-14-15-17
3	1-2-3-5-6-8-9-11-13-14-16-17
4	1-2-3-5-6-8-10-11-17
5	1-2-3-5-6-8-10-11-13-14-15-17
6	1-2-3-5-6-8-10-11-13-14-16-17
7	1-2-3-5-7-8-9-11-12-17
8	1-2-3-5-7-8-9-11-13-14-15-17
9	1-2-3-5-7-8-9-11-13-14-16-17
10	1-2-3-5-7-8-10-11-12-17
11	1-2-3-5-7-8-10-11-13-14-15-17
12	1-2-3-5-7-8-10-11-13-14-16-17
13	1-2-4-5-6-8-9-11-12-17
14	1-2-4-5-6-8-9-11-13-14-15-17
15	1-2-4-5-6-8-9-11-13-14-16-17
16	1-2-4-5-6-8-10-11-12-17
17	1-2-4-5-6-8-10-11-13-14-15-17
18	1-2-4-5-6-8-10-11-13-14-16-17
19	1-2-4-5-7-8-9-11-12-17
20	1-2-4-5-7-8-9-11-13-14-15-17
21	1-2-4-5-7-8-9-11-13-14-16-17
22	1-2-4-5-7-8-10-11-12-17
23	1-2-4-5-7-8-10-11-13-14-15-17
24	1-2-4-5-7-8-10-11-13-14-16-17

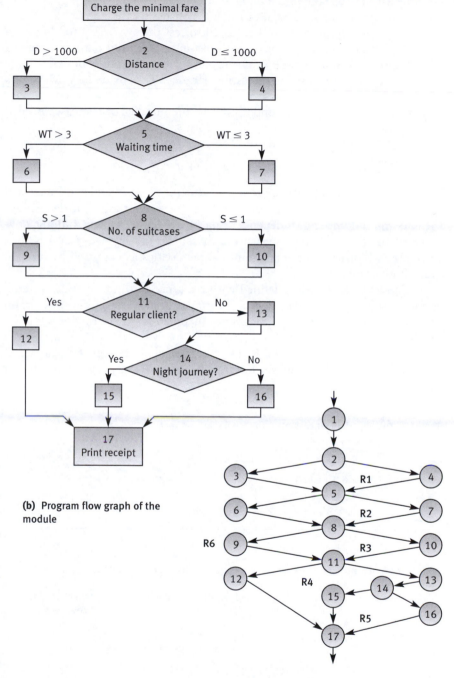

(a) Flow chart of the module

(b) Program flow graph of the module

Figure 9.3: The ITS taxi fare calculation process – flow chart and program flow graph

In contrast, the program flow graph allows us to observe that full line coverage of the ITS software module can be reached by inspecting the minimum number of paths – a total of three – as listed in Table 9.4.

The proportion of test cases required to test the system by full line coverage of three test cases (by basic path testing) versus full path coverage of 24 test cases is 1:8! This ratio grows rapidly with program complexity.

Support for the basic path testing strategy is provided by McCabe's cyclomatic complexity metrics, which besides being software complexity metrics also serve to give an upper limit to the number of test cases needed for full line coverage.

9.4.4 McCabe's cyclomatic complexity metrics

The cyclomatic complexity metrics developed by McCabe (1976) measures the complexity of a program or module at the same time as it determines the maximum number of independent paths needed to achieve full line coverage of the program. The measure is based on graph theory and is thus calculated according to the program characteristics as captured by its program flow graph.

An independent path is defined with reference to the succession of independent paths accumulated, that is: "Any path on the program flow graph that includes at least one edge that is not included in any of the former independent paths".

To illustrate this definition, let us refer once again to Figure 9.3. A set of independent paths that achieves full line coverage of the program is listed in Table 9.5.

Table 9.4: The Imperial Taxi example – the minimum number of paths

No.	The path
1	1-2-3-5-6-8-9-11-12-17
23	1-2-4-5-7-8-10-11-13-14-15-17
24	1-2-4-5-7-8-10-11-13-14-16-17

Table 9.5: The ITS example – the set of independent paths to achieve full coverage

Path no.	The path	Edges added by the path	Number of edges added by the path
1	1-2-3-5-6-8-9-11-12-17	1-2, 2-3, 3-5, 5-6, 6-8, 8-9, 9-11, 11-12, 12-17	9
2	1-2-3-5-6-8-9-11-13-14-15-17	11-13, 13-14, 14-15, 15-17	4
3	1-2-3-5-6-8-9-11-13-14-16-17	14-16, 16-17	2
4	1-2-4-5-7-8-10-11-13-14-15-17	2-4, 4-5, 5-7, 7-8, 8-10, 10-11	6

As mentioned above, the cyclomatic complexity metric $V(G)$ also determines the maximum number of independent paths that can be indicated in the program flow graph.

The cyclomatic complexity metric ($V(G)$) is expressed in three different ways, all of which are based on the program flow graph:

(1) $V(G) = R$
(2) $V(G) = E - N + 2$
(3) $V(G) = P + 1$

In these equations R is the number of regions in the program flow graph. Any enclosed area in the graph is considered a region. In addition the area around the graph not enclosed by it is counted as one additional region. E is the number of edges in the program flow graph, N is the number of nodes in the program flow graph, and P is the number of decisions contained in the graph, represented by nodes having more than one leaving edge.

Example

Applying the above to the ITS taximeter module example described above, we can obtain the values of the above parameters from Figure 9.3. We find that $R = 6$, $E = 21$, $N = 17$, and $P = 5$. Substituting these values into the metrics formulae we obtain:

(1) $V(G) = R = 6$
(2) $V(G) = E - N + 2 = 21 - 17 + 2 = 6$
(3) $V(G) = P + 1 = 5 + 1 = 6$

The resulting metrics calculations indicate that the maximum number of independent paths in the example is six. One realization of a maximal set of six independent paths is shown in Table 9.6.

Several empirical studies of the relationships between the cyclomatic complexity metrics and quality and testability characteristics have been car-

Table 9.6: The ITS example – the maximum set of independent paths

Path no.	The path	Edges added by the path	Number of edges added by the path
1	1-2-3-5-6-8-9-11-12-17	1-2, 2-3, 3-5, 5-6, 5-8, 8-9, 9-11, 11-12, 12-17	9
2	1-2-4-5-6-8-9-11-12-17	2-4, 4-5	2
3	1-2-3-5-7-8-9-11-12-17	5-7, 7-8	2
4	1-2-3-5-6-8-10-11-12-17	8-10, 10-11	2
5	1-2-3-5-6-8-9-11-13-14-15-17	11-13, 13-14, 14-15, 15-17	4
6	1-2-3-5-6-8-9-11-13-14-16-17	14-16, 16-17	2

ried out over the years. Some of the findings are summarized by Jones (1996) as follows: "Empirical studies reveal that programs with cyclomatic complexities of less than 5 are generally considered simple and easy to understand. Cyclomatic complexities of 10 or less are considered not too difficult; if 20 or more, the complexity is perceived as high. When the McCabe value exceeds 50, the software for practical purposes becomes untestable." Other publications report no confirmation of the relationship between the cyclomatic complexity metrics and the quality of the software, or that the relationships found have not been supported statistically (Fenton, 1995, pp. 279–281).

9.4.5 Software qualification and reusability testing

Software qualification testing

Although the subject of qualification was discussed in Section 7.3, the topic was not exhausted. Qualification testing is of crucial importance for coding in the development as well as maintenance stages. To quickly review, software that qualifies is coded and documented according to standards, procedures and work instructions. This makes it easier for the team leader to check the software, for the replacement programmer to comprehend the code and continue coding tasks, and for the maintenance programmer to correct bugs and/or update or change the program upon request.

Software qualification testing ascertains whether software development responded positively to questions reflecting a specific set of criteria:

- Does the code fulfill the code structure instructions and procedures, such as module size, application of reused code, etc.?
- Does the coding style fulfill coding style procedures?
- Do the internal program documentation and "help" sections fulfill coding style procedures?

Specialized software packages (called code auditors) can now perform a portion of the qualification tests by listing instances of non-conformity to coding standards, procedures and work instructions. Other tests continue to rest on trained personnel for their manual execution.

Software reusability testing

Software reusability substantially reduces project resources requirements and improves the quality of new software systems. In doing so, reusability shortens the development period, which by itself benefits the software development organization. Reusability testing supports these functions by determining whether the packaging and documentation of the programs and modules listed for reuse conform to the standards and procedures demanded for inclusion in the reusable software library. Reusability testing is actually one of the tools supporting the growth of software reuse.

The main advantages of white box testing are:

■ Direct statement-by-statement checking of code enables determination of software correctness as expressed in the processing paths, including whether the algorithms were correctly defined and coded.

■ It allows performance of line coverage follow-up (applying specialized software packages) that provides the tester with lists of lines of code that have not yet been executed. The tester can then initiate test cases to cover these lines of code.

■ It ascertains quality of coding work and its adherence to coding standards.

The main disadvantages of white box testing are:

■ The vast resources utilized, much above those required for black box testing of the same software package.

■ The inability to test software performance in terms of availability (response time), reliability, load durability, and other testing classes related to operation, revision and transition factors.

The characteristics of white box testing limit its use to software modules of very high risk and very high cost of failure, where it is highly important to identify and fully correct as many of the software errors as possible.

9.5 Black box testing

Black box testing allows us to perform output correctness tests and most classes of tests as shown in Table 9.2. Apart from output correctness tests (if you are prepared to pay the extra costs, these could be performed by white box data processing and calculation correctness tests) and maintainability tests (that could be performed by white box tests), most of the other testing classes are unique to black box testing. This explains the importance of black box testing. Still, due to the special characteristics of each testing strategy and the test classes unique to white box testing, black box testing cannot automatically substitute for white box testing.

This section will thus deal with the following issues:

■ Equivalence classes and their effect on the number of test cases required for output correctness test.
■ Performance methodology for other classes of black box tests.
■ Advantages and disadvantages of black box testing.

For additional material on black box testing, Beizer (1995) is one of the major sources available.

9.5.1 Equivalence classes for output correctness tests

Output correctness tests are, in most cases, among the tests that consume the greater part of testing resources. In those frequent cases where output correctness tests alone are performed, they consume all testing resources. Implementation of other classes of tests depends on the nature of the software product and its future users as well as on the developer's procedures and decisions.

The output correctness tests apply the concept of test cases. Improved choice of test cases can be achieved by the efficient use of equivalence class partitioning, a method to be discussed here.

Equivalence class partitioning is a black box method aimed at increasing the efficiency of testing and, at the same time, improving coverage of potential error conditions. An equivalence class (EC) is a set of input variable values that produce the same output results or that are processed identically. EC boundaries are defined by a single numeric or alphabetic value, a group of numeric or alphabetic values, a range of values, and so on. An EC that contains only valid states is defined as a "valid EC", whereas an EC that contains only invalid states is defined as an "invalid EC". In cases where a program's input is provided by several variables, valid and invalid ECs should be defined for each variable.

According to the equivalence class partitioning method, test cases are defined so that each valid EC and each invalid EC are included in at least one test case. Test cases are defined separately for the valid and invalid ECs. In defining a test case for the valid ECs, we try to cover as many as possible "new" ECs (i.e., classes not included in any of the former test cases) in that same test case. Test cases are added as long as there are uncovered ECs. As a result of this process, the total number of required test cases to cover the valid ECs is equal to and in most cases significantly below the number of valid ECs. Note that in defining invalid ECs, we must assign one test case to each "new" invalid EC, as only one invalid EC can be included in a test case. A test case that includes more than one invalid EC may not allow the tester to distinguish between the program's separate reactions to each of the invalid ECs. Hence, the number of test cases required for the invalid ECs equals the number of invalid ECs.

Compared to the use of a random sample of test cases, equivalence classes save testing resources because they eliminate duplication of the test cases defined for each EC. Importantly, as the equivalence class method is a black box method, equivalence class partitioning is based on software specification documentation, not on the code. Systematic constructing of equivalence classes for a program's input variables increases the coverage of possible valid and error conditions of input and thus improves the testing plan's effectiveness. Further improvement of testing effectiveness and efficiency is achieved by testing for the boundary values of ECs, a subject we elaborate next.

Test cases and boundary values

According to the definition of equivalence classes, one test case should be sufficient for each class. However, when equivalence classes cover a range of values (e.g. monthly income, apartment area), the tester has a special interest in testing border values when these are considered to be error prone. In these cases, the preparation of three test cases – for mid range, lower boundary and upper boundary values – is recommended.

Example – the Golden Splash Swimming Center

The following example illustrates the definition of (valid and invalid) equivalence classes and the corresponding test case values. The software module in question calculates entrance ticket prices for the Golden Splash Swimming Center.

The Center's ticket price depends on four variables: day (weekday, weekend), visitor's status (OT = one time, M = member), entry hour (6.00–19.00, 19.01–24.00) and visitor's age (up to 16, 16.01–60, 60.01–120). The entrance ticket price table is shown in Table 9.7.

The equivalence classes and the corresponding test case values for the above example are presented in Tables 9.8 and 9.9.

A total of 15 ECs were defined for the ticket price module: nine valid ECs and six invalid ECs. The test cases that correspond to these ECs apply the representing values listed in Table 9.8. The test cases for these ECs, including their boundary values, are presented in Table 9.9.

A total of 15 test cases cover all the defined ECs, including the respective EC boundary values:

■ Three test cases for the valid ECs (for our example a total of nine valid ECs were defined).

■ Six test cases for the boundary value ECs (in our example, boundary testing is applicable for only two of the four input variables).

■ Six test cases for invalid ECs (for our example a total of six invalid ECs were defined).

Table 9.7: Entrance ticket price table – the Golden Splash Swimming Center

	Mon, Tue, Wed, Thurs, Fri				Sat, Sun			
Visitor's status	OT	OT	M	M	OT	OT	M	M
Entry hour	6.00–19.00	19.01–24.00	6.00–19.00	19.01–24.00	6.00–19.00	19.01–24.00	6.00–19.00	19.01–24.00
	Ticket prices – $							
Visitor's age								
0.0–16.00	5.00	6.00	2.50	3.00	7.50	9.00	3.50	4.00
16.01–60.00	10.00	12.00	5.00	6.00	15.00	18.00	7.00	8.00
60.01–120.00	8.00	8.00	4.00	4.00	12.00	12.00	5.50	5.50

Table 9.8: Equivalence classes – the Golden Splash Swimming Center ticket price module

Variable	Valid equivalence classes	Representing values		Invalid equivalence classes	Representing values for invalid ECs
		Values for valid ECs	Boundary values		
Day of week	(1) Mon, Tue, Wed, Thurs, Fri	Mon		(1) Any alpha-numeric value (not a day)	Mox
	(2) Sat, Sun	Sat			
Visitor's status	(1) OT	OT		Other than OT or M	88
	(2) M	M			
Entry hour	(1) 6.00–19.00	7.55	6.00, 19.00	(1) Hours < 6.00	4.40
	(2) 19.01–24.00	20.44	19.01, 24.00	(2) Any alpha-numeric values (not time)	&@
Visitor's age	(1) 0.0–16.00	8.4	0.0, 16.00	(1) Any alpha-numeric value (not an age)	TTR
	(2) 16.01–60.00	42.7	16.01, 60.00		
	(3) 60.01–120.00	65.0	60.01, 120.00	(2) Ages > 120.0	150.1

Table 9.9: Test cases – the Golden Splash Swimming Center ticket price module

Test case type	Test case no.	Day of week	Visitor's status	Entry hour	Visitor's age	Test case results
For valid ECs	1	Mon	OT	7.55	8.4	$5.00
	2	Sat	M	20.44	42.7	$8.00
	3	Sat	M	22.44	65.0	$5.50
	4	Sat	M	6.00	0.0	$3.50
	5	Sat	M	19.00	16.00	$3.50
	6	Sat	M	19.01	16.01	$8.00
	7	Sat	M	19.01	60.00	$8.00
	8	Sat	M	24.00	60.01	$5.50
	9	Sat	M	24.00	120.0	$5.50
For invalid ECs	10	Mox	OT	7.55	8.4	Invalid day
	11	Mon	88	7.55	8.4	Invalid visitor status
	12	Mon	OT	4.40	8.4	Invalid entry hour
	13	Mon	OT	&@	8.4	Invalid entry hour
	14	Mon	OT	7.55	TTR	Invalid visitor age
	15	Mon	OT	7.55	150.1	Invalid visitor age

Though the equivalence class method is applied mainly with correctness tests, it may be used for other operation factor testing classes as well as for revision and transition factor testing classes.

9.5.2 Other operation factor testing classes

Apart from output correctness tests, operation factor testing classes include the following classes of tests:

Quality requirements factor	Test class
Correctness	(1) Documentation tests
	(2) Availability (reaction time) tests
Reliability	Reliability tests
Efficiency	Stress tests (load and durability tests)
Integrity	Software system security tests
Usability	(1) Training usability tests
	(2) Operational usability tests

Documentation tests

Documentation testing, though neglected in many cases, should be considered as important as code testing or design documents inspections. An erroneous user manual or programmer manual can lead to mistakes during program operation and maintenance that may incur damages equivalent in severity to those caused by software bugs.

Common components of documentation, supplied by the developer, are:

- **Functional descriptions of the software system.** This overview enables the potential user to decide whether the system is suitable for his needs or not.

- **Installation manual.** This document includes a detailed description of the installation process and hardware requirements as well as instructions for interfacing with equipment and with other software packages – if such interfaces are part of the system specifications. In commercial software packages (COTS software), the installation manual usually includes also customization instructions.

- **User manual.** "How to get started" instructions, detailed instructions for applying the various system functions, recovery instructions for common operator mistakes and system errors are all covered in the user manual. In many cases, the user manual is supplied as a computerized help manual.

- **Programmer manual.** This type of documentation is supplied for custom-made software. It includes the information required for maintaining the system (bug corrections, adaptation to changing requirements and software improvement), program structure, description of program logic including algorithms, and so on. Users and customers of COTS software do not require a programmer's manual as they do not carry out maintenance individually.

Document testing plans should include the following three components:

- **Document completeness check**. Based on the requirements specification and the detailed design reports, its purpose is to check whether all the required documents have been completed as specified and as intended by the designer.
- **Document correctness tests**. Correctness tests determine whether the instructions listed in the user document are correct. Implementation of correctness tests requires designing a test case file in a manner that closely resembles the methodology of output correctness tests discussed in Section 9.5.1.
- **Document style and editing inspection**. Refers to document clarity and its agreement with documentation standards in cases this requirement is specified in the contract.

Availability tests

Availability is defined as *reaction time* – the time needed to obtain the requested information or the time required for firmware installed in computerized equipment to react. Availability is of highest importance in on-line applications of frequently used information systems. The failure of firmware software to meet availability requirements (i.e., retarded reaction time) can make the equipment useless.

It is relatively difficult to test availability, especially for information systems planned to serve a large population of users, and for real-time systems planned to treat high-frequency events. This difficulty stems from the need to carry out the tests under regular operation load as well as under maximal load conditions as specified in the requirement specifications. It should be noted that the availability requirements for regular and maximal workloads are usually different. The required characteristics of the availability testing environment support combining of this class of tests with load tests (stress tests) and performing the adjusted computerized combined tests. (For discussion of load tests, see below.)

Reliability tests

The software system reliability requirement deals with features that can be translated as events occurring over time, such as average time between failures (e.g., 500 hours), average time for recovery after system failure (e.g., 15 minutes), or average downtime per month (e.g., 30 minutes per month). Reliability requirements are to be in effect during regular full-capacity operation of the system. It should be noted that in addition to the software factor, reliability tests also relate to the hardware, the operating system and the data communication system effects.

Like availability testing, reliability testing is especially difficult as it requires operation of the full range of software applications conducted under regular workload conditions. To be practical, such tasks should be carried out only after computerized simulations have been run to obtain average values, and only once the system is completed. With respect to resources, the major constraint on performing tests of this type is the scope of resources required, which is vast as testing may continue for hundreds of hours and a comprehensive test case file must be constructed.

Statistical reliability testing offers a much less expensive and much speedier option for the assessment of reliability on the basis of statistical models. Much literature is available on the subject, just a few major sources being Myers (1976), Musa *et al.* (1990) and Musa (1998). However, despite their widespread use and practical benefits, statistical reliability tests have been subjected to criticism ever since their emergence. The main issue debated is the extent to which statistical models represent real-life software system operation.

Stress tests

The class of stress tests subsumes two main types of tests: load tests and durability tests. It is possible to perform these tests only subsequent to software system completion. Durability tests, however, can generally be carried out only after the firmware or the information system software has been installed and is ready for testing.

Stress tests: load tests

Load tests relate to the functional performance of the system under maximal operational load: maximal transactions per minute, hits per minute to an Internet site and the like. Load tests, which are usually conducted for loads higher than those indicated in the requirements specification, are of utmost importance for software systems planned to serve simultaneously a large population of users. In most working software systems, the maximal load figure combines several types of transactions. Due to its variability, the best way to explain the process is through an example.

Example

"Music in the Air", a network of music stores, run a service on the Internet that registers requests for price quotations and orders. On weekdays, the average rate of customer hits is 10 per minute for orders and 20 per minute for price quotations. The maximum loads recorded on Saturday afternoon are 30 per minute for orders and 100 per minute for price quotations. The maximal load defined in the software specifications, which takes future growth into account, is 60 per minute for orders and 200 per minute for price quotation. The loads for which the program will be tested are 75 per minute for orders and 250 per minute for price quotations. So, this explains how the test loads were chosen for the example.

Manual performance of load tests is impractical for most software systems, and is therefore carried out by computerized tests based on comprehensive simulations of high loads, again similar to the procedures adapted for availability testing. These load simulations enable us to measure the expected reaction times as a function of a range of loads. They thus allow us to ascertain whether upgrading is necessary and which changes should be made to allow the software system to meet the planned requirements. For more about computerized load testing, see Section 10.3 in the next chapter which deals with computerized software testing.

Stress tests: durability tests

Durability tests are carried out in physically extreme operating conditions such as high temperatures, humidity, and high-speed driving along unpaved rural roads, as detailed in the durability specification requirements. Hence, these durability tests are typically required for real-time firmware integrated into systems such as weapon systems, long-distance transport vehicles, and meteorological equipment. Durability issues for firmware include firmware responses to climatic effects such as extreme hot and cold temperatures, dust, road bumps, and extreme operation failures resulting from sudden electrical failure, voltage "jumps" in the supply mains, sudden cutoffs in communications, and so on. Information system software durability tests focus on operation failures resulting from sudden electrical failures, voltage "jumps" in the supply mains and sudden cutoffs in communications.

Software system security tests

Software security components of software systems are aimed at preventing unauthorized access to the system or parts of it, detection of unauthorized access and the activities performed by the penetration, and the recovery of damages caused by unauthorized penetration cases.

The main security issues dealt with by these tests are:

- Access control, where the usual requirement is for control of multi-level access (usually by a password mechanism). Of special importance here are the firewall systems that prevent unauthorized access to Internet sites.
- Backup of databases and software files and recovery in cases of system failure.
- Logging of transactions, system usage, access trials, and so forth.

The challenge of creating and breaking into security systems has bred a special brand of delinquent, the hacker. Often very young, these enthusiasts find their ultimate pleasure first and foremost by breaking into complex computer systems, sometimes accompanied by system disruption, or creation of the viruses that incapacitate others. Their success has been astounding in some cases (e.g. national banks, US military security systems, etc.), and embarrassing to the same extent. One "payoff" of their success is that it is no longer rare to find hackers invited to join tester teams, especially for software systems where security requirements are high.

Training usability tests

When large numbers of users are involved in operating a system, training usability requirements are added to the testing agenda. The scope of training usability is defined by the resources needed to train a new employee, in other words, how many hours of training are required for a new employee to achieve a defined level of acquaintance with the system or to reach a defined hourly production rate. The details of these tests, like any other, are based on system characteristics but, more importantly here, on employee characteristics. The results of the tests should inspire a sophisticated plan of training courses and follow-up as well as improved directions for software system operation.

Operational usability tests

The focus of this class of tests is the operator's productivity, that is, those aspects of the system that affect the performance regularly achieved by system operators, or that are applied mainly for information systems that serve many users. These tests are of high importance in cases where the workings of the system can affect substantially the productivity of its users.

The implementation of this class of tests deals mainly with the productivity, quantitatively and qualitatively. Naturally these aspects are highly important for systems that serve as the main vocational tools for a large group of users.

Operational usability tests can be performed manually by means of time studies. In addition to productivity data, these manual tests provide some insight into the reasons for (high or low) performance levels and initiate ideas for improvements. Accurate performance records can be achieved by automated follow-up software that records all user activities throughout their shift. Software packages of this type supply performance statistics and comparative figures for different variables, such as specific activity, time period, and industry.

Comprehensive discussion of usability testing issues and detailed examples can be found in Rubin (1994).

9.5.3 Revision factor testing classes

Easy revision of software is a fundamental factor assuring a software package's successful, long service and its successful sales to larger user populations. Related to these features are the revision testing classes discussed in this section:

- Maintainability tests
- Flexibility tests
- Testability tests.

Maintainability tests

The importance of software maintenance and maintainability can never be overestimated; consider the fact that these functions consume more than 60% of total design and programming resources invested in a software system throughout its life cycle (Pressman, 2000). Although estimates of the share of maintenance resources vary – from over 50% as reported by Lientz and Swanson (1980) and 65–75% as reported by McKee (1984) – their significance remains undeniable.

Maintainability tests relate mainly to these issues:

(1) The system structure abides by the standards and development procedures imposed on the specific components for support of future maintenance activities, including the modular structure of self-contained modules and module size.

(2) The programmer's manual is prepared according to approved documentation standards and provides complete system documentation.

(3) The internal documentation incorporated in the software code is prepared according to coding procedures and conventions and fully covers the system's documentation requirements.

Software qualification testing is the software quality assurance tool preferred for checking adherence to maintainability requirements as in issue (1) above (see Section 9.4.4). Testing adherence to the requirements of issues (2) and (3) fall in the scope of programmer's documentation testing and are performed unless included in the user documentation tests (see Section 9.5.2).

Flexibility tests

Software system flexibility refers to the system's capabilities, based on its structural and programming characteristics. These factors significantly affect the efforts required to adapt the software to the variety of customer needs as well as to introduce changes initiated by customers and maintenance teams for the purpose of improving system functionality.

Flexibility tests are intended to test the software characteristics that support flexibility, such as adequate modular structure and application of parametric options to provide a wide range of possible applications.

Testability tests

Testability requirements deal with the ease of testing the software system. Thus, testability here relates to the addition of special features in the program that help the testers in their work, such as the possibility of obtaining intermediate results for certain checkpoints and predefined log files. Although often overlooked, these special testing support features should be specified in the requirements document as integral to the functional software requirements.

Another objective of testability deals with diagnostic tool applications implemented for the analysis of the system performance and the report of any failure found. Some features of this kind are activated automatically when starting the software package or during regular operation and report whenever conditions warranting alarm arise. Other features of this type may be activated by the operator or maintenance technician. Testability is particularly crucial for support of control rooms of large operating systems (e.g., electricity plants) and for maintenance teams, especially with respect to diagnosis of failures. Maintenance support applications of this type may be activated at the customer site and/or at some remote help desk support center.

Testability tests will be carried out for applications of both types, as noted in the requirement specifications. The tests should relate mainly to aspects of correctness, documentation and availability, as already discussed.

9.5.4 Transition factor testing classes

The software characteristics required to be operative, with minor adaptations, in different environments, and those needed to incorporate reused modules or to permit interfacing with other software packages are all among the transition features required from a software system, especially for commercial software packages aimed at a wide range of customers. Hence, the following testing classes, discussed in this section, must be applied:

(1) Portability tests
(2) Reusability tests
(3) Tests for interoperability requirements:
   - Software interfacing tests
   - Equipment interfacing tests.

Portability tests
Portability requirements specify the environments (or environmental conditions) in which the software system has to be operable: the operating systems, hardware and communication equipment standards, among other variables. The portability test to be carried out will verify, validate and test these factors as well as estimate the resources required for transfer of a software system to a different environment.

Reusability tests
Reusability defines which parts of the program (modules, integrations and the like) are to be developed for future reuse in other software development projects, whether already planned or not. These parts should be developed, packaged and documented according to reused software library procedures. Reusability requirements are of special importance for object-oriented software projects. Tests are therefore devised to examine whether reusability standards were indeed adhered to.

Software interoperability tests

Software interoperability deals with software capabilities of interfacing equipment and other software packages, to enable them to operate jointly as one complex computerized system. The requirements list delineates the specific equipment and/or software interfaces to be tested, as well as the applicable data transfer and interfacing standards. A growing share of commercial over-the-counter (COTS) software packages as well as custom-made software packages are now required to have interoperability capabilities, that is, to display the capacity to receive inputs from equipment firmware and/or other software systems and/or to send outputs to other firmware and software systems. These software capabilities are carried out under rigid data transfer standards, international and global or industry-oriented interoperability standards, and tested accordingly.

Equipment interoperability tests

Equipment interoperability deals with the equipment's firmware interfacing other equipment units and /or software packages, where the requirements list the specified interfaces, including with interfacing standards. The relevant tests should examine implementation of the equipment interoperability requirements throughout the system.

9.5.5 Advantages and disadvantages of black box testing

The main advantages of black box testing are:

■ Black box testing allows us to carry out the majority of testing classes, most of which can be implemented solely by black box tests. Of the test classes unique to black box testing, of special importance are system performance tests such as load tests and availability tests.

■ For testing classes that can be carried out by both white and black box tests, black box testing requires fewer resources than those required for white box testing of the same software package.

The main disadvantages of black box testing are:

■ Possibility that coincidental aggregation of several errors will produce the correct response for a test case, and prevent error detection. In other words, black box tests do not readily identify cases of errors that counteract each other to accidentally produce the correct output.

■ Absence of control of line coverage. In cases where black box testers wish to improve line coverage, there is no easy way to specify the parameters of the test cases required to improve coverage. Consequently, black box tests may not execute a substantial proportion of the code lines, which are not covered by a set of test cases.

■ Impossibility of testing the quality of coding and its strict adherence to the coding standards.

(1) Explain testing objectives.

One should distinguish between direct and indirect testing objectives. The direct objectives are:

■ To identify and reveal as many errors as possible in the tested software

■ To bring the tested software to an acceptable quality level

■ To perform the required testing in an efficient and effective way, within budget and scheduling limitations.

The indirect objective:

■ To supply records of software errors to be used for error prevention.

(2) Discuss the differences between the various testing strategies, their advantages and disadvantages.

There are basically two testing strategies:

■ "Big bang testing": tests the software as a whole, once the completed package is available.

■ "Incremental testing": tests the software piecemeal – software modules are tested as they are completed (unit tests), followed by groups of modules composed of tested modules integrated with newly completed modules (integration tests). Once the entire package is completed, it is tested as a whole (system test).

There are two basic incremental testing strategies: bottom-up and top-down. In top-down testing, the first module tested is the main module, the highest level module in the software structure; the last modules to be tested are the lowest level modules. In bottom-up testing, the order of testing is reversed: the lowest level modules are tested first, with the main module tested last.

■ **Big bang vs. incremental testing.** Unless the program is very small and simple, applying the "big bang" testing strategy presents severe disadvantages. Identification of error in the entire software package when perceived as one "unit" is very difficult and, in spite of the vast resources invested, is not very effective. Moreover, performing perfect correction of an error in this context is frequently laborious. Obviously, estimates of the required testing resources and testing schedule tend to be rather fuzzy. In contrast, the advantages of incremental testing, because it is performed on relatively small software units, yields higher percentages of identified errors and facilitates their correction. As a result, it is generally accepted that incremental testing should be preferred.

■ **Bottom-up vs. top-down.** The main advantage of the bottom-up strategy is its relative ease of performance, while its main disadvantage is the lateness of the stage at which it is possible to observe the program as a whole. The main advantage of the top-down strategy is the early stage at which it is possible to demonstrate the program as a whole, a condition that supports early identification of analysis and design errors. The main disadvantage of the approach is the comparative difficulty of its performance.

(3) Describe the concepts of black box testing and white box testing, and discuss their advantages and disadvantages.

- **Black box testing** identifies bugs only according to malfunctioning of the software as revealed from its outputs, while disregarding the internal paths of calculations performed by the software.
- **White box testing** examines the internal paths of calculations in order to identify bugs.

The main advantages of black box testing are:
- It allows the tester to carry out almost all test classes.
- For test classes that can be carried out by both white and black box testing, black box testing requires considerably fewer resources.

The main disadvantages of black box testing are:
- It allows for identification of coincidental errors as correct.
- It lacks control of line coverage.
- It lacks possibilities to test the quality of coding work.

The main advantages of white box testing are:
- It permits direct checking of processing paths and algorithms.
- It provides line coverage follow-up that delivers lists of lines of code that have not yet been executed.
- It is capable of testing the quality of coding work.

The main disadvantages of white box testing are:
- It requires vast resources, much above those required for black box testing.
- It cannot test the performance of software in terms of availability, reliability, stress, etc.

(4) Define path coverage vs. line coverage.

"Path coverage" is defined as the percentage of possible paths of software processing activated by the test cases. "Line coverage" is defined as the percentage of executed lines of code examined during the tests.

   The concepts of path testing and line coverage are applicable for estimating white box testing coverage only. In most cases, the achievement of full path coverage is impractical because of the scope of resources required for its implementation.

(5) Describe the various types of black box tests.

The black box tests are classified into three groups:
- Operation factor testing classes
- Revision factor testing classes
- Transition factor testing classes.

Operation factor testing classes include:
(1) Output correctness tests – in most cases, the class of tests that consume the largest weight of testing resources
(2) Documentation tests (for correctness)
(3) Availability (reaction time) tests (for correctness)
(4) Reliability tests

(5) Stress tests (load tests, durability tests) (for efficiency)

(6) Software system security tests

(7) Training usability tests (for usability)

(8) Operational usability tests (for usability).

Revision factor testing classes include:

(1) Maintainability tests

(2) Flexibility tests

(3) Testability tests.

Transition factor testing classes include:

(1) Portability tests

(2) Reusability tests

(3) Software interfacing tests (for interoperability)

(4) Equipment interfacing tests (for interoperability).

Selected bibliography

1. Beizer, B. (1984) *Software System Testing and Quality Assurance*, Van Nostrand Reinhold, New York.
2. Beizer, B. (1995) *Black Box Testing – Techniques for Functional Testing of Software and Systems*, John Wiley & Sons, New York.
3. Fenton, N. E. (1995) *Software Metrics – A Rigorous Approach*, International Thomson Press, London.
4. Hamlet, D. and Maybee, J. (2001) *The Engineering of Software – Technical Foundation for the Individual*, Addison-Wesley-Longman, Boston, MA.
5. IEEE (1990) "IEEE Std 610.12-1990 – IEEE Standard Glossary of Software Engineering Terminology", in *IEEE Software Engineering Standards Collection*, The Institute of Electrical and Electronics Engineers, New York.
6. Jones, C. (1996) *Applied Software Measurement – Assuring Productivity and Quality*, 2nd edn, McGraw-Hill, New York.
7. Jorgensen, P. C. (1995) *Software Testing – A Craftsman's Approach*, CRC Press, Boca Raton, FL.
8. Kaner, C., Falk, J. and Nguyen, H. Q. (1999) *Testing Computer Software*, 2nd edn, John Wiley & Sons, New York.
9. Kit, E. (1995) *Software Testing in the Real World – Improving the Process*, Addison-Wesley, Wokingham, UK.
10. Lientz, B. P. and Swanson, E. B. (1980) *Software Maintenance Management*, Addison-Wesley, Reading, MA.
11. McCabe, T. J. (1976) "A software complexity measure", *IEEE Transactions on Software Engineering*, 2(6), 308–320.
12. McKee, J. R. (1984) "Maintenance as a function of design", AFIPS National Computer Conference, Las Vegas, NV.
13. Musa, J. D. (1998) *Software Reliability Engineering: More Reliable Software, Faster Development and Testing*, McGraw-Hill, New York.
14. Musa, J. D., Iannino, A. and Okumoto, K. (1990) *Software Reliability – Measurement, Prediction, Application*, Professional Edition, McGraw-Hill, New York.
15. Myers, G. J. (1976) *Software Reliability – Principles and Practices*, John Wiley & Sons, New York.

16. Perry, W. (1996) *Effective Methods for Software Testing*, John Wiley and Sons, New York.
17. Perry, W. E. and Rice, R. W. (1997) *Surviving the Top Ten Challenges of Software Testing – A People-Oriented Approach*, Dorset House Publishing, New York.
18. Pressman, R. S. (2000) *Software Engineering – A Practitioner's Approach*, European adaptation by D. Ince, 5th edn, McGraw-Hill International, London.
19. Rubin, J. (1994) *Handbook of Usability Testing*, John Wiley & Sons, New York.
20. Sommerville, I. (2001) *Software Engineering*, 6th edn, Addison-Wesley, Harlow, Essex, UK.

Review questions

9.1 Not a few software industry professionals maintain that the main goal of software testing is "to prove that the software package is ready".

(1) Explain in your own words why this is not a suitable goal for software testing.
(2) What other goals might replace the goal mentioned above, and what gains in the effectiveness of the testing team can be expected from this change?

9.2 Explain in your own words why big bang testing is inferior to any method of incremental testing conducted for software packages that are not small.

9.3 Module G12 is coupled with seven lower-level modules and only one upper-level module.

(1) Discuss how the number of couplings affects the efforts required for incremental testing strategy.
(2) Consider the case described above. What are the effects of module G12's specific coupling situation on the resources required to perform unit tests according to the top-down strategy and the bottom-up strategy?

9.4 Section 9.4 mentions the terms *path coverage* and *line coverage*.

(1) Explain in your own words what the terms mean and list the main differences between these coverage metrics.
(2) Explain why the implementation of path coverage is impractical in most test applications.

9.5 Bengal Tours is a city center travel agency that specializes in tours and vacations in Canada. The agency regularly employs 25 permanent employees. During the spring and summer, the agency employs an additional 20–25 temporary staff, mostly senior citizens and students. The agency is considering purchasing the right to use the software system "Tourplanex", which supports the planning with flight and vacation site vacancies and price information. If purchased, the software will become the main working tool for the agency staff.

(1) Discuss the importance of the training usability and operational usability tests to be performed by the agency before it purchases "Tourplanex".
(2) Suggest to Bengal Tours management that they should apply training usability and operational usability tests to be performed on the program.

9.1 Bhealthy Ltd is a medical insurance company that reimburses the cost of drugs and various other medical expenses to its customers. According to current procedures, customers are asked to present receipts of drug purchases together with the relevant physician prescriptions and other medical documents. Reimbursement is calculated according to the insurance agreement stipulations:

■ Two lists of drugs are in effect for the purpose of reimbursement: class A and class B.
  - Class A: 90% of the costs of each purchased drug are reimbursed by Bhealthy after a minimum customer participation of $5. For example, a $10 drug is reimbursed by $4.50 and an $85 drug is reimbursed by $72.
  - Class B: 50% of the costs of each purchased drug are reimbursed by Bhealthy (no access).

■ A check is prepared and sent to the customer. The insurance agreement states the period of 45 days for the company to complete the reimbursement.
■ For some class A drugs the customer should prefer to buy the medications as a private customer as no reimbursement is expected (the drug's price is below $5).

The procedure described proved to be very expensive for Bhealthy at the same time that it provoked much subscriber dissatisfaction. The growth in the number of subscribers as well as the problems of complying with the current procedure motivated a new agreement with the licensed pharmacies. The agreement authorized the licensed pharmacy to deduct the reimbursement sums from the drug invoices; Bhealthy will then reimburse the pharmacies monthly for the deducted sums.

Bhealthy decided to prepare a special pharmacy software package that combines regular pharmacy sales operations with the operations required by its agreement with the licensed pharmacies and its subscribers.

Consider the invoicing module that prepares invoices for Bhealthy prescriptions as well as for regular sales of prescriptions and other items at a licensed pharmacy.

(1) Prepare a flow chart for the module.
(2) Prepare a program flow graph for the module.
(3) Calculate the cyclomatic complexity for the module.
(4) Prepare the maximal set of independent paths according to (3). Document the basic paths and indicate the added edges of each independent path.

9.2 "Police Star 1000 System" is the new prestigious software system for recording all the verbal communication (line telephone, cellular telephone and wireless) nationwide to be instituted by the police force. One feature of the system is its ability to supply any voice record completed in the last 12 months within 15 minutes in 98% of the applications. The system is planned to be operative within 10 months.

(1) Discuss the importance of conducting comprehensive load tests for the system.
(2) Suggest the recommended guidelines for these load tests.
(3) What basic data about police activities would you recommend to collect in order to plan the load test according to your recommended guidelines?

9.3 "Super Saving Light" is a new software system for control of street illumination and enhancement of its economy, developed for municipality maintenance departments. Among its functions are:

■ Commencement and conclusion of street lighting according to daily timetable, scheduled annually.

■ Partial illumination (only one of each two lights will be activated) during the first and last 15 minutes of each illumination period activated by (1).

■ Measurement of natural light conditions by special sensors to ascertain whether natural lighting is insufficient (e.g., on cloudy days), leading to earlier commencement of street illumination and later conclusion of illumination. In these cases, only one of a trio of streetlights will be activated.

■ Reduction of illumination time according to traffic density, monitored by a traffic sensor installed at every road section, which will reduce illumination as follows: if traffic density is below one vehicle per minute, only half of the street lights in the road section will be activated; if traffic density is below 0.3 vehicles per minute, only one-third of the lights will be activated.

Mr Jones, head of the testing team, claims that black box testing is insufficient and that white box tests are necessary for testing "Super Saving Light".

Support Mr Jones's claim with three software error examples based on the illumination rules described above. In the examples you choose, black box test results will be "OK", while white box testing of the same example will detect at least one error. For each example, explain why errors undetected by black box testing will be detected by white box testing.

9.4 Based on the "Super Saving Light" case described above:

(1) What input variables are required for test cases and what are the required output variables?

(2) Suggest three to five simple test cases having low potential to identify errors.

(3) Suggest three to five test cases that you believe contain serious potential for error.

(4) Suggest three to five test cases to deal with boundary value situations.

9.5 Referring to the "Bhealthy" case discussed in Topic 9.1, the following is the list price for a sample of 12 medications, including the cases' reimbursement class:

Medication name code	Medication classification according to Bhealthy	Price ($)
101	Not included	$3.45
102	Class B	$10.60
103	Class A	$5.50
104	Class A	$19.50
105	Class A	$4.50
106	Class B	$28.00
107	Not included	$74.99
108	Class B	$8.30
109	Class A	$3.90
110	Class B	$22.70
111	Class A	$5.20

(1) Based on the above price list, prepare the set of test cases required for implementing the maximal set of independent paths appropriate for your solution to Topic 9.1 question (4).

(2) Assume that Bhealthy changes its minimum subscriber participation for class A medications from $5 to $6. Will the test cases in (1) have to be changed? If yes, make the necessary changes and present the updated test case file.

Software testing – Implementation

The main issues to be raised with respect to testing implementation are test effectiveness and efficiency. In other words, constant efforts are to be directed to reduction of the percentage of undetected errors remaining in the software or system tested on the one hand, and to performance of those tests with fewer resources on the other.

Despite the vast resources invested in defect identification, it is commonly accepted that software free of defects is still an unrealizable task. This situation has inspired testing professionals to stress the issues of effectiveness and efficiency at every opportunity. The two main routes taken toward improvement involve upgrading the effectiveness of the test cases applied during testing, and development of automatic software testing.

The processes of designing, planning and carrying out tests at the various levels – unit tests, integration test and system test – are discussed in the first section of this chapter.

An improved test case file exhibits fewer repetitions of test cases covering the same situation and covers the vast space of possible software
implementations more thoroughly and accurately. Accordingly, improvements in this area are expected to improve test efficiency by reducing the
total number of required test cases and, at the same time, increasing test
effectiveness. Section 10.2 expands on this issue.

As to the second improvement route, we are gradually realizing the
potential of automated computerized testing. A discussion of this subject is
presented in Section 10.3.

An additional informal route for error detection of the software is based
on the contribution of future users to its quality through alpha and beta sites.
This option is discussed in Section 10.4.

Valuable sources for additional material on test implementation can be
found in books dealing with software testing, such as Perry (1995), Kit
(1995), Kaner *et al.* (1999) and Perry and Rice (1997). Other sources are
books on software engineering and software quality assurance such as
Pressman (2000) and Sommerville (2001), as are standards such as ISO/IEC
9000-3 (ISO/IEC, 2001), IEEE Std 829 (IEEE, 1998a), IEEE Std 1012 (IEEE,
1998b) and IEEE Std 12207 (IEEE, 1996, 1997a, 1997b), to cite some of the
major documents in this category.

After completing this chapter, you will be able to:

- Describe the process of planning and designing tests.
- Discuss the sources for test cases, with their advantages and disadvantages.
- List the main types of automated software tests.
- Discuss the advantages and disadvantages of automated computerized
  testing as compared to manual testing.
- Explain alpha and beta site test implementation and discuss their advan-
  tages and disadvantages.

10.1 The testing process

Planning, design and performance of testing are carried out throughout the
software development process. These activities are divided in phases, beginning in the design stage and ending when the software is installed at the
customer's site. The testing process is illustrated in Figure 10.1.

10.1.1 Determining the test methodology phase

The main issues that testing methodology has to contend with are:

- The appropriate required software quality standard
- The software testing strategy.

Decisions about these two issues are fundamental and must be made before
planning begins.

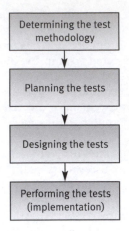

Figure 10.1: The testing process

Determining the appropriate software quality standard

The level of quality standard selected for a project depends mainly on the characteristics of the software's application.

■ Example 1: A software package for a hospital patient bed monitor requires the highest software quality standard considering the possibly severe consequences of software failure.

■ Example 2: A package developed for handling feedback information for an organization's internal employee training program could make do with a medium-level software quality standard, assuming that the cost of failure is relatively low (or much lower than that of Example 1).

■ Example 3: A software package has been developed for sale to a broad range of organizations. The sales prospects justify higher quality standards than would a custom-made software package having similar characteristics yet developed to serve a single customer.

These examples illustrate the main criterion to be applied when choosing the software quality standard: the evaluation of the nature and magnitude of expected damages in case of system failure. These damages may affect the customers and users on one hand, and the developer on the other. In general, the higher the expected level of damage resulting from failure, the higher the appropriate standard of software quality.

Typical types of damage to customers and users as well as to developers are listed in Table 10.1 (see also Table 8.1).

(a) Damage to customers and users	
Type of damage	**Examples**
1. Endangers the safety of human lives	▪ Hospital patient monitoring systems ▪ Aeronautical and aerospace systems ▪ Weapons systems
2. Affects accomplishment of an essential organizational function; no system replacement capability available	▪ E-business sales ▪ Nationwide multi-warehouse inventory systems
3. Affects the functioning of firmware, causing malfunction of an entire system	▪ Household appliances ▪ Automobiles ▪ Computerized electronic equipment
4. Affects accomplishment of an essential organizational function but a replacement is available	▪ Front-desk sales systems that can be replaced by manual mechanisms
5. Affects proper functioning of software packages for business applications	▪ Slow response time for a point-of-sale (POS) transaction ▪ Because of a fault, information that is regularly supplied on one screen is distributed among three different displays
6. Affects the proper functioning of software packages for a private customer	▪ Computer games ▪ Educational software ▪ Word processors
7. Affects functioning of a firmware application but without affecting the entire system	▪ Blackout of the control board of a household appliance without harming its functionality ▪ Failure of secondary systems (e.g., the outside temperature display found in some automobiles)
8. Inconveniences the user but does not prevent accomplishment of the system's capabilities	▪ Distorted but not misleading displays ▪ Inability to produce the output listed although alternative routes to obtaining the required information or performing the same operation are available

(b) Damage to the software developer	
Type of damage	**Examples**
1. Financial losses	▪ Damages paid for physical injuries ▪ Damages paid to organizations for malfunctioning of software ▪ Purchase cost reimbursed to customers ▪ High maintenance expenses for repair of failed systems
2. Non-quantitative damages	▪ Expected to affect future sales ▪ Substantially reduced current sales

Determining the software testing strategy

The issues that have to be decided include:

- The testing strategy: should a big bang or incremental testing strategy be adopted? If incremental testing is preferable, should testing be performed bottom-up or top-down?
- Which parts of the testing plan should be performed according to the white box testing model?
- Which parts of the testing plan should be performed according to the automated testing model?

10.1.2 Planning the tests

The tests to be planned include:

- Unit tests
- Integration tests
- System tests.

While unit tests deal with small units of software or modules, integration tests deal with several units that combine into a subsystem. System tests refer to the entire software package/system.

It is incumbent upon planners to consider the following issues before initiating a specific test plan:

- What to test?
- Which sources to use for test cases?
- Who is to perform the tests?
- Where to perform the tests?
- When to terminate the tests?

These five issues will be discussed in this section. The last subject of the section will be devoted to documentation.

What to test?

A straightforward approach to perfect testing would recommend a full and comprehensive software test plan that requires performing unit tests for all the individual units, integration tests for all the unit integrations, and a system test to test the software package as a whole. Implementing this "straightforward" plan ensures top quality software but requires the investment of vast resources and an extended timetable.

Relatedly, certain questions will undoubtedly arise with respect to common situations that pertain to the benefits of such an approach. For instance:

- Is it justified to perform unit tests for a module composed of 98% reused software?
- Is a unit test mandatory for a simple module that represents the 12th version of a basic module repeatedly applied by the development team over the last three years?

Only in rare cases it is justified to test "everything". Usually, the feasibility of testing "everything" is highly limited. Apart from performance of the list of tests specified in the contract or required by the developer's procedures (e.g. load tests for the system as a whole), several considerations order our preferences for the tests to be applied. The factors to be decided revolve around:

- Which modules should be unit tested
- Which integrations should be tested
- The priorities determining allocation of testing resources to the individual software system applications. As a result, low-priority applications are tested by only some types of tests or not included in the system test at all.

In determining what is to be included and what excluded from the system tests, the unit and integration tests already planned should be considered.

For the software quality of applications and modules not covered by the unit, integration and system tests, we rely on the code checks done by the programmer and his team leader and on code inspections and walkthroughs initiated by the development team.

Rating units, integrations and applications

The methods for rating units (modules), integrations and applications to determine their priority in the testing plan are based on two factors:

- Factor A: **Damage severity level.** The severity of results in case the module or application fails. Table 10.1 can serve as a guideline to estimate severity.
- Factor B: **Software risk level.** The level of risk represents the probability of failure. In order to determine the risk level of a module, unit, integration or application, the issues affecting risk require examination. These issues can be classified as module/application issues and programmer issues (see Frame 10.1).

Frame 10.1 **Issues affecting software risk level**

Module/application issues

- Magnitude
- Complexity and difficulty
- Percentage of original software (vs. percentage of reused software)

Programmer issues

- Professional qualifications
- Experience with the module's specific subject matter
- Availability of professional support (backup of knowledge and experience)
- Acquaintance with the programmer and the ability to evaluate his or her capabilities.

It is important to note that the issues raised represent a specific case of the general problem of determining the adequate intensity of quality assurance activities discussed in Section 7.2. Therefore, their underlying logic reaches beyond software testing priorities.

Generating a combined rating based on the two factors

The combined rating C will be based on the ratings for A (the damage severity grading) and B (the risk severity grading). C can be calculated in a variety of ways, for instance:

$$C = A + B$$
$$C = k \times A + m \times B$$
$$C = A \times B$$

where k and m are constants. The inclusion of a unit, integration or application in a testing plan and the amount of resources allocated to each test depend on priorities as expressed in the combined rating. In order to determine these priorities, initial calculation of the ratings is necessary. As a rule, the higher the rating, the higher the testing priority and the greater the allocation for testing resources.

Implementation tip

Changes may be required in the testing plan as a result of:

■ Unavailability of resources.

■ Time requirements are too long and will cause the project to go beyond its completion schedule.

■ Disagreements may arise about the evaluations of the expected damage and risk severity levels and/or about estimates of time and resources required for the testing activities.

The final testing plan will be completed only after these issues are resolved. Of course, the plan may need to be updated as the project proceeds, to reflect changes in conditions, including delays in project implementation.

Example

Super Teacher is a software package designed to support teachers in managing the grades of elementary school pupils. The package includes eight applications. Ratings are required in order to plan the allocation of testing resources for each application. Applications 7 and 8 are based on high percentages of reused code. Application 2 was developed by team C, composed of new employees. A five-level scale is used for rating damage severity (Factor *A*) as well as software risk severity level (Factor *B).*

The combined rating for the application is calculated according to three different methods:

(1) $C = A + B$
(2) $C = 7 \times A + 2 \times B$
(3) $C = A \times B$

The applications and their single-factor and combined ratings, are presented in Table 10.2.

When examining the results, it is noteworthy that the two highest priorities were both determined in the same order by all three methods of calculating the combined rating.

Which sources to use for test cases?

The planners should consider which of the two main sources of test cases – samples of real-life test cases and/or synthetic test cases – are most appropriate to their needs. Each component of the testing plan, dealing with unit,

Table 10.2: *Super Teacher* – results of alternative combined rating methods

Application	Damage severity level A	Risk severity level B	Combined rating method*		
			A + B	7 × A + 2 × B	A × B
1. Input of test results	3	2	5 (4–5)	25 (5)	6 (4)
2. Interface for input and output of pupils' data to and from other teachers	4	4	8 (1)	36 (1)	16 (1)
3. Preparation of lists of low achievers	2	2	4 (6–7)	18 (7)	4 (5-6)
4. Printing letters to parents of low achievers	1	2	3 (8)	11 (8)	2 (8)
5. Preparation of reports for school principal	3	3	6 (3)	27 (4)	9 (3)
6. Display of a pupil's achievements profile	4	3	7 (2)	34 (2)	12 (2)
7. Printing of pupil's term report card	3	1	4 (6–7)	23 (6)	3 (7)
8. Printing of pupil's year-end report card	4	1	5 (4–5)	30 (3)	4 (5–6)

*The figures in brackets in the combined rating columns represent the application preferences.

integration or the system test, requires an individual decision about the respective test cases and their source:

- The use of a single or combined source of test cases or both
- How many test cases from each source are to be prepared
- The characteristics of the test cases.

We shall return to the subject of test cases later (see Section 10.2).

Who performs the tests?
Who will perform the various tests is determined at the planning stage:

- Integration tests, but especially unit tests, are generally performed by the software development team. In some instances it is the testing unit that performs the tests.
- System tests are usually performed by an independent testing team (internal testing team or external testing consultants team).
- In cases of large software systems, more than one testing team can be employed to carry out the system tests. The prerequisite decision to be made in such cases concerns the allocation of system tests between the internal and the external testing teams.

In small software development organizations, where a separate testing team does not exist, the following testing possibilities nonetheless exist:

- Testing by another development team. Each development team will serve as the testing team for projects developed by other teams.
- Outsourcing of testing responsibilities.

Where to perform the tests?
Unit and integration testing are naturally carried out at the software developer's site. Location becomes important only when system tests are concerned: should they be performed at the developer's site or at the customer's site (the "target site")? If system testing is to be performed by external testing consultants, a third option arises: the consultant's site. The choice depends on the test's or system's computerized environment: as a rule, the computerized environment at the customer's site differs from that at the developer's site, despite efforts to "simulate" that environment. In such situations, apprehension regarding the occurrence of unpredicted failures once the system is installed at the customer's site is reduced as long as the customer is content with the system tests and plans no acceptance tests.

The decision about the stage at which software testing should be terminated is meaningful mainly with respect to system tests. The following five alternative routes are available, each chosen on the basis of different criteria.

(1) The completed implementation route. According to this route, testing is terminated once the entire test plan has been carried out and error free ("clean") results are achieved for all the required regression tests. This alternative applies the perfection approach, which disregards budget and timetable constraints.

(2) The mathematical models application route. When following this route, mathematical models are applied to estimate the percentage of undetected errors, based on the rate of error detection. Testing would be terminated once the error detection rate declines below the rate that corresponds to a predetermined level of undetected errors which is considered an acceptable software quality standard. The disadvantage of this route is that the mathematical model chosen may not fully represent the project's characteristics; hence, reliance on this model may undermine the usefulness of the tests because they will be terminated either too early or too late. Another deficiency of this approach arises when the model either chosen or available does not supply estimates about the severity of the undetected errors.

(3) The error seeding route. According to this approach, errors of various types are seeded (hidden) in the tested software prior to the outset of testing. The underlying assumption of this route is that the percentage of discovered seeded errors will correspond to the percentage of real errors detected. Accordingly, testing will terminate once the residual percentage of undetected seeded errors reaches a predefined level considered acceptable for "passing" the system. Besides the additional workload for the testers, the main deficiency of this approach lies in the experience upon which it is based. While the testers are expected to face "new and original" errors in every new project, the seeding plan is totally based on past experience. As experience with each system differs, the seeding method can not accurately estimate the residual rate of undetected errors in unfamiliar systems.

(4) The dual independent testing teams route. If this route is adopted, two teams implement the testing process independently. By comparing the lists of detected errors provided by each team, the number of errors left undetected is estimated as follows.

The teams' achievements yield:

Na = number of errors detected by team A
Nb = number of errors detected by team B.

The following count of detected errors is arrived at after comparison of the lists:

Nab = number of errors detected by both team A and team B.

We would expect to find:

Pa = proportion of errors detected by team A

Pb = proportion of errors detected by team B

Pab = proportion of errors detected by both team A and team B

P(a)(b) = proportion of errors undetected by both teams

N(a)(b) = number of errors undetected by both teams

N = total number of errors in the software package/program.

Assuming statistically independent testing by the teams and random detection of errors, simple probability equations can be applied that yield estimates of P(a)(b), N and N(a)(b). For this purpose we define:

(1) $Pab = Pa \times Pb = Nab/N$

(2) $Pa = Na/N$

(3) $Pb = Nb/N$

(4) $P(a)(b) = (1 - Pa) \times (1 - Pb)$

Simple mathematical manipulation of equations (1), (2), (3) and (4) above yields the following results:

(5) $N = Na \times Nb \,/\, Nab$

(6) $Pa = Nab \,/\, Nb$

(7) $Pb = Nab \,/\, Na$

(8) $P(a)(b) = (1 - Pa) \times (1 - Pb) =$

$\qquad = (Na - Nab) \times (Nb - Nab) \,/\, (Na \times Nb)$

(9) $N(a)(b) = (Na - Nab) \times (Nb - Nab) \,/\, Nab$

Example: The developers of *Super Magic*, an electronic game for children aged 4–7, have decided to employ the dual test method. They determined their testing termination level to be residual undetected errors of 2.5%. As a complementary "tool" for identifying the undetected errors, they planned wide application of beta site testing (see Section 10.4) before beginning the marketing of *Super Magic*.

The testing teams summarized their achievements after eight weeks of testing and regression testing as follows:

Team A detected 160 errors (Na = 160)

Team B detected 180 errors (Nb = 180).

Comparison of the detected errors of the two teams yielded the following result:

$Nab = 144$

Application of the probabilistic model (equations. (8), (9) and (5) above) yields:

$P(a)(b) = 16 \times 36 / (160 \times 180) = 0.02$
$N(a)(b) = 16 \times 36 / 144 = 4$
$N = 160 \times 180 / 144 = 200$

According to the above results, only 2% of the total number of errors were undetected; testing may therefore be terminated at this stage.

Applying equations (6), (7), (9) and (5) yields the following results: team A detected 80% of the total number of 200 program errors, while team B detected 90% of the total number of errors. Together, the two teams successfully detected 196 out of the estimated total number of 200 errors, leaving four undetected errors.

The main deficiency of the dual testing method is that, by definition, it can be applied only to projects where two independent testing teams are employed for the same project. Another deficiency lies in the assumption of random detection of errors. Its methodological basis may be questioned in some cases, especially where both teams share similar testing experience and employ the same testing methodology.

(5) **Termination after resources have petered out.** Termination of this type occurs when budgets or the time allocated for testing run out. This situation, unfortunately not uncommon in the software industry, is, of course, undesirable.

Implementation tip

Once you consider terminating testing, whether on the basis of a mathematical model, the error seeding route, or the dual testing teams route, validation of the accuracy of the results within your organization's testing environment is of highest importance.

Systematic follow-up is required for validation:

(1) **Data collection.** Collection of quality data on the errors detected in the project: total number of code errors = errors detected in the testing process + errors detected by the customer and the maintenance team during the first 6 or 12 months of regular software use.

(2) **Analysis of the error data.** The analysis will compare estimates suppliedby the models with the real figures.

(3) **Comparative analysis of severity of errors.** Errors detected in the testing process are compared to errors detected by the customer and the maintenance team during the first 6 or 12 months of regular software use.

Test planning documentation

The planning stage of the software system tests is commonly documented in a "software test plan" (STP). A template for the STP is presented in Frame 10.2.

10.1.3 Test design

The products of the test design stage are:

- Detailed design and procedures for each test
- Test case database/file.

Frame 10.2 **The software test plan (STP) – template**

1 Scope of the tests

1.1 The software package to be tested (name, version and revision)
1.2 The documents that provide the basis for the planned tests (name and version for each document)

2 Testing environment

2.1 Testing sites
2.2 Required hardware and firmware configuration
2.3 Participating organizations
2.4 Manpower requirements
2.5 Preparation and training required of the test team

3 Test details (for each test)

3.1 Test identification
3.2 Test objective
3.3 Cross-reference to the relevant design document and the requirement document
3.4 Test class
3.5 Test level (unit, integration or system tests)
3.6 Test case requirements
3.7 Special requirements (e.g., measurements of response times, security requirements)
3.8 Data to be recorded

4 Test schedule (for each test or test group) including time estimates for the following:

4.1 Preparation
4.2 Testing
4.3 Error correction
4.4 Regression tests

The test design is carried out on the basis of the software test plan as documented by STP. The test procedures and the test case database/file may be documented in a "software test procedure" document and "test case file" document or in a single document called the "software test description" (STD). A template for the STD is presented in Frame 10.3.

Frame 10.3 **Software test descriptions (STD) – template**

1 Scope of the tests

1.1 The software package to be tested (name, version and revision)
1.2 The documents providing the basis for the designed tests (name and version for each document)

2 Test environment (for each test)

2.1 Test identification (the test details are documented in the STP)
2.2 Detailed description of the operating system and hardware configuration and the required switch settings for the tests
2.3 Instructions for software loading

3 Testing process

3.1 Instructions for input, detailing every step of the input process
3.2 Data to be recorded during the tests

4 Test cases (for each case)

4.1 Test case identification details
4.2 Input data and system settings
4.3 Expected intermediate results (if applicable)
4.4 Expected results (numerical, message, activation of equipment, etc.)

5 Actions to be taken in case of program failure/cessation

6 Procedures to be applied according to the test results summary

---

10.1.4 Test implementation

Commonly, the testing implementation phase activities consist of a series of tests, corrections of detected errors and re-tests (regression tests). Testing is culminated when the re-test results satisfy the developers. The implementation phase process is illustrated in Figure 10.2.

The tests are carried out by running the test cases according to the test procedures. Documentation of the test procedures and the test case database/file comprises the "software test description" (STD), presented in Frame 10.3.

Re-testing (also termed "regression testing") is conducted to verify that the errors detected in the previous test runs have been properly corrected, and that no new errors have entered as a result of faulty corrections. It is

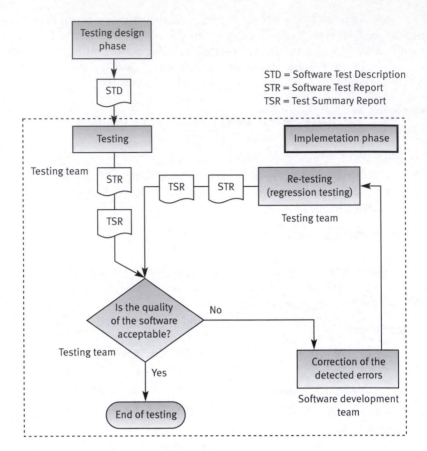

Figure 10.2: Implementation phase activities

quite common to find that the correction-regression testing sequence is repeated two to four times before satisfactory test results are achieved. Usually, it is advisable to re-test according to the original test procedure. However, in many cases, especially in manual software tests, only a portion of the original test procedure is re-tested to save testing resources and shorten re-testing duration. The parts of the software system omitted are those where no errors were detected or where all the detected errors were properly corrected at a previous point. Partial reruns of the test procedure save resources and time but involve the risk of not detecting new errors unintentionally introduced in the omitted parts during erroneous correction of the errors found in other parts of the software. The results of the individual tests and re-tests are documented in a "software test report" (STR). A template for the STR is presented in Frame 10.4.

The summary of the set of tests planned for a software package (or software development project) is documented in the "test summary report" (TSR).

Frame 10.4   Software test report (STR) – template

1 Test identification, site, schedule and participation

1.1 The tested software identification (name, version and revision)
1.2 The documents providing the basis for the tests (name and version for each document)
1.3 Test site
1.4 Initiation and concluding times for each testing session
1.5 Test team members
1.6 Other participants
1.7 Hours invested in performing the tests

2 Test environment

2.1 Hardware and firmware configurations
2.2 Preparations and training prior to testing

3 Test results

3.1 Test identification
3.2 Test case results (for each test case individually)
    3.2.1 Test case identification
    3.2.2 Tester identification
    3.2.3 Results: OK / failed
    3.2.4 If failed: detailed description of the results/problems

4 Summary tables for total number of errors, their distribution and types

4.1 Summary of current tests
4.2 Comparison with previous results (for regression test summaries)

5 Special events and testers' proposals

5.1 Special events and unpredicted responses of the software during testing
5.2 Problems encountered during testing
5.3 Proposals for changes in the test environment, including test preparations
5.4 Proposals for changes or corrections in test procedures and test case files

Correction of detected errors, as carried out by the software developers, is a highly controlled process. Follow-up of the process is performed to ensure that all the errors listed in the STR have been corrected.

10.2 Test case design

10.2.1 Test case data components

A test case is a documented set of the data inputs and operating conditions required to run a test item together with the expected results of the run. The tester is expected to run the program for the test item according to the test case documentation, and then compare the actual results with the expected results noted in the documents. If the obtained results completely agree with the expected results, no error is present or at least has been identified. When some or all of the results do not agree with the expected results, a potential error is identified. The equivalence class partitioning method, discussed in Section 9.5.1, is applied to achieve efficient and effective definition of the test cases, as sets, to be used for black box testing.

Example

Consider the following test cases for the basic annual municipal property tax on apartments. The basic municipal property tax (before discounts to special groups of city dwellers) is based on the following parameters:

S, the size of the apartment (in square yards)

N, the number of persons living in the apartment

A, B or C, the suburb's socio-economic classification.

The municipal property tax (MPT) is calculated as follows:

For class A suburbs: $MPT = (100 \times S) / (N + 8)$

For class B suburbs $MPT = (80 \times S) / (N + 8)$

For class C suburbs $MPT = (50 \times S) / (N + 8)$

The following are three test cases for the software module used to calculate the basic municipal property tax on apartments:

	Test case 1	Test case 2	Test case 3
Size of apartment – (square yards), S	250	180	98
Suburb class	A	B	C
No. of persons in the household, N	2	4	6
Expected result: **municipal property tax (MPT)**	**$2500**	**$1200**	**$350**

Application of the test case will produce one or more of the following types of expected results:

- Numerical
- Alphabetic (name, address, etc.)
- Error message. Standard output informing user about missing data, erroneous data, unmet conditions, etc.

With real-time software and firmware, the expected results can be of one or more of the following types:

- Numerical and/or alphabetic messages displayed on a monitor screen or on the equipment display.
- Activation of equipment or initiation of a defined operation.
- Activation of an operation, a siren, warning lamps and the like as a reaction to identified threatening conditions.
- Error message. Standard output to inform the operator about missing data, erroneous data, etc.

Implementation tip

It is highly important that the test case file include items where the expected result is an error message, as well as non-standard items and items displaying undesirable operation conditions, and so forth. Only by testing the software for non-regular conditions can we be assured that it will remain under control should undesirable situations arise. In such cases, the software is expected to activate pre-defined reactions, alarms, operator flags, and so forth – all in ways appropriate to system and customer needs. See Section 9.5.1 for invalid equivalence classes.

10.2.2 Test case sources

There are two basic sources for test cases:

- **Random samples of real life cases.** Examples:
  - A sample of urban households (to test a new municipal tax information system)
  - A sample of shipping bills (to test new billing software)
  - A sample of control records (to test new software for control of manufacturing plant production)
  - A recorded sample of events that will be "run" as a test case (to test online applications for an Internet site, and for real-time applications).
- **Synthetic test cases** (also called "simulated test cases") prepared by test designers. This type of test case does not refer to an existing customer, shipment or product but to combinations of the system's operating

conditions and parameters (defined by a set of input data). These combinations are designed to cover all known software operating situations or at least all situations that are expected to be in frequent use or that belong to a high error probability class. For the equivalence class method, see Section 9.5.1.

The implications of using each test case source are summarized and compared in Table 10.3.

In most cases, the test case file preferred should combine sample cases with synthetic cases so as to overcome the disadvantages of a single source of test cases and to increase the efficiency of the testing process. In the case of combined test case files, test plans are often carried out in two stages: in the first stage, synthetic test cases are used. After correction of the detected errors, a random sample of test cases is used in the second stage.

Table 10.3: Comparison of test data sources

Implication	Type of test case source	
	Random sample of cases	Synthetic test cases
Effort required to prepare a test case file	Low effort, especially where expected results are available and need not be calculated	High effort; the parameters of each test case must be determined and expected results calculated
Required size of test case file	Relatively high as most cases refer to simple situations that repeat themselves frequently. In order to obtain a sufficient number of non-standard situations, a relatively large test case file needs to be compiled	Relatively small as it may be possible to avoid repetitions of any given combination of parameters
Efforts required to perform the software tests	High efforts (low efficiency) as tests must be carried out for large test case files. The low efficiency stems from the repetitiveness of case conditions, especially for the simple situations typical to most real-life case files	Low efforts (high efficiency) due to the relatively small test case file compiled so as to avoid repetitions
Effectiveness – probability of error detection	▪ Relatively low – unless the test case files are very large – due to the low percentage of uncommon combinations of parameters ▪ No coverage of erroneous situations ▪ Some ability to identify unexpected errors for unlisted situations	▪ Relatively high due to good coverage by design ▪ Good coverage of erroneous situations by test case file design ▪ Little possibility of identifying unexpected errors as all test cases are designed according to predefined parameters

Substantial improvement in the efficiency of random sampling of test cases is achieved by using a stratified sampling procedure rather than standard random sampling of the entire population. Stratified sampling allows us to break down the random sample into sub-populations of test cases, thereby reducing the proportion of the majority "regular" population tested while increasing the sampling proportion of small populations and high potential error populations. This method application minimizes the number of repetitions at the same time that it improves coverage of less frequent and rare conditions.

As an example, Garden City's population of about 100 000 households is divided between the city itself (70%), suburb Orange (20%), suburb Lemon (7%) and suburb Apple (3%). The suburbs and the city differ substantially in the characteristics of their housing and socio-economic status. Some 5% of the households, the great majority of them city dwellers, enjoy tax reductions entailing 40 different types of discounts (disabled, very large families, low-income single-parent families with more than six children, etc.). Originally, the standard 0.5% sample had been planned. It was later replaced by the following stratified random sample:

	Households (no.)	Standard sampling (no.)	Stratified sampling (no.)
Regular households	65 000	325	100
Households enjoying discounts	5 000	25	250
Suburb A	20 000	100	50
Suburb B	7 000	35	50
Suburb C	3 000	15	50
Total	100 000	500	500

Test cases for reused software.
It is quite common for reused software to include many applications not required for the current software system in addition to the required applications. In situations of this kind, planners should consider which reused software modules should be tested. Other modules of the reused software will not be tested.

10.3 Automated testing

Automated testing represents an additional step in the integration of computerized tools into the process of software development. These tools have joined computer aided software engineering (CASE) tools in performing a growing share of software analysis and design tasks.

Several factors have motivated the development of automated testing tools: anticipated cost savings, shortened test duration, heightened thoroughness of the tests performed, improvement of test accuracy, improvement of result reporting as well as statistical processing and subsequent reporting. The possibility of efficiently performing various classes of tests previously not feasible or impossible to perform manually, such as load tests, has likewise propelled the drive for investment in automating testing development.

Valuable sources for additional material on automated testing can be found in books such as Buwalda *et al.* (2002), Fewster and Graham (1999) and Dustin *et al.* (1999), as well as in other publications.

This section covers:

- The process of automated testing
- The types of automated tests
- The advantages and disadvantages of automated tests.

10.3.1 The process of automated testing

Typically, automated software testing requires test planning, test design, test case preparation, test performance, test log and report preparation, re-testing after correction of detected errors (regression tests), and final test log and report preparation including comparison reports. The last two activities may be repeated several times.

At this stage of its development, the planning, design and test case preparation of automated testing require substantial investment of professional manpower. It is the computerized test performance and the reporting that yield the main economic, quality and timetable advantages of the process. The availability of the required professional manpower and the extent they are to be used represent the main factors to be considered before initiating automation of software tests.

To better understand the issues, a comparison of automated and manual testing is presented in Table 10.4.

10.3.2 Types of automated tests

Numerous types of automated tests are available; some have become more or less routine. The more established automated tests are mainly those employed for testing tasks that have a high number of regression tests and those performing test classes not feasible for manual testing such as load testing. The main types of automated tests currently used are listed in Frame 10.5.

Code auditing

This test performs automated qualification testing. The computerized code auditor checks the compliance of code to specified standards and procedures of coding. The auditor's report includes a list of the deviations from the standards and a statistical summary of the findings.

Table 10.4: A comparison of automated and manual testing by phase

Testing process phases	Automated testing		Manual testing	
	Automated/ manual performance	Comments	Automated/ manual performance	Comments
Test planning	M	Preparing test plan	M	Preparing test plan
Test design	M	Preparing test database	M	Preparing testing procedure
Preparing test cases	M	Preparing test cases and their recording into test case database	M	Preparing test cases
Performance of the tests	A	Computerized running the tests	M	Performing tests with testers
Preparing test log and test reports	A	Computerized output	M	Prepared by testers
Regression tests	A	Computerized running the tests	M	Performing tests by testers
Preparing test log and test reports including comparative reports	A	Computerized output	M	Prepared by testers

---

Frame 10.5	**The main types of automated tests**

- Code auditing
- Coverage monitoring
- Functional tests
- Load tests
- Test management

A code auditor can verify the following:

- Does the code fulfill code structure instructions and procedures?
  - Module size. Some code auditors calculate for the tested code complexity metrics, such as McCabe's cyclomatic complexity metrics
  - Levels of loop nesting
  - Levels of subroutine nesting
  - Prohibited constructs, such as GOTO.

■ Does the coding style follow the coding style procedures?
   – Naming conventions for variables, files, etc.
   – Unreachable code lines of program or entire subroutines.
■ Do the internal program documentation and help support sections follow the coding style procedures?
■ Format and size of comments:
   – Location of comments in the file
   – Help index and presentation style.

Coverage monitoring

Coverage monitors produce reports about the line coverage achieved when implementing a given test case file. The monitor's output includes the percentage of lines covered by the test cases as well as listings of uncovered lines. These features make coverage monitoring a vital tool for white-box tests.

Functional tests

Automated functional tests often replace manual black-box correctness tests. Prior to performance of these tests, the test cases are recorded into the test case database. The tests are then carried out by executing the test cases through the test program. The test results documentation includes listings of the errors identified in addition to a variety of summaries and statistics as demanded by the testers' specifications.

After the corrections have been completed, re-testing the whole program or parts of it ("regression tests") is commonly required. Automated regression tests performed for the whole program verify that the error corrections have been performed satisfactorily and that the corrections have not unintentionally introduced new errors in other parts of the program. The regression tests themselves are performed with the existing test case database; hence, these tests can be executed with minimal effort or professional resources. An additional automated testing tool that supports functional tests, the output comparator, is of great help in the regression test stage. The automated comparison of outputs of successive tests, together with the results of the functional testing tools, enables testers to prepare an improved analysis of the regression test results and to help developers to discover the causes of the errors detected in those tests. It is quite common for a program to require three or four regression tests before its quality level is considered satisfactory.

Load tests

The history of software system development contains many sad chapters of systems that succeeded in correctness tests but severely failed – and caused enormous damage – once they were required to operate under standard full load. The damage in many cases was extremely high because the failure occurred "unexpectedly", when the systems were supposed to start providing their regular software services. The most spectacular failures tend to take place in very large information systems that serve large numbers of users at any one time or in real-time firmware systems that handle a high volume of simultaneous events.

For load tests to be performed, the maximal load environment must first be created. If executed manually, the tests must be conducted when the system is under maximal user load, a condition that is impractical in most cases and impossible in others. Therefore the only way to carry out load tests for medium-sized and large systems is by means of computerized simulations that can be programmed to closely approach real load conditions.

The load tests themselves are based on scenarios of the maximal load situations – composed of events or transactions and their frequencies – that the software system is expected to confront and deal with. This allows automated load testing (stress tests) to be combined with availability and efficiency tests, which likewise require maximal load environment for their execution.

At this point, "virtual users and virtual events" come into play. For operating scenarios devised for load testing, virtual users and virtual events are generated and operated in a hardware and communication environment defined by the system planner. A virtual user or event emulates the behavior of a human user or a real event. Its behavior is "constructed" by applying real outputs captured from real user applications, that are then used as inputs for the simulation. The simulation's required loads and frequencies are also created by computerization. The simulation then produces outputs similar to those captured from real-life users at the frequencies and with the user mix defined by the scenario. These outputs serve as inputs for the tested software. The tests are carried out with the final approved version of software and with the planned hardware and communication configuration.

The computerized monitoring of the load tests produces software system performance measurements in terms of reaction time, processing time, and other desired parameters. These are compared with the specified maximal load performance requirements in order to evaluate how well the software system will perform when in daily use. Usually, a series of load tests is conducted, with the load gradually increased to the specified maximal load and beyond. This step enables a more thorough study of system performance under full load. The computer-produced tables and graphs, based on the performance measurement information, allow the tester to decide what changes are to be introduced into each simulation for each test iteration. For example, the tester may wish to:

- Change the hardware, including the communication system, to allow the software system to fulfill its performance requirements at each load level.
- Change the scenario in order to reveal the load contributed by each user or event.
- Test an entirely different scenario.
- Test new combinations of hardware and scenario components.

The tester will continue his iterations till he finds the appropriate hardware configuration.

Example

The "Tick Ticket" is a new Internet site planned to meet the following requirements:

- The site should be able to handle up to a maximum of 3000 hits per hour.
- Average reaction time required for the maximal load of 3000 hits per hour is 10 seconds or less.
- Average reaction time required for the regular load of 1200 hits per hour is 3 seconds or less.

The plan: The load tests were planned for the following series of hit frequencies (hits per hour): 300, 600, 900, 1200, 1500, 1800, 2100, 2400, 2700, 3000, 3300 and 3600. An initial hardware configuration was defined, to be adapted according to the load test results.

Implementation: Three series of load tests were run before the adequate hardware and communication software configuration was determined. After the first and second series of load tests, the hardware configuration was changed to increase the system's capacity so as to achieve the required reaction times. The second configuration fulfilled the reaction time requirements for the average load but not for the maximal load. Therefore, capacity was further increased. In its final configuration, the software system could satisfactorily handle loads 20% higher than the originally specified maximal load. See Table 10.5 for the average reaction times measured at each round of load testing.

Table 10.5: Tick ticket load tests – measured reaction times

Hit frequency (hits per hour)	Average reaction time (seconds) for load tests		
	Series I (hardware configuration I)	Series II (hardware configuration II	Series III (hardware configuration III)
300	2.2	1.8	1.5
600	2.5	1.9	1.5
900	3.0	2.0	1.5
1200	3.8	2.3	1.6
1500	5.0	2.8	1.8
1800	7.0	3.5	2.2
2100	10.0	4.5	2.8
2400	15.0	6.5	3.7
2700	22.0	10.5	4.8
3000	32.0	16.0	6.3
3300	55.0	25.0	7.8
3600	95.0	38.5	9.5

Testing involves many participants occupied in actually carrying out the tests and correcting the detected errors. In addition, testing typically monitors performance of every item on long lists of test case files. This workload makes timetable follow-up important to management. Computerized test management supports these and other testing management goals. In general, computerized test management tools are planned to provide testers with reports, lists and other types of information at levels of quality and availability that are higher than those provided by manual test management systems.

Automated test management software packages provide features applicable for manual as well as automated testing and for automated tests only. The inputs the testers key in, together with the software package's capabilities, determine the application's scope. Especially important here is the package's interoperability with respect to the automated testing tools.

Frame 10.6 provides a concise summary of the features offered by automated test management software packages.

Frame 10.6	Automated test management packages – main features

Type of feature	Automated/manual testing
A. Test plans, test results and correction follow-up	
Preparation of lists, tables and visual presentations of test plans	A, M
List of test case	A, M
Listing of detected errors	A, M
Listing of correction schedule (performer, date of completion, etc.)	A, M
Listing of uncompleted corrections for follow-up	A, M
Error tracking: detection, correction and regression tests	A, M
Summary reports of testing and error correction follow-up	A, M
B. Test execution	
Execution of automated software tests	A
Automated listing of automated software test results	A
Automated listing of detected errors	A
C. Maintenance follow-up	
Correction of errors reported by users	A, M
Summary reports for maintenance correction services according to customer, software system applications, etc.	A, M

The availability of automated testing tools

Most of the automated testing tools are specialized, and planned for use in specific areas of programming and system applications: client/server systems, C/C++, UNIX applications, a specific software house's ERP (Enterprise Resource Planning) applications, to cite just a few. The variety of tools currently offered covers most prevailing programming areas and applications, and they are readily available from the software development companies specializing in automated testing tools.

10.3.3 Advantages and disadvantages of automated tests

The decision to employ automated testing tools is difficult to make because of the substantial investments involved in purchasing the tools and in adequately training a team for their effective and efficient implementation.

The first part of this section presents a comprehensive qualitative comparison of automated testing and manual testing, conducted by listing the advantages and disadvantages of automated testing. A quantitative comparison, especially an economic analysis based on empirical data, is sorely needed to support the qualitative comparison. The second part of the section deals with some early quantitative findings that point to the economic advantages of using automated testing tools.

The main advantages of automated tests are:

(1) **Accuracy and completeness of performance.** Computerized testing guarantees – to the maximum degree possible – that all tests and test cases are carried out completely and accurately. Manual testing suffers from periods of tester weariness or low concentration, traits that induce inaccurate keying-in of the test case, omissions, and so forth.

(2) **Accuracy of results log and summary reports.** Automated tests are programmed for accuracy of reporting of errors detected. In contrast, the testers who perform manual tests occasionally do not recognize errors and may overlook others in their logs and summaries.

(3) **Comprehensiveness of information.** Naturally, once the test data – including test results – are stored in a database, queries and reports about the test and its results are incomparably more available than the same items would be after performance of manual tests. Besides supporting testing and correction follow up, the improved error information enhances the input needed for preventive and corrective actions (see Chapter 16).

(4) **Few manpower resources required to perform tests.** Manual performance of testing, in comparison, is a major consumer of manpower resources.

(5) **Shorter duration of testing.** The duration of computerized testing is usually far shorter than that of manual testing. In addition, automated tests can be carried out, uninterrupted, 24 hours a day, seven days a week, in

contrast to manual testing, which might require one testing team to work a three-shift day or, alternatively, to employ three testing teams, both being rather impractical in most cases.

(6) **Performance of complete regression tests.** Because of the shortage of time and manpower resources, manual regression tests tend to be conducted on only a relatively small portion of the software package. Hence, the advantages of automated testing: the minimal time and manpower resources required make it possible to rerun tests based on previous results. This option *substantially* reduces the risk of not detecting any errors introduced during the previous round of corrections.

(7) **Performance of test classes beyond the scope of manual testing.** Computerization enables the tester to perform, for example, load tests, availability tests and efficiency tests for medium- and large-scale systems. These tests are almost impossible to perform manually on systems of greater than small size.

The main disadvantages of automated testing are:

(1) **High investments required in package purchasing and training.** An organization that decides to implement automated testing must invest in software packages and additional training to qualify its staff to perform those tests. Despite the claims of the software package developers, although the amount of training varies by software package, it is still long and thus expensive.

(2) **High package development investment costs.** In cases where available automated testing packages do not fully suit the system's requirements, custom-made packages must be developed.

(3) **High manpower requirements for test preparation.** The human resources required for preparing an automated test procedure are usually substantially higher than those required for preparing a manual procedure for the same software package.

(4) **Considerable testing areas left uncovered.** At present, automated software testing packages do not cover the entire variety of development tools and types of applications either available manually or still needed. This forces testers to mix manual and automated testing in their test plans.

The advantages and disadvantages of automated software testing are presented in Frame 10.7.

Quantitative comparison – empirical findings
Dustin *et al.* (1999) report the findings of a study carried out during 1997–1998, initiated by the European Systems and Software Institute (ESSI). Graphical user interface (GUI) software was chosen to be tested. The study comprised 10 comparative experiments, with parallel manual testing and

Frame 10.7 Automated software testing: advantages and disadvantages

Advantages

1. Accuracy and completeness of performance

2. Accuracy of results log and summary reports

3. Comprehensive information

4. Few manpower resources for test execution

5. Shorter testing periods

6. Performance of complete regression tests

7. Performance of test classes beyond the scope of manual testing

Disadvantages

1. High investments required in package purchasing and training

2. High package development investment costs

3. High manpower resources for test preparation

4. Considerable testing areas left uncovered

automated testing performed in each experiment. A summary of the results is presented in Table 10.6.

The study results conform with qualitative evaluations, meaning that the average preparation time for automated testing is substantially more than that for manual testing of a similar software system, with 65% more resources consumed, on average, in preparation for the automated testing. Also as anticipated, the tester's run execution time for automated testing is much less than that for manual testing, or 18.7 times more, on average, than the time testers need to invest in automated test runs. Based on these figures, the study's authors estimated N – the minimum number of test runs (the first test run and subsequent regression runs) that economically justify application of automated testing (the "break-even point"). Assuming that the resources invested in regression tests, manual as well as automated, are

Table 10.6: Automated versus manual testing – GUI testing experiment results

| | Preparation time | | | Tester's run execution time | | |
| | | Time range | | | Time range | |
	Average (hours)	Min. (hours)	Max. (hours)	Average (hours)	Min. (hours)	Max. (hours)
Automated testing	19.2	10.6	56.0	0.21	0.1	1.0
Manual testing	11.6	10.0	20.0	3.93	0.5	24.0

Source: Adapted from Dustin *et al.* (1999)

similar to those invested in the first test run, N can be derived according to the following equation:

$$19.2 + 0.21 \times N = 11.6 + 3.93 \times N$$
$$N = 2.04$$

Based on this model, if the testing process requires more than one regression test run, automated testing is to be preferred.

Some reservations, including those mentioned by Dustin *et al.* (1999), are evident:

- The break-even point model ignores or considers negligible the heavy investments required for acquiring automated testing capabilities and its regular upgrading.

- Manual regression test runs, especially second, third and later regression runs, are usually partial, therefore requiring only a portion of the resources consumed during the first test run.

- Automated test runs are carried out without any human interaction during the run.

- No modifications (preparation effort) are required in the automated test files for performing regression tests.

It should be emphasized that even if considering the above reservations would change N to be $N = 4$ or more, the important qualitative advantages of automated testing would lead us to prefer it to manual testing in many cases.

Much additional research is needed to construct a comprehensive integrated model for the comparison, quantitative and qualitative, of the two testing approaches. The research efforts should be directed to collecting sufficient empirical data and to developing models capable of quantifying a good portion of the qualitative advantages of automated testing.

10.4 Alpha and beta site testing programs

Alpha site and beta site tests are employed to obtain comments about quality from the package's potential users. They are additional commonly used tools to identify software design and code errors in software packages in commercial over-the-counter sale (COTS). In a way, alpha and beta site tests replace the customer's acceptance test, a test that is impractical under the conditions of commercial software package development. However, an analysis of the characteristics of these tests leads one to conclude that in no case should they replace the formal software tests performed by the developer.

Alpha site tests

"Alpha site tests" are tests of a new software package that are performed at the developer's site. The customer, by applying the new software to the specific requirements of his organization, tends to examine the package from angles not expected by the testing team. The errors identified by alpha site tests are expected to include the errors that only use by a real user can reveal, and thus should be reported to the developer.

Beta site tests

Beta site tests are much more commonly applied than are alpha site tests. The beta site test process can be described as follows. Once an advanced version of the software package is available, the developer offers it free of charge to one or more potential users. The users install the package in their sites (usually called the "beta sites"), with the understanding that they will inform the developer of all the errors revealed during trials or regular usage. Participants in beta site testing are often users of previously released packages, sophisticated software professionals and the like. Because beta site tests are considered to be a valuable tool, some developers involve hundreds or even thousands of participants in the process.

The main advantages of beta site tests are:

■ **Identification of unexpected errors.** Users usually examine software in an entirely different way and, of course, apply it in ways far from those anticipated in the developer's scenarios. Consequently, they reveal errors of a type that professional testers rarely identify.

■ **A wider population in search of errors.** The wide range of participants involved in beta site testing contributes a scope of software usage experience and potential for revealing hidden errors that go beyond those available at the developer's testing site.

■ **Low costs.** As the participants are not paid for their participation or for error information they report, the only costs encountered are the price of the package and its delivery free of charge to the customer. In most cases these costs, including the loss of sales, are relatively low.

The main disadvantages of beta site tests are:

■ **A lack of systematic testing.** As participants in beta site tests are in no way obligated to prepare orderly reports, they tend to report scattered experience and leave untouched applications as well as segments of those applications.

■ **Low quality error reports.** Participants are not professional testers; hence, their error reports are often faulty (some report no errors at all), and it is frequently impossible to reconstruct the error conditions they report.

■ **Difficult to reproduce the test environment.** Beta site testing is usually performed in an uncontrolled testing environment, a fact that creates difficulties when attempting to identify the causes of the reported errors.

■ **Much effort is required to examine reports.** A relatively high investment of time and human resources is needed when examining reports due to the frequent repetitions and low quality of reporting.

Alpha site testing enjoys the same advantages and displays the same disadvantages as beta site testing. Alpha site tests are usually more difficult to organize than beta site tests, but tend to be fruitful.

Implementation tip

Testers and developers should be especially cautious when applying beta site testing. Beta site testing of pre-matured software may detect many software errors but can result in highly negative publicity among potential customers. In some cases, these negative impressions can reach the professional journals and cause substantial market damage. We therefore recommend that alpha site testing be initiated first, and that beta site testing be delayed until the alpha site tests have been completed and their results analyzed.

Summary

(1) Describe the process of planning and designing tests.

The planning activities include:
- Determining the test methodology
- Planning unit and integration tests
- Planning the system test
- Designing the tests.

Determining the test methodology deals mainly with decisions about the required software quality standard and the software strategy: big bang or incremental testing (bottom-up or top-down), and the extent of automated testing.

Planning unit and integration tests. Prior to planning the tests, preferences must be established as to which unit and integration test will be carried out, based on the system's characteristics.

Planning the system test. Planners focus on the following main issues:
- What to test?
- Which types of sources are to provide the test cases?
- Who performs the tests?
- Where will the tests be performed?
- When to terminate the tests?

Designing the tests. The products of the test design stage are:
- Detailed design and procedure for each test,
- Test case database/file.

(2) Discuss the sources for test cases and their advantages and disadvantages.

There are basically two types of test case sources:
- Random samples of real-life cases
- Synthetic test cases ("simulated test cases") prepared by the test designers.

Comparison of the advantages and disadvantages of each source yields:

■ The effort required to prepare a test case file is low for random samples, high for synthetic cases.

■ The required size of test case is relatively high for random samples, relatively low for synthetic cases. Efforts required to perform the software tests are relatively high for relatively large random samples, relatively low for the relatively small synthetic cases.

■ Effectiveness (the probability of revealing errors) is relatively low for random samples unless the files are very large and relatively high for synthetic cases due to the good coverage of regular and erroneous situations as designed by the test designers. Moreover, in random sampling, although no coverage is provided for invalid situations, the probability of identifying unexpected errors for valid situations exists, a quality that, by definition, is excluded from the coverage built into the synthetic cases.

■ The performance of the random sample test cases can be substantially improved by employing stratified sampling. In most cases, the preferred test case file will combine random sample test cases with synthetic cases so as to overcome the disadvantages of a single source.

(3) List the main types of automated software tests.

The main types are:

■ **Code auditors.** The code auditor checks the compliance of code to specified standards and procedures of coding. This is an automated type of qualification testing. The auditor's report includes a list of the deviations from the standards and a statistical summary of the findings.

■ **Coverage monitors** produce reports about the line coverage achieved by implementing a given test case file.

■ **Functional tests.** Automated functional tests replace manual black-box correctness tests. The first test runs as well as the regression test runs, applied with the same test files and the same test cases, are performed by a computer program that replaces the "classic" tester.

■ **Load tests.** The load tests are based on simulated scenarios of maximal load situations the software system will confront. An automated testing system enables measurement of the expected performance of the software system under various load levels .

■ **Test management.** The main objectives of these automated tools are to provide comprehensive follow-up and reporting of the testing and correction of detected errors.

(4) Discuss the advantages and disadvantages of automated computerized testing compared to manual testing.

The main advantages of automated tests are:

■ Accuracy and completeness of performance

■ Accuracy of results log and summary reports

■ Ability to obtain much more comprehensive information

■ Performance requires few manpower resources
■ Shorter testing periods
■ Performance of complete regression tests
■ Performance of test classes beyond the reach of manual testing.

The main disadvantages of automated tests are:
■ High investments required in package purchasing and training
■ High manpower tester resources for preparing the tests
■ Considerable testing areas not covered by automated testing.

(5) **Explain the inplementation of alpha and beta site test and discuss their advantages and disadvantages.**

Alpha site testing is a method by which customers try out the new software package at the developer's site. Beta site testing is a method by which a selected group of users or customers receive an advanced version of the software to be installed in their sites, and report the errors they find in the process of their experiments with the program and the program's regular use.

The main advantages of beta site testing are:
■ Identification of unexpected errors
■ Wide scope of coverage in search for errors
■ Low costs.

The main disadvantages of beta site tests are:
■ Lack of systematic testing
■ Error reports of low quality
■ Much human effort expended to examine participants' reports.

Selected bibliography

1. Buwalda, H., Jenssen, D. and Pinkster, I. (2002) *Integrated Test Design and Automation Using the TestFrame Method*, Addison-Wesley-Longman, Reading, MA.
2. Dustin, E., Rashka, J. and Paul, J. (1999) *Automated Software Testing–Introduction, Management and Performance*, Addison-Wesley-Longman, Reading, MA.
3. Fewster, M. and Graham, D. (1999) *Software Test Automation-Effective Use of Test Execution Tools*, ACM Press, New York.
4. IEEE (1996) "IEEE/EIA Std 12207.0-1996 – IEEE/EIA Standard – Industry Implementation of International Standard ISO/IEC 12207:1995", in *IEEE Software Engineering Standards Collection*, The Institute of Electrical and Electronics Engineers, New York, NY, USA.
5. IEEE (1997a) "IEEE/EIA Std 12207.1-1997 – IEEE/EIA Guide – Industry Implementation of International Standard ISO/IEC 12207:1995, Software Life Cycle Processes – Life Cycle Data", in *IEEE Software Engineering Standards Collection*, The Institute of Electrical and Electronics Engineers, New York.
6. IEEE (1997b) "IEEE/EIA Std 12207.1-1997 – IEEE/EIA Guide – Industry Implementation of International Standard ISO/IEC 12207:1995, Software Life

Cycle Processes – Implementation Considerations", in *IEEE Software Engineering Standards Collection*, The Institute of Electrical and Electronics Engineers, New York.

7. IEEE (1998a) "IEEE Std 829-1998 – IEEE Standard for Software Test Documentation", in *IEEE Software Engineering Standards Collection*, The Institute of Electrical and Electronics Engineers, New York.

8. IEEE (1998b) "IEEE Std 1012-1998 – IEEE Standard for Software Verification and Validation", in *IEEE Software Engineering Standards Collection*, The Institute of Electrical and Electronics Engineers, New York.

9. ISO/IEC (2001) "ISO 9000-3:2001 Software and System Engineering – Guidelines for the Application of ISO 9001:2000 to Software, Final draft", International Organization for Standardization (ISO), Geneva, unpublished draft, December 2001.

10. Kaner, C., Falk, J. and Nguyen, H. Q. (1999) *Testing Computer Software*, 2nd edn, John Wiley & Sons, New York.

11. Kit, E. (1995) Software *Testing in the Real World – Improving the Process*, Addison-Wesley, Wokingham, UK.

12. Perry W. (1995) *Effective Methods for Software Testing*, John Wiley & Sons, New York, N.Y.

13. Perry, W. E. and Rice, R. W. (1997) *Surviving the Top Ten Challenges of Software Testing – a People-Oriented Approach*, Dorset House Publishing, New York, N.Y.

14. Pressman, R. S. (2000) *Software Engineering – A Practitioner's Approach*, European adaptation by D. Ince, 5th edn, McGraw-Hill International, London.

15. Sommerville I. (2001) *Software Engineering*, 6th edn, Addison-Wesley, Harlow, Essex, UK

Review questions

10.1 "Alpha phone" is a software package that includes the following among its features:

- It manages a household phone address book.
- It produces printouts of the phone book according to a variety of classifications.
- It analyzes the monthly traffic of incoming and outgoing phone calls according to the classifications mentioned above.

You are called to perform a documentation test of the very elegant "alpha phone" users' manual. List at least five types of possible documentation errors in the manual.

10.2 "MPT star" is a program for calculating the annual municipal property taxes, based on the neighborhood, the type of property (house, store, apartment, etc.), the size of the property, the discounts to which the owner is entitled (pensioners, low-income large family, single-parent family, etc.).

Suggest a framework for stratified sampling test cases from the citizens' file. List your assumptions about the population's distribution.

10.3 "In most cases, the test case file preferred should combine sample cases with synthetic cases so as to overcome the disadvantages of a single source of test cases and to increase the efficiency of the testing process." Taken from Section 10.2.2.

(1) Elaborate on how applying a mixed-source methodology overcomes the disadvantages of a single-source methodology.
(2) Elaborate on how applying a mixed-source methodology enhances testing efficiency. Provide a hypothetical example.

10.4 Software testing experts claim that applying a stratified sample of real-life test cases is more effective for identifying errors and more efficient than regular random sampling.

(1) If you agree, list your arguments.
(2) If you disagree, list your contradictory arguments.

10.5 Reviewing the advantages and disadvantages of automated software testing:

(1) Explain the main advantages and disadvantages of automated tests in your own words.
(2) Referring to your answer to (1), suggest what project characteristics are most suitable for automated testing. List your assumptions.
(3) Referring to your answer to (1) suggest what project characteristics are most unsuitable for automated testing. List your assumptions.

10.6 Mr Aleppo, the head of the software development department, claims that beta site tests should always be carried out as early as possible in the development process as there are no disadvantages in this method.

(1) Are beta site tests really a "disadvantage free" method? If not, what are their main disadvantages and risks?
(2) Recommend guidelines that will minimize the risks and disadvantages in applying beta site tests as listed in (1).

Topics for discussion

10.1 RSM–Real Time Software Magicians Ltd signed a contract with defense authorities for development of "Light in the Darkness", an advanced night vision system for infantry use. The system is based on a comprehensive pattern recognition model, whose development was completed last year at a prestigious university. It is expected to identify the presence of a human, standing, sitting or lying, from a distance of 100 meters. The system to be used by the soldier ("soldier's set") contains a unit for geographic identification based on the satellite GPS technology, and includes a ciphered communication system linking the soldier to headquarters.

Headquarters' central unit for processing the data received from the night vision system (from the front line) is not part of the "Light in the Darkness" project.

The "Light in the Darkness" system is constructed of four subsystems (integrations) and 13 units (modules) as shown in Table 10.7.

Table 10.7: Structure of "Light in the Darkness" system

Subsystems (integrations)	Units (modules)
1. Subsystem for night recognition of humans	1.1 Unit that identifies humans according to a mathematical pattern recognition model 1.2 Unit for display of the identified humans on the screen of the "soldier's set" 1.3 Unit for calculating and displaying on the screen the distance to the identified humans 1.4 Unit for creating a display on the soldier's screen of the combined identification data from all the unit's soldiers 1.5 Unit for warning the soldier according to the combined identification data
2. Subsystem for ciphered communication	2.1 Unit for communicating the geographic location of the military unit 2.2 Unit for communicating the identification of the observed human figures 2.3 Unit for performing the ciphered communication according to military communication standards
3. Subsystem for documentation of the soldiers sets' usage	3.1 Unit for recording set usage time by the soldier 3.2 Unit for daily reporting of the soldier's set usage according to the soldier's set identification number 3.3 Unit for producing notices about soldier's sets that exceed 1000 hours of usage (for preventative maintenance)
4. Subsystem for recording of communication times of the military units	4.1 Unit for recording communication times from the units 4.2 Unit for processing daily reports of when communications were received

Due to timetable and budget considerations, it was decided to carry out only five unit tests and only two integration tests on the new system.

(1) Provide support for the RSM–Real Time Software Magicians testing team by planning a comprehensive method to determine the priorities of the different modules to be included in the unit testing plan. The priorities will be based on two criteria:

■ Severity level: the severity of the damages anticipated if this module fails during real application of the system

■ Risk level: the probability that the module will fail if it is not tested and corrected accordingly.

(2) Apply the method suggested in (1) to rank the priorities of the 13 modules of "Light in the Darkness" described above. List your assumptions.

(3) Adapt the same method to determine the priorities of the integrations to be tested as listed in the description of the example.

(4) Considering that the modules have already been included in the unit test plan, does this fact change the method for determining the priorities you

reached with respect to integrations in (3)? Applying the updated method to the integrations of "Light in the Darkness", is there any change in the resulting priorities?

10.2 H.C. – Hardware Center Ltd – has developed a new billing software system to bill regular customers and H.C. credit cardholders, who include private as well as corporate customers. Regular customers are billed as they complete their purchase; they are not entitled to discounts. All H.C. cardholders are entitled to a 4%–10% discount, depending on the purchase sum and the items, and are billed monthly. Corporate customers are entitled to an additional 1%–5% discount, depending on their total purchases during the previous year.

The average monthly total number of bills is 30 000; 92% of the bills are regular customer purchase bills, 6% are monthly bills for private H.C. cardholder, and the rest are monthly bills for corporate H.C. cardholder. The testing unit has decided to use a regular random sample of 1000 bills for its test of the new billing software. Mr Evans, the head of the SQA group, claims that a stratified random sample of 400 bills would be more effective for revealing the software errors and much cheaper to perform.

(1) Do you agree with Mr Evans' claim? List your arguments.
(2) If you agree with Mr Evans, describe the stratified sampling you would suggest and list your arguments for this choice.
(3) List the assumptions that guided you in making your decisions.

10.3 Imagine the results of software system failure.

(1) What are the main issues causing higher severity of failure?
(2) Referring to your answer to (1), give three examples of software development projects that display the lowest severity of failure.

10.4 Chapter 2 of the STD (software test description) is dedicated to the test environment (see Frame 10.3).

(1) Discuss the alternative settings the planner can use, and explain the importance of professional planning of the test environment.
(2) Suggest the risks incurred by inappropriate planning of the test environment.

10.5 One would expect the STR (software test report) to be limited to a list of test results and some statistical summaries of the results. However, Chapters 1 and 2 of the report (see template in Frame 10.4) are divided into not less than nine subsections devoted to the comprehensive description of the test, its site, the participants, and the test environment.

(1) Refer to the nine sections and explain the importance of the information to be reported in each.
(2) Some of these sections provide information that could jeopardize the applicability of the test results. List the subjects and the circumstances in which doubt could be raised.

chapter 11

Assuring the quality of software maintenance components

The major part of the software life cycle is the operation period, usually lasting for 5 to 10 years, although cases of software being operational for 15 years and even more are not rare. What makes one software package capable of reaching "old age" with satisfied users, while another package, serving almost the same population, "perishes young"? The main factor responsible for long and successful service is the quality of maintenance. Just how important software maintenance is can be surmised by the attention given the subject in the ISO 9000-3 Standard (see ISO (1997), Sec. 4.19 and ISO/IEC (2001), Sec. 7.5), IEEE (1998) and Oskarsson and Glass (1996).

This chapter will therefore pursue the following quality assurance issues as they relate to software maintenance:

- The foundations for high quality maintenance
- Pre-maintenance software quality components
- SQA tools for corrective maintenance
- SQA tools for functionality improvement maintenance
- Infrastructure SQA tools for software maintenance
- Managerial control SQA tools for software maintenance.

After completing this chapter, you will be able to:

- List software maintenance components and explain their distinction.
- Explain the foundations of high quality maintenance.
- Describe and explain pre-maintenance software quality components.
- List the infrastructure tools that support maintenance quality assurance.
- List the managerial tools for controlling software maintenance quality and explain their importance.

11.1 Introduction

The following three components of maintenance service are all essential for success:

- **Corrective maintenance** – user support services and software corrections.
- **Adaptive maintenance** – adapts the software package to differences in new customer requirements, changing environmental conditions and the like.
- **Functionality improvement maintenance** – combines (1) **perfective maintenance** of new functions added to the software so as to enhance performance, with (2) **preventive maintenance** activities that improve reliability and system infrastructure for easier and more efficient future maintainability.

The inclusion of user support services ("user support centers") in corrective maintenance may need some clarification. User support services is the address for solution of all user difficulties arising when using the software system; software correction services are usually integrated in this service. The user's difficulties may have been caused by:

- Code failure (usually termed "software failure").
- Documentation failure in the user's manual, help screens or other form of documentation prepared for the user. In this case, the support service can provide the user with correct instructions (although no correction of the software documentation itself is performed).
- Incomplete, vague or imprecise documentation.
- User's insufficient knowledge of the software system or his or her failure to use the documentation supplied. In these situations no software system failure is encountered.

The first three of the above causes are considered software system failures. In addition, integration of user support services and software correction services is generally accomplished in close cooperation, with much sharing of information. The other components of maintenance services – functionality improvement and adaptive maintenance – tend not to be initiated by the user support services. In most cases, the functionality improvement and adaptive tasks display the characteristics of a small or large project, depending on the customer's needs. This being the case, these tasks can be performed by a software development unit as well. Considering the above, it is reasonable to include user support services among the corrective maintenance activities.

Generally, one may say that while corrective maintenance ensures that current users can operate the system as specified, adaptive maintenance enables expansion of the user population, while functionality improvement maintenance extends the package's service period.

As mentioned in previous chapters, the combination of the three components of software maintenance consumes more than 60% of total design and programming resources invested in a software system throughout its life cycle (Pressman, 2000). Others estimate that the share of maintenance resources ranges from over 50% (Lientz and Swanson, 1980) to about 65–75% (McKee, 1984) of total project development resources.

The distribution of maintenance resources to the various maintenance services is estimated as follows:

Maintenance service	Lientz and Swanson (1980)	Oskarsson and Glass (1996)
Corrective maintenance	22%	17%
Adaptive maintenance	24%	23%
Functionality improvement maintenance	54%	60%

Surveys of this issue are rare; however, the figures reported by Nosek and Palvia (1990) do not significantly diverge from the estimates shown here. It is believed that the 1980 figures, with minimal changes, continue to represent actual distribution.

The objectives of software maintenance QA activities are presented in Frame 11.1 (repeated from Frame 2.7).

As the nature of the different types of software maintenance components varies substantially, so do the required quality assurance tools. In general, functionality improvement maintenance activities, most adaptive maintenance activities and the software development process basically share the same software quality assurance tools. However, SQA tools employed for corrective maintenance tend to display some unique characteristics. It is important to remember that corrective maintenance activities are service activities and that, unlike functionality improvement and adaptive tasks, they are performed under the close supervision of the user/customer. Management of corrective maintenance services focuses mainly on the availability of services

| Frame 11.1 | Software maintenance QA activities: objectives |

1. Assure, with an accepted level of confidence, that the software maintenance activities conform to the functional technical requirements.

2. Assure, with an accepted level of confidence, that the software maintenance activities conform to managerial scheduling and budgetary requirements.

3. Initiate and manage activities to improve and increase the efficiency of software maintenance and SQA activities. This involves improving the prospects of achieving functional and managerial requirements while reducing costs.

and their quality (measured by time to solution, percentage of cases of correction failures, etc.) rather than on the budgetary and timetable controls typically applied when managing functionality improvement and adaptive maintenance tasks.

General discussion of a variety of software maintenance issues took place at the IEEE International Conference in Oxford, England (IEEE Computer Society, 1999).

11.2 The foundations of high quality

It goes without saying that the quality of the software package to be maintained is perhaps the single most important foundation underlying the quality of maintenance services. Another critical foundation is maintenance policy. The discussion of these subjects follows.

11.2.1 Foundation 1: software package quality

The quality of the software package that is to be maintained clearly stems from the expertise and efforts of the development team as well as the SQA activities performed throughout the development process. If the quality of the package is poor, maintenance will be poor or ineffective, almost by definition. In light of this fundamental insight, we choose to stress here those seven of the original 11 quality assurance factors (see Chapter 3) that have a direct impact on software maintenance. Specifically, we will be discussing two of the five product operation factors, all three product revision factors and two of the three product transition factors.

The two product operation factors are as follows.

(1) **Correctness** – includes:

■ **Output correctness:** The completeness of the outputs specified (in other words, no pre-specified output is missing), the accuracy of the outputs (all system's outputs are processed correctly), the up-to-datedness of the outputs (processed information is up to date as specified) and the availability of the outputs (reaction times do not exceed the specified maximum values, especially in online and real-time applications).

■ **Documentation correctness.** The quality of documentation: its completeness, accuracy, documentation style and structure. Documentation formats include hard copy and computer files – printed manuals as well as electronic "help" files – whereas its scope encompasses installation manuals, user manuals and programmer manuals.

■ **Coding qualification.** Compliance with coding instructions, especially those that limit and reduce code complexity and define standard coding style.

(2) **Reliability.** The frequency of system failures as well as recovery times.

The three product revision factors are as follows.

(1) **Maintainability.** These requirements are fulfilled first and foremost by following the software structure and style requirements and by implementing programmer documentation requirements.

(2) **Flexibility.** Achieved by appropriate planning and design, features that provide an application space much wider than necessary for the current user population. In practice, this means that room is left for future functional improvements.

(3) **Testability.** Testability includes the availability of system diagnostics to be applied by the user as well as failure diagnostics to be applied by the support center or the maintenance staff at the user's site.

Lastly, the two product transition factors are as follows.

(1) **Portability.** The software's potential application in different hardware and operating system environments, including the activities that enable those applications.

(2) **Interoperability.** The package's capacity to interface with other packages and computerized equipment. High interoperability is achieved by providing capacity to meet known interfacing standards and matching the interfacing applied by leading manufacturers of equipment and software.

To sum up – the efforts to assure the quality of maintenance services should begin early in the software development phase, when each of the quality factors reviewed above is specified in the project requirements and again later, when integrated in the project design.

The above seven factors and their distinctive impact on the various software maintenance components are presented in Table 11.1.

Table 11.1: Quality factors: impacts on software maintenance components

Quality factor	Quality sub-factors	Software maintenance components		
		Corrective	Adaptive	Functionality improvement
Correctness	Output correctness	High		
	Documentation correctness	High	High	High
	Coding qualification	High	High	High
Reliability		High		
Maintainability		High	High	High
Flexibility			High	
Testability		High		
Portability			High	
Interoperability			High	

11.2.2 Foundation 2: maintenance policy

The main maintenance policy components that affect the success of software maintenance are the version development and change policies to be applied during the software's life cycle.

Version development policy

This policy relates mainly to the question of how many versions of the software should be operative simultaneously. While it is clear that this is not an issue for custom-made software that serves one organization, the number of versions becomes a major issue for COTS software packages that are planned to serve a large variety of customers. The version development policy for the latter can take a "sequential" or "tree" form. When adopting a *sequential* version policy, only one version is made available to the entire customer population. This version includes a profusion of applications that exhibit high redundancy, an attribute that enables the software to serve the needs of all customers. The software must be revised periodically but once a new version is completed, it replaces the version currently used by the entire user population.

When adopting a *tree* version policy, the software maintenance team supports marketing efforts by developing a specialized, targeted version for groups of customers or a major customer once it is requested. A new version is inaugurated by adding special applications or omitting applications, depending on what is relevant to customer needs. The versions vary in complexity and level of application – targeted industry-oriented applications and so forth. If this policy is adopted, the software package can evolve into a multi-version package after several years of service, meaning it will resemble a tree, with several main branches and numerous secondary branches, each branch representing a version with specialized revisions. As opposed to sequential version software, maintenance and management of tree version software is much more difficult and time-consuming. Considering these deficiencies, software development organizations try to apply a *limited tree* version policy, which allows only a small number of software versions to be developed.

Example: After a few years of application, *Inventory Perfect*, an inventory management package developed according to the tree policy, has evolved into a seven-version software package with these main branches: Pharmacies, Electronics, Hospitals, Bookstores, Supermarkets, Garages–Auto Repairs, and Chemical Plants. Each of the branches includes four or five secondary branches that vary by number of software modules, level of implementation or specific customer-oriented applications. For example, the Bookstores version has the following five secondary branches (versions): bookstore chains, single bookstores, advanced management bookstores, and special versions for the LP bookstore chain and for CUCB (City University Campus Bookstores). The software maintenance team tends to a total of 30 different versions of the software package simultaneously, with each version revised periodically according to customer requests and the team's technical innovations.

The daily experience of the maintenance team therefore includes overcoming hardships created by the version structure of the package that go beyond those related to the software itself:

■ Faulty corrections caused by inadequate identification of the module structure of the current version used by the specific customer.

■ Faulty corrections caused by incorrect replacement of a faulty module by a module of another version that later proved to be inadequate for integration into the customer's package version.

■ Efforts invested to convince customers to update their software package by adding newly developed modules or replacing current module versions by a new version. Following successful efforts to persuade customers to update their software package, the problems and failures incurred when attempting to integrate newly developed modules or to replace current with advanced versions of the modules.

The head of the maintenance team has often mentioned that she envies her colleague, the head of *Inventory Star*'s maintenance team, who had insisted that the software package developed by his firm was to offer only one comprehensive version for all customers.

It is clear that the sequential policy adopted by *Inventory Star* requires much less maintenance; as only one version has to be maintained, it is much easier to maintain its quality level.

Change policy

Change policy refers to the method of examining each change request and the criteria used for its approval. It is clear that a permissive policy, whether implemented by the CCB (the Change Control Board) or any other body authorized to approve changes, contributes to an often-unjustified increase in the change task load. A balanced policy, one that requires thorough examination of change requests, is to be preferred as it allows staff to focus on the most important and beneficial changes, as well as those that they will be able to perform within a reasonable time and according to the required quality standards. This policy will, of course, culminate in the approval of only a small proportion of change requests.

For more about change control, see Chapter 18.

11.3 Pre-maintenance software quality components

Like pre-project SQA components, the pre-maintenance SQA activities to be completed prior to initiating the required maintenance services are of utmost importance. These entail:

- Maintenance contract review
- Maintenance plan construction.

11.3.1 Maintenance contract review

When considering the maintenance contract, a broad perspective should be embraced. More than anything else, decisions are required about the categories of services to be contracted. These decisions depend on the type of customers served: customers for whom a custom-made package has been developed, customers who purchased a COTS software package, and internal customers. So, before commencing to supply software maintenance services to any of these customers, an adequate maintenance contract should be finalized that sets down the total range of maintenance obligations according to the relevant conditions.

Implementation tip

Maintenance services to internal customers are often not contracted. In a typical situation, some of the services provided during the running-in period are continued, with no one bothering to determine the binding obligations for continuation of these services. In such situations, dissatisfaction is expected on both sides: the internal customers feel that they need to ask for favors instead of receiving the regular service that they deserve, whereas the development team eventually experiences requests to perform maintenance tasks as intrusions once they have begun work on another project.

To prevent these tensions, an "internal service contract" should be written. In this document, the services to be provided by the internal maintenance team to the internal customer are clearly defined. By eliminating most of the misunderstanding related to these vital services, such a contract can serve as the basis for satisfactory maintenance to internal customers.

The maintenance contract review activities include proposal draft reviews as well as contract draft reviews. Naturally, the objectives and implementation of maintenance contract reviews follow the lines of pre-project contract reviews (see Chapter 5). We next list the major objectives of software maintenance contract reviews.

(1) **Customer requirements clarification**

The following issues deserve special attention:

- Type of corrective maintenance services required: list of remote services and on-site services to be provided, hours of service, response time, etc.
- Size of the user population and the types of applications to be used.
- Location of users, especially of long-distance (or overseas) sites and the types of applications installed in each.
- Adaptive and functionality improvement maintenance to be provided and procedures for submission of requests for service as well as proposing and approving performance of these services.

(2) **Review of alternative approaches to maintenance provision**

The following options deserve special consideration:

- Subcontracting for sites or type of service
- Performance of some services by the customer himself with support from supplier's maintenance team.

(3) **Review of estimates of required maintenance resources**

First, these estimates should be examined on the basis of the required maintenance services, clarified by the proposal team. Then, the company's capacity to meet its commitments with respect to professional competence as well as availability of maintenance teams should be analyzed.

(4) **Review of maintenance services to be provided by subcontractors and/or the customer**

This review refers to the definition of the services provided by each participant, payments to subcontractors, quality assurance and follow-up procedures to be applied.

(5) **Review of maintenance costs estimates**

These estimates should be reviewed on the basis of required resources.

11.3.2 Maintenance plan

Maintenance plans should be prepared for all customers, external and internal. The plan should provide the framework within which maintenance provision is organized. Hence, as anticipated, the maintenance and development plans (see Chapter 6) are based on similar concepts.

The plan includes the following:

(1) **A list of the contracted maintenance services**

- The internal and external customers, the number of users, the locations of each customer site.

■ The characteristics of corrective maintenance services (remote and on site).

■ The obligations for adaptive and functional improving maintenance service provision for each customer.

(2) **A description of the maintenance team's organization**

The maintenance team organization plan focuses on manpower requirements, which should be carefully considered according to these criteria:

■ The number of required team members. If services are to be provided from several facilities, the team requirement for each facility.

■ The required qualifications for team members according to the maintenance tasks, including acquaintance with the software package(s) to be maintained.

■ Organizational structure of the maintenance teams, including names of team leaders.

■ Definition of tasks (responsibility for customers, types of applications, etc.) for each team.

■ Training needs.

Implementation tip

In determining the maintenance team and its organization, one should consider preparing for peak demand for corrective maintenance services. The support in peak situations can be based on temporary use of development and other maintenance teams located at the same or other facilities. It should be emphasized that effective peak-load support is based on pre-planning, which includes training. Maintenance teams require regular training for these tasks; on-the-spot improvised solutions may prove to be harmful rather than helpful.

(3) **A list of maintenance facilities**

Maintenance facilities – the infrastructure that makes it possible to provide services – include:

■ The maintenance support center with its installed hardware and communication equipment to provide user support and software correction services.

■ A documentation center containing a complete set of documents (in printed or electronic format):

- The software documentation, including the development documentation
- The service contracts
- The software configurations for each customer and versions of the software packages installed at each site, provided by configuration management
- The maintenance history records for each user and customer.

(4) **A list of identified maintenance service risks**

Maintenance service risk relates to situations where failure to provide adequate maintenance is anticipated. These risks include:

■ Staff shortages, whether throughout the organization's maintenance services, in a specific maintenance support center or for a specific application.

■ Inadequate qualifications or acquaintance with part of the relevant software packages for performing user support services and/or corrective maintenance tasks.

■ Insufficient team members qualified to perform functional improvement as well as adaptive tasks, in cases where a customer places an order of a significant size.

(5) **A list of required software maintenance procedures and controls**

Most of the required procedures refer to the processes implemented by the corrective maintenance teams and by the user support center. These procedures typically deal with:

■ Handling customers' applications
■ Handling a software failure report
■ Periodic reporting and follow-up of user support services
■ Periodic reporting and follow-up of corrective maintenance services
■ Training and certification of maintenance team members.

For more about software quality procedures, see Chapter 14.

(6) **The software maintenance budget**

The estimates used in the corrective maintenance budget are based on the manpower organization plan, required facilities and investments needed to establish these facilities, team training needs and other tasks. They can be prepared once the manpower, facilities and procedures have been defined. Estimates for adaptive and functionality improvement maintenance tasks are prepared according to the expected workload induced by the changes and improvements to be carried out.

11.4 Maintenance software quality assurance tools

A great variety of software quality assurance tools are used throughout the operational period of the software life cycle. The specific nature of each component of software maintenance – corrective maintenance, adaptive maintenance and functionality improvement maintenance – demands that different sets of SQA tools be used for each. Furthermore, the operational period of the software typically makes intensive use of infrastructure SQA tools and managerial control tools more probable.

Some indication of the extent of resources invested in SQA during maintenance has been prepared by Perry (1995). In a survey he carried out in November 1994, the participants reported that based on their experience,

31% of their maintenance schedules were dedicated to quality assurance (reviews and testing tasks).

The next sections are dedicated to the following subjects:

- SQA tools for corrective maintenance
- SQA tools for functionality improvement maintenance
- SQA infrastructure tools for software maintenance
- SQA tools for managerial control of software maintenance.

11.4.1 SQA tools for corrective maintenance

Corrective maintenance activities entail primarily (a) user support services and (b) software corrections (bug repairs). *User support services* deal with cases of software code and documentation failures, incomplete or vague documentation; they may also involve instruction of users who have insufficient knowledge of the software or fail to use the available documentation. *Software correction services* – bug repairs and documentation corrections – are called for in cases of software failures, and are typically provided during the initial period of operation (despite the efforts invested in testing) and continue to be required, though in lower frequency. As the two types of service are inherently different, distinctive sets of quality assurance tools are used irrespective of the shared focuses on quality of service. Nonetheless, in many cases the same team performs both types of corrective maintenance.

In addition to infrastructure and management control SQA tools (discussed later in this section), most bug repair tasks require the use of *mini life cycle* SQA tools, mainly mini-testing. Mini-testing procedures are required to handle *repair patch* (small-scale) tasks, characterized by a small number of coding line changes together with intense pressure to complete the corrections rapidly. The implications of delayed repair are such that an abridged – mini – form of testing is often employed. However, use of these mini testing tools should be retained to avoid compromise situations of no testing.

In order to assure "mini testing" quality, these guidelines should be adhered to:

- Testing is to be performed by a qualified tester, not by the programmer who carried out the repair.
- A testing procedure document (in most cases 2–3 pages long) should be prepared. Included in the document are a description of the anticipated effects of the repair, the scope of corrections and a list of test cases to be activated. A re-testing procedure document, similar to the testing procedure document, should be also be prepared to handle testing of repairs of errors detected in previous tests.
- A test report fully documenting the errors detected in each stage of testing and re-testing should be completed.
- The head of the testing team is to review the testing documentation for the scope of corrections, the adequacy of the test cases and the testing

results. Responsibility for approval of the repaired software for operational (sometimes termed "production") use rests with the team's head.

■ For repairs considered "simple and trivial", especially for those performed at the customer's site, mini-testing may be avoided.

Subcontracting (outsourcing) maintenance services, especially user support services, has become quite common whenever it is too troublesome or uneconomic for the maintenance contractor to directly provide these services. The main tool to assure the quality of the subcontractor's maintenance services and pave the way for smooth relations is the contractor–subcontractor contract. The SQA tools integrated into the contract focus on:

■ Procedures for handling a specified range of maintenance calls.

■ Full documentation of the service procedures.

■ Availability of records documenting professional certification of the subcontractor's maintenance team members, for contractor review.

■ Authorization for the contractor to carry out periodic review of the maintenance services as well as customer satisfaction surveys.

■ Quality-related conditions requiring imposition of penalties and termination of the subcontracting contract in extreme cases.

Once maintenance becomes operative, the contractor should regularly conduct the agreed-upon reviews of maintenance service and customer satisfaction surveys.

Implementation tip

Many of the bitter failures experienced with software maintenance contracts are due to subcontracting. Failures often result from lax control over the subcontractor's performance, not from the absence of software quality assurance clauses from the contract. The reasons for subcontracting, such as a shortage of maintenance professionals at the remotely located customer's site that consumes the subcontracted services, may induce faulty control over the subcontractor's services. In other words, successful subcontracting requires adequate organization and procedures to implement proper control over performance.

More about subcontracting may be found in Chapter. 12.

11.4.2 SQA tools for functionality improvement maintenance

Due to the similarity of functionality improvement maintenance tasks to software development project tasks, project life cycle tools (reviews and testing) are regularly applied for functionality improvement maintenance. These same tools are also regularly implemented for large-scale adaptive maintenance tasks where, again, the task characteristics resemble those of functionality improvement tasks.

For a detailed general discussion of reviews and testing, see Chapters 8, 9 and 10.

Additional SQA tools implemented for functionality improvement maintenance are infrastructure and management control tools, discussed later in this section.

11.4.3 SQA infrastructure components for software maintenance

Software quality assurance infrastructure tools, discussed in Part IV of the book (Chapters 14 to 19), are vital components of software maintenance. A great proportion of the array of infrastructure SQA tools are of a general nature and implemented throughout the life cycle of the software system. In addition, the similarity of the software functionality improvement and software development processes enables both processes to share the same infrastructure SQA tools with minor changes. Specialized infrastructure tools are required for corrective maintenance activities, due to the special characteristics of these activities. Adaptive maintenance activities are served by infrastructure SQA tools, according to their characteristics. The most frequently employed tools are functional improvement SQA tools, followed by corrective maintenance SQA tools.

Actually, the contribution of infrastructure SQA tools to maintenance does not begin with the onset of the maintenance process. Obviously, adequate application of SQA infrastructure tools by the software development teams contributes substantially to the efficiency and effectiveness of maintenance team activities. In other words, these tools contribute to maintenance quality assurance in two ways: first, by supporting the software development teams when producing high-quality software, and second, by supporting the maintenance teams responsible for the maintenance of the same software product.

Specialized SQA infrastructure tools are required for software maintenance processes, especially corrective maintenance, displaying special characteristics. Here we focus on specialized SQA infrastructure tools of the following classes:

- Maintenance procedures and work instructions
- Supporting quality devices
- Training and certification of maintenance teams
- Preventive and corrective actions
- Configuration management
- Documentation and quality record control.

Maintenance procedures and work instructions
Most specialized maintenance procedures and work instructions are applied for corrective maintenance and user support activities, for example:

- Remote handling of requests for service in cases of software failure
- On-site handling of customer requests for service in cases of software failure
- User support service
- Quality assurance control of software correction and user support activities
- Customer satisfaction surveys
- Certification of corrective maintenance and user support team members.

Supporting quality devices

The maintenance department is expected to develop specialized devices to support software correction and user support activities: templates, checklists and the like. Such devices may include:

- Checklists for location of causes for a failure – to be applied by the maintenance technician.

- Templates for reporting how software failure were solved, including findings of the correction process.

- Checklists for preparing a mini testing procedure document.

Training and certification of maintenance teams

Training of maintenance teams that deal with functional improvement tasks does not differ substantially from training of other software development teams. However, special training and certification are crucial for corrective maintenance teams.

Training of corrective maintenance professionals is motivated by the need to supply the services specified in maintenance contracts (or agreements, in cases of internal customers) on a continuous basis. Thus, the training plan should provide solutions to staffing needs during peak load periods and the organization's need to replace, at short notice, retiring, resigning or discharged personnel. In many cases, general training of these "reserve" maintenance personnel is insufficient, and training in specific systems must be added. In other words, rigorous training programs are required to enable the organization to cope with the contracted level of service specified for peak-load periods and in situations of maintenance personnel changes, for whatever reason.

Certification requirements for software correction and user support personnel are rooted in the characteristics of these services. Special attention should be given to certification of software correction professionals, who usually perform their tasks under heavy time pressures, work alone, and in many cases work at the customer's site, where the availability of professional support from the team leader or others is limited.

Preventive and corrective actions

The operative phase of the software life cycle produces highly valuable information: records of software failures and their repair as well as records of user support requests can lead to preventive and corrective actions and thereby contribute to improvement of existing and new software systems. For the process to be effective, there need to be adequate processes for screening the collected information, reviewing and analyzing findings, and devising recommendations for improvements of relevant development and maintenance processes. These SQA activities are directed and controlled by an internal committee – the CAB (Corrective Action Board), found in major software development organizations.

Issues typically forwarded to the Board for review include:

- Changes in content and frequency of customer requests for user support services
- Increased average time invested in complying with customer's user support requests
- Increased average time invested in repairing customer's software failures
- Increased percentage of software correction failures.

Configuration management

The maintenance teams represent the groups most dependent on configuration management. This dependence results from their intimate involvement with servicing software packages over many years, during which new versions are added, old versions replaced and many new installations and changes of software performed.

Two common applications relying on configuration management are (1) failure corrections and (2) "group" replacement of the currently used version of the software by a new version, initiated by the maintaining organization.

(1) **Failure repair.** In the course of software failure repairs, reliable and updated support is needed in the form of:

- Information regarding the version of the software system installed at the customer's site
- A copy of the current code and its documentation.

The contribution to software quality is achieved by fewer errors in failure correction trials and reduced resources invested in the corrections.

(2) **Group replacement.** The term "group" in the SQA context refers to all those customers having the same software version installed at their sites. Hence, "group" replacement indicates that all the customers using the stated version will receive the newly developed or updated version of the software at more or less the same time. Configuration management support for group replacement, based on information about the members of a customer group, entails:

- Decision making about the advisability of performing a group replacement, based on the extent of the replacement and the type of contracts signed with the customers.
- Planning the group replacement, allocating resources and determining the timetable.

The contribution to software quality is achieved by replacement of the current software version with an improved version that is usually less prone to software failure and requires less support. The improved quality also contributes to software maintenance efficiency as fewer resources are required for corrective maintenance.

Maintenance documentation and quality records

The specialized requirements for documentation and quality records are most closely related to software correction and user support activities. Documentation and quality records are prepared in order to:

- Supply vital data for preventive and corrective actions (as mentioned earlier)
- Support the handling of future customer failure reports and user support requests
- Provide evidence in response to future customer claims and/or complaints.

The documentation requirements listed in the various maintenance procedures should respond to all of these documentation needs.

11.4.4 Managerial control SQA tools for software maintenance

While specialized managerial control SQA tools are required for corrective maintenance activities, the similarity in the software processes characterizing functionality improvement and adaptive maintenance and software development enables these processes to employ the same managerial tools. Specifically, managerial SQA components are meant to improve control of maintenance by creating early alarms that signal reduced quality of service and increasing rates of service failures.

The remainder of this section is dedicated to special managerial control issues, mainly those touching upon software correction and user support services:

- Performance controls for corrective maintenance services
- Quality metrics for corrective maintenance
- Costs of software maintenance quality.

For more about managerial control SQA tools, see Part V of the book (Chapters 20–22).

Performance controls for software maintenance services

Managerial performance controls of corrective maintenance services differ when applied to software correction (failure repair) services and to user support services. The managerial control tools yield, beside periodic performance information, alarms for management attention, such as the following:

(1) **Software correction**

- Increased resources utilization
- Decreased rate of remote failure repairs (low cost repairs) versus customer's on-site repairs
- Increased rate of on-site repairs at long-distance locations and overseas services
- Increased percentage of failures to meet repair schedule requirements
- Increased rate of faulty repairs, and list of specific "model" cases of extreme failure situations
- Lower customer satisfaction based on customer satisfaction surveys.

(2) **User support**

- Increased rates of requests for service for a specific software system, for service type, etc.
- Increased resource utilization in user support services
- Increased rate of failures to provide requested consulting services
- Increased rate of faulty consulting, and specific cases of "outstanding" failures
- Customer satisfaction information based on customer satisfaction surveys.

These managerial failure repair controls (that are expected to yield alarms) are carried out through periodic reporting, regularly scheduled staff meetings, visits to the maintenance support center providing the services, and analysis of reports dealing with software maintenance metrics and maintenance quality costs. The accumulated information supports managerial decisions regarding the planning and operation of corrective maintenance.

Quality metrics for software maintenance

Software maintenance quality metrics are used mainly to identify trends in maintenance efficiency, effectiveness and customer satisfaction. The software quality assurance unit usually processes the metrics. Changes in trends, negative as well as positive, provide the quantitative basis for managerial decision making regarding:

- Estimation of resource requirements when preparing maintenance plans for the next period
- Comparison of methods of operation
- Initiation of preventive and corrective actions
- Estimation of resource requirements as a basis for proposals for new or adjusted maintenance services.

For examples of quality metrics of software correction and user support services, see Section 21.4.

Costs of software maintenance quality

As in the former sections, we refer here only to corrective maintenance issues. As will be shown in Chapter 22, the quality costs of corrective maintenance are classified into six classes. Following are definitions for each class and examples.

■ **Costs of prevention** – Costs of error prevention, i.e. costs of instruction and training of maintenance team, costs of preventative and corrective actions.

■ **Costs of appraisal** – Costs of error detection, i.e. costs of review of maintenance services carried out by SQA teams, external teams and customer satisfaction surveys.

■ **Costs of managerial preparation and control** – Costs of managerial activities carried out to prevent errors, i.e. costs of preparation of maintenance plans, maintenance team recruitment and follow-up of maintenance performance.

■ **Costs of internal failure** – Costs of software failure corrections initiated by the maintenance team (prior to receiving customer complaints).

■ **Costs of external failure** – Costs of software failure corrections initiated by customer complaints.

■ **Costs of managerial failure** – Costs of software failures caused by managerial actions or inaction, i.e. costs of damages resulting from shortage of maintenance staff and/or inadequate maintenance task organization.

After reviewing these classes of software quality costs, defined according to the classic as well as the extended model, as will be discussed in Chapter 22, we find that the general considerations for defining classes of cost of software quality, as discussed in Chapter 22, apply nicely to all but one class of cost of software maintenance quality. Special definitions are required for external failure costs at the maintenance phase. This issue will be discussed next.

Costs of external failure of software corrective maintenance activities

In order to define external failure costs, the two maintenance periods must be considered separately. These are: (a) the warranty period (usually 3–12 months after the software is installed) and (b) the contracted maintenance services period, which begins at the end of the warranty period. The issue here requires a decision as to what situation should be considered an external failure; only after making this decision can the quality costs be identified and estimated. Suggested definitions of external failure costs and their supporting arguments for software correction and user support services follow.

(1) **For software corrections:**

■ All costs of software correction initiated by users during the warranty period are external quality costs because they are considered to result directly from software development failures; hence, the developer is responsible for their correction during this period.

- Software corrections performed during the contracted maintenance period are considered part of regular service, as the responsibility of the developer for corrections is limited to the warranty period. As such, the costs of these services are considered regular service costs and not quality costs.
- During the contracted maintenance period, only costs of re-correction after failure of the initial correction efforts are considered external failure costs as the software technician failed in his regular maintenance service.

(2) **For user support services:**

- During the warranty period, user support services are considered to be an inherent part of the instruction effort, and therefore should not be considered external failure costs.
- During the contracted maintenance period, all types of user support services, whether dealing with an identified software failure or consultations about application options, are all part of regular service, and their costs are not considered external failure costs.
- During both maintenance periods, an external failure is defined as a case where a second consultation is required after the initial consultation proves to be inadequate. The costs of furnishing the second and further consultations for the same case are considered external failure costs.

As in the general case, maintenance quality cost information, together with the other managerial control information, is expected to assist management in making decisions regarding:

- Directions for investment in the improvement of maintenance services by indicating weak points of extremely high quality costs and strong points of extremely low quality costs.
- Development of an improved version of the software (in the case of custom-made software) or replacement of a purchased software package.

Summary

(1) List the components of software maintenance and explain their distinctiveness.

There are three components of software maintenance, each doing the following:
- **Corrective maintenance** of software corrections and user support services.
- **Adaptive maintenance** adjusts the software package to the requirements of new customers and changing environmental conditions.
- **Functionality improvement maintenance** combines maintenance activities with improvement of software performance and reliability.

(2) Describe the foundations of high quality maintenance.

Two factors are considered to be the foundations of high quality maintenance: the software package's quality and the maintenance policy applied. It is clear that the first could be guaranteed by implementing SQA activities throughout the development process, and should begin in the earliest phases of software development (including the pre-project phase).

The main constituents of maintenance policy are version policy and change policy. As to version policy, a "strictly one active version" policy is quite preferable to a "multi-version policy". The former policy saves the resources needed to cope with maintenance of several versions and allows the team to focus on effective, reliable corrective and adaptive maintenance in addition to the development of a comprehensive improved version of the original package. As to change policy, the "balanced" policy that approves only a small proportion of worthwhile changes as a result of its focus on the most important, beneficial changes is preferable to a "permissive" policy that approves every change requested.

(3) Describe and explain the pre-maintenance software quality components.

The pre-maintenance software quality assurance components include (a) maintenance contract review and (b) preparation of a maintenance plan. Some of the objectives of these activities are customer requirements clarification, review of alternative approaches to providing the services and review of resource and costs estimates. The maintenance plan's crucial elements are definition of the maintenance services to be provided, manpower requirements, maintenance service risks, maintenance procedures, controls to be applied, and costs.

(4) List the infrastructure tools that support maintenance quality assurance.

The major SQA maintenance infrastructure tools are:
- Software maintenance procedures and work instructions
- Training and certification of maintenance teams
- Quality-supporting devices
- Preventive and corrective actions
- Configuration management
- Software maintenance documentation and quality records.

(5) List the main managerial tools for controlling software maintenance quality and explain their importance.

The main managerial SQA components for corrective maintenance are:
- Performance controls – implemented by means of periodic reporting, regular staff meetings and visits to maintenance support centers
- Quality metrics for corrective maintenance
- Quality costs of corrective maintenance.

The managerial control of functionality improvement and adaptive maintenance tasks applies mainly to the tools used for controlling software development projects.

As in the software development phase, managerial SQA tools for the maintenance phase are planned to assist management in making decisions regarding:
- Directions for investment in the improvement of maintenance services by analyzing the weak and strong points of extremely high as well as extremely low quality costs.

■ Development of an improved version of the software exhibiting extremely high quality problem indications or replacement of such purchased software packages with other packages.

■ Comparison of methods of operation.

■ Estimation of resource requirements as a basis for preparation of proposals for new or adjusted maintenance services.

Selected bibliography

1. IEEE (1998) "IEEE Std 1219-1988 – IEEE Standard for Software Maintenance", in *IEEE Software Engineering Standards Collection*, The Institute of Electrical and Electronics Engineers, New York.

2. IEEE Computer Society (1999) *"Proceedings of the IEEE International Conference on Software Maintenance – 1999 (ICSM99) Software Maintenance for Business Change"*, IEEE Computer Society Press, Los Alamitos, CA, USA.

3. ISO (1997) *ISO 9000-3:1997(E), Quality Management and Quality Assurance Standards – Part 3: Guidelines for the Application of ISO 9001:1994 to the Development, Supply, Installation and Maintenance of Computer Software*, 2nd edn, International Organization for Standardization (ISO), Geneva.

4. ISO/IEC (2001) "ISO 9000-3:2001 Software and System Engineering – Guidelines for the Application of ISO 9001:2000 to Software, Final draft", International Organization for Standardization (ISO), Geneva, unpublished draft, December 2001.

5. Lientz, B. P. and Swanson, E. B. (1980) *Software Maintenance Management*, Addison-Wesley, Reading, MA.

6. McKee, J. R. (1984) "Maintenance as a function of design", AFIPS National Computer Conference, Las Vegas, NV.

7. Nosek, J. T. and Palvia, P. (1990) "Software maintenance management: changes in the last decade", *Software Maintenance: Research and Practice*, 2(3), 157–174.

8. Oskarsson O. and Glass R. L. (1996) *An ISO 9000 Approach to Building Quality Software*, Prentice Hall, Upper Saddle River, NJ.

9. Perry, W. (1995) *Effective Methods for Software Testing*, John Wiley & Sons, New York.

10. Pressman, R. S. (2000) *Software Engineering – A Practitioner's Approach*, European adaptation by D. Ince, 5th edn, McGraw-Hill International, London.

Review questions

11.1 Refer to Section 11.2 on the foundations of software quality assurance.

(1) Explain in your own words the importance of the first foundation.

(2) List and explain the importance of the various factors affecting the first foundation.

(3) Explain in your own words the second foundation and how it affects the quality of software maintenance services.

11.2 A company is anxious to sign a three-year maintenance contract for an ERP (Enterprise Resource Planning) software package for a multinational organization that employs 6000 people in eight countries. The company has already acquired experience in the maintenance of the ERP package. The multinational organization suggests paying a lump sum for corrective and adaptive maintenance tasks, and separate payment for functional improvements, based on the characteristics of each request. The Sales Department's pressure for immediate signing of the contract leaves little time for preparation of a proposal and practically no time for maintenance contract review.

(1) What risks are entailed with neglect of the contract review?
(2) What subjects would you recommend for contract review in this case?
(3) If required maintenance of a similar nature was requested by an internal customer (to serve employees of the same company), would you recommend carrying out a contract review? List your arguments.

11.3 Refer to Section 11.3 on maintenance plans.

(1) What are the basic elements of a maintenance plan? Explain the importance of each element in your own words.
(2) Who, do you think, should be responsible for preparing the plan? Who should approve it? List your arguments.
(3) What difficulties would you expect to arise if no plan is prepared?

11.4 Five guidelines are suggested in Section 11.4.1 for testing small repairs of software performed by a software maintenance team member.

(1) Explain the importance of each of the guidelines for achieving adequate quality of software repairs.
(2) Explain how the guidelines cope with the special characteristics of small repairs ("patches").

11.5 The six issues to be stipulated in a contract for subcontracting software maintenance services are mentioned in Section 11.4.1.

(1) Explain the importance of each issue in your own words.
(2) Suggest how the subcontractor could benefit from full implementation of the control clauses included in the contractor's contract with the customer.

11.6 It is claimed that higher standards are needed for training and certification of maintenance team members than for development team members.

(1) Do you agree or disagree with this statement? List your arguments.
(2) If you agree with the above, what component of software maintenance (corrective, adaptive or functionality improvement) do you consider most suitable for the above statement?

11.7 Most software corrective maintenance procedures require extensive documentation of the activities performed.

(1) List the main uses for the various types of corrective maintenance documentation.
(2) Explain the importance of the required documentation in your own words.

11.8 Refer to Section 11.4.4 on managerial control of software maintenance services.

    (1)   List the main issues dealt with by managerial maintenance control.

    (2)   Once management receives proper reporting from the maintenance teams, is there a need for meetings and visits? What additional contributions to managerial control might be achieved by meetings and visits? List your arguments.

Topics for discussion

11.1 A lecturer in a SQA conference concluded his talk by recommending that a software maintenance specialist participate in the quality assurance activities carried out during the development process.

    (1)   Do you agree with the lecturer?

    (2)   List your arguments for and against this suggestion.

    (3)   Do you support "reverse" cooperation, where a development specialist participates in quality assurance activities of the maintenance team? List your arguments for and against this position.

11.2 Mr Steve Barber, a software maintenance expert, was recruited to serve as leader of the team providing maintenance services for Hotelex, a hotel management software package, after the former team leader resigned. The package had been on the market for six months and the team has already installed and maintained four different versions of Hotelex in seven hotels. The company is in the first stages of developing packages for sports clubs and community centers. The software maintenance team is expected to serve the customers of all three packages. During the team's monthly meeting, Mr Barber mentioned that after a month in service, he found that the foundations for maintaining Hotelex are inadequate, causing the high software maintenance costs. While nothing could be done in relation to the software package's quality (the first maintenance foundation) at this point, he hoped to improve maintenance policy (the second foundation) within the next three months. In general, he declared that he would act to assure proper foundations for the two new software packages being currently developed.

    (1)   Suggest what findings regarding the maintenance of Hotelex had brought Mr Barber to his negative evaluation of its maintenance according to its two foundations.

    (2)   Suggest what could still be altered, and how to do so.

    (3)   Suggest what actions Mr Barber might plan to assure proper foundations for the two new packages.

11.3 The weekly customers' complaints that were piled on the desk of the head of the Operations Department included the following:

    ■ A complaint repeated by several customers: the software maintenance technician, who was unable to solve the problem on site at the scheduled time, claimed that he was unaware that he was required to carry the software programmers' manual with him at all times; therefore, he could not solve the problem on time.

- A complaint by the Operations Manager of a supermarket chain: the software maintenance team had unsuccessfully tried to correct the software three times; as a result, several crucial functions could not be activated for four days.
- A customer's angry letter complaining about an unfair cost estimate for a requested minor improvement: 60 man-days. He quoted the head of the Software Functional Improvement Team, who had said that the high estimate was the outcome of missing documentation and non-standard coding of the original package.

Analyze each of the cases and then:

(1) Suggest the reasons for each of the maintenance team's failures.
(2) Suggest the steps to be taken in each case to prevent the failures mentioned in (1).

11.4 At a recent SQA conference, a speaker mentioned the following costs as maintenance quality costs:

- High operating costs due to unanticipated high frequency of overseas service calls. It has been found that the overseas branches of a firm employ six times more employees than were estimated by software suppliers' sales departments at the time the proposals were prepared.
- Damages to the Software Development Department due to increasing difficulties in sales and higher rates of tender losses after two leading customers had decided not to renew their maintenance contracts, claiming inadequate quality of maintenance services.
- Increased penalties paid to customers during a two-month period in which the maintenance team was short of three team members.

(1) Can all the costs in the three cases mentioned above be considered maintenance quality costs? Analyze each case separately. List your arguments.
(2) How would you classify each of quality costs described in the above cases according to the classic and extended models (see Sections 22.2 and 22.3)? List your arguments.

chapter 12

Assuring the quality of external participants' contributions

Evidence for the importance of assuring the quality of external participants' contributions is found in the ISO 9000-3 Standard (see ISO, 1997, Sec. 4.6 and ISO/IEC, 2001, Sec. 7.4), IEEE Std 1062 (IEEE, 1998) and the software quality assurance literature (see Basili and Boehm, 2001; Oskarsson and Glass, 1996).

After completing this chapter, you will be able to:

■ Explain the difference between contractors and external participants.
■ List the types of external participants, and explain the benefits they provide to the contractor.
■ Describe the risks for the contractor associated with turning to external participants.
■ List the SQA tools appropriate for use with external participants and add short statements regarding the risks they help to eliminate or reduce.

12.1 Introduction: the HealthSoft case

The RedAid Health Insurance tender presented a real challenge for HealthSoft, a software house that specialized in hospital and pharmacy software. The tender's main item was an integrative nationwide system for online handling of fees charged by hospitals for services, by pharmacies for prescriptions, by physicians for clinic visits and by medical laboratories for tests. The tender also included a comprehensive patient's personal health information service to be made available through the Internet. The customer's Management Information System (MIS) Department was to develop the home office modules, based on the existing software. In addition, the MIS Department will purchase and install the hardware and communication equipment according to the contractor's specifications, see to the computerized interfacing agreements required with RedAid's suppliers of health services, and instruct RedAid personnel in the new system's operation. All the systems were to be under tight security, with high reliability requisite for all the components. The system was to become fully operative not later than 13 months after signing the contract, with the contractor fully responsible for the quality and timely completion of all system parts.

Already at the beginning of preparing the RedAid tender proposal, the HealthSoft tender team realized that they needed the professional support of companies that specialize in software security and data communication. The size of the anticipated programming load led the team to decide that a subcontractor would carry out 60%–70% of the programming load. Cape-Code, a very small software house located in a nearby suburb, was chosen as the programming subcontractor on the basis of the lowest price proposed. Some "breathing space" when preparing the proposal was obtained when the team discovered that the new enhanced Medal Software's product Version 5E of the widely used Medal Version 5, a laboratory accounting software program, included important new modules. These new modules for online external authorization of patient credit and for the preparation of monthly accounts for organizational customers like RedAid suited the tender requirements. Medal's developers had stressed the wide variety of their package's interfacing capabilities, which were touted as suited to almost any requirements. The integration of Medal's 5E version into the proposed software solved one of the remaining difficulties hampering completion of the proposal and enabled substantial reduction of development costs. Finally, HealthSoft signed agreements with all the potential external participants – Lion Securities, Comcom and Cape-Code, subcontractors for security, communication and programming, respectively – that framed its responsibility for financial issues as well as coordination between the various organizations.

The day HealthSoft was announced winner of the tender was one of satisfaction and joy for the company. Within a few days, all the project teams were working "at full speed". Monthly coordination meetings were conducted regularly. The subcontractors reported satisfactory progress according to the project schedule. The first signs of alert appeared in the tenth meeting. Comcom, the communication subcontractor, reported that some of RedAid's major suppliers had refused to supply the information needed for planning the communication equipment to be installed on their premises as they had not reached an agreement with RedAid on the issue. As expected, Lion Securities, the security subcontractor, faced similar difficulties. Both subcontractors declared that even if full cooperation was to be achieved within a week, a one-month delay in completion of the project was inevitable. Yet, Cape-Code people continued to express their satisfaction with the progress of the development tasks they had undertaken. The next coordination meeting was a special meeting, called after only two weeks, to discuss the severe delays that had appeared in Cape-Code's schedule. The delays had been discovered by a HealthSoft team when it tried to coordinate a planned integration test. At this late stage, HealthSoft found out that Cape-Code had subcontracted the development task to another small software house. It became clear that all the previous calming reports had not been based on actual information; they were fabrications, meant to satisfy HealthSoft people (and ensure regular income to Cape-Code).

Integration tests of the Cape-Code modules, begun 10 weeks behind schedule, identified many more faults – of all kinds – than anticipated. Correction time required exceeded that planned. About the same time, the team assigned to integrate the Medal Version 5E software into the system realized that the enhanced version was not operative for all new modules, particularly the online external authorization of patients' credit status. In addition, the interfacing trials with other system modules failed. Medal Software assigned a special team to complete the development of the missing module parts and perform the necessary corrections. Though their efforts were visible, successful completion of the software integration tests was accomplished almost 20 weeks behind schedule.

The system test started 19 weeks behind schedule, with the same severity of quality problems that had been observed at the integration phase. Finally, about five months late, it became possible to install the hardware and software equipment in RedAid's main office and at its suppliers' sites.

The three-week conversion phase of the project, begun 23 weeks behind schedule, was, surprisingly, a great success, with no major faults discovered and immediate repair of all faults that were revealed. However, the implementation phase was a colossal failure: only one-third of the staff listed for training actually participated in the instruction courses, and the majority of those participating displayed insufficient preliminary knowledge of the new systems. Success with supplier personnel was even lower. Only eight weeks later could regular operation of the system begin, but with only about half of RedAid's suppliers integrated into the new system.

The project, a frustrating one for all who participated, ended with a series of court claims. RedAid sued HealthSoft, and HealthSoft sued RedAid, Cape-Code and Medal Software, the developers of the Medal software package. Lion Securities and Comcom decided not to sue HealthSoft – despite the extra costs they had incurred following RedAid's lack of cooperation and the subsequent obstacles raised to efficient performance of their parts in the project – in expectation of continuing cooperation with HealthSoft on future projects. The trials lasted for years. The only consolation was that the new software, once in operation, was a great success, with many of RedAid's management admitting that the system worked well beyond their expectations.

You may ask yourself:

■ Could the final gratifying results have been achieved without the "mess" experienced during the course of the project?

■ Could they have been achieved without the major losses faced by all the participants?

■ Was the HealthSoft method of choosing subcontractors satisfactory?

■ Was the method of purchasing COTS software appropriate?

■ Was the method of controlling the implementation of the customer's contribution to the project adequate?

■ Was HealthSoft's control over its external participants adequate?

Whatever your responses to the specific questions, we can readily claim that had HealthSoft properly implemented SQA activities, problems like those described could have been avoided. Prevention of such troubles is the subject of this chapter.

12.2 Types of external participants

The partners to a software development project – the organization that is interested in the software system (the "customer") and the organization that undertakes to carry out the development (the "contractor") – are nowadays often not the only participants in the project. The external participants involved in a software development project contribute to the project but are not contractors, nor are they the contractor's partners. Their contributions to the project are structured through agreements with the contractor (subcontractors and suppliers of COTS software) or through those clauses of the project contract that state what parts of the project will be performed by the customer himself. The larger and more complex the project, the greater the likelihood that external participants will be required, and the larger the proportion of work to be transmitted or parceled out. The motivation for turning to external participants rests on several factors, ranging from the economic to the technical and to personnel-related interests, and reflects a growing trend in the allocation of the work involved in completing complex projects.

External participants can be classified into three main groups:

(1) **Subcontractors** (currently called "outsourcing" organizations) that undertake to carry out parts of a project, small or large, according to circumstances. Subcontractors usually offer the contractor at least one of the following benefits: staff availability, special expertise or low prices.

(2) **Suppliers of COTS software and reused software modules.** The advantages of integrating these ready elements are obvious, ranging from timetable and cost reductions to quality. One expects that integration of these ready-for-use elements will achieve savings in development resources, a shorter timetable and higher quality software. Software of higher quality is expected as these components have already been tested and corrected by the developers as well as corrected according to the faults identified by previous customers. The characteristics of COTS software and quality problems involved in their use are discussed by Basili and Boehm (2001).

(3) **The customer themselves as participant in performing the project.** It is quite common for a customer to perform parts of the project: to apply the customers' special expertise, respond to commercial or other security needs, keep internal development staff occupied, prevent future maintenance problems and so forth. This situation does have drawbacks in terms of the customer–supplier relationship necessary for successful performance of a project, but they are overweighed by the inputs the customer makes. Hence, the inevitability of this situation has become a standard element of many software development projects and contractual relations.

Typical contracting structures of projects are presented in Figure 12.1.

12.3 Risks and benefits of introducing external participants

The main risks to project quality associated with introducing external participants within the framework of the project are as follows.

(1) **Delays in completion of the project.** In those cases where external participants are late in supplying their parts to the software system, the project as a whole will be delayed. These delays are typical for subcontractors'

(a) "Simple" contracting project
(no external participants)

(b) "Compound" contracting project
(with external participants)

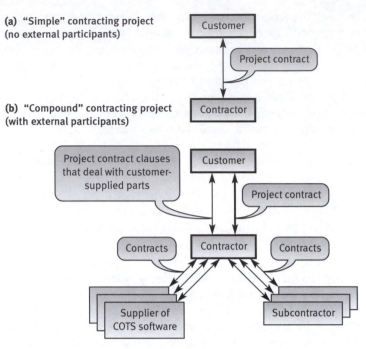

Figure 12.1: Software development projects: typical contracting structures

parts and customers' parts but less so for COTS software suppliers. In many cases the control over subcontractors' and the customers' software development obligations is loose, a situation that causes tardy recognition of expected delays and leaves no time for the changes and reorganization necessary to cope with the delays and to limit their negative effects on the project.

Implementation tip

Purchasing a software package for integration into a newly developed software system usually entails substantial savings of development resources, including budgeted funds. This is especially true when the relevant software has been tested and currently serves a substantial population of users. In some cases the contractor is persuaded to purchase a new, supposedly advanced version of an accepted software package, soon to be put on the market and touted as better suited to his/her requirements. However, it has become common to discover just a week or two later that the version's release is (unexpectedly) delayed – and repeatedly. More thorough investigation into the status of the new version, including requests for information from customers, may also reveal that vital parts – for instance, development of equipment and software interfaces or an advanced application – have been shifted to a later stage.

(2) **Low quality of project parts supplied by external participants.** Quality problems can be classified as (a) defects: a higher than expected number of defects, often more severe than expected; and (b) non-standard coding and documentation: violations of style and structure in instructions and procedures (supposedly stipulated in any contract). Low quality and non-standard software are expected to cause difficulties in the testing phase and later in the maintenance phase. The extra time required to test and correct low-quality software can cause project delays even in cases when external participants complete their tasks on time.

(3) **Future maintenance difficulties.** The fact that several organizations take part in development but only one of them, the contractor, is directly responsible for the project creates two possibly difficult maintenance situations:

   (a) One organization, most probably the contractor, is responsible for maintenance of the whole project, the arrangement commonly stipulated in the tender itself. The contractor may then be faced with incomplete and/or non-standard coding and documentation supplied by the external participants, causing lower-quality maintenance service delivered by the maintenance team and higher costs to the contractor.

   (b) Maintenance services are supplied by more than one organization, possibly the subcontractors, suppliers of COTS software and occasionally the customer's software development department. Each of these bodies takes limited responsibility, a situation that may force the customer to search for the body responsible for a specific software failure once discovered.

Damages caused by software failures are expected to grow in "multi-maintainer" situations. Neither of these situations contributes to good and reliable maintenance unless adequate measures are taken in advance, during the project's development and maintenance planning phases.

(4) **Loss of control over project parts.** Whether intentionally or not, the control of software development by external bodies may produce an unrealistically optimistic picture of the project's status. Communication with external participants' teams may be interrupted for several weeks, a situation that prevents assessment of the project's progress. As a result, alerts about development difficulties, staff shortages and other problems reach the contractor belatedly. The possibilities for timely solution of the difficulties – whether by adaptations or other suitable changes – are thereby often drastically reduced.

Before entering into these agreements, the contractor must consider the associated benefits and risks of introducing external participants in a project. These are summarized in Frame 12.1.

Frame 12.1	Introduction of external participants: benefits and risks

Benefits

For the contractor:

1. Budget reductions
2. Remedy of professional staff shortages
3. Shorter project schedule
4. Acquisition of expertise in specialized areas

For the customer (as external participant):

1. Protecting the customer's commercial secrets
2. Provision of employment to internal software development department
3. Acquisition of project know-how for self-supplied maintenance
4. Project cost reductions

Risks

For the contractor and the customer:

1. Delayed completion of the project caused by delays in completion of parts supplied by external participants
2. Low quality of parts supplied by external participants
3. Increased probability of difficulties in maintaining parts supplied by external participants
4. Loss of control over development of specific project parts

12.4 Assuring the quality of external participants' contributions: objectives

What are the objectives to be obtained by application of SQA tools in the case of parts supplied by external participants? These objectives can be derived directly from the risks listed in Frame 12.1:

(1) To prevent delays in task completion and to ensure early alert of anticipated delays.
(2) To assure acceptable quality levels of the parts developed and receive early warnings of breaches of quality requirements.
(3) To assure adequate documentation to serve the maintenance team.
(4) To assure continuous, comprehensive and reliable control over external participants' performance.

12.5 SQA tools for assuring the quality of external participants' contributions

We can expect external participants to operate their own SQA systems that include the tools necessary for achieving acceptable quality levels for their own software products and services. The tools mentioned here are those that contractors can apply *vis-à-vis* their external participants. For this purpose, the issues of quality and timetable are the most important to be addressed.

The main SQA tools to be applied before and during incorporation of external participants in a software development project are listed in Frame 12.2.

Frame 12.2 **SQA tools applied to external participants in a software development project**

- Requirements document reviews
- Evaluation of choice criteria regarding external participants
- Establishment of project coordination and joint control committee
- Participation in design reviews
- Participation in software testing
- Formulation of special procedures
- Certification of supplier's team leaders and members
- Preparation of progress reports of development activities
- Review of deliverables (documents) and acceptance tests

12.5.1 Requirements document reviews

Requirements documents provide the formal basis for the contracts signed between the contractor and subcontractors as well as for the contract clauses dealing with the customer's obligations to carry out parts of the project. The requirements document is vital for the examination of proposals presented by suppliers of COTS software and the subsequent negotiations regarding their participation. Hence, review of the requirements documents to be presented to external participants is meant to assure their correctness and completeness. The principles guiding the review are similar to those of contract reviews, adjusted to the different role of the contractor in this case – as the customer.

In general, the requirements documents presented by contractors to external participants should be correlated with the customer's requirements. The main issues to be dealt with in a requirements document are presented in Table 12.1.

Table 12.1: Requirements list presented to external participants

Requirements type	Requirements subject
Software functionality	(1) Functional requirements (related to the customer's requirements) (2) Interfaces between the external participant's part and other parts of the project (3) Performance, availability, usability and reliability (related to the customer's requirements) (4) Maintenance services that will be required
Formal and staff	(1) Required qualifications of team leaders and members, including certification where applicable (2) Establishment of coordination and joint control committee including procedures for handling complaints and problems (3) List of documents to be delivered by the external participant (4) Criteria for completion of external participant's part (5) Financial arrangements, including conditions for bonuses and penalties
SQA	(1) Requirements regarding participation in the external participant's design reviews (2) Requirements regarding participation in the external participant's software testing

Implementation tip

One of the main surprises encountered by contractors is the revelation that the subcontractor – without any authorization or prior consent – has subcontracted his task to another company. Whatever the reason or justification for this step, it usually leads to a loss of contractor control over project quality, with the subsequent delays and non-compliance with quality requirements.

Contract clauses dealing with these issues are often inadequate to prevent such behavior. Improved prospects for elimination of such behavior can be achieved only by combining stringent contractual clauses with strict implementation controls.

12.5.2 Choice of external participants

While it is clear that the case of customer participation in a project is difficult if not impossible to circumscribe or prevent, a good degree of choice is available with respect to the other external participants: subcontractors and suppliers of COTS software. General quality assurance procedures, with the appropriate adaptations, can be applied in this situation as well. Any choice of external participants requires collection of information about the candidates, their products and team qualification, and evaluation of that information.

The main tools that support choice are:

- Contractor's information about suppliers and subcontractors based on previous experience with their services
- Auditing the supplier's or subcontractor's quality assurance system
- Survey of opinions regarding the external participants from outside sources.

(1) **Use of contractor's internal information about suppliers and subcontractors.** An external participant (subcontractor or supplier) file, that records past performance, is the main source of information for the contractor. Such an information system is based on cumulative experience with tasks performed by the subcontractor or supplier of COTS software, as well as on information gathered for evaluation of their past proposals. Implementation of this tool requires systematic reporting, based on SQA procedures, by the departments involved:

- Teams of committees that evaluate suppliers' proposals
- User representatives and coordination committee members who are responsible for project follow-up
- "Regular" users who have identified software faults or have gained experience with the supplier's products and maintenance service.

Implementation tip

Two issues impinging on the adequacy of a "Suppliers' File" should be considered:

(a) Individuals evaluating a proposal like to receive full documentation on the organization's past experience with a prospective subcontractor/supplier together with information gathered in the past from various outside sources. Yet, these same individuals are likely to neglect preparing records related to their own experience with an external participant.

(b) Difficulties often result from unstructured reporting to the Suppliers' File. If the information is not properly structured, evaluation and comparison of suppliers become taxing, if not impossible.

The answer to these difficulties frequently lies in the procedures applied and forms used. Procedures that define who should report what and in which situations can limit the reporting burden. A structured reporting form, supported by unstructured descriptions, can be helpful in responding to both issues.

(2) **Auditing the supplier's quality system.** Auditing the supplier's SQA system is often encouraged by the suppliers themselves in an effort to promote acceptance of their proposals. In some cases such an audit is part of the tender requirements. The auditors should take care that the audited features are relevant to the project in its content, magnitude and complexity. Another issue to be considered is the demonstration project and team, which are usually chosen by the supplier. The preferred route is, of course, for the auditors to randomly choose the project and team from a list of relevant projects and teams. This approach is, however, rarely adopted due to objections voiced openly or implicitly by subcontractor and/or supplier.

(3) **Opinions of regular users of the supplier's products.** Opinions can be gathered from internal units that used the supplier's services in the past, from other organizations that have experienced the supplier's services in the past, from professional organizations that certified the supplier as qualified to specialize in the field, and from firms that have had professional dealings with the potential subcontractor or supplier. The purpose of this step is also to ascertain reliability, among other variables that may affect contractual relations.

Systematic evaluation of the suppliers

Evaluation and comparison of potential external participants should be carried out according to procedures adequate to their purpose. Among the factors set down in the procedure are designation of the evaluation committee or responsible manager and the process of evaluation, including the method for defining the relative importance attached to each item and source of information.

12.5.3 The project coordination and joint control committee

The scope of this committee's activities and responsibilities varies in direct relation to the part the external participant will play in the project. Naturally, these will be rather limited in the case of purchased COTS software or reused software in cases where the required supplier's support is minimal and no maintenance is required. Alternatively, substantial coordination and progress control are demanded when subcontractors are to carry out major parts of the project.

The committee's main activities are:

■ Confirmation of the project timetable and milestones
■ Follow-up according to project progress reports submitted to the committee
■ Meeting with team leaders and others in the field in severe situations
■ Making decisions about solutions to timetable and resource shortage problems arising during the project that have been identified during follow-up

- Making decisions regarding solution of problems identified in design reviews and software tests

- Solving disagreements about contract implementation.

Application of the specific SQA procedure that regulates follow-up of external participants' work activities can be of great help.

12.5.4 Participation in design reviews

The extent to which contractors' participation is required in subcontractors' design reviews or customers' reviews of other development activities depends on the nature of the project parts provided by the external participants. When the contractor participates, we can expect him or her to act as a full member of the review. In other words, he or she will read and review the documents before the team's meeting and participate in the team's discussions as well as in the decision taken at the end of the review.

12.5.5 Participation in software testing

Participation in software testing, when required, should include all the stages of the testing process: design reviews of the planning and design of the tests, reviews of the test results, follow-up meetings for the corrections and regression testing. That is, the character of participation in the testing process is sufficiently comprehensive to enable the contractor's representative to intervene, if necessary, to obtain assurance of the quality demanded of the supplied software and the expected timetable for completion of the testing (and correction) process.

12.5.6 Specialized procedures

The specialized procedures that regulate SQA activities within the context of contractual relations with external organizations (i.e., organizations that are not partners in the project contract) have already been mentioned in this chapter. These special procedures are usually adaptations of procedures applied in projects that the organization has carried out. Here, these procedures are mentioned in greater detail. Usually, they are supported by templates, checklists and forms that attach extra value to the fundamental procedures. The main objectives of specialized procedures are:

- Preparation of requirements documents for external participants
- Choice of a subcontractor or supplier of COTS software
- Audit of the subcontractor's SQA system
- The Suppliers' File, its sources of information and mode of operation

- Appointment of the coordination and joint control committee for project parts to be carried out by external participants and preparation of instructions for its operation
- Progress reporting requirements for project parts carried out by external participants.

12.5.7 Certification of external participants' team leaders and other staff

Qualification and certification of the external participants' team leaders and other staff are intended to ensure an acceptable level of professional work *as required by the project or the customer*. This requirement is not to be belittled, for the quality of staff is the heart of any contractual relationship. The SQA activities required here are:

- Qualification and certification of staff should be listed as a contractual requirement
- Implementation of these clauses is to be confirmed by the contractor at the outset of the work
- Changes and replacement of the respective team members are to be approved by the contractor
- Implementation of these clauses by the contractor is to be periodically reviewed.

Implementation tip

Subcontractors under pressure from other projects or for other reasons frequently try to replace qualified and professional certified team members needed elsewhere with staff who are not fully qualified and/or lack certification. "Partial" violations – with the team leader or team member allocating his or her time, without approval, on more than one project – are also common. The control activities mentioned should deter the subcontractor from changing staff in this manner and help the contractor quickly identify violations should they occur.

12.5.8 Progress reports

When external participants share the project's workload, the main progress reports prepared for the coordination and joint progress control committee are as follws:

- **Follow-up of the risks identified in the project work.** This report describes the current status of the risks identified in previous reports, such as shortage of professionals having special expertise, shortage of equipment, and difficulties in development of a module. For risks still unsolved, the report should discuss possible remedial actions. The new risks identified in the period covered by the report, as well as the actions to be taken and their prospects, should also be mentioned.

■ **Follow-up of the project's schedule.** This report focuses on activities that are behind schedule, and milestones expected to be reached later than scheduled. The report describes the actions taken to minimize delays and suggests further actions and changes in plans to be approved by the committee.

Two other issues to be covered in progress reports are:

■ The follow-up of the usage of resources
■ The follow-up of the project budget.

In most of the cases where subcontractors or suppliers of COTS software perform their parts as fixed-price tasks, these issues seem to be of importance mainly to the external participants. However, it is clear that an unfavorable situation regarding these two issues can affect the project's quality, an event that makes them of immediate concern to the contractor.

12.5.9 Review of deliverables (documents) and acceptance tests

Two of the most powerful tools for assuring the quality of external participants, primarily subcontractors and customer-supplied software, are thorough review of software development documents ("deliverables") by the contractor and acceptance tests, planned, designed and carried out by the contractor. These tools provide independent and direct review of development documents and testing of the software components of the external participant's products.

It has been suggested that the presence of the subcontractor's representative in design review teams could replace the contractor's independent review of deliverables and acceptance tests. In many cases, cost and timetable considerations force contractors to be satisfied with participation in the system testing process carried out by the subcontractor. Decisions regarding these options should be taken very carefully.

Summary

(1) Explain the difference between contractors and external participants.

Software development contractors are organizations or groups of organizations that are contracted by a customer in a project contract to develop a software system. External participants are organizations that participate in the development process, performing small to large parts of the work, but are not legally designated sides in the project's contract.

(2) List the types of external participants, and explain the benefits they provide to the contractor.

The external participants can be categorized into three main groups:
- Subcontractors
- Suppliers of COTS software and reused software modules
- The customer themselves as an active participant in performing parts of the project.

The main benefits to the contractor of using external organizations are:
- **Overcoming shortages of professional staff** by transferring parts of the project to be carried out to firms employing staff having those skills.
- **Potentially shorter project schedules,** achieved by purchasing COTS software and reused software rather than developing the software.
- **Expertise acquired in areas that need specialization** through the participation of owners – the subcontractor or the customer's development department – of that expertise.
- **Saved budget,** achieved when subcontractors offer prices below those incurred by performing the project internally, and by the use of COTS and reused software.

(3) Describe the risks for the contractor associated with turning to external participants.

- **Delays in completion of the project parts** due to the external participants' competing interests, given that the contractor is the only party committed to living up to schedule demands as stated in the project contract signed with the customer. Even the customer – as supplier for their own project – might prefer another project and delay completion of their part.
- **Low quality of project parts** caused by insufficient capabilities, attempts to save resources, or other factors.
- **Future maintenance difficulties** due to low quality or non-standard software and/or incomplete or poor documentation of parts carried out by external participants.
- **Loss of control over parts of the project** instigated by periods of cut-off communication, whether intentionally or inadvertently initiated.

(4) List the SQA tools appropriate for use with external participants and add short statements regarding the risks they help to eliminate or reduce.

- **The requirements document review** assures a correct and complete list of the requirements related to software functionality, to formal and staff aspects of the project and to SQA issues; it contributes mainly to delay reduction and fewer cases of low quality.
- **Choice of external participants,** if done properly, reduces all types of risks, especially those related to low quality.
- **The project coordination and joint control committee,** if it operates properly, discovers anticipated as well as unanticipated delays, quality problems and potential for loss of control over the project at early stage. Early alerts and cooperation can reduce and even eliminate these risks. The committee's suggested solutions to quality problems, especially those related to documentation, also reduce future maintenance difficulties.

- **Participation in design reviews** provides an excellent opportunity to examine the real quality of a subcontractor's work and to introduce corrections where necessary. The review's main contribution is to low-quality product reduction.
- **Participation in software testing,** like participation in design reviews, contributes to the reduction of low-quality products. Furthermore, such participation enables the contractor to be alerted about possible delays in the work schedule, and can help reduce the effects of those delays.
- **Specialized procedures** are part of the contractors' SQA infrastructure and are meant to handle all kinds of risky situations.
- **Qualification and certification of the supplier's team leaders and other staff** assure the professional capacities of the project teams, and contribute to reduction of low-quality products.
- **Progress reports of external participants' development activities** are prepared mainly in order to reduce the risk of delays.
- **Review of deliverables (documents) and acceptance tests** is aimed at assuring the quality of the work performed by the external participant and consequently reduces the risks of future maintenance difficulties.

Selected bibliography

1. Basili, V. R. and Boehm, B. (2001) "COTS-based systems Top 10 list", *Computer*, 34(5), 91–93.
2. IEEE (1998) "IEEE Std 1062-1998–IEEE Recommended Practices for Software Aqcuisition", in *IEEE Software Engineering Standards Collection*, The Institute of Electrical and Electronics Engineers, New York.
3. ISO (1997) *ISO 9000-3:1997(E), Quality Management and Quality Assurance Standards – Part 3: Guidelines for the Application of ISO 9001:1994 to the Development, Supply, Installation and Maintenance of Computer Software*, 2nd edn, International Organization for Standardization (ISO), Geneva.
4. ISO/IEC (2001) "ISO 9000-3:2001 Software and System Engineering – Guidelines for the Application of ISO 9001:2000 to Software, Final draft", International Organization for Standardization (ISO), Geneva, unpublished draft, December 2001.
5. Oskarsson, O. and Glass, R. L. (1996) *An ISO 9000 Approach to Building Quality Software*, Prentice Hall, Upper Saddle River, NJ.

Review questions

12.1 Customers as suppliers of parts of the project are listed as one of the three types of external participants. Compared to subcontractors and suppliers of COTS software, the customer as supplier causes special difficulties to the contractor before and during implementation of the project.

   List these special difficulties and explain their possible effects on the project.

12.2 External participants introduce four main risks into the project's quality.

   List the main risks and explain in your own words the implications of each.

12.3 Employing external participants provides the contractor with four major benefits with respect to carrying out a project.

List the main benefits to the contractor and explain in your own words the implications of each.

12.4 The customer enjoys four principal benefits from the employment of external participants when carrying out a project.

List the main benefits to the customer and explain in your own words the implications of each.

12.5 Qualifications and certification requirements for team leaders and team members are included in many subcontracting contracts.

(1) Can you suggest examples of project team functions and list some relevant qualification and certification requirements?
(2) What do contractors expect to gain from qualification and certification requirements?

12.6 For contractors, project adherence to schedule and discovery of hitherto unknown project risks are the main areas of their interest in progress reports.

Explain in your own words what actions are to be taken and what information items are to be required to assure that progress reports comply with these two demands.

Topics for discussion

12.1 Refer to the HealthSoft case (Section 12.1).

(1) List the errors made by Healthsoft in the proposal preparation stage.
(2) List the errors committed by HealthSoft during performance of the project.
(3) Suggest SQA tools that could have prevented the above errors.

12.2 A nationwide furniture store chain has issued a tender for the development of its new generation software system, integrating advanced data communication systems, online applications and a new feature – an Internet site – to display the chain's products. The chain received several proposals, two of which were chosen for the last stage of the tender. Both contenders were well-established software houses, experienced in large-scale projects and enjoying good professional reputations. Both proposals fully cope with the tender schedule and other organizational demands, as well as with the software specification requirements. The difference in price between the proposals is negligible.

■ **Proposal A:** The "in-house proposal", based on entirely in-house development, would integrate various company teams. The company declared that substantial parts of the project will be based on reused software modules taken from the company's reused software library.

■ **Proposal B:** The "big coalition proposal" is based on six external participants, half of them suppliers of reused software, the others subcontractors that are leading specialists in their field of expertise.

You have been appointed to present your recommendations regarding the final choice between the final proposals.

(1) Which of the two final proposals do you recommend?
(2) List your arguments for and against your preferred proposal.
(3) Given that the cost of the proposal not preferred (not recommended in question (1) is 10% lower than the preferred proposal, would you consider changing your recommendation? What are your arguments?

12.3 In Topic 12.2, three sources of information are reviewed in the process of choosing external participants.

(1) List each source of information and explain in your own words the contribution of each.
(2) Why is it important to use all three types of sources?
(3) What are the difficulties involved in employing each type of information source?

12.4 Some professionals claim that in cases where the contract specifies review of deliverables and acceptance tests of project parts carried out by external participants, the contractor has no justification to participate in design reviews and software tests.

(1) Do you agree with the professionals? List your arguments.
(2) Do you agree with others who suggest that there is no need to carry out acceptance tests in cases where comprehensive participation in design reviews and software tests has been executed? List your arguments.

chapter 13

CASE tools and their effect on software quality

An increasing variety of specialized computerized tools (actually software packages) have been offered to software engineering departments since the early 1990s. The purpose of these tools is to make the work of development and maintenance teams more efficient and more effective. Collectively named CASE (computer-aided software engineering) tools, they offer:

- Substantial savings in resources required for software development
- Shorter time to market
- Substantial savings in resources required for maintenance
- Greater reuse due to increased standardization of the software systems
- Reduced generation of defects coupled with increased "interactive" identification of defects during development.

It is clear that this last characteristic is the one most attracting the interest of software quality analysts to CASE tools.

In light of their characteristics, CASE tools serve as a source for easing the amount of effort expended on development of increasingly complex and large software systems.

The following sections will deal with the subjects:

- What is a CASE tool?
- How can CASE tools contribute to the improved quality of software products?

- How can CASE tools contribute to the improved quality of software maintenance?
- How and to what extent can CASE tools contribute to maintaining development process timetables and keeping with budgets?

After completing this chapter, you will be able to:

- Explain the difference between "classic" and "real" CASE tools and provide examples of each.
- Explain the contribution of CASE tools to software development.
- List the main contributions of real CASE tools to product quality.
- Explain the contribution of CASE tools to software quality maintenance.

13.1 What is a CASE tool?

Frame 13.1 contains the basic definition of a CASE tool.

> **Frame 13.1   CASE tools – definition**
>
> CASE tools are computerized software development tools that support the developer when performing one or more phases of the software life cycle and/or support software maintenance.

The definition's generality allows compilers, interactive debugging systems, configuration management systems and automated testing systems to be considered as CASE tools. In other words, well-established computerized software development support tools (such as interactive debuggers, compilers and project progress control systems) can readily be considered *classic* CASE tools, whereas the new tools that support the developer for a succession of several development phases of a development project are referred to as real CASE tools. When referring to *real* CASE tools, it is customary to distinguish between *upper* CASE tools that support the analysis and design phases, and *lower* CASE tools that support the coding phase (where "upper" and "lower" refer to the location of these phases in the Waterfall Model – see Section 7.1), and *integrated* CASE tools that support the analysis, design and coding phases.

The main component of real CASE tools is the *repository* that stores all the information related to the project. The project information accumulates in the repository as development proceeds and is updated as changes are initiated during the development phases and maintenance stage. The repository of the previous development phase serves as a basis for the next phase. The accumulated development information stored in the repository provides support for the maintenance stage in which corrective, adaptive and functionality improvement tasks are performed. The computerized management of the repository guarantees the information's consistency and its compliance with project methodology as well as its standardization according to style and structure procedures and work instructions. It follows that CASE tools are capable of producing full and updated project documentation at any time. Some lower CASE and integrated CASE tools can automatically generate code based entirely on the design information stored in the repository. Reverse engineering (re-engineering) tools are also considered to be real CASE tools. Based on the system's code, these tools are applied mainly for recovery and replication of (now non-existing) design documents for currently used, well-established software systems ("legacy" software). In other words, reverse engineering CASE tools operate in the opposite direction of "regular" CASE tools: instead of creating system code on the basis of design information, they automatically create complete, updated repository and design documents on the basis of system code.

Figure 13.1 describes the application of CASE tools in the development process in comparison to the traditional development process.

The support that CASE tools provide the developer can be in one or more of the following areas, listed in Table 13.1.

Table 13.1: CASE tools and the support they provide to developers

Type of CASE tool	Support provided
Editing and diagramming	Editing text and diagrams, generating design diagrams according to repository records
Repository query	Display of parts of the design texts, charts, etc.; cross-referencing queries and requirement tracing
Automated documentation	Automatic generation of requested documentation according to updated repository records
Design support	Editing design recorded by the systems analyst and management of the data dictionary
Code editing	Compiling, interpreting or applying interactive debugging code for specific coding language or development tools
Code generation	Transformation of design records into prototypes or application software compatible with a given software development language (or development tools)
Configuration management	Management of design documents and software code versions, control of changes in design and software code*
Software testing	Automated testing, load testing and management of testing and correction records, etc.
Reverse engineering (re-engineering)	Construction of a software repository and design documents, based on code: the "legacy" software system. Once the repository of the legacy software is available, it can be updated and used to automatically generate new versions of the system. As new re-engineered software version is generated, it can be easily maintained and its documentation automatically updated
Project management and software metrics	Support progress control of software development projects by follow-up of schedules and calculation of productivity and defects metrics

* For more about configuration management, see Chapter 18.

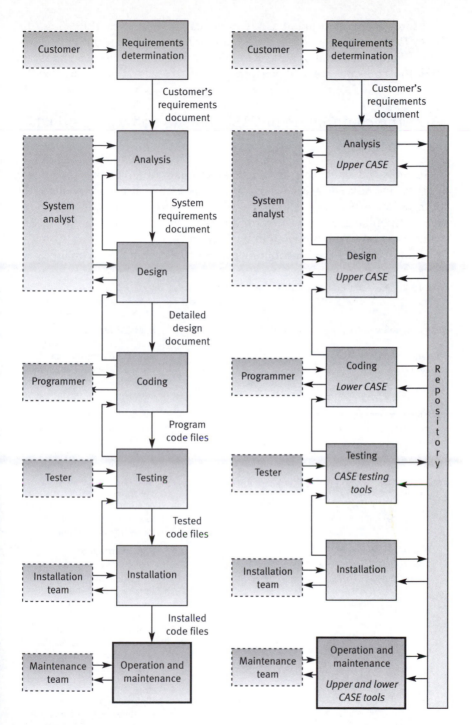

(a) Traditional development life cycle   (b) Real CASE tool-supported development life cycle

Figure 13.1: Traditional vs. CASE-supported development life cycle

More information about CASE tools can be found in IEEE Std 1462 (IEEE, 1998) and in the software engineering literature, particularly Pressman (2000), Sommerville (2001) and Kendall and Kendall (1999). The impact of CASE tools on software quality assurance is discussed by McManus (1999).

13.2 The contribution of CASE tools to software product quality

CASE tools contribute to software product quality by reducing the number of errors introduced in each development phase. In order to evaluate this contribution, we now examine the quality improvements anticipated for each of the nine causes of software errors listed in Section 2.3. We include classic and real CASE tools in our evaluation.

Table 13.2 lists the contributions CASE tools can make to quality.

Table 13.2: CASE tools and the quality of software products

Cause of software errors	Extent and manner of contribution to quality	
	Classic CASE tools	Real CASE tools
1. Faulty requirements definition		**Almost no contribution** Computerized examination of requirements consistency or correctness is rarely possible.
2. Client–developer communication failures		**Almost no contribution** In most cases, computerized identification of communication failures is impossible. Communication failures can be located or prevented only when a change or other information is found to be inconsistent with repository information.
3. Deliberate deviations from software requirements		**High contribution** Based on information stored in the repository, deviations from recorded requirements are identified as inconsistent and labeled as errors. Such deviations can also be identified by repository-based requirements tracing tools and cross-referenced query tools.
4. Logical design errors		**High contribution** (1) Re-engineering enables automated generation of the design of legacy systems and their recording in a repository.

Cause of software errors	Extent and manner of contribution to quality	
	Classic CASE tools	Real CASE tools
4. Logical design errors		**High contribution** (2) Use of the repository is expected to identify design omissions, changes and additions inconsistent with repository records.
5. Coding errors	**Very high contribution** Application of compilers, interpreters and interactive debuggers.	**Very high contribution** Application of lower CASE tools for automated code generation achieves full consistency with the design recorded in the repository. In addition, as coding is automatic, no coding errors are expected.
6. Non-compliance with coding and documentation instructions	**Limited contribution** Use of text editors and code auditing supports the standardization of structure and style of texts and code and facilitates identification of non-compliance.	**Very high contribution** Application of lower CASE tools for automated code generation assures full compliance with documentation and coding instructions.
7. Shortcomings in the testing process	**High contribution** Automated testing tools perform full regression and automated load testing. Computerized management of testing and corrections reduces errors by improvement follow-up.	**High contribution** Application of lower CASE but especially of integrated CASE tools prevents coding errors and reduces design errors. Application of repository tools (cross-referenced queries and performance consistency checks) to corrections and changes during the development process prevent most software errors.
8. Procedural errors	**High contribution** Control of versions, revisions and software installation by means of software configuration management tools.	**Limited contribution** Use of updated and full documentation is expected to prevent many of the maintenance errors caused by incomplete and/or inaccurate documentation, especially if the design has been revised several times.
9. Documentation errors	**Limited contribution** Application of text editors only	**High contribution** Use of repository automatically generates full and updated documentation prior to each correction or change.

13.3 The contribution of CASE tools to software maintenance quality

Classic but especially real CASE tools contribute to the various types of software maintenance quality in several ways.

Corrective maintenance:

■ CASE-generated full and updated documentation of the software enables easier and more reliable identification of the cause for software failure.

■ Cross-referenced queries enable better identification of anticipated effects of any proposed correction.

■ Correction by means of lower CASE or integrated CASE tools provides automated coding, with no expected coding errors as well as automated documentation of corrections.

Adaptive maintenance:

■ Full and updated documentation of the software by CASE tools enables thorough examination of possible software package adaptations for new users and applications.

Functional improvement maintenance:

■ Use of the repository enables designers to assure consistency of new applications and improvements with existing software systems.

■ Cross-referenced repository queries enable better planning of changes and additions.

■ Changes and additions carried out by means of lower CASE or integrated CASE tools enable automated coding, with no expected coding errors as well as automated documentation of the changes and additions.

13.4 The contribution of CASE tools to improved project management

Let us compare two projects of similar nature and magnitude: Project A is carried out by conventional methods, Project B by advanced CASE tools. The following results were obtained after comparison of the planning and implementation phases:

Method of development	Project A Conventional tools	Project B CASE tools
Planned resources (man-months)	35	20
Actual resources invested	42	27
Planned completion time (months)	15	9
Actual completion time	18	12

Two items quickly attract our attention:

(1) The advanced CASE method was much more economical than the conventional method.

(2) The quality of management in both projects was similar, with resources and schedule estimated at below the required levels.

In general, application of CASE tools is expected to reduce project budgets and development time ("shorter time to market"). However, the contribution made by CASE tools to the quality aspects of project management, namely budget control and timetables, is the focus of our interest. At the moment, it appears that use of real CASE tools does substantially reduce deviations from the implementation budget and planned schedule from the plan, especially because they prevent high error rates and provide for easier and shorter error correction when required.

For project management to be improved still further, project control tools (considered here under the category of classic CASE tools) and improved budget and time estimation methodologies must be developed.

Summary

(1) Explain the contribution of CASE tools to software development.

A major contribution of CASE tools to software development is improvement of the developer's productivity and shortening of the development period. Even more impressive is the contribution to productivity and quality of software maintenance. Another highly relevant contribution is software reuse, supported by the complete, updated documentation and maximum standardization. Last, but not least important is the contribution to software quality attained through substantial reduction of errors.

(2) Explain the difference between classic and real CASE tools and provide some examples.

Classic CASE tools are long-established computerized tools that support developers (and maintenance teams) in one of several development phases. Compilers, graphical editors and automated testing tools are examples of these tools. *Real* CASE tools are "new" tools that apply repositories for storage of software development information that can be applied for several development phases. Cross-referencing tools based on repository data, integrated CASE tools and reverse engineering tools are examples of real CASE tools.

(3) List the main contributions of real CASE tools to product quality.

- Identification of deviations from design requirements.
- Identification of design inconsistencies.
- Automated generation of code based on the repository design records, with no expected errors.

- Full compliance with design and coding documentation instructions achieved by the automated coding and the repository-based documentation.
- High quality corrections and changes made during development due to the repository tools support.
- Automated generation of a repository of legacy systems by CASE reverse engineering tools enables efficient development of new generations of the software system with maximal assurance of software quality.

(4) Explain the contribution of CASE tools to the quality of software maintenance.

Application of CASE tools affects quality issues for all maintenance service components:

- The full and updated documentation provided by CASE repositories assures the consistency of repairs, changes and additions within the existing system and enables thorough examination of applications of the existing system.
- The cross-referencing repository tool facilitates planning and prevents a significant proportion of design errors.
- The automated coding carried out by CASE tools eliminates coding errors.

Selected bibliography

1. IEEE (1998) "IEEE Std 1462-1998 – Information Technology – Guidelines for the Evaluation of CASE Tools", in *IEEE Software Engineering Standards Collection*, The Institute of Electrical and Electronics Engineers, New York.
2. Kendall, K. E. and Kendall, J. E. (1999) *Systems Analysis and Design*, 4th edn, Prentice Hall, Upper Saddle River, NJ.
3. McManus, J. I. (1999) "Software Quality Assurance CASE Tools", in G. G. Schulmeyer and J. I. McManus (eds), *Handbook of Software Quality Assurance*, 3rd edn, Prentice Hall, Upper Saddle River, NJ, pp. 381–402.
4. Pressman R. S. (2000) *Software Engineering – A Practitioner's Approach*, European adaptation by D. Ince, 5th edn, McGraw-Hill International, London.
5. Sommerville, I. (2001) *Software Engineering*, 6th edn, Addison-Wesley, Harlow, Essex, UK.

Review questions

13.1 Explain in your own words the expected benefits of using CASE tools for software system developers and software maintenance teams.

13.2 "The main component of real CASE tools is the repository."

(1) Define "repository" in your own words.

(2) List the functions a repository fulfills and explain their impact on software development productivity.

(3) List the functions a repository serves and explain their impact on software quality.

13.3 Software development and functional improvement maintenance are said to have much in common.

    (1) Discuss their similarities regarding quality assurance and application of CASE tools. List and explain which CASE tools, if any, can be applied in common.

    (2) Discuss the special quality assurance problems typical of functional improvement maintenance and how CASE tools can be applied in their correction.

13.4 The contribution of real CASE tools to the quality of project management is debatable.

    (1) Describe the quality aspects of project management.

    (2) Discuss what contributions real CASE tools can make to the quality of project management and why.

Topics for discussion

13.1 It has been claimed that "the availability of full and updated documentation provided by an Integrated CASE (I-CASE) system is of higher value for a maintenance team than for a development team."

    (1) Discuss the above statement as it relates to the team's productivity.

    (2) Discuss the above statement as it relates to the quality of the work performed by the teams.

13.2 The Shureshure/Ashure Insurance Company has just marked completion of a re-engineering project that generated a new version of its main legacy software system. The budget for the re-engineered alternative was 30% below the budget estimated for development of a similar but new software system. The re-engineered version, which includes a list of additions and changes, was developed by applying a fourth generation lower CASE tool that replaced the third generation language of the legacy system. The project, planned to take six months, was completed one week earlier than scheduled.

The company's monthly magazine dedicated two pages to a report of the event. In its description of the satisfaction felt from the project, the following statements were made:

> ". . . The management expressed their full satisfaction from the project's budget and their admiration of the team's punctuality."

> ". . . The leaders of the quality assurance and software maintenance teams declared that the new software version is a real success. It can be maintained more easily and with fewer failures when compared to the former legacy system."

> ". . . The only staff disappointed with the system were the managers of the Operations and Local Branches Departments. They claimed that the users they represent are highly dissatisfied with the new version."

(1) Why was the software maintenance team leader satisfied with the system? Try to list his arguments.

(2) Why was the software quality assurance team leader satisfied with the system? Try to list her arguments.

(3) Can you suggest why users were dissatisfied with the re-engineered version?

part IV

Software quality infrastructure components

Some software quality assurance components are of a general nature; they are common to many projects and maintenance activities, to all design reviews, to all testing routines. Components of this nature represent "the infrastructure of software quality assurance". As infrastructure, they are the main tools employed to prevent software errors and promote the quality level of the entire organization. The responsibility for their development, updating, maintenance, and distribution is usually laid in the hands of the quality assurance team.

What are typical infrastructure components?

- Procedures and work instruction
- Quality support devices like templates and checklists
- Staff SQA training and certification activities
- Preventive and corrective actions
- Software configuration management
- Documentation and quality records control.

The elements comprising these components, their development, updating and use, are the subjects of the chapters found in Part IV of this book.

Procedures and work instructions

A *procedure* is "a particular way of accomplishing something or of acting" (Webster's New College Dictionary). In other words, procedures, as transmitted in documents, are the detailed activities or processes to be performed according to a given method for the purpose of accomplishing a task. The procedures adopted by an organization are considered to be binding on that organization's employees, meaning that each employee is to perform his or her tasks according to the steps appearing in the relevant procedure document, often bearing the name of the designated task. Procedures also tend to be universal within the organization, meaning that they are applied whenever the task is performed, irrespective of the person performing the task or the organizational context.

Work instructions are used mainly in cases where a uniform method of performing the task throughout the organization is either impossible or undesirable. As a result, work instructions are specific to a team or department; they supplement procedures by providing explicit details that are suitable solely to the needs of one team, department, or unit.

The software quality assurance procedures and work instructions of special interest to us are those that affect the quality of a software product, software maintenance or project management.

Professionally developed and maintained SQA procedures are required to conform to the organization's quality policy but also tend to conform to international or national SQA standards. An important point to bear in mind when preparing them is that procedural conformity with an SQA standard supports certification of the organization's SQA system (see Part VI). The ISO 9000-3 standard (ISO, 1997; ISO/IEC, 2001) is one of the main certification standards that guide the preparation of procedures. Smith and Edge (1991) present examples of procedures.

Figure 14.1 presents a conceptual hierarchy frequently used to govern development of procedures and work instructions.

This chapter's sections will discuss the following:

■ The need for SQA procedures

■ Procedures and procedure manuals

■ Work instructions and work instruction manuals

■ The organizational framework for preparing, implementing and updating procedures and work instructions.

After completing this chapter, you will be able to:

■ Explain the contribution of procedures to software quality assurance

■ Explain the difference between procedures and work instructions

■ List the activities involved in maintaining an organization's procedures manual.

14.1 The need for procedures and work instructions

■ "Why should we use SQA procedures and work instructions?"

■ "Wouldn't it be better if every professional relied on his own experience and performed his task the best way he knows?"

■ "What are the benefits to the organization of forcing me to perform a task only in the way chosen by them?"

Figure 14.1: A conceptual hierarchy for development of procedures and work instructions

Questions like these are frequently voiced by staff in most organizations. The answers uncover the challenge to be met by procedures and work instructions: application of the organization's accumulated know-how, experience and expertise.

SQA procedures and work instructions aim at:

- Performance of tasks, processes or activities in the most effective and efficient way without deviating from quality requirements.

- Effective and efficient communication between the separate staffs involved in the development and maintenance of software systems. Uniformity in performance, achieved by conformity with procedures and work instructions, reduces the misunderstandings that lead to software errors.

- Simplified coordination between tasks and activities performed by the various bodies of the organization. Better coordination means fewer errors.

14.2 Procedures and procedures manuals

Procedures

Procedures supply all the details needed to carry out a task according to the prescribed method for fulfilling that task's function. These details can be viewed as responding to five issues, known as the *Five W's*, listed in Frame 14.1.

Frame 14.1	The Five W's: issues resolved by procedures

- **W**hat activities have to be performed?
- Ho**W** should each activity be performed?
- **W**hen should the activity be performed?
- **W**here should the activity be performed?
- **W**ho should perform the activity?

Standardization – the application of a fixed format and structure – is the principle applied to all SQA procedures. A typical example for a fixed table of contents that can be used for all the organization's procedures is presented in Frame 14.2.

Although they are not mandatory features, appendices are commonly used to present reporting forms and documentation related to the activities included in a procedure. Other appendices provide tables and lists that support choice of the appropriate sequence of activities among the options, if any, defined by the procedure.

An example of this approach is presented in Appendix 14A. The method chapter of the procedure reproduced employs a table format. The main advantage of a table format as compared with textual descriptions is clarity of presentation of responsibilities and the activity's documentation requirements. The annex to this sample procedure presents the form to be used when preparing a design review report.

Frame 14.2   **Fixed table of contents for procedures**

1 Introduction *

2 Purpose

3 Terms and abbreviations *

4 Applicable documents

5 Method

6 Quality records and documentation

7 Reporting and follow-up *

8 Responsibility for implementation *

9 List of appendices *

Appendices *

* Sections included only if applicable

Implementation tip

Constructing and choosing appendices

Documentation and report forms, but especially tables or lists of conditions that determine alternative sequences of activities and tables that define limits to authority, tend to change frequently in response to external developments or internal modifications of the product or task. Most such changes do not reflect any inherent modification of the procedure. Appendices that provide these details simply provide a handy way to introduce changes without interfering with the procedure itself.

The procedures manual

The collection of all SQA procedures is usually referred to as the *SQA procedures manual*. The contents of any one organization's procedures manual varies according to:

■ The types of software development and maintenance activities carried out by the organization

■ The range of activities belonging to each activity type

■ The range of customers (e.g., internal, customers of custom-made software, COTS software customers) and suppliers (e.g., self-development and maintenance, subcontractors, suppliers of COTS software and reused software modules)

■ The conceptions governing the choice of method applied by the organization to achieve desired SQA objectives.

How are these differences expressed in the SQA procedures manual? While one organization may require a broad range of procedures, another organization may be satisfied with a limited range of procedures. However, the specific number of procedures and their structure considerably depend on editorial and style decisions, not just type of procedure.

A useful approach for defining the structure of the table of contents of the SQA procedures manual is to use the table of contents of the related SQA standard as a skeleton. Table 14.1 presents an example of applying this approach. As we can readily see, the organization's manual divides procedures into categories according to the corresponding ISO standard sections (in the table, the table of contents found in ISO 9000-3 is used for illustrative purposes).

Table 14.1: SQA procedures manual: table of contents

ISO 9000.3 – table of contents	SQA procedures manual – table of contents
4.1 Managerial responsibility	1.1 The company's SQA policy 1.2 Management quality review
4.2 Quality system	2.1 The SQA organization 2.2 Procedures and work instructions – preparation, approval and distribution 2.3 The annual quality planning
4.3 Contract review	3.1 Contract review
4.4 Design control	4.1 Development and quality plans 4.2 Quality assurance of the design
4.5 Document and data control	5.1 Document control
4.6 Purchasing	6.1 Subcontractors and suppliers file management 6.2 Pre-contract review for subcontractor proposal 6.3 Acceptance tests for subcontracted software
4.7 Control of customer-supplied products	7.1 Acceptance tests for customer-supplied software
4.8 Product identification and traceability	8.1 Configuration management
4.9 Process control	9.1 Software development process
4.10 Inspection and testing	10.1 Unit tests and integration tests 10.2 Software system tests 10.3 Customer's acceptance tests
4.11 Control of inspection, measuring and test equipment	— Not applicable
4.12 Inspection and test status	12.1 Progress control for software development project
4.13 Control of non-conforming product	13.1 Control of design and code corrections
4.14 Corrective and preventive actions	14.1 Corrective and preventive actions
4.15 Handling, storage, packaging, preservation and delivery	15.1 Installation and delivery
4.16 Control of quality records	16.1 Control of quality records

Table 14.1: Continued

ISO 9000.3 – table of contents	SQA procedures manual – table of contents
4.17 Internal quality audits	17.1 Internal quality audits
4.18 Training	18.1 Training and certification of employees
4.19 Servicing	19.1 Maintenance plan
	19.2 Change requests management
	19.3 Dealing with customers' complaints
4.20 Statistical techniques	20.1 Quality metrics
	20.2 Quality assurance costs

14.3 Work instructions and work instruction manuals

As mentioned above, work instructions deal with the application of procedures, adapted to the requirements of a specific project team, customer, or other relevant party. While general methodology is defined in a procedure, the precise details that allow its application to a specific project or unit are often laid out in a work procedure. In no case can work instructions contradict their parent procedure, although several instructions can be associated with any given procedure. This means that one can add, change or cancel work instructions without altering the respective procedure.

Examples of work instructions, summarized in their titles, are found in Frame 14.3.

Frame 14.3   SQA work instructions subjects – examples

Departmental work instructions

- Audit process for new software development subcontractors (supplier candidates)
- Priorities for handling corrective maintenance tasks
- Annual evaluation of software development subcontractors
- On-the-job instructions and follow-up for new team members
- Design documentation templates and their application
- C++ (or other language) programming instructions

Project management work instructions

- Coordination and cooperation with the customer
- Weekly progress reporting by team leaders
- Special design report templates and their application in the project
- Follow-up of beta site reporting
- Monthly progress reporting to the customer
- Coordination of installation and customer's team instructions

An "active" SQA procedures manual conceals numerous, often ongoing activities that guarantee the procedures' continued applicability: for instance, preparation of the procedures, their implementation and regular updating. These ongoing activities performed by SQA team members together with members of the teams and organizational units involved, assure that the procedures are properly adapted to changes in technology as well as clientele and competition.

Preparation of new procedures

The initial steps taken in development of a new SQA procedures manual should deal with the conceptual and organizational frameworks that determine the menu of the proposed procedures and who will be responsible for their preparation, updating and approval. This framework is usually also formulated as a procedure (frequently called *the procedure of procedures*). The subsequent steps will, naturally, deal with specific procedures. A common approach to preparation of procedures is the appointment of an *ad hoc* committee of professionals working in the units involved, SQA unit members and experts in the respective topics to be dealt with. The committee pours over the proposed drafts until a satisfactory version is reached, and ceases its work only after the procedure is approved by the authorized person(s). An alternative approach to procedure manual preparation is dependence on consulting, where an outside expert is assigned the responsibility of preparing one procedure, some procedures or the complete manual. The main advantages of employing a consultant are found in the added value of his or her expertise and experience in other organizations, the reduced burden on the organization's senior professionals as well as the shortened task completion timetable. The main disadvantage experienced with this approach is reduced applicability due to the organization's unique characteristics.

Implementation of new or revised procedures

Approval of a new or revised procedure says little about the ease of that procedure's implementation, which is a separate and often difficult issue. In many cases, distribution of the material in printed or e-mail form and instruction of the team or unit are insufficient to assure full or nearly full conformity. The fact that members of a team or department were involved in the procedure's preparation helps convince their colleagues to abide by the new requirements but this, too, is often inadequate. Follow-up and individual instruction of those who lack or disregard the new procedure is mandatory for the procedure's integration within daily routines.

Updating procedures

The motivation to update existing procedures is based, among other things, on the following:

- Technological changes in development tools, hardware, communication equipment, etc.
- Changes in the organization's areas of activity
- User proposals for improvement
- Analysis of failures as well as successes
- Proposals for improvements initiated by internal audit reports
- Learning from the experience of other organizations
- Experiences of the SQA team

Implementation tip

A procedure (as well as a work instruction) that has not been updated for a considerable period (e.g. three years) is, in most cases, obsolete: it is no longer needed or, more commonly, simply ignored. Both situations justify review of the procedure and its implementation environment. Periodic review of "neglected" (i.e., unused) procedures can generally remedy this situation by initiating updating or removal of the procedures from the manual.

Once the need to update is recognized, a mechanism similar to that applied when preparing new procedures can be put into operation: an *ad hoc* team is convened to prepare the updated version, followed by authorization and implementation activities. This implies that updating should be viewed as a stage integral to software quality assurance, as important as preparing new procedures.

Summary

(1) Explain the contribution of procedures to software quality assurance.

SQA procedures are assumed to reflect the most adequate method known to date for the performance of design and maintenance activities. SQA procedures that are up-to-date and fully implemented by developers and maintenance teams assure conformity of their activities to the software's quality requirements and performance of the associated activities in an efficient and effective performance. At the same time, uniform development and maintenance enables easier and more effective professional review together with better communication with the maintenance team. It likewise facilitates cooperation and coordination between all the bodies, internal and external, involved in the project. Not less important is the reduction in errors made possible by uniformity.

(2) Explain the difference between procedures and work instructions.

Procedures define the activities performed in order to achieve given tasks, where performance is universal to the entire organization. Work instructions are complementary tools, used to define local variations in the application of the procedures by specific teams and/or departments. Work instructions, however detailed and targeted, cannot contradict the organization's procedures.

(3) List the activities involved in maintaining an organization's procedures manual.

The activities involved include the activities for preparing new procedures, updating existing procedures and implementing new and updated procedures. Involved in these efforts are the organization's SQA team members in addition to members of *ad hoc* committees gathered to prepare a new or update an existing procedure. Participants in the implementation process include unit leaders and SQA trustees.

Selected bibliography

1. ISO (1997) *ISO 9000-3:1997(E), Quality Management and Qualtity Assurance Standards – Part 3: Guidelines for the Application of ISO 9001:1994 to the Development, Supply, Installation and Maintenance of Computer Software*, 2nd edn, International Organization for Standardization (ISO), Geneva.
2. ISO/IEC (2001) "ISO 9000-3:2001 Software and System Engineering – Guidelines for the Application of ISO 9001:2000 to Software, Final draft, International Organization for Standardization (ISO), Geneva, unpublished draft, December 2001.
3. Smith, D. J. and Edge, J. S. (1991) *Quality Procedures for Hardware and Software*, Elsevier Applied Science, Barking, Essex, UK.

Review questions

14.1 Figure 14.1 presents a conceptual hierarchy for development of SQA procedures and work instructions.

(1) Describe each of the components of the diagram in your own words.
(2) Explain the meaning of each of the hierarchical relationships defined in the diagram in your own words.

14.2 List the benefits of implementing an SQA procedures manual in an organization.

14.3 The table of contents suggested in Frame 14.2 includes an optional section, "Terms and abbreviations".

(1) Do you recommend including terms like software program, printed output, configuration management or ATM in this section? List your arguments.
(2) What criteria should be applied when including a term or abbreviation? List your arguments.

14.4 Some software quality experts claim that a standard procedures manual with no changes or adaptations can serve 90% of the organization.

Do you agree with this statement? List your arguments.

Topics for discussion

14.1 "The Software Lions" recently completed compilation of their SQA procedures manual. The following are the "purpose" and "method" sections taken from the "certification of professional employees" procedure.

2. Purpose

2.1. To determine the professional positions that require certification and the respective updating processes.

2.2. To define the process by which a candidate is certified.

5. Method

5.1. Candidates for a position that requires certification, whether new or long-term employees, must successfully pass the relevant certification examination before entry into the position.

5.2. The content and format of the certification examinations will be prepared by the Quality Assurance Unit after consultation with the Chief Software Engineer. The certification examinations will be approved by the General Manager of the company.

5.3. A list of Examiners will be determined for every position that requires certification.

5.4. A candidate for a position that requires certification will be directed to one of the listed Examiners.

5.5. The Examiner will report the results of the certification examinations to the Quality Assurance Unit. The candidate will be able to appeal against the results. In special circumstances, the candidate can be re-examined.

5.6. The department that is interested in a candidate's appointment will be informed about the certification examination results.

5.7. The Quality Assurance Unit will update the content and format of the certification examinations in response to organizational changes and information technology developments.

5.8. Management will receive a summary report of the certification examinations and their results.

(1) Read the sections of the proposed procedure carefully and list your comments while referring to any defects and shortcomings (usually incomplete sections).

(2) For each item listed in question (1), suggest an appropriate change, addition or deletion in order to correct the detected defects or shortcomings.

14.2 "Wild Solutions" is a medium-sized software house, employing about 250 staff. The new SQA manager has decided to prepare several new procedures to replace very old and outdated procedures. You are asked to join him in his efforts and prepare a draft for the procedure entitled "Progress control of software development projects".

The procedure should deal with the following subjects:

(a) Preparation of a timetable, manpower resources usage plan and budget

(b) Progress reporting for those parts of the project carried out by the company

(c) Progress reporting for those parts of the project carried out by subcontractors, partners and the customer(s)

(d) Control process for progress reporting

(e) Updating of the timetable, manpower resources usage plan and budget

(f) Responses to deviations from the timetable, manpower resources usage plan and budget in parts carried out by the company

(g) Responses to deviations from the timetable, manpower resources usage plan and budget in parts carried out by subcontractors

(h) Responses to deviations from the timetable, manpower resources usage plan and budget in parts carried out by partners or customers.

(1) Sketch what you imagine to be the company's organizational chart. The chart will serve for your procedure draft.

(2) Prepare a draft of the "Progress control of software development projects" procedure. The procedure should cover all eight subjects listed above. Add appendices if required.

(3) List your assumptions regarding the procedure.

14.3 As an SQA unit member, you are required to prepare the first draft of a new procedure.

(1) Suggest what sources of information may be used to prepare the draft.

(2) Mark those sources mentioned in your answer to (1) that are essential for a good draft.

14.4 It is recommended that the new and updated procedures be prepared by an *ad hoc* committee rather than by an expert member of the SQA unit or a consultant.

(1) List the expected advantages of the "committee" option in preparing new and updated procedures. Does reliance on "expert" option have any advantages at this stage?

(2) List the expected advantages of the "committee" option to be realized in the implementation stage.

Appendix 14A   Design review procedure

Bla-Bla Software Industries Ltd	SQA procedures
SQA Procedure 8-09: Design reviews	Revision 8 (8 May 2003)

1 Introduction

Design reviews are carried out throughout software development projects according to the project's quality plan, as defined in procedure 8-02.

2 Purpose

To define the method for carrying out design reviews in software development projects.

3 Scope

The Procedure will apply to all software development projects, excluding minor projects carried out according to procedure 8-17.

4 Applicable documents

Procedure 8-02: Project quality plan for software development projects.
Procedure 8-17: Minor software development projects.

5 Method

No.	Step	Activity	Responsibility: performer / approval	Documentation	Notes
5.1	Preparation of design documents	Preparation of complete draft of design documents	Perf: project leader Approval: not required	Drafts of design documents	
5.2	Coordination of DR meeting	(1) Define list of participants	Perf: project leader Approval: Development dept. manager	(1) List of participants	(1) See project quality plan for preliminary list of participants
		(2) Coordination of DR meeting	Perf: DR team leader Approval: not required	(2) DR invitation letters to DR team members	(2) See contract for customer's participation
		(3) Delivery of documents to DR team members	Perf: DR team leader Approval: not required		(3) Delivery of documents in printed or electronic form at least 48 hours before DR meeting
5.3	DR meeting	Agenda: – Presentation (concise) – DR team comments and discussion – Definition of action items (AI)	Perf: DR team members Approval: not required	DR minutes	See DR report template in Annex to the procedure

Bla-Bla Software Industries Ltd
SQA Procedure 8-09: Design reviews

SQA procedures
Revision 8 (8 May 2003)

323

Appendix 14A Design review procedure

No.	Step	Activity	Responsibility: performer / approval	Documentation	Notes
5.3	DR meeting	Agenda: – Designation of AIs schedule and person responsible for their execution – Designation of DR member responsible for follow-up of corrections – DR team decision about continuation of development work	Perf: DR team	DR minutes	See DR report
5.4	DR report	(1) Preparation of DR report	Perf: DR team leader Approval: DR team members	DR report	The report should be completed and signed within 48 hours of the meeting
		(2) Distribution of report to participants as well as chief software engineer, development dept. manager, head of quality assurance unit	Perf: DR team leader. Approval: not required		
5.5	Implementation of DR decisions	(1) Implementation of required corrections included in AIs list	Perf: project team Approval: project leader	Re manual preparation ents	
		(2) Examination of corrections and approval by DR team member	Perf: DR team member Approval: not required	(1) Approval of each correction (2) Approval of completion of all corrections	

Prepared by: Dave Towers   QA engineer   Date: 3 April 2002   Signed: Dave Towers
Approved: Barry Hotter   Head, QA unit   Date: 2 May 2002   Signed: Barry Hotter

Annex: DR report form

DR report

Date of the DR: _____ Project title: _____

Participants: _____

_____

DR type: _____

Documents reviewed

Document title	Version and revision

Action items (AIs)

No.	Description of AI	Responsibility	Scheduled completion	Approval of completion	
				Completion date	Signed

Decisions: ( ) Approved

( ) Approval conditional upon completion of all AIs

( ) Corrected document should be submitted for repeated review
     The repeated DR will be on _____

( ) Other: _____

_____

DR team member responsible for follow up: _____

Signed: _____   _____   _____   _____   _____

Name: _____   _____   _____   _____   _____

Date: _____   _____   _____   _____   _____

              DR leader   Member   Member   Member   Member

Supporting quality devices

We often refer to documents prepared in the past to save time and confirm that nothing has been forgotten. For example, we scan old reports in order to apply their tables of contents to the current report we are about to compile. In other situations, we look for lists of previously asked questions prior to preparing a design review session. In still other cases we wonder why no form can be found for a quite common reporting task. The element common to all these situations is the savings in time we expect to realize by using simple support devices for repetitive tasks.

In addition to saving time, these simple tools – especially templates and checklists – contribute to software quality assurance in various ways. This chapter deals with the contributions made by these devices, considered as infrastructure tools, and the organizational aspects related to their preparation, implementation and revision.

After completing this chapter, you will be able to:

- Explain the main contribution of templates to software quality assurance.
- Explain the main contribution of checklists to software quality assurance.
- List the activities involved in maintaining templates and checklists.

15.1 Templates

In other areas of work, a *template* is "a gauge, pattern or mold (as a thin plate or board) used as a guide to the form of a piece being made" (Webster's New College Dictionary). When applied to software engineering, the term template refers to a format (especially tables of contents) created by units or organizations, to be applied when compiling a report or some other type of document. Application of templates may be obligatory for some documents and elective for others; in some cases, only part of a template (e.g., specific chapters or general structure) is demanded.

Three examples of templates are presented in the following frames:

- Frame 10.2: Software test plan (STP)
- Frame 10.3: Software test description (STD)
- Frame 10.4: Software test report (STR).

Additional examples of templates appear in Chapter 18:

- Frame 18.4: Software change request (SCR)
- Frame 18.6: Documentation of software configuration release.

A comprehensive collection of templates was developed by the US Department of Defense for use with documents to be completed by software development contractors according to the military standard MIL–STD–498 (DOD, 1994). The military standard uses the term DID – Data Item Description – in place of template. The DIDs provide the very detailed tables of contents suitable for the documentation required in the large-scale software development contracts typical of military projects. In addition to section titles, the DIDs include explanations of the contents expected in each section of the report. A total of 22 DIDs are available for the users of MIL-STD-498, for instance:

- Software Requirements Specification (SRS)
- System/Subsystem Design Description (SSDD)
- Computer Operator Manual (COM)
- Interface Design Description (IDD)
- Software Test Plan (STP)
- Software Version Description (SVD).

The next section deals with the contribution of templates to software quality and the efforts required for producing, maintaining and implementing templates.

15.1.1 The contribution of templates to software quality

Template use is quite advantageous to development teams and to review teams. For development teams, template use:

- **Facilitates the process of preparing documents** by saving the time and energy required to elaborate the report's structure. Most organizations allow templates to be copied from a SQA public file or downloaded from the organization's intranet files, which even saves keying the table of contents to the new document.

- **Ensures that documents prepared by the developer are more complete** as all the subjects to be included in the document have already been defined and repeatedly reviewed by numerous professionals over the course of the template's use. Common errors, such as overlooking a topic, are less likely to occur.

- **Provides for easier integration of new team members** through familiarity. The document's standard structure, prepared according to templates that may be known to the new member from previous work in another of the organization's units or teams, makes finding information much easier. It also smoothes ongoing document preparation in cases where parts of the document have been prepared by another team member who may or may not have left.

- **Facilitates review of documents** by eliminating the need to study a document's structure and confirm its completeness, if the document is based on the appropriate template. It also simplifies review of the completed document as its structure is standard and reviewers are familiar with its expected contents (chapters, sections and appendices). As a result of this consistency, the review is expected to be more thorough yet less time-consuming.

For software maintenance teams, template use:

- **Enables easier location of the information** required for performing maintenance tasks.

15.1.2 The organizational framework for preparing, implementing and updating templates

Organizations tend to save their internal resources, which often means employing successful reports prepared for one department or purpose as models for the entire organization. Thus, if Mr Brown's or Mr Johnson's reports have acquired a reputation as comprehensive and highly professional, their tables of contents may be used as templates by their colleagues. One disadvantage of this situation is that not everyone who can benefit from these templates is aware of their existence. Another disadvantage is that further improvement of the templates, accomplished through their review by professional teams, may be thwarted.

The SQA unit is usually responsible for preparing professional templates of the more common types of reports and documents required of the organization's staff. Informal initiatives from the field may spur the SQA unit to action, but developing the general infrastructure for use of templates, the subject of this section, is inherent in the unit's mission.

Preparation of new templates

Development of a template infrastructure naturally centers on the work of a group of professionals devoted to the task. This group (or committee) should include senior staff who represent the various software development lines, the department's chief software engineer and SQA unit members. Informal developers of "template services" should likewise be encouraged to join the group.

One of the group's first tasks is to compile a target list of templates to be developed. Once the list is accepted, priorities must be set. Higher priority should be given to templates of the most commonly prepared documents as well as to "informal" templates already in use (it is estimated that only minimal efforts are required for their completion and authorization). Subcommittees are then assigned the task of preparing the first drafts. An SQA unit member can be anticipated to undertake the task of leading the group, but a template "freak" who is also a member of the committee may just as readily be chosen for the job. Irrespective of who the group's head may be, he or she must see to the distribution of template drafts among members, the organization of meetings and the follow-up of progress made by template preparation subcommittees. Distribution of template drafts among team leaders for their comments can yield important improvements and at the same time promote the templates' future use.

The most common information sources used in preparing a template are as follows:

- Informal templates already in use in the organization
- Template examples found in professional publications
- Templates used by similar organizations

Application of templates

Several fundamental decisions are involved in the implementation of new or updated templates:

- What channels should be used for advertising the templates?
- How should the templates be made available to the organization's internal "consumers"?
- Which templates will be compulsory and how can their application be enforced?

All professional internal means of communication can be used for advertising templates internally within the organization: leaflets, e-mail, SQA intranet as well as short presentations at meetings.

One of the most efficient methods of making templates available to the organization is the internal net (**intranet**), to be preferred to any paper-based route. Distribution through the internal net ensures user choice of the updated version of the template needed and, at the same time, saves keying in (required for paper-based templates) of the document's table of contents.

Directions regarding compulsory use of specific templates are generally found in the organization's procedures or work instructions. The chief software engineer or another senior staff member is usually authorized to determine the list of compulsory templates appropriate to the selected procedure, although we can expect the template group to submit its own recommended list.

Updating templates

The decision to update an existing template may be considered a reactive measure, stemming from any of the following:

- User proposals and suggestions
- Changes in the organization's areas of activity
- Proposals initiated by design review and inspection teams based on their review of documents prepared according to the templates
- Analysis of failures as well as successes
- Other organizations' experience
- SQA team initiatives.

The process of updating templates is quite similar to that of template preparation.

15.2 Checklists

The checklist used by software developers refers to the list of items specially constructed for each type of document, or a menu of preparations to be completed prior to performing an activity (e.g., installing a software package at the customer site). Checklists are planned to be comprehensive if not complete. Usually, checklist use tends to be considered an optional infrastructure tool, depending mainly on the list's professional attributes, user acquaintance with the list and availability.

Some checklists have dual purposes: while providing a complete list of items to be verified, they also provide space for documenting findings of the checks performed. Figure 15.1 presents an example of a dual-purpose checklist, applied for design reviews of requirement specification documents.

Two additional examples of checklists can be found in Chapter 5:

- Appendix 5A: Proposal draft reviews – Subjects checklist
- Appendix 5B: Contract draft review – Subjects checklist

Several examples of comprehensive and detailed checklists may be found in Perry (1995). For example, one such checklist is entitled "Work Paper 5.1: Requirement Phase Test Process" (pp. 84–98).

Next we deal with the contribution of checklists to software quality and the efforts required for establishing, maintaining and applying those lists.

Goldenbug Ltd
Checklist for requirement specification report

Project name: _____

The reviewed document: _____ Version: _____

Item no.	Subject	Yes	No	N.A.*	Comments
1	**The document**				
1.1	Prepared according to configuration management requirements				
1.2	Structure conforms to the relevant template				
1.3	Reviewed document is complete				
1.4	Proper references to former documents, standards, etc.				
2	**Specifying the requirements**				
2.1	Required functions were properly defined and clearly and fully phrased				
2.2	Designed inputs conform with required outputs				
2.3	Software requirement specifications conform with product requirements				
2.4	Required interfaces with external software packages and computerized equipment are fully defined and clearly phrased				
2.5	GUI interfaces are fully defined and clearly phrased				
2.6	Performance requirements – response time, input flow capacity, storage capacity – are correctly defined and fully and clearly phrased				
2.7	All error situations and required system reactions are correctly defined and fully and clearly phrased				
2.8	Data interfaces with other existing or planned software package or products components are correctly defined and fully and clearly phrased				
2.9	Procedures to test fulfillment of the specified requirement are correctly and fully defined and clearly phrased				
3	**Project feasibility**				
3.1	Are the specified requirements feasible considering the project's resources, budget and timetable?				
3.2	Are the specified performance requirements (see 2.6) feasible considering the constraints imposed by other system components and by external systems interfaced with the system?				

Comments: *N.A. = Not applicable

Signed: Name: _____Date: _____ Signature: _____

Figure 15.1: Dual-purpose checklist – DR checklist for requirement specification documents

Like templates, checklists provide many benefits to development teams, software maintenance teams and document quality.

The advantages to development teams are as follows:

- **Helps developers carrying out self-checks of documents or software code** prior to document or software code completion and formal design reviews or inspections. Checklists are expected to help the developer discover incomplete sections as well as detect overlooked lapses. Checklists are also expected to contribute to the quality of documents or software code submitted for review as the quality issues to be surveyed by the review team are already listed in the checklist.

- **Assists developers in their preparations for tasks** such as installation of software at customer sites, performance of quality audits at subcontractors' sites or signing contracts with suppliers of reused software modules. Checklists are expected to help the developers be better equipped for task performance.

The advantages to review teams are:

- **Assures completeness of document reviews by review team members** as all the relevant review items appear on the list.

- **Facilitates improves efficiency of review sessions** as the subjects and order of discussion are defined and well known in advance.

15.2.2 The organizational framework for preparing, implementing and updating checklists

Though highly recommended, the use of checklists remains discretionary. Checklist preparation and updating, like promotion of their use, are usually assigned to the SQA unit. A "checklist group", headed by a SQA unit member, can undertake the task of maintaining a collection of updated lists. The participation of other staff interested in promoting the use of checklists in the group is also voluntary; in some cases, however, the assistance of an SQA consultant is recommended. In the remainder of this section, we describe the processes required to maintain a checklist infrastructure: preparation of new checklists, promotion of their use and updating.

Preparation of new checklists

One of the first tasks awaiting the "checklist group" is compilation of a list of checklists targeted for development, followed by definition of a common format for all the checklists released by the group.

The first checklists approved by the group are usually informal checklists already in use by some development team members and reviewers. In most cases, a few changes and adaptations of these checklists are sufficient to satisfy the format and contents defined by the group. Preparation of new checklists as well as improvement of informal checklists is supported by the following sources of information:

- Informal checklists already in use in the organization
- Checklist examples found in books and other professional publications
- Checklists used by similar organizations.

The process of preparing a new checklist is similar to that for templates.

Promotion of checklist use

As the use of checklists is rarely mandatory, promotion of their use is based on advertising and guaranteed availability. All internal channels of communication can be used for publicizing the checklists: leaflets, e-mail, SQA intranet as well as professional meetings. The internal net remains, however, the preferred and most efficient method for making checklists available to the organization's internal "consumers".

Updating checklists

Like templates and procedures, initiatives to update an existing checklist generally flow from the following sources:

- User proposals and suggestions
- Changes in technology, areas of activity and clientele
- Proposals initiated by design review and inspection teams emanating from document reviews
- Analysis of failures as well as successes
- Other organizations' experience
- SQA team initiatives.

The process of updating checklists is quite similar to their preparation.

Summary

(1) Explain the main contribution of templates to software quality assurance.

- Documents submitted for review tend to be more complete. As a result, review teams can direct their efforts to further improvement of the final product.
- Document reviews are facilitated as their structure is standard and well known among reviewers. Freed of structural concerns, reviewers can focus on issues of document content.

(2) Explain the main contributions of checklists to software quality assurance.

- Checklists support document completeness and improve document quality as all the relevant items and quality issues to be reviewed are already listed.
- Conduct of review sessions becomes less problematic when topics and their order of priority are defined and well known. An efficient session is expected to carry out a thorough analysis of comments by reviewers.

(3) List the activities involved in maintaining templates and checklists.

The activities involved in maintaining state-of-the-art compilations of template and checklist collections include preparation, implementation and updating. The preparation and updating for both types of document is the work of groups of interested staff, including those who have already offered informal templates and checklists to their colleagues. Leadership of the group is usually an SQA unit obligation. The group members decide on target lists of templates and checklists, which they later try to complete. Drafts are prepared with the assistance of informal templates and checklists, releases found in the professional literature and collections used in similar organizations. Team members, SQA unit members and others, especially those in the field, can readily initiate updating efforts. Updates are meant to improve current releases on the basis of team and external experience, cope with organizational changes, altered consumer tastes, failure analysis results, and so forth.

The implementation of templates and checklist is successful when the majority of users or the relevant internal consumers apply them regularly. Successful application is based on promotion activities and on ready availability. Promotion is based on advertising, especially along internal communication networks, while easy access is usually achieved through the internal net. In many organizations, use of some or all templates is compulsory, a situation that demands adequate procedures and/or work instructions.

Selected bibliography

1. DOD (1994) *MIL-STD-498 DIDs*, US Department of Defense.
2. ISO (1997) *ISO 9000-3:1997(E)*, *Quality Management and Quality Assurance Standards – Part 3: Guidelines for the Application of ISO 9001:1994 to the Development, Supply, Installation and Maintenance of Computer Software*, 2nd edn, International Organization for Standardization (ISO), Geneva.
3. ISO/IEC (2001) "ISO 9000-3:2001 Software and System Engineering – Guidelines for the Application of ISO 9001:2000 to Software, Final draft", International Organization for Standardization (ISO), Geneva, unpublished draft, December 2001.
4. Perry, W. (1995) *Effective Methods for Software Testing*, John Wiley & Sons, New York.

Review questions

15.1 Explain the advantages of templates in your own words.

15.2 The SQA unit has prepared a list of eight new additional templates awaiting preparation.

(1) Whom do you recommend for participation in an *ad hoc* committee for preparing the templates?

(2) The head of the SQA unit is considering hiring an SQA consultant to join the committee. Is this advisable? List your arguments.

(3) If you agree with the unit's head, what tasks would you prefer the consultant to attend to? List your arguments.

15.3 Explain the advantages of the use of checklists in your own words.

Topics for discussion

15.1 Mr John Bogart, head of the SQA unit, has decided that henceforth it will be mandatory for all developers to apply the templates included in the well-known *Templates Manual for the SQA Professional*. A procedure has been prepared to enforce adherence to the templates. The Manager of the Software Development Department is asked to approve the procedure.

(1) Would you recommend that the manager approve the procedure? List your arguments.
(2) If your recommendation is against approval of the procedure, suggest how the department's informal templates, if deemed more suitable than the *Manual*'s templates, can be adopted.

15.2 Tommy, a software development team leader, tends to delete standard (i.e., template) sections and chapters that are not applicable from the tables of contents of the documents he compiles. He claims that by doing this the documents "look nicer".

(1) Do you agree with this method of adapting templates to current application?
(2) What are the disadvantages of "template editing" by the team leader? What do you recommend doing in cases of inapplicable template chapters or sections?

15.3 An SQA professional claims that the availability of design review checklists makes the DR redundant.

(1) Do you agree with this claim? List your arguments.
(2) Compare the expected situation in the following two DR sessions: the first, when the designers do not use a checklist, and second, when designers make use of a DR document checklist.

15.4 It is suggested that the revised edition of the *Templates and Checklists Procedure* include the following section: "If a template or checklist has not been updated or changed for a period of 36 months, a team should be nominated to check these templates and checklists and recommend the required changes and updates. The SQA unit is responsible for performing the needed review at least semi-annually. A committee, nominated by the head of the Software Development Department, should submit its recommended changes and updates not later than six months after their nomination."

(1) Is the proposed procedure for updating templates and checklists justified or a waste of time?
(2) Suggest situations where templates and checklists, accepted as proper and highly professional when released, deserve to be changed.

15.5 It is recommended that an *ad hoc* committee (or group) rather than an expert member of the SQA unit or a consultant prepare a new and updated checklist file.
List the expected advantages and disadvantages of the committee/group option for performing this task.

Staff training and certification

It goes without saying that keeping staff abreast of the latest professional knowledge available is the key to achieving quality in development and maintenance. Moreover, it is generally accepted that regular professional training, retraining and updating are mandatory if the gap between required and current professional knowledge is to be kept as narrow as possible. Internal certification (hereinafter just "certification") of staff members assigned to key software development and maintenance positions is another, complementary tool for assuring professional quality. Internal certification of staff should not, however, be confused with the certification awarded by the American Society for Quality (ASQ), which confers CSQE status (see below) in addition to other types of certification, or the professional certification granted by commercial organizations such as Microsoft or Novell.

The importance of professional training as a vital component of any SQA system is stressed in ISO 9000-3 as well as the CMM Guidelines (see ISO, 1997; ISO/IEC, 2001; Paulk *et al.*, 1995). Job descriptions and training program development for SQA personnel are discussed by Mendis (1999).

Also of interest is the program for certified software quality engineers (CSQE) delivered by the American Society for Quality (ASQ), described by Hamilton (1999) and an ASQ brochure (ASQ, 1999).

The training and certification process and the activities that comprise it are dealt with in the different sections of this chapter.

After completing this chapter, you will be able to:

- Explain the main objectives of training and certification.
- Discuss what is needed to prepare a training and updating program.
- List the main components of a certification program.
- Explain the objectives of follow-up of trained and certified staff performance and the main sources of the follow-up data.

16.1 Introduction: surprises for the "3S" development team

Team 7 of "3S – Sahara Software Specialists" started a new project for Apollo Ltd three weeks late because of delays in completion of the previous project. Severely pressured for time, the team leader decided to cancel the scheduled five-day training course on the new Athena application generator to be used for subsystem F, as required by the contract. He believed that the concise Athena manuals supplied by the customer would be an adequate substitute for the course. This decision proved to be very costly. The two team members responsible for subsystem F found it very difficult to apply a generator they had never used. In addition to the three days spent receiving expert advice, they were forced to spend 25 working days more than were scheduled to complete the subsystem. At this point, the project was two weeks behind schedule, yet some hope still existed that they could close the gap during the 18 weeks left to complete the package prior to the system tests. Then, within the space of two weeks, two of the team's six programmers abruptly resigned and left. As no programmers could be shifted in-house, management turned to an employment agency and requested that they find replacements as quickly as possible. The team leader was relieved as the urgently needed programmers were located and recruited, on a temporary basis, within a few days. Both new team members were experienced programmers and almost never troubled the other team members with requests for assistance or instruction. This arrangement seemed to suit the situation wonderfully as it did not interfere with the intensive efforts exerted to complete the project with minimal delay.

Considering the project's unexpected difficulties – the Athena application problems and the resignation of the two programmers – the team felt very lucky to manage to complete the programming stage by 11 November, only 11 days behind schedule.

The team's troubles began in earnest with the issuance of the testers' report three weeks later. Together with a long list of minor defects, the report mentioned numerous severe faults in units A2, A6, A7, A9 and A11 of sub-system A and in F5 and F7 of subsystem F. Although correction of the faults detected in units F5 and F7 required only five days of programmer time, correction of the faults found in the other units proved to be a different story. All five units of subsystem A were programmed by John Abrams, one of the temporary programmers recruited by the agency, who had already left the company. The two team members who were directed to repair the units were confronted with unexpected difficulties: in addition to grave programming errors and incorrect understanding of the relevant design documents, the coding did not comply with any company coding procedures or work instructions. When describing the situation, they jokingly stated that they felt more like archeologists than programmers. Later, they concluded that John Abrams' professional qualifications were far below those claimed in his letters of recommendation. After investing several days in attempts to correct the errors, four out of the five units were recoded because all efforts to repair the existing code came to naught. In the end, six exhausting weeks were spent on bringing these units up to shape.

At this point, seven weeks behind schedule, the team leader concluded that the "super saver strategy" applied to training, as well as the "super short-cut procedure" implemented in recruitment, instruction and follow-up, had proven to be quite costly.

16.2 The objectives of training and certification

The objectives of training and certification are listed in Frame 16.1.

Frame 16.1 **The objectives of training and certification**

- To develop the knowledge and skills new staff need to perform software development and maintenance tasks at an adequate level of efficiency and effectiveness. Such training facilitates integration of new team members.

- To assure conformity to the organization's standards for software products (documents and code) by transmitting style and structure procedures together with work instructions.

- To update the knowledge and skills of veteran staff in response to developments in the organization, and to assure efficient and effective performance of tasks as well as conformity to the organization's style and structure procedures and work instructions.

- To transmit knowledge of SQA procedures.

- To assure that candidates for key software development and maintenance positions are adequately qualified.

These **objectives** conform with the general **goals** of software quality assurance by inspiring management to persistently nurture the level of knowledge and skills displayed by staff and to improve their efficiency and effectiveness (for more about SQA goals, see Section 2.5.3).

16.3 The training and certification process

The operation of a successful training and certification system demands that the following activities be regularly performed:

- Determine the professional knowledge requirements for each position
- Determine the professional training and updating needs
- Plan the professional training program
- Plan the professional updating program
- Define positions requiring certification
- Plan certification processes
- Deliver training, updating and certification programs
- Perform follow-up of trained and certified staff.

All these activities converge into an integrated process in which feedback from past activities and information about professional developments stimulate a cycle of continuous training, certification and adaptation to changing quality requirements.

Training and certification activities are meant to fill the needs of veteran staff and new employees. Comprehensive follow-up of the outcomes of current programs as well as keeping track of developments in the profession are required to make sure that programs are adequately up-to-date. A detailed discussion of each of these activities is presented in the next sections.

The training and certification process is displayed in Figure 16.1.

16.4 Determining professional knowledge requirements

The most common positions in a software development and maintenance organization are those of systems analyst, programmer, software development team leader, programming team leader, software maintenance technician, software tester, and software testing team leader. Most organizations set education and experience requirements for each of these positions. Staff members who fulfill education requirements still need additional "local" or "internal" knowledge and skills, related to specific development and maintenance procedures. This specialized knowledge can be grouped into two categories:

- Knowledge and skills of software engineering topics, such as software development tools, programming language versions, and CASE tool versions applied by the specific organization or unit. The relevant procedures and work instructions that were compiled for their implementation also belong to this category.

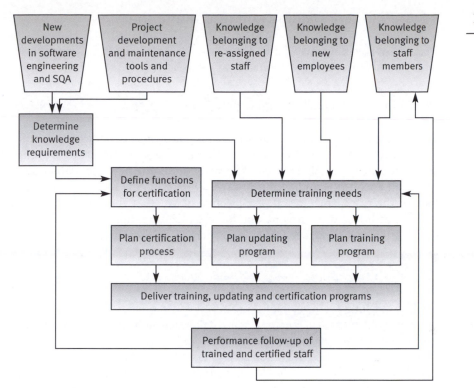

Figure 16.1: The training and certification process

■ Knowledge of SQA topics, such as the procedures pertaining to the various development and maintenance activities, assigned to be performed by the individual occupying a specific position.

16.5 Determining training and updating needs

Training and updating needs are determined by comparison of the staff's current knowledge with the updated knowledge requirements. The type of training is adapted to the needs of three distinct groups of staff:

■ Training: for new employees, according to their designated assignment
■ Retraining: for employees assigned to new positions or receiving new assignments
■ Updating: for staff members as demanded by their position.

The need to update staff should be assessed regularly to facilitate planning of the required programs.

Finally, follow-up of staff performance in the wake of training and updating provides major input to be used in redefining training needs.

16.6 Planning training and updating programs

Practically speaking, two basic programs should be devised – one for software engineering topics and one for SQA topics.

Planning training and updating programs for software engineering topics

The timing of many training and retraining activities cannot be determined in advance because new personnel are recruited and veteran staff are shifted often after relatively short notice. However, updating activities can be scheduled well ahead (the audience is known), with contents finalized close to the date of their implementation. Irrespective of whether the programs are carried out in-house or by an outsourcing organization, high-level staff, such as the chief software engineer, usually participate in their preparation.

Implementation tip

Unless the software development organization is rather large, it often happens that only one or a small number of new staff needs to be trained or retrained. Moreover, as new employees may be recruited to a variety of different positions, the training program may have to be highly differentiated. When the same training program applies to the entire staff, the training is frequently inappropriate for carrying out specific tasks, with the subsequent negative implications on software quality. On-the-job as well as computer-aided training (e-learning) can provide appropriate solutions in such situations.

Planning training and updating programs for SQA topics

Training programs for SQA topics include training for new employees as well as updating for veteran staff members. The general characteristics of SQA training programs allow them to be organized periodically, every one or two months, and delivered to all new staff recruited in the interim. Typical SQA updating programs are carried out once a year or once every six months, depending on the pace of change. The SQA unit or others responsible for SQA issues in the organization usually prepare these training and updating programs.

16.7 Defining positions requiring certification

It is commonly accepted that assignment of personnel to key positions in software development and maintenance organizations requires extreme care. One of the procedures used to guarantee the suitability of candidates is certification. Examples of positions frequently requiring certification of their occupants are software development team leader, programming team leader, software testing team leader, software maintenance technician and internal quality auditor. The last two positions are particularly sensitive because their occupants' activities are usually performed by one staff member, acting alone, and subject to little close control or support by superiors.

A certification committee (or a designated senior staff member) defines the list of positions that require certification and whether the certification will be effective permanently or for a limited period. Considering the volatility of the profession, this list should be revised periodically. Renewal of limited period certification demands that staff members demonstrate up-to-date knowledge and skills according to the current certification requirements.

The list of positions that require certification naturally varies by firm or organization. Some use certification sparingly while others apply this tool on a large scale, even to standard programmers.

16.8 Planning the certification processes

Certification is intended to provide a framework for the thorough investigation of a candidate's qualifications and a demonstration of his or her professional knowledge and skills. The details of the certification process are unique to the organization; they reflect its special characteristics, areas of specialization, software development and maintenance tools, customers and so on. Because the process is geared toward the needs and decisions of specific organizations, internal certification cannot be automatically substituted by the general certification that is granted by professional societies and leading suppliers of development tools and network communication software or their equivalents.

The certification process, in every detail and for every position, requires approval as defined in the certification procedure.

Typical certification requirements

For the individual undergoing certification, a typical certification process entails meeting some or even all of the following requirements:

- Professional education: academic or technical degrees and in some cases certification by a professional organization or by a leading commercial software producer
- Internal training courses
- Professional experience in the organization (may be partially or completely replaced by experience in other organizations)
- Assessment of achievements and ability as noted in periodic performance appraisals
- Evaluation by the candidate's direct superior (often by completion of a special questionnaire)

- Demonstration of knowledge and skills by means of a test or a project
- Mentor's supervision for a specified period of time.

Functions of the certification committee
Similar to the pattern recommended for training and retraining programs, the person or committee members responsible for certification are usually senior software development and maintenance staff. The responsibilities of the certifying body include:

- To perform the certification process on the basis of requests made by individual applicants or units and grant certification to those who qualify
- To follow up certification activities (such as mentoring) carried out by others
- To update certification requirements in response to developments in the organization as well as the profession
- To revise the list of positions requiring certification.

> **Implementation tip**
>
> An additional task to be performed by those responsible for certification is the active search for qualified personnel who can be encouraged to become certified for a future position. The latter may then serve as a "reservoir of certified candidates".

Example: Certification requirements at SKF Advanced Software
SKF Advanced Software is a medium-sized software house. The firm's certification requirements document for programming team leader is presented in Frame 16.2.

16.9 Delivery of training and certification programs

Training and updating can cover topics such as software engineering, software quality assurance and management skills (within the framework of certification or for general information), all of which are coordinated with the organization's or firm's needs. How training and updating are carried out varies accordingly. Courses can be transmitted in formats that range from short lectures and demonstrations, often lasting only half a day, to lengthy courses held over several weeks or months. These may be conducted in-house, by the organization's training unit, or externally, by vocational or academic institutions that prepare programs attuned to the organization's requirements.

More about organizing and delivering training and certification programs can be found in the human resources management literature.

Frame 16.2	SKF Advanced Software – position certification document (example)

SKF Advanced Software

Position Certification Document

Position 11.3 – Programmer team leader

Version 5 Valid as from 1.4.2002

Approved by C. Haley   Position: Chief software engineer   Date of approval: 3 March 2002

Certification requirements

- *Professional education*. Two options – (a) BA or BSc in software engineering or an equivalent degree, or (b) Technician or equivalent degree in software engineering granted by a recognized school.

- *Internal training courses*. Two required courses – (1) Project management: 5-day course. (2) Advanced project management: 5-day course.

- *Professional experience in the organization*. For candidates holding a technician's degree – three years of experience as a programmer in SKF. For candidates holding an academic degree – two years of experience as a programmer in SKF. For candidates having over five years of recognized experience as a programmer or programming team leader in another organization – half the respective period of experience in SKF.

- *Periodic performance appraisal*. The average score of each of the last two semi-annual performance appraisals will not fall below 3.8 (out of a maximum of 5).

- *Targeted evaluation by candidate's direct superior*. The score of each of the eight items in the questionnaire will be no less than 3 (out of 5), with an average score of all items of at least 3.8.

- *Demonstration of knowledge and skill by means of a test or project*. Eight-hour test of programming skills according to a specially selected software design document. Minimum grade: 80.

- *Mentor's supervision for a designated period*. Mentor supervision and on-the-job instruction by a senior programming team leader for a period of 6 months.

Responsibility for certification

- *Overall responsibility*. Chief software engineer.

- *Responsibility for skill demonstration test*. Manager of the relevant software development or software maintenance department (preparation of the candidate's test/task and its evaluation).

16.10 Follow-up subsequent to training and certification

Managers and software professionals often express doubts about the effectiveness of training and certification in general or of one of the associated activities. They question whether the substantial resources and efforts invested in training are really worthwhile. To assuage these doubts, systematic follow-up is necessary to provide feedback to the professional units. Such feedback indicates whether the training efforts were justified at the same time that it assures continuous improvement of training and certification activities. The information provided by follow-up relates to:

■ All training activities and certification procedures conducted – records of the performance of the participants in the program.

■ Information about special cases of training activities that proved to be either highly successful or clearly unsuccessful in improving staff performance.

■ Information about proven cases of failures of certified staff in the performance that point to clearly inadequate certification requirements.

Analysis of the data accumulated following a training course provides the information necessary to revise programs by guiding the modification, addition and deletion of identified activities and materials. Meaningful follow-up of training requires performance information collected prior as well as subsequent to training. As for certification follow-up, comparisons of the performance of non-certified with certified staff holding the same principle of information collection is impossible because non-certified staff are not expected to hold positions that require certification. Instead, we can base our follow-up on performance comparisons of certified staff whose achievements in the certification process were high with certified staff whose achievements were substantially lower. Given these constraints, the units responsible for training and certification should regularly perform follow-up using instruments such as the following.

■ Collection of regular performance metrics – such as errors and productivity statistics, corrective maintenance statistics and resources invested – prepared by the respective units. For a discussion of software quality metrics in general and the specific issue of performance metrics, see Chapter 21.

■ Questionnaires completed by staff members who received training, their superiors, customers and others.

■ Analysis of outstanding achievements as well as failures.

■ Specialized review of software products (documents and code) prepared by certified and trained employees.

The Corrective Action Board (CAB), based on follow-up subsequent to training and certification and other sources of information, may initiate training and/or updating activities subsequent to analysis of the cases presented to it.

For more about corrective and preventive actions in the context of training 345
and other issues, see Chapter 17.

Summary

Summary

(1) Explain the main objectives of training and certification.

- To develop the knowledge and skills needed by new employees and to update the knowledge and skills of veteran employees so as to assure efficient and effective task performance.
- To impart knowledge of style and structure procedures and work instructions to assure conformity of software products to the organization's standards.
- To impart knowledge of SQA procedures.
- To assure that the qualifications of candidates for key professional positions conform to the position's requirements.

(2) Discuss what is needed to prepare a training and updating program.

The three activities to be performed prior to planning a program are as follows.
- **Determine the knowledge requirements for each position.** These include knowledge obtained while acquiring a general professional education with the addition of the internally generated knowledge and skills required within the organization.
- **Determine training and professional updating needs.** These needs are ascertained through comparisons of the staff's knowledge with the state of the art. These should be specified for three populations:
  - New employees (training)
  - Employees assigned to new position (retraining)
  - Other staff (professional updating).

Training and updating needs should also be determined by performance requirements, based on feedback transmitted by the organization's various units.
- **Plan training and updating programs.** These programs will respond to the following issues:
  - The use of in-house training teams and facilities or outsourcing
  - The timing of the training and updating activities (whenever possible)
  - The use of e-learning programs.

(3) List the main components of a certification program.

A certification program defines position requirements and responsibilities for carrying out the program and its revision. Certification requirements may include some or even all of the following components, depending on their relevance to the task or position:
- Professional education
- Internal training courses
- Professional experience in the current organization or another organization
- Evaluation of the candidate's achievements and ability as found in periodic performance assessments

- Evaluation by the candidate's direct superior
- Demonstration of knowledge and skills by means of a test or a project
- Mentor's supervision for a specified period.

Certification responsibilities include:
- Response to requests made by applications or the organization
- Conduct of follow-up
- Revision of certification requirements according to technological developments
- Revision of the list of positions requiring certification.

(4) Explain the objectives of follow-up of trained and certified staff performance and main sources of the follow-up data.

Follow-up is meant to provide the information necessary to initiate revisions of the training and certification programs based on performance data. Sources for performance data include:
- Regular performance metrics – such as errors and productivity statistics – prepared by the individual units
- Questionnaires completed by trainees, their superiors and others
- Analysis of outstanding achievements as well as failures
- Specialized review of software products (documents and code) produced by certified and trained employees.

Selected bibliography

1. ASQ (1999) *Certified Software Quality Engineer* (brochure), American Society for Quality (ASQ), Milwaukee, WI.
2. Hamilton, D. H. (1999) "American Society for Quality (ASQ) Software Quality Engineer Certification Program", in G. G. Schulmeyer and J. I. McManus (eds), *Handbook of Software Quality Assurance*, 3rd edn, Prentice Hall, Upper Saddle River, NJ, pp. 171–194.
3. ISO (1997) *ISO 9000-3:1997(E)*, *Quality Management and Quality Assurance Standards – Part 3: Guidelines for the Application of ISO 9001:1994 to the Development, Supply, Installation and Maintenance of Computer Software*, 2nd edn, International Organization for Standardization (ISO), Geneva.
4. ISO/IEC (2001) "ISO 9000-3:2001 Software and System Engineering – Guidelines for the Application of ISO 9001:2000 to Software, Final draft", International Organization for Standardization (ISO), Geneva, unpublished draft, December 2001.
5. Mendis, K. S. (1999) "Personnel requirements to make software quality assurance work", in G. G. Schulmeyer and J. I. McManus (eds), *Handbook of Software Quality Assurance*, 3rd edn, Prentice Hall, Upper Saddle River, NJ, pp. 147–170.
6. Paulk, M. C., Weber, C. V. Curtis, B. and Chrissis, M. B. (1995) *The Capability Maturity Model: Guidelines for Improving the Software Process*, Addison-Wesley, Reading, MA.

16.1 It has been claimed that training and certification objectives conform to SQA objectives (see Section 2.5.3).

Review each of the SQA objectives and explain, in your own words, how they conform to the relevant training and certification objectives.

16.2 The main tasks of training are classified into professional training and updating. Discuss the main characteristics differentiating the two types of tasks.

16.3 Consider the certification requirement "mentor's supervision".

(1) Explain, in your own words, the unique contribution of supervision to the success of the certification process.
(2) Can you suggest certification requirements that can be replaced, wholly or partially, by a mentor's supervision? List your arguments.

16.4 The Certification Committee of SKF Advanced Software has decided to enlarge the list of positions requiring certification. The following positions were added:

- C++ programmer
- Automated testing planner
- Testers' team leader.

Prepare a proposal for a position certification document (see Frame 16.2) for one of the above positions.

Topics for discussion

16.1 Refer to the "3S" development team case in the Introduction.

(1) List the decisions made by the team leader that created the problematic situation.
(2) Can you suggest procedures that could have eliminated or reduced the risk of arriving at a situation similar to that found in "3S"? Explain, in a few sentences, how each of your proposed procedures can contribute to eliminating these risks.

16.2 In the last few years, many human resource management departments and staff training units have invested substantial resources in computer-aided training.

(1) Discuss the advantages of computer-aided training and retraining.
(2) Discuss the advantages of computer-aided training for professional updating.
(3) Discuss the disadvantages of computer-aided training for professional training, retraining and updating.
(4) Suggest ways to overcome the above disadvantages.

16.3 New Ventures Bank (NVB) operates 87 branches throughout the state. The Software Development and Maintenance Department employs a professional staff of 350. Lately, the Bank's General Manager, who has often expressed his dissatisfaction with the performance of NVB's certification processes, divested the Manager of the Software Development Department of the responsibility for staff certification. A day later, he assigned to Raphael Jones, the very successful Head of the Finance Department, the responsibility for the staff certification process.

(1) Do you expect the new choice to be successful? List your arguments in each direction.

(2) Some senior staff members of the Development Department had suggested that Victoria McFaden, a senior software development consultant, well experienced with training and certification, be appointed Head of the new Certification Committee to be established. Do you agree with this recommendation? List your arguments and compare this solution to the appointment of Mr Jones.

16.4 The managers of a software development department have decided that all training and certification programs will be delivered only by members of the department's staff. They explained that the decision is based on the importance of "local color" in any training and certification activity, and stressed that economic considerations did not play any role in the decision.

(1) Discuss the appropriateness of the decision.

(2) Suggest ways for improving the decision.

16.5 Follow-up of training, updating and certification, discussed in Section 16.10, rests on four different sources of information. An SQA expert claims that the quantitative information provided by performance metrics is sufficient, and that collecting additional information is unnecessary and may very well be a waste of resources.

(1) Do you agree with the claim? List your arguments for and against.

(2) If you disagree, discuss the unique contribution of each source of information to a successful feedback process.

Corrective and preventive actions

Systematic activities that implement organization-wide improvements of effectiveness and operational efficiency fall under the heading of *corrective and preventive actions* (CAPA). These are activities that are not intended to deal with immediate correction of detected defects but to eliminate the causes of those defects throughout software development departments.

By promoting continuous improvement of effectiveness and efficiency, the CAPA process has became one of the main tools used to achieve the performance-oriented objective of SQA: fulfillment of functional and managerial requirements while reducing the costs of carrying out software development, maintenance and quality assurance activities. For more about SQA objectives, see Section 2.5.3.

The CAPA process is the subject of this chapter. The last section presents illustrations of its implementation.

The importance of CAPA in any SQA system is emphasized by the ISO 9000–3 standard (see ISO, 1997, Section 4.14 and ISO/IEC, 2001, Sections 8.5.2 and 8.5.3). The principles underlying the process are major elements of the CMM Guidelines (they appear under the heading "defect prevention") summarized by Paulk *et al.* (1995).

After completing this chapter, you will be able to:

- Explain the difference between defect correction and corrective and preventive actions.
- List the main types of internal sources for CAPA process.
- List and explain the main approaches for introduction of CAPA.
- Explain the main CAPA follow–up tasks.
- List the participants in the CAPA process and their contributions to its successful implementation.

17.1 Introduction: the "3S" development team revisited

We illustrate corrective and preventive actions by continuing the case of the "3S" project for Apollo Ltd from Chapter 16. This project, completed by Team 7, had been operative for about seven months but the team's troubles continued. Keeping its previous experience in mind, the Development Department's manager felt that the causes of the Team's difficulties should be analyzed. He believed that some of the conclusions reached might be appropriately applied throughout the Department.

Participants at the meeting organized by the Department's manager included the Team 7 leader, the head of the SQA unit and the head of the Human Resources Department. They defined their objective as: "To detect systematic causes for the improper functioning of Team 7 and to devise measures to prevent its recurrence". They raised the cancellation of the Athena application generator training and the unsuccessful recruitment of a replacement programmer. In addition to some personal conclusions, the participants recommended that the following actions be taken:

(1) The training procedure should be updated to include a clause that requires a special consultant or mentor to support team members in case of inability to undergo needed training prior to the introduction of new applications.

(2) Programmers should be added to the list of positions requiring certification (a certification procedure appendix).

(3) Appointment of a mentor for a minimum period of three months for new department employees and two months for employees changing positions should be added to the recruiting procedure. Modification of the mentoring period requires approval of the Department manager.

(4) The new Focus Version 6.1 was found to far exceed the previous Version 5.1 in terms of quality and productivity. It was decided that all the Department's teams would begin to use Version 6.1 within the next three months. The recommended action was based on a comparison of the performance of Version 6.1 Focus application generator (used for Integrations B, C, D, E and G) to that of Version 5.1 (used for Integrations A and F), both versions having been applied regularly by Team 7 for the last 10 months.

Before closing the meeting, one of the participants commented that the subject of their meeting should have been treated long ago by the CAB

(Corrective Action Board), the committee charged with reviewing such incidents and initiating actions in cases similar to the Apollo project. Other participants agreed. A short investigation revealed that the firm's CAB committee had been inactive since the resignation of its last head and his departure from "3S" some 17 months ago. They also found that no internal auditing had ever reviewed the CAB's activities although company procedures require it to do so. Therefore, the participants added two action items to their list of recommendations:

(5) To "reactivate" the Committee by, first of all, finding a proper candidate to head the CAB and renew its paralyzed activities.

(6) To prepare a new appendix to the internal quality auditing procedure to deal with CAB activities.

The above six recommendations are examples of *corrective and preventive actions* (CAPA).

17.2 Corrective and preventive actions – definitions

Frame 17.1 presents the standard, most inclusive definitions of corrective and preventive actions with respect to software development and maintenance.

Frame 17.1   Corrective and preventive actions – definitions

■ **Corrective actions:** A regularly applied feedback process that includes collection of information on quality non-conformities, identification and analysis of sources of irregularities as well as development and assimilation of improved practices and procedures, together with control of their implementation and measurement of their outcomes.

■ **Preventive actions:** A regularly applied feedback process that includes collection of information on potential quality problems, identification and analysis of departures from quality standards, development and assimilation of improved practices and procedures, together with control of their implementation and measurement of their outcomes.

■ **Sources of CAPA information:** Quality records, service reports, internal quality audits, project risk reviews, software risk management reports, etc.

It should be emphasized that the analytic distinction between corrective and preventive actions is somewhat artificial, as can be seen by the analogous elements in their definitions. This means that certain items of information may support both corrective and preventive actions. Furthermore, it should be remembered that the two aspects of CAPA create, in practice, a joint response; therefore, they will be treated as one in the remainder of the chapter.

It is noteworthy that changes in training and certification occupy a major place in the CAPA process (see Chapter 16).

17.3 The corrective and preventive actions process

Successful operation of a CAPA process includes the following activities:

■ Information collection
■ Analysis of information
■ Development of solutions and improved methods
■ Implementation of improved methods
■ Follow-up.

The process is regularly fed by the flow of information from a variety of sources. In order to estimate the success of the process, a closed feedback loop is applied to control the flow of information, implementation of the resulting changes in practices and procedures together with measurement of the outcomes.

A schematic overview of the CAPA process is shown in Figure 17.1. Each of its stages will be discussed in a separate subsection of this chapter.

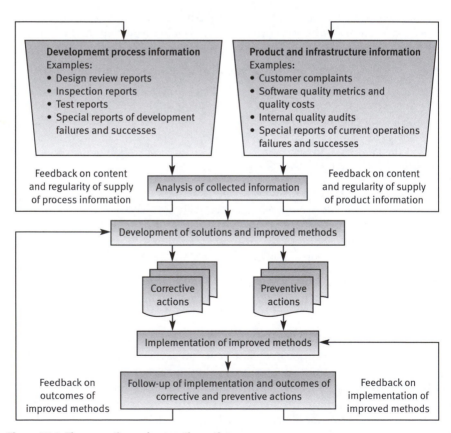

Figure 17.1: The corrective and preventive action process

The variety of information sources, internal and external, that serve the CAPA process is quite remarkable. Following this internal/external dichotomy, the four main internal sources of information are the (1) Software development process, (2) Software maintenance, (3) SQA infrastructure and (4) Software quality management procedures. External sources of information are mainly customers' application statistics and customer complaints. This classification, as it pertains to CAPA, is presented in Frame 17.2.

Frame 17.2	Information used for corrective and preventive actions by source and document

Internal information sources

Software development process

- Software risk management reports
- Design review reports
- Inspection reports
- Walkthrough reports
- Experts' opinion reports
- Test reviews
- Special reports on development failures and successes
- Proposals suggested by staff members.

Software maintenance

- Customer applications statistics
- Software change requests initiated by customer applications
- Software change requests initiated by maintenance staff
- Special reports on maintenance failures and successes
- Proposals suggested by staff members.

SQA infrastructure class of sources

- Internal quality audit reports
- External quality audit reports
- Performance follow-up of trained and certified staff
- Proposals suggested by staff members.

▶

Software quality management procedures class of sources

■ Project progress reports

■ Software quality metrics reports

■ Software quality cost reports

■ Proposals of staff members.

External information sources

■ Customer complaints

■ Customer service statistics

■ Customer-suggested proposals.

An alternative classification of information sources (as shown in Figure 17.1) distinguishes between the development process-related and product and infrastructure-related (including managerial and maintenance) sources of information.

Implementation tip

The initiation of inquiries into major project failures is almost instinctive. The conclusions reached by these inquiries affect a project's immediate environment; in many cases they also contribute to improved practices and procedures through the application of CAPA.

Success stories, however, are rarely investigated. Although the staff immediately responsible for the success are usually rewarded, the likelihood of applying a CAPA analysis is low. Such a process can yield meaningful information about which aspects of the process led to the project's success as well as identify elements that could benefit from further improvement.

The analysis of the accumulated information as reported in different documents is the subject of the next section.

17.5 Analysis of collected information

Regular operation of the CAPA process is expected to create a massive flow of documents related to a wide range of information.

Analysis involves:

■ **Screening the information and identifying potential improvements.** Documents received from the various sources of information are reviewed by professionals in order to identify potential opportunities for CAPA.

This stage includes comparison of documents of the same type received from various units as well as comparison of documents of different types related to the same case.

- **Analysis of potential improvements**. Efforts are directed to determine:
  - Expected types and levels of damage resulting from the identified fault.
  - Causes for faults. Typical causes are non-compliance with work instructions and procedures, insufficient technical knowledge, extreme time and/or budget pressures due to unrealistic estimates, and lack of experience with new development tools.
  - Estimates of the extent of organization-wide potential faults of each type. This information is needed to estimate the total damage expected and to determine the priority of each fault case.
- **Generating feedback** on the content and regularity of information received from the designated information sources.

Two opposing requirements affect responses at this stage – comprehensive analysis of masses of information conflicting with the need for swift reactions to a fault. Resolution of this conflict lies in organization and methods. A team of professionals assigned to deal with incoming information without delay should be created forthwith. This team will set priorities for solution of identified faults, with low-priority cases being delayed or even not treated at all.

Implementation tip

The staff responsible for information analysis are expected to face mounds of documents, making it unfeasible for all the documents to be screened. One approach to reduce the load is to report only those cases that the units believe are amenable to initiation of a CAPA process. This approach can induce a situation of "no fault" reporting through use of the "no importance" excuse. Another approach is to ask the units to indicate the priority of each case in their reports. This information will induce the CAPA team to deal with the high-priority items first. A third approach is to sample the fault documents. Application of random sampling to each type of information and document can reduce the load to a manageable level and increase the probability of identifying the most important cases. Sampling can also be used in combination with the second approach, where it is applied to low- and medium-priority cases. A combination of the second and third approaches is preferable in most instances.

17.6 Development of solutions and their implementation

17.6.1 Development of solutions

Solutions to identified causes of recurrent software systems faults are required to:

- Eliminate recurrence of the types of faults detected
- Contribute to improved efficiency by enabling higher productivity and shorter schedules.

Several directions for solutions are commonly taken:

- Updating relevant procedures. Changes may refer to a spectrum of procedures, from those related to specific stages of software development or maintenance (e.g., changes in style of software comments, changes of contract review procedure in clauses dealing with proposals for small projects) to procedures of a general nature (e.g. changes of employee recruitment procedures, changes of the maximum and minimum number of participants in a formal design review).
- Changes in practices, including updating of relevant work instructions (if any exist).
- Shifting to a development tool that is more effective and less prone to the detected faults.
- Improvement of reporting methods, including changes in report content, frequency of reporting and reporting tasks. This direction is expected to improve prospects for identification of software system faults and their earlier detection, both resulting in substantial reductions in damages.
- Initiatives for training, retraining or updating staff. This direction is taken only in cases when the same training deficiencies are found in several teams.

It is worth noting that:

- In many cases, the recommended solutions combine several action items, from one or several directions.
- Changing and updating of procedures and work instructions need to be discussed and approved by the bodies assigned to their development and maintenance.

Returning to our example, the "3S" case displays six instances of CAPA:

- Updating of existing procedure (recommendations (1), (2), (3) and (6))
- Replacement of development tools of low efficiency and effectiveness by better tools (recommendation (4))
- Improvement in the operation of SQA infrastructure tools (recommendation (5)).

To clarify the point being made, two further examples may be helpful.

Analysis of software quality metrics for the Development Department of "Peak Performance Software Ltd" identified a high proportion of high-severity software defects in the projects completed by two of its six teams. It was also found that the resources these teams required to correct the defects were substantially higher in comparison to other teams.

The analysis was based on documented information related to the two teams' current as well as former projects, in addition to projects performed by the four "healthy" teams. The findings revealed that the characteristic common to most of the faulty modules was the presence of algorithms of medium to high complexity. Inquiries related to the SQA tools applied by all the teams revealed a meaningful difference in the number of applications inspected, especially in the analysis and design stages. While the "healthy" teams treated inspection as a more-or-less standard procedure for the more complicated modules, the other teams used inspections rather sparingly. The recommended CAPA solution was to introduce definitions of the module types requiring inspection within the inspection work instructions.

The second example illustrates how a CAPA process can produced unexpected findings and recommendations.

Example B: Increase in help desk calls that require service at the customer's site

The "Perfect Programming Company" regularly operates two help desk teams to support users of its two most popular software products: Team 1 specializes in point of sale (POS) packages, Team 2 in accountancy packages. The Help Desk Unit's management devised some new quality metrics to support control of the teams' effectiveness and efficiency. These new metrics emphasized control of services performed at the customer's site, due to their high costs, and kept track of two variables (metrics), namely, percentage of customer site visits and average technician time per site visit. The quarterly metrics reports for the two help desk teams are shown in Table 17.1.

The report for the fourth quarter ignited a warning signal among company management. Whereas Team 2 showed stability in its performance, a

Table 17.1: Help desk quarterly report – fourth quarter emphasized

The HD team	Quality metrics	I Quarter	II Quarter	III Quarter	IV Quarter
Team 1 POS packages	Number of packages installed	2105	2166	2200	**2223**
	% of customer's site visits	8.5%	8.7%	12.8%	**20.3%**
	Average technician time per site visit (hours)	2.8	2.6	3.3	**3.8**
Team 2 Accountancy packages	Number of packages installed	987	1011	1011	**1189**
	% of customer's site visits	10.5%	10.1%	10.4%	**10.2%**
	Average technician time per site visit (hours)	2.9	2.7	2.8	**2.8**

dangerous change in Team 1's performance was observed. Management was very concerned by the substantial increase in the percentage of customer's site visits and average technician time per site visit. A corrective and preventive action team (CAPA team) headed by an SQA unit staff member was appointed. The CAPA team held three long meetings devoted to interviewing the help desk team leaders, reviewing a sample of their customer's site visit reports and examining their detailed monthly statistical reports. The team also observed the help desk teams at work during one afternoon.

The CAPA team discovered that while the previous year was one of conservative operations for Team 2, displaying some regression in their efficiency, it had been a year of major changes in the operations of Team 1. During the first and second quarters, the team had invested substantial efforts in improvement of the user interface of the POS package and added several helpful error messages. In addition, a revised user manual had been issued. All these improvements were included in the new Version 6.4 that replaced the Version 6.3 of the POS packages that had served the company for the last 20 months. Version 6.4 had been installed by most users during the third quarter.

Analysis of the monthly operations statistics revealed that the currently used quarterly reports were misleading. Unexpectedly, it soon became obvious that in the last two quarters Team 1 had actually achieved a substantial reduction of total help desk efforts, as measured in hours of help desk service per customer. Moreover, a dramatic decrease in the number of user calls was observed, evidently as a result of the new friendlier and more proficient version of the packages. The increase in average time spent at a customer's site visit was due to the higher percentage of services now given to new customers. The CAPA team based its conclusions on a revised, extended quarterly report, presented in Table 17.2. Application of the revised help desk quarterly report for Team 2 figures revealed a constant decrease in the efficiency and effectiveness of the team's HD services.

Two corrective actions were proposed by the CAPA team:

(1) To replace the currently used quarterly report by a more comprehensive one, based on the lines of Table 17.2.

(2) An inquiry into the practices implemented by Team 2 was suggested to achieve a substantial improvement in the team's performance.

17.6.2 Implementation of a CAPA process

Implementation of CAPA solutions relies on proper instructions and often training but most of all on the cooperation of the relevant units and individuals. Therefore, successful implementation requires that targeted staff members be convinced of the appropriateness of the proposed solution. Without cooperation, the contribution of a CAPA can be undermined.

Table 17.2: Revised help desk quarterly report – fourth quarter emphasized

The HD team	Quality metrics	I Quarter	II Quarter	III Quarter	IV Quarter
Team 1 POS packages	Number of packages installed	2105	2166	2200	**2223**
	Total number of customer's calls	1454	1433	872	**517**
	Number of phone service calls	1330	1308	755	**412**
	Average technician time per phone service call	0.21	0.22	0.18	**0.15**
	Number of customer's site calls	124	125	117	**105**
	% of customer's site calls	8.5%	8.7%	13.4%	**20.3%**
	Average technician time per customer's site call (hours)	2.8	2.6	3.3	**3.8**
	Average HD hours per customer	0.536	0.495	0.379	**0.286**
Team 2 Accountancy packages	Number of packages installed	987	1001	1011	**1089**
	Total number of customer's calls	585	604	615	**698**
	Number of phone service calls	524	543	551	**627**
	Average technician time per phone service call	0.28	0.29	0.31	**0.30**
	Number of customer's site calls	61	61	64	**71**
	% of customer's site calls	10.4%	10.1%	10.4%	**10.2%**
	Average technician time per customer's site call (hours)	2.9	2.7	2.8	**2.8**
	Average HD hours per customer	0.610	0.589	0.650	**0.690**

17.7 Follow-up of activities

Three main follow-up tasks are necessary for the proper functioning of a corrective and preventive action process in any organization:

- **Follow-up of the flow of development and maintenance CAPA records** from the various sources of information. This enables feedback that reveals cases of no reporting as well as low-quality reporting, where important details are missing or inaccurate. This type of follow-up is conducted mainly through analysis of *long-term* activity information, which generates feedback to the CAPA information sources.

- **Follow-up of implementation.** This activity is intended to indicate whether the designated actions – training activities, replacement of development tools, procedural changes (after approval) – have been performed in practice. Adequate feedback is delivered to the bodies responsible for implementation of the corrective and preventive actions.

- **Follow-up of outcomes.** Follow-up of the improved methods' actual outcomes, as observed by project teams and organizational units, enables assessment of the degree to which corrective or preventive actions have achieved the expected results. Feedback on the outcomes is delivered to the improved methods' developers. In cases of low performance, formulation of a revised or new corrective action is needed, a task undertaken by the CAPA team.

Obviously, regular follow-up activities that promptly examine incoming information and initiate adequate flows of feedback are an essential link in the CAPA chain of activities.

17.8 Organizing for preventive and corrective actions

Proper performance of these CAPA activities depends on the existence of a permanent core organizational unit as well as many *ad hoc* team participants. This nucleus, generally known as the Corrective Action Board (CAB) committee, although it may have other titles in different organizations, promotes the CAPA cause within the organization. Its tasks include:

■ Collecting CAPA records from the various sources

■ Screening the collected information

■ Nominating entire *ad hoc* CAPA teams to attend to given subjects, or heading some of the teams

■ Promoting implementation of CAPA in units, projects, etc.

■ Following up information collection, data analysis, progress made by *ad hoc* teams and implementation as well as outcomes of improved CAPA methods.

Members of the SQA unit, top-level professionals and development and maintenance department managers are the natural candidates for membership in a CAB committee.

A complementary group of potential participants, taken from regular staff, join CAPA efforts as members of *ad hoc* CAPA teams. They regularly focus on:

■ Analysis of the information related to the team's topic

■ Initiation of additional observations and inquiries

■ Identification of the causes for the faults

■ Development of solutions and the relevant corrective and preventive actions

■ Preparation of proposed implementation revisions

■ Analysis of the CAPA implementation outcomes and CAPA revision if necessary.

Most members of the CAPA *ad hoc* team are department members, experienced in the subject matter. In cases where localized knowledge is inadequate, other internal or sometimes external experts are asked to join the team.

(1) Explain the difference between defect correction and corrective and preventive actions.

- **Defect correction** is a limited activity directed toward immediate solution of the defects detected in a project or a software system.
- **Corrective and preventive actions** are wider in scope; they are meant to initiate and guide performance of organization-wide actions that will eliminate the causes of known or potential faults.

(2) List the main types of internal sources for CAPA processes.

There are four main information source types that support and feed CAPA processes:
- Software development process
- Software maintenance
- SQA infrastructure procedures
- Software quality management procedures.

(3) List and explain the main approaches for introduction of CAPA.

Five approaches are commonly used:
- Updating relevant procedures.
- Changing software development or maintenance practices and updating work instructions.
- Changing current to more effective software development tools that are less prone to faults.
- Improving reporting methods by revising task content and reporting frequencies. This approach is meant to achieve earlier detection of faults and thus reduce damages.
- Initiating training, retraining and updating of staff.

(4) Explain the main CAPA follow-up tasks.

Three main follow-up tasks necessary for successful CAPA processes are:
- **Follow-up of the flow of development and maintenance CA records** enables feedback regarding cases of no reporting or low-quality reporting.
- **Implementation follow-up** determines whether a CAPA has been performed as required.
- **Outcomes follow-up** ascertains the degree to which a CAPA has achieved the expected results.

(5) List the participants in the CAPA process and their contribution to its successful implementation.

The CAPA process is carried out by the joint efforts of a permanent CAPA body together with *ad hoc* team participants. The permanent CAPA body, commonly called the CAB, activates the CAPA process by screening information, appointing members of targeted *ad hoc* CAPA teams, promoting implementation and following up the process. The *ad hoc* CAPA team's task is to analyze information about a given topic in addition to developing solutions and a CAPA process. The team members are expected to implement the CAPA and use CAB-provided assistance, if needed. Most members of *ad hoc* CAPA teams are department staff members experienced in the subject matter.

Selected bibliography

1.   ISO (1997) *ISO 9000-3:1997(E), Quality Management and Quality Assurance Standards – Part 3: Guidelines for the Application of ISO 9001:1994 to the Development, Supply, Installation and Maintenance of Computer Software*, 2nd edn, International Organization for Standardization (ISO), Geneva.
2.   ISO/IEC (2001) "ISO 9000-3:2001 Software and System Engineering – Guidelines for the Application of ISO 9001:2000 to Software, Final draft", International Organization for Standardization (ISO), Geneva, unpublished draft, December 2001.
3.   Paulk, M. C., Weber, C. V., Curtis, B. and Chrissis, M. B. (1995) *The Capability Maturity Model: Guidelines for Improving the Software Process*, Addison-Wesley, Reading, MA.

Review questions

17.1   Analysis of the cases discussed in Section 17.5 involves identifying the causes of the defects but also determining the types and levels of damage expected from an identified fault, followed by preparation of estimates of those damages and organization-wide distribution of information about the respective defects and damages.

(1)   Some SQA professionals believe that analysis of the case should be limited to identifying the causes of the defects. Do you agree?

(2)   List your arguments.

17.2   Improved reporting methods are mentioned (in Section 17.6) as possible solutions for an identified defect, though no change of performance practices is recommended in the associated CAPA.

(1)   Some SQA professionals believe that a CAPA has no place for changes in reporting methods. Do you agree? List your arguments.

(2)   If you do not agree, list possible contributions a CAPA can make based on changed reporting methods.

17.3   Section 17.7 lists three main tasks of CAPA follow-up.

(1)   List the three tasks.

(2)   Explain, in your own words, the importance of the follow-up tasks to the success of the process.

17.4 Section 17.5 lists the following typical causes for defects that should be treated by CAPA: (1) lack of adherence to work instructions and procedures, (2) insufficient knowledge, (3) extreme time and/or budget pressures due to unrealistic estimates, and (4) lack of sufficient experience with new development tools. Section 17.6 presents five possible approaches to their solution.

Examine the feasibility of applying each of the five directions to each typical cause of defects.

Topics for discussion

17.1 Frame 17.2 lists four different types of internal CAPA information sources.

(1) Considering the multitude of internal CAPA information sources, are external information sources necessary?
(2) If you believe that external information sources are required, list your arguments and explain their special contribution to the CAPA process.

17.2 Statement Software Ltd is a software house that specializes in development of custom-made billing systems for the manufacturing industry. A common "Statement Software" contract offers the customer 12 months of guarantee services. The company's help desk (HD) supplies solutions to customers' calls by phone or on site. The last quarter's performance report indicates a decline in service quality, a trend that also characterized the last two quarters. This trend was identified by the following four help desk quality metrics:

■ Percentage of recurrent calls: the percentage of customer's site calls that required a recurrent call to deal with a defect supposedly solved by the prior call.

■ Average reaction time to customer's site calls (working days).

■ Average hours invested in customer's site calls, including travel time.

■ Customer satisfaction computed from a quarterly customer satisfaction questionnaire, using a scale from 0–10.

The SQA metrics	I Quarter	II Quarter	III Quarter	IV Quarter
Percentage of recurrent calls	12%	13%	19%	21%
Average reaction time (days) to customer's site calls	0.7	0.8	1.7	1.8
Average hours per site call	4.7	4.9	3.3	3.1
Customer satisfaction	8.3	8.4	6.7	6.5

The *ad hoc* CAPA team appointed to deal with the subject decided that each member would prepare his own list of possible causes for the decline in the quality of HD services before an analysis of the collected information and complementary observations was begun.

(1) Can you list possible causes for the recorded phenomenon?
(2) Indicate possible solutions for each of the causes proposed in (1).

17.3 The head of the *ad hoc* CAPA team became quite angry and offended when it was discovered that the team's recommendations regarding two procedures, sent to the Procedures Committee five months ago, had not yet been approved; he subsequently forwarded his protest to the Procedures Committee. In reply to the angry letter, the Procedures Committee head mentioned that the committee had already dedicated two of its meetings to the subject and hoped to finalize the issue in their next meeting.

(1) Is it reasonable for a Procedures Committee to require such a lengthy period of time to approve a recommended CAPA?

(2) Suggest reasons where such a delay might be justified.

(3) Suggest changes to the route taken by the head of the CAPA team and the Procedures Committee which could have improved the process in this and similar situations.

17.4 The head of the CAB suggested adding three new members, and believes that the extended CAB will be able to handle all the tasks currently carried out by *ad hoc* teams. He believes that his proposed change will substantially reduce the difficulties accompanying the operation of *ad hoc* teams.

(1) Do you support the change proposal of the CAB's head? List your arguments.

(2) If you disagree, discuss the advantages of *ad hoc* teams.

Configuration management

- "What is the correct version of the software module that I have to continue its coding?"
- "Who can provide me with an accurate copy of last year's version 4.1 of the TMY software system?"
- "What version of the design document matches the software version we are currently adapting to a new customer's requirements?"
- "What version of the software system is installed at ABC Industries?"
- "What changes have been introduced in the version installed at the ABC Industries' site?"

- "What changes have been introduced in the new version of the software?"
- "Where can I find the full list of customers that use version 6.8 of our software?"
- "Can we be sure that the version installed at Top Com Ltd does not include undocumented changes (and changes that have not been approved)?"

These and many similar questions reflect the fact that an active software system is a system that is in constant change. Even a medium-sized software system, serving only one organization, typically undergoes tens to hundreds of changes annually; quality assurance steps must therefore be planned to provide accurate responses to a wealth of questions similar to our examples. If the software package serves a variety of customers, the number of changes and questions it must respond to will multiply considerably.

Clearly, the need to cope with rapid software changes is one of the more important tasks of software systems development and maintenance teams. The task encompasses adequate quality assurance of all changes performed and their proper documentation as well as identification of the software version (or release) installed by each customer. The efforts required to document the various items as well as the benefits of proper documentation can be appreciated only at the end of the service period because software systems must be maintained for years, regardless of changing technological environments and staff turnover.

Software configuration management (SCM) is the SQA component assigned to manage changes and supply accurate answers to inquiries of the types mentioned above. SCM deals with all the issues related to control of software changes, proper documentation of changes, registering and storing the approved software versions, provision of the relevant information and supply of copies of registered versions throughout the software system's life cycle.

The importance of SCM is stressed by ISO 9000–3 standards (see ISO, 1997; ISO/IEC, 2001), as they are in the CMM Guidelines summarized by Paulk *et al.* (1995). IEEE dedicates a standard to SCM issues (IEEE, 1998). Leon (1999) and Siegel and Donaldson (1999) are only two of the books and numerous papers dedicated to the subject. Chapters dedicated to SCM are likewise found in software engineering texts such as Van Vliet (2000) and Pressman (2000), to mention just two.

After completing this chapter, you will be able to:

- Define the concept *software configuration version*.
- Explain the objectives of software configuration management.
- Explain the objectives of software change management.
- Explain the difference between baseline and intermediate software configuration versions.
- Explain the objectives of software configuration management plans.
- Explain the nature of the tasks fulfilled by software configuration management audits.

18.1 Software configuration, its items and its management

The definitions of software configuration items and software configuration versions are presented in Frame 18.1.

Frame 18.1 **Software configuration items and software configuration versions – definitions**

■ **Software configuration item (SCI) or configuration item (CI)**
An approved unit of software code, a document or piece of hardware that is designed for configuration management and treated as a distinct entity in the software configuration management process.

■ **SCI version**
The approved state of an SCI at any given point of time during the development or maintenance process.

■ **Software configuration version**
An approved selected set of documented SCI versions that constitute a software system or document at a given point of time, where the activities to be performed are controlled by software configuration management procedures. The software configuration versions are released according to the cited procedures.

A unit of software code, a document or piece of hardware is defined as an SCI if it is assumed that it may be needed for further development of the software system and/or its maintenance. In other words, the main criterion governing a non-code item's classification as an SCI and its inclusion in a software configuration version is its potential contribution to the software development and maintenance process.

A software configuration is composed of as many SCIs as the developers assume will be needed in the future, with each SCI approved, identified and registered. The SCIs aggregated in each software configuration version naturally correspond to the software components and software definitions reviewed in Section 2.1. The SCIs are generally placed into four classes, as follows:

■ Design documents
■ Software code
■ Data files, including files of test cases and test scripts
■ Software development tools.

A list of common types of SCIs is presented in Frame 18.2.

Frame 18.2   Common types of software configuration items

Design documents

- Software development plan (SDP)
- System requirements document
- Software requirements document (SRD)
- Interface design specifications
- Preliminary design document (PDD)
- Critical design document (CDD)
- Database description
- Software test plan (STP)
- Software test procedure (STPR)
- Software test report (STR)
- Software user manuals
- Software maintenance manuals
- Software installation plan (SIP)
- Software maintenance requests (including problem reports)
- Software change requests (SCRs) and software change orders (SCOs)
- Version description document (VDD)

Software code

- Source code
- Object code
- Prototype software

Data files

- Test cases and test scripts
- Parameters, codes, etc.

Software development tools

(the versions applied in the development and maintenance stages)

- Compilers and debuggers
- Application generators
- CASE tools

To illustrate the process, see Table 18.1, which shows two software configuration versions of the *Pepper Mountain Travel* software package and the versions of the SCIs included in each configuration.

The SQA component under whose heading all the activities necessary to attend to the availability and accuracy of information regarding all aspects of a software configuration is called *software configuration management* (SCM), sometimes referred to simply as configuration management (CM). Its definition is presented in Frame 18.3.

Frame 18.3	Software configuration management – definition

An SQA component responsible for applying (computerized and non-computerized) technical tools and administrative procedures that enable completion of the tasks required to maintain SCIs and software configuration versions.

18.2 Software configuration management – tasks and organization

18.2.1 The tasks of software configuration management

The tasks of software configuration management may be classified into four groups:

- Control software change
- Release of SCI and software configuration versions

Table 18.1: Pepper Mountain Travel (PMT) – software configuration versions, including SCI versions

SCI version	Release and release date	
	PMT Version 6.0 January 6, 2002 SCI version in the release	PMT Version 7.0 January 22, 2003 SCI version in the release
SRD	Ver. 1	Ver. 1
CDD	Ver. 3	Ver. 4
STP	Ver. 3	Ver. 4
SIP	Ver. 2	Ver. 2
VDD	Ver. 6	Ver. 7
Code Module 1	Ver. 3	Ver. 5
Code Module 2	Ver. 8	Ver. 8
Code Module 3	Ver. 2	Ver. 2
Test cases file	Ver. 3	Ver. 4
CL compiler	Ver. 5	Ver. 7
Software user manual	Ver. 6	Ver. 7

■ Provision of SCM information services
■ Verification of compliance to SCM procedures.

A summary list of SCM tasks, with respect to software configuration items and software configurations, is presented in Table 18.2.

18.2.2 The software configuration authority

It is practically self-evident that an authority to oversee implementation of the above tasks is vital in software developing and/or maintaining organizations. SCM procedures specify who is responsible for SCM issues. This responsibility is usually assigned to a senior professional or a committee dedicated to SCM issues. In many organizations, software change control is

Table 18.2: Summary of configuration management systems tasks

Task	Applicable to SCIs	Applicable to software configurations
(1) Software change control		
■ Grant approval to carry out changes	+	+
■ Control the changes and assure the quality of approved changes	+	+
■ Document the approved changes	+	+
■ Apply mechanisms that coordinate the changes made to the SCI by preventing more than one team from simultaneously introducing changes into the same SCI	+	
(2) Release of SCI and software configuration versions		
■ Approve the release of new versions		+
■ Document the configuration of each released software configuration version		+
■ Document the sites where software configuration versions are installed		+
■ Secure the version source and documentation files from changes, deletions and other damages	+	+
(3) Provision of SCM information services		
■ Information about the status of changes	+	+
■ Information about versions installed at a site as well as about the site itself		+
■ Version history list	+	+
■ Accurate copies of given versions	+	+
■ Supply copies of documentation	+	+
(4) Verification of compliance to SCM procedures		
■ Audit compliance to SCM procedures.	+	+
■ Initiate updating and change of SCM procedures	+	+

dealt with by a special committee set up for such matters, commonly called the software change control authority (SCCA) or the software change control board (SCCB). This body is frequently called the change control authority (CCA) or the change control board (CCB). During the development stage, the project manager may be charged with the authority to carry out SCM responsibilities.

The activities involved in realizing each of the above objectives are discussed in Sections 18.3 to 18.6. Section 18.7 deals with computerized SCM tools.

18.3 Software change control

Software change management controls the process of introducing changes mainly by doing the following:

- Examining change requests and approving implementation of appropriate requests.
- Assuring the quality of each new version of software configuration before it becomes operational.

18.3.1 Approval to carry out proposed changes

Once the baseline version of the software system becomes operational, it is just a matter of time before proposals for changes begin to flow. These initiatives may relate to one or several SCIs. In order to coordinate the efforts invested and guarantee that the changes follow project or customer priorities, an authorized body must analyze the requests and make the necessary decisions.

The factors affecting the decision whether to implement a proposed change include:

- Expected contribution of the proposed change
- Urgency of the change
- Effect of the proposed change on project timetables, level of service, etc.
- Efforts required in making the change operational
- Required software quality assurance efforts
- Estimated required professional resources and cost of performing the change.

The information items required before any decision about a change proposal can be made are reflected in the contents of a typical software change request (SCR) form. (The same information can be phrased as a change request – CR – or engineering change request – ECR.) See Frame 18.4 for an example.

Despite the perceived urgency of the change, a favorable decision is not automatically given to its initiator. The CCA may approve the request for immediate implementation, delay or deny it.

| Frame 18.4 | Software change request (SCR) document – a template |

(1) Change principles

■ The initiator

■ The date the SCR was presented

■ The character of the change

■ The goals

■ The expected contribution to the project/system

■ The urgency of performance

(2) Change details

■ Description of the proposed change

■ A list of the SCIs to be changed

■ Expected effect on other SCIs

■ Expected effect on interfaces with other software systems and hardware firmware

■ Expected delays in development completion schedules and expected disturbances to services to customers

(3) Change timetable and resources estimates

■ Timetable for implementation

■ Estimated required professional resources

■ Other resources required

■ Estimated total cost of the requested change

For each SCR approved for immediate implementation, a software change order (SCO) (in some organizations, called a change order (CO) or engineering change order (ECO)) is issued. The SCO provides the change details and their schedule, which may differ from the original request because the authority is free to exercise its discretion on the related issues (e.g., the list of changes and schedules).

18.3.2 Quality assurance of software changes

While change efforts are directed to one or several SCIs, the user experiences the changes indirectly, through application of the revised version of the software system. The goal of software quality assurance is to assure that the quality of the new software system version does not fall below that of the previous version.

Quality assurance efforts are required at two levels:

■ Quality assurance of each of the changed SCIs
■ Quality assurance of the entire new software system version (that includes changed SCIs).

Quality assurance of the changed SCIs

This requires preparation of a reviews and testing plan at a magnitude appropriate to the character of the change. As mentioned in earlier chapters, it is most important that reviews and testing be carried out by professional testers and not by the SCI's developer. The process of reviews and testing, corrections and retesting (regression testing) the changed SCIs is expected to conclude with their approval.

Quality assurance of the entire new software system version

A new version of the software is considered to have been completed once the changed SCIs replace the former SCIs. Although one might expect the new version of the software system to function perfectly and certainly better than the old original version, many new versions, especially of complex software systems, actually fail. These system failures generally occur as a result of damage done to interfaces between the changed SCIs and other SCIs left unchanged and not retested because they were not expected to be affected by the changes performed. Unless the entire new version, or at least all the whole software parts that might be affected, is tested to identify unexpected interface defects, prospects are meager that the software system will function properly.

18.4 Release of software configuration versions

The need to release a new software configuration version usually stems from one or more of the following conditions:

■ Defective SCIs
■ Special features demanded by new customers
■ The team's initiatives to introduce SCI improvements.

A discussion of the following issues, all of which are part of the process of software configuration version release, occupy the remainder of this section:

■ Types of software configuration releases
■ Software configuration management plans (SCMPs)
■ Software configuration evolution models
■ Documentation of software configuration versions.

18.4.1 Types of software configuration releases

Among software configuration releases, baseline versions, intermediate versions and revisions are considered to be the three main types of release.

Baseline versions

Baseline software configuration versions are planned early, during a system's development or operating stage. As part of the process, they are reviewed, tested and approved, as are their SCIs. Baseline versions serve as milestones in the software system's life cycle, and represent the foundations for further system development.

Intermediate versions

When problems arise that require immediate attention – such as the need to correct defects identified in an important SCI, or perform immediate adaptations as defined in a contract with a new customer – an intermediate version of the software is often prepared.

Usually, intermediate versions serve only a portion of a firm's customers, and then for a limited period, until replaced by a new baseline version. Naturally, we can expect that these versions will not receive the attention and investment of efforts usually devoted to the release of baseline versions. An intermediate software configuration version can thus serve as a "pilot" or springboard to the next baseline version.

Revisions

Revisions introduce minor changes and corrections to a given software configuration version. In some cases, several successive revisions are released before a new baseline version is released.

Numeration conventions for identification of SCI and software versions

Numeration conventions have been formulated to identify SCIs; the most commonly used is decimal numeration, which indicates the successive version and revision numbers and is registered accordingly. For example, an SCI design document captioned DD-7 may have several versions and revisions, identified as DD-7 Ver.1.0, DD-7 Ver.1.1, DD-7 Ver.2.0, DD-7 Ver.3.0, DD-7 Ver.3.1, DD-7 Ver.3.2, etc., where the first number represents the version and the second the revision. Put simply, an SCI is identified by its name in combination with its version and revision numbers.

A similar numeration convention is applied for software configurations. Each software configuration version (identified by version and revision numbers) is composed of SCIs, each of which is identified by its own version and revision numbers. Examples of such numeration applications are presented later in Tables 18.3 and 18.4.

The numeration conventions can likewise be used to identify firmware to be embedded in a variety of product lines and models, but these may require special adaptations.

The main objective of a software configuration management plan (SCMP) is to plan ahead the schedule of baseline version releases and the required resources to carry out all the activities required for the software configuration releases. An additional objective of the SCMP is to enable one to follow up the progress of activities involved in software version release. SCMPs are required during the development stage as well as the operation (maintenance) stage. Accordingly, an SCMP usually includes:

■ An overview of the software development project or existing software system.
■ A list of scheduled baseline version releases.
■ A list of SCIs (documents, code, etc.) to be included in each version.
■ A table identifying the relationship of software development project plans and maintenance plans to scheduled releases of new SCIs or SCI versions.
■ A list of assumptions about the resources required to perform the various activities required by the SCMP.
■ Estimates of the human resources and budget needed to perform the SCMP.

SCMP for the development stage

Based on the project plan, the SCMP sets the release dates of baseline versions, which usually coincide with the conclusion of one or more of the following three events: the design stage, the coding stage and the system test stage. Quite commonly, these plans represent a segment of the entire system's development plans, prepared at a project's initiation. External participants in the project are required to comply with the SCMP or to suggest an alternative SCMP that is appropriate for their part of the project, contingent on its acceptance by the project manager.

All the instructions and procedures necessary for performing SCM tasks at this stage are documented in the SCMP. The project manager is usually the person responsible for carrying out these tasks.

SCMP for the operation (maintenance) stage

During the operation (maintenance) stage, further releases of software baseline versions are required in order to introduce improved software versions released after accumulation of SCI changes made during regular customer use. The plan generally schedules new baseline releases periodically, either annually, semi-annually, or according to the anticipated number of accumulated changes in SCIs. The periodic releases will include corrected as well as new versions of SCIs, each of which will contain the adaptations and/or improvements initiated by the company. Only SCIs for which changes have been completed and approved by the targeted release date can be included in new software configuration versions.

All the instructions and procedures for performing SCM tasks during the operation (maintenance) stage are likewise documented in the respective SCMP. This stage's SCMP may be incorporated in the comprehensive SCMP that covers the system's entire life cycle, prepared at the project's initiation. The plan also leaves room for release of intermediate software versions and revisions, as need arises.

18.4.3 Software configuration evolution models

Successive development or evolution of a software system's configuration versions should be undertaken according to a route that is planned in advance by the system's developer. The choice of routes depends on the system's characteristics, the customer population and the firm's intentions regarding the system's market. Two fundamental software configuration evolution models – the line model and the tree model – are generally applied. We discuss these next.

■ **The linear evolution model**

According to the linear model, only one unique software system's configuration version serves all customers at any given time. Each new configuration version then replaces the prior version. This model is the natural choice for software systems developed to serve a single organization. The model is also applied to popular software packages, which tend to be uniform in structure, where the need to meet a wide range of maintenance demands for a single version is a great advantage.

■ **The tree evolution model**

According to this model, several parallel versions of the software are developed to serve the needs of different customers simultaneously throughout the system's life cycle. Tree models are typically applied in firmware configuration versions, where each branch serves a different product or product line.

Tables 18.3 and 18.4 illustrate application of the linear and tree evolution models respectively. In both examples, decimal numeration is implemented, with the type of configuration version – baseline or intermediate – clearly marked. Table 18.3 documents the configuration versions of an accounting software system throughout its development and operation stages. Table 18.4 presents the format for documenting configuration versions of a system developed for printer firmware, where separate versions were developed for the printer-fax and regular printer software. Further development of the product line resulted in two separate configuration versions, one for black-ink printer and one for color. In this case, the first baseline software configuration version was defined at the end of the development stage.

Note that Version 1.0 is a *design baseline* version and Version 2.0 is the *final software product baseline* version. Version 2.1 is an intermediate version released with only one SCI, SM–4, which was changed to replace its faulty Version 1.2. Baseline Version 4.0 introduces a new software module, SM–5, to respond to a new accounting regulation. The version of the commercial CASE tool that was applied for the development and maintenance, Version 6.03, has been replaced with the more advanced Version 7.0, beginning with Version 3.0 of our software system.

Table 18.3: Application of the linear evolution model – the accounting software package
example

SCI name	Software configuration version (BL = baseline, IN = intermediate)						
	1.0 BL	2.0 BL	2.1 IN	2.2 IN	3.0 BL	4.0 BL	4.1 IN
Design document DD–1	1.3	1.3	1.3	1.3	1.4	1.4	1.4
Design document DD–2	1.1	1.2	1.2	1.2	1.3	1.4	1.4
Design document DD–3	1.2	1.4	1.4	1.5	1.5	1.6	1.6
Software module SM–1	—	1.0	1.0	1.1	1.2	1.4	1.4
Software module SM–2	—	1.3	1.3	1.5	1.5	1.5	1.5
Software module SM–3	—	1.3	1.3	1.4	1.7	1.8	1.9
Software module SM–4	—	1.2	1.4	1.4	1.4	1.4	1.5
Software module SM–5	—	—	—	—	—	1.0	1.1
Test case file TC	—	1.2	1.2	1.2	1.2	1.3	1.3
User manual UM	—	1.0	1.0	1.0	2.0	3.0	3.0
CASE tool CA	—	6.03	6.03	6.03	7.0	7.0	7.0

Table 18.4: Application of the tree evolution model – the printer firmware example

SCI name	Software configuration version (BL = baseline, IN = intermediate)									
	General	Printer		Black printer		Color printer		Printer–fax		
	a1.0 BL	b1.0 BL	b1.1 IN	d1.0 BL	d1.1 IN	e1.0 BL	e1.1 IN	c1.0 BL	c1.1 IN	c2.0 BL
Design document DD–1	1.3	1.3	1.3	1.4	1.4	1.4	1.4	1.3	1.3	1.4
Design document DD–2	1.1	1.1	1.1	1.1	1.3	2.0	2.4	1.2	1.2	2.4
Design document DD–3	1.2	1.3	1.3	1.3	1.5	1.6	1.6	2.0	2.3	2.6
Design document DD–4	—	—	—	—	—	—	—	1.0	1.1	1.3
Design document DD–5	—	—	—	—	—	1.0	1.1	—	—	1.1
Software module SM–1	1.0	1.2	1.3	1.4	1.2	1.4	1.4	1.3	1.4	1.4
Software module SM–2	1.0	1.0	1.1	1.2	1.5	1.5	1.6	1.1	1.1	1.5
Software module SM–3	1.0	1.1	1.1	1.1	1.7	3.0	3.0	2.0	2.1	2.2
Software module SM–4	1.0	1.2	1.2	1.4	1.4	3.0	3.1	2.0	2.2	2.2
Software module SM–5	1.4	1.4	1.4	1.5	1.5	3.0	3.0	1.4	1.4	1.6
Software module SM–6	—	—	—	—	—	—	—	1.0	1.1	1.2
Software module SM–7	—	—	—	—	—	1.0	1.3	—	—	1.3
Test case file TC	1.0	1.0	1.0	3.0	3.0	4.0	4.0	2.0	2.0	2.1
User manual UM	1.0	1.1	1.1	1.2	2.0	3.0	3.0	2.0	2.0	2.1
Development tool DT	2.3	2.3	2.3	2.3	2.3	3.0	3.0	2.3	2.3	3.0

Table 18.4 illustrates evolution of software configurations at the development stage according to the tree model. The letters mark the branch of the evolution tree. In this case, parallel firmware configuration versions evolved so as to serve three product lines: regular printers, color printers and printer–fax units. The three firmware configuration versions replace one general firmware configuration. The table displays two version partitions: first, general baseline version a1.0 is partitioned into printer version b1.0 and printer–fax version c1.0; second, printer baseline version b1.0 is partitioned into black printer version d1.0 and color printer version e1.0. It also displays the SCIs common to the firmware of more than one product in addition to the unique SCIs included in the firmware of only one product. We can assume that different test procedures, different test case files and different user manuals serve the respective product–line firmware. Special attention should be paid to the fact that printer–fax firmware version c2.0 serves a color printer-fax product; as such, it shares the SCIs DD-1, DD-2, DD-5, SM-2 and SM-7 with the color printer firmware version e1.1.

18.4.4 Documentation of software configuration versions

Within the framework of software configuration management, the project manager must see to it that all documentation tasks are properly performed. Two of these tasks – documentation of SCI versions and documentation of software configuration releases (versions and revisions) – represent the two main types of tasks to be completed.

The information items required for documentation of an SCI version are listed in Frame 18.5.

Frame 18.5 **SCI version document – a template**

Identification

- SCI Version number

- Name(s) of software engineer(s) who implemented the change

- Date the new version was completed and approved

Changes in the new version

- Former SCI version number

- Short description of the introduced changes

- List of other SCIs that had to be changed as a result of the current changes

- List of SCOs included in the new version

- List of software problem reports resolved by the new version

- Operational as well as other implications of the changes introduced in the new version

The documentation for a new SCI version may be submitted as a document or as part of the code (i.e., as "release notes" in the code listing).

Documentation of software configuration releases includes the same information items listed in Frame 18.6, and is often referred to as a *version description document* (VDD).

Frame 18.6 **Software configuration release documentation – VDD template**

Identification and installations

- Release version and revision number

- Date of the new version's release

- List of installations where the release was entered (site, date, name of technician who installed the version), if applicable

Configuration of the released version

- List of SCIs in the released version, including identification of each SCI version

- List of hardware configuration items required for operating the specified version, including specification of each hardware configuration item

- List of interfacing software systems (including version) and hardware systems (including model)

- Installation instructions for the new release

Changes in the new version

- Previous software configuration version

- List of SCIs that have been changed, new SCIs introduced for the first time, and deleted SCIs

- Short description of introduced changes

- Operational and other implications of changes introduced in the new release

Further development issues

- List of software system problems that have not been solved in the new version

- List of SCRs and proposals for development of the software system for which implementation of development was delayed

18.5 Provision of SCM information services

The SCM is required to provide information to professionals, mainly developers, maintenance teams and customer representatives, who have requested that changes be introduced in a software system.

The information provided may be classified into information related to software change control and information dealing with SCI and software configuration versions.

Information related to software change control

■ Change request status information – based on records for every submission of an SCR and the decisions made.

■ Change order progress information – based on records for every approved SCO, its schedule, implementation progress and test results. Information about delays in performance may also be supplied.

Information about SCIs and software configuration versions

■ Accurate copies of SCI versions (code SCIs, document SCIs, etc.) and entire software configuration versions.

■ Full reports of changes introduced between successive releases (versions and/or revisions) of code SCIs as well as between successive releases of other types of SCIs.

■ Copies of SCI version documentation and software configuration version documentation (VDDs).

■ Detailed version and revision history for SCIs and software configurations for any specific SCI or software system.

■ Progress information about planned versions and releases (usually included in the SCMP).

■ Information correlated about versions installed at a given site and about the site itself.

■ List of sites where a given software configuration version is installed.

Provision of the above information services is practically impossible for manual SCM systems. Only a computerized service is expected to cope with this task effectively and reliably. For more about this subject, see Section 18.7.

18.6 Software configuration management audits

SCM involves the execution of a great variety of tasks by the SCM authority, the CCB and many others involved in software development and maintenance. All the respective tasks are defined in the SCM procedures. SCM audits are performed by the SCM authority and the CCB in order to control compliance with SCM procedures. SCM audits may be combined with internal quality issues (see Chapter 27), and are expected to initiate updates and changes of SCM procedures and instructions. Hence, SCM audits check whether and how these tasks were performed for samples of change requests, SCIs, and software configuration versions. SCM audits may be also performed for a sample of planned releases, as specified in the SCMP. However, although we may expect SCM audits to yield information regarding the level of compliance to SCM procedures (including typical failures of those procedures), they cannot serve as compliance enforcement tools.

The following is a list of typical bits of control information that SCM audits are meant to discover and transmit to management:

- Percentage of unapproved changes introduced in the system during development or operation.
- Percentage of SCOs not carried out according to instructions and not fully complying with procedures.
- Percentage of design reviews and software tests of changed SCIs that have not been performed according to the relevant procedures.
- Percentage of SCOs that have been completed on schedule.
- Percentages of cases where SCIs affected by changes have not been checked, with some necessary changes not implemented.
- Percentages of properly documented new SCIs and software configuration versions.
- Percentage of properly documented installations of new software configuration versions.
- Percentage of cases of failure to transmit all version–related information to the customer.
- Number of cases recorded annually where the SCI work coordination mechanisms failed (i.e., did not prevent different teams from simultaneously introducing changes in the same SCI).

18.7 Computerized tools for managing software configuration

Computerized SCM tools have been on the market for many years. These computerized tools differ in their level of comprehensiveness, flexibility of application and ease of use. More comprehensive tools can supply most or almost all of the SCM information services listed in Section 18.5.

It is expected that a computerized tool will be able to comply with the required level of accuracy and completeness of information, and with the required level of availability (measured by the response time from request of information to its provision).

The computerized SCM tools also operate the mechanisms coordinating the work on an SCI's changes and prevent different teams from simultaneously introducing changes in the same SCI.

An additional benefit of the use of a computerized SCM system is the high security level it is able to provide:

- It secures the code version and documentation files versions by protecting them from any changes, deletions and other damages.
- It activates back-up procedures required for safe SCM file storage.

Current enhanced tools are characterized by easier input capacities, coordination of SCM support teams operating in different development environments, including geographically distributed teams, and provision of an expanded variety of reporting options.

Summary

(1) Define software configuration version.

A software configuration version is an approved set of the SCI versions that constitute a documented software system at a given point of time. The respective activities are controlled by *software configuration management* procedures.

(2) Explain the tasks of software configuration management.

Software configuration management tasks are classified into the following four groups:
- Control of software change
- Release of SCI and software configuration versions
- Provision of SCM information services
- Verification of compliance to SCM procedures.

(3) List the main tasks of software change control.

The main tasks of software change management can be described as:
- Examining change requests and approving implementation those requests that qualify.
- Controlling the changes and assuring the quality of approved changes.
- Documenting the approved changes.
- Applying mechanisms that prevent more than one team from simultaneously introducing changes into the same SCI.

(4) Explain the difference between baseline and intermediate software configuration versions.

Baseline versions are configuration versions that are planned ahead, during a system's development or operating stage. As part of the process, baseline versions are also reviewed and approved. As a rule, they serve as milestones in the software system's life cycle.

Intermediate versions are software configuration versions released, in most cases, to respond to immediate needs. These may range from correction of defects identified in an important SCI to swift introduction of adaptations to meet a new customer's requirements. As expected, intermediate versions will not receive the attention and efforts typically invested in baseline versions.

(5) Explain the objectives of software configuration management plans.

The main objective of a software configuration management plan (SCMP) is to plan ahead the required resources to carry out all the activities required for the software configuration releases. An additional objective of the SCMP is to enable one to follow up the progress of activities involved in software version release. SCMPs are required during the development stage as well as the operation (maintenance) stage.

(6) Describe the nature of the tasks performed in software configuration management audits.

SCM audits are based on checking the tasks performed for samples of change requests, SCIs, and software configurations. Typical checks included in SCM audits include the percentage of cases of compliance with procedures or, alternatively, of failure to comply with procedures.

Selected bibliography

1. IEEE (1998) "IEEE Std 828–1998–IEEE Standard for Software Configuration Management Plans", in *IEEE Software Engineering Standards Collection*, The Institute of Electrical and Electronics Engineers, New York.
2. ISO (1997) *ISO 9000–3:1997(E), Quality Management and Quality Assurance Standards – Part 3: Guidelines for the Application of ISO 9001:1994 to the Development, Supply, Installation and Maintenance of Computer Software*, 2nd edn, International Organization for Standardization (ISO), Geneva, paragraph 4.8.
3. ISO/IEC (2001) "ISO 9000–3:2001 Software and System Engineering – Guidelines for the Application of ISO 9001:2000 to Software, Final draft", International Organization for Standardization (ISO), Geneva, unpublished draft, December 2001.
4. Leon, A. (1999) *A Guide to Software Configuration Management*, Artech House, Boston, MA.
5. Paulk, M. C., Weber, C. V., Curtis, B. and Chrissis, M. B. (1995) *The Capability Maturity Model: Guidelines for Improving the Software Process*, Addison-Wesley, Reading, MA, pp. 180–191.
6. Pressman, R. S. (2000) *Software Engineering – A Practitioner's Approach*, European adaptation by D. Ince, 5th edn, McGraw-Hill International, London.
7. Siegel, G. S. and Donaldson S. D. (1999) "Software configuration management – a practical look", in G.G. Schulmeyer and J. I. McManus (eds), *Handbook of Software Quality Assurance*, 3rd edn, Prentice Hall, Upper Saddle River, NJ, pp. 255–290.
8. Van Vliet, H. (2000) *Software Engineering Principles and Practices*, Ch. 4, John Wiley & Sons, New York.

Review questions

18.1 One of the tasks of an SCM is to supply information about sites where a given software configuration version is installed (Table 18.2).

Explain potential uses for this type of information and its contribution to software quality.

18.2 Design documents or source code files are identified and stored as SCIs (see Frame 18.2) for obvious reasons: further development of the software system or its correction can not take place without accurate copies of these items.

Explain in your own words why the following should be identified and stored as SCIs:

(1) Test cases
(2) Compiler
(3) Software installation plans
(4) Software change request files.

18.3 An SCR relating to only two of the software source SCIs has been approved. However, the software test plan prepared by the Testing Unit mentioned nine of the system's software source SCIs.

Explain in your own words why it may not be sufficient to test the two SCIs specified in the SCR after they were changed.

18.4 It is mentioned that a version history of a software system configuration includes baseline, intermediate and revision version releases.

(1) Explain in your own words the function of each type of release.
(2) Explain in your own words the special importance of baseline versions.

18.5 Frame 18.6 is a template that lists the information items necessary for software configuration version documentation (VDD).

List possible uses for each of the information items mentioned in the template.

18.6 The SCM Authority is expected to spend a significant part of its resources in carrying out software configuration audits.

(1) List the main SQM audit tasks.
(2) Explain the contribution of each task to software quality.

Topics for discussion

18.1 One of the tasks of SCM is to: "Apply mechanisms that coordinate the changes made to an SCI by preventing more than one team from simultaneously introducing changes into the same SCI".

(1) Explain in your own words the importance of this task and its contribution to software quality.
(2) Supply an example that illustrates the consequences of failure of SCM to effectively implement this objective.

18.2 The success of an SQA system depends to a great extent on compliance to SCM procedures.

(1) Referring to the software change control tasks of SCM, explain in your own words the risks incurred to software quality by partial compliance to SCM procedures.

(2) Referring to the release of new versions of the software system, explain in your own words the risks incurred to software quality by partial compliance to SCM procedures.

(3) What tools are available for verification of compliance to SCM procedures?

18.3 Two SCRs have been placed before the CCB for a decision. Some of their characteristics are:

SCR–1:

- Expected to contribute substantially to the sales of the company's leading software package
- Essence of the change: introduction of new software functions
- Changes in two software SCIs are required
- Other SCIs expected to be affected by the requested change – none
- Estimate of required professional resources – 40 man-days
- Estimated timetable for implementation – 2 months.

SCR–2:

- Expected to save substantial help desk resources, due to the improved user interface
- Essence of the change: improvement of the user interface to make it easier and more user-friendly
- Changes in 11 software SCIs are required
- Other SCIs expected to be affected by the requested change – 8
- Estimate of required professional resources – 15 man-days
- Estimated timetable for implementation – 2 months.

(1) Can you determine which of the requests deserves the higher priority? What are your supporting arguments?

(2) If you find it difficult to decide the priorities, what additional information do you require to prioritize the SCRs?

18.4 "Audit trails" are basic requirements of proper SQA documentation. In order for a document to comply with audit trail requirements, the documentation has to provide information enabling identification of the source for each event and/or item recorded. This information enables future location of the source according to document reference, name of programmer who coded the software unit, and so forth.

(1) List at least two audit trails required within the framework of SQM and show how the required audit trail information is meant to become available.

(2) Explain how the audit trails you described in (1) contribute to software quality.

18.5 Software houses that develop and maintain COTS software packages to serve large customer populations are recommended to adopt the line evolution model for their packages rather than the tree evolution model.

(1) Describe the principles of the line and tree evolution models and the environments in which they are used.

(2) Do you agree with the above recommendation? List your arguments for and against.

(3) What consequences for the structure and size of the COTS software packages would follow from adopting this recommendation?

(4) What are the consequences of this recommendation from the user's perspective?

18.6 The software maintenance department provides services to 215 customers that use one or more of the company's three popular software packages. From time to time a maintenance team discovers that the software version installed in a customer's site includes unrecorded changes, never requested by an SCR nor approved as part of an SCO.

(1) Who do you believe inserted the unrecorded changes and under what conditions could this occur?

(2) What effect could this event have on maintenance performance, and what is its expected influence on software quality from the perspective of the customer?

(3) What measures could be taken to make sure that no such unauthorized changes occur?

18.7 The VDD document (see Frame 18.6) includes a list of unsolved problems pertaining to a released software version.

Discuss the justification for including this type of information in a VDD.

18.8 Most SCM systems are operated nowadays by specialized software packages.

Explain the special features offered effectively and efficiently only by computerized management software packages and explain their contribution to software quality.

Documentation control

Software development and maintenance processes involve production and use of a multitude of documents; some are vital immediately while others may become vital for software quality assurance over the life cycle of the system. Special procedures for documentation control (usually called *documentation procedures, documentation control procedures* or *control of documents procedures*) are therefore introduced to indicate which documents are indeed expected to be vital at some point and to assure their appropriate preparation and availability. Documents that display these characteristics and that are treated according to these procedures are called *controlled documents*. One type of controlled document – *quality records* – is aimed mainly to provide evidence that the development and maintenance processes were performed in conformity to requirements and that the software quality system is operating fully and effectively.

The issues of documentation control together with the characteristics of controlled documents and quality records are the subject of this chapter. Documentation control, controlled documents and quality records are important components of the SQA system, as indicated by the ISO 9000-3 standard conception: see ISO (1997), ISO/IEC (2001) and IEEE/EIA

Std 12207 (IEEE/EIA, 1996, 1997). A number of specialized documentation standards, such as IEEE Std 1063 (IEEE, 2001), have been constructed to this end.

After completing this chapter, you will be able to:

■ Explain the objectives of controlled documents.

■ Describe the tasks involved in establishment and maintenance of a controlled documents list.

■ Discuss the issues covered by documentation control procedures.

19.1 Introduction: where is the documentation?

Jeff, Head of the Legal Department, was obviously furious when he entered the office of Roberto, the Software Development Department's Manager. Ignoring preliminaries, he stated: "You can't imagine the difficulties I am having while trying to collect evidence to support our case in the Margaret Gardens claim. Jerry, who directed the development project, mentioned lots of documents that could have supported me. You know, the project was completed just 16 months ago yet so many important documents are already unavailable or flawed:

■ The minutes of the joint meetings held with the customer to discuss our proposal prior to signing the contract, during which some major changes were agreed to, were thrown out or shredded two months ago.

■ A software change request form submitted last August by Margaret Gardens is available but, unbelievably, it is unsigned. The requested change was implemented just four months ago; however, the respective SCO (software change order) as well as the test report for the completed change are missing.

■ Some of the major claims relate to software design. I managed to find the minutes of only one of the three design review sessions attended by customer representatives. Another review session report, located in the unit's filing system, was not signed by the customer's representatives.

■ Lastly, the summary test report issued by the joint testing committee, with Margaret Gardens participating, is missing. The Testing Unit's secretary believes that the document is in the possession of Ted James, who left us a year ago and moved to Indiana.

Once Jeff left, Roberto called Martin, his deputy, into his office. "Jeff just left after voicing some serious complaints. As you remember, quite similar complaints have frequently been heard from our development and maintenance team leaders. Please prepare a proposal, including the necessary procedures, to solve these documentation problems."

In this section, we present a detailed definition of controlled documents and quality records, the objectives of their management, the authority established for this purpose and the compliance required.

19.2.1 Definitions and objectives

Let us first discuss controlled document and quality records, as defined in Frame 19.1.

Frame 19.1 **Controlled document and quality record – definitions**

Controlled document

A document that is currently vital or may become vital for the development and maintenance of software systems as well as for the management of current and future relationships with the customer. Hence, its preparation, storage, retrieval and disposal are controlled by documentation procedures. The main objectives for managing controlled documents are:

- To assure the quality of the document.

- To assure its technical completeness and compliance with document structure procedures and instructions (use of templates, proper signing, etc.).

- To assure the future availability of documents that may be required for software system maintenance, further development, or responses to the customer's (tentative) future complaints.

- To support investigation of software failure causes and to assign responsibility as part of corrective and other actions.

Quality record

A quality record is a special type of controlled document. It is a customer-targeted document that may be required to demonstrate full compliance with customer requirements and effective operation of the software quality assurance system throughout the development and maintenance processes.

Frame 19.2 presents an overview of the types of documents that may be categorized as controlled documents. An examination of the document list reveals that a good number of the controlled documents may be classified as quality records. The magnitude of the list and its composition vary between organizations and depend on the characteristics of the customers in addition to those of the software packages. Contracts for large-scale "custom-made" software projects usually require quite different lists of controlled documents than do COTS software packages.

Frame 19.2   Typical controlled documents (including quality records)

Pre-project documents

- Contract review report
- Contract negotiation meeting minutes
- Software development contract
- Software maintenance contract
- Software development subcontracting contract
- Software development plan

Project life cycle documents

- System requirements document
- Software requirements document
- Preliminary design document
- Critical design document
- Database description
- Software test plan
- Design review report
- Follow-up records of design review action items
- Software test procedure
- Software test report
- Software user manuals
- Software maintenance manuals
- Software installation plan
- Version description document
- Software change requests
- Software change orders
- Software maintenance requests
- Maintenance services reports
- Records of subcontractor evaluations

SQA infrastructure documents

- SQA procedures
- Template library
- SQA forms library
- CAB meeting minutes

Software quality management documents

- Progress reports
- Software metrics reports

SQA system audit documents

- Management review report
- Minutes of management review meeting
- Internal quality audit report
- External SQA certification audit report

Customer documents

- Software project tender documents
- Customer's software change requests

The document types listed in Frame 19.2 are produced during the implementation of a variety of SQA processes, to mention but a few:

- Contract and negotiation process
- Development process
- Software change process
- Maintenance services
- Software quality metrics
- Internal quality audits.

Many of the processes listed above are readily recognized as SQA processes, while many of the controlled documents listed in Frame 19.2 are products of those processes. As other chapters of the book deal with the specific processes, they need not be discussed here.

19.2.2 Documentation control procedures

The SQA tools that regulate the handling of a controlled document from its creation to its final disposal are called *documentation control procedures*. Typical components of such procedures are presented in Frame 19.3.

| Frame 19.3 | **Typical components of documentation control procedures** |

- Definition of the list of the document types and updates to be controlled
- Document preparation requirements
- Document approval requirements
- Document storage and retrieval requirements, including controlled storage of document versions, revisions and disposal

Naturally, documentation control procedures vary among organizations according to the nature of their software products and maintenance services, their customers, their structure and their size, among other characteristics. In other words, one organization's procedures might be totally inadequate for a different organization.

Two documentation control tasks – namely, storage and retrieval – are included among the organization's software configuration management procedures and performed with a variety of software configuration management tools. Yet, special efforts are still needed to coordinate documentation procedures with those of software configuration management.

It should be noted that documentation requirements are integral parts of most SQA procedures. Therefore, coordination of these requirements with documentation control procedure requirements is of utmost importance.

Implementation tip

The use of subcontractors in the development and in some cases the maintenance of software systems is the source of various documentation control procedures to be applied with subcontractors. These procedures should assure that subcontractors' documents – such as design documents – comply with the contractor's documentation procedures. Communication difficulties as well as negligence often result in a subcontractor's partial compliance. The damages caused by such lapses may become apparent months or even years later, when a vital document is missing or is discovered to provide inadequate or only partial information. Prevention of such situations can be achieved by appropriate contract clauses as well as by continuous follow-up of subcontractor compliance with documentation requirements.

The following sections are dedicated to the components of the documentation control procedure, namely:

- The controlled documents list
- Controlled document preparation
- Controlled document approval issues
- Issues of controlled document storage and retrieval issues.

19.3 The controlled documents list

The key to management of controlled documents (including quality records) is the controlled document types list. Proper construction of the list is based on the establishment of an authority to implement the concept, whether embodied in a person or a committee. Specifically, this authority is responsible for:

- Deciding which document type is to be categorized as a controlled document and which controlled document types are to be classified as quality records.

- Deciding whether the level of control is adequate for each document type categorized as a controlled document.

- Following up of compliance with the controlled document types list. This subject can be incorporated in the internal quality audits plan (see Chapter 26).

- Analyzing follow-up findings and initiating the required updates, changes, removals and additions to the controlled documents types list.

Most controlled document types are documents created internally by the organization itself. Nonetheless, a substantial number of external document types, such as contract documents and minutes of joint committee meetings, also fall into this category.

The documentation requirements involved in the creation of a new document or the revision of an existing document focus on completeness, improved readability and availability. These requirements are realized in the documents:

- Structure
- Identification method
- Standard orientation and reference information.

The document's **structure** may be free or defined by a template. Templates and their contribution to software quality are discussed in Section 15.1.

An **identification method** is devised to provide each document, version and revision with a unique identity. The method usually entails notation of (a) the software system or product name or number, (b) the document (type) code and (c) the version and revision number. The method can vary for different types of documents.

The document's **orientation and reference information** may be required as well. Orientation and reference information support future access of required documents by supplying information about the content of the document and its suitability to the needs of the future user. Depending on the document type, a greater or smaller proportion of the following information items is commonly required:

- The document's author(s)
- Date of completion
- Person(s) who approved the document, including position(s) held
- Date of approval
- Signature(s) of the author(s) and person(s) who approved it
- Descriptions of the changes introduced in the new release
- List of former versions and revisions
- Circulation list
- Confidentiality restrictions.

The relevant documentation procedures and work instructions pertain to paper as well as electronic documents (e.g., e-mail and intranet applications).

19.5 Issues of controlled document approval

Certain documents require approval while others may be exempt from the associated review. For those documents that must be approved, the relevant procedures indicate the position of the person(s) authorized to do so for each type of document and the details of the process implemented.

Approval can be granted by a person, several persons, or a committee – such as a formal design review (FDR) committee – according to the type of document and the organization's preferences. The holders of the positions authorized by the documentation control procedures are expected to have the experience and technical expertise sufficient to the task of document review.

The approval process

Approval of documents is required for reasons that go beyond assuring the documents' quality; approval is also aimed at detecting and preventing professional inadequacies together with deviations from the document template. In cases where FDR approval is required, the appropriate review procedures should be applied (see Section 8.2).

Implementation tip

Observation of the approval process frequently reveals instances of rubber-stamping, that is, situations where the process does not contribute to the document's quality due to the absence or neglect of thorough document review. Some claim that formal approval actually reduces a document's quality because the person(s) authorized to approve the document, by the very act of approval, become directly responsible for its quality. Accordingly, two options may be considered for the relevant document types: (a) exemption of the document type from approval, meaning that full responsibility is returned to the author, or (b) implementation of an approval process that assures thorough review of the document. In other words, the implied solution to rubber-stamping is either revision of the approval process or its total elimination.

19.6 Issues of controlled document storage and retrieval

Requirements pertaining to controlled storage and retrieval of documents are set mainly to assure a document's security and its continued availability. The same requirements should apply to paper documents as well as electronic and other media. They refer to:

- Document storage *per se*
- Circulation and retrieval of documents
- Document security, including document disposal.

Document storage requirements apply to (1) the number of copies to be stored, (2) the unit responsible for storage of each copy, and (3) the storage medium. Storage on electronic media is usually much more efficient and more economical than storage on paper. Still, paper originals of certain documents are kept in compliance with legal stipulations. In these cases, an image processing copy is stored in addition to the paper original.

Circulation and retrieval of documents requirements refer to (1) instructions for circulating a new document, on time, to the designated recipients, and (2) efficient and accurate retrieval of copies, in full compliance with security restrictions. The procedures should apply to the circulation of paper documents as well as use of e-mail, intranet and the Internet.

Document security, including document disposal requirements, (1) provide restricted access to document types, (2) prevent unauthorized changes to stored documents, (3) provide back-up for stored paper as well as electronic files, and (4) determine the storage period. At the end of a specified storage period, documents may be discarded or removed to lower-standard storage containers, a shift that usually reduces availability. While paper files are prone to fire and flood damage, modern electronic storage is subject to electronic risks. The planned method for back-up storage reflects the level of these risks and the relative importance of the documents.

Summary

(1) Explain the objectives of controlled documents.

The main objectives for managing controlled documents are:
- To assure the quality of the document.
- To assure the document's technical completeness, compliance with approved document structure and use instructions (use of templates, proper signing, etc.).
- To assure future availability of documents that may be required for maintenance, further development of the software system or responding to the customer's complaints.
- To support investigation of software failure causes and to assign responsibility as part of corrective and other actions.

(2) Describe the tasks involved in establishment and maintenance of a controlled documents list.

The objectives of this component of the documentation procedure are fulfilled by a defined authority whose responsibilities entail:
- Deciding which document types are to be categorized as controlled documents and which controlled document types are to be classified as quality records.
- Deciding the level of control adequate for each type of document.
- Following up of compliance with the controlled documents list. This task may be introduced into the internal quality audits plan.
- Analyzing follow-up findings and initiating the required updates, changes, removals and additions to the controlled documents list.

(3) Discuss the issues covered by documentation control procedures.

The issues related to controlled documents and quality records covered by documentation procedures are:

■ Definition of the types of documents to be controlled
■ Document preparation requirements
■ Document approval requirements
■ Document storage and retrieval requirements.

Definition of the list of controlled documents and their maintenance is carried out by authorized person(s) responsible for carrying out the activities mentioned above.

Document preparation issues include document structure and identification as well as standard orientation and reference information.

Document approval issues include designation of the organizational position of the person(s) authorized to approve a document and delineation of the approval process that assures the document's quality and completeness.

Document storage requirements apply to paper documents as well as electronic media. The main issues involved are the documents' circulation, assurance of future availability and retrieval, and security, including disposal at the appropriate time.

Selected bibliography

1. IEEE (2001) "IEEE Std 1063-2001 – IEEE Standard for Software User Documentation", in *IEEE Software Engineering Standards Collection*, The Institute of Electrical and Electronics Engineers, New York.
2. IEEE/EIA (1996) "IEEE/EIA Std 12207.0-1996 – IEEE/EIA Standard – Industry Implementation of International Standard ISO/IEC 12207:1995", in *IEEE Software Engineering Standards Collection*, The Institute of Electrical and Electronics Engineers, New York, paragraph 6.1.
3. IEEE/EIA (1997) "IEEE/EIA Std 12207.1–1997 – IEEE/EIA Guide – Industry Implementation of International Standard ISO/IEC 12207:1995, Software Life Cycle Processes – Implementation Considerations", in *IEEE Software Engineering Standards Collection*, The Institute of Electrical and Electronics Engineers, New York, paragraph 6.1.
4. ISO (1997) *ISO 9000–3:1997(E), Quality Management and Quality Assurance Standards – Part 3: Guidelines for the Application of ISO 9001:1994 to the Development, Supply, Installation and Maintenance of Computer Software*, 2nd edn, International Organization for Standardization (ISO), Geneva, paragraph 4.16.
5. ISO/IEC (2001) "ISO 9000-3:2001 Software and System Engineering – Guidelines for the Application of ISO 9001:2000 to Software, Final draft", International Organization for Standardization (ISO), Geneva, unpublished draft, December 2001, paragraph 4.2.

19.1 The following documents are listed in Frame 19.2:

■ Software development contract
■ Design review report
■ Software metrics report.

(1) Which of the above documents do you believe should be defined as controlled documents, and why?
(2) Which of the documents that you have defined as controlled documents do you believe should also be classified as quality records and why?
(3) Suggest an imaginary situation that illustrates the control of a document belonging to each of the types you specified.

19.2 Choose six of the document types listed in Frame 19.2 (one from each group).

(1) Which of the above document types do you believe should be defined as controlled documents? List your arguments.
(2) Which of the document types that you defined as controlled documents do you believe should also be classified as quality records? List your arguments.
(3) Which of the listed objectives of controlled documents may be achieved by the use of documents of the specified types you have chosen?

19.3 Section 19.3 discusses the procedure component that manages the controlled documents list.

(1) Describe in your own words the tasks to be performed by the authority appointed to implement this component and discuss their importance.
(2) Explain the contribution of controlled documents and quality records to software quality assurance.

19.4 It has been said that documentation procedures are the main tool for implementing the objectives of controlled documents and quality records.

(1) Explain in your own words the issues addressed by these procedures.
(2) Discuss how each of the procedural issues mentioned in (1) contributes to achievement of the objectives of controlled documents and quality records while indicating the associated objectives.
(3) List other procedures involved in documentation control issues.

Topics for discussion

19.1 The introduction presents four examples of documentation system failure in a software development company.

(1) Examine each of the examples and determine what type of failure it is – a controlled document failure or a quality record failure? Explain your answer.
(2) For each of the above examples, describe the lapse in implementation of documentation control procedures that caused the failure.

19.2 The handling of several types of documents requires compliance to SCM (see Chapter 18) and documentation procedures simultaneously.

(1) Explain in your own words whether the requirements are contradictory or complementary.
(2) Suggest directions for coordination between documentation control and SCM procedures.

19.3 Section 19.3 discusses the tasks to be performed in order to provide an updated controlled documents list and the responsibilities of the appointed authority that carries out the tasks.

(1) Explain the need for such an authority and why the local solutions proposed by unit leaders, department managers and so forth are to be rejected.
(2) Who do you think should be appointed as the authority? Refer to specific organizational positions and explain their suitability for the assignment.

19.4 Paper-based storage systems can be used alongside electronic systems to serve an organization's documentation requirements.

Compare the two storage technologies and list, for each, their advantages and disadvantages for performing the various tasks required by the documentation control procedure.

part V

Management components of software quality

As the previous chapters have indicated, the SQA system also includes tools to be applied by management. The three basic SQA management tools offered here are:

- Project progress control
- Software quality metrics
- Software quality costs.

The first managerial SQA tool, project progress control, enables management to oversee each project and initiate, when required, changes and improvements in how a project is performed. Software quality metrics and software quality costs provide overviews of the headway made in assuring software quality by identifying evolving trends. A fourth category of managerial SQA tools, those available for control of software maintenance, have already been discussed in Chapter 11.

Prior to reviewing these managerial SQA tools, we should ourselves ask a fundamental question: does application of these managerial SQA tools promote management's contribution to the achievement of software quality assurance objectives?

The reasons for our response – a qualified "yes" – can be found in Frame 2.7, which presents a comprehensive list of software quality assurance objectives. Here we cite the following, which are specific to software development:

- Conformity to functional technical requirements
- Conformity to scheduling and budgetary requirements
- Initiation of improvements to the software development process (including SQA activities).

A detailed "snapshot" of these contributions, summarized in Table V.1, reveals that the SQA tools mentioned above provide good coverage for most managerial SQA objectives. Project process control is, however, the most encompassing of these tools.

Table V.1: The contributions of managerial SQA tools

Objectives of software quality assurance in the software development process	Managerial SQA tools		
	Project progress control	Software quality metrics	Software quality costs
Conformity to functional technical requirements	+		
Conformity to scheduling and budgetary requirements	+		
Initiation of improvements to the software development process	+	+	+

Project progress control

Months of delay in completing project phases and budget overruns exceeding tens of percents are "red flags" for project management. These events, which are mainly failures of management itself, are caused by situations such as:

■ Overly or even blindly optimistic scheduling and budgeting (often beginning earlier, during the proposal development stage).

■ Unprofessional software risk management expressed as tardy or inappropriate reactions to software risks.

■ Belated identification of schedule and budget difficulties and/or underestimation of their extent.

Situations of the first type can be prevented by using contract review and project planning tools. Project progress control is expected to prevent situations of the second and third types.

While design reviews, inspections and software tests focus on a project's professional (technical–functional) aspects, project progress control deals mainly with its managerial aspects, namely scheduling, human and other resources, budget and risk management.

The importance of using managerial SQA tools during software development is underscored by the consequences of their neglect: the relatively higher risks of delayed project completion and budget deviations, especially when compared to other industries (e.g., civil engineering). The seriousness of these outcomes is directly related to the special characteristics exhibited by software development projects (see Chapter 1).

The components of project progress control and their implementation are discussed in this chapter. Special attention is assigned to the difficulties entailed with controlling external participants and internal projects. Another section deals with tools for project progress control.

Management's control over maintenance contracts is discussed in Section 11.4.4, within our comprehensive discussion of quality assurance of software maintenance (see Chapter 11). Several software maintenance activities, especially perfective maintenance, include tasks that are similar to software development tasks. Hence, progress control of these tasks can be performed by applying the progress control components discussed in this chapter.

The place of project progress control is attested to in SQA general life cycle standards: the ISO 9000-3 Standard (ISO (1997) Sec. 4.9 and ISO/IEC (2001) Sec. 7.5) and the IEEE/EIA Std 12207 (IEEE/EIA 1996, 1997a, 1997b). It is also the subject of specialized standards: see IEEE Std 1058 (IEEE, 1998a) and IEEE Std 1490 (IEEE, 1998b).

After completing this chapter, you will be able to:

■ Explain the components of project progress control.
■ Explain the implementation issues involved in project progress control.

20.1 The components of project progress control

Project progress control (CMM uses the term "software project tracking") has one immediate objective: early detection of irregular events. Detection promotes the timely initiation of problem-solving responses. The accumulated information on progress control as well as successes and extreme failures also serve a long-term objective: initiation of corrective actions.

The main components of project progress control are:

■ Control of risk management activities
■ Project schedule control
■ Project resource control
■ Project budget control.

Control of risk management activities
This refers to the software development risk items identified in the pre-project stage, those listed in contract review and project plan documents, together with other risk items identified throughout the project's progress (see Appendix 6A). The software development team copes with software risk items by applying systematic risk management activities. Control of the progress of risk management begins with the preparation of periodic assess-

ments about the state of software risk items and the expected outcomes of the risk management activities performed in their wake. Based on these reports, project managers are expected to intervene and help arrive at a solution in the more extreme cases. Several standards and many books and articles deal with software project risks, e.g., IEEE (2001) and Jones (1994), to mention just two.

Project schedule control

This deals with the project's compliance with its approved and contracted timetables. Follow-up is based mainly on milestones, which are set (in part) to facilitate identification of delays in completion of planned activities. Milestones set in contracts, especially dates for delivery of specified software products to the customer or completion of a development activity, generally receive special emphasis. Although some delay can be anticipated, management will focus its control activities on critical delays, those that may substantially affect final completion of the project. Much of the information needed for management project progress control is transmitted by means of milestone reports and other periodic reports. In response to this information, management may intervene by allocating additional resources or even renegotiating the schedule with the customer.

Project resource control

This focuses on professional human resources but it can deal with other assets as well. For real-time software systems and firmware, software development and testing facilities resources typically demand the most exacting control. Here as well, management's control is based on periodic reports of resource use that compare actual to scheduled utilization because, it should be stressed, the true extent of deviations in resource use can be assessed only from the viewpoint of the project's progress. In other words, a project displaying what appears to be only slight deviations in resource utilization when considering the resources scheduled used up to a specific point of time (e.g., 5%) may actually experience severe cumulative deviations (e.g., 25%) if severe delays in its progress are suffered.

Another aspect of resource control is internal composition or allocation. For example, management may find that no deviations have taken place in total man-months allocated to system analysts. However, review of itemized expenditures may disclose that instead of the 25% of man-months originally allocated to senior system analysts, 50% was actually spent, a step that may eventually undermine the planned budget. Although project budget controls also reveal deviations of this type, they do so at a much later stage of the project, a fact that impedes introduction of remedial actions. If the deviations are justified, management can intervene by increasing the resources allocated; alternatively, management can shift resources by reorganizing the project teams, revising the project's plan, and so forth.

Project budget control
This is based on the comparison of actual with scheduled expenditures. As in resource control, a more accurate picture of budget deviations requires that the associated delays in completion of activities be taken into consideration. The main budget items demanding control are:

- Human resources
- Development and testing facilities
- Purchase of COTS software
- Purchase of hardware
- Payments to subcontractors.

Again, like resource control, budget control is based on milestones and the periodic reports that facilitate early identification of budget overruns. In cases of deviations by internal bodies, the menu of optional interventions is similar to that applied in project resource control. In deviations by external participants, legal and other measures may also be applied.

Budget control is obviously of the highest priority to management because of its direct effect on project profitability. Managers therefore tend to neglect other components of project progress control, especially if they are under serious constraints imposed by monitoring staff. Neglect of other components of project progress control naturally reduces the effect of control in general. This is regrettable because if applied correctly and in a timely manner, these other progress control tools can reveal unresolved software risk items, delays in completion of activities and excessive use of resources at a much earlier stage in the project life cycle. This means that reliance solely on budget control activities may be more costly in the long run than application of the full spate of project progress control activities because implementation of effective solutions to problems may be delayed.

20.2 Progress control of internal projects and external participants

Project progress control is initiated in order to provide management with a comprehensive view of all the software development activities carried out in an organization. Nevertheless, in most organizations, project control provides, for different reasons, a limited view of the progress of internal software development and an even more limited view of the progress made by external participants. Control over internal projects and external participants tends to be somewhat flawed, as we will describe.

Internal projects, such as those undertaken for other departments or projects dealing with software packages for the general software market, exclude, by definition, the option of external customers. These projects thus tend to occupy a lower place among management's priorities. The inadequate attention awarded is often accompanied by inappropriate or lax follow-up on the part of the internal customer. (Similar tendencies are observed in the earlier pre-project stage, in preparation development plans; see Sections 5.5 and 6.4.2.) Typically, this situation results in tardy identification of adverse delays and severe budget overruns, with the ensuing limited correction of the problems encountered. The inevitable solution to this situation is the imposition of the full range of project progress controls to internal projects as well.

External participants include subcontractors, suppliers of COTS software and reused software modules and, in some cases, the customer himself (see Section 12.5.8). The more sizeable and complex the project, the greater the likelihood that external participants will be required, and the larger the proportion of work allocated to them. Management turns to external participants for any number of reasons, ranging from economic to technical to personnel-related interests, and this trend has been growing in project contracting and subcontracting. Moreover, the agreements entered into by the participants in a project have become so intricate that communication and coordination have become problematic for the project team as well as for management. In response, more significant efforts are called for in order to achieve acceptable levels of control. Hence, project progress control of external participants must focus mainly on the project's schedule and the risks identified in planned project activities.

For a comprehensive discussion of the subject of assuring quality in projects with external participants, see Chapter 12.

20.3 Implementation of project progress control regimes

Project progress control is usually based on procedures that determine:

■ The allocation of responsibility for performance of the process control tasks that are appropriate for the project's characteristics, including size:
  - The person or management unit responsible for executing progress control tasks
  - The frequency of reporting required from each of the project's units and administrative level
  - The situations requiring project leaders to report immediately to management
  - The situations requiring lower management to report immediately to upper management.
■ Management audits of project progress, which deal mainly with: (1) how well progress reports are transmitted by project leaders and by lower- to upper-level managers, and (2) the specific management control activities to be initiated.

In large software development organizations, project progress control may be conducted on several managerial levels, such as software department management, software division management and top management. Although each level is expected to define its own project progress control regime, one that reflects the parameters considered adequate for assessing the project's progress from that particular location, coordination among the various levels is mandatory for progress control to be effective.

The entire reporting chain transmits information culled from the lowest managerial level – the project leader's periodic progress report – which summarizes the status of project risks, project schedule and resources utilization, that is, the first three components of progress control. The project leader bases his or her progress report on information gathered from team leaders. An example of a project leader's project progress report is presented in Figure 20.1.

20.4 Computerized tools for project progress control

Computerized tools for software project progress control are a clear necessity given the increasing size and complexity of projects on one hand, and the benefits they bring with them on the other. The comprehensive project management tools that have been available in the market for many years can serve most of the control components of software projects quite effectively and efficiently. The majority of these general-purpose packages apply PERT/CPM analysis so that the resulting reports take the interactions between activities and the criticality of each activity into account. These packages are usually readily adaptable to specific cases due to the great variety of options that they offer.

Examples of services that computerized tools can provide are as follows.

Control of risk management activities
- Lists of software risk items by category and their planned solution dates.
- Lists of exceptions of software risk items – overrun solution dates that can affect the project completion date.

Project schedule control
- Classified lists of delayed activities.
- Classified lists of delays of critical activities – delays that can, if not corrected, affect the project's completion date.
- Updated activity schedules generated according to progress reports and correction measures applied – for teams, development units, etc.
- Classified lists of delayed milestones.
- Updated milestone schedules generated according to progress reports and applied correction measures – for teams, development units, etc.

Project Leader's Progress Report

For the period: _____

The project: _____

1 Status of software risks

No.	Risk item	Activities involved	Other projects involved	Solved	Risk severity	Comments
1						
2						
3						
4						
5						
6						

Risk severity: 1 – Solution expected within one month. 2 – Solution expected within 3 months. 3 – Solution expected within 6 months. 4 – Solution directions are available, good success prospects. 5 – All trials failed, no possible solution is identified.

2 Status of resources use

No.	Activity	Hours Worked				Percent of activity completed	Comments
		Planned	Used prior to report period	Invested during report period	Total invested		
1							
2							
3							
4							
5							
6							
7							
8							
9							
10							
11							

3 Project completion estimates (mark the most probable estimate)

Human resources	Completed with less than planned	No additional resources required	10% Excess	20% Excess	30% Excess	40% Excess	50% Excess or more
Timetable	Completed before planned date	Completed on time	2 weeks delay	1 month delay	2 months delay	4 months delay	6 months delay and more

Comments:

Signed: Name:_____ Date:_____ Signature:_____

Figure 20.1: Project leader's progress report – example

Project resource control

■ Project resources allocation plan – for activities and software modules, for teams, development units, designated time periods, etc.

■ Project resources utilization – by period or accumulated – as specified above.

■ Project resources utilization exceptions – by period or accumulated – as specified above.

■ Updated resources allocation plans generated according to progress reports and correction measures applied.

Project budget control

■ Project budget plans – by activity and software module, for teams, development units, designated time periods, etc.

■ Project budget utilization reports – by period or accumulated – as specified above.

■ Project budget utilization deviations – by period or accumulated – as specified above.

■ Updated budget plans generated according to progress reports and correction measures applied.

Summary

(1) Explain the components of management's control of project progress.

There are four main components of project progress control. Management is expected to intervene and contribute to arriving at solutions in extreme cases.

(a) **Control of risk management activities** refers to actions taken with respect to software risk items identified in the contract review and project plan documents as well as to risk items identified later, during the project's progress. In practice, the software development team attempts to reduce risk by applying systematic risk management activities. Management controls these efforts through review of periodic reports and evaluation of progress information. This component of progress control directly contributes to achievement of the project's functional and technical objectives.

(b) **Project schedule control** deals with compliance with the project's approved and contractual timetables. Follow-up is based on milestones in addition to periodic reports, which together enable identification of delays in completion of planned activities. Special emphasis is given to customer-demanded milestones, as noted in the contract. Management tends to focus control on those critical delays that threaten to substantially interfere with project completion dates.

(c) **Project resource control** focuses on professional human resources; it also deals with software development and testing facilities, typically required by real-time software systems and firmware. Management exercises control on the basis of periodic reports of resources used, which should be viewed in terms of actual project progress.

(d) **Project budget control** is based on comparison of actual with scheduled costs. The main budget items to be controlled are:
- Human resources
- Development and testing facilities
- Purchase of COTS software
- Purchase of hardware
- Payments to subcontractors.

Budget control requires input transmitted by milestone as well as periodic reports. These reports permit early identification of the budget overruns that affect project profitability. Ignorance of the other components of progress control is expected to substantially reduce the effectiveness of project progress control. The other components of process control are expected to identify deviant situations earlier than budget control is capable of doing.

(2) Explain the implementation issues associated with project progress control.

The implementation of project progress control requires:
- The following to be defined for each project:
  - Person or management unit responsible for progress control
  - Frequency of progress reports required from the various project management levels
  - Situations where project leaders are required to report immediately to management
  - Situations where lower-level management is required to report immediately to upper-level management.
- Management audits of project progress which deal with how well reporting by project leaders and other managers, as well as management project control activities, are functioning.

Selected bibliography

1. IEEE (1998a) "IEEE Std 1058-1998 – IEEE Standard for Software Project Management Plans", in *IEEE Software Engineering Standards Collection*, The Institute of Electrical and Electronics Engineers, New York.
2. IEEE (1998b) "IEEE Std 1490-1998 – IEEE Guide – Adoption of PMI Standard – A Guide to the Project Management Body of Knowledge", in *IEEE Software Engineering Standards Collection*, The Institute of Electrical and Electronics Engineers, New York.
3. IEEE (2001) "IEEE Std 1540-2001 – IEEE Standard for Software Life Cycle Processes – Risk Management", in *IEEE Software Engineering Standards Collection*, The Institute of Electrical and Electronics Engineers, New York.
4. IEEE/EIA (1996) "IEEE/EIA Std 12207.0-1996 – IEEE/EIA Standard – Industry Implementation of International Standard ISO/IEC 12207:1995", in *IEEE Software Engineering Standards Collection*, The Institute of Electrical and Electronics Engineers, New York.
5. IEEE/EIA (1997a) "IEEE/EIA Std 12207.1-1997 – IEEE/EIA Guide – Industry Implementation of International Standard ISO/IEC 12207:1995 – Software Life

Cycle Processes – Life Cycle Data", in *IEEE Software Engineering Standards Collection*, The Institute of Electrical and Electronics Engineers, New York.

6. IEEE/EIA (1997b) "IEEE/EIA Std 12207.1-1997 – IEEE/EIA Guide – Industry Implementation of International Standard ISO/IEC 12207:1995 – Software Life Cycle Processes – Implementation Considerations", in *IEEE Software Engineering Standards Collection*, The Institute of Electrical and Electronics Engineers, New York.

7. ISO (1997) *ISO 9000-3:1997(E), Quality Management and Quality Assurance Standards – Part 3: Guidelines for the Application of ISO 9001:1994 to the Development, Supply, Installation and Maintenance of Computer Software*, 2nd edn, International Organization for Standardization (ISO), Geneva, paragraph 4.16.

8. ISO/IEC (2001) "ISO 9000-3:2001 Software and System Engineering – Guidelines for the Application of ISO 9001:2000 to Software, Final draft", International Organization for Standardization (ISO), Geneva, unpublished draft, December 2001, paragraph 4.2.

9. Jones, C. (1994) *Assessment and Control of Software Risks*, Yourdon Press, Prentice Hall, Upper Saddle River, NJ.

Review questions

20.1 The introduction of the chapter presents three examples of situations that can cause managerial failure in the control of a software development project.

(1) What measures could management have taken to prevent each of these adverse situations?

(2) Which of these adverse situations could have been detected by audits of project progress control procedures?

20.2 In April, the project progress control system identified an unexpected delay of three months in the project's delivery date (originally planned for October), causing that date to be postponed to the following January.

(1) List your proposed interventions in this situation, including the assumptions underlying each proposal.

(2) Would you alter your proposals if the project were an internal project for development of a computer game software package scheduled for the pre-Christmas market?

20.3 A project progress control process has been planned to involve two levels: (1) Management of the Development Department, which regularly operates six to eight software development teams, and (2) Management of the Software Development Division, which covers three software development departments.

Consider the case of a standard one-year software development project.

(1) Inform the project leader of your suggestions for the proper progress reporting frequencies and conditions for immediate reporting to departmental management.

(2) Inform the departmental manager of your suggestions for the proper progress reporting frequencies and conditions for immediate reporting to divisional management.

(3) What type of progress-related information would you recommend be reported to divisional management?

Topic for discussion

20.1 The "Golden Bridge" software development project was scheduled to be completed in about 12 months. Two to six team members were planned to work on the project. Project progress control was based on a monthly report that would refer to each of the 32 activities to be performed and to the components (1) risk item management, (2) timetable, and (3) project's human resources utilization.

The first three monthly progress reports submitted to management did not indicate any deviation from the plan. The fourth progress report presented a substantial overrun in terms of human resources utilization (overtime, etc.) as well as a one-month delay in the expected completion dates for some of the activities.

(1) Can you suggest possible reasons for the relatively late detection of the deviations from the plan?
(2) For each of the above three components, describe the measures that could have prevented deviations and their adverse effects.
(3) Suggest some interventions that management could have introduced to compensate for the project's failures, including the assumptions behind each intervention.

Software quality metrics

Tom DeMarco's statement has become the motto for software quality experts trying to develop and apply quality metrics in the software industry.

Two alternative but complementary definitions (IEEE, 1990) describe quality metrics as a category of SQA tools:

(1) A quantitative measure of the degree to which an item possesses a given quality attribute.

(2) A function whose inputs are software data and whose output is a single numerical value that can be interpreted as the degree to which the software possesses a given quality attribute.

That is, the second definition refers to the process that produces quality metrics whereas the first refers to the outcome of the above process.

It is commonly believed that quality metrics should be included in software, as in other industries, among the fundamental tools employed to assist management in three basic areas: control of software development projects and software maintenance, support of decision taking, and initiation of corrective actions. Statistical analysis of metrics data is expected to pinpoint (descriptively and statistically significant) changes initiated as a result of application of new development tools, changed procedures, and other interventions.

The scope of software quality metrics (hereinafter "metrics") has expanded considerably over the past few decades. We will review some of those most pertinent software development and maintenance issues at the heart of this chapter. Metrics as a quality assurance tool has not, unfortunately, been applied at an adequate level in the software industry. Nor have they provided benefits at the anticipated levels. Only a small portion of software development organizations apply software quality metrics systematically, and few of these report successful use of the results of their efforts. Some of the reasons for this situation and prospects for the future are discussed in the last part of the chapter.

Experience with metrics in the field has not threatened its potential significance, attested to by the ISO 9000-3 standard (see ISO/IEC (1997) Sec. 4.20 and ISO (2001) Sec. 8). Software quality metrics are also an important part of the CMM guidelines (see Paulk *et al.*, 1995).

Several books, chapters in books, and numerous journal as well as conference papers have been dedicated to this subject. Some are listed in the bibliography at the end of this chapter. In addition, IEEE offers some software quality metrics criteria within its software engineering standards (IEEE 1988, 1998). A comprehensive discussion of metrics for software reuse, including their economic implications, is presented by Poulin (1997).

After completing this chapter, you will be able to:

■ Explain the objectives of software quality metrics.
■ List the requirements to be fulfilled by successful software quality metrics.
■ Explain how software quality metrics are categorized.
■ Compare the KLOC and function point measures for the size of a software system.
■ Describe the process of defining a new software quality metrics.
■ Explain the reasons for limitations characterizing some software quality metrics.

21.1 Objectives of quality measurement

Software quality and other software engineers have formulated the main objectives for software quality metrics, presented in Frame 21.1.

Frame 21.1   **Main objectives of software quality metrics**

(1) **To facilitate management control as well as planning and execution of the appropriate managerial interventions.** Achievement of this objective is based on calculation of metrics regarding:

■ Deviations of actual functional (quality) performance from planned performance

■ Deviations of actual timetable and budget performance from planned performance.

(2) **To identify situations that require or enable development or maintenance process improvement in the form of preventive or corrective actions introduced throughout the organization.** Achievement of this objective is based on:

■ Accumulation of metrics information regarding the performance of teams, units, etc.

Comparison provides the practical basis for management's application of metrics and for SQA improvement in general. The metrics are used for comparison of performance data with *indicators*, quantitative values such as:

■ Defined software quality standards
■ Quality targets set for organizations or individuals
■ Previous year's quality achievements
■ Previous project's quality achievements
■ Average quality levels achieved by other teams applying the same development tools in similar development environments

- Average quality achievements of the organization
- Industry practices for meeting quality requirements.

In order for the selected quality metrics to be applicable and successful, both general and operative requirements, as presented in Frame 21.2, must be satisfied.

Frame 21.2	**Software quality metrics – requirements**

General requirements	Explanation
Relevant	Related to an attribute of substantial importance
Valid	Measures the required attribute
Reliable	Produces similar results when applied under similar conditions
Comprehensive	Applicable to a large variety of implementations and situations
Mutually exclusive	Does not measure attributes measured by other metrics

Operative requirements	Explanation
Easy and simple	The implementation of the metrics data collection is simple and is performed with minimal resources
Does not require independent data collection	Metrics data collection is integrated with other project data collection systems: employee attendance, wages, cost accounting, etc. In addition to its efficiency aspects, this requirement contributes to coordination of all information systems serving the organization
Immune to biased interventions by interested parties	In order to escape the expected results of the analysis of the metrics, it is expected that interested persons will try to change the data and, by doing so, improve their record. Such actions obviously bias the relevant metrics. Immunity (total or at least partial) is achieved mainly by choice of metrics and adequate procedures

21.2 Classification of software quality metrics

Software quality metrics can fall into a number of categories. Here we use a two-level system.

The first classification category distinguishes between life cycle and other phases of the software system:

- Process metrics, related to the software development process (see Section 21.3)
- Product metrics, related to software maintenance (see Section 21.4).

The second classification category refers to the subjects of the measurements:

- Quality
- Timetable
- Effectiveness (of error removal and maintenance services)
- Productivity.

These items are dealt with in the respective sections.

A sizeable number of software quality metrics involve one of the two following measures for system size:

- **KLOC** – this classic metric measures the size of software by thousands of code lines. As the number of code lines required for programming a given task differs substantially with each programming tool, this measure is specific to the programming language or development tool used. Application of metrics that include KLOC is limited to software systems developed using the same programming language or development tool.
- **Function points** – a measure of the development resources (human resources) required to develop a program, based on the functionality specified for the software system (see Appendix 21A).

Customer satisfaction metrics are excluded from our presentation; the reader can find wide coverage of this topic in the marketing literature.

21.3 Process metrics

Software development process metrics can fall into one of the following categories:

- Software process quality metrics
- Software process timetable metrics
- Software process productivity metrics.

21.3.1 Software process quality metrics

Software process quality metrics may be classified into three classes:

- Error density metrics
- Error severity metrics
- Error removal effectiveness metrics.

Another group of indirect metrics that relates to software process quality is the McCabe's cyclomatic complexity metrics (see Section 9.4.4).

A discussion of the above three classes follows.

This section describes six different types of metrics. Calculation of error density metrics involves two measures: (1) software volume, and (2) errors counted.

Software volume measures. Some density metrics use the number of lines of code while others apply function points. For a comparison of these measures, see Section 21.2.

Errors counted measures. Some relate to the number of errors and others to the weighted number of errors. Weighted measures that ascertain the severity of the errors are considered to provide more accurate evaluation of the error situation. A common method applied to arrive at this measure is classification of the detected errors into severity classes, followed by weighting each class. The weighted error measure is computed by summing up multiples of the number of errors found in each severity class by the adequate relative severity weight. Department of Defense standard MIL-STD-498, presented in Table 8.1, describes a commonly used five-level severity classification system. It should be noted that application of weighted measures can lead to decisions different than those arrived at with simple (unweighted) metrics: weighted measures are assumed to be better indicators of adverse situations.

Example 1. This example demonstrates the calculation of the number of code errors (NCE) and the weighted number of code errors (WCE). A software development department applies two alternative measures, NCE and WCE, to the code errors detected in its software development projects. Three classes of error severity and their relative weights are also defined:

Error severity class	Relative weight
Low severity	1
Medium severity	3
High severity	9

The code error summary for the department's Atlantis project indicated that there were 42 low severity errors, 17 medium severity errors, and 11 high severity errors. Calculation of NCE and WCE gave these results:

Error severity class	Calculation of NCE (number of errors)	Calculation of WCE	
a	b	Relative weight c	Weighted errors $D = b \times c$
Low severity	42	1	42
Medium severity	17	3	51
High severity	11	9	99
Total	70	—	192
NCE	70	—	—
WCE	—	—	192

Table 21.1: Error density metrics

Code	Name	Calculation formula
CED	Code Error Density	$CED = \dfrac{NCE}{KLOC}$
DED	Development Error Density	$DED = \dfrac{NDE}{KLOC}$
WCED	Weighted Code Error Density	$WCED = \dfrac{WCE}{KLOC}$
WDED	Weighted Development Error Density	$WDED = \dfrac{WDE}{KLOC}$
WCEF	Weighted Code Errors per Function point	$WCEF = \dfrac{WCE}{NFP}$
WDEF	Weighted Development Errors per Function point	$WDEF = \dfrac{WDE}{NFP}$

Key:
- NCE = number of code errors detected in the software code by code inspections and testing. Data for this measure are culled from code inspection and testing reports.
- KLOC = thousands of lines of code.
- NDE = total number of design and code errors detected in the software development process. Data for this measure are found in the various design and code reviews and testing reports conducted.
- WCE = weighted code errors detected. The sources of data for this metric are the same as those for NCE.
- WDE = total number of design and code errors detected in development of the software. The sources of data for this metric are the same as those for NDE.
- NFP = number of function points required for development of the software. Sources for the number of function points are professional surveys of the relevant software.

Table 21.1 (above) displays six error density metrics.

Example 2. This example follows Example 1 and introduces the factor of weighted measures so as to demonstrate the implications of their use. A software development department applies two alternative metrics for calculation of code error density: CED and WCED. The unit determined the following indicators for unacceptable software quality: CED > 2 and WCED > 4. For our calculations we apply the three classes of quality and their relative weights and the code error summary for the Atlantis project mentioned in Example 1. The software system size is 40 KLOC. Calculation of the two metrics resulted in the following:

Measures and metrics	Calculation of CED (Code Error Density)	Calculation of WCED (Weighted Code Error Density)
NCE	70	—
WCE	—	192
KLOC	40	40
CED (NCE/KLOC)	1.75	—
WCED (WCE/KLOC)	—	4.8

The conclusions reached after application of the unweighted versus weighted metrics are different. While the CED *does not* indicate quality *below* the acceptable level, the WCED metric *does* indicate quality *below* the acceptable level (in other words, if the error density is too high, the unit's quality is not acceptable), a result that calls for management intervention.

Error severity metrics

The metrics belonging to this group are used to detect adverse situations of increasing numbers of severe errors in situations where errors and weighted errors, as measured by error density metrics, are generally decreasing. Two error severity metrics are presented in Table 21.2.

Error removal effectiveness

Software developers can measure the effectiveness of error removal by the software quality assurance system after a period of regular operation (usually 6 or 12 months) of the system. The metrics combine the error records of the development stage with the failures records compiled during the first year (or any defined period) of regular operation. Two error removal effectiveness metrics are presented in Table 21.3.

Table 21.2: Error severity metrics

Code	Name	Calculation formula
ASCE	Average Severity of Code Errors	$ASCE = \dfrac{WCE}{NCE}$
ASDE	Average Severity of Development Errors	$ASDE = \dfrac{WDE}{NDE}$

Table 21.3: Error removal effectiveness metrics

Code	Name	Calculation formula
DERE	Development Errors Removal Effectiveness	$DERE = \dfrac{NDE}{NDE + NYF}$
DWERE	Development Weighted Errors Removal Effectiveness	$DWERE = \dfrac{WDE}{WDE + WYF}$

Key:
- NYF = number of software failures detected during a year of maintenance service.
- WYF = weighted number of software failures detected during a year of maintenance service.

21.3.2 Software process timetable metrics

Software process timetable metrics may be based on accounts of success (completion of milestones per schedule) in addition to failure events (non-completion per schedule). An alternative approach calculates the average delay in completion of milestones. The metrics presented here are based on the two approaches illustrated in Table 21.4.

The TTO and ADMC metrics are based on data for all relevant milestones scheduled in the project plan. In other words, only milestones that were designated for completion in the project plan stage are considered in the metrics' computation. Therefore, these metrics can be applied throughout development and need not wait for the project's completion.

21.3.3 Software process productivity metrics

This group of metrics includes "direct" metrics that deal with a project's human resources productivity as well as "indirect" metrics that focus on the extent of software reuse. Software reuse substantially affects productivity and effectiveness.

An additional term – "benchmarking software development productivity" – has recently entered the list of metrics used to measure software process productivity (see Maxwell, 2001; Symons, 2001).

Four process productivity metrics, direct and indirect, are presented in Table 21.5.

21.4 Product metrics

Product metrics refer to the software system's operational phase – years of regular use of the software system by customers, whether "internal" or "external" customers, who either purchased the software system or con-

Table 21.4: Software process timetable metrics

Code	Name	Calculation formula
TTO	Time Table Observance	$TTO = \dfrac{MSOT}{MS}$
ADMC	Average Delay of Milestone Completion	$ADMC = \dfrac{TCDAM}{MS}$

Key:
- MSOT = milestones completed on time.
- MS = total number of milestones.
- TCDAM = total Completion Delays (days, weeks, etc.) for All Milestones. To calculate this measure, delays reported for all relevant milestones are summed up. Milestones completed on time or before schedule are considered "0" delays. Some professionals refer to completion of milestones before schedule as "minus" delays. These are considered to balance the effect of accounted-for delays (we might call the latter "plus" delays). In these cases, the value of the ADMC may be lower than the value obtained according to the metric originally suggested.

Table 21.5: Process productivity metrics

Code	Name	Calculation formula
DevP	Development Productivity	$DevP = \dfrac{DevH}{KLOC}$
FDevP	Function point Development Productivity	$FDevP = \dfrac{DevH}{NFP}$
CRe	Code Reuse	$CRe = \dfrac{ReKLOC}{KLOC}$
DocRe	Documentation Reuse	$DocRe = \dfrac{ReDoc}{NDoc}$

Key:
- DevH = total working hours invested in the development of the software system.
- ReKLOC = number of thousands of reused lines of code.
- ReDoc = number of reused pages of documentation.
- NDoc = number of pages of documentation.

tracted for its development. In most cases, the software developer is required to provide customer service during the software's operational phase. Customer services are of two main types:

- **Help desk services (HD)** – software support by instructing customers regarding the method of application of the software and solution of customer implementation problems. Demand for these services depends to a great extent on the quality of the user interface (its "user friendliness") as well as the quality of the user manual and integrated help menus.

- **Corrective maintenance services** – correction of software failures identified by customers/users or detected by the customer service team prior to their discovery by customers. The number of software failures and their density are directly related to software development quality. For completeness of information and better control of failure correction, it is recommended that all software failures detected by the customer service team be recorded as corrective maintenance calls.

Commonly, all customer services – namely, HD and corrective maintenance services – are provided to customers/users by a software support center (the "customer service center", among the many titles given to this service). It is expected that very few customer calls will be related to identified failures. In other words, most of the software support center's customer calls will be "non-failure" calls. For those calls that deal with an identified failure and for cases where the maintenance team has detected a failure, a failure report is expected.

HD metrics are based on all customer calls while corrective maintenance metrics are based on failure reports. Product metrics generally rely on performance records compiled during one year (or any other specified period of time). This policy enables comparisons of successive years in addition to comparisons between different units and software systems.

The array of software product metrics presented here is classified as follows:

- HD quality metrics
- HD productivity and effectiveness metrics
- Corrective maintenance quality metrics
- Corrective maintenance productivity and effectiveness metrics.

It should be remembered that software maintenance activities include:

- Corrective maintenance – correction of software failures detected during regular operation of the software.
- Adaptive maintenance – adaptation of existing software to new customers or new requirements.
- Functional improvement maintenance – addition of new functions to the existing software, improvement of reliability, etc.

In the metrics presented here we limit our selection to those that deal with corrective maintenance. For other components of software maintenance, the metrics suggested for the software development process (*process metrics*) can be used as is or with minor adaptations.

21.4.1 HD quality metrics measures

The types of HD quality metrics discussed here deal with:

- HD calls density – the extent of customer requests for HD services as measured by the number of calls.
- The severity of the HD issues raised.
- HD success – the level of success in responding to these calls. A success is achieved by completing the required service within the time determined in the service contract.

HD calls density metrics

This section describes six different types of metrics. Some relate to the number of the errors and others to a weighted number of errors. As for size/volume measures of the software, some use number of lines of code while others apply function points. The sources of data for these and the other metrics in this group are HD reports. Three HD calls density metrics for HD performance are presented in Table 21.6.

Severity of HD calls metrics

The metrics belonging to this group of measures aim at detecting one type of adverse situation: increasingly severe HD calls. The computed results may contribute to improvements in all or parts of the user interface (its "user friendliness") as well as the user manual and integrated help menus. We have

Table 21.6: HD calls density metrics

Code	Name	Calculation formula
HDD	HD calls Density	$HDD = \dfrac{NHYC}{KLMC}$
WHDD	Weighted HD calls Density	$WHDD = \dfrac{WHYC}{KLMC}$
WHDF	Weighted HD calls per Function point	$WHDF = \dfrac{WHYC}{NMFP}$

Key:
- NHYC = number of HD calls during a year of service.
- KLMC = thousands of lines of maintained software code.
- WHYC = weighted HD calls received during one year of service.
- NMFP = number of function points to be maintained.

selected one metric from this group for demonstration of how the entire category is employed. This metric, the **Average Severity of HD Calls (ASHC)**, refers to failures detected during a period of one year (or any portion thereof, as appropriate):

$$ASHC = \frac{WHYC}{NHYC}$$

where WHYC and NHYC are defind as in Table 21.6.

Success of the HD services

The most common metric for the success of HD services is the capacity to solve problems raised by customer calls within the time determined in the service contract (*availability*). Thus, the metric for success of HD services compares the actual with the designated time for provision of these services.

For example, the availability of help desk (HD) services for an inventory management software package is defined as follows:

- The HD service undertakes to solve any HD call within one hour.
- The probability that HD call solution time exceeds one hour will not exceed 2%.
- The probability that HD call solution time exceeds four working hours will not exceed 0.5%.

One metric of this group is suggested here, **HD Service Success (HDS)**:

$$HDS = \frac{NHYOT}{NHYC}$$

where NHYOT = number of HD calls per year completed on time during one year of service.

21.4.2 HD productivity and effectiveness metrics

Productivity metrics relate to the total of resources invested during a specified period, while effectiveness metrics relate to the resources invested in responding to a HD customer call.

HD productivity metrics

HD productivity metrics makes use of the easy-to-apply KLMC measure of maintained software system's size (see Table 21.6) or according to function-point evaluation of the software system. Two HD productivity metrics are presented in Table 21.7.

HD effectiveness metrics

The metrics in this group refer to the resources invested in responding to customers' HD calls. One prevalent metric is presented here, **HD Effectiveness (HDE):**

$$HDE = \frac{HDYH}{NHYC}$$

where HDYH and NHYC are as defined in Tables 21.7 and 21.6 respectively.

21.4.3 Corrective maintenance quality metrics

Software corrective maintenance metrics deal with several aspects of the quality of maintenance services. A distinction is needed between software system failures treated by the maintenance teams and failures of the maintenance service that refer to cases where the maintenance failed to provide a repair that meets the designated standards or contract requirements. Thus, software maintenance metrics are classified as follows:

■ **Software system failures density metrics** – deal with the extent of demand for corrective maintenance, based on the records of failures identified during regular operation of the software system.

■ **Software system failures severity metrics** – deal with the severity of software system failures attended to by the corrective maintenance team.

Table 21.7: HD productivity metrics

Code	Name	Calculation formula
HDP	HD Productivity	$HDP = \dfrac{HDYH}{KLMC}$
FHDP	Function point HD Productivity	$FHDP = \dfrac{HDYH}{NMFP}$

Key:
■ HDYH = total yearly working hours invested in HD servicing of the software system.
■ KLMC and NMFP are as defined in Table 21.6.

- **Failures of maintenance services metrics** – deal with cases where maintenance services were unable to complete the failure correction on time or that the correction performed failed.

- **Software system availability metrics** – deal with the extent of disturbances caused to the customer as realized by periods of time where the services of the software system are unavailable or only partly available.

Software system failures density metrics

The software system failures density metrics presented here relate to the number and/or weighted number of failures. The size of the maintenance tasks is measured by the total number of code lines of the maintained software as well as by the function point evaluation. The sources of data for these metrics are software maintenance reports. Three software system failures density metrics are presented in Table 21.8.

Software system failures severity metrics

Metrics of this group detect adverse situations of increasingly severe failures in the maintained software. Results may trigger retesting of all or parts of the software system. The events measured relate either to the disturbances and damages caused to the customer (representing the customer's point of view) or to the resources required to resolve the failure (representing the interests of the maintenance team). The metric presented here can be used for both purposes, that is, to apply weights that refer to the severity of the disturbances and damages experienced by the customer, or to the extent of resources required by the maintainer. This metric, the **Average Severity of Software System Failures (ASSSF)**, refers to software failures detected during a period of one year (or alternatively a half or a quarter of a year, as appropriate):

$$ASSSF = \frac{WYF}{NYF}$$

Table 21.8: Software system failures density metrics

Code	Name	Calculation formula
SSFD	Software System Failure Density	$SSFD = \dfrac{NYF}{KLMC}$
WSSFD	Weighted Software System Failure Density	$WSSFD = \dfrac{WYF}{KLMC}$
WSSFF	Weighted Software System Failures per Function point	$WSSFF = \dfrac{WYF}{NMFP}$

Key:
- NYF = number of software failures detected during a year of maintenance service.
- WYF = weighted number of yearly software failures detected during a year of maintenance service.
- KLMC = thousands of lines of maintained software code.
- NMFP = number of function points designated for the maintained software.

Failures of maintenance services metrics

As mentioned above, maintenance services can fail either because they were unable to complete the failure correction on time or when the correction performed failed and a repeated correction is required. The metrics presented here relate to the second type of maintenance failure.

A customer call related to a software failure problem that was supposed to be solved after a previous call is commonly treated as a maintenance service failure. For practical purposes, many organizations limit the time frame for the repeat calls to three months, although the period can vary by type of failure or some other organizational criterion. The metric, **Maintenance Repeated repair Failure (MRepF)**, is defined as follows:

$$MRepF = \frac{RepYF}{NYF}$$

where RepYF is the number of repeated software failure calls (service failures).

Software system availability metrics

User metrics distinguish between:

- Full availability – where all software system functions perform properly
- Vital availability – where no vital functions fail (but non-vital functions may fail)
- Total unavailability – where all software system functions fail.

The source for all availability metrics is user failure records. The latter specify the extent of damage (non-vital failure, vital failure and total system failure) as well as duration (hours) for each failure. Three software system availability metrics are presented in Table 21.9.

21.4.4 Software corrective maintenance productivity and effectiveness metrics

While corrective maintenance productivity relates to the total of human resources invested in maintaining a given software system, corrective maintenance effectiveness relates to the resources invested in correction of a single failure. In other words, a software maintenance system displaying higher productivity will require fewer resources for its maintenance task, while a more effective software maintenance system will require fewer resources, on average, for correcting one failure. Three software corrective maintenance productivity and effectiveness metrics are presented in Table 21.10.

Table 21.9: Software system availability metrics

Code	Name	Calculation formula
FA	Full Availability	$FA = \dfrac{NYSerH - NYFH}{NYSerH}$
VitA	Vital Availability	$VitA = \dfrac{NYSerH - NYVitFH}{NYSerH}$
TUA	Total Unavailability	$TUA = \dfrac{NYTFH}{NYSerH}$

Key:
- NYSerH = number of hours software system is in service during one year. For an office software system that is operating 50 hours per week for 52 weeks per year, NYSerH = 2600 (50×52). For a real-time software application that serves users 24 hours a day, NYSerH = 8760 (365×24).
- NYFH = number of hours where at least one function is unavailable (failed) during one year, including total failure of the software system.
- NYVitFH = number of hours when at least one vital function is unavailable (failed) during one year, including total failure of the software system.
- NYTFH = number of hours of total failure (all system functions failed) during one year.
- $NYFH \geq NYVitFH \geq NYTFH$.
- $1 - TUA \geq VitA \geq FA$.

Table 21.10: Software corrective maintenance productivity and effectiveness metrics

Code	Name	Calculation formula
CMaiP	Corrective Maintenance Productivity	$CMaiP = \dfrac{CMaiYH}{KLMC}$
FCMP	Function point Corrective Maintenance Productivity	$FCMP = \dfrac{CMaiYH}{NMFP}$
CMaiE	Corrective Maintenance Effectiveness	$CMaiE = \dfrac{CMaiYH}{NYF}$

Key:
- CMaiYH = total yearly working hours invested in the corrective maintenance of the software system.
- KLMC = thousands of lines of maintained software code.
- NMFP = number of function points designated for the maintained software.
- NYF = number of software failures detected during a year of maintenance service.

21.5 Implementation of software quality metrics

The application of software quality metrics in an organization requires:

- Definition of software quality metrics – relevant and adequate for teams, departments, etc.
- Regular application by unit, etc.
- Statistical analysis of collected metrics data.

■ Subsequent actions:

  – Changes in the organization and methods of software development and maintenance units and/or any other body that collected the metrics data
  – Change in metrics and metrics data collection
  – Application of data and data analysis to planning corrective actions for all the relevant units.

The technical aspects of Nokia's experience in applying metrics are summarized by Kilpi (2001). Unfortunately, this paper does not explore Nokia's application of metrics to decision making in such areas as productivity, effectiveness and so forth.

21.5.1 Definition of new software quality metrics

The definition of metrics involves a four–stage process:

(1) Definition of attributes to be measured: software quality, development team productivity, etc.

(2) Definition of the metrics that measure the required attributes and confirmation of its adequacy in complying with the requirements listed in Frame 21.2.

(3) Determination of comparative target values based on standards, previous year's performance, etc. These values serve as *indicators* of whether the unit measured (a team or an individual or a portion of the software) complies with the characteristics demanded of a given attribute.

(4) Determination of metrics application processes:

  – Reporting method, including reporting process and frequency of reporting
  – Metrics data collection method.

The new metrics (updates, changes and revised applications) will be constructed following analysis of the metrics data as well as developments in the organization and its environment. The software quality metrics definition process is described in Figure 21.1.

21.5.2 Application of the metrics – managerial aspects

The process of applying a metric or a set of metrics is similar to the implementation of new procedures or methodologies. It involves:

■ Assigning responsibility for reporting and metrics data collection.
■ Instruction of the team regarding the new metrics.
■ Follow-up includes:
  – Support for solving application problems and provision of supplementary information when needed.
  – Control of metrics reporting for completeness and accuracy.
■ Updates and changes of metrics definitions together with reporting and data collection methods according to past performance.

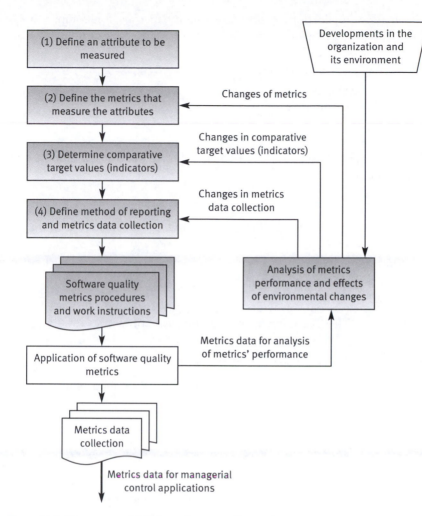

Figure 21.1: The process of defining software quality metrics

Implementation tip

Not a few of the currently applied software quality metrics procedures and work instructions omit the third stage of the metrics definition process: setting target values (indicators). In other words, no target values for the metrics are to be found in the procedure or its appendices, the accompanying work instructions or any other document. In most cases this situation reflects a lack of serious commitment to metrics use in managerial control, the major reason for applying metrics in the first place. When application of metrics goes beyond lip service, target values should be set even if updates of these values are expected soon after their first application.

An interesting application of software quality metrics for comparison of national software industries is presented in the following example.

Example – Comparison of US and Japanese software industries
Cusumano (1991) makes use of three metrics in a comparison of the US and Japanese software industries:

■ Mean productivity
■ Failure density (based on measurements during the first 12 months after system delivery)
■ Code reuse.

These metrics are presented in Table 21.11, and Cusumano's results are presented in Table 21.12.

21.5.3 Statistical analysis of metrics data

Analysis of metrics data provides opportunities for comparing a series of project metrics. These certainly include comparison of metrics results against

Table 21.11: US and Japanese software industries – metrics

Name	Calculation formula
Mean productivity (similar to DevP, Table 21.5)	$\dfrac{KNLOC}{WorkY}$
Failure density (similar to SSFD, Table 21.8)	$\dfrac{NYF}{KNLOC}$
Code reuse (similar to CRe, Table 21.5)	$\dfrac{ReKNLOC}{KNLOC}$

Key:
■ KNLOC = thousands of non-comment lines of code.
■ WorkY = human work-years invested in the software development.
■ ReKNLOC = thousands of reused non-comment lines of code.

Source: Based on Cusumano (1991)

Table 21.12: US and Japanese software industries – comparison of three software quality metrics

Software quality metrics	United States	Japan
Mean productivity	7290	12447
Failure density	4.44	1.96
Code reuse	9.71%	18.25%
N – (number of companies)	20	11

Source: Cusumano (1991)

predefined indicators, as well as comparisons with former projects or team performance at different periods of time, and so on. Another important comparison relates to the effectiveness with which the metrics themselves fulfill their respective aims. The following questions are just a sample of those that can be asked with respect to the metrics portion of the SQA process.

- Are there significant differences between the HD teams' quality of service?
- Do the metrics results support the assumption that application of the new version of a development tool contributes significantly to software quality?
- Do the metrics results support the assumption that reorganization has contributed significantly to a team's productivity?

For the metrics data to be a valuable part of the SQA process, statistical analysis is required of the metrics' results. Statistical tools provide us with two levels of support, based on the type of statistics used:

- Descriptive statistics
- Analytical statistics.

Descriptive statistics

Descriptive statistics, such as the mean, median and mode as well as use of graphic presentations such as histograms, cumulative distribution graphs, pie charts and control charts (showing also the indicator values) to illustrate the information to which they relate, enable us to quickly identify trends in the metrics values. Exaggerated trends, identified by the appearance of acute deviations from target values, may indicate the need for corrective actions or, alternatively, to continue or expand application of a successful innovation. Because these statistics are so basic to quality assurance, the majority of the popular software statistical packages (*statistical tools*) available generally provide a rather complete menu of graphic presentations, including the ones mentioned above. However, it should be stressed that descriptive statistics, however sophisticated, are not intended to analyze the statistical significance – how much the observed trends are the result of chance rather than substantive processes – of the events.

Analytical statistics

Description is not always enough. To determine whether the observed changes in the metrics are meaningful, whatever the direction, the observed trends must be assessed for their significance. This is the role of analytic statistics (e.g., regression tests, analysis of variance, or more basic tests such as the T-test and Chi-square test). However, the application of statistical analysis to software system performance metrics is relatively difficult, which is one outcome of the complexity of software systems development and maintenance, discussed in the introduction to this book. For further study of the subject the reader is referred to the literature on statistical analysis.

What should be noted here is the fundamental difference between statistical analysis of production line metrics by application of classical SPC (statistical process control) methods and of software development and maintenance. While production line activities are repetitive, the development activities, by definition, vary from one project to the next; they are never repetitive in the SPC sense. Although the statistical methods applied may be similar, the subject matter differs, as may the implications of the statistical results.

21.5.4 Taking action in response to metrics analysis results

The actions taken in response to metrics analysis can be classified as direct actions if initiated by the project or team management or indirect actions if initiated by the Corrective Action Board. The CAB indirect actions are a result of analysis of metrics data accumulated from a variety of projects and/or development departments.

Examples of the direct changes initiated by management include reorganization, changes in software development and maintenance methods, and revision of the metrics computed. For a comprehensive discussion of indirect actions as initiated by the Corrective Action Board, see Chapter17.

21.6 Limitations of software metrics

Application of quality metrics is strewn with obstacles. These can be grouped as follows:

- Budget constraints in allocating the necessary resources (manpower, funds, etc.) for development of a quality metrics system and its regular application.
- Human factors, especially opposition of employees to evaluation of their activities.
- Uncertainty regarding the data's validity, rooted in partial and biased reporting.

These difficulties are fairly universal and, as such, apply to software quality metrics too. However, additional obstacles may appear that are uniquely related to the software industry. These are discussed in this section. (For an up-to-date discussion in the literature see Rifkin (2001), McGarry (2001), Maxwell (2001) and Symons (2001), who discuss the difficulties in applying software quality metrics, especially for decision making in the context of software development.)

The unique barriers associated with the application of software quality metrics are rooted in the attributes measured. As a result, most commonly used metrics suffer from low validity and limited comprehensiveness. Examples of the software metrics that exhibit severe weaknesses are:

- Parameters used in development process metrics: KLOC, NDE, NCE
- Parameters used in product (maintenance) metrics: KLMC, NHYC, NYF.

The main factors affecting development process measuress, especially their magnitude, are:

(1) Programming style: strongly affects software volume, where "wasteful" coding may double the volume of produced code (KLOC).

(2) Volume of documentation comments included in the code: affects volume of the code. The volume of comments is usually determined by the programming style (KLOC).

(3) Software complexity: complex modules require much more development time (per line of code) in comparison to simple modules. Complex modules also suffer from more defects than simple modules of similar size (KLOC, NCE).

(4) Percentage of reused code: the higher the percentage of reused code incorporated into the software developed, the greater the volume of code that can be produced per day as well as the lower the number of defects detected in reviews, testing and regular use (NDE, NCE).

(5) Professionalism and thoroughness of design review and software testing teams: affects the number of defects detected (NCE).

(6) Reporting style of the review and testing results: some teams produce concise reports that present the findings in a small number of items (small NCE), while others produce comprehensive reports, showing the same findings for a large number of items (large NDE and NCE).

The main factors affecting the magnitude of the product (maintenance) parameters are:

(1) Quality of installed software and its documentation (determined by the quality of the development team as well as the review and testing teams): the lower the initial quality of the software, the greater the anticipated software failures identified and subsequent maintenance efforts (NYF, NHYC).

(2) Programming style and volume of documentation comments included in the code: as in the development stage, both strongly affect the volume of the software to be maintained, where wasteful coding and documentation may double the volume of code to be maintained (KLMC).

(3) Software complexity: complex modules require investment of many more maintenance resources per line of code than do simple modules, and suffer from more defects left undetected during the development stage (NYF).

(4) Percentage of reused code: the higher the percentage of reused code, the lower the number of defects detected in regular use as well as the fewer required corrective maintenance and HD efforts (NYF).

(5) Number of installations, size of the user population and level of applications in use: affect the number of HD calls as well as the number of defects detected by users during regular use (NHYC, NYF).

By affecting the magnitude of the parameters, these factors distort the software product quality metrics on which they are based. The inevitable result is that a major portion of the metrics we have discussed do not reflect the real productivity and quality achievements of development or maintenance teams in what may be the majority of situations. In other words, many of the metrics reviewed here, like the metrics applied in other industries, most of which are characterized by relative simplicity of application, are characterized by low validity and limited comprehensiveness.

Substantial research efforts are needed in order to develop metrics appropriate to the software industry. The function point method is an example of a successful methodological development aimed at replacing the problematic KLOC metric. For a comprehensive discussion of the function point method, see Appendix 21A.

Summary

(1) Explain the objectives of software quality metrics.

Software quality metrics are implemented:
- To support control of software development projects and software maintenance contracts. Their aim is to provide management with information regarding:
  - Compliance with functional (quality) performance requirements
  - Compliance with project timetable and budget.
- To deliver the metrics accumulated and analyzed by the CAB. Use of these metrics data is aimed at enabling preventive and corrective actions throughout the organization.

(2) List the requirements for successful software quality metrics.

Applicability of quality metrics is determined by the degree to which the following general and operative requirements are fulfilled:

General requirements
- Relevant – measures an attribute of considerable importance
- Valid – measures the required attribute
- Reliable – produces similar results when applied in similar conditions
- Comprehensive – applicable to a large variety of situations
- Mutually exclusive – does not measure attributes already measured by other metrics.

Operative requirements
- Easy and simple – data collection is implemented with minimal resources
- Does not require independent data collection – metrics data collection is based on currently employed data collection systems, e.g. employee attendance records, cost accounting methods
- Immune to biased interventions by interested parties (team members and others).

(3) Explain how software quality metrics are categorized.

A two-level system of categories is used here. The first level distinguishes between two categories:
- Process metrics, related to the software development process
- Product metrics, related to software maintenance.

Each first-level category is broken down into one of three sub-categories :
- Software process quality metrics
- Software process timetable metrics
- Software process productivity metrics.

The software product metrics are classified into four HD and corrective maintenance sub-categories:
- HD quality metrics
- HD productivity and effectiveness metrics
- Software corrective maintenance quality metrics
- Software corrective maintenance productivity and effectiveness metrics.

(4) Compare the KLOC and function points measures for the size of a software system.

A significant number of the metrics presented here use one of two measures for software system size, which are compared according to the following criteria:
- **Dependency on the development tool, programming language, or programmer style.** KLOC depends heavily on the development tool's characteristics and on the programmer's style. Alternatively, although the function point method does not depend on either of these factors, it does depend to some extent on the function point instruction manual used. It should also be noted that most successful implementations and research supporting the results of the function point method are related to data processing systems, whereas only limited experience has been gained in other areas of software systems.
- **Professional experience required for implementation.** Relatively little experience is required for counting KLOC, while relatively great experience is needed to evaluate function points.
- **Amount of professional work required.** Relatively little for KLOC; far more work for evaluation of function points.
- **Subjective factors.** Estimation of KLOC requires little subjective judgment, whereas the opposite is true for function points because subjective evaluations are required for determining the weight and relative complexity factors for each software system component, as required by the function point method.
- **Pre-project estimates.** Pre-project estimates are unavailable for KLOC but available for function points as the latter can be based on requirement specification documents.

(5) Describe the process of defining a new software quality metric.

The definition of metrics involves a four-stage process:
(a) Definition of attributes to be measured: software quality, development team productivity, etc.

(b) Formulation of the metric and assessment of its adequacy with respect to metrics requirements.

(c) Determination of comparative target values (indicator) to enable the evaluation of the performance measured by the metrics.

(d) Determination of the metrics application process:
   – Reporting method
   – Metrics data collection method.

(6) Explain the reasons for limitation characterizing some software quality metrics.

A unique difficulty faced by use of software quality metrics is rooted in the measures (parameters) that comprise many software quality metrics. As a result, a large proportion of software metrics, including most of the commonly used metrics, suffer from low validity and limited comprehensiveness. Examples of metrics that exhibit severe weaknesses are:

■ Software development metrics that are based on measures such as KLOC, NDE and NCE

■ Product (maintenance) metrics that are based on measures such as KLMC, NHYC and NYF.

For example, the KLOC measure is affected by the programming style, the volume of documentation comments included in the code and the complexity of the software. NYF is affected by the quality of the installed software and its documentation as well as the percentage of reused code, among the other factors affecting maintenance.

Selected bibliography

1. Albrecht, A. J. (1979) "Measuring Application Development Productivity", in *Process Joint SHARE/GUIDE/IBM Application Development Smposium*, October 1979, 34–43.
2. Albrecht, A. J. and Gaffney, J. E. (1983) "Software Functions, Source Lines of Code and Development Efforts Prediction: A Software Science Validation", *IEEE Transactions on Software Engineering*, SE–9, Nov. 1983, 639–648.
3. Caldiera, G., Antoniol, G., Fiutem, R. and Lokan, C. (1998) "Definition and experimental evaluation of function points for object-oriented systems", in IEEE Computer Society, *Proceedings of the Fifth International Software Metrics Symposium, Metrics 1998*, 20–21 November 1998, Bethesda, MD, IEEE Computer Society Press, Los Alamitos, CA, pp. 167–178.
4. Cusumano, M. A. (1991) *Japan's Software Factories – A Challenge to U.S. Management*, Oxford University Press, New York.
5. Davis, D. B. (1992) "Develop applications on time, every time", *Datamation*, 1 Nov, 85–89.
6. DeMarco, T. (1982) *Controlling Software Projects: Management, Measurement and Estimation*, Yourdon Press, New York.
7. Fenton, N. E. (1995) *Software Metrics – A Rigorous Approach*, International Thomson Press, London.
8. Fenton, N. E. and Pfleger, S. L. (1998) *Software Metrics – A Rigorous and Practical Approach*, 2nd edn, International Thomson Press, London.

9. Grable, R., Jernigan, J., Pogue, C. and Davis, D. (1999) "Metrics for small projects: experience at the SED", *IEEE Software*, 16(2), 21–29.

10. Gramus, D. and Herron, D. (1996) *Measuring the Software Process – A Practical Guide to Functional Measurements*, Yourdon Press, Prentice Hall, Upper Saddle River, NJ.

11. Henderson-Sellers, B. (1996) *Object-Oriented Metrics – Measures of Complexity*, Prentice Hall, Upper Saddle River, NJ.

12. IEEE (1988) "IEEE Std 982.1-1988 – IEEE Standard Dictionary of Measures to Produce Reliable Software", in *IEEE Software Engineering Standards Collection*, The Institute of Electrical and Electronics Engineers, New York.

13. IEEE (1990) "IEEE Std 610.12-1990 – IEEE Standard Glossary of Software Engineering Terminology", in *IEEE Software Engineering Standards Collection*, The Institute of Electrical and Electronics Engineers, New York.

14. IEEE (1998) "IEEE Std 14143.1-2000 – Implementation Note for IEEE Adoption of ISO/IEC 14143:1998 Information Technology – Software Measurement – Functional Size Measurement – Part 1: Definition of Concept", in *IEEE Software Engineering Standards Collection*, The Institute of Electrical and Electronics Engineers, New York.

15. IEEE (2000) "IEEE Std 1061-1998 – Standard for Software Quality Metrics Methodology", in *IEEE Software Engineering Standards Collection*, The Institute of Electrical and Electronics Engineers, New York.

16. IEEE Computer Society (1994) *Proceedings of the 2nd International Software Metrics Symposium*, IEEE Computer Society Press, Los Angeles, CA.

17. IEEE Computer Society (1998) *Proceedings of the Fifth International Software Metrics Symposium, Metrics 1998*, Bethesda, MD, IEEE Computer Society Press, Los Alamitos, CA.

18. ISO (1997) *ISO 9000-3:1997(E), Quality Management and Quality Assurance Standards – Part 3: Guidelines for the Application of ISO 9001:1994 to the Development, Supply, Installation and Maintenance of Computer Software*, 2nd edn, International Organization for Standardization (ISO), Geneva.

19. ISO/IEC (2001) "ISO 9000-3:2001 Software and System Engineering – Guidelines for the Application of ISO 9001:2000 to Software, Final draft", International Organization for Standardization (ISO), Geneva, unpublished draft, December 2001.

20. Jeffery, D. R., Low, G. C. and Barnes, M. (1993) "A comparison of function point counting techniques", *Transactions on Software Engineering*, 19(5), 529–532.

21. Jones, C. (1996) *Applied Software Measurement – Assuring Productivity and Quality*, 2nd edn, McGraw-Hill, New York, Sec. 3.

22. Jones, C. (1998) *Estimating Software Costs*, McGraw-Hill, New York.

23. Kautz, K. (1999) "Making sense of measurement for small organizations", *IEEE Software* 16(2), 14–20.

24. Kan, S. H. (1995) *Metrics and Models in Software Quality Engineering*, Addison Wesley, Reading, MA.

25. Kilpi, T. (2001) "Implementing a software metrics program at Nokia", *IEEE Software*, 18(6), 72–77.

26. Lowe, G. C. and Jeffery, D. C. (1990) "Function Points in the Estimation and Evaluation of the Software Process", *IEEE Transactions on Software Engineering*, 16(1), 64–71.

27. Maxwell, K. D. (2001) "Collecting data for comparability: benchmarking software development productivity", *IEEE Software*, 18(5), 22–25.

28. McGarry, J. (2001) "When it comes to measuring software, every project is unique", *IEEE Software*, 18(5), 19, 21.

29. Mendes, E., Mosley, N. and Counsell, S. (2001) "Web metrics – estimating design and authoring efforts", *IEEE Multimedia*, 8(1), 50–57.

30. Moller, K. H. and Paulish, D. L. (1993) *Software Metrics – A Practitioner's Guide to Improved Product Development*, IEEE Computer Society Press and Chapman & Hall, London.

31. Oman, P. and Pfleeger S. L. (eds) (1997) *Applied Software Metrics*, IEEE Computer Society Press, Los Alamitos, CA.

32. Paulk, M. C., Weber, C. V., Curtis, B. and Chrissis, M. B. (1995) *The Capability Maturity Model: Guidelines for Improving the Software Process*, Addison-Wesley, Reading, MA.

33. Poulin, J. S. (1997) *Measuring Software Reuse – Principles, Practices and Economic Models*, Addison-Wesley, Reading, MA.

34. Pressman, R. S. (2000) *Software Engineering – A Practitioner's Approach*, European adaptation by D. Ince, 5th edn, McGraw-Hill, International, London, Chs 4, 19 and 24.

35. Rifkin, S. (2001) "What makes measuring software so hard?", *IEEE Software*, 18(3), 41–45.

36 Schulmeyer, G. G. (1999) "Software quality assurance metrics", in G. G. Schulmeyer and J. I. McManus (eds), *Handbook of Software Quality Assurance*, 3rd edn, Prentice Hall, Upper Saddle River, NJ, 403–443.

37 Sedigh-Ali, S., Ghafoor, A. and Paul, R. (2001) "Software engineering metrics for COTS-based systems", *IEEE Computer*, 34(5), 44–50.

38 Shoval, P. and Feldman, O. (1997) "A combination of the Mk-II function points software estimation method with the ADISSA methodology for systems analysis and design", *Information and Software Technology*, 39, 855–865.

39 Simmons, P. (1994) "Measurement and the evaluation of I.T. investment", in IEEE Computer Society, *Proceedings of the 2nd International Software Metrics Symposium*, 24–26 October, 1994, IEEE Computer Society Press, Los Angeles, CA.

40 Symons, C. R. (1991) *Software Sizing and Estimating – Mk II FPA (Function Point Analysis)*, John Wiley, Chichester, UK.

41 Symons, C. (2001) "Software benchmarking: serious management tool or a joke", *IEEE Software*, 18(5), 18, 20.

Review questions

21.1 Section 21.3.1 describes the following three code-error density metrics: CED, WCED and WCEF.

(1) Compare CED and WCED including references to their managerial application characteristics as well as to their validity.

(2) Compare WCED and WCEF including references to their managerial implementation characteristics as well as to their validity.

(3) Which of the above metrics would you prefer? List your arguments.

21.2 Section 21.3.3 describes the following two development productivity metrics: DevP and FDevP.

(1) Compare DevP and FDevP including references to their managerial implementation characteristics as well as to their validity.
(2) Which of the above metrics would you prefer? List your arguments.

21.3 Section 21.4 lists metrics for HD and corrective maintenance services.

(1) Explain the difference between these services.
(2) Justify the separate metrics categories and the actions based on their differences.

21.4 Section 21.4.3 describes two maintenance failure density metrics – WSSFD and WSSFF.

(1) Evaluate each of the above metrics as to the degree they fulfill the requirements for software quality metrics as listed in Frame 21.2.
(2) Indicate the expected direction of distortion for each of the metrics.

21.5 HD services are vital for successful regular use of a software system.

(1) Suggest situations where the HD service is a failure.
(2) What metrics can be applied for the failure situations mentioned in (1)?

21.6 Section 21.3 describes several measures used to construct the software development metrics presented in this section.

Based on the listed measures, suggest two new process quality metrics and two new process productivity metrics.

21.7 Section 21.4 describes several measures used to construct the HD and corrective maintenance metrics presented in this section.

Based on the listed measures, suggest three new product quality metrics and two new product productivity metrics.

21.8 Choose one of the product metrics described in Section 21.4 that includes NYF as one of its measures.

(1) Examine the five factors affecting the maintenance measures listed in Section 21.6, indicate in what direction each of them might bias the metrics you have chosen, and indicate how that bias affects the metric's validity.
(2) Examine the above five factors and indicate how each of them may limit the comprehensiveness of the metrics you have chosen.

21.9 A human resources software system requires 15000 lines of Visual Basic code and 5000 lines of SQL code.

(1) Estimate the number of function points required for the software system.
(2) Estimate the number of lines of C code required for the software system.

21.10 Analysis of the requirement specifications for a tender for development of *The Buyers Club CRM System* has been publicized in a professional journal.

ABC Software Labs is considering participating in the tender. The team appointed to prepare the tender analyzed its requirement specifications and obtained the following results:

- Number of user inputs – 28
- Number of user outputs – 36
- Number of user online queries – 24
- Number of logical files – 8
- Number of external interfaces – 12.

The team estimated that 50% of the components are simple, 25% average and 25% complex. The team also evaluated the project's complexity, with an estimated RCAF = 57.

(1) Compute the function points estimate for the project.
(2) Mr Barnes, the Chief Programmer, estimated that 3500 lines of C++ code will be required for the project. Based on the result for (1), do you agree with his estimate?

Topics for discussion

21.1 Two versions for the measure of software system size – KLOC – are applied: one version counts every code line, while the other counts only the non-comment lines of code.

(1) Discuss the advantages and disadvantages of each version. Refer to the validity of both versions.
(2) Try to suggest an improved version that will comply with the arguments you mentioned in your answer to (1).

21.2 *Money-Money*, a software package for financial management of medium-to-small businesses developed by Penny-Penny Ltd, captured a substantial share of the market. The Penny-Penny help desk (HD) has gained a reputation for its high level of professional service to customers who use the software package. During the third and fourth quarters of 2002, the company invested substantial efforts in preparing an improved user manual. Its distribution to customers was completed during December 2002.

The following table presents HD data summarizing the firm's HD activities for the first quarters of 2002 and 2003.

Data	Code	1st Quarter 2002	1st Quarter 2003
Number of customers	A	305	485
Total number of calls received during the quarter	B	2114	2231
Number of HD calls requiring visit to customer's site	C	318	98
Average time for customer calls served by phone (in minutes)	D	9.3	8.8
Average time for customer calls served by visits to customer's site (in minutes)	E	95	118
Number of customer complaints	F	38	41

No.	Quality metrics	Calculation formula

(2) Calculate the value of the quality metrics according to the data presented in the above for each quarter, under the following headings.

No.	Quality metrics	Quality metrics for 1st Quarter 2002	Quality metrics for 1st Quarter 2003

(3) Evaluate the changes in the service quality according to the metrics you suggested.

(4) Can the investments made to improve the user's manual be justified? List your arguments.

21.3 The selection of quality metrics presented in Sections 21.3 and 21.4 include several severity metrics for errors and failures (e.g., ASCE and ASHC).

(1) Explain the importance of these metrics and list the managerial needs not covered by the other metrics.

(2) Suggest situations where such metrics are unjustified.

21.4 Examine the metrics described in Sections 21.3 and 21.4.

(1) Analyze the measures (parameters) that comprise the respective metrics and decide whether they are objective or subjective, where objective measures are based on reliable counts and subjective measures are partly or totally determined by professional evaluation.

(2) Compare the attributes of objective and subjective measures.

(3) List the advantages and disadvantages of the two types of measures.

21.5 The two Software Development Department teams have recently completed their projects. Both applied the same development tool and similar programming style, where comments comprise about a quarter of the total number of lines of code. The following metrics were supplied:

	Team A	Team B
NCE	15.4	9.1
NDE	22.3	20.6

(1) What additional data would you require to determine which of the teams achieved better quality results?

(2) After examining the metrics, what differences in software quality conception held by the team leaders may be concluded from the results?

21.6 Choose one of the process metrics described in Section 21.3 that includes KLOC as one of the constituent measures.

   (1) Examine the three factors listed in Section 21.6 affecting KLOC (as a measure of the software development process) and indicate in what direction each of them might bias the metrics you have chosen and how this would affect its validity.
   (2) Examine the above three factors and indicate the way by which each of them may limit the comprehensiveness of the metrics you have chosen.

21.7 Comparison revealed 188 errors detected during the development process for a team's recently completed project compared with 346 errors during the team's previous project.

   (1) What additional data would you require to determine whether real progress in software quality has been achieved (as claimed by the team leader)?
   (2) Which software quality metrics would you use to examine the team leader's claim?

21.8 Statistical analysis software packages enable the user to calculate descriptive and analytical statistics.

   (1) Explain in your own words the difference between descriptive statistics and analytical statistics.
   (2) Explain the differences in the making and implementing decisions based on each type of statistical tool.

Appendix 21A The function point method

21A.1 Introduction

An important attribute of the function point method is its capacity to provide pre-project estimates of project size, stated in terms of required development resources. These estimates represent one major basis for the resource estimates a firm uses in preparing its tender proposals and project plans. Use of such a tool prevents or at least reduces substantially the risk of managerial failure incurred by underestimating (or overestimating, which is less likely) the expected project costs.

It is clear that KLOC measurement for software size does not possess this attribute as the number of code lines may be counted only after programming completion, which occurs at a very late stage of the project. An alternative measure – the *function point method* – possesses the desired attribute. It measures project size by functionality, indicated in the customer's or tender requirement specification. More accurate estimates are produced as the analysis phase progresses and the software system functions and components are thoroughly studied.

An inherent attribute of KLOC use (not shared by the function point method) is dependence on the programming language or development tool. This attribute limits the comprehensiveness of the KLOC measure as it limits its applicability to comparisons based on the same development tool – unless a conversion factor is used. The extreme differences in the number of lines of code needed for function points is illustrated by the averages presented by Jones (1998).

The estimates for the average number of lines of code (LOC) required for programming a function point are the following:

Programming language/development tool	Average LOC
C	128
C++	64
Visual Basic	32
Power Builder	16
SQL	12

It should be noted that the number of function points for a given software system depends to some extent on the function point counting instruction manual used (the ones most commonly used currently are IFPUG 3, IFPUG 4 and Mark II).

The methodology was first presented in 1979 (Albrecht, 1979; Albrecht and Gaffney, 1983). The function point method is already in wide commercial use but is still considered experimental by many professionals. A wide range of research and tool development activity has been carried out. The main research efforts were directed to validating the method, to improve and adapt it to special areas of software such as real-time software systems and object-oriented software systems. Tool development efforts focus on function point application manuals (especially on function point counting methods) and applications to large-scale software systems. Here we mention just a few of the numerous publications: Gramus and Herron (1996), IEEE (2000), Jeffery *et al.* (1993), Low and Jeffery (1990), Symons (1991), Davis (1992), Caldiera *et al.* (1998), Henderson-Sellers (1996) and Shoval and Feldman (1997).

21A.2 The function point method

The function point method for estimating project size is conducted as follows:

- **Stage 1:** Compute crude function points (CFP). The number of software system functional components are first identified, followed by evaluation of each component as "simple", "average" or "complex". At this point we are able to apply weighting factors to the system components and compute their weighted value. The sum of the weighted values for the software system is the CFP.

- **Stage 2:** Compute the relative complexity adjustment factor (RCAF) for the project. The RCAF varies between 0 and 70.
- **Stage 3:** Compute the number of function points (FP):

$$FP = CFP \times (0.65 + 0.01 \times RCAF)$$

Stage 1: Calculation of crude function points

The method relates to the following five types of software system components:

- Number of user inputs – distinct input applications, not including inputs for online queries.
- Number of user outputs – distinct output applications such as batch processed reports, lists, customer invoices and error messages (not including online queries).
- Number of user online queries – distinct online applications, where output may be in the form of a printout or screen display.
- Number of logical files – files that deal with a distinct type of data and may be grouped in a database.
- Number of external interfaces – computer–readable output or inputs transmitted through data communication, on CD, diskette, etc.

The function point method applies weight factors to each component according to its complexity; the form shown in Table 21A.1 can assist in computation of the CFP.

Table 21A.1: Crude Function Points (CFP) – calculation form

Software System Component	Complexity level									Total CFP
	Simple			Average			Complex			
	Count	Weight factor	Points	Count	Weight factor	Points	Count	Weight factor	Points	
	A	B	C= A×B	D	E	F= D×E	G	H	I= G×H	J=C+F+I
User inputs		3			4			6		
User outputs		4			5			7		
User online queries		3			4			6		
Logical files		7			10			15		
External interfaces		5			7			10		
Total CFP										

Stage 2: Calculating the relative complexity adjustment factor (RCAF)

The relative complexity adjustment factor (RCAF) summarizes the complexity characteristics of the software system by assigning grades (0 to 5) to the 14 subjects that substantially affect the required development efforts. The list of subjects is presented in the RCAF calculation form; see Table 21A.2.

Table 21A.2: Relative Complexity Adjustment Factor (RCAF) – calculation form

No.	Subject	Grade
1	Requirement for reliable backup and recovery	0 1 2 3 4 5
2	Requirement for data communication	0 1 2 3 4 5
3	Extent of distributed processing	0 1 2 3 4 5
4	Performance requirements	0 1 2 3 4 5
5	Expected operational environment	0 1 2 3 4 5
6	Extent of online data entries	0 1 2 3 4 5
7	Extent of multi-screen or multi-operation online data input	0 1 2 3 4 5
8	Extent of online updating of master files	0 1 2 3 4 5
9	Extent of complex inputs, outputs, online queries and files	0 1 2 3 4 5
10	Extent of complex data processing	0 1 2 3 4 5
11	Extent that currently developed code can be designed for reuse	0 1 2 3 4 5
12	Extent of conversion and installation included in the design	0 1 2 3 4 5
13	Extent of multiple installations in an organization and variety of customer organizations	0 1 2 3 4 5
14	Extent of change and focus on ease of use	0 1 2 3 4 5
	Total = RCAF	

Stage 3: Computing the number of function points (FP)

The function point value for a given software system is computed according to the results of stages 1 and 2, by applying the following formula:

$$FP = CFP \times (0.65 + 0.01 \times RCAF)$$

21A.3 Example – the *Attend-Master* software system

Attend-Master is a basic employee attendance system that is planned to serve small to medium-sized businesses employing 10–100 employees. The system is planned to have interfaces to the company's other software packages: *Human-Master*, which serves human resources units, and *Wage-Master*, which serves the wages units. Attend-Master is planned to produce several reports and online queries. The scheme of the planned software system is found in the data flow diagram (DFD) shown in Figure 21A.1.

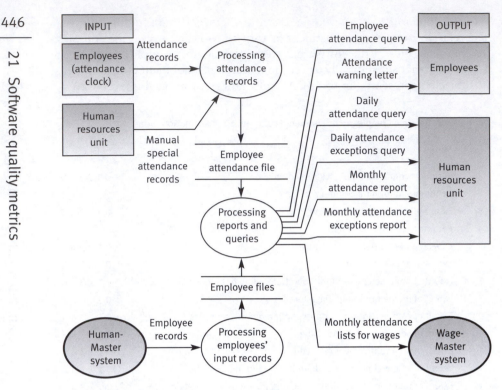

Figure 21A.1: The *Attend-Master* data flow diagram

Let us now compute the function point value for the proposed Attend-Master software system.

Stage 1: Calculation of crude function points

Analysis of the software system as presented in the DFD summarizes the number of the various components:

- Number of user inputs – 2
- Number of user outputs – 3
- Number of user online queries – 3
- Number of logical files – 2
- Number of external interfaces – 2.

The degree of complexity (simple, average or complex) was evaluated for each component (see Table 21A.3), after which CFP calculations were performed.

Software System Component	Compexity level									Total CFP
	Simple			Average			Complex			
	Count	Weight factor	Points	Count	Weight factor	Points	Count	Weight factor	Points	
	A	B	C= A×B	D	E	F= D×E	G	H	I= G×H	J=C+F+I
User inputs	1	3	3	----	4	----	1	6	6	9
User outputs	----	4	----	2	5	10	1	7	7	17
User online queries	1	3	3	1	4	4	1	6	6	13
Logical files	1	7	7	----	10	----	1	15	15	22
External interfaces	----	5	----	----	7	----	2	10	20	20
Total CFP										81

Stage 2: Calculating the relative complexity adjustment factor (RCAF)

The evaluation of the complexity characteristics of *Attend-Master* and calculation of the relative complexity adjustment factor (RCAF) are presented in Table 21A.4.

Table 21A.4: Attend-Master RCAF – calculation form

No.	Affecting subjects	Grade
1	Requirement for reliable backup and recovery	0 1 2 3 4 ⑤
2	Requirement for data communication	⓪ 1 2 3 4 5
3	Extent of distributed processing	⓪ 1 2 3 4 5
4	Performance requirements	0 1 2 3 4 ⑤
5	Expected operational environment	⓪ 1 2 3 4 5
6	Extent of online data entries	0 1 2 3 ④ 5
7	Extent of multi-screen or multi-operation online data input	0 1 ② 3 4 5
8	Extent of online updating of master files	0 1 ② 3 4 5
9	Extent of complex inputs, outputs, online queries and files	0 1 2 3 ④ 5
10	Extent of complex data processing	0 1 2 3 ④ 5
11	Extent that currently developed code can be designed for reuse	0 1 2 ③ 4 5
12	Extent of conversion and installation included in the design	0 1 ② 3 4 5
13	Extent of multiple installations in an organization and variety of customer organizations	0 1 2 3 4 ⑤
14	Extent of change and focus on ease of use	0 1 2 3 4 ⑤
	Total = RCAF	**41**

Stage 3: Competing the number of function points (FP)

After applying the stated formula, the calculation was performed as follows:

$$FP = CFP \times [0.65 + 0.01 \times RCAF) = 81 \times (0.65 + 0.01 \times 41) = 85.86$$

21A.4 Function point advantages and disadvantages

Main advantages:

- Estimates can be prepared at the pre-project stage and therefore can support the management in its project preparation efforts.
- As it is based on requirement specification documents (i.e., function points are not dependent on development tools or programming languages), the method's reliability is relatively high.

Main disadvantages:

- To some extent, FP results depend on the function point counting instruction manual used by the professionals who prepare the estimates.
- Estimates need to be based on detailed requirements specifications or software system specifications, which are not always available at the pre-project stage.
- The entire process requires an experienced function point team and devotion of substantial resources prior to computation of the FP.
- The many evaluations required result in subjective results.
- Most successful applications and research results are related to data processing systems. Other areas of software system require specialized adaptations. In other words, the function point method cannot be universally applied.

Costs of software quality

More and more, management – whether of commercial companies or public organizations – is requiring economic evaluation of their quality assurance systems. Accordingly, it is becoming ever more likely for proposals for development of new quality assurance tools or investment in improved and expanded operation of existing systems to be examined through an "economic" microscope. Quality assurance units are thus being forced to demonstrate the potential profitability of any request they may make for the substantial funds required to finance additional system infrastructure or operating costs.

We would claim that *cost of software quality* – the economic assessment of software quality development and maintenance – is just another class of software quality metrics, where financial values are used as the measuring tool. However, whereas quality metrics and costs of quality both support management control and decision making, *costs of quality* is a metric displaying a unique characteristic. Application of common financial measures enables management to obtain the type of general overview of all software quality assurance activities unavailable with any other metrics.

The unique features of costs of software quality discussed in this chapter reflect the special characteristics of SQA, characteristics that are absent from quality assurance in manufacturing industry (see Section. 1.1).

The cost of software development has been the subject of many research projects, books and articles in the last two decades (e.g., Boehm, 1981, 2000; Jones, 1998; Dobbins, 1999; Hale *et al.*, 2000); publications dedicated to the cost of software quality are nevertheless rare. One indication of the subject's importance is the appearance of publications dedicated to colossal software system failures. These works make it clear that the quality system applied in the projects rested at the heart of the failures (Glass, 1998; Montealegre and Keil, 2000). We can assume that a regularly implemented, effective software quality assurance system could have prevented or drastically reduced the immense damages involved in these now "classic" cases.

This chapter discusses the classic model of cost of software quality, which applies the general costs of quality model to the software industry. An additional model, the *extended costs of software quality model*, proposed by the author, is presented as an alternative that more effectively captures features specific to the software industry. The concluding part of the chapter deals with application of a costs of software quality system and the problems raised in the process.

After completing this chapter, you will be able to:

■ Explain the objectives of costs of software quality measurements.
■ Compare the classic model to the extended model.
■ Justify development of a unique quality cost model for software development.
■ Describe the process of implementation of a costs of software quality system.
■ Explain the "standard" and unique difficulties arising in application of cost of software quality systems.

22.1 Objectives of cost of software quality metrics

Frame 22.1 presents the main objectives to be achieved by application of cost of software quality metrics.

Managerial control over the cost of software quality is achieved by comparison of actual performance figures with:

■ Control budgeted expenditures (for SQA prevention and appraisal activities)
■ Previous year's failure costs

<table>
<tr><td>Frame 22.1</td><td>Cost of software quality metrics – objectives</td></tr>
</table>

Application of cost of software quality metrics enables management to achieve economic control over SQA activities and outcomes. The specific objectives are:

■ Control organization-initiated costs to prevent and detect software errors

■ Evaluation of the economic damages of software failures as a basis for revising the SQA budget

■ Evaluation of plans to increase or decrease SQA activities or to invest in a new or updated SQA infrastructure on the basis of past economic performance

■ Previous project's quality costs (control costs and failure costs)
■ Other department's quality costs (control costs and failure costs).

After introducing changes in SQA procedures or SQA infrastructure, the following relations may provide better indications of the success of an SQA plan than those just mentioned:

■ Percentage of cost of software quality out of total software development costs
■ Percentage of software failure costs out of total software development costs
■ Percentage of cost of software quality out of total software maintenance costs
■ Percentage of cost of software quality out of total sales of software products and software maintenance.

22.2 The classic model of cost of software quality

The classic quality cost model, developed in the early 1950s by Feigenbaum and others (see Feigenbaum, 1991), provides a methodology for classifying the costs associated with product quality assurance from an economic point of view. Developed to suit the quality situations found in manufacturing organizations, the model has since been widely implemented.

The model classifies costs related to product quality into two general classes:

■ **Costs of control** include costs that are spent to prevent and detect software errors in order to reduce them to an accepted level.

■ **Costs of failure of control** include costs of failures that occurred because of failure to prevent and detect software errors. The model further subdivides these into subclasses.

Costs of control are assigned to either the prevention or the appraisal costs subclass:

■ **Prevention costs** include investments in quality infrastructure and quality activities that are not directed to a specific project or system, being general to the organization.

■ **Appraisal costs** include the costs of activities performed for a specific project or software system for the purpose of detecting software errors.

Failures of control costs are further classified into internal failure costs and external failure costs:

■ **Internal failure costs** include costs of correcting errors that have been detected by design reviews, software tests and acceptance tests (carried out by the customer) and completed before the software is installed at customer sites.

■ **External failure costs** include all costs of correcting failures detected by customers or the maintenance team after the software system has been installed.

The classic model of cost of software quality is presented in Figure 22.1.

Although attempts to apply the classic model to software development and maintenance have been reported, success has been very partial. Reasons for the difficulties confronted are discussed later in the chapter. But before doing so, the model is reviewed.

22.2.1 Prevention costs

Prevention costs include investments in establishing a software quality infrastructure, updating and improving that infrastructure as well as performing the regular activities required for its operation. A significant share of the

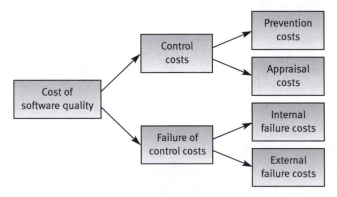

Figure 22.1: The classic model of cost of software quality

activities performed by the SQA team is preventive in character, as reflected in the SQA budget. Typical preventive costs include:

(1) Investments in development of new or improved SQA infrastructure components or, alternatively, regular updating of those components:
- Procedures and work instructions
- Support devices: templates, checklists, etc.
- Software configuration management system
- Software quality metrics.

(2) Regular implementation of SQA preventive activities:
- Instruction of new employees in SQA subjects and procedures related to their positions
- Instruction of employees in new and updated SQA subjects and procedures
- Certification of employees for positions that require special certification
- Consultations on SQA issues provided to team leaders and others.

(3) Control of the SQA system through performance of:
- Internal quality reviews
- External quality audits by customers and SQA system certification organizations
- Management quality reviews.

22.2.2 Appraisal costs

Appraisal costs are devoted to detection of software errors in specific projects or software systems. Typical appraisal costs cover:

(1) Reviews:
- Formal design reviews (DRs)
- Peer reviews (inspections and walkthroughs)
- Expert reviews.

(2) Costs of software testing:
- Unit tests
- Integration tests
- Software system tests
- Acceptance tests (participation in tests carried out by the customer).

(3) Costs of assuring quality of external participants, primarily by means of design reviews and software testing. These activities are applied to the activities performed by:
- Subcontractors
- Suppliers of COTS software systems and reusable software modules
- The customer as a participant in performing the project.

22.2.3 Internal failure costs

Internal failure costs are those incurred when correcting errors that have been detected by design reviews, software tests and acceptance tests performed before the software has been installed at customer sites. In other words, internal failure costs represent the costs of error correction subsequent to formal examinations of the software during its development, prior to the system's installation at the customer's site. It should be noted that corrections and changes resulting from team leader checks or other team-initiated reviews are generally not considered internal failure costs because they are conducted informally. Typical costs of internal failures are:

■ Costs of redesign or design corrections subsequent to design review and test findings

■ Costs of re-programming or correcting programs in response to test findings

■ Costs of repeated design review and re-testing (regression tests). Importantly, although the costs of regular design reviews and software tests are considered appraisal costs, any repeated design reviews or software tests directly resulting from poor design and inferior code quality are considered internal failure costs.

22.2.4 External failure costs

External failure costs entail the costs of correcting failures detected by customers or maintenance teams after the software system has been installed at customer sites. These costs may be further classified into "overt" external failure costs and "hidden" external failure costs. In most cases, the extent of hidden costs is much greater than that of overt costs. This gap is caused, not least, by the difficulty of estimating hidden external failure costs in comparison to overt external failure costs, which are readily recorded or estimated. In addition, the estimates obtained are frequently disputed among the professionals involved. Hidden external failure cost estimation is rarely undertaken as a result. Therefore, we will use the term external failure costs to refer exclusively to overt failure costs. Typical external failure costs cover:

■ Resolution of customer complaints during the warranty period. In most cases, this involves a review of the complaint and transmission of instructions. In most cases, complaints result from failure of the "help" function or the guidelines found in the instruction manual.

■ Correction of software bugs detected during regular operation. Those involving correction of code (including tests of the corrected software) followed by installation of the corrected code or replacement of the erroneous version by the correct version are often performed at the customer's site.

■ Correction of software failures after the warranty period is over even if the correction is not covered by the warranty.

- Damages paid to customers in case of a severe software failure detected during regular operation.
- Reimbursement of customer's purchase costs, including handling, in case of total dissatisfaction (relates to COTS software packages as well as to custom-made software).
- Insurance against customer's claims in case of severe software failure.

The listed items reflect only overt external failure costs, costs that represent a small proportion of the full range of external failure costs. These costs are directly incurred by software failures detected and recorded during regular operation of the software. The greater proportion of external failure costs – hidden costs – reflect the indirect damages suffered by the software development organization as a result of those same failures. Typical examples of hidden external failure costs are:

- Damages of reduction of sales to customers suffering from high rates of software failures
- Severe reduction of sales motivated by the firm's damaged reputation
- Increased investment in sales promotion to counter the effects of past software failures
- Reduced prospects to win a tender or, alternatively, the need to under-price to prevent competitors from winning tenders.

22.3 An extended model for cost of software quality

Analysis of the software quality costs defined by the classic model reveals that several costs of substantial magnitude are excluded. These costs are either unique to the software industry or negligible for other industries. For example, typical software quality failure costs include:

- Damages paid to customers as compensation for late completion of the project due to unrealistic scheduling
- Damages paid to customers in compensation for late completion of the project as a result of failure to recruit sufficient staff.

The element common to these two failures is that they result not from any particular action of the development team or any lack of professionalism; they are actually outcomes of *managerial failure*.

Management can perform several activities to prevent or reduce the costs that result from the types of failure particular to its functions:

- Contract reviews (proposal draft review and contract draft review). The cost of these reviews is usually negligible for contracts in the manufacturing industries. However, in the software industry, considerable professional work is required to assure that a project proposal is based on sound estimates and comprehensive evaluations. The significant difference in required resources results from the nature of the product and the production process covered by the contract. While a typical contract in the manufacturing industry deals with repeated manufacturing of catalog-listed products, a typical contract in the software industry deals with development of a new, unique software system (see Chapter 1).

■ Thorough appropriate progress control of the software project. While production control carried out in the manufacturing industry is a repetitive task that can, in most cases, be performed automatically by machines, software development progress control supervises task design and coding activities performed for the first time by the development team.

The important effect of management on the cost of software quality is reflected by the title of Flowers' book: *Software Failure: Management Failure* (Flowers, 1996). In this book Flowers describes and analyzes several colossal software project failures; he concludes by discussing the critical managerial failures at their root and suggests ways to prevent or reduce them.

The *extended cost of software quality model*, as proposed by the author of this volume, extends the classic model to include management's "contributions" to the total cost of software quality. According to the extended model, two subclasses are added to complete the model's coverage: managerial preparation and control costs, and managerial failure costs. The extended cost of software quality model is shown in Figure 22.2. In the sections below, the new cost subclasses are discussed in full.

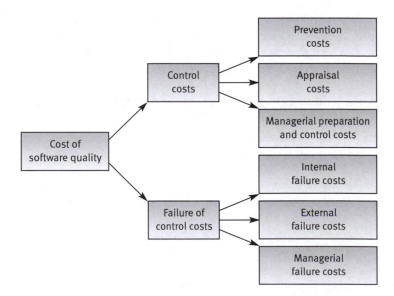

Figure 22.2: The extended cost of software quality model

22.3.1 Managerial preparation and control costs

Managerial preparation and control costs are associated with activities performed to prevent managerial failures or reduce prospects of their occurrence. Several of these activities have already been discussed in previous chapters related to various SQA frameworks. Typical managerial preparation and control costs include:

- Costs of carrying out contract reviews (proposal draft and contract draft reviews) – see Chapter 5.
- Costs of preparing project plans, including quality plans and their review – see Chapter 6.
- Costs of periodic updating of project and quality plans.
- Costs of performing regular progress control of internal software development efforts – see Chapter 20.
- Costs of performing regular progress control of external participants' contributions to the project – see Chapter 12.

22.3.2 Managerial failure costs

Managerial failure costs can be incurred throughout the entire course of software development, beginning in the pre-project stage. They are most likely to crop up in connection with failed attempts to estimate the appropriate project schedule and budget as well as detect in a timely fashion those deviations and problems that demand management intervention. Several of these activities have already been discussed previously and are repeated here for the sake of completeness. Typical managerial failure costs include:

- Unplanned costs for professional and other resources, resulting from underestimation of the resources upon which the submitted proposals are based.
- Damages paid to customers as compensation for late completion of the project, a result of the unrealistic schedule presented in the company's proposal.
- Damages paid to customers as compensation for late completion of the project, a result of management's failure to recruit sufficient and appropriate team members.
- *Domino effect*: damages to other projects performed by the same teams involved in the delayed projects. These damages should be considered managerial failure costs of the original project, whose scheduling problems interfered with the progress of other projects. Should it materialize, we can expect a domino effect to obstruct the progress of several other company projects and induce considerable hidden external failure costs.

22.4 Application of a cost of software quality system

In order to apply a cost of software quality system in an organization, the following are required:

■ Definition of a cost of software quality model and array of cost items specifically for the organization, department, team or project. Each of the cost items that constitute the model should be related to one of the subclasses of the chosen cost of software quality model (the classic model or the extended model).

■ Definition of the method of data collection.

■ Application of a cost of software quality system, including thorough follow-up.

■ Actions to be taken in response to the findings produced.

22.4.1 Definition of a cost of software quality model

At a preliminary stage in a project, the organization has to choose its preferred type of cost model – the classic or the extended model. Whichever model is selected, its effectiveness is determined to a great degree by its suitability for the organization or project of the cost items designed to be measured for the model. In other words, these model items are defined specifically for the case involved, a process that requires determination of a list of the software quality cost items considered relevant to the organization's budgeted expenditures. Each item should belong to one of the subclasses comprising the cost model. Classification of cost items along the lines set in Section 22.3 is strongly recommended.

Example
The SQA unit of the Information Systems Department of a commercial company adopted the classic model as its cost of software quality model. The SQA unit defined about 30 cost items to comprise the model. Some of the cost items are listed in Table 22.1 including their cost subclass.

Implementation tip

The software development and maintenance departments should agree upon the structure of the cost of software quality model and the related cost items. It is preferable to omit those items over which agreement is difficult to reach, even at the expense of reduced coverage of quality costs.

Some software quality cost items may be shared by several departments or projects. In such cases, the rules determining allocation of costs should be as simple as possible and should be agreed by all the relevant parties.

Cost item	Cost of quality subclass
Head of SQA Unit (personnel costs)	50% prevention costs, 50% internal failure costs
SQA team member reviewing compliance with instructions (personnel costs)	Prevention costs
Other team SQA members (personnel costs)	Prevention and appraisal costs according to monthly personnel records
Development and maintenance team participation in internal and external SQA audits (personnel costs)	Prevention costs – recorded time spent on audits
Testing team – first series of tests (personnel costs)	Appraisal costs – recorded time spent
Testing team – regression tests (personnel costs)	Internal failure costs – recorded time spent
Development and maintenance team correction of errors identified by the testing team (personnel costs)	Internal failure costs – recorded time spent
Maintenance team correction of software failures identified by the customer (personnel costs + traveling costs to the customer's site)	External failure costs – recorded time spent
Regular visits of unit's SQA consultant (standard monthly fee)	Prevention costs
Unit's SQA consultant's participation in external failure inquiries (special invoices)	External failure costs
SQA journals, seminars, etc.	Prevention costs

Updates and changes of the quality cost items can be expected. These are based on analyses of the cost of software quality reports as well as on changes in the organization's structure and environment.

22.4.2 Definition of the cost data collection method

The method of cost data collection is a key (although regularly underestimated) factor in the success or failure of the cost of software quality system.

Once the list of software quality cost items is finalized, a method for collecting the relevant data must be determined. One of the major issues raised at this stage is whether to develop an independent system for collecting data or to rely on the currently operating management information system (MIS). After some adaptations, the MIS is usually capable of serving the needs of data collection for the chosen cost model. For instance, its human resources costing system can record working hours invested in quality issues. Relatively simple changes in ledger categories enable the accounting system to record the costs of external services and purchases for the SQA system as well as damages paid to customers. In general, use of MIS systems in place is preferable to creating new systems. To be more precise, the reasons for preferring the existing system are:

- Expected savings in costs by running a working data collection system already operating instead of creating and running an independent system.
- Avoidance of disagreements in interpretation of the data provided by the MIS versus the data provided by the independent system, typical events when operating an independent data collection system. Disagreements of this type reduce the reliability of the software quality cost results.

22.4.3 Implementation of a cost of software quality system

Like any other new procedure, implementation of a new cost of software quality system involves:

- Assigning responsibility for reporting and collecting quality cost data.
- Instruction of the team in the logic and procedures of the new system.
- Follow-up:
  - Support for solving implementation problems and providing supplementary information when needed
  - Review of cost reporting, proper classification and recording
  - Review of the completeness and accuracy of reports by comparing them with records produced by the general MIS system and the cost and activity records from previous periods. This task requires special efforts during the initial implementation period.

- Updating and revising the definitions of the cost items together with the reporting and collecting methods, based on feedback.

22.4.4 Actions taken in response to the model's findings

Most of the actions taken in response to the model's findings – that is, the results obtained after analysis of the software quality reports based on comparisons with previous periods, with other units, etc. – are rooted in the application of the *cost of software quality balance* concept. According to this concept, an increase in control costs is expected to yield a decrease in failure of control costs and vice versa: a decrease in control costs is expected to lead to an increase in failure of control costs. Moreover, the effect of changes in control costs is expected to vary by the desired software quality level. This relationship is expected to yield a minimal total cost of software quality, a cost that is achievable at a specified quality level – the optimal software quality level. See Figure 22.3 for a graphic illustration of the cost of software quality balance concept and the relationships between control and failure of control costs for all the quality levels.

Management is usually interested in minimal total quality costs rather than in control or failure of control cost components. Therefore, managers tend to focus on the optimal quality level and apply this concept when budgeting the annual SQA activity plan as well as when budgeting a project.

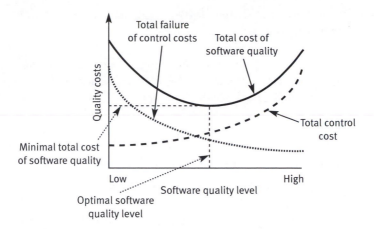
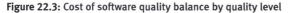

Figure 22.3: Cost of software quality balance by quality level

Examples of typical decisions taken in the wake of cost of software quality analysis and their expected results are shown in Table 22.2.

In addition to the direct actions taken by management, other actions can be initiated by the Corrective Action Board, which bases its analysis of the accumulated cost of quality data on factors other than those considered by management. A comprehensive discussion of such indirect actions is found in Chapter 17.

Table 22.2: Cost of software quality analysis – typical actions and expected results

No.	Action	Expected results
1	Improvement of software package's help function	Reduction of external failure costs
2	Increased investment of resources in contract review	Reduction of managerial failure costs
3	Reduction in instruction activities yielding no significant improvement	Reduction of prevention costs with no increase in failure costs
4	Increased investment in training inspection team members and team leaders	Reduction of internal and external failure costs
5	Adoption of more intensive project progress control procedures	Reduction of managerial failure costs
6	Construction of certified list of subcontractors allowed to participate in the company's projects	Reduction of failure costs, especially of external failure costs
7	Introduction of automated software tests to replace manual testing with no substantial increase in testing costs	Reduction of internal and external failure costs

22.5 Problems in the application of cost of software quality metrics

Application of a cost of software quality model is generally accompanied by problems to be overcome, whatever the industry. These impinge upon the accuracy and completeness of quality cost data caused by:

■ Inaccurate and/or incomplete identification and classification of quality costs

■ Negligent reporting by team members and others

■ Biased reporting of software costs, especially of "censored" internal and external costs

■ Biased recording of external failure costs due to indirect if not "camouflaged" compensation of customers for failures (e.g., discounted future services, delivery of free services, etc.) whose implications remain unrecorded as external failure costs.

The above-mentioned problems do arise within the context of the software industry but there are others as well, some of which are unique to software. We shall focus on the problems faced when recording managerial preparation and control costs and managerial failure costs because these items significantly affect the validity and comprehensiveness of the total cost of software quality, especially when the extended cost of software quality model is applied.

Problems arising when collecting data on managerial preparation and control costs include:

■ Contract review and progress control activities are performed in many cases in a "part-time mode", and in addition they are subdivided into several disconnected activities of short duration. The reporting of time invested in these activities is usually inaccurate and often neglected.

■ Many participants in these activities are senior staff members who are not required to report use of their time resources.

Problems encountered in collection of data on managerial failure costs, especially schedule failures include:

■ Determination of responsibility for schedule failures. These costs may be assigned to the customer (in which case the customer is required to compensate the contractor), the development team (considered as an external failure cost), or management (considered as a managerial failure cost). Schedule failure costs are frequently deliberated for lengthy periods because their direct causes or the specific contributions of each participant to the initial failures are difficult to pinpoint. Table 22.3 shows examples of typical causes for delays and the associated quality costs.

Table 22.3: Typical causes for delays and associated costs

Cause for deviation from schedule	Class of quality costs
1. Changes introduced in the project's specifications during development	No internal failure costs; customer responsibility for failure costs
2. Customer-delayed installation of communication and other hardware, and/or delays in staff recruitment and training	No internal failure costs, customer responsibility for failure costs
3. Poor performance by development team, requiring extensive rework and corrections of software	External failure costs
4. Project proposal based on unrealistic schedules and budgets	Managerial failure costs
5. Late or inadequate recruitment of staff or reliance on company professionals whose release from other projects does not meet project needs	Managerial failure costs

■ Payment of overt (not "camouflaged") and formal compensation usually occurs quite some time after the project is completed, and much too late for efficient application of the lessons learned. This tardiness opens up the question of whether the failure was managerial or external.

Summary

(1) Explain the objectives of cost of software quality measurements.

The objectives of cost of software quality measurements relate to management interventions on the basis of economic data:
- ■ To control the costs associated with error prevention (prior to occurrence) and detection of errors (once they occur).
- ■ To evaluate the extent of economic damages of software failures and prevention and appraisal costs as a basis for revising and updating the SQA budget.
- ■ To facilitate economic evaluation of planned increases or decreases in SQA activities or investment in new or updated SQA infrastructure, based on past economic performance.

(2) Compare the classic software quality costs model with the extended model.

The classic model for quality costs delivered by Feigenbaum and others in the early 1950s presents a general concept that classifies manufacturing quality costs into two classes: **costs of control** (prevention costs and appraisal costs) – costs controlled by the organization and expended to prevent and detect failures so as to reduce total failures to an acceptable level; and **costs of failure of control** (internal failure costs and external failure costs) – costs of failures, regarded as consequences, caused by failure to prevent and detect software errors.

The extended model expands the scope of the classic model by introducing factors related to management's contribution to project success and failure. The subclasses added are managerial preparation and control costs (a third subclass to the costs of control class), and managerial failure costs (a third subclass to the costs of failure of control class).

(3) Justify the formulation of a unique quality cost model for software development.

The need for the extended cost of software quality model, unique to the software industry, is justified by its inclusion of managerial quality costs. While managerial costs – i.e., managerial preparation and control costs and managerial failure costs – as a proportion of quality costs are usually negligible in manufacturing, they may be quite considerable in software development. The extent of losses (failure costs) incurred by management's erroneous actions and decisions or by its failure to act on time can be colossal. Also, as preparations and progress control involve much effort, the associated costs are very high. This situation stems from the special characteristics of the software industry as described in Chapter 1.

(4) Describe the implementation of a cost of software quality system.

Implementation of a cost of software quality system in an organization requires:
- Delineation of the cost of software quality model for the particular organization, with each quality cost item related to one of the model's cost subclasses.
- Determination of the method of cost data collection for each cost item.
- Institution of the planned cost of software quality system, including follow-up procedures.
- Taking actions on the basis of the cost model's findings.

(5) Explain the standard and unique problems involved in implementing a cost of software quality system.

Implementation of such a system for software is generally confronted by problems as in other industries. The standard difficulties that affect accuracy and completeness of quality cost data are:
- Inaccurate and incomplete identification and classification of quality costs
- Negligent reporting
- Human tendency for biased reporting, especially of internal and external costs
- Biased external failure cost records due to indirect if not "camouflaged" compensation of customers that is not officially recorded as external failure costs.

These problems also impinge on the cost of software quality, to which obstacles unique to the software industry must be added. Together they significantly affect the validity and comprehensiveness of the collected cost of software quality data.

Typical difficulties in collecting quality costs on managerial preparation and control costs include:
- Segmentation of contract review and progress control activities into several short and disconnected activities, which interferes with accurate reporting of time invested.
- Many senior staff members are not required to report their use of time resources.

Typical difficulties in collecting managerial failure cost data, especially regarding schedules, are:

- Difficulties in determining the responsibility for schedule failures. The costs of such failures may be assigned to the customer (in which case the customer is required to compensate the contractor), the development team (classified as external failure costs) or management (classified as managerial failure costs).
- Compensation often occurs too late in the process for the lessons learnt to be applied. Still, in most cases, determination of responsibility for failure costs remains problematic; in other words, the debate remains open as to whether they are managerial or external failures.

Selected bibliography

1. Boehm, B. W. (1981) *Software Engineering Economics*, Prentice Hall, Upper Saddle River, NJ.
2. Boehm, B. W. (2000) *"Safe and simple software cost analysis"*, IEEE Software, 17(5), 14–17.
3. Crosby, P. B. (1992) *Quality is Free*, McGraw-Hill, New York.
4. Dobbins, J. H. (1999) "The cost of software quality" in G. G. Schulmeyer, and J. I. McManus, (eds), *Handbook of Software Quality Assurance*, 3rd edn, Prentice Hall, Upper Saddle River, NJ, pp. 403–443.
5. Feigenbaum, A. V. (1991) *Total Quality Control*, 3rd edn, McGraw-Hill, New York.
6. Flowers, S. (1996) *Software Failure: Management Failure*, John Wiley & Sons, Chichester, West Sussex, UK.
7. Glass, R. L. (1998) *Software Runaways*, Prentice Hall, PTR, Upper Saddle River, NJ.
8. Hale, J., Parrish, A., Dixon B. and Smith, R. K. (2000), "Enhancing the Cocomo estimation models", IEEE Software, 17(6), 45–49.
9. ISO (1997) *ISO 9000-3:1997(E), Quality Management and Quality Assurance Standards – Part 3 Guidelines for the Application of ISO 9001:1994 to the Development, Supply, Installation and Maintenance of Computer Software*, 2nd edn, International Organization for Standardization (ISO), Geneva.
10. Jones, C. (1998) *Estimating Software Costs*, McGraw-Hill, New York.
11. Montealegre, R. and Keil, M. (2000) "De-escalating information technology projects: lessons from the Denver International Airport", *MIS Quarterly*, 24(3), 417–447.

Review questions

22.1 Section 22.1 presents the classic cost of software quality model. It classifies quality costs into four classes: prevention costs, appraisal costs, internal failure costs and external failure costs.

(1) Explain in your own words the main characteristics of each class of costs and indicate the differences between them.

(2) Suggest three items for each class.

22.2 Both cost of software quality models, the classic and the extended, assign costs to two main classes: costs of control and costs of failure of control.

(1) Explain in your own words the nature of each class.
(2) What would you consider to be the idea guiding this classification and what are its managerial aspects?

22.3 Section 22.2 presents the extended cost of software quality model.

(1) Explain the difference between the classic and the extended models in your own words.
(2) Justify the formulation of a special extended cost of quality model for software. Base your arguments on a comparison of the characteristics of the software development project environment with those of industrial manufacturing companies.

22.4 The annual report issued by Leonard Software Inc. includes several expenditure items as listed in Table 22.4.

(1) Indicate the subclass of cost of software quality to which each of the following expenditures belongs: prevention costs, appraisal costs, managerial preparation and control costs, internal failure costs, external failure costs, managerial failure costs. In case an expenditure item is not a software quality cost, mark "X" in the "Non-software quality cost" column.
(2) For each software quality cost, indicate the expected direction of reporting distortions: upward, downward or none.

Table 22.4: Leonard Software Inc.: expenditure

No.	Expenditure item	Subclass of software quality cost	Expected direction of reporting distortions	Non-software quality cost
1	Working hours spent installing software in customer's site in Singapore			
2	Customer's debt as agreed in compromise following software failures detected in the installed software			
3	Payment for Dr Jacobs' participation in a design review			
4	Payments made to King SQA Consultants for preparing the new version of the software quality procedures			
5	Repair of a color printer			
6	Participation in monthly meetings of the Coordination and Control Committee headed by the Department Manager, total hours			

No.	Expenditure item	Subclass of software quality cost	Expected direction of reporting distortions	Non-software quality cost
7	Travel to Switzerland for examination of advanced software testing system offered to company			
8	Purchase of barcode stickers software package to be integrated in the inventory management software system			
9	Working hours spent in correcting errors listed in a design review report			
10	Customer's compensation for delay in schedule resulting from the company's inability to recruit sufficient professional manpower for the development team			
11	Working hours spent by the Chief Software Engineer and Senior Project Manager in examining the schedule estimates for the "Top Assets" tender			
12	Preparation of an updated version of Leonard Software's *C Programming Instructions*			
13	Working hours spent by programmer in correcting program bugs detected by her team leader in their weekly meeting			

22.5 Leonard Software's last year's annual costs of software quality are shown in Table 22.5.

Table 22.5: Leonard Software Inc.: costs of software quality

Cost of software quality class	Previous year's annual costs, $000s
Prevention costs	1238
Appraisal costs	3450
Managerial preparation and control costs	300
Internal failure costs	4243
External failure costs	2890
Managerial failure costs	6444

The Software Quality Assurance Manager has proposed a dramatic change in Leonard Software's software quality expenditures policy that is expected to reduce failure costs by significant percentages, as follows: internal failure costs by 10%, external failure costs by 25%, and managerial failure costs by at least 25%.

The SQA manager's proposal involves increasing expenditures as follows: prevention costs by $400 000, appraisal costs by $1 100 000, and managerial preparation and control costs by $900 000.

The company's management commented about the proposed fourfold expenditures on its preparations and control, but promised to seriously evaluate the proposal. You were asked to evaluate for the management the SQA manager's proposal.

(1) Examine the proposal and calculate its results from the financial point of view.
(2) Explain, in your own words, how this dramatic program's additional funds should be utilized in order to bring about the expected reduction in failure costs.
(3) Can you list any hidden costs of failure that have not been mentioned in the program but which are expected to be reduced as a result of implementing the proposal?

Topics for discussion

22.1 *Software Runaways* by Glass (1998) is dedicated to the description and analysis of software development projects that ended in catastrophic failure.

(1) Choose one of the projects described in the book and try to determine the extent of the project's failure costs. What do you think was management's contribution to these failure costs?
(2) List the management decisions, activities and oversights that caused the colossal failure.
(3) Try to suggest an improved mode of management practice that could have minimized or even prevented the failure costs.

22.2 In their paper "De-escalating information technology projects: lessons from the Denver International Airport", Montealegre and Keil (2000) analyze the colossal failure of the Denver International IT project and suggest improvements in management's reactions.

(1) Based on the paper, how do you think management contributed to the failure costs of the project?
(2) Summarize the Denver Airport management's erroneous reactions and the project's management suggestions in your own words.
(3) Classify management's erroneous reactions by project stage. What should management have done at each stage?

22.3 A good part, if not the majority, of external failure costs are "hidden" costs.

(1) List some examples of hidden failure costs. For each example, indicate for what type of software development organization and situation these failure costs could become extremely high.
(2) Explain the difficulties faced in estimating the extent of failure costs for each of the examples mentioned in (1).

22.4 Xrider, a leading software house, employs 500 professionals distributed among five departments, each of which carries out 20–30 software development projects simultaneously. The company's new cost of software quality system has successfully completed its second year of operation. The periodic cost of software quality report produces data on departments, teams and projects.

(1) Suggest a systematic method, based on the compiled data, for comparing the system's achievements.
(2) Discuss the limitations of some or all of the comparisons suggested in (1) and propose checks to be carried out to prevent reaching erroneous conclusions based on questionable comparisons.

22.5 The SQA unit of AB Dynamics has summarized its "seven years of success" in a colorful brochure. One of the brochure's tables (Table 22.6) presents the unit's SQA achievements by summarizing the cost of software quality over the period.

Table 22.6: AB Dynamics: cost of software quality and annual sales – 1996–2002

| Year | Cost of software quality, $000s | | | | | Total annual sales, $millions |
| | Prevention costs | Appraisal costs | Internal failure costs | External failure costs | Total cost of software quality | |
A	B	C	D	E	F	G
1996	380	2200	930	1820	5330	38
1997	680	2270	760	1140	4850	43
1998	840	2320	500	880	4540	49
1999	1200	2020	490	700	4410	56
2000	1110	2080	420	640	4250	58
2001	1170	2080	400	510	4160	66
2002	1330	2120	410	450	4310	76

(1) Analyze the data in the above table regarding the progressively higher efficiency and effectiveness achieved by the SQA system during the period 1996–2002.
(2) Draw a diagram displaying the cost of software quality balance by quality level (see Figure 22.3), based on the data in the above table. For this purpose, assume **quality cost** to be the cost of quality per $1 million of sales, calculated by applying the formula F/G. **Software quality level** is inversely proportional to the percentage of external failure costs out of annual sales, calculated by applying the formula $(10 \times F)/(D + E)$. The lower the percentage of external failure costs, the higher the quality level.
(3) Analyze the data in the diagram drawn in (2) according to the cost of software quality balance concept.

22.6 The classic cost of software quality model employs – unchanged – the general quality cost model applied in manufacturing industries.

(1) Compare the characteristics of prevention costs for software development with any manufacturing industry (e.g. wood product industry, metal products industry).

(2) Compare the characteristics of appraisal costs for software development with any manufacturing industry.

(3) Compare the characteristics of internal failure costs for software development with any manufacturing industry.

(4) Compare the characteristics of external failure costs for software development with any manufacturing industry.

part VI

Standards, certification and assessment

One can easily imagine professionals asking themselves these questions: Why should SQA standards be implemented in our organization and software projects? Wouldn't it be preferable to apply our experience and professional knowledge and continue enjoying the best procedures and methodologies that best suit our organization?

Despite the legitimacy of pondering such issues, it is widely accepted that the benefits gained from standardization are far beyond those reaped from professional independence.

To introduce the subject, let us refer to the following issues:

- The benefits of use of standards
- The organizations involved in standards development
- The ways in which SQA standards contribute to SQA
- The classification of standards.

VI.1 The benefits of use of standards

The main benefits gained by use of standards (benefits that are not expected in "professionally independent" organizations) are listed in Frame VI.1.

Frame VI.1   The benefits of use of standards

- The ability to apply software development and maintenance methodologies and procedures of the highest professional level

- Better mutual understanding and coordination among development teams but especially between development and maintenance teams

- Greater cooperation between the software developer and external participants in the project

- Better understanding and cooperation between suppliers and customers, based on the adoption of known development and maintenance standards as part of the contract

These advantages, together with the growing complexity and scope of software projects, have prompted wider application of standards in the industry.

VI.2 The organizations involved in standards development

Development of SQA standards has been undertaken by several national and international standards institutes, professional and industry-oriented organizations that invest remarkable amounts of resources in these projects.

The following institutes and organizations, among the most prominent developers of SQA and software engineering standards, have gained international reputation and standing in this area:

- IEEE (Institute of Electrical and Electronics Engineers) Computer Society
- ISO (International Organization for Standardization)
- DOD (US Department of Defense)
- ANSI (American National Standards Institute)
- IEC (International Electrotechnical Commission)
- EIA (Electronic Industries Association).

VI.3 The ways in which organizations contribute to SQA

International and national professional organizations contribute to software quality assurance in a variety of ways. One avenue involves provision of updated international standards for use by professionals and managers of SQA activities. These activities contribute to the quality of the professional and managerial activities performed in software development and maintenance organizations. Among the organizations that contribute in this way we should mention the ISO (for its SQA management standards) and the IEEE (for its SQA/software engineering professional standards).

Another avenue taken by international organizations is SQA certification, provided through independent professional quality audits. These external audits assess achievements in the development of SQA systems and their implementation. Certification, which is granted after the periodic audits, is considered valid only until the next audit, and therefore must be renewed. At present, the ISO 9000 Certification Service is the most prominent provider of SQA certification in Europe and other countries.

Yet another important way is the professional support. International and other organizations provide the tools for "self-assessment" of an organization's SQA system and its operation. The detailed documentation provided by assessment programs serves as "manuals" for SQA system development. The Capacity Maturity Model (CMM) developed by the Software Engineering Institute (SEI), Carnegie Mellon University, and ISO/IEC Std 15504 are the best-known examples of this approach.

Software quality assurance standards can be classified into two main classes:

- Software quality assurance management standards, including certification and assessment methodologies (*quality management standards*)
- Software project development process standards (*project process standards*).

Quality management standards

These focus on the organization's SQA system, infrastructure and requirements, while leaving the choice of methods and tools to the organization. By complying with quality management standards, organizations can steadily assure that their software products achieve an acceptable level of quality. ISO 9000-3 and the Capability Maturity Model (CMM) are, respectively, examples of a standard and a methodology belonging to this class.

Some current software development tenders require participants to be certified according to one of the quality management standards.

Project process standards

These focus on the methodologies for carrying out software development and maintenance projects, that is, on "how" a software project is to be implemented. These standards define the steps to be taken, design documentation requirements, the contents of design documents, design reviews and review issues, software testing to be performed and testing topics, and so forth.

Naturally, due to their characteristics, many SQA standards in this class can serve as software engineering standards and vice versa.

The characteristics of these two classes of standards are summarized in Table VI.1.

Table VI.1: Classes of SQA standards – comparison

Characteristics	Quality management standards	Project process standards
The target unit	Management of software development and/or maintenance and the specific SQA units	A software development and/or maintenance project team
The main focus	Organization of SQA systems, infrastructure and requirements	Methodologies for carrying out software development and maintenance projects
The standard's objective	"What" to achieve	"How" to perform
The standard's goal	Assuring supplier's software quality and assessing its software process capability	Assuring the quality of a specific software project
Examples	ISO 9000-3 SEI's CMM	ISO/IEC 12207 IEEE Std 1012-1998

As might be anticipated, standards vary in their scope, from comprehensive standards that cover all (or almost all) aspects to specialized standards that deal with one area or issue. ISO 9000-3 and IEEE/IEA 12207 are examples of comprehensive standards that cover all aspects of software quality management and the software development life cycle, respectively. Examples of specialized standards of both classes may be found in IEEE software engineering standards, such as IEEE Std 730-1998 for software quality assurance plans, IEEE Std 1012-1998 for software verification and validation, and IEEE Std 1045-1992 for software productivity metrics.

The 1990s was a decade of rapid development in international SQA standards, expressed in increasing coverage of topics and greater comprehensiveness. Another development was the growing tendency for standards-developing organizations to issue joint standards, a trend that promotes internationalization of standards. Examples of such "joint ventures" are the standards issued by the IEEE/ANSI, the ISO/IEC and the IEEE/ISO. An example of a "merger" covering five institutes is standard ISO/IEC 12207:1995, adopted in 1996 by the IEEE, the EIA and ANSI, now referred to as IEEE/EIA 12207. Further movement in this direction was the DOD's decision to cancel MIL-STD-498 and replace it by IEEE/EIA 12207. Another parallel and growing trend is the adoption of international standards as national standards by national standards institutes. This trend further supports internationalization.

The above developments inaugurated a trend toward application of software industry standards worldwide. This trend, as observed at the time of writing, is directed toward three complementary directions, so as to guarantee that the following standards become universally accepted tools:

- ISO/IEC 9000-3 – Quality certification standards for software development and maintenance organizations
- ISO/IEC 15504 – Organizational software process capability/capacity assessment
- ISO/IEC/IEEE 12207 – Software development practices.

The next two chapters discuss some of the most commonly used software quality assurance standards belonging to each of the two classes. Chapter 23 is dedicated to quality management standards, including certification and assessment of SQA systems based on these standards. Chapter 24 is dedicated to project process standards.

Quality management standards

Quality management standards and methodologies focus on the software quality assurance system – its organization, infrastructure and requirements – yet leave the choice of the methods and tools to be used in the hands of the organization. In other words these standards focus on the "what" of SQA and not its "how". Compliance to quality management standards supports the organization's steady efforts to assure an acceptable quality level for its software products. Standards belonging to this class, especially ISO 9000-3, structure the SQA certification procedures that are applied to organizations developing software. Some standards and methodologies of this class, to mention only the Capability Maturity Model (CMM), Bootstrap and ISO/IEC 15504, serve mainly for assessment of the organization's SQA achievements while they guide development of its SQA system.

One indication of the importance of standards is the current trend in software development tenders, which requires certification of participants according to at least one of the dominant quality management standards.

The first section of this chapter describes the scope of certification and assessment standards. The sections that follow present some of the most common and important standards.

The references to the main standards mentioned in this chapter are included in the bibliography. Many publications – El Emam (1998), Ince (1994), Jung (2001), Jung *et al.* (2001), Kahoe and Jarvis (1995), Oskarsson and Glass (1996) – limit themselves to a discussion of just one standard, although several others are dedicated to the review and comparison of several standards, e.g. Tingey (1997) and Paulk (1999), to mention just two. Schulmeyer (1999) presents a general review of SQA standards from the perspective of development.

After completing this chapter, you will be able to:

- Explain the benefits of using SQA standards.
- Describe the contributions made by use of standards.
- Describe the general principles underlying quality management according to ISO 9000-3.
- Describe the ISO 9000-3 certification process.
- Describe the principles embodied in the CMM.
- Describe the principles underlying ISO/IEC 15504.

23.1 The scope of quality management standards

Certification standards vary from assessment standards by content as well as by emphasis.

The scope of certification standards is determined by the aims of certification, which are to:

- Enable a software development organization to demonstrate consistent ability to assure that its software products or maintenance services comply with acceptable quality requirements. This is achieved by certification granted by an external body.

- Serve as an agreed basis for customer and supplier evaluation of the supplier's quality management system. This may be accomplished by customer performance of a quality audit of the supplier's quality management system. The audit will be based on the certification standard's requirements.

- Support the software development organization's efforts to improve quality management system performance and enhance customer satisfaction through compliance with the standard's requirements.

The scope of assessment standards is also determined by the aims fo assessment, which are to:

- Serve software development and maintenance organizations as a tool for self-assessment of their ability to carry out software development projects.

- Serve as a tool for improvement of development and maintenance processes. The standard indicates directions for process improvements.

- Help purchasing organizations determine the capabilities of potential suppliers.

- Guide training of assessors by delineating qualifications and training program curricula.

To sum up, while the certification standards emphasis is external – to support the supplier–customer relationships – the emphasis of the assessment standards is internal because it focuses on software process improvement.

23.2 ISO 9001 and ISO 9000-3

ISO 9000-3, the Guidelines offered by the International Organization for Standardization (ISO), represent implementation of the general methodology of quality management ISO 9000 Standards to the special case of software development and maintenance. Both ISO 9001 and ISO 9000-3 are reviewed and updated once every 5–8 years, with each treated separately. As ISO 9000-3 adaptations are based on those introduced to ISO 9001, publication of the revised Guidelines follows publication of the revised Standard by a few years. For example, the 1997 edition of ISO 9000-3 (ISO, 1997) relies on the 1994 edition of ISO 1994 (ISO, 1994). At the time of writing, the 2000 edition of ISO 9001 (ISO, 2000a) has been issued, but only the final just-completed draft of ISO 9000-3 (ISO/IEC, 2001) is awaiting approval.

The current 1997 edition of ISO 9000-3 Guidelines integrates ISO 9001 with its specialized ISO 9000-3 Guidelines into one "all inclusive" standard for the software industry. In other words, from the 1997 edition on, the ISO 9000-3 will represent the stand-alone ISO standard for the software industry. The new version of ISO 9000-3 follows this lead and will also serve as an "all-inclusive" standard for the software industry. Hence, the ISO 9000-3 Standard for the software industry can be considered to provide the requirements for ISO 9000-3 certification.

The new ISO/IEC 9000-3 version (expected to be issued in 2003) is planned to serve the entire population of software development and maintenance organizations by adopting a policy of comprehensiveness and standard redundancy. The individual user is expected to tailor the standard to specific needs. These features facilitate achievement of the universality that allows ISO/IEC 9000-3 to fit the immense variety of organizations belonging to the software industry: big or small, developers of tailor-made software or COTS software packages, developers of real-time application software, embedded software or management information systems, etc.

The 2000 edition of ISO 9001 as well as the new edition of ISO 9000-3 are supported by two additional conceptual standards: ISO 9000 (ISO, 2000b), which deals with fundamental concepts and terminology, and ISO 9004 (ISO, 2000c), which provides guidelines for performance improvement.

In the following sections, the principles underlying ISO 9000-3 (Section 23.2.1) are reviewed; in addition, the structure of the new version is compared with that of the current versions (Section 23.2.2) to illuminate their expanded applications. The last part of this section (Section 23.2.3) is dedicated to TickIT, an organization that significantly contributed to the adoption of ISO 9000-3.

23.2.1 ISO 9000-3 quality management system: guiding principles

Eight principles guide the new ISO 9000-3 standard; these were originally set down in the ISO 9000:2000 standard (ISO, 2000b), as follows:

(1) **Customer focus.** Organizations depend on their customers and therefore should understand current and future customer needs.

(2) **Leadership.** Leaders establish the organization's vision. They should create and maintain an internal environment in which people can become fully involved in achieving the organization's objectives via the designated route.

(3) **Involvement of people.** People are the essence of an organization; their full involvement, at all levels of the organization, enables their abilities to be applied for the organization's benefit.

(4) **Process approach.** A desired result is achieved more efficiently when activities and resources are managed as a process.

(5) **System approach to management.** Identifying, understanding and managing processes, if viewed as a system, contributes to the organization's effectiveness and efficiency.

(6) **Continual improvement.** Ongoing improvement of overall performance should be high on the organization's agenda.

(7) **Factual approach to decision making.** Effective decisions are based on the analysis of information.

(8) **Mutually supportive supplier relationships.** An organization and its suppliers are interdependent; a mutually supportive relationship enhances the ability of both to create added value.

The current standard edition of ISO, 9000-3 (ISO 1997) includes 20 requirements that relate to the various aspects of software quality management systems. The new ISO 9000-3 (ISO/IEC, 2001) offers a new structure, with its 22 requirements classified into the following five groups:

- Quality management system
- Management responsibilities
- Resource management
- Product realization
- Management, analysis and improvement.

The new structure is presented in Table 23.1. The new structure realizes a change in emphasis among the various subjects that make up the requirements, a totally new classification of SQA topics into standard sections and revision of requirement section titles. These changes reflect a gradual rather than a radical change of concepts as presented in the updated guiding principles (see Section 23.2.1). Table 23.2 compares ISO 9000-3:1997 edition with those of the upcoming edition for a sample of requirement subjects, one for each requirement class.

Table 23.1: ISO 9000-3 new edition – Requirements and their classification

Requirement class	Requirement subjects
4. Quality management system	4.1 General requirements 4.2 Documentation requirements
5. Management responsibilities	5.1 Management commitments 5.2 Customer focus 5.3 Quality policy 5,4 Planning 5.5 Responsibility, authority and communication 5.6 Management review
6. Resource management	6.1 Provision of resources 6.2 Human resources 6.3 Infrastructure 6.4 Work environment
7. Product realization	7.1 Planning of product realization 7.2 Customer-related processes 7.3 Design and development 7.4 Purchasing 7.5 Production and service provision 7.6 Control of monitoring and measuring devices
8. Measurement, analysis and improvement	8.1 General 8.2 Monitoring and measurement 8.3 Control of non-conforming product 8.4 Analysis of data 8.5 Improvement

Source: ISO (2000a)

Table 23.2: Current ISO 9000-3:1997 vs. new edition – requirements comparison (sample)

ISO 9000-3: new edition Requirement class and subject	ISO 9000-3:1997 edition Requirement subjects
Requirement class 4 (Quality management system) Subject 4.2 Documentation requirements	4.2 Quality system 4.5 Document and data control 4.16 Control of quality records
Requirement class 5 (Management responsibilities) Subject 5.4 Planning	4.1 Management responsibility 4.2 Quality system
Requirement class 6 (Resource management) Subject 6.3 Infrastructure	4.9 Process control
Requirement class 7 (Product realization) Subject 7.5 Production and service provision	4.7 Control of customer-supplied product 4.8 Product identification and traceability 4.9 Process control 4.10 Inspection and testing 4.12 Inspection and test status 4.15 Handling, storage, packaging, preservation and delivery 4.19 Servicing
Requirement class 8 (Measurement, analysis and improvement) Subject 8.3 Control of non-conforming product	4.13 Control of non-conforming product

Source: Adapted from ISO (2000a)

23.2.3 ISO 9001 – application to software: the TickIT initiative

TickIT was launched in the late 1980s by the UK software industry in cooperation with the UK Department for Trade and Industry to promote development of
a methodology for adapting ISO 9001 to the characteristics of the software
industry known as the *TickIT initiative*. At the time of its launch, ISO 9001 had
already been successfully applied in manufacturing industry; however, no significant methodology for its application to the special characteristics of the software
industry was yet available. In the years to follow, the TickIT initiative, together
with the efforts invested in development of ISO 9000-3, achieved this goal.

TickIT is, additionally, a leading provider of ISO 9001 certification, specializing in information technology (IT); it covers the entire range of
commercial software development and maintenance services. TickIT, now
managed and maintained by the DISC Department of BSI (the British
Standards Institute), is accredited for certification of IT organizations in the
UK and Sweden. In June 2002, TickIT reported a clientele of 1252 organizations in 42 countries, the majority in the UK (882), Sweden (54) and the
United States (109). TickIT is currently authorized to accredit other organizations as certification bodies for the software industry in the UK.

TickIT activities include:

■ Publication of the *TickIT Guide*, that supports the software industry's
efforts to spread ISO 9001 certification. The current guide (edition 5.0,
TickIT, 2001), which includes references to ISO/IEC 12207 and ISO/IEC
15504, is distributed to all TickIT customers.

- Performance of audit-based assessments of software quality systems and consultation to organizations on improvement of software development and maintenance processes in addition to their management.
- Conduct of ISO 9000 certification audits.

TickIT auditors who conduct audit-based assessments and certification audits are registered by the International Register of Certificated Auditors (IRCA). Registered IRCA auditors are required, among other things, to have experience in management and software development; they must also successfully complete an auditors' course. Registered lead auditors are required to have demonstrated experience in conducting and directing TickIT audits.

23.3 Certification according to ISO 9000-3

The ISO 9000-3 certification process verifies that an organization's software development and maintenance processes fully comply with the standard's requirements.

As ISO 9000 standards have been adopted as national standards in many countries, there is growing worldwide interest in certification according to ISO 9000 by organizations in many industries, including the software industry. The certification service is organized by the International Organization for Standardization (ISO) through a worldwide network of certification services that are authorized by means of *accreditation bodies and certification bodies*. Each accreditation body is licensed by ISO to authorize other professional organizations as certification bodies. Certification bodies, whose number may vary by country, perform the actual certification audits and certify those organizations that qualify.

Organizations wishing to obtain ISO 9000-3 certification are required to complete the following:

- Develop the organization's SQA system
- Implement the organization's SQA system
- Undergo certification audits.

Fulfillment of these requirements demands thorough planning of the structures and resources necessary to perform the activities culminating in certification.

This process may vary somewhat from one organization to another, depending on the characteristics of its design and maintenance activities as well as by the certification bodies. Its basic form parallels the process demanded by other certification standards. Certification is discussed in greater detail in the next four sections and is illustrated in Figure 23.1.

23.3.1 Planning the process leading to certification

Once management has made its decision to obtain ISO 9000-3 certification for its software development and maintenance activities, an action plan is needed.

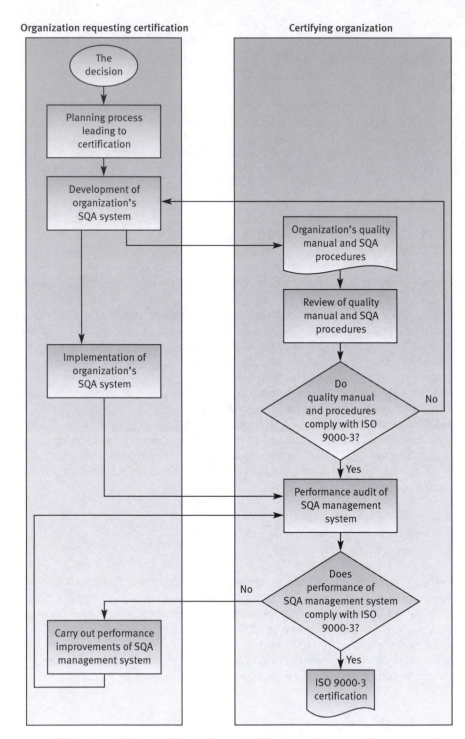

Figure 23.1: The ISO 9000-3 certification process

An internal survey of the current SQA system and how it is implemented is a good place to begin. The survey should supply information about:

- Gaps between currently employed SQA and required procedures: missing procedures in addition to inadequate procedures.
- Gaps between staff know-how and knowledge required regarding SQA procedures and SQA tools.
- Gaps regarding documentation of development as well as maintenance activities.
- Gaps or lack of parity regarding software configuration system capabilities and implementation.
- Gaps regarding managerial practices demanded for project progress control.
- Gap regarding SQA unit organization and its capabilities.

After completing the previous analysis, the plan for obtaining certification can be constructed. It should include:

- A list of activities to be performed, including timetables
- Estimates of resources required to carry out each activity
- Organizational resources: (a) internal participants – SQA unit staff (including staff to be recruited) and senior software engineers; (b) SQA consultants.

23.3.2 Development of the organization's SQA system

Before proceeding, the organization's SQA management system should be developed to a level adequate to meet ISO 9000-3 requirements. These efforts should include:

- Development of a quality manual and a comprehensive set of SQA procedures.
- Development of other SQA infrastructure:
    - Staff training and instruction programs, including staff certification programs
    - Preventive and corrective actions procedures, including the CAB committee
    - Configuration management services, including a software change control management unit
    - Documentation and quality record controls.
- Development of a project progress control system.

23.3.3 Implementation of the organization's SQA system

Once the components of the SQA management system conform to certification demands, efforts are shifted towards implementing the system. These include setting up a staff instruction program and support services appropriate to the task of solving problems that may arise when implementing SQA tools. These arrangements are targeted especially at team leaders and unit managers, who are expected to follow up and support the implementation efforts made by their units.

Throughout this stage, internal quality audits are carried out to verify the success in implementation as well as to identify units and SQA issues that require additional attention. The internal quality audit findings will enable determination of whether the organization has reached a satisfactory level of implementation.

23.3.4 Undergoing the certification audits

The certification audits are carried out in two stages:

(1) *Review of the quality manual and SQA procedures developed by the organization.* The review ascertains completeness and accuracy. In cases of non-compliance with standards, the organization is obligated to complete the corrections prior to advancing to the second stage of certification.

(2) *Verification audits of compliance with the requirements defined by the organization in its quality manual and SQA procedures.* The main questions to be answered are:

- Have the staff been adequately instructed on SQA topics and do they display a satisfactory level of knowledge?
- Have the relevant procedures – project plans, design reviews, progress reports, etc. – been properly and fully implemented by the development teams?
- Have documentation requirements been fully observed?

The main sources of information for certification audits are (a) interviews with members of the audited unit, and (b) review of documents such as project plans, design documents, test plans and procedures, and design review records. In order to assure reliable results and avoid biased conclusions, audits are based on a random selection of projects and/or teams.

23.3.5 Procedures for retaining ISO certification

Periodic re-certification audits, usually carried out once or twice a year, are performed to verify continued compliance with ISO 9000-3 requirements. During these audits, the organization has to demonstrate continuing development of its SQA management system, which is expressed in quality and productivity performance improvements, regular updates of procedures to reflect technological changes, and process improvements.

Carnegie Mellon University's Software Engineering Institute (SEI) took the initial steps toward development of what is termed a *capability maturity model* (CMM) in 1986, when it released the first brief description of the maturity process framework. The initial version of the CMM was released in 1992, mainly for receipt of feedback from the software community. The first version for public use was released in 1993 (Paulk *et al.*, 1993, 1995; Felschow, 1999).

23.4.1 The principles of CMM

CMM assessment is based on the following concepts and principles:

■ Application of more elaborate management methods based on quantitative approaches increases the organization's capability to control the quality and improve the productivity of the software development process.

■ The vehicle for enhancement of software development is composed of the five-level capability maturity model. The model enables an organization to evaluate its achievements and determine the efforts needed to reach the next capability level by locating the process areas requiring improvement.

■ Process areas are generic; they define the "what", not the "how". This approach enables the model to be applied to a wide range of implementation organizations because:
   – It allows use of any life cycle model
   – It allows use of any design methodology, software development tool and programming language
   – It does not specify any particular documentation standard.

The CMM and its key process areas (KPAs) are presented in Figure 23.2.

23.4.2 The evolution of CMM

After 1993, the SEI expanded the original Software Development and Maintenance Capability Maturity Model (SW-CMM) through diversification. Its main structure was retailored to fit a variety of specialized capability maturity models. The following variants have been developed:

■ **System Engineering CMM (SE-CMM)** focuses on system engineering practices related to product-oriented customer requirements. It deals with product development: analysis of requirements, design of product systems, management and coordination of the product systems and their integration. In addition, it deals with the production of the developed product: planning production lines and their operation.

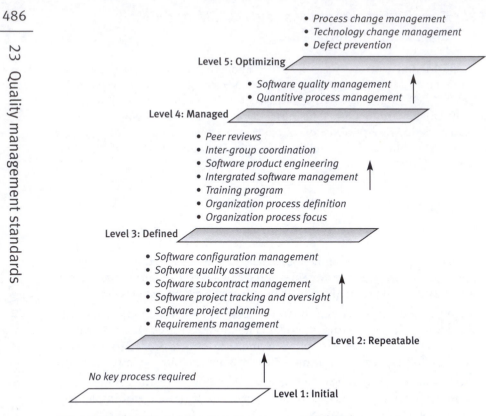

- *Process change management*
- *Technology change management*
- *Defect prevention*

Level 5: Optimizing

- *Software quality management*
- *Quantitive process management*

Level 4: Managed

- *Peer reviews*
- *Inter-group coordination*
- *Software product engineering*
- *Intergrated software management*
- *Training program*
- *Organization process definition*
- *Organization process focus*

Level 3: Defined

- *Software configuration management*
- *Software quality assurance*
- *Software subcontract management*
- *Software project tracking and oversight*
- *Software project planning*
- *Requirements management*

Level 2: Repeatable

No key process required

Level 1: Initial

Figure 23.2: The CMM model levels and key process areas (KPAs)
Source: After Paulk *et al.* (1995)

- **Trusted CMM (T-CMM)** was developed to serve sensitive and classified software systems that require enhanced software quality assurance.

- **System Security Engineering CMM (SSE-CMM)** focuses on security aspects of software engineering and deals with secured product development processes, including security of development team members.

- **People CMM (P-CMM)** deals with human resource development in software organizations: improvement of professional capacities, motivation, organizational structure, etc.

- **Software Acquisition CMM (SA-CMM)** focuses on special aspects of software acquisition by treating issues – contract tracking, acquisition risk management, quantitative acquisition management, contract performance management, etc. – that touch on software purchased from external organizations.

- **Integrated Product Development CMM (IPD-CMM)** serves as a framework for integration of development efforts related to every aspect of the product throughout the product life cycle as invested by each department.

Practically speaking, this CMM overlaps key processes of SW-CMM and SE-CMM rather considerably, hence its elements were integrated into a CMMI model (see the following) and its development was discontinued.

For an expanded discussion of the diversity of CMM applications, see Johnson and Brodman (2000).

Capability Maturity Model Integration (CMMI)

In the late 1990s a new developmental direction was taken – development of integrated CMM models. Development of specialized CMM models involved development of different sets of key processes for model variants for different departments that exhibited joint processes. In practice, this created a situation where departments that applied different CMM variants in the same organization faced difficulties in cooperation and coordination. The CMMI approach solved these problems at the same time as the moduals better conformed to the emerging ISO/IEC 15504 standard (see Royce, 2002).

At the beginning of 2002, SEI could offer the 1.1 version of three CMMI models, with each model presenting different integrated components:

■ CMMI-SE/SW integrates the system engineering and selected aspects of software.
■ CMMI-SE/SW/IPPD/SS integrates system engineering, software and integrated product/process aspects.
■ CMMI-SE/SW/IPPD integrates system engineering, software, integrated product/process and supplier sourcing aspects.

23.4.3 The CMMI structure and processes areas

The CMMI model, like the original CMM models, is composed of five levels. The CMMI capability levels are the same as those of the original, apart from a minor change related to capability level 4, namely:

■ Capability maturity level 1: Initial
■ Capability maturity level 2: Managed
■ Capability maturity level 3: Defined
■ Capability maturity level 4: Quantitatively managed
■ Capability maturity level 5: Optimizing.

A substantial change has nonetheless evolved with respect to the processes included in the models. The 18 key process areas of CMM (frequently referred to as *KPAs*) were replaced by 25 process areas (PAs). The PAs are classified by the capability maturity level that the organization is required to successfully perform. For each process area, objectives, specific practices and procedures are defined.

Appendix 23A presents the revised process areas and their descriptions.

23.4.4 CMM implementation experience

At this point it is worthwhile to quickly review some success stories reported by companies that achieved level 5 assessment according to CMM, the efforts invested and benefits gained. For two of the companies, ISO 9000 certification represented a preparatory step for their final goal of achieving CMM level 5 assessment. In addition, we relay some of the experience accumulated with CMM implementation by a consulting firm.

The following cases are presented:

- Boeing's Space Transportation Systems Software
- Tata Consultancy Services (TCS)
- Telcordia Technologies
- Gartner Inc.

Boeing's Space Transportation Systems Software

Wigle and Yamamura (1999) discuss the three-year process of gradual quality assurance improvements that finally yielded the CMM level 5 for Boeing. The improvements realized in level 5 projects included:

- A substantial shift in defect detection, from 89% late detection by testing to 83% early detection by application of various review methods.
- Earlier detection of defects caused a 31% decrease of rework efforts.
- Elimination of defects prior to version release increased from 94% to almost 100%.
- A 140% increase in general productivity.

Tata Consultancy Services (TCS)

TCS's quality project, summarized by Keeni (2000), was implemented by a South Asian company employing a staff of 14 000. For TCS the CMM project was a natural continuation of its successful adoption of ISO 9000 standards. It required two years (1992–1994) for the company to adapt its procedures and entire quality management system (QMS), which culminated in ISO certification of all the company's major centers. After the new QMS was firmly established, the company continued on to the CMM project in 1996. As TCS was ISO 9000 certified, very few practices needed adaptation to achieve the CMM level 3 assessment. The next phase involved a pilot project, initiated in one of TCS's centers (professional staff of 1000). The pilot project's goal was to achieve level 4 assessment for the center, which was achieved in 1998. Similar projects were launched in 1997 in two additional centers; their target – level 5 assessment – was achieved in 1999. In 1998, TCS decided to expand its CMM project to embrace 17 of its development centers in India. By 2000, a significant proportion of those centers had achieved level 5 assessment, while others had reached level 4 assessment.

One of the company's major efforts was certification of the software quality assurance professionals who were to lead the ISO 9000 and CMM quality projects. The SQA professionals certified included:

- Three authorized CMM lead assessors
- Some 77 internally trained CMM assessors
- Some 678 certified quality analysts
- Over 300 quality auditors.

Among the main benefits listed by the company are the following improvements, achieved during 1996–2000:

(1) Reduction of average percentage of rework from 12% to about 4%
(2) Reduction of percentage of project schedule slippage from over 3% to less than 2.5%
(3) Increase in overall review effectiveness from 40% to 80% defect detection
(4) Decreases of 5% in management efforts and of 24% in change request implementation efforts.

Telcordia Technologies

Telcordia Technologies traveled a remarkable journey from low quality software development to ISO 9000 certification and CMM level 5 assessment, as analyzed by Pitterman (2000). Development efforts by the company's software quality assurance system and progress control teams (about 2% of overall software development staff) began in 1994. As its goals, the software quality assurance team set ISO 9000 certification as its primary objective, followed by CMM assessment. All company software development units were ISO 9000 certified by September 1996.

The now well-established quality system required relatively limited additional efforts to achieve CMM level 3 assessment, achieved in December 1996. However, the next stage, CMM level 5 assessment, required substantial efforts for development of quantitative quality assurance tools and further development of the QMS. In May 1999, eight development units, employing more than 3500 software engineers, had successfully realized this goal.

Among the main benefits garnered by Telcordia during its six-year quality journey, we can cite:

- A 94% reduction in the field faults (release faults) density
- Percentage of on-schedule major releases reached 98%
- Overall customer satisfaction rose from 60% in 1962 and 80% in 1994 to over 95% in 1997.

Gartner Inc.

Gartner Inc. is a consulting firm that specializes in CMM implementation. A report (Gartner Inc., 2001) summarizing the firm's accumulated experience presents some quantitative data to support its claims. Of special interest are the results dealing with the benefits of CMM application and the time required for progress from one capability level to the next. The data should, however, be treated with some reservations as the total number of organizations observed and the period over which the data were collected are not mentioned.

The mean time required for progress from one CMM assessment level to the next is shown in Table 23.3.

One of the expected benefits is improved effectiveness of development efforts. This benefit, which naturally also involves substantial software development cost reductions, is expressed in reduced time spent on reworking and the subsequent retesting and quality assurance. The Gartner paper quotes the impressive changes experienced by Raytheon in this respect (see Table 23.4) as the company progressed up the capability level ladder.

23.5 The Bootstrap methodology

The Bootstrap Institute, a non-profit organization that operates in Europe as part of the European Strategic Program for Research in Information Technology (ESPRIT) in cooperation with the European Software Institute (ESI), offers another route for professional SQA support to organizations, based on its Bootstrap methodology.

The Bootstrap Institute provides various types of support to its licensed members:

(1) Access to the Bootstrap methodology for assessment and improvement of software development processes. The Institute constantly updates and improves its methodology.

Table 23.3: Time required to progress to the next CMM assessment level (Gartner Inc., 2001)

Capability level transition	Mean time (months)	No. of organizations
Level 1 to level 2	24	125
Level 2 to level 3	21.5	124
Level 3 to level 4	33	18
Level 4 to level 5	18	19

Table 23.4: Project resources distribution by CMM capability level – the case of Raytheon

| CMM capability level | Percentage of project resources | | |
	Original work	Reworking	Testing and quality assurance
1	34	41	25
2	55	18	27
3	67	11	22
4	76	7	17

(2) Training and accreditation of assessors.

(3) Access to the Bootstrap database.

The Bootstrap methodology measures the maturity of an organization and its projects on the basis of 31 quality attributes grouped into three classes: process, organization and technology. A five-grade scale is applied to each of the quality attributes separately. The methodology facilitates detailed assessment of the software development process by evaluating its achievements with respect to each attribute and indicates the improvements required in the software development process and in projects. The assessment options include:

- Evaluation of the current position of the software quality assurance system as a basis for improvement initiation
- Evaluation of level of achievements according to the Capability Maturity Model (CMM)
- Evaluation of achievements according to ISO 15504 (the SPICE project)
- ISO 9000-3 gap assessment to support preparations for a certification audit.

Bootstrap trains three levels of registered assessors, namely trained assessor, assessor and lead assessor. A person can become a registered lead assessor, having overall responsibility for planning and performing a Bootstrap assessment, only after successfully performing as a trained and then a registered assessor. In order to become a trained assessor, a person has to successfully complete a basic assessor training program, after which she or he can participate in Bootstrap assessments. Trained assessors who have demonstrated knowledge in performance of assessments and been recommended by a registered lead assessor may qualify as a registered assessor. Registered assessors are likewise required to demonstrate knowledge and competence in carrying out higher-level assessments in addition to participation in a lead assessors' training course. Only then can they applying for acceptance as lead assessors. The process is illustrated in Figure 23.3.

The Bootstrap database contains the findings of Bootstrap assessments conducted for its member organizations. Although the sources of the data are kept anonymous, the assessment results are classified according to type of organization, country, type of product or service, market and development effort. Members can obtain the following types of information:

- Member's own assessments, retrieved from the database
- Aggregate assessment results from comparable organizations
- Data for surveys and research of software development to improve development processes and product quality.

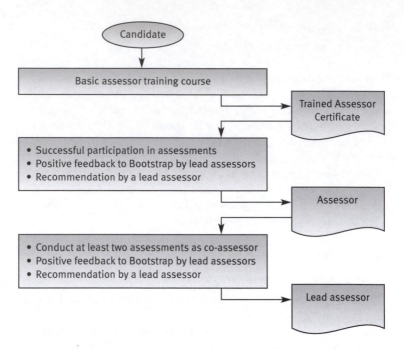

Figure 23.3: Bootstrap assessor accreditation process

23.6 The SPICE project and the ISO/IEC 15504 software process assessment standard

The parallel development of several software process assessment methodologies raised difficulties of non-standardization. A joint initiative by ISO and IEC, the SPICE (Software Process Improvement for Capability Determination) Project was established in 1993 to overcome this problem by developing a standard software process assessment methodology.

The SPICE Project released its Version 1.0 report in 1995, which became the basis for the development of the TR (technical report) version of the ISO/IEC 15504 Standard released in 1998.

The next stage in the development of the ISO/IEC 15504 Standard will be its release as an international standard. An ISO/IEC working group has been assigned the responsibility of introducing the revisions required to transform the standard from technical report status to international standard status. The working group has solicited revision proposals from the public (through a special website) as well as from national bodies. Another route taken to identify features demanding revision was the conduct of a major three-phase trial within the framework of the SPICE Project.

The next sections are dedicated to the following subjects:

■ Principles behind the ISO/IEC 15504 assessment model
■ Structure of the ISO/IEC 15504 assessment model
■ Content of the ISO/IEC 15504 assessment model

23.6.1 Principles behind the ISO/IEC 15504 assessment model

The initiators of the SPICE project and the ISO/IEC standard have defined the following guiding principles for the new assessment model:

- Harmonize the many existing "independent" assessment methodologies by providing a comprehensive framework model (instruct the users in "what" has to be accomplished rather than on "how" it has to be done).
- Be universal to serve all or almost all categories of software suppliers and customers as well as software categories.
- Be highly professional.
- Aim at reaching international acceptance to emerge as a real world standard. Becoming a world standard is expected to save suppliers' resources by eliminating the need to perform several different capability assessments simultaneously in response to different customer requirements.

23.6.2 Structure of the ISO/IEC 15504 assessment model

The assessment model is composed of six levels of capability, where level 0 is the lowest and level 5 the highest. The model defines which process attributes have to be attained to achieve each capability level. Process attributes are generic, defining "what", not "how", in order to allow conformity of existing assessment models to the ISO/IEC standard. Comparative studies have already proved high conformity of the ISO/IEC 15504 standard with the CMM model (Paulk, 1999) and Bootstrap model.

The model is composed of:

- Capability levels and process attribute requirements for each level
- An achievement grade scale for process attributes
- Accumulative achievement requirements for each capability level.

Capability levels and process attribute requirements

Level 0: Incomplete. No process attributes are expected. There is no (or only little) implementation of any planned or identified process.

Level 1: Performed process. Process attribute: **Process performance** includes identifying processes and their inputs and outputs.

Level 2: Managed process. Process attributes:

(a) **Performance management** – processes performed according to procedures; their progress is controlled.
(b) **Work products management** – work products are controlled and documented; their compliance is verified.

Level 3: Established process. Process attributes:

(a) **Process definition** – the organization applies well-defined processes throughout. Processes tailored to any specific project originate in standard processes.

(b) **Process resources** – the organization controls use of project resources: human resources, infrastructure resources, etc.

Level 4: Predictable process. Process attributes:

(a) **Measurement** – performance measurement supports achievement of project goals.

(b) **Process contro**l – the organization controls processes by collection of data on performance and product measures, analysis and implementation of needed corrections of process performance to achieve process goals.

Level 5: Optimizing process. Process attributes:

(a) **Process change** – the organization initiates and controls processes and managerial systems to improve its effectiveness and efficiency for achievement of its business goals.

(b) **Continuous improvement** – the organization persistently monitors the changes implemented through quantitative measurement to assure continuous improvement of processes and management.

The model and the process attributes required for each level are illustrated in Figure 23.4.

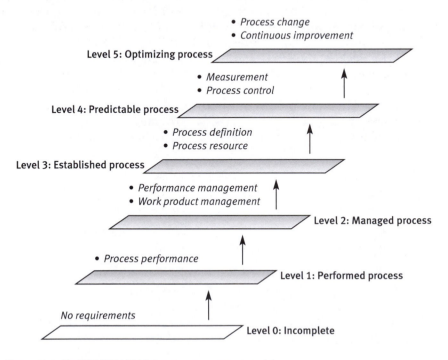

Figure 23.4: The ISO/IEC 15504 process assessment model

Achievement grades scale

Table 23.5 shows the achievement grades scale applied in association with the ISO/IEC 15504 process attributes described above.

Accumulative achievement requirements

The ISO/IEC 15504 model likewise determines the achievements required for each of the relevant process attributes. The accumulated requirements for each of the capability levels are presented in Table 23.6.

Table 23.5: Achievement grades scale for ISO/IEC 15504 process attributes

Grade	Rating	Achievements
F (Fully achieved)	86–100%	Systematic and complete or almost complete performance of process attributes
L (Largely achieved)	51–85%	Significant achievement and systematic approach are evident. Some areas of low performance exist
P (Partially achieved)	16–50%	Some achievements and partial adoption of systematic approach are evident. Other aspects of process attributes are uncontrolled
N (Not achieved)	0–15%	Little or no achievement of the process attributes

Source: After Jung *et al.* (2001)

Table 23.6: Accumulated achievements required for an ISO/IEC 15504 capability level

Capability level	Process attributes	Grades required
1	Process attributes of level 1	F or L
2	Process attributes of level 2	F or L
	Process attributes of level 1	F
3	Process attributes of level 3	F or L
	Process attributes of levels 1 and 2	F
4	Process attributes of level 4	F or L
	Process attributes of levels 1, 2 and 3	F
5	Process attributes of level 5	F or L
	Process attributes of levels 1, 2, 3 and 4	F

Source: After Jung *et al.* (2001)

23.6.3 Content of the ISO/IEC 15504 assessment model

The comprehensive ISO/IEC 15504 standard consists of nine parts, as detailed in Frame 23.1.

Frame 23.1 **The ISO/IEC TR 15504 Standard – structure**

ISO/IEC TR 15504: 1998 Standard. Information technology – Software process assessment:

■ Part 1: Concepts and introductory guide

■ Part 2: A reference model for processes and process capability

■ Part 3: Performing an assessment

■ Part 4: Guide to performing an assessment

■ Part 5: An assessment model and indicator guide

■ Part 6: Guide to competency of assessors

■ Part 7: Guide for use in process improvement

■ Part 8: Guide for use in determining supplier process capability

■ Part 9: Vocabulary

23.6.4 ISO/IEC 15504 processes

The ISO/IEC 15504 includes 29 processes that the organization has to perform successfully to reach capability level 5. The processes are grouped into the following five subject areas:

Subject area	No. of processes
Customer–supplier (CUS)	5
Engineering (ENG)	7
Support (SUP)	8
Management (MAN)	4
Organization (ORG)	5

The subject areas correspond to the generic process attributes mentioned above, where each process or subprocess corresponds to a certain process attribute. In general, several processes and subprocesses correspond to any single process attribute.

The 29 processes are listed in Appendix 23B. Subprocesses as well as the correspondence table of the processes and the process attributes are not shown in the Appendix.

The SPICE project management planned a large-scale trial of the ISO/IEC 15504 technical report version to facilitate its transformation into an effective standard. The trials had three goals:

- To validate the model's conformity with current standards
- To verify its usability in determining whether software satisfies user requirements
- To gain experience in applying the model.

The trial's findings were expected to contribute to significant improvement of the SPICE 1995 report and the 1998 version 1.0 of the standard ISO/IEC TR 15504.

The three phases of the trial were carried out during 1995–2000. The required database was built on data collected during full-scale assessments performed in real organizational environments. An assessment team included at least one qualified assessor. Each organization, which had volunteered to participate, agreed to carry out at least one full-scale assessment. Special efforts were invested to create a diversified database, including participants from every continent and a variety of software specializations. During these trials, more than 200 full-scale assessments were carried out, with the SPICE report applied in phases 1 and 2 and the 1998 technical report version of 15504 for phase 3. Detailed descriptions of some of the findings can be found in El Emam (1998), Jung (2001) and Jung *et al.* (2001).

Summary

(1) Explain the benefits of the use of SQA standards.

- The ability to make use of the most sophisticated and comprehensive professional methodologies and procedures
- Better understanding and cooperation between users of the same standards:
  - Between team members and between project teams
  - Between software developers and external participants in the project
  - Between suppliers and customers.

(2) Describe the contributions made by the use of standards.

- Provision of superior professional methodologies for use in the development process and for its management
- Provision of SQA certification services based on independent professional quality audits
- Provision of tools for "self-assessment" of achievements in planning and operating an organization's SQA system.

(3) Describe the general principles underlying quality management according to ISO 9000-3.

- Customer focus – understanding a customer's current and future needs
- Leadership exercised in the creation and maintenance of a positive internal environment in order to achieve the organization's objectives
- Involvement of people at all levels to further organizational goals
- Process approach – activities and related resources perceived and managed as a process
- Systems approach to management – managing processes as a system
- Continual improvement of the organization's overall performance
- Factual approach to decision-making – decisions based on the analysis of data and information
- Mutually beneficial supplier relationships – emphasis on coordination and cooperation.

(4) Describe the ISO 9000-3 certification process.

To acquire ISO 9000-3 certification, organizations must:
- Plan the organization's activities for gaining certification
- Develop the organization's SQA system, including procedures
- Obtain approval of procedures by the certifying organization
- Implement the organization's SQA system
- Undergo certification audits of actual performance of the SQA system.

(5) Describe the principles embodied in the Capability Maturity Model (CMM).

- Application of more highly elaborated software quality management methods increases the organization's capability to control quality and improve software process productivity
- Application of the five levels of the CMM enables the organization to evaluate its achievements and determine what additional efforts are needed to reach the next capability level
- Process areas are generic, with the model defining "what" and leaving the "how" to the implementing organizations, i.e., the choice of life cycle model, design methodology, software development tool, programming language and documentation standard.

(6) Describe the principles that guided the developers of ISO/IEC 15504.

- Harmonization of independent assessment methodologies by providing a conceptual framework based on "what", not "how."
- Universality of applicability to all or almost all categories of software suppliers and customer organizations as well as software categories
- Professionalism
- Worldwide acceptance.

1. El Emam, K. (1998) *The Internal Consistency of the ISO/IEC 15504 Software Process Capability Scale*, International Software Engineering Research Network Technical Report ISEERN-98-06.
2. Felschow, A. (1999) "Understanding the Capability Maturity Model (CMM) and the role of SQA in the software development maturity", in G. G. Schulmeyer and J. I. McManus (eds), *Handbook of Software Quality Assurance*, 3rd edn, Prentice Hall, Upper Saddle River, NJ, pp. 329–350.
3. Gartner Inc. (2001) "Describing the Capability Maturity Model", *Measure, Special Edition 2001*, Gartner Inc., http//www.gartner.com/measurements.
4. IEEE (1992) "IEEE Std 1045–1992 – IEEE Standard for Software Productivity Metrics", in *IEEE Software Engineering Standards Collection*, The Institute of Electrical and Electronics Engineers, New York.
5. IEEE (1998a) "IEEE Std 1012–1998 – IEEE Standard for Software Verification and Validation", in *IEEE Software Engineering Standards Collection*, The Institute of Electrical and Electronics Engineers, New York.
6. IEEE (1998b) "IEEE Std 730–1998 – IEEE Standard for Software Quality Assurance Plans", in IEEE *Software Engineering Standards Collection*, The Institute of Electrical and Electronics Engineers, New York.
7. IEEE/EIA (1996) "IEEE/EIA Std 12207.0-1996 – IEEE/EIA Standard – Industry Implementation of International Standard ISO/IEC 12207:1995", in *IEEE Software Engineering Standards Collection*, The Institute of Electrical and Electronics Engineers, New York.
8. Ince, D. (1994) *ISO 9001 and Software Quality Assurance*, McGraw-Hill, Maidenhead, Berkshire, UK.
9. ISO (1994) *ISO 9001:1994 Quality Systems – Model for Quality Assurance in Design, Development, Production, Installation and Servicing*, International Organization for Standardization (ISO), Geneva.
10. ISO (1997) *ISO 9000-3:1997(E), Quality Management and Quality Assurance Standards – Part 3: Guidelines for the Application of ISO 9001:1994 to the Development, Supply, Installation and Maintenance of Computer Software*, 2nd edn, International Organization for Standardization (ISO), Geneva.
11. ISO (2000a) *ISO 9000:2000 Quality Management Systems – Requirements*, International Organization for Standardization (ISO), Geneva.
12. ISO (2000b) *ISO 9000:2000 Quality Management Systems – Fundamentals and Vocabulary*, International Organization for Standardization (ISO), Geneva.
13. ISO (2000c) *ISO 9000:2000 Quality Management Systems – Guidelines for Performance Improvements*, International Organization for Standardization (ISO), Geneva.
14. ISO/IEC (1998) *ISO/IEC TR 15504 Parts 1–9:1998 Information Technology – Software Process Assessment*, International Organization for Standardization (ISO), Geneva.
15. ISO/IEC (2001) "ISO 9000-3:2001 Software and System Engineering – Guidelines for the Application of ISO 9001:2000 to Software, Final draft", International Organization for Standardization (ISO), Geneva, unpublished draft, December 2001.
16. Johnson, D. L. and Brodman, J. G. (2000) "Applying CMM project planning practices to diverse environments", *IEEE Software*, 17(4), 79–88.
17. Jung, H-W. (2001) "Rating the process attribute utilizing AHP in SPICE-based process assessment", *Software Process Improvement and Practice*, 7(6), 112–122.

18. Jung, H.-W. Hunter, R., Goldenson, D. R. and El-Emam, K. (2001) "Findings from Phase 2 of the SPICE trials", *Software Process Improvement and Practice*, 7(6), 205–242.
19. Kahoe, R. and Jarvis, A. (1995) ISO 9000-3 – A Tool for *Software Product and Process Improvement*, Springer, New York.
20. Keeni, G. (2000) "The evolution of quality processes at Tata Consultancy Services", *IEEE Software*, 17(4), 79–88.
21. Oskarsson, O. and Glass, R. L. (1996) *An ISO 9000 Approach to Building Quality Software*, Prentice Hall, Upper Saddle River, NJ.
22. Paulk, M. C. (1999) "Analyzing the conceptual relationship between ISO/IEC 15504 (Software Process Assessment) and the Capability Maturity Model for software, *Proceedings of the 1999 International Conference on Software Quality*, Cambridge, MA, 1–11.
23. Paulk, M. C. (2001) "Extreme programming from a CMM perspective", *IEEE Software*, 18(6), 19–25.
24. Paulk, M. C., Curtis B., Chrissis, M. B. and Weber, C. V. (1993) *Capability Maturity Model for Software, Version 1.1*, CMU/SEI-93-TR-24, ESC-TR-93-177, Software Engineering Institute, Carnegie Mellon University, Pittsburgh, PA.
25. Paulk, M. C., Weber, C. V. Curtis, B., Chrissis, M. B. (1995) *The Capability Maturity Model: Guidelines for Improving the Software Process*, Addison-Wesley, Reading, MA.
26. Pitterman, B. (2000) "Telcordia Technologies: the journey to high maturity", *IEEE Software*, 17(4), 89–96.
27. Royce, W. (2002) *CMM vs. CMMI: From Conventional to Modern Software Management*, Rational Edge, Rational Software Inc., http//www.therationaledge.com.
28. Schulmeyer, G. G. (1999) "Standardization of software quality assurance – where is it all going?", in G. G. Schulmeyer and J. I. McManus (eds), *Handbook of Software Quality Assurance*, 3rd edn, Prentice Hall, Upper Saddle River, NJ, pp. 91–113.
29. TickIT (2001) *The TickIT Guide, A Guide to Software Quality Systems Construction and Certification Using ISO 9001:2000*, 5.0 edition, BSI DISC TickIT Office, London.
30. Tingey, M. O. (1997) *Comparing ISO 9000, Malcolm Baldridge, and the SEI CMM for Software: A Reference and Selection Guide*, Prentice Hall, Upper Saddle River, NJ.
31. Wigle, G. B. and Yamamura G. (1999) "SEI CMM Level 5: Boeing Space Transportation systems software", in G. G. Schulmeyer and McManus J. I. (eds) *Handbook of Software Quality Assurance*, 3rd edn, Prentice Hall, Upper Saddle River, NJ, pp. 351–380.

Review questions

23.1 The introduction to Part VI presents the four main benefits of SQA/software engineering standards.

(1) Explain, in your own words, the benefits of using standards for a software developer.
(2) Explain, in your own words, the benefits of using standards from the vantage point of customers of software development services.

23.2 National and international SQA standards contribute to organizations due to their distribution along three different ways.

Describe these routes in your own words and explain their importance.

23.3 The introduction to Part VI presents classes of SQA standards.

(1) Define the various classes of SQA standards.
(2) Explain the differences between the classes.

23.4 Section 23.1 presents classes of software quality management standards.

(1) Explain the differences between the two classes.
(2) Compare the scope of the two classes and discuss their differences with respect to the goals of software quality assurance.

23.5 The evolution and diversification of the CMM methodology have produced several specialized CMM products that were offered to the software industry. At a certain point, SEI moved toward creation of integrated CMM models.

(1) Explain the reasons for this move.
(2) List some arguments against integration.

23.6 One of the main activities of the Bootstrap Institute is training and accreditation of assessors.

(1) Describe the accreditation process in your own words and explain the importance of each level of the accreditation process.
(2) Discuss the special role of assessors in implementing the Bootstrap methodology.

23.7 The SPICE project performed a comprehensive trial for the early versions of the ISO/IEC 15504 Standard.

Explain, in your own words, the contribution of the trial to development of the standard.

Topics for discussion

23.1 Two ISO/IEC standards were completed during the last few years: a new version of 9000-3 and the TR version of 15504. Study these standards.

(1) Compare the 9000-3 requirements with the processes to be assessed according to 15504. Discuss differences in subject matter as well as approach.
(2) Present three examples of standard subject to demonstrate your conclusions.

23.2 ISO/IEC 9000-3 serves as a certification standard for interested software development organizations throughout the world.

(1) The ISO and the IEC are neither capable of nor interested in carrying out certification audits. How are standards organizations assuring the performance of audits conducted with the same method and requiring the same level of achievement in the same subjects for organizations worldwide?

(2) Describe, in your own words, certification of an organization.

(3) Explain the unique importance of each stage of a certification audit.

23.3 CMM and CMMI are both composed of almost identical capability maturity models. While CMM bases its assessments on 18 key process areas, CMMI employs 24 process areas.

(1) Explain the differences between the CMM and CMMI process areas in relation to the respective subject matter.

(2) Indicate which of the capability levels have been substantially changed.

(3) Can you characterize the observed changes?

23.4 Section 23.4.4 describes the CMM implementation experience of four organizations.

(1) Discuss the common experience of these organizations.

(2) What additional information (excluded from the section and the referenced papers) could be helpful for the successful completion of an evaluation?

23.5 Appendix 23B lists the ISO/IEC 15504 process areas. A parallel list of CMMI process areas classified into capability maturity levels is provided in Appendix 23A.

(1) Discuss the differences between the ISO/IEC 15504 and the CMMI process areas in relation to their subject matter.

(2) Regarding the CMMI capability levels, try to relate the ISO/IEC 15504 processes to the appropriate CMMI capability level. Indicate which of the CMMI capability levels reveal substantial differences in the allocated processes and which reveal similarity.

(3) Can you pinpoint differences between the models?

Appendix 23A CMMI process areas

Table 23A.1: CMMI process areas

PA code	Process area name	Process area description
Capability maturity level 1: Initial		
—		No process area is required.
Capability maturity level 2: Managed		
RM	Requirements Management	Analyzes requirements of the project's products and verifies that project plans and products of planned activities conform to requirements.
PP	Project Planning	Plans project activities: resources, schedules and outputs are to achieve approval and commitment of all levels involved in the project.
PMC	Project Monitoring and Control	Performs project's progress control: initiates changes and corrections to solve problems and update plans.

PA code	Process area name	Process area description
Capability maturity level 2: Managed (Cont.)		
SAM	Supplier Agreement Management	Manages acquisition of products and services from suppliers and subcontractors: contracts, progress control and quality assurance.
MA	Measurement and Analysis	Develops, initiates and completes measurements and analyses required to support management progress control and fulfill other information needs.
PPQA	Process and Product Quality Assurance	Develops, implements and follows up application of quality assurance tools for processes and software products.
CM	Configuration Management	Develops implements and operates a configuration management system: assures integrity of work products, configuration status accounting, etc.
Capability maturity level 3: Defined		
RD	Requirements Development	Prepares and analyzes product component requirements as required for development and cooperation with customers.
TS	Technical Solution	Introduces solutions to requirements: analyses, designs and implements the solutions for the product as a whole or its individual components.
PI	Product Integration	Integrates systems and product components developed by different teams into a completed product that functions according to the specified requirements.
VER	Verification	Assures that the product and its components comply with specifications.
VAL	Validation	Assures that the product and its components fulfill the customer's actual use needs.
OPF	Organizational Process Focus	Develops and maintains the organization's understanding of its process and procedures infrastructure and the activities for initiation of corrective actions and process improvements throughout the organization.
OPD	Organizational Process Definition	Develops and maintains an adequate infrastructure of organizational processes and procedures.
OT	Organizational Training	Identifies the skills and knowledge needs of people so they can effectively and efficiently carry out their professional tasks.
IPM	Integrated Project Management	Adapts the organization's management methodology to the project environment so that all the managerial levels are coordinated and share the project's goals, planning and progress control processes.

Table 23A.1: Continued

PA code	Process area name	Process area description
Capability maturity level 3: Defined (Cont.)		
IT	Integrated Teaming	Organizes stakeholder teams that collaborate to support the project team in achieving project goals.
RM	Risk Management	Implements continuous activities to identify project risks and potential risks, prevent potential risks and eliminate or reduce damages.
DAR	Decision Analysis and Resolution	Establishes structured decision-making for selection of project implementation alternatives, based on evaluation of alternatives according to defined criteria.
OEI	Organizational Environment for Integration	Establishes approach and infrastructure for integration of teams, implements said approach.
Capability maturity level 4: Quantitatively managed		
OPP	Organizational Process Performance	Develops, implements and maintains quantitative projects quality and performance objectives that conform with organization's objectives.
QPM	Quantitative Project Management	Applies quantitative management of project's defined process and product metrics to control performance and identify improvement needs and opportunities.
Capability maturity level 5: Optimizing		
OID	Organizational Innovation and Deployment	Initiates development and implementation of selected incremental productivity and quality improvements in organization's processes and technologies.
CAR	Causal Analysis and Resolution	Systematically operates corrective and preventive actions: analyzes failure and success data, develops and implements preventive and corrective actions, follows up results.

Source: Based on *Compusol News*, August 21, 2002, compusolsoftware.com/gocmmi.htm.

Table 23B.1: ISO/IEC 15504 model processes

Process code	Process name	Process description
CUS.1	Acquire software	Activities required for a customer to obtain contracted software, including requirements specification, contracting the supplier, follow-up of development process (if any) and acceptance testing.
CUS.2	Manage customer needs	Establish and maintain the customer's software requirements file; update files according to changing customer's needs.
CUS.3	Supply software	Deliver and install at customer's site a software package that conforms with all specified quality requirements.
CUS.4	Operate software	Operate installed software correctly and efficiently.
CUS.5	Provide customer service	Provide an acceptable level of support services to enable effective use of software by the customers.
ENG.1	Develop system requirements and design	Analyze and define system requirements; allocate each requirement to a system element, including delay of implementation to later releases.
ENG.2	Develop software requirements	Analyze and define system's software requirements.
ENG.3	Develop software design	Prepare a software design that fully complies with software requirements.
ENG.4	Implement software design	Produce the software unit code, perform unit tests and complete necessary corrections.
ENG.5	Integrate and test software	Perform unit integration and integration tests. Perform entire software integration and test the software system. Complete integration and software system corrections.
ENG.6	Integrate and test system	Perform product system integration of software and non-software components. Perform system test and corrections of detected defects.
ENG.7	Maintain system and software	Perform corrective maintenance according to user calls; perform adaptive and functional maintenance according to customer requests.
SUP.1	Develop documentation	Develop and implement documentation procedure for process activities.
SUP.2	Perform configuration management	Develop and maintain software configuration procedures to assure integrity of software products and support development and maintenance processes.

Table 23 B.1: Continued

Process code	Process name	Process description
SUP.3	Perform quality assurance	Establish software quality assurance system to assure that software products comply with requirements and standards.
SUP.4	Perform work product verification	Verify that each product of a process fully complies with its specified requirements.
SUP.5	Perform work product validation	Confirm that the work product fulfills the requirements of the system's intended user.
SUP.6	Perform joint reviews	Together with customer, maintain joint follow-up of contract implementation; reach understanding about required actions and process changes to satisfy customer.
SUP.7	Perform audits	Perform independent reviews and audits of processes and work products to assure conformity with project requirements.
SUP.8	Perform problem resolution	Analyze all problems detected and assure their removal; perform preventive actions in cases of identified recurrent problems.
MAN.1	Manage the project	Prepare project plan, including required resources; coordinate and manage project to produce the required project products.
MAN.2	Manage quality	Define quality of project products and/or services to fulfill quality requirements and assure customer satisfaction.
MAN.3	Manage risk	Perform periodic risk surveys to detect risks, analyze their expected impact and carry out necessary actions to eliminate risks and reduce damages.
MAN.4	Manage subcontractors	Select qualified subcontractors, assure adequate contract terms, control their performance and quality of products.
ORG.1	Engineer the business	Establish an organizational environment that supports team members in their efforts; encourage professional achievements and improved effectiveness and efficiency.
ORG.2	Define the process	Support teams' performance by defining procedures, standards and library of reused software code and design modules.
ORG.3	Improve the process	Invest constant effort to improve process effectiveness and efficiency and control implementation.
ORG.4	Provide skilled human resources	Provide adequate training and instruction to assure that the organization's human resources acquire required professional skills and knowledge.
ORG.5	Provide software engineering infrastructure	Provide professional teams with adequate integrative software tools and hardware environments that suit their software development and maintenance projects.

SQA project process standards – IEEE software engineering standards

Project process standards focus on methodologies for carrying out software development and maintenance – on the "how" of software development project implementation. A project process standard is devised by delineating each step of a process and its attendant requirements, design documentation and contents, design review and review issues, software testing and its objectives, and so forth.

The main benefits gained by use of project process standards are:

- The ability to apply the most professional software development and maintenance methodologies available.
- The ability to apply state-of-the-art project process procedures.
- Better mutual understanding and coordination among teams, especially between development and maintenance teams.
- Greater cooperation between the software developer and external participants in the project.
- Better understanding and cooperation between suppliers and customers, based on incorporation of known standards within the contract.

To better acquaint the reader with the issues involved, the benefits of standards use, the organizations involved in standards development and the ways in which standards contribute to SQA are discussed in the introduction to Part VI.

Due to their comparable characteristics, many SQA project process standards naturally operate as software engineering standards and vice versa.

Many organizations – international standards organizations, national standards institutes, professional organizations and industry organizations, among others – are occupied in developing, adapting and enforcing SQA project process standards. A 1997 survey quoted by Moore (1999) lists 315 software standards developed by 46 different organizations. There is a growing tendency among these organizations to abandon local standards and join in efforts to create international standards, as discussed in the introduction to Part VI of this book.

One of the organizations leading this trend is the American Institute of Electrical and Electronics Engineers (IEEE), and the associated IEEE Computer Society. One of IEEE's main contributions lies in the generation, promulgation and promotion of standards use. A subgroup of the IEEE standards working group was formed in 1976 to develop SQA standards, later published as the *IEEE Software Engineering Standard Collection* (in regularly updated editions). These standards, most of which may be classified as project process standards, become a major source for international standards. For this reason – as well as space limitations – this chapter is devoted to IEEE software engineering standards, a small sample of which will be reviewed. The complete list of standards available at the time of writing is presented in Appendix 24A.

For discussions of the directions taken by SQA standardization and the range of applications, see Schulmeyer (1999) and Heil (1999), respectively.

The chapter deals with the following topics:

- The structure and content of the IEEE software engineering standards
- IEEE/EIA Std 12207 (the framework standard)
- IEEE Std 1012 (on verification and validation)
- IEEE Std 1028 (on reviews).

After completing this chapter, you will be able to:

- Explain the concepts embodied in IEEE/EIA Std 12207.
- Explain the concepts embodied in IEEE Std 1012.
- Explain the essence of the SVVP as required by IEEE Std 1012.
- Explain the concepts embodied in IEEE Std 1028.

24.1 Structure and content of IEEE software engineering standards

IEEE standards may be allocated to three main classes:

(1) **Conceptual standards.** These set forth the guiding principles and overall approach to be applied. Examples:

- IEEE 610.12 – Glossary of Software Engineering Terminology
- IEEE 1061 – Software Quality Metrics Methodology
- IEEE 1320.2 – Conceptual Modeling Language, Syntax and Semantics for IDEF1X97
- IEEE 1420.1a – Software Reuse, Data Model for Reuse Library Interoperability: Assets Certification Framework
- IEEE/EIA 12207.0 – Information Technology Software Life Cycle Processes.

(2) **Prescriptive standards of conformance.** These standards address the requirements to which a software developer must conform. A major portion of the standards collection belongs to this class. Examples:

- IEEE 828 – Software Configuration Plans
- IEEE 829 – Software Test Documentation
- IEEE 1012 – Software Verification and Validation
- IEEE 1028 – Software Reviews
- IEEE 1042.1 – Software Reuse – Model for Reuse Library Interoperability: Basic Interoperability Data Model (BIDM).

(3) **Guidance standards.** These apply mainly to implementation of Class b standard conformance requirements. Examples:

- IEEE 1233 – Guide for Developing System Requirement Specifications
- IEEE/EIA 12207.1 – Guide, Information Technology – Software Life Cycle Processes – Life Cycle Data
- IEEE/EIA 12207.2 – Guide, Information Technology – Software Life Cycle Processes – Implementation Technology

The 2002 list of active IEEE standards appears in Appendix 24A.

24.2 IEEE/EIA Std 12207 – software life cycle processes

IEEE/EIA Std 12207 provides a framework that incorporates the entire spectrum of software life cycle processes. In this capacity, it refers the reader to other IEEE standards as sources for specialized details and prescriptive requirements.

Evolution of the standard

IEEE/EIA Std 12207 is the product of intensive cooperative efforts exerted by several major standards organizations for the purpose of developing a global software life cycle processes standard. The main contributors were: (1) the US Department of Defense (MIL-STD-498:1994), (2) ANSI, IEEE and EIA (Joint Standard 016 (J-Std-016-1995)) and (3) the International Organization for Standardization (ISO) and the International Electrotechnical Commission (IEC) (ISO/IEC 12207 Standard). ISO/IEC 12207 was adopted by IEEE and EIA under the title IEEE/EIA Std 12207. The initial step was followed by adaptation of portions of J-Std-016 in the development of a guide for the implementation of the 12207 standard, and additions to the original 12207. The supplements, a product of IEEE and EIA collaboration, transformed ISO/IEC 12207 into a three-part standard:

- IEEE/EIA Std 12207.0-1996 (IEEE/EIA, 1996): includes the original ISO/IEC 12207 and new Appendices (also called annexes) contributed by IEEE/EIA.
- IEEE/EIA Std 12207.1-1997 (IEEE/EIA, 1997a): Guide – Life Cycle Data, entirely developed by IEEE/EIA.
- IEEE/EIA Std 12207.2-1997 (IEEE/EIA, 1997b): Guide – Implementation Considerations, entirely developed by IEEE/EIA.

A further step was taken with the US Department of Defense's May 1998 decision to replace its MIL-STD-498 with IEEE/EIA Std 12207. As both standards share the same concepts and cover similar areas, the DOD's decision facilitated coordination between military software developers and customers and the civil software industry; at the same time, it enabled implementation of an updated and comprehensive standard. Although MIL-STD-498 was cancelled, its comprehensive and highly valued collection of templates for software development process reports (termed "DIDs" – Data Item Descriptions) remained available. These DIDs are listed in Appendix 24B.

24.2.1 Purpose

The purposes of IEEE/EIA Std 12207, as determined by the IEEE and EIA, can be summarized thus:

- To establish an internationally recognized model of common software life cycle processes that can be referenced by the software industry worldwide.
- To promote understanding among business parties by application of commonly recognized processes, activities and tasks.

The software life cycle architecture outlined in the standard is structured as a four-level tree composed of:

(1) Process classes
(2) Processes
(3) Activities
(4) Tasks.

The three process classes are:

(1) Primary life cycle processes ("Primary processes")
(2) Supporting life cycle processes ("Supporting processes")
(3) Organizational life cycle processes ("Organizational processes").

The two upper levels of the standard's process architecture, namely the process classes and their constituent processes, can be illustrated in a fishbone diagram: see Figure 24.1.

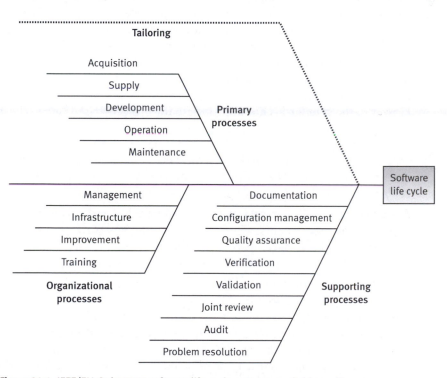

Figure 24.1: IEEE/EIA Std 12207 software life cycle processes – fishbone diagram
Source: IEEE (1992). From IEEE Std 1045-19992. Copyright 1992 IEEE. All rights reserved.

The standard provides comprehensive definitions of the tasks comprising each activity. Comprehensiveness is realized in the number of tasks assigned to each activity and the level of detail characterizing the descriptions. A task definition can be of any length from one to 32 lines (almost a full page). Additional details regarding data and task implementation are found in the standard's two guides (IEEE/EIA, 1997a, 1997b). Users are also directed by the 12207 Guides to other IEEE standards, the majority of which present prescriptive requirements related to the original task.

The detailed division of activities into tasks and the standard's tree structure, demonstrated in an example (primary processes), are presented in Appendix 24C.

24.2.3 Underlying concepts

Annex E of IEEE/EIA Std 12207.0 (IEEE/EIA, 1996) presents the standard's basic concepts, which can be classified into two groups: general concepts and task-related concepts.

General concepts
(1) **Applicability of the standard in general and its adaptation by tailoring**. Tailoring the standard allows it to be applicable to a large variety of software projects: large, highly complex as well as small, simple projects, stand-alone projects, and projects that represent parts within extensive systems. A standard should be planned to fit all parties, whether external customers (within the customer–supplier relationship) or internal customers (developed for other departments within the organization). However, the standard is not appropriate for projects based on purchase of COTS software products because, as a rule, no software development process is involved after purchases of this type. Organizations are encouraged to tailor the standard to their needs by omitting irrelevant or unsuitable elements. The remaining processes, activities and tasks thus become the standard for that particular project.

(2) **Applicability for all participants in the software life cycle**. The standard applies to all participants who have a role in the software life cycle: acquirers, suppliers, developers, operators and maintainers. It provides separate definitions of processes, activities and tasks for each.

(3) **Flexibility and responsiveness to technological change**. The standard instructs its users in "how to do", not "exactly how to do", that is, it leaves room for users to choose their own life cycle model, development tools, software metrics, project milestones and documentation standards. Despite this freedom, the standard's highly detailed tasks as well as required level of conformance to its principles are firmly imposed. Benefits of the "how to do" approach include reduction of the user's dependence on a specific technology, a property that introduces flexibility and

enhances responsiveness to changes in information technology (software and hardware).

(4) **Software links to the system.** The standard establishes strong links between the software and the system it belongs to (which may be constructed from several software components and several hardware components). These connections are to be implemented at each phase of the software's life cycle.

(5) **TQM consistency.** The standard is consistent with Total Quality Management concepts, particularly:

- Quality is integral to every software process.
- Each process includes "built-in" quality components to be applied by the teams responsible for each phase of the process.
- SQA processes are dedicated to achievement of conformance with specific quality requirements coupled with organizational freedom to affect conformity and initiate corrective actions of their choice if necessary.

(6) **No certification requirements.** The standard does not require certification of the developer organization, a fact that supports its worldwide acceptance. It should be noted that ISO/IEC 9000-3 is closely coordinated with ISO 12207 (adopted by IEEE and EIA as IEEE/EIA Std 12207).

(7) **Baselining.** The standard requires that software and hardware baseline configuration versions be prepared in tandem with the project schedule so as to establish successively improved versions of the project that can, in turn, serve as foundations for further software development and maintenance.

Task-related concepts

(1) **Responsibility for activities and tasks.** Responsibility for performance of each activity and task is assigned to a specific unit or an individual member of the organization.

(2) **Modularity of components of the software life cycle.** The components of the software life cycle architecture, especially activities and tasks, are structured to be modular, as cohesive as possible.

(3) **Levels of required conformance.** The standard defines four levels of required conformance to the standard. They are, in descending order, "will", "shall", "should" and "may", where "will" and "shall" refer to required activities, "should" to those recommended and "may" to those permissible.

(4) **Nature of evaluation task.** The standard requires evaluations of entities with given purposes against defined criteria. Examples of entities are process, activity, agreement, report and plan. Examples of criteria are traceability for requirement specifications and correctness of design.

24.2.4 Contents

The standard's contents reflect the processes that appear throughout the software's life cycle:

- Description of the primary life cycle processes
- Definitions of supporting life cycle processes
- Definitions of organizational life cycle processes
- Six (out of the standard's 10) Annexes, each dealing with the following issues:
  - Annexes A and B: The tailoring process
  - Annex E: Discussion of the standard's concepts
  - Annex G: Objectives of the life cycle processes
  - Annex H: Objectives of the life cycle data
  - Annex I: Roles and relationships of the following standards: IEEE Std 1074, ISO/IEC 12207, IEEE Std 1498 and ISO 9001.

24.3 IEEE Std 1012 – verification and validation

The IEEE Std 1012-1998 (IEEE, 1998) deals with the processes for determining whether a software product conforms to its requirements specifications (verification) and whether it satisfies the objectives of its intended use (validation). The standard adopts a broad range of applications, as demanded by the variety of verification and validation (V&V) methods available for use throughout the software life cycle. In response to developments in the field, the current standard has been substantially expanded from the 1986 version.

24.3.1 Purpose

The purposes of IEEE 1012-1998 are:

- To establish a common framework for V&V activities and tasks for all software life cycle processes
- To define V&V requirements, including their inputs and outputs
- To define software integrity levels and the V&V tasks appropriate for each
- To define the content of a SVVP (Software V&V Plan) document.

24.3.2 Underlying concepts

The concepts expressed in IEEE 1012-1998 respond to 10 basic issues:

(1) **Broad definition of V&V activities**. This enables the standard to embrace all the checking and investigative activities performed throughout the software life cycle: review, testing, method evaluation, hazard identification and risk analysis, among others.

(2) **Software integrity levels and their V&V requirements**. The standard defines four integrity levels according to the criticality of a software function, module or unit, as follows:

- ■ "High" – a function that affects critical system performance
- ■ "Major" – a function that affects important system performance
- ■ "Moderate" – a function that affects system performance; however, availability of an alternative method of operation enables the system to overcome the associated difficulties
- ■ "Low" – a function that affects system performance only by inconveniencing the user.

IEEE 1012–1998 grades V&V requirements according to the integrity level; see Table 2 of the standard for the minimum V&V requirements assigned to each level. The standard also requires that when preparing the software verification and validation plan (SVVP), integrity levels be assigned to each component of the product.

(3) **Prescriptive requirements**. IEEE Std 1012–1998 is a prescriptive standard in that it lists the tasks that shall be performed in the course of every activity initiated during the software life cycle. For each of these tasks, the standard provides the following information:

- ■ Detailed description of the performance methodology
- ■ Required inputs
- ■ Required outputs
- ■ Definition of integrity levels for which performance of the task is not mandatory
- ■ Optional V&V tasks to be performed during selected life cycle process.

(4–6) **Independence of V&V activities**. To fulfill their objectives, V&V are to be undertaken as independent activities (IV&V), classified as managerial, technical and financial functions.

Managerial independence (issue 4) requires that responsibility for performance of IV&V activities be separated from responsibility for the general management of the development project. The IV&V team independently decides which V&V methods are to be applied; accordingly, it bears sole responsibilities for evaluation of the results. This means that at least in theory, the team is insulated from any pressure that may be exerted by project management.

Technical independence (issue 5) refers to the status of the V&V team together with the analytic tools employed. Technical independence demands that the persons belonging to the team not be involved in the software's development, a requirement aimed at allowing them to formulate an independent understanding of the project, "a fresh viewpoint". It requires also that the V&V team develops its own analysis and testing tools, separate from those used by the development team.

Financial independence (issue 6) requires that control over the V&V budget not be vested in the development department but determined as an independent part of the budget defined in the project plan.

Even superficial observation of real-life software development projects discloses a variety of independent components and associated levels of independence. Hence, to avoid confusion and minimize *ad hoc* decision making, the standard requires that the degree of V&V independence be determined in advance, as part of the SVVP.

(7) **Compliance and compatibility with international standards.** Compliance and compatibility with international and IEEE standards, especially with IEEE/EIA Std 12207.0-1996 and ISO/IEC 12207:1995, where IEEE Std 1012-1998 complements the tasks designated in 12207, is essential. (In Appendix A of the IEEE 1012, ISO/IEC 12207 V&V requirements and IEEE 1074 V&V requirements are mapped in relation to IEEE Std 1012 activities and tasks.)

We should note that special standard IEEE Std 1012a-1998 is dedicated to mapping the conformance of IEEE Std 1012-1998 to IEEE/EIA Std 12207.1-1997 and IEEE/EIA Std 12207.0-1996.

(8) **Special characteristics of reusable software V&V.** IEEE 1012-1998 presents the difficulties of performing V&V activities for reusable software (software from a software library, COTS software, etc.). It also indicates possible directions to facilitate performance of these activities.

(9) **Application of V&V metrics.** According to IEEE 1012-1998, two classes of metrics are to be performed:

- Metrics for evaluation of software development processes and products
- Metrics for evaluation of the quality and coverage of V&V activities.

While the first class of metrics measures the development process and its products, the second is dedicated to exploring features such as the effectiveness of V&V activities as well as metrics that belong to the first class.

(10) **Quantitative criteria for V&V tasks.** A list of quantitative criteria for evaluation of V&V tasks, including correctness, consistency, completeness, accuracy, readability and testability, is defined by the standard.

24.3.3 The standard's content

The main body of IEEE 1012-1998 is dedicated to:

- Specification of verification and validation (V&V) software integrity levels.
- Delineation of V&V processes.
- Itemization of V&V reporting, administrative and documentation requirements.
- Explication of the software V&V plan (SVVP) outline.

■ Eight informative annexes that provide details to the standard's chapters. Four of the most important of these annexes are:
  - Annex A: Mapping ISO/IEC V&V requirements to IEEE Std 1012 V&V activities and tasks
  - Annex C: V&V of reusable software
  - Annex D: V&V metrics
  - Annex G: Optional V&V task descriptions.

The software life cycle architecture presented in the standard is structured as a three-level tree composed of:

(1) Processes

(2) Activities

(3) Tasks.

The six processes covered by the standard are:

(1) Management

(2) Acquisition

(3) Supply

(4) Development

(5) Operation

(6) Maintenance.

The description of each process includes the requisite one to six activities, while three to ten tasks are assigned to each task.

Table 24.1 presents the structure of the V&V architecture in terms of processes, activities and tasks, and demonstrates that the higher the integrity level, the greater the number of tasks assigned to the pertinent activity.

Table 24.1: IEEE Std 1012 V&V processes, activities and tasks structure

V&V processes	V&V activities	Number of V&V tasks at integrity level:			
		Low 1	Moderate 2	Major 3	High 4
1. Management	1.1 Management of V&V				
	1.1.1 Acquisition	—	1	2	2
	1.1.2 Supply	—	1	2	2
	1.1.3 Development				
	1.1.3.1 Concept	2	2	4	5
	1.1.3.2 Requirements	1	2	4	4
	1.1.3.3 Design	1	2	4	4
	1.1.3.4 Implementation	1	2	4	4
	1.1.3.5 Test	1	2	4	4
	1.1.3.6 Installation and checkout	1	2	4	4
	1.1.4 Operation	1	2	4	4
	1.1.5 Maintenance	2	2	5	5

Table 24.1: Continued

V&V processes	V&V activities	Number of V&V tasks at integrity level:			
		Low 1	Moderate 2	Major 3	High 4
2. Acquisition	2.1 Acquisition support V&V	1	3	3	3
3. Supply	3.1 Supply support V&V	—	1	1	2
4. Development	4.1 Concept V&V	1	4	6	7
	4.2 Requirements V&V	2	6	9	9
	4.3 Design V&V	2	6	9	9
	4.4 Implementation V&V	3	7	9	9
	4.5 Test V&V	2	5	7	7
	4.6 Installation and checkout V&V	—	1	5	5
5. Operation	5.1 Operation V&V	—	2	5	5
6. Maintenance	6.1 Maintenance V&V	2	5	9	9

For the SVVP to conform with the standard's requirements, planners have to thoroughly understand the software system and ascertain the professional, administrative and resource issues implicit in the V&V project as planned. The scope of the required SVVP is demonstrated by its outline (template). Frame 24.1 duplicates the SVVP shown in standard IEEE Std 1012.

Frame 24.1 **IEEE Std 1012's SVVP outline (template)**

1 Purpose

2 Referenced Documents

3 Definitions

4 V&V Overview
  4.1 Organization
  4.2 Master Schedule
  4.3 Software Integrity Level Scheme
  4.4 Resources Summary
  4.5 Responsibilities
  4.6 Tools, Techniques, and Methods

5 V&V Processes
  5.1 Process: Management
  5.2 Process: Acquisition
  5.3 Process: Supply
  5.4 Process: Development
  5.5 Process: Operation
  5.6 Process: Maintenance

6 V&V Reporting Requirements

7 V&V Administrative Requirements
  7.1 Anomaly Resolution and Reporting
  7.2 Task Iteration Policy
  7.3 Deviation Policy
  7.4 Control Procedures
  7.5 Standards, Practices and Conventions

8 V&V Documentation Requirements

For each section and subsection of the SVVP outline, the IEEE 1012 supplements provide detailed definitions of the requisite contents.

24.4 IEEE Std 1028 – reviews

IEEE Std 1028-1997 (IEEE, 1997) limits itself to the technical issue of "how to perform a systematic review". According to the standard, a systematic review is defined as a review performed by a team according to a documented procedure that produces documented results. Methodological issues, such as when to carry out a review or what type of review is most appropriate, are sidestepped, to be determined by other standards or by project management.

The five types of systematic reviews covered are:

- Management reviews
- Technical reviews (referred to as "formal design reviews" in this book)
- Inspections
- Walkthroughs
- Audits.

24.4.1 Purpose

The purpose of IEEE Std 1028-1997 is to define systematic review procedures that:

- Are applicable for reviews performed throughout the software life cycle
- Conform with the review requirements defined by other standards.

24.4.2 Underlying concepts

Three underlying concepts characterize the standard:

(1) **High formality.** The standard's high formality is manifested throughout, especially by requirements for authorization and documentation.

(2) **Follow-up.** The standard demands incorporation of follow-up and performance approval for corrections made in all its review activities.

(3) **Compliance with international and IEEE standards.** IEEE Std 1028-1997 complies with other IEEE standards and international standards (e.g., ISO/IEC 9000-3) that prescribe performance of reviews). Especially noteworthy are IEEE/EIA Std 12207.0-1996, ISO/IEC 12207:1995 and IEEE Std 1012-1998, discussed earlier in the chapter. Appendix A of the standard presents its relationship to several other standards applied in the software industry.

24.4.3 The standard's content

The main portion of IEEE Std 1028-1997 entails:

■ Detailed definition of review requirements
■ An appendix that shows the standard's relationships to life cycle processes described in IEEE 730-1989, IEEE 1012-1998, IEEE 1074-1995 and ISO/IEC 12207:1995.

The standard devotes one chapter each (Chapters 4–8) to five types of reviews. It also applies the identical nine-component structure to all the requirements of the various review types, although the number of components varies according to the review's characteristics. For instance, the last two components of this structure, namely "data collection recommendation" and "improvement", are mentioned only in the chapters dealing with inspections and walkthroughs.

The components of the basic review requirement structure are:

(1) **Introduction**

■ Purposes of each type of review
■ Typical examples of each type of software product.

(2) **Responsibilities**. The responsibilities section deals with participants in the review and the role of each. The standard provides a list of participants, some of whom are mandatory and others optional. For example, the mandatory participants of a technical review are decision-maker, review leader, recorder and technical staff. Optional participants are management staff, other team members and customer or user representatives.

No optional participants are listed for inspections and walk-throughs, as these are peer reviews, or for audits, as this type of review depends solely on the auditors' professional qualifications.

(3) **Input**. This section deals with data inputs. Data are divided into mandatory and optional items, and vary with review type. The mandatory data items are common to all review types, as might be expected. They focus on a statement of the review's objectives and the software products to be reviewed.

For example, the data items mandatory for a walkthrough are:

■ A statement of objectives
■ The software product being examined
■ Standards in effect for the acquisition, supply, development, operation, and/or maintenance of the software product.

Optional data items are:

■ Regulations, standards, guidelines, plans and procedures against which the software product is to be examined
■ Anomalies.

(4) **Entry criteria.** The review's authorization and performance preconditions represent what are otherwise known as entry criteria. Criteria common to all review types entail:

- A statement of the review's objectives
- Availability of the required input data.

(5) **Procedure.** Review procedures are required to include:

- Management preparations
- Planning of the review
- Preparation by team members
- Examination of the software product, including determination of required reworked software and corrections
- Follow-up of performance of corrective activities.

(6) **Exit criteria.** The exit criteria specify what must be accomplished before the review can be officially concluded. These criteria include:

- Completion of procedural activities
- Follow-up and approval of satisfactory completion of action items or corrective and preventive actions
- Completion of required review documentation.

(7) **Output.** The standard specifies the mandatory output items for each type of review. Additional items may be required by the organization, other local procedures, or specific cases.

(8) **Data collection recommendations.** It is recommended that inspection and walkthrough teams collect data related to anomalies encountered, where each case is classified and ranked according to its severity. This data will then be used to study the effectiveness and efficiency of current practices; they are also expected to stimulate improvements of methods and procedures.

(9) **Improvements.** The accumulated inspection and walkthrough data shall be analyzed in order to:

- Formulate improved procedures
- Update checklists used by the participants
- Improve software development processes.

Summary

(1) Explain the concepts underlying IEEE/EIA Std 12207.

The concepts may be classified into general concepts and task-related concepts as follows:

General concepts

(a) **Applicability of the standard and its adaptation by tailoring**
The standard is applicable to projects that vary by size, complexity and user. Much of its broad applicability is due to tailoring within the limits allowed to users.

(b) **Applicability for all participants in the software life cycle**
The standard serves all the participants of the software life cycle – acquirers, suppliers, developers, operators and maintainers – and provides separate sections for each participant.

(c) **Flexibility and responsiveness to technological changes**
The standard instructs "how to do" and not "exactly how to do" a project; hence, users can choose their life cycle model, development tools, software metrics, project milestones and product and documentation standards. As a consequence, this approach contributes to reduced dependence on specific technologies coupled with increased responsiveness to technological change.

(d) **Software links with its system**
For each phase of the life cycle, the standard establishes strong links between the software and the system of which it is a part.

(e) **TQM consistency**
The standard is consistent with Total Quality Management concepts.

(f) **No certification of developer organizations**
The standard does not require certification of the developer organization.

(g) **Baselining**
The standard requires that the software and hardware baseline configuration versions be prepared according to the project schedule.

Task-related concepts

(a) **Allocation of responsibility for activities and tasks**
The performance of each process, activity and task is assigned to a unit or individual.

(b) **Modularity of software life cycle components**
Components of the software life cycle, especially activities and tasks, are to be modular as much as possible.

(c) **Levels of required conformance to tasks**
The standard defines four levels of required conformance, in descending order: "will", "shall", "should" and "may".

(d) **Nature of evaluation tasks**
The standard requires that evaluation of entities (process, activity, report, etc.) with given purpose be conducted against their defined criteria.

(2) Explain the concepts underlying IEEE Std 1012.

(a) **A broad definition of V&V activities**
The standard views V&V activities broadly, to be performed throughout the software life cycle. These include reviews, tests, evaluations, risk analyses, hazard analyses, retirement assessments, etc.

(b) **Software integrity levels and adapted V&V requirements**
The standard distinguishes four integrity levels – high, major, moderate and low – according to the criticality of the software function, module or unit. Graded requirements are attuned to the integrity level. The standard requires that integrity levels shall be assigned to components as early as the SVVP.

(c) **Prescriptive standard requirements**
The IEEE Std 1012-1998 is a prescriptive standard that lists the tasks to be performed for every activity throughout the software life cycle.

(d) **Required independence of V&V activities**
Independent V&V (IV&V) are defined in the standard as managerial, technical and financial independence in the performance of the V&V process. The degree of independence will be determined in the SVVP as part of the V&V organization plan.

(e) **Compliance with international and IEEE standards**
The standard requires compliance with international and IEEE standards, especially IEEE/EIA Std 12207.0-1996.

(f) **Recognition of special characteristics of V&V of reusable software**
The difficulties of performing V&V activities for reusable software are recognized, and possible directions to performing V&V activities are shown.

(g) **Application of V&V metrics**
The Standard requires two classes of metrics:
- Metrics for evaluation of software development process and products
- Metrics for quality and coverage evaluation of V&V activities.

(h) **Detailed quantitative criteria for V&V tasks**
Specific quantitative criteria for V&V tasks – including correctness, consistency, completeness, accuracy, readability and testability – are defined.

(3) Explain the essence of the SVVP as required by IEEE Std 1012.

The SVVP is designed to thoroughly delineate a plan for V&V activities that will include all aspects of their performance, including the schedule, resources, responsibilities, tools and techniques to be used. In addition, the SVVP documents administrative directions concerning anomaly-resolution procedures, task iteration and deviation policies, performance control procedures and the standard practices and conventions that have to be applied. Special instructions are given for documentation.

(4) Explain the concepts underlying IEEE Std 1028.

The standard applies the following concepts:

(a) **High formality**
Review processes are formal, as realized in authorization and documentation contents requirements.

(b) **Follow-up**
The standard extends the review process to include follow-up and approval of satisfactory performance of the required corrections listed in the review document, irrespective of the type of review.

(c) **Compliance with international and IEEE standards**
The Standard complies with other IEEE standards and international standards, e.g., ISO/IEC 9000-3, pertaining to performance of reviews.

Selected bibliography

1. Heil J. H. (1999) "Practical application of software quality assurance to mission critical software", in G. G. Schulmeyer, and J. I. McManus (eds), *Handbook of Software Quality Assurance*, 3rd edn, Prentice Hall, Upper Saddle River, NJ, pp. 445–512.
2. IEEE (1997) "IEEE Std 1028-1997 – IEEE Standard for Software Reviews", in *IEEE Software Engineering Standards Collection*, The Institute of Electrical and Electronics Engineers, New York.
3. IEEE (1998) "IEEE Std 1012-1998 – IEEE Standard for Software Verification and Validation", in *IEEE Software Engineering Standards Collection*, The Institute of Electrical and Electronics Engineers, New York.
4. IEEE/EIA (1996) "IEEE/EIA Std 12207.0-1996 – IEEE/EIA Standard – Industry Implementation of International Standard ISO/IEC 12207:1995", in *IEEE Software Engineering Standards Collection*, The Institute of Electrical and Electronics Engineers, New York.
5. IEEE/EIA (1997a) "IEEE/EIA Std 12207.1-1997 – IEEE/EIA Guide – Industry Implementation of International Standard ISO/IEC 12207:1995, Software Life Cycle Processes – Life Cycle Data", in *IEEE Software Engineering Standards Collection*, The Institute of Electrical and Electronics Engineers, New York.
6. IEEE/EIA (1997b) "IEEE/EIA Std 12207.1-1997 – IEEE/EIA Guide – Industry Implementation of International Standard ISO/IEC 12207:1995, Software Life Cycle Processes – Implementation Considerations", in *IEEE Software Engineering Standards Collection*, The Institute of Electrical and Electronics Engineers, New York.
7. Moore, J. W. (1999) "An integrated collection of software engineering standards", *IEEE Software*, 16(6), 51–57.
8. Schulmeyer, G. G. (1999) "Standardization of software quality assurance – where is it all going?", in G. G. Schulmeyer, and J. I. McManus (eds) *Handbook of Software Quality Assurance*, 3rd edn, Prentice Hall, Upper Saddle River, NJ, pp. 91–113.

Review questions

24.1 IEEE/EIA Std 12207 is considered an international standard. Explain, in your own words, why this status is warranted.

24.2 Consider the purpose of the two standards IEEE Std 1012 and IEEE Std 1028.

(1) Explain, in your own words, the purpose of each of the standards.
(2) In what way do the standards complement each other?

24.3 The 1998 version of IEEE Std 1012 introduces the notion of "V&V metrics" in one of its Annexes. This notion was absent from the 1986 version (reaffirmed 1992).

(1) Explain, in your own words, the notion of "V&V metrics" and how it should be implemented.
(2) Describe the two classes of metrics defined in the Annex.
(3) Discuss the contribution of V&V metrics to software quality and to the effectiveness of V&V activities.

24.4 The "master schedule", a document that describes the project life cycle and its milestones together with the planned V&V activities, is one of the IEEE Std 1012 requirements for a SVVP (see Frame 24.1).

(1) Describe, in your own words, the coordination activities that the master schedule's planner has to perform in the process of preparing the document.
(2) Discuss the importance of the master schedule and its contribution to the project's success.

24.5 "Task iteration policy", which refers to the criteria and procedure applied to determine which V&V tasks shall be repeated in case of changes in input or changes in V&V procedures, is another of the IEEE Std 1012 administrative requirements for an SVVP (see Frame 24.1).

(1) Describe two situations where you would expect a decision to be made about repeating a V&V task.
(2) Explain, in your own words, the importance of task iteration policy in such cases.

Topics for discussion

24.1 The 10 concepts at the foundation of IEEE/EIA Std 12207 are listed in Section 24.2.2.

Examine the concepts and determine which of these contributes the most to the standard's wide applicability. Explain your choice.

24.2 IEEE/EIA Std 12207 sets levels of conformance to meet the standard's requirements.

(1) List the four levels of conformance and explain, in your own words, the significance of each level.
(2) Discuss the contribution made by clear definition of these levels.

24.3 IEEE Std 1012 dedicates a special Appendix to V&V of reusable software.

(1) List the kinds of software that are considered to be "reusable".
(2) Explain the special characteristics of "reusable software" in relation to V&V activities.
(3) List what you consider to be options for overcoming the difficulties inherent in performing V&V of "reusable software".

24.4 IEEE Std 1028 requires the review team to determine the needed rework and corrections, and include these requirements in the review documentation. It also requires that the review team follow up the corrections and approve their satisfactory completion.

(1) Detail the activities that reviewers are expected to perform when conducting the follow-up.
(2) Explain, in your own words, the importance of follow-up within the framework of software quality assurance.

24.5 Some senior system analysts claim that as a result of their experience, the SVVP required in IEEE Std 1012 is simply a "waste of time", and that a development (project) plan should suffice.

(1) Do you agree with this claim?

(2) List the arguments backing up your position. Base them on a comparison of the contents of the two documents (an SVVP and a project plan).

24.6 The 1998 version of IEEE Std 1012 introduces the notion "level of integrity", absent from the 1986 version (reaffirmed 1992).

(1) Address the contribution of "level of integrity" to the effectiveness of the standard's prescribed V&V activities.

(2) How does your response to (1) influence the standard's applicability?

24.7 IEEE Std 1012-1998 defines the term "independence of V&V" (absent from the 1986 version).

(1) Explain, in your own words, the three components of V&V and how independence is measured.

(2) Discuss the contribution of greater V&V independence to software quality.

(3) Suggest three (real-life or imaginary) examples of organizations that carry out V&V activities of software development projects. Define the managerial, technical and financial degree of independence based on the conditions surrounding each example.

(4) Try to grade your examples according to their integrity level. Support your grading with the appropriate arguments.

(5) Discuss the contribution of this addition of V&V independence to software quality.

Appendix 24A IEEE Software Engineering Standards

Updated July 2002

610.12-1990	IEEE Standard Glossary of Software Engineering Terminology
730-1998	IEEE Standard for Software Quality Assurance Plans
828-1998	IEEE Standard for Software Configuration Management Plans
829-1998	IEEE Standard for Software Test Documentation
830-1998	IEEE Recommended Practice for Software Requirements Specifications
982.1-1988	IEEE Standard Dictionary of Measures to Produce Reliable Software
1008-1987 (R1993)	IEEE Standard for Software Unit Testing
1012-1998	IEEE Standard for Software Verification and Validation
1012a-1998	IEEE Standard for Software Verification and Validation – Supplement to 1012-1998 – Content Map to IEEE 12207.1
1016-1998	IEEE Recommended Practice for Software Design Descriptions
1028-1997	IEEE Standard for Software Reviews
1044-1983	IEEE Standard Classification for Anomalies
1045-1992	IEEE Standard for Software Productivity Metrics
1058-1998	IEEE Standard for Software Project Management Plans
1058.1-1987 (R1993)	IEEE Standard for Software Project Management Plans
1061-1998	IEEE Standard for Software Quality Metrics Methodology

1062-1998	IEEE Recommended Practice for Software Acquisition (includes IEEE 1062a)
1063-2001	IEEE Standard for Software User Documentation
1074-1997	IEEE Standard for Developing Software Life Cycle Processes
1219-1998	IEEE Standard for Software Maintenance
1220-1998	IEEE Standard for the Application and Management of the Systems Engineering Process
1228-1994	IEEE Standard for Software Safety Plans
1233-1998	IEEE Guide for Developing System Requirements Specifications (including IEEE 1233a)
1320.1-1998	IEEE Standard for Functional Modeling Language – Syntax and Semantics for IDEF0
1320.2-1998	IEEE Standard for Conceptual Modeling Language – Syntax and Semantics for IDEF1X97 (IDEF object)
1362-1998	IEEE Guide for Information Technology – System Definition – Concept of Operation Document
1420.1-1995	IEEE Standard for Information Technology – Software Reuse – Data Model for Reuse Library Interoperability: Basic Interoperability Data Model (BIDM)
1420.1a-1996	IEEE Supplement to Standard for Information Technology – Software Reuse – Data Model for Reuse Library Interoperability: Asset Certification Framework
1420.1b-1999	IEEE Trial-use Supplement to IEEE Standard for Information Technology – Software Reuse – Data Model for Reuse Library Interoperability: Intellectual Property Rights Framework
1462-1998	Information Technology – Guideline for the Evaluation and Selection of CASE tools
1465-1998	(ISO/IEC 12119:1998) Information Technology – Software Packages – Quality Requirements and Testing
1471-2000	IEEE Recommended Practice for Architectural Description of Software Incentive Systems
1490-1998	IEEE Guide (©IEEE) – Adoption of PMI Standard – A Guide to the Project Management Body of Knowledge (©PMI)
1517-1999	IEEE Standard for Information Technology – Software Life Cycle processes – Reuse Processes
1540-2001	IEEE Standard for Software Life Cycle Processes – Risk Management
J-Std-016-1995	EIA/IEEE Interim Standard for Information Technology – Software Life Cycle Processes – Software Development Acquirer – Supplier Agreement (Issued for Trial Use)
12207.0-1996	IEEE/EIA Standard: Industry Implementation of International Standard ISO/IEC 12207:1995 Standard for Information Technology – Software Life Cycle Processes
12207.1-1997	IEEE/EIA Standard: Industry Implementation of International Standard ISO/IEC 12207:1995 Standard for Information Technology – Software Life Cycle Processes – Life Cycle Data
12207.2-1997	IEEE/EIA Standard: Industry Implementation of International Standard ISO/IEC 12207:1995 Standard for Information Technology – Software Life Cycle Processes – Implementation Considerations
14143.1-2000	Implementation Note for IEEE Adoption of ISO/IEC 14143–1:1998, Information Technology – Software Measurement – Functional Size Measurement – Part 1: Definition of Concepts

Appendix 24B MIL-STD-498: list of Data Item Descriptions (DIDs)

DID code	DID name
COM	Computer Operator Manual
CPM	Computer Programming Manual
DBDD	DataBase Design Description
FSM	Firmware Support Manual
IDD	Interface Design Description
IRS	Interface Requirements Specification
OCD	Operational Concept Description
SCOM	Software Center Operator Manual
SDD	Software Design Description
SDP	Software Development Plan
SIOM	Software Input/Output Manual
SIP	Software Installation Plan
SPS	Software Product Specification
SRS	Software Requirements Specification
SSDD	System/Subsystem Design Description
SSS	System/Subsystem Specification
STD	Software Test Description
STP	Software Test Plan
STR	Software Test Report
STRP	Software TRansition Plan
SUM	Software User Manual
SVD	Software Version Description

Appendix 24C Task structure for a primary process according to IEEE/EIA Std 12207 – example

Table 24C.1 demonstrates the structure of a process class by presenting the processes, activities and tasks of the primary process affected. The table was prepared according to Sections 5.1 to 5.5 of the standard (IEEE/EIA, 1996).

Note that whenever "software development" is mentioned, it refers also to "software services" as found in the original. Also conformance levels are indicated by the wording.

Process	Activities	Tasks
1. Acquisition – performed by the acquirer	1.1 Initiation	1.1.1 Acquirer will describe a concept or need for the system or software product requested. 1.1.2 Acquirer will define and analyze the system requirements. 1.1.3 If the requirement definition and analysis are performed by the supplier, the acquirer will approve. 1.1.4 The requirement definition and analysis may be performed by the acquirer or the supplier. 1.1.5 The development process defined in the Table's Section 3 should be applied when performing 1.1.2 and 1.1.4. 1.1.6 Acquirer will consider options for acquisition and analyze each option. 1.1.7 For COTS software options, specified conditions will be satisfied. 1.1.8 Acquirer should prepare an acquisition plan including specified subjects. 1.1.9 Acquirer should define and document the acceptance strategy, including acceptance criteria.
	1.2 Request for proposal preparation (RFP)	1.2.1 Acquirer should prepare an RFP for the acquisition option selected in 1.1.6 to include specified subjects. 1.2.2 Acquirer should tailor the standard's processes, activities and tasks. The acquirer should specify the applicable supporting processes and their performing organizations to be considered in the suppliers' proposals. 1.2.3 Acquirer will define milestones as part of acquisition monitoring. 1.2.4 The RFP should be given to the organization performing the project.
	1.3 Contract preparation and updating	1.3.1 Acquirer should establish procedures for supplier selection and proposal evaluation. 1.3.2 Acquirer should select supplier based on supplier's proposal, capabilities and other factors. 1.3.3 Acquirer will tailor the standard to the contract and attach it as a reference. 1.3.4 Acquirer will negotiate details of the contract. 1.3.5 Acquirer will control contract changes during negotiations according to agreed mechanism. Proposed changes shall be explored prior to their introduction.

Table 24C.1: Continued

Process	Activities	Tasks
1. Acquisition – performed by the acquirer	1.4 Supplier monitoring	1.4.1 Acquirer will monitor supplier's activities according to joint review, audit, verification and validation processes. 1.4.2 Acquirer will cooperate with supplier for timely provision of information and resolution of pending items.
	1.5 Acceptance and completion	1.5.1 Acquirer should prepare for acceptance, including detailed test procedures and test cases. 1.5.2 Acquirer will conduct acceptance activities for all deliverable software products. 1.5.3 Acquirer should take responsibility for configuration management of accepted software products.
2. Supply – performed by the supplier	2.1 Initiation	2.1.1 Supplier conducts review of RFP according to its policies and other regulations. 2.1.2 Supplier should decide whether to bid or accept the contract.
	2.2 Preparation of response	2.2.1 Supplier should prepare response to RFP, including recommended tailoring of standard to response conditions.
	2.3 Contract	2.3.1 Supplier shall negotiate and enter into a formal contract with acquirer. 2.3.2 Supplier may request changes in contract in accordance with agreed change control mechanism.
	2.4 Planning	2.4.1 Supplier shall review requirements and define framework for assuring quality of products, including management of SQA process. 2.4.2 If not stipulated by the contract, supplier shall define the appropriate life cycle model and map the standard-required processes, activities and tasks onto the model. 2.4.3 Supplier shall establish requirements for management and quality assurance plan, including resources and acquirer involvement. 2.4.4 Supplier shall consider software product development options following risk analysis of each option. 2.4.5 Supplier shall prepare project management plans based on the selected development options.

Process	Activities	Tasks
2. Supply – performed by the supplier	2.5 Execution and control	2.5.1 Supplier shall execute the project management plans. 2.5.2 Supplier shall develop the software product in accordance with development, operation and maintenance processes. 2.5.3 Supplier shall monitor and control the progress of development and quality of software products, including problem identification, analysis and resolution. 2.5.4 Supplier shall monitor and control subcontractors in accordance with the acquisition contract, relevant parts of which have been transferred from the primary contract to the subcontractor's contract. 2.5.5 Supplier shall interface with an independent verification, validation or test agent as specified in the contract. 2.5.6 Supplier shall interface with other parties specified in the contract and project plan.
	2.6 Review and evaluation	2.6.1 Supplier should coordinate contract review of activities, interfaces and communication with the acquirer. 2.6.2 Supplier shall conduct or support informal meetings, acceptance reviews, acceptance testing and audits as specified in the project and project plans. 2.6.3 Supplier shall perform verification and validation to demonstrate that the software products fully satisfy the requirements. 2.6.4 Supplier shall make available reports of evaluations, reviews, audits, testing and problem resolution as specified in the contract with the acquirer. 2.6.5 Supplier shall provide acquirer access to its and subcontractor's facilities for review of software product as specified in the contract and project plans. 2.6.6 Supplier shall perform the specified software quality assurance activities.
	2.7 Delivery and completion	2.7.1 Supplier shall deliver the software products as specified in the contract. 2.7.2 Supplier shall assist the acquirer in support of delivered software products as specified in the contract.

Table 24C.1: Continued

Process	Activities	Tasks
3. Development – performed by the developer	3.1 Process implementation	3.1.1 If not stipulated in the contract, developer shall select an appropriate life cycle and map the standard's activities and tasks onto the model. 3.1.2 Developer shall place outputs under configuration management, perform change control, resolve problems and non-conformance of software products, and document outputs, problems and resolutions. 3.1.3 Developer shall select, tailor and use those standards, methods and development tools appropriate for performance and documentation of the project. 3.1.4 Developer shall plan the conducting of the development activities: specific methods, tools, actions and responsibilities. Plans are to be documented and executed. 3.1.5 Non-deliverable items may be employed during the development process, but must be independent of any deliverable item. If such item is not independent it should be delivered.
	3.2 System requirements analysis	3.2.1 Developer shall analyze the intended use of the system to specify the system requirements, that fully describe system functions and capabilities. System requirements specifications are to be documented. 3.2.2 System requirements shall be evaluated according to listed criteria; results will be documented.
	3.3 System architectural design	3.3.1 Top-level system architecture shall be established, identifying hardware items, software and manual-operation items to ensure full coverage of requirements. The architectural items and their requirements shall be documented. 3.3.2 System architecture and requirements for the items shall be evaluated according to listed criteria; results shall be documented.
	3.4 Software requirements analysis	3.4.1 Developer shall establish and document software requirements including quality specifications that are defined according to listed characteristics. 3.4.2 Developer shall evaluate the software requirements according to listed criteria and document the results.

Process	Activities	Tasks
3. Development – performed by the developer		3.4.3 Developer shall conduct joint review of requirements. A baseline for the requirements shall be established after the review.
	3.5 Software architectural design	3.5.1 Top-level software architecture of the software shall be established, software components identified and full coverage of requirements ensured. Software components shall be refined to detailed design and documented. 3.5.2 Developer shall develop and document top-level design for the interfaces. 3.5.3 Developer shall develop and document top-level design for the database. 3.5.4 Developer should develop and document preliminary versions of user documentation. 3.5.5 Developer shall develop and document preliminary test requirements and software integration schedules. 3.5.6 Developer shall evaluate the architectural items and design performed according to listed criteria and document the results. 3.5.7 Developer shall conduct joint reviews.
	3.6 Software detailed review	3.6.1 Developer shall perform detailed design for each software component and refine it to lower levels, including software units to be coded as units. Developer shall ensure full coverage of software requirements and document the detailed design. 3.6.2 Developer shall develop and document detailed design for the interfaces. 3.6.3 Developer shall develop and document detailed design for the database. 3.6.4 Developer shall update user documentation as necessary. 3.6.5 Developer shall define and document test requirements and schedule for unit testing. Testing requirements include stress testing of units. 3.6.6 Developer shall update test requirements and schedule for software integration.

Table 24C.1: Continued

Process	Activities	Tasks
3. Development – performed by the developer	3.6 Software detailed review	3.6.7 Developer shall evaluate detailed design and test requirements according to listed criteria and document the results. 3.6.8 Developer shall conduct joint reviews.
	3.7 Software coding and testing	3.7.1 Developer shall develop and document software units, database and the required test procedures. 3.7.2 Developer shall test each unit and database, ensure that all requirements are satisfied and document the results. 3.7.3 Developer shall update user documentation as necessary. 3.7.4 Developer shall update test requirements and schedule for software integration. 3.7.5 Developer shall evaluate software code and test results according to listed criteria and document the results.
	3.8 Software integration	3.8.1 Developer shall develop and document integration plan for software units and components. 3.8.2 Developer shall integrate software units and components into aggregates and tests the aggregates. Developer shall document the integration test results. 3.8.3 Developer shall update user documentation as necessary. 3.8.4 Developer shall develop and document software qualification test procedures, including sets of tests, test cases and procedures. 3.8.5 Developer shall evaluate integration plan, design, code, test and test results, and user documentation according to listed criteria, and document the results. 3.8.6 Developer shall conduct joint reviews.
	3.9 Software qualification testing	3.9.1 Developer shall conduct and document qualification tests, and ensure that each requirement is tested for compliance. 3.9.2 Developer shall update user documentation as necessary. 3.9.3 Developer shall evaluate design, code, test and test results and user documentation according to listed criteria and document the results. 3.9.4 Developer shall support audits and document the results.

Process	Activities	Tasks
3. Development – performed by the developer	3.9 Software qualification testing	3.9.5 Upon successful audits, developer shall update and prepare the deliverable software products and establish a baseline for the design and code of the software item.
	3.10 System integration	3.10.1 Software configuration items shall be integrated with hardware and other system configuration items and manual operations into the system. System integration shall be tested and the results documented. 3.10.2 Test set, test cases and test procedure shall be developed for each system qualification requirement. 3.10.3 The integrated system shall be evaluated according to listed criteria and the results documented.
	3.11 System qualification testing	3.11.1 System qualification testing shall be conducted to ensure full coverage of system requirements until the system is ready for delivery. Test results shall be documented. 3.11.2 System shall be evaluated according to the listed criteria and the results shall be documented. 3.11.3 Developer shall support audits and document the results. 3.11.4 Upon successful audits, developer shall update and prepare the deliverable software products for installation and support acceptance testing, as well as establish baselines for the design and code for each software configuration item.
	3.12 Software installation	3.12.1 Developer shall develop and document plans to install software products in the target environment according to the contract. Developer shall support acquirer in setup and parallel ongoing activities as required by the contract. 3.12.2 Developer shall install software products according to plans, including database initialization as specified by the contract. Installation events shall be documented.
	3.13 Software acceptance support	3.13.1 Developer shall support acquirer's acceptance reviews and tests of software products, considering the joint reviews, audits and software and system qualification testing. The results shall be documented.

Table 24C.1: Continued

Process	Activities	Tasks
3. Development – performed by the developer	3.13 Software acceptance support	3.13.2 Developer shall complete and deliver software products according to the contract. 3.13.3 Developer shall provide training and support the acquirer as specified in the contract.
4. Operation processes – performed by the operator	4.1 Process implementation	4.1.1 Operator shall develop plan and operational standards for performing activities and tasks. Plans shall be documented and executed. 4.1.2 Operators shall establish procedures for operation, including problem resolution and feedback. Problems are to be recorded and treated by the problem resolution process. 4.1.3 Operator shall establish test procedures for testing software products in the operational environment and for handling problem reports, and modification requests and release of software products for operational use.
	4.2 Operational testing	4.2.1 Operator shall perform operational testing for new releases of software products. On satisfying the specified criteria, the new software product will be released for operational use. 4.2.2 Operator shall ensure that software code and database initialize, execute and terminate as planned.
	4.3 System operation	4.3.1 The system shall operate in its intended environment according to user documentation.
	4.4 User support	4.4.1 Operator shall provide assistance and consultation to the users as requested. Requests and their handling process shall be recorded and monitored. 4.4.2 Operator shall forward modification requests for resolution. The resulting planned actions shall be reported to the originator of the request, and resolutions shall be monitored. 4.4.3 If a temporary problem-resolving action has been initiated, system improvements shall be applied before a permanent solution is implemented.
5. Maintenance processes – performed by maintainer	5.1 Process implementation	5.1.1 Maintainer shall develop, document and execute plans and procedure for conducting maintenance activities and tasks.

Process	Activities	Tasks
5. Maintenance processes – performed by maintainer	5.1 Process implementation	5.1.2 Maintainer shall establish procedures for handling problem reports, and modification requests and feedback to users. Problems shall be recorded and treated by the problem resolution process. 5.1.3 Maintainer shall implement configuration management system for managing modifications.
	5.2 Problem and modification analysis	5.2.1 Maintainer shall analyze problem reports and modification requests for their impact on the organization. Systems shall be interfaced according to listed criteria. 5.2.2 Maintainer shall replicate or verify the problem. 5.2.3 Maintainer shall consider options for implementing modifications. 5.2.4 Maintainer shall document the problem reports and modification requests. 5.2.5 Maintainer shall obtain approval for modifications according to contract.
	5.3 Modification implementation	5.3.1 Maintainer shall conduct analysis to determine which documentation, software units and software versions demand modification. Results shall be documented. 5.3.2 Maintainer shall use development process to implement modifications. Modification requirements shall include test and evaluation criteria. Correct and complete modification shall be assured, as will original unmodified and unaffected parts. The test results shall be documented.
	5.4 Maintenance review/ acceptance	5.4.1 Maintainer shall review modification together with the modifications authorizer. 5.4.2 Maintainer shall obtain approval of satisfactory completion of the modifications.
	5.5 Migration	5.5.1 If software product is migrated to a new operational environment, it shall be assured that software product, data produced or modified during migration conforms with the standard. 5.5.2 A migration plan shall be developed, documented and executed. 5.5.3 Users shall be notified of the migration plan, including the reason for migration, description of the new environment and support available for the previous environment once item is removed.

▶

Table 24C.1: Continued

Process	Activities	Tasks
5. Maintenance processes – performed by maintainer	5.5 Migration	5.5.4 Parallel operation of new and old environments may be conducted to assure that smooth transition and training are provided during this period. 5.5.5 All concerned persons shall be notified about arriving migration. Previous environment's documentation, logs and code should be archived. 5.5.6 A post-migration review shall be performed to assess results of changing environments. Results of review shall be sent to appropriate authority for information, guidance and action. 5.5.7 Data used in previous environment shall be accessible according to contract requirements.
	5.6 Software retirement	5.6.1 A retirement plan to remove active support by the operations and maintenance organization shall be developed, documented and executed. 5.6.2 Users shall be notified about retirement plan and activities, including retirement description, reasons for software product and description of alternative. 5.6.3 Parallel operation of the retired and new software products should be conducted to assure smooth transition. Training shall be provided during the transition period. 5.6.4 All concerned persons shall be notified about impending retirement. Previous documentation, logs and code should be archived. 5.6.5 Data used in the retired software product shall be accessible according to contract requirements.

part VII

Organizing for quality assurance

Previous parts of this book dealt with a panoply of SQA components: pre-project components, project life cycle components, infrastructure components, management components, and standards and certification components. But who initiates, activates and operates all those components? Who is responsible for all the activities needed to run an effective and efficient SQA system? Partial answers to these questions are sprinkled throughout the various chapters. In this part, we take an integrated look at the quality assurance system from the point of view of the people who create, develop and make sure that system functions properly, to wit, the managers and team members who implement the quality assurance organizational framework.

VII.1 The software development organizational structure

Regarding software development organizations one may generalize by assuming three levels of management structure, found in most organizations of this type. These three levels are top management, middle management, and project management. Top management includes the general manager and executives of the organization. Middle management's internal structure is the most susceptible to variation by organizational type and, of course, by organization size. It can include several roles and levels: department managers and division managers, among others. Project management likewise varies; depending on the project and its scale, it consists of project managers, project section managers, team leaders, and so forth.

For the purposes of our discussion, we consider the classic, basic three-level structure of software development organizations that is found among many medium to small organizations of the industry. Three managerial levels are considered:

- **Top management**, including the organization's general manager and its executives (CEOs).
- **Department managers**, including managers of software development, maintenance and software testing departments.
- **Project managers** and team leaders of development projects and maintenance services.

The quality assurance organizational framework described in the next section is adapted to the organizational structure outlined above.

VII.2 The quality assurance organizational framework

In order for a software quality assurance system to operate successfully, many or even all of the organization's employees have to contribute their share to the quality of the organization's software products and/or services. This goal is achieved by their diligent compliance to SQA procedures and work instructions, and certainly by the professional performance of their tasks. Special mention should be made of the individuals – managers and other employees – who people the *quality assurance organizational framework*: those professionals whose software quality assurance tasks represent the substance of their positions and those whose participation in SQA activities represents extensions of their tasks' formal definitions. The quality assurance organizational framework that operates within the organizational structure with which we are concerned includes the following participants ("actors"), whom we group into the categories of managers, testers and SQA professionals and interested practitioners:

(1) **Managers:**
   - Top management executives, especially the executive directly in charge of software quality assurance
   - Software development and maintenance department managers
   - Software testing department managers
   - Project managers and team leaders of development and maintenance projects
   - Leaders of software testing teams.

(2) **Testers:**
   - Members of software testing teams.

(3) **SQA professionals and interested practitioners:**
   - SQA trustees
   - SQA committee members
   - SQA forum members
   - SQA unit team members.

Of all the above actors in the quality assurance organizational framework, only members of the SQA unit, managers and employees of the software testing department are occupied full time in the performance of SQA tasks. The others dedicate part of their time to quality issues, whether during fulfillment of their managerial functions or professional tasks, or as volunteers in others, most often a SQA committee, a SQA forum, or as SQA trustees.

Figure VII.1 shows a schematic organizational chart associated with the SQA framework. This displays the SQA framework found in the typical

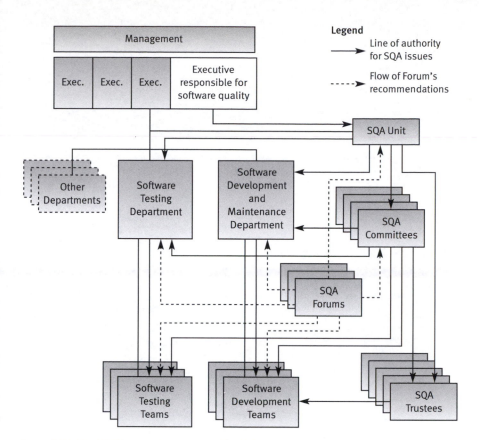

Figure VII.1: The SQA framework – organizational chart

organization. Expanded structures that include divisional managers and team leaders as well as divisional or departmental SQA units may be appropriate to larger organizations. Organizations whose projects include international and overseas software development and maintenance may find it necessary to adopt far more complex SQA frameworks. As it is beyond the scope of this book to deal with the full range of SQA organizational issues arising in the different contexts, we limit ourselves to a presentation of the main issues.

Chapter 25 focuses on the contributions made to quality assurance by the three main managerial levels – top management, department management and project management.

Chapter 26 dwells on SQA professionals and interested practitioners, namely SQA unit members and, in addition, SQA committees, trustees and forums.

Management and its role in software quality assurance

For the purposes of our discussion, we refer to three levels of management found in many software development organizations:

- Top management
- Department management
- Project management.

It is beyond the scope of this book to deal with the full range of SQA organizational structures and to issues arising in the different contexts. We limit ourselves here to a presentation of the main issues, with implications for specific organizations left to the reader.

A good many quality assurance managerial tasks are shared by managers of the same level or of more than one level, with each manager taking on the responsibilities suitable to his or her level of authority and expertise. Among these tasks, project progress control was comprehensively discussed in Chapter 20. Others were mentioned briefly. This chapter provides an overview of the managerial tasks specifically related to compliance with functional requirements, schedules and budget, and continuous improvement of the system's productivity and effectiveness.

After completing this chapter, you will be able to:

- List the actors of a typical quality assurance organizational framework.
- Describe top management's responsibilities regarding software quality.
- Describe the software system-related responsibilities of the executive in charge of software quality issues.
- Describe the main objectives of management reviews.
- Explain the SQA-related responsibilities of department management.
- List the SQA professional hands-on tasks required of project managers.

25.1 Top management's quality assurance activities

Among its other responsibilities, top management is also responsible for software quality. This level's overall responsibilities in this area are summarized in Frame 25.1.

Frame 25.1 **Top management's overall responsibilities for software quality**

- Assure the quality of the company's software products and software maintenance services

- Communicate the importance of product and service quality in addition to customer satisfaction to employees at all levels

- Assure satisfactory functioning and full compliance with customer requirements

- Ensure that quality objectives are established for the organization's SQA system and that its objectives are accomplished

- Initiate planning and oversee implementation of changes necessary to adapt the SQA system to major internal as well as external changes related to the organization's clientele, competition and technology

- Intervene directly to support resolution of crisis situations and minimize damages

- Ensure availability of resources required by SQA systems

The three main tools available to top management for fulfillment of its responsibilities are:

- Establishment and updating of the organization's software quality policy
- Assignation of one of the executives in charge of software quality issues (e.g., Vice President for SQA)

■ Conduct of regular *management reviews* of performance with respect to software quality issues.

The next three sections deal with these tools.

ISO 9000-3 relates to management commitment and its translation into action as major components of the software quality assurance system (ISO, 1997, Sec. 4.1; ISO/IEC, 2001, Ch. 5).

25.1.1 Software quality policy

The organization's software quality policy, though very general in its contents and their statement, should communicate the following requirements:

■ Conformity to the organization's purpose and goals
■ Commitment to general software quality assurance concepts
■ Commitment to the quality standards adopted by the organization
■ Commitment to allocate adequate resources for software quality assurance
■ Commitment to continuous improvement of the organization's quality and productivity.

An example of a software quality policy, formulated by (the fictional) Lion Quality Software (LQS) Ltd, is presented in Frame 25.2.

Frame 25.2   **Lion Quality Software (LQS) Ltd – software quality policy**

The Company's Quality Goal

The principal goal of Lion Quality Software is to provide software products and software maintenance services that fully comply with customer requirements and expectations, at the scheduled time and according to the agreed budget.

The Company's Quality Policy

The quality policy adopted by LQS supports this goal by:

■ Assigning maximum priority to customer satisfaction by promptly fulfilling requirements and expectations and requests and complaints.

■ Involving employees in determination of quality objectives and commitment to their achievement.

■ Performing development and maintenance tasks correctly the first time around and minimizing the need for rework and correction.

■ Assuring the high and adequate professional and managerial level of its employees, a value maintained by offering incentives and encouragement for its employees to achieve professional excellence.

▶

- Performing quality assurance activities throughout the software life cycle to ensure the achievement of the required quality objectives.

- Applying its quality assurance standards to subcontractors and suppliers. Only those that qualify will be incorporated in the Company's development projects and maintenance services.

- Aiming at continuous improvement of development and maintenance productivity as well as SQA effectiveness and efficiency.

- Allocating all the organizational, physical and professional resources necessary to realize software quality assurance objectives.

Lionel Johnson

L. T. Johnson, President

Marcel Talbot

M. Talbot, General Manager

Industrial Park, CA, February 12, 2003

The organization's software quality policy, as might be anticipated, is stated in general terms. So, it is quite common to find that one organization's software quality policy declaration can be easily transferred to another organization "as is" or with only minor change.

25.1.2 The executive in charge of software quality

The responsibilities of the executive in charge of software quality issues may be classified as follows:

- Responsibility for preparation of an annual SQA activities program and budget
- Responsibility for preparation of SQA system development plans
- Overall control of implementation of the annual SQA regular activities program and planned SQA development projects
- Presentation and advocacy of SQA issues to executive management.

The details of these responsibilities will now be discussed in greater detail.

Responsibility for preparation of an annual SQA activities program and budget
This requires the executive to:

- Establish the system's SQA objectives for the coming year
- Review proposals prepared by the SQA unit for the annual activities program and verify the proposals' potential to fulfill the objectives set for the SQA system

- Determine whether the activities program is adequate to the characteristics and scope of subcontractor services and software purchases planned for the coming year
- Determine the adequacy of the manpower and other resources planned for implementation of the SQA program
- Approve the final version of the annual SQA activities program and budget.

Responsibility for preparation of SQA system development plans
Such plans must be able to cope with technological changes as well as shifts in customer demands and competition. The associated responsibilities include:

- Review of trends that are expected to affect the organization's software quality in the near future.
- Review proposals for SQA adaptations. For example, attempts to penetrate a new market induced introduction of new software development tools and the need to comply with software quality standards never before applied by the company. The adaptation of the SQA system included:
  - Preparation of new procedures appropriate to the new tools and SQA standards
  - Preparation of training programs for veteran software development teams and newly recruited team members
  - Development of software quality metrics appropriate for evaluating the new tools and standards as well as the success of the training programs.
- Approval of the final version of the planned SQA development projects, including their schedules and budgets.

Overall control of implementation of the annual SQA program and planned projects
The executive in charge is responsible for:

- General supervision of the annual activities program
- Review of progress of the SQA adaptation projects
- General supervision of actions taken to realize the quality achievements dictated by the teams' objectives (based on periodic reports)
- Review of compliance with SQA procedures and standards (based on internal quality audits)
- General follow-up of compliance to software development project schedules and budgets
- General follow-up of provision of quality maintenance services to external and internal customers.

Presentation and advocacy of SQA issues to executive management
In order to promote quality and resolve SQA system difficulties requires:

■ Presentation for final approval of the proposed annual activities program and budget

■ Presentation for final approval of planned SQA adaptation projects together with the corresponding budgets

■ Initiation and leadership of periodic management review meetings dedicated to the organization's software quality policy and attendant SQA system issues, summarized in a report on the subjects covered (see Section 25.1.3)

■ Initiation of management-level discussions dedicated to special software quality events, such as severe quality failures, threats to the successful completion of projects due to severe professional staff shortages, managerial crises in the SQA unit, and so on.

25.1.3 Management review

Management review is the name given to the periodic meeting convened to allow executives to obtain an overview of their organization's software quality issues. Management reviews tend to be scheduled for once or twice a year.

A *management review report*, prepared by the SQA unit, sets the stage for the discussions by providing items that appear on the meeting's agenda. A sample of typical items is presented in Frame 25.3.

Frame 25.3 **Typical items contained in management review reports**

■ Progress reports regarding recommendations for implementation made at previous management review meetings

■ Periodic performance reports, including quality metrics

■ Customer satisfaction feedback

■ Assessment of successes/failures in achieving quality objectives, staying within the budget, etc.

■ Follow-up reports for SQA annual regular activity program and SQA projects

■ Summary of special quality events related to customers, suppliers, subcontractors, etc.

■ Review of significant findings of internal and external quality audits as well as special surveys

■ Identification of new software quality risks and unsolved pre-existing risks

■ Recommendations for improvements to be introduced in the software quality management system (e.g., development of new SQA components, purchase of tools, invitation of consultant) to be submitted for final approval

The main objectives of management reviews are to assess the SQA system's compliance with the organization's quality policy, that is, to:

- Assess achievement of the quality objectives set for the organization's software quality management system
- Initiate updates and improvements of the software quality management system and its objectives
- Outline directions for remedying major SQA deficiencies and software quality management problems
- Allocate additional resources to the software quality management system.

Decisions made during management reviews are expected to guide and direct the operation of the software quality management system for the subsequent period, ending at the next review.

25.2 Department management responsibilities for quality assurance

Middle management's quality assurance responsibilities include management of the software quality management system (*quality system-related tasks*) and the tasks related to the projects and services performed by units or teams under the specific manager's authority (*project-related tasks*).

Quality system-related responsibilities
These include SQA activities to be performed on the department level:

- Preparation of the department's annual SQA activities program and budget, based on the recommended program prepared by the SQA unit
- Preparation of the department's SQA systems development plans, based on the recommended plan prepared by the SQA unit
- Control of performance of the department's annual SQA activities program and development projects
- Presentation of the department's SQA issues to top management, in the person of the executive in charge of software quality.

Project-related responsibilities
These vary according to the organization's procedures and distribution of authority; they usually involve:

- Control of compliance to quality assurance procedures in the department's units, including CAB, SCM and SCCA bodies
- Detailed follow-up of contract review results and proposal approvals

review of unit performance of planned review activities; approval of project documents and project phase completion

- Follow-up of software tests and test results; approval of project's software products
- Follow-up of progress of software development project schedules and budget deviations
- Advice and support to project managers in resolving schedule, budget and customer relations difficulties (e.g., during negotiations with the customer, when recruitment issues arise)
- Follow-up of quality of maintenance services provision
- Detailed follow-up of the project risks and their solutions
- Follow-up of project's compliance with customer requirements and customer's satisfaction
- Approval of large software change orders and significant deviations from project specifications.

25.3 Project management responsibilities for quality assurance

Most project management responsibilities are defined in procedures and work instructions; the project manager is the person in charge of making sure that all the team members comply with the said procedures and instructions. His tasks include professional hands-on and managerial tasks, particularly the following.

Professional hands-on tasks

- Preparation of project and quality plans and their updates
- Participation in joint customer–supplier committee
- Close follow-up of project team staffing, including attending to recruitment, training and instruction.

Management tasks

Project managers address the follow-up issues:

- Performance of review activities and the consequent corrections, including participating in some reviews
- Software development and maintenance units' performance with respect to development, integration and system test activities as well as corrections and regression tests
- Performance of acceptance tests
- Software installation in customer sites and the running-in of the software system by the customer

- SQA training and instruction of project team members
- Schedules and resources allocated to project activities (may intervene to correct deviations)
- Customer requests and satisfaction
- Evolving project development risks, application of solutions and control of results (implementation of the risk management process – see Appendix 6A).

Summary

(1) List the actors in a typical quality assurance organizational framework.

The actors in the SQA framework include employees whose software quality assurance tasks comprise all or part of their position's functions as well as others who contribute to the SQA system beyond the confines of their regular position. The actors are grouped into managers, testers and SQA professionals and interested practitioners. A typical list includes the following.

- **Managers**
  - Top management executives, especially the executive directly in charge of software quality assurance
  - Software development and maintenance department managers
  - Software testing department managers
  - Project managers and team leaders of development and maintenance projects
  - Leaders of software testing teams.
- **Testers**
  - Members of software testing teams.
- **SQA professionals and interested practitioners**
  - SQA trustees
  - SQA committee members
  - SQA forum members
  - SQA unit team members.

(2) Describe top management responsibilities regarding software quality.

Top management is responsible for:
- Assuring the quality of the company's software products and software maintenance services
- Communicating to all employees the importance of product and service quality as well as customer satisfaction
- Assuring satisfactory functioning and full compliance with customer requirements
- Ensuring that SQA system objectives are established and realized
- Planning and controlling implementation of changes necessary to adapt the SQA system to organizational transformations as well as changes in clientele, competition and technology

- Intervening to resolve and minimize damages in severe quality failures and other crisis situations
- Ensuring availability of the resources required by the SQA systems.

(3) Describe the software system-related responsibilities of the executive in charge of software quality issues.

The executive in charge is required to do the following:
- Be responsible for preparation of an SQA annual activities program and budget, for final approval by senior management
- Be responsible for preparation of SQA development plans to respond to changes in the organization's internal and external environments
- Have overall control for the implementation of the annual SQA regular activities program and SQA development projects
- Present and advocate SQA issues to the organization's executive management

(4) Describe the main objectives of management reviews.

Management reviews are instruments that enable the organization's executives to:
- Assess the compliance of the SQA system with the organization's quality policy
- Assess the achievement of quality objectives
- Initiate changes and improvements to the software quality management system
- Outline directions for solution of major deficiencies and problems in the organization's software quality management system
- Allocate additional resources for software quality activities when necessary.

(5) Explain the SQA system-related responsibilities of department management.

These responsibilities relate to department-level SQA tasks:
- Preparation of the department's annual SQA activities program and budget
- Preparation of the department's SQA system development plans
- Control of performance of the department's annual SQA activities program and development projects
- Presentation of the department's SQA issues to top management, in the person of the executive in charge of software quality.

(6) List the SQA professional hands-on tasks required of project managers.

- Preparation of project and quality plans and their updates
- Participation in joint customer–supplier committee
- Review of staffing of project teams including recruitment and training.

Selected bibliography

1. ISO (1997) *ISO 9000-3:1997(E), Quality Management and Quality Assurance Standards – Part 3: Guidelines for the Application of ISO 9001:1994 to the Development, Supply, Installation and Maintenance of Computer Software*, 2nd edn, International Organization for Standardization (ISO), Geneva.

2. ISO/IEC (2001) "ISO 9000-3:2001 Software and System Engineering – Guidelines for the Application of ISO 9001:2000 to Software, Final draft", International Organization for Standardization (ISO), Geneva, unpublished draft, December 2001.

Review questions

25.1 The top management contributes to software quality by employing three main managerial tools.

   (1) List the tools applied by top management to achieve its software quality objectives.

   (2) Describe each tool in your own words and explain how it affects software quality.

25.2 Refer to the software quality policy document presented in Frame 25.2.

   (1) List the policy clauses and explain their meanings in your own words.

   (2) Explain how each policy clause contributes to the achievement of the company's quality goals.

25.3 Refer to the LQS Ltd software quality policy document presented in Frame 25.2.

   (1) Examine each clause of the policy document and identify the SQA components directly referred to in those clauses.

   (2) Examine the document and identify those components of the SQA system indirectly addressed by the policy document.

   (3) List the SQA components not referred to at all.

25.4 The executive in charge of software quality issues is responsible for the preparation of the annual SQA activities program and budget.

   (1) Describe in your own words the activities the executive has to perform to prepare the mentioned program and budget.

   (2) Refer to Chapter 26 and describe the participation of the heads of the SQA unit and sub-units in the preparation of the program and budget.

25.5 The executive in charge of software quality issues is responsible for overall control of the performance of SQA activities.

   (1) List the types of SQA activities under the executive's responsibility.

   (2) Describe in your own words the activities the executive has to perform to control the SQA activities listed in (1).

25.6 Nine typical items contained in a management review report are mentioned in Frame 25.3.

   (1) List at least five of these items.

   (2) Suggest possible decisions that can be taken, based on the items listed in (1).

25.7 The responsibilities of department management may be classified into quality system related responsibilities and project-related responsibilities.

List the project-related tasks and explain in your own words the objective of each task.

25.8 The responsibilities of project management may be classified into hands-on professional tasks and project follow-up tasks.

List the project manager's follow-up tasks and explain the objective of each task in your own words.

Topics for discussion

25.1 It is commonly agreed that "SQA objectives are achieved through the cooperation and integrated activities of all actors involved in the quality assurance organizational framework".

(1) Define in your own words who should be considered an actor in a quality assurance organizational framework, and provide a list of typical actors.

(2) Explain the unique contribution of each actor to the SQA system.

25.2 The organization's software quality policy should conform to the organization's purposes and goals.

Suggest at least one example where an organization's software quality policy does not conform to the organization's purpose and goals.

25.3 "Alpha Software" is a medium-sized software house specializing in telecom real-time software, employing about 180 professionals. As no executive volunteered for the position of "executive in charge of software quality", the general manager of Alpha Software did not insist on nominating an executive to this position. Moreover, he did not assign any great importance to issuing a quality policy document because, as he claimed, "the company is anyway committed to quality"; hence, there was no need for any written document. This situation continued for about two years without any critical failure.

(1) Suggest what unnoticed and undesired events may have resulted from this position.

(2) Suggest what an executive in charge of software quality, in addition to an adequate and updated policy document, could contribute to company product quality.

chapter 26

The SQA unit and other actors in the SQA system

We would like to assume that most if not all of an organization's staff are expected to contribute their share to the quality of the organization's software products and/or services. In the previous chapter, Chapter 25, we discussed the contributions made by management as actors in the *software quality assurance framework*. In this chapter, we turn to the SQA professionals and interested practitioners found among the software development and maintenance staff. That is, we refer here to those staff members whose SQA activities represent all or part of their standard assignments or whose participation in SQA bodies goes beyond their regular activities, namely:

- SQA unit members
- SQA trustees

- SQA committee members
- SQA forum members.

Among the above actors, only members of the SQA unit dedicate all their work-related activities to the SQA; that is, they can be considered as "full-time SQA staff". The others either have part-time responsibilities or are, like most trustees and members of SQA committees and forums, employees who volunteer their time due to their interest in quality.

After completing this chapter, you will be able to:

- Describe the SQA unit's tasks according to the proposed Organizational Structure Model.
- Describe the typical tasks of the head of an SQA unit.
- Describe typical project life cycle tasks.
- Describe the types of audits performed by the SQA unit.
- Describe the development and maintenance tasks associated with SQA standards and procedures.
- Describe the tasks of SQA trustees.
- Describe and compare the types of SQA committees.
- Describe SQA forum characteristics: scope and participants.

26.1 The SQA unit

SQA unit structure varies by type and, of course, size of the organization. As it is impossible to describe all the optional arrangements, the chapter presents a model whose structure and task distribution are readily adaptable to the characteristics and procedures characterizing the internal environment of a spate of major organizations. The model is shown in Figure 26.1.

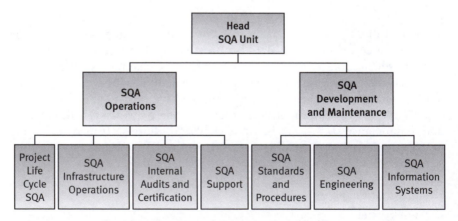

Figure 26.1: Proposed model for an SQA unit's organizational structure

We first list the tasks typically assigned to the SQA unit head (Section 26.1.1) followed by the sub-units, as indicated in the model (Sections 26.1.2 to 26.1.8).

26.1.1 Tasks performed by the head of the SQA unit

The head of the SQA unit is responsible for all the quality assurance tasks performed by the SQA unit and its sub-units. In addition, some SQA tasks are assigned only to him: this allocation reflects the manager's professional experience and administrative position.

The typical tasks performed by an SQA unit head may be classified into the following categories:

- Planning
- Management of the unit
- Tasks related to contacts with customers and other external bodies as well as with the executive in charge of software quality
- SQA professional activities.

Planning tasks

- Preparation of proposed annual activity program and budget for the unit
- Planning and updating the organization's software quality management system
- Preparation of recommended annual SQA activities programs for the software development and maintenance departments; assistance from SQA sub-units may be requested when performing this task
- Preparation of recommended SQA systems development plans for the software development and maintenance departments; assistance from SQA sub-units may be requested when performing this task.

Management tasks

- Management of the SQA team's activities
- Monitoring implementation of the SQA activity program
- Nomination of team members, SQA committee members and SQA trustees
- Preparation of special and periodic reports, e.g., status of software quality issues within the organization and monthly performance reports.

Contacts with customers and other external bodies and the executive in charge of software quality

- Serving as the customer's address for software quality issues
- Outreach to customers with respect to quality of software products and services supplied

- Representation of the organization before external bodies regarding software quality issues
- Drafting the management review reports required for management review meetings
- SQA organizational issues, preparing requested material, and so forth, for top management's consideration (done through the executive in charge of software quality).

SQA professional activities

- Participation in project joint committees
- Participation in formal design reviews
- Review and approval of deviations from specifications (when required by procedures)
- Consultation with project managers and team leaders
- Participation in SQA committees and forums.

26.1.2 SQA sub-unit tasks related to the project life cycle

The SQA tasks related to the project life cycle sub-unit may be classified into two groups:

- "Pure" managerial follow-up and approval tasks (*project life cycle control* tasks)
- "Hands-on" or active participation in project team SQA activities, where professional contributions are required (*participation* tasks).

Project life cycle control tasks

- Follow-up of development and maintenance teams' compliance with SQA procedures and work instructions
- Approval or recommendation of software products (design reports and code) according to the relevant procedures
- Monitoring delivery of software maintenance services to internal and external customers
- Monitoring customer satisfaction (by means of surveys, etc.) and maintaining contact with customers' quality assurance representatives.

Participation tasks

These tasks include participation in:

- Contract reviews
- Preparation and updating of project and project quality plans
- Formal design reviews

- Subcontractors' formal design reviews
- Software testing, including customer acceptance tests
- Software acceptance tests of subcontractors' software products
- Installation of new software products.

26.1.3 SQA sub-unit infrastructure operations tasks

As discussed in Part IV, SQA systems employ a variety of infrastructure components to operate smoothly, namely:

- Procedures and work instructions
- Supporting quality devices (templates, checklists)
- Staff training, instruction and certification
- Preventive and corrective actions
- Configuration management
- Documentation control.

More specifically, the SQA sub-unit's tasks regarding these components include:

- Publication of updated versions of procedures, work instructions, templates, checklists, and so forth, together with their circulation in hard copy and/or by electronic means
- Transmission of training and instruction regarding adherence to and application of SQA procedures, work instructions and similar items to new and current staff
- Instruction of SQA trustees regarding new and revised procedures as well as development tools and methods, among other components
- Monitoring and supporting implementation of new and revised SQA procedures
- Follow-up of staff certification activities
- Proposal of subjects requiring preventive and corrective actions, including participation in CAB committees
- Follow-up of configuration management activities, including participation in CCA committees
- Follow-up of compliance with documentation procedures and work instructions.

26.1.4 SQA sub-unit audit and certification tasks

The types of SQA audits carried out in or by software organizations can be classified as follows:

- Internal audits
- Audits of subcontractors and suppliers to evaluate their SQA systems

- External audits performed by certification bodies
- External audits performed by customers who wish to evaluate the SQA system prior to accepting the organization as a supplier.

The first two classes of audits are initiated and performed by the SQA sub-unit, the last two by external bodies. Descriptions of the activities performed by the sub-unit, by audit type, follow.

Internal SQA audits demand that the following tasks be completed by the SQA unit:

- Preparation of annual programs for internal SQA audits
- Performance of internal SQA audits
- Follow-up of corrections and improvements to be carried out by the audited teams and other units
- Preparation of periodic summary reports of status of audit findings, including recommendations for improvements.

SQA audits of subcontractors and suppliers demand that the following tasks be carried out by the SQA unit:

- Preparation of the annual program for SQA audits of subcontractors and suppliers
- Performance of SQA audits of subcontractors and suppliers
- Follow-up of corrections and improvements to be carried out by the audited subcontractors and suppliers
- Collection of data on the performance of subcontractors and suppliers from internal as well as external sources
- Periodic evaluation of the organization's certified subcontractors' and suppliers' SQA systems based on audit reports and information collected from other internal and external sources. The evaluation report includes recommendations regarding certification of subcontractors and suppliers.

External audits performed by certification bodies involve the following tasks:

- Coordination of the certification audit's contents and schedule
- Preparation of documents specified by the certification bodies
- Instruction of the audited teams and performance of the preparations necessary for certification audits
- Participation in certification audits
- Ensuring that required corrections and improvements are performed.

SQA audits performed by the organization's customers entail these tasks:

- Coordination of the audit's contents and schedule
- Preparation of documents specified by the customer's auditor

- Instruction of the audited teams and performance of the preparations necessary for SQA audits by the organization's customers
- Participation in the audits
- Ensuring that required corrections and improvements are performed.

Table 26.1 compares the SQA activities required for the various types of audits.

26.1.5 SQA sub-unit support tasks

Most of the consumers of SQA support services are located within the organization: project managers, team leaders and SQA trustees. The support they need revolves around implementation of SQA procedures, for example:

- Preparation of project plans and project quality plans
- Staffing review teams
- Choice of development methodologies and tools that reflect the failure experience data accumulated by the SQA unit
- Choice of measures to solve identified software development risks
- Choice of measures to solve schedule delays and budget overruns
- Choice of SQA metrics and software costs components
- Use of SQA information systems.

Table 26.1: Comparison by audit type of SQA sub-unit's tasks

Task	Class of audits			
	Internal audits	Audits of subcontractors and suppliers	Certification audits	Audits by customers
Preparation of annual programs for SQA audits	+	+	–	–
Performance of SQA audits	+	+	–	–
Follow-up of corrections	+	+	+	+
Preparation of periodic summary reports	+	–	–	–
Collection of data on the performance of the audited organization from internal and external sources	–	+	–	–
Periodic evaluation of the audited organization	–	+	–	–
Coordination of the external audit's contents and schedule	–	–	+	+
Preparation of documents as specified by external auditors	–	–	+	+
Instruction of the audited teams and performance of preparations for external audits	–	–	+	+
Participation in the audit	–	–	+	+

26.1 The SQA unit

26.1.6 SQA sub-unit standards and procedures: development and maintenance tasks

The SQA sub-unit is intimately involved in deciding which SQA standards will be adopted as well as developing and maintaining the organization's procedures. To fulfill the attendant obligations, the SQA unit is required to:

- Prepare an annual program for development of new procedures and procedure updates, including responsibility for development of new procedures and procedure updates, with participation in appropriate committees and forums

- Follow-up of developments and changes in SQA and software engineering standards; introduction of additional procedures and changes relevant to the organization

- Initiation of updates and adaptations of procedures in response to changes in professional standards, including adoption or deletion of standards applied by the organization.

26.1.7 SQA sub-unit engineering development and maintenance tasks

Follow-up of professional advances, solution of operational difficulties and expert analysis of failures are the immediate objectives of this SQA sub-unit. Hence, the main engineering tasks involved cover the following:

- Testing quality and productivity aspects with respect to new development tools and new versions of currently used development tools

- Evaluation of quality and productivity of new development and maintenance methods and method improvements

- Development of solutions to difficulties confronted in application of currently used software development tools and methods

- Development of methods for measuring software quality and team productivity

- Provision of technological support to CAB committees during analysis of software development failures and formulation of proposed solutions.

26.1.8 SQA sub-unit information system tasks

SQA information systems are meant to facilitate and improve the functioning of SQA systems. The tasks involved include:

- Development of SQA information systems for software development and maintenance units for collection of activity data and processing of, for example, periodic reports, lists, exception reports and queries

- Development of SQA information systems facilitating the SQA unit's processing of information delivered by software development and maintenance units (e.g., data analysis, report preparation, etc.), including estimates of software quality metrics and software quality costs

- Updating of SQA information systems
- Development and maintenance of the organization's SQA Internet /intranet site.

26.2 SQA trustees and their tasks

SQA trustees are staff members who, being strongly interested in software quality, volunteer part of their time to promoting quality. They are frequently instructed on subjects of interest by the SQA unit. As SQA "agents", trustees are expected to provide the internal support necessary to successfully implement SQA components.

Trustees' tasks vary substantially among organizations. Tasks may be unit-related and/or organization-related, and include some or all of the following activities.

Unit-related tasks
- Support their colleagues' attempts to solve difficulties arising in the implementation of software quality procedures and work instructions
- Help their unit manager in performing his or her SQA tasks (e.g., preparation of a project's work instructions, collection of data for calculating SQA metrics)
- Promote compliance and monitor implementation of SQA procedures and work instructions by colleagues
- Report substantial and systematic non-compliance events to the SQA unit
- Report severe software quality failures to the SQA unit.

Organization-related tasks
- Initiate changes and updates of *organization-wide* SQA procedures and work instructions
- Initiate organization-wide improvements of development and maintenance processes and applications to the CAB for solutions to recurrent failures observed in their units
- Identify organization-wide SQA training needs and propose an appropriate training or instruction program to be carried out by the SQA unit.

26.3 SQA committees and their tasks

SQA committees can be either permanent or *ad hoc*. The subjects dealt with, authority as well as division of tasks between permanent and *ad hoc* committees, vary considerably among organizations and over time.

Permanent committees commonly deal with SCC (software change control), CA (corrective actions), procedure s, method development tools and quality metrics. *Ad hoc committees* commonly deal with specific cases of more general interest such as updates of a specific procedure, analysis and solution of a software failure, elaboration of software metrics for a targeted process or product, updating software quality costs and data collection methods for a specific issue.

Permanent SQA committees are integral parts of the SQA organizational framework; their tasks and operation are usually defined in the organization's SQA procedures. In contrast, *ad hoc* committees are established on a short-term per-problem basis, with members nominated by the executive responsible for software quality issues, the head of the SQA Unit, the SQA sub-units, the permanent SQA committees, or any other body that initiated its formation and has an interest in the work it is to do. This body also defines the *ad hoc* committee's tasks.

26.4 SQA forums – tasks and methods of operation

SQA forums are informal components of the SQA organizational framework; they are established by volunteers and display some features of a community. The forums operate rather freely, not being subject to any standard requirements or procedures. A forum's subjects, activities and participants vary from one organization to another and reflect, more than anything else, the individuals belonging to the organization's software quality community who are eager to create a meeting place for the exchange of SQA experiences and ideas. An organization generally benefits from the activities of its SQA forums, which can function independently or in some kind of cooperative relationship.

Members of an SQA forum usually define its scope and mode of operation, which can be limited or broad in scope. The forum can meet regularly or sporadically, and can define its preferred means of communication (Internet, intranet, electronic mail, etc.).

SQA forums typically focus on:

- SQA procedure improvements and implementation
- Quality metrics
- Corrective actions – analysis of failure and success cases
- Quality system issues – development and implementation of new tools
- Quality line management problems – daily operational software quality problems brought before it by quality managers from every level.

Participation in SQA forums may be closed (e.g., limited to quality line managers) or open to all. Members of an open forum may include:

- SQA unit members
- SQA trustees
- Software development and maintenance staff

- SQA and software engineering consultants/experts
- Customer representatives.

Forums also maintain the option of publication. Publications can include newsletters to members, periodic reviews of SQA issues, reports of professional task force or special forum committees. In addition to describing and analyzing a quality issue, reports may include recommendations for corrective actions. The forum also decides upon a distribution list, and whether its publications are limited to its members or extended to other members of the organization.

An example of a forum operating for several years in a well-known software house was the "Template Forum". Four team leaders, two of whom had a reputation of being outstanding report writers, established the forum, whose sole objective was to prepare a set of templates for the 11 teams working within the framework of the Software Development Department. On average, membership of the forum was 8–11 members, but membership never exceeded 15. During the forum's three years of activity, about 20 different templates were issued, most of which were also updated at least once during this period. The templates were publicized in the department's data communication network and were defined as the department's standard in the space of about a year. The forum discontinued its activities after two of its initiators left the firm. Several attempts by the SQA unit to renew the forum's activities failed in the absence of a staff member to drive its reactivation.

Summary

(1) Describe the SQA unit's tasks according to the proposed Organizational Structure Model.

The tasks of the SQA unit are grouped into SQA operations functions and SQA development and maintenance functions.

SQA operations functions:

- Project life cycle SQA: performs tasks such as contract reviews, formal design reviews and software testing.
- SQA infrastructure operations: performs tasks such as publication of updated versions of SQA procedures, SQA training activities and follow-up of staff certification.
- SQA audits and certification, including internal SQA audits, SQA audits of subcontractors, external audits performed by certification bodies and external audits performed by customers.
- SQA support: performs tasks such as consultations related to project quality plan, choice of development methodology and implementation of SQA procedures.

SQA development and maintenance functions:

- SQA standards and procedures: tasks such as development and updating of procedures, adaptations to changes in professional standards and recommendations for adoption of additional standards.

- SQA engineering: tasks such as evaluation of quality and productivity of new development tools, development of solutions to difficulties encountered in application of software development tools, and development of methods for measuring software quality.
- SQA information system: tasks such as development of software development and maintenance unit-level SQA information systems, development of systems for receipt and processing of data by the SQA Unit, and maintenance of the SQA Internet/intranet site.

(2) Describe the typical tasks of the head of an SQA unit.

- Planning tasks include preparation of proposed SQA annual activity program and budget for the SQA unit, planning of the organization's software quality management system, and preparation of recommended SQA activities programs and SQA system development plans for the software development departments.
- Management tasks include monitoring implementation of the annual SQA activities program, appointment of SQA committee members, and preparation of the unit's periodic summary reports.
- Maintaining contacts with customers and other external bodies and the executive in charge of software quality.
- SQA professional activities include participation in project joint committees, formal design reviews, and consultations with project managers, software development team leaders and others.

(3) Describe typical project life cycle tasks.

- **Control tasks**: follow-up of compliance with SQA procedures, approval or recommendations for approval of software products and monitoring performance of software maintenance services.
- **Follow-up and participation tasks**: contract reviews, review activities, subcontractors' formal design reviews and software testing, including customer acceptance tests.

(4) Describe the audit types the SQA unit is involved with.

Organizations carry out four types of SQA audits, two of which are performed by the SQA unit:
- Internal SQA audits
- SQA audits of the organization's subcontractors and suppliers to evaluate their SQA systems.

The other two audits, performed by other bodies, are:
- External audits performed by certification bodies to obtain SQA certification (e.g., ISO 9001 certification)
- External audits performed by customers who wish to evaluate their suppliers' SQA systems.

(5) Describe the development and maintenance tasks associated with SQA standards and procedures.

The tasks associated with the standards adopted by the organization include follow-up of developments and changes in SQA and software engineering standards and recommending adoption of additional standards.

The tasks associated with the organization's SQA procedures include coordination and participation in development, maintenance and updating of procedures as well as preparation of an annual program for development of new procedures.

(6) Describe the tasks of SQA trustees.

SQA trustees are involved in unit-related tasks and organization-related tasks, which vary considerably among organizations.

- **Typical unit-related tasks**: support other unit/team members in solving difficulties in implementation of software quality procedures, help their unit manager in performing his SQA tasks, and report to the SQA unit on substantial and systematic non-compliance situations and severe software quality failures.
- **Typical organization-related tasks**: initiation of changes and updates of SQA procedures, initiation of organization-wide improvements of development and maintenance processes and applications to the CAB, identification of SQA training needs and preparation of proposals for appropriate training and/or instruction programs.

(7) Describe and compare the types of SQA committees.

SQA committees may be permanent or *ad hoc*. The subjects, membership criteria and authority of permanent SQA committees are usually defined by SQA procedures. *Ad hoc* committees are quite different: establishment of *ad hoc* committees and their task definitions are initiated by various bodies, according to circumstances and current needs. Members of *ad hoc* committees are chosen by their availability; their authority is adjusted to the committee initiators' needs. One may expect great variation among the *ad hoc* committees nominated for the same task by different initiators and at different times.

(8) Describe SQA forum characteristics: scope and participants.

SQA forums are informal components of the SQA organizational framework. They are established, operated and developed freely.

The scope of SQA forums is limited or broad. Forum subjects, activities and participants vary by organization and typically relate to SQA procedure improvements and implementation, quality metrics, development of software engineering tools and implementation of new tools.

Participation in SQA forums may be closed or open. Participants of open SQA forums can include SQA unit members, SQA trustees, members of software development and maintenance teams, customer representatives and software engineering consultants.

Review questions

26.1 The organizational structure of an SQA unit according to a model presented in Figure 26.1 includes four sub-units that deal with SQA operations.

(1) List the four sub-units.
(2) Describe in your own words the tasks performed by each.

26.2 According to a model presented in Figure 26.1, the organizational structure of an SQA unit includes three sub-units that deal with SQA development and maintenance.

(1) List the three sub-units.
(2) Describe in your own words the tasks performed by each.

26.3 Project life cycle SQA tasks include project life cycle control tasks and participation tasks.

(1) List at least four participation tasks.
(2) Indicate the unique contribution of an SQA unit member's participation for each of the tasks listed in (1).

26.4 SQA infrastructure operations tasks refer to the seven SQA infrastructure components discussed in Part IV of the book.

(1) Describe in your own words the SQA infrastructure operations tasks.
(2) Indicate at least one task that relates to each of the infrastructure components.

26.5 The typical SQA unit dedicates a great part of its resources to SQA audits.

(1) Describe the types of SQA audits performed by the SQA unit.
(2) Describe the tasks involved in performing each of the audits listed in (1) and indicate the differences between them.

26.6 It has become customary in recent years for external bodies to perform SQA audits of a supplier's SQA system.

(1) Describe the types of SQA audits performed by external bodies.
(2) Describe the SQA tasks involved in each of the external audits listed in (1) and indicate the differences between them.

Topics for discussion

26.1 Computerized SQA information systems are already available in most organizations. The SQA tasks related to the information system are meant to make the SQA system more effective and efficient.

(1) Describe in your own words the SQA tasks related to the SQA information system.
(2) Improvements of the SQA information systems are expected to contribute to reduction of failure rates and quality costs. If you agree, give two or three examples of such reductions.

(3) Suggest types of information services to be provided by an SQA intranet site and list the advantages for the SQA system of intranet-based systems over the classic paper-based systems.

26.2 SQA trustees are expected to be SQA agents in their teams/units and provide the internal support for successful implementation of SQA components.

(1) Explain how SQA trustees complement the formal activities performed by SQA units and unit managers.

(2) Evaluate the contributions of SQA trustees to software quality.

26.3 The permanent Software Metrics Committee of Venus Software has identified a significant increase in two failure-related software quality metrics for the new version 6.1 of its popular "Customer-Venus" software package, used by about 2500 consumer clubs all around the country. The Committee decided to establish an *ad hoc* committee to contend with the failures.

(1) Suggest a list of tasks for the *ad hoc* committee.

(2) Suggest who should be invited onto the *ad hoc* committee and who should head it.

(3) List the assumptions on which you based your answers to (1) and (2).

26.4 SQA forum activities are conducted entirely informally. For instance, participants may join and leave the forum whenever they wish and they may undertake or refuse to perform tasks of interest to the forum. Accordingly, some SQA experts tend to consider forums to be worthless.

(1) Do you agree with this opinion? If not, list your arguments.

(2) In what ways can an organization promote and encourage SQA forum activities?

The future of SQA

Current SQA systems apply a considerable array of components to achieve an acceptable level of software quality. Yet, despite all the SQA components employed and the vast resources invested in assuring the quality of software developer will declare a product as "free of defects". This reticence reflects reality: it is far from rare for severe defects to be identified in new software products, new versions of software packages or firmware of reputable developers.

If such is the case, what can we expect in the future?

■ Will future SQA methodologies enjoy the pleasures of "defect free" software?

■ Or, alternatively, will the rapidly growing demands made of new software packages cause a decline in achievable software quality?

In the following we attempt to anticipate the future of SQA according to current trends in software engineering and software quality assurance. In other words, we present:

■ The growing future challenges for SQA, expected in response to changes in software development requirements.

■ These are balanced by a forecasting regarding the growing capabilities of SQA tools for overcoming the new challenges.

Facing the future: SQA challenges

The challenges SQA will face in the future can be outlined in terms of already observable software engineering trends:

- Growing complexity and size of software packages
- Growing integration and interface requirements
- Shorter project schedules
- Growing intolerance of defective software products.

Growing complexity and size of software packages

Some of the pivotal trends responsible for the growing complexity and size of software packages include:

- Incorporation of increasingly complex algorithms. The algorithms are based on a larger number of inputs and make use of more complicated calculations.

- Expansion in the number of output categories, based on multiplying sources of inputs, targeted to more and larger groups of users. For instance, sales and inventory systems, traditionally internal systems, nowadays also serve customers, who use the systems to record orders and check shipment schedules.

- Demands for greater accuracy, more complete information and shorter reaction times.

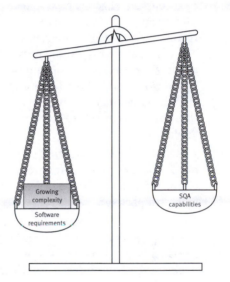

Examples

(a) *Military radar-driven systems*. Although the algorithms are more complex, reaction times for military radar-driven systems are required to be much shorter than previously in order to respond to the higher speed and maneuverability of aircraft and missiles.

(b) *Municipal tax collection information systems*. Systems that were once allowed to produce notifications of unpaid property tax within not later than 30 days after payment due date with errors not exceeding 0.5% are now required to process the same notifications within 7 days but with errors not exceeding 0.1%.

Growing integration and interface requirements

New software systems are clearly characterized by growing integration and interface requirements:

■ *Internal intra-organizational integration.* Representative examples are ERP (Enterprise Resources Planning) software packages that combine the functions of several intra-organizational software systems such as production planning and control, sales, inventory management and financial systems in one program. Other examples are CRM (Customer Relations Management) systems that deal with all customer-related systems: purchase records, payments, complaints, services provided, consumer socio-economic characteristics, etc. The same trend is observed in firmware and embedded software applications.

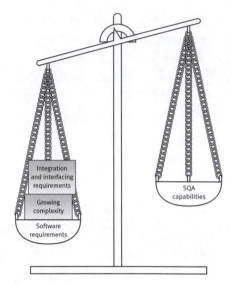

■ *Internal interface capabilities among the same developer's software products.* For example, software packages for management of consumer clubs are increasingly required to interface with CRM *and* accounting software packages.

■ *External interfaces, namely software–software, software–firmware and firmware–firmware interfaces.* Different developers supply the respective interfacing software and firmware packages. It is imperative for software packages to fully interface with leading software packages or firmware embedded in equipment manufactured by principal manufacturers.

Examples

(a) A new wage-management software system must interface with a list of leading attendance and human resources software packages.

(b) Patient monitoring software systems need to interface with many patient vital-sign monitoring devices, that is, devices attached to the patient that record heartbeat, blood pressure, etc. Requirements of this type are in many cases set by marketing experts.

Shorter project schedules

Shorter project scheduling is typical of COTS software packages as well as custom-made software. Competition has shortened the lead times for developing new versions of software packages; requests for proposals (RFPs) for custom-made software cite shorter and shorter completion times. It is estimated that project schedules have been cut by 50% every 2–3 years. The implications of this trend on SQA, irrespective of other, simultaneously realized trends, are dramatic:

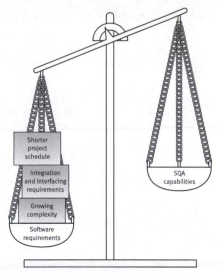

- *Employment of larger development teams*. This creates greater coordination and cooperation difficulties and, quite likely, more severe quality problems.
- *Much less time available for review and testing activities*. Again, quality is expected to suffer.

Growing intolerance of defective software products

As software systems become more comprehensive and sophisticated, users – whether organizations or individuals – become increasingly dependent on software products; the subsequent damage from software failures grows accordingly. As a result, customer sensitivity to software damages has reduced tolerance of software defects, with even less tolerance of critical defects. This trend places greater demands on SQA as pressure intensifies for failure-resistant software. In other words, quality levels acceptable in the past are expected to be unacceptable in the future.

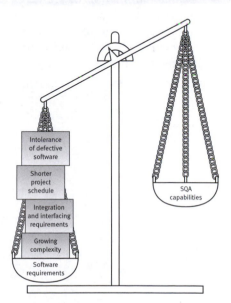

To sum up: the combined effects of the four trends characterizing software engineering frame vital challenges for software quality assurance in the near future. Notwithstanding the obstacles, can any trends in improved SQA capabilities be expected to offset these difficulties?

Facing the future: SQA capabilities

We can expect SQA to meet the challenges outlined in terms of already observable software engineering trends:

- Extended use of CASE tools
- Expanded use of professional standards
- Extended use of automated testing
- Expanded software reuse.

Extended use of CASE tools

Progress in upgrading currently used and potentially new CASE tools in the next few years will support the features that have already been proven crucial to SQA. These tools:

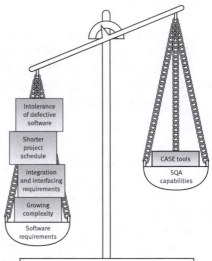

- *Provide updated accurate documentation* to support development of the interfaces and integrated systems that are of special importance for large-scale software systems.
- *Support coordination of large teams* by providing updated documentation and online logical, linguistic and other checks of design and code products.
- *Enable automation* of segments of the development process (especially by ICASE), thereby shortening schedules and reducing the number of defects.
- *Support maintenance* by updating documentation and automating activities.

Expanded use of professional standards

The emergence of international professional standards and their spread is expected to affect software development by:

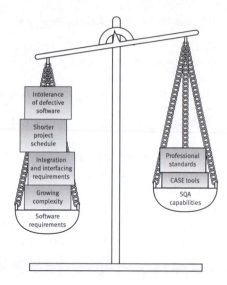

- *Simplifying communication and coordination* between software developers in the same organization but especially from different organizations.

- *Facilitating mobility and absorption* of software professionals between teams. In addition to contributing to the reduction of errors made by new team members, replacement or addition of team members will become easier. The smoother staffing transitions, in turn, curtail the likelihood of non-compliance with short schedules.

- *Simplify reuse of code*, whether the code is the developer's own or that of others (e.g., software taken from reused code libraries).

Extended use of automated testing

Automated testing is expected to offer improved SQA tool effectiveness and efficiency and expand the variety of testing activities covered. As a result, we will witness a much higher rate of use. The characteristics of automated testing contributing to this trend are improved performance accuracy, comprehensiveness of records and statistics, efficiency and speed of regression tests, and reusable testing programs.

Automated testing contends with SQA challenges in several ways:

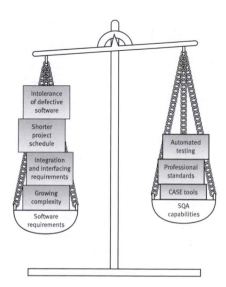

- It provides *effective and efficient tools* for dealing with large-scale, complex software systems, especially by regression testing and comprehensive test records and summaries produced.

- Its capacity for *regression testing and testing program reuse* supports efforts to comply with shorter schedules.

Expanded software reuse

The capacity to incorporate reused software – that is, software that has already been tested and corrected according to defects identified in previous tests as well as by users during regular application – in new systems seems to be a very effective if not the most effective response to SQA's future challenges:

- Significant application of reused software *substantially reduces development efforts* to make meeting short project schedules conceivable.

- Reused software *minimizes efforts needed to test and correct the new software system* (most defects have already been identified by previous applications). These contribute, again, to shorter project schedules.

- Software reuse is expected to *increase standardization*, resulting in smoother interface development and system integration.

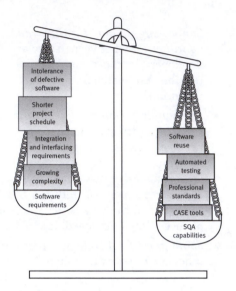

The anticipated combined outcome of trends already prevalent in SQA development is impressive. Yet, the basic questions remains: will they be adequate to the challenges? The assumption guiding preparation of this text is that "Yes" is the proper answer.

Author index

Subject index